Lecture Notes in Computer Science 10695

Commenced Publication in 1973
Founding and Former Series Editors:
Gerhard Goos, Juris Hartmanis, and Jan van Leeuwen

More information about this series at http://www.springer.com/series/7408

Bor-Yuh Evan Chang (Ed.)

Programming Languages and Systems

15th Asian Symposium, APLAS 2017
Suzhou, China, November 27–29, 2017
Proceedings

 Springer

Editor
Bor-Yuh Evan Chang
University of Colorado
Boulder, CO
USA

ISSN 0302-9743   ISSN 1611-3349   (electronic)
Lecture Notes in Computer Science
ISBN 978-3-319-71236-9   ISBN 978-3-319-71237-6   (eBook)
https://doi.org/10.1007/978-3-319-71237-6

Library of Congress Control Number: 2017959598

LNCS Sublibrary: SL2 – Programming and Software Engineering

Printed on acid-free paper

This Springer imprint is published by Springer Nature
The registered company is Springer International Publishing AG
The registered company address is: Gewerbestrasse 11, 6330 Cham, Switzerland

Preface

This volume contains the proceedings of the 15th Asian Symposium on Programming Languages and Systems (APLAS 2017), held in Suzhou, China during November 27–29, 2017. APLAS aims to stimulate programming language research by providing a forum for the presentation of latest results and the exchange of ideas in programming languages and systems. APLAS is based in Asia but is an international forum that serves the worldwide programming languages community.

APLAS 2017 solicited submissions in two categories: regular research papers and tool demonstrations. The conference solicits contributions in, but is not limited to, the following topics: semantics, logics, and foundational theory; design of languages, type systems, and foundational calculi; domain-specific languages; compilers, interpreters, and abstract machines; program derivation, synthesis, and transformation; program analysis, verification, and model-checking; logic, constraint, probabilistic and quantum programming; software security; concurrency and parallelism; and tools for programming and implementation.

New to APLAS in 2017, the conference employed a double-blind reviewing process with an author-response period. Within the review period, APLAS 2017 used an internal two-round review process where each submission received three first-round reviews to drive the possible selection of additional expert reviews as needed before the author response period. All submissions received at least three reviews with nearly half of the submissions receiving four or five reviews. The author response period was followed by a two-week Program Committee discussion period with over 425 comments generated and culminating in a synchronous, virtual Program Committee meeting on August 11, 2017, to finalize the selection of papers.

This year APLAS received 56 submissions. After thoroughly evaluating the relevance and quality of each paper, the Program Committee decided to accept 24 contributions. We were also honored to include four invited talks by distinguished researchers:

- Gilles Barthe (IMDEA, Spain) on "Relational Verification of Higher-Order Probabilistic Programs"
- Ron Garcia (University of British Columbia, Canada) on "Gradual Enforcement of Program Invariants"
- Sumit Gulwani (Microsoft Research, USA) on "Programming by Examples: PL Meets ML"
- Naijun Zhan (Chinese Academy of Sciences, China) on "Synthesizing SystemC Code from Delay Hybrid CSP"

This program would not have been possible without the substantial efforts of many people, whom I sincerely thank. The Program Committee, sub-reviewers, and external expert reviewers worked tirelessly to select the strongest possible program while simultaneously offering constructive and supportive comments in their reviews.

Xinyu Feng (University of Science and Technology of China) serving as general chair of APLAS 2017 ensured that all aspects of the conference planning were addressed. I also graciously thank the APLAS Steering Committee for their leadership, as well as APLAS 2016 PC chair Atsushi Igarashi (Kyoto University, Japan) for timely advice.

Lastly, I would like to acknowledge the organizers of the associated events that makes APLAS a truly exciting event: the Poster Session and Student Research Competition (Yu Zhang, University of Science and Technology of China) and the APLAS Workshop on New Ideas and Emerging Results (Wei-Ngan Chin, National University of Singapore and Zhenjiang Hu, National Institute of Informatics, Japan).

September 2017   Bor-Yuh Evan Chang

Organization

General Chair

Xinyu Feng   University of Science and Technology of China

Program Chair

Bor-Yuh Evan Chang   University of Colorado Boulder

Program Committee

Andreas Abel	Gothenburg University, Sweden
Aws Albarghouthi	University of Wisconsin-Madison, USA
Sam Blackshear	Facebook, USA
Yu-Fang Chen	Academia Sinica, Taiwan
Yuting Chen	Shanghai Jiao Tong University, China
Stephen Chong	Harvard University, USA
Vijay D'Silva	Google, USA
Benjamin Delaware	Purdue University, USA
Rayna Dimitrova	The University of Texas at Austin, USA
Cezara Dragoi	Inria, ENS, CNRS, France
William Harris	Georgia Institute of Technology, USA
Guoliang Jin	North Carolina State University, USA
Akash Lal	Microsoft Research, India
Vu Le	Microsoft, USA
Akimasa Morihata	The University of Tokyo, Japan
Sergio Mover	University of Colorado Boulder, USA
Santosh Nagarakatte	Rutgers University, USA
Hakjoo Oh	Korea University, South Korea
Bruno C.D.S. Oliveira	The University of Hong Kong, SAR China
Xiaokang Qiu	Purdue University, USA
Arjun Radhakrishna	University of Pennsylvania, USA
Aseem Rastogi	Microsoft Research, India
Sukyoung Ryu	KAIST, South Korea
Ilya Sergey	University College London, UK
Makoto Tatsuta	National Institute of Informatics, Japan
Tachio Terauchi	Waseda University, Japan
Bow-Yaw Wang	Academia Sinica, Taiwan
Yingfei Xiong	Peking University, China
Kwangkeun Yi	Seoul National University, South Korea

Danfeng Zhang   Pennsylvania State University, USA
Xin Zhang   Georgia Institute of Technology, USA
Kenny Zhu   Shanghai Jiao Tong University, China

Poster Chair

Yu Zhang   University of Science and Technology of China

Workshop on New Ideas and Emerging Results Organizers

Wei-Ngan Chin   National University of Singapore
Zhenjiang Hu   National Institute of Informatics, Japan

Asian Association for Foundation of Software Executive Committee

Co-chairs

Wei-Ngan Chin   National University of Singapore
Zhenjiang Hu   National Institute of Informatics, Japan

Members

Xinyu Feng   University of Science and Technology of China
Yuxi Fu   Shanghai Jiao Tong University, China
Jacques Garrigue   Nagoya University, Japan
Atsushi Igarashi   Kyoto University, Japan
Ranjit Jhala   University of California, San Diego, USA
Yukiyoshi Kameyama   University of Tsukuba, Japan
Naoki Kobayashi   The University of Tokyo, Japan
Shin-Cheng Mu   Academia Sinica, Taiwan
Sungwoo Park   Pohang University of Science and Technology,
                           South Korea
Chung-chieh Shan   Indiana University, USA
Zhong Shao   Yale University, USA
Harald Sondergaard   The University of Melbourne, Australia
Kazunori Ueda   Waseda University, Japan
Hongseok Yang   KAIST, South Korea
Kwangkeun Yi   Seoul National University, South Korea

Additional Reviewers

Brotherston, James
Chen, Yifan
Docherty, Simon
Dodds, Mike
Dolby, Julian
Enea, Constantin
Hammer, Matthew
Hong, Chih-Duo
Jia, Limin
Kang, Jeehoon
Kedia, Piyus
Kimura, Daisuke
Kwang, Jeehoon

López Juan, Víctor
Nakazawa, Koji
Nordvall Forsberg, Fredrik
Ramyaa, Ramyaa
Rennela, Mathys
Sankaranarayanan, Sriram
Sjöberg, Vilhelm
Tang, Hao
Tzevelekos, Nikos
Vazou, Niki
Xie, Ningning
Yang, Yanpeng
Zhang, Weixin

Abstracts of Invited Talks

Relational Verification of Higher-Order Probabilistic Programs

Gilles Barthe

IMDEA Software Institute, Madrid, Spain

Hyperproperties go beyond the traditional formulation of program verification by considering sets of sets of traces—in contrast to program properties which consider sets of traces. Common instances of hyperproperties include robustness, information flow security, and for probabilistic programs differential privacy. These latter properties are instances of the more restricted class of 2-properties, which contemplate related executions of the same program, or executions of two different programs. These properties can be formally established using lightweight type systems, which are tailored to enfore specific classes of properties, relational program logics, which are tailored to reason about relations between two programs, or product programs which construct from each pair of programs a single product program that emulates their behavior. One challenge, independently of the approach chosen, is to develop methods that support syntax-directed reasoning that is traditionally favoured in standard verification and yet provides sufficient flexibility to accommodate programs that are structurally different or have diverging control flow on different but related inputs.

The talk shall present and compare the different approaches, including Relational Higher-Order Logic [1]. Moreover, it will present several applications, including relational cost and security.

Reference

1. Aguirre, A., Barthe, G., Gaboardi, M., Garg, D., Strub, P.-Y.: A relational logic for higher-order programs. PACMPL 1(ICFP), 21:1–21:29 (2017)

Programming by Examples: PL Meets ML

Sumit Gulwani[1] and Prateek Jain[2]

[1] Microsoft Corporation, Redmond, USA
sumitg@microsoft.com
[2] Microsoft Research, Bangalore, India
prajain@microsoft.com

Abstract. Programming by Examples (PBE) involves synthesizing intended programs in an underlying domain-specific language from example-based specifications. PBE systems are already revolutionizing the application domain of data wrangling and are set to significantly impact several other domains including code refactoring.

There are three key components in a PBE system. (i) A search algorithm that can efficiently search for programs that are consistent with the examples provided by the user. We leverage a divide-and-conquer-based deductive search paradigm that inductively reduces the problem of synthesizing a program expression of a certain kind that satisfies a given specification into sub-problems that refer to sub-expressions or sub-specifications. (ii) Program ranking techniques to pick an intended program from among the many that satisfy the examples provided by the user. We leverage features of the program structure as well of the outputs generated by the program on test inputs. (iii) User interaction models to facilitate usability and debuggability. We leverage active-learning techniques based on clustering inputs and synthesizing multiple programs.

Each of these PBE components leverage both symbolic reasoning and heuristics. We make the case for synthesizing these heuristics from training data using appropriate machine learning methods. This can not only lead to better heuristics, but can also enable easier development, maintenance, and even personalization of a PBE system.

Gradual Enforcement of Program Invariants

Ronald Garcia

University of British Columbia, Vancouver, British Columbia, Canada
rxg@cs.ubc.ca

Abstract. Static and dynamic techniques have long been used to check and enforce properties of program executions. They are often seen as diametrically opposed, as exemplified by the long-running kerfuffle over the merits and deficits of static versus dynamic type checking.

Recently, PL researchers and designers have sought to bridge the divide between these approaches to program checking and analysis. In particular, *gradual typing* sets out to seamlessly combine static and dynamic checking of how closely programs adhere to standard typing disciplines from the literature. In this context, static and dynamic checking and enforcement are treated as complementary rather than conflicting.

In this talk I will discuss the theory and practice of gradual typing. Both have undergone significant development in the last few years. These advances in language design change not only how dynamic and static checking can work together, but also change how we think about each individually.

Synthesizing SystemC Code from Delay Hybrid CSP

Gaogao Yan[1,2], Li Jiao[1], Shuling Wang[1], and Naijun Zhan[1,2]

[1] State Key Laboratory of Computer Science, Institute of Software, Chinese
Academy of Sciences, Beijing, China
{yangg,ljiao,wangsl,znj}@ios.ac.cn
[2] University of Chinese Academy of Sciences, Beijing, China

Abstract. Delay is omnipresent in modern control systems, which can prompt oscillations and may cause deterioration of control performance, invalidate both stability and safety properties. This implies that safety or stability certificates obtained on idealized, delay-free models of systems prone to delayed coupling may be erratic, and further the incorrectness of the executable code generated from these models. However, automated methods for system verification and code generation that ought to address models of system dynamics reflecting delays have not been paid enough attention yet in the computer science community. In our previous work, on one hand, we investigated the verification of delay dynamical and hybrid systems; on the other hand, we also addressed how to synthesize SystemC code from a verified hybrid system modelled by Hybrid CSP (HCSP) without delay. In this paper, we give a first attempt to synthesize SystemC code from a verified delay hybrid system modelled by Delay HCSP (dHCSP), which is an extension of HCSP by replacing ordinary differential equations (ODEs) with delay differential equations (DDEs). We implement a tool to support the automatic translation from dHCSP to SystemC.

Contents

Numerical Reasoning

Invited Contributions

Programming by Examples: PL Meets ML

Sumit Gulwani[1($\boxtimes$)] and Prateek Jain[2]

[1] Microsoft Corporation, Redmond, USA
sumitg@microsoft.com
[2] Microsoft Research, Bangalore, India
prajain@microsoft.com

Abstract. Programming by Examples (PBE) involves synthesizing intended programs in an underlying domain-specific language from example-based specifications. PBE systems are already revolutionizing the application domain of data wrangling and are set to significantly impact several other domains including code refactoring.

There are three key components in a PBE system. (i) A search algorithm that can efficiently search for programs that are consistent with the examples provided by the user. We leverage a divide-and-conquer-based deductive search paradigm that inductively reduces the problem of synthesizing a program expression of a certain kind that satisfies a given specification into sub-problems that refer to sub-expressions or sub-specifications. (ii) Program ranking techniques to pick an intended program from among the many that satisfy the examples provided by the user. We leverage features of the program structure as well of the outputs generated by the program on test inputs. (iii) User interaction models to facilitate usability and debuggability. We leverage active-learning techniques based on clustering inputs and synthesizing multiple programs.

Each of these PBE components leverage both symbolic reasoning and heuristics. We make the case for synthesizing these heuristics from training data using appropriate machine learning methods. This can not only lead to better heuristics, but can also enable easier development, maintenance, and even personalization of a PBE system.

1 Introduction

Program Synthesis is the task of synthesizing a program that satisfies a given specification [1]. The traditional view of program synthesis has been to synthesize programs from logical specifications that relate the inputs and outputs of the program. Programming by Examples (PBE) is a sub-field of program synthesis, where the specification consists of input-output examples, or more generally, output properties over given input states [2]. PBE has emerged as a favorable paradigm for two reasons: (i) the example-based specification in PBE makes it more tractable than general program synthesis. (ii) Example-based specifications are much easier for the users to provide in many scenarios.

© Springer International Publishing AG 2017
B.-Y.E. Chang (Ed.): APLAS 2017, LNCS 10695, pp. 3–20, 2017.
https://doi.org/10.1007/978-3-319-71237-6_1

2   Applications

The two killer applications for programming by examples today are in the space of data transformations/wrangling and code transformations.

2.1   Data Wrangling

Data Wrangling refers to the process of transforming the data from its raw format to a more structured format that is amenable to analysis and visualization. It is estimated that data scientists spend 80% of their time wrangling data. Data is locked up into documents of various types such as text/log files, semi-structured spreadsheets, webpages, JSON/XML, and pdf documents. These documents offer their creators great flexibility in storing and organizing hierarchical data by combining presentation/formatting with the underlying data. However, this makes it extremely hard to extract the underlying data for several tasks such as processing, querying, altering the presentation view, or transforming data to another storage format. PBE can make data wrangling a delightful experience for the masses.

Extraction: A first step in a data wrangling pipeline is often that of ingesting or extracting tabular data from semi-structured formats such as text/log files, web pages, and XML/JSON documents. These documents offer their creators great flexibility in storing and organizing hierarchical data by combining presentation/formatting with the underlying data. However, this makes it extremely hard to extract the relevant data. The FlashExtract PBE technology allows extracting structured (tabular or hierarchical) data out of semi-structured documents from examples [3]. For each field in the output data schema, the user provides positive/negative instances of that field and FlashExtract generates a program to extract all instances of that field. The FlashExtract technology ships as the ConvertFrom-String cmdlet in Powershell in Windows 10, wherein the user provides examples of the strings to be extracted by inserting tags around them in test. The FlashExtract technology also ships in Azure OMS (Operations Management Suite), where it enables extraction of custom fields from log files.

Transformation: The Flash Fill feature, released in Excel 2013 and beyond, is a PBE technology for automating syntactic string transformations, such as converting "FirstName LastName" into "LastName, FirstName" [4]. PBE can also facilitate more sophisticated string transformations that require lookup into other tables [5]. PBE is also a very natural fit for automating transformations of other data types such as numbers [6] and dates [7].

Formatting: Another useful application of PBE is in the space of formatting data tables. This can be useful to convert semi-structured tables found commonly in spreadsheets into proper relational tables [8], or for re-pivoting the underlying hierarchical data that has been locked into a two-dimensional tabular format [9]. PBE can also be useful in automating repetitive formatting in a powerpoint slide deck such as converting all red colored text into green, or switching the direction of all horizontal arrows [10].

2.2 Code Transformations

There are several situations where repetitive code transformations need to be performed and examples can be used to automate this tedious task.

A standard scenario is that of general code refactoring. As software evolves, developers edit program source code to add features, fix bugs, or refactor it for readability, modularity, or performance improvements. For instance, to apply an API update, a developer needs to locate all references to the old API and consistently replace them with the new API. Examples can be used to infer such edits from a few examples [11].

Another important scenario is that of *application migration*—whether it is about moving from on prem to the cloud, or from one framework to another, or simply moving from an old version of a framework to a newer version to keep up with the march of technology. A significant effort is spent in performing repetitive edits to the underlying application code. In particular, for database migration, it is estimated that up to 40% of the developer effort can be spent in performing repetitive code changes in the application code.

Yet another interesting scenario is in the space of feedback generation for programming assignments in programming courses. For large classes such as massive open online courses (MOOCs), manually providing feedback to different students is an unfeasible burden on the teaching staff. We observe that student submissions that exhibit the same fault often need similar fixes. The PBE technology can be used to learn the common fixes from corrections made by teachers on few assignments, and then infer application of these fixes to the remaining assignments, forming basis for automatic feedback [11].

3   PL Meets ML

It is interesting to compare PBE with Machine learning (ML) since both involve example-based training and prediction on new unseen data. PBE learns from very few examples, while ML typically requires large amount of training data. The models generated by PBE are human-readable (in fact, editable programs) unlike many black-box models produced by ML. PBE generates small scripts that are supposed to work with perfect precision on any new valid input, while ML can generate sophisticated models that can achieve high, but not necessarily perfect, precision on new varied inputs. Hence, given their complementary strengths, we believe that PBE is better suited for relatively simple well-defined tasks, while ML is better suited for sophisticated and fuzzy tasks.

Recently, *neural program induction* has been proposed as a fully ML-based alternative to PBE. These techniques develop new neural architectures that learn how to generate outputs for new inputs by using a latent program representation induced by learning some form of neural controller. Various forms of neural

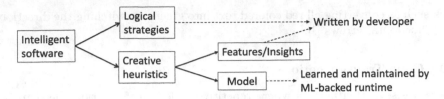

Fig. 1. A proposal for development of intelligent software that facilitates increased developer productivity and increased software intelligence.

controllers have been proposed such as ones that have the ability to read/write to external memory tape [12], stack augmented neural controller [13], or even neural networks augmented with basic arithmetic and logic operations [14]. These approaches typically involve developing a continuous representation of the atomic operations of the network, and then using end-to-end training of a neural controller or reinforcement learning to learn the program behavior. While this is impressive, these techniques aren't a good fit for the PBE task domains of relatively simple well-defined tasks. This is because these techniques don't generate an interpretable model of the learned program, and typically require large computational resources and several thousands of input-output examples per synthesis task. We believe that a big opportunity awaits in carefully combining ML-based data-driven techniques with PL-based logical reasoning approaches to improve a standard PBE system as opposed to replacing it.

3.1 A Perspective on PL Meets ML

AI software often contains two intermingled parts: logical strategies + creative heuristics. Heuristics are difficult to author, debug, and maintain. Heuristics can be decomposed into two parts: insights/features + model/scoring function over those features. We propose that an AI-software developer refactors their intelligent code into logical strategies and declarative features while ML techniques are used to evolve an ideal model or scoring function over those insights with continued feedback from usage of the intelligent software. This has two advantages: (i) Increase in developer's productivity, (ii) Increase in system's intelligence because of better heuristics and those that can adapt differently to different workloads or unpredictable environments (a statically fixed heuristic cannot achieve this).

Figure 1 illustrates this proposed modular construction of intelligent software. Developing an ML model in this framework (where the developer authors logical strategies and declarative insights) poses several interesting open questions since traditional ML techniques are not well-equipped to handle such declarative and symbolic frameworks. Moreover, even the boundary between declarative insights and ML-based models may be fluid. Depending on the exact problem setting as well as the domain, the developer may want to decide which part of the system should follow deterministic logical reasoning and which part should be based on data-driven techniques.

3.2   Using ML to Improve PBE

There are three key components in a PBE engine: search algorithm, ranking strategy, and user interaction models. Each of these components leverage various forms of heuristics. ML can be used to learn these heuristics, thereby improving the effectiveness and maintainability of the various PBE components. In particular, ML can be used to speed up the search process by predicting the success likelihood of various paths in the huge search space. It can be used to learn a better ranking function, allowing users to provide fewer examples and thus increasing usability. It can be used to cluster test data and associate confidence measure over the outputs generated by the synthesized program to drive an effective active-learning session with the user for debuggability.

4   Search Algorithm

Figure 2 shows the architecture of a PBE system. The most involved technical component is the search algorithm, which we discuss in this section. Sections 4.1 and 4.2 describe the two key PL ingredients that form the foundation for designing this search algorithm that is based on logical/symbolic reasoning. Section 4.3 then discusses and speculates how ML can further build over the traditional PL-style logical reasoning to obtain an even more efficient, real-time search algorithm for PBE.

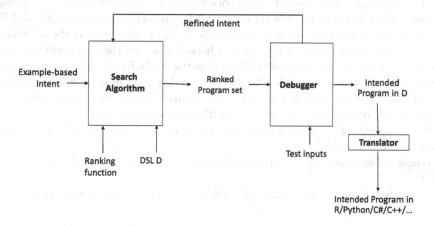

Fig. 2. Programming-by-Examples Architecture. The search algorithm, parameterized by a domain-specific language (DSL) and a ranking function, synthesizes a ranked set of programs from the underlying DSL that are consistent with the examples provided by the user. The debugging component, which leverages additional test inputs, interacts with the user to refine the specification, and the synthesis process is repeated. Once an intended program has been synthesized, it can be translated to a target language using standard syntax-directed translation.

String Expression E:=concat(E_1, E_2) | substr(x, P_1, P_2) | conststr($String$)
Position P:= $Integer$ | pos(x, R_1, R_2, k)

Fig. 3. An example domain-specific language. substr, concat are string operators and conststr represents a constant string constructor. pos operator identifies position of a particular pattern in the input x. $String$ is any constant string and $Integer$ is an arbitrary integer that can be negative as well.

4.1   Domain-Specific Language

A key idea in program synthesis is to restrict the search space to an underlying domain-specific language (DSL) [15,16]. The DSL should be expressive enough to represent a wide variety of tasks in the underlying task domain, but also restricted enough to allow efficient search. We have designed many functional domain-specific languages for this purpose, each of which is characterized by a set of operators and a syntactic restriction on how those operators can be composed with each other (as opposed to allowing all possible type-safe composition of those operators) [2]. A DSL is typically specified as a context-free grammar that consists of one or more production rules for each non-terminal. The right hand side of a production rule can be a non-terminal, an explicit set of program expressions, or a program operator applied to some non-terminals or expressions.

For illustration, we present an extremely simple string manipulation grammar in Fig. 3; this DSL is a heavily stripped down version of the Flash Fill DSL [4]. The language has two key operators for string manipulations: (a) substr operator which takes as input a string x, and two position expressions P_1 and P_2 that evaluate to positions/indices within the string x, and returns the substring between those positions, (b) concat which concatenates the given expressions. The choice for position expression P includes the pos(x,R_1,R_2,k) operator, which returns the kth position within the string x such that (some suffix of) the left side of that position matches with regular expression R_1 and (some prefix of) the right side of that position matches with regular expression R_2.

For example, the following program maps input "evan chang" into "evanchang@cs.colorado.edu".

concat(substr(Input, ϵ, " ", 1), substr(Input, " ", ϵ, −1), conststr("@cs.colorado.edu"))

Note that we overload concat operator to allow for more than 2 operands.

4.2   Deductive Search Methodology

A simple search strategy is to enumerate all programs in order of increasing size by doing a bottom-up enumeration of the grammar [15]. This can be done by maintaining a graph of reachable values starting from the input state in the user-provided example. This simply requires access to the executable semantics of the operators in the DSL. Bottom-up enumeration is very effective for small grammar fragments since executing operators forward is very fast. Some techniques have been proposed to increase the scalability of enumerative search: (i) divide-and-conquer method that decomposes the problem of finding programs that satisfy all examples to that of finding programs, each of which satisfies some subset, and then combining those programs using conditional predicates [17]. (ii) operator-specific lifting functions that can compute the output set from input sets more efficiently than point-wise computation. Lifting functions are essentially the forward transformer for an operator [18].

Unfortunately, bottom-up enumeration does not scale to large grammars because there are often too many constants to start out with. Our search methodology combines bottom-up enumeration with a novel top-down enumeration of the grammar. The top-down enumeration is goal-directed and requires pushing the specification across an operator using its inverse semantics. This is performed using *witness functions* that translate the specification for a program expression of the kind $F(e_1, e_2)$ to specifications for what the sub-expressions e_1 and e_2 should be. The bottom-up search first enumerates smaller sub-expressions before enumerating larger expressions. In contrast, the top-down search first fixes the top-part of an expression and then searches for its sub-expressions.

The overall top-down strategy is essentially a divide-and-conquer methodology that recursively reduces the problem of synthesizing a program expression e of a certain kind and that satisfies a certain specification ψ to simpler sub-problems (where the search is either over sub-expressions of e or over sub-specifications of ψ), followed by appropriately combining those results. The reduction logic for reducing a synthesis problem to simpler synthesis problems depends on the nature of the involved expression e and the inductive specification ψ. If e is a non-terminal in the grammar, then the sub-problems correspond to exploring the various production rules corresponding to e. If e is an operator application $F(e_1, e_2)$, then the sub-problems correspond to exploring multiple sub-goals for each parameter of that operator. As is usually the case with search algorithms, most of these explorations fail. PBE systems achieve real-time efficiency in practice by leveraging heuristics to predict which explorations are more likely to succeed and then either only explore those or explore them preferentially over others.

Machine learning techniques can be used to learn such heuristics in an effective manner. In the next subsection, we provide more details on one such investigation related to predicting the choice over exploring multiple production rules for a grammar non-terminal. In particular, we describe our ML-based problem formulation, our training data collection process as well as some preliminary results.

4.3   ML-Based Search Algorithm

A key ingredient of the top-down search methodology mentioned above is grammar enumeration where while searching for a program expression e of the non-terminal kind, we enumerate all the production rules corresponding to e to obtain a new set of search problems and recursively solve each one of them. The goal of this investigation is to determine the best production rules that we should explore while ignoring certain production rules that are unlikely to provide a desired program. Now, it might seem a bit outlandish to claim that we can determine the correct production rule to explore before even exploring it!

However, many times the provided input-output specification itself provides clues to make such a decision accurately. For example, in the context of the DSL mentioned in Fig. 3, lets consider an example where the input is "evan" and the desired output is "evan@cs.colorado.edu". In this case, even before exploring the productions rules, it is fairly clear that we should apply the concat operator instead of substr operator; a correct program is concat(Input, const-str("@cs.colorado.edu")). Similarly, if our input is "xinyu feng" and the desired output is "xinyu" then it is clear that we should apply the substr operator; a correct program is substr(Input, 1, pos(Input, Alphanumeric, " ", 1)).

But, exploiting the structure in input-output examples along with production rules is quite challenging as these are non-homogeneous structures without a natural vector space representation. Building upon recent advances in natural language processing, our ML-based approach uses a version of neural networks to exploit the structure in input-output examples to estimate the set of best possible production rules to explore. Formally, given the input-output examples represented by ψ, and a set of candidate production rules $P_1, P_2, \ldots, P_k$ whose LHS is our current non-terminal e, we compute a score $s_i = score(\psi, P_i)$ for each candidate rule P_i. This score reflects the probability of synthesis of a desired program if we select rule P_i for the given input-output examples ψ. Note that input-output example specification ψ changes during the search process as we decompose the problem into smaller sub-problems; hence for recursive grammars, we need to compute the scores every time we wish to explore a production rule.

For learning the scoring model, similar to [19], our method embeds input-output examples in a vector space using a popular neural network technique called LSTM (Long Short-Term Memory) [20]. The embedding of a given input-output specification essentially captures its critical features, e.g., if input is a substring of output or if output is a substring of input etc. We then match this embedding against an embedding of the production rule P_i to generate a joint embedding of (ψ, P_i) pair. We then learn a neural-network-based function to map this joint embedding to the final score. Now for prediction, given scores $s_1, s_2, \ldots, s_k$, we select branches with top most scores with large enough margin, i.e., we select rules $P_{i_1}, \ldots, P_{i_\ell}$ for exploration where $s_{i_1} \geq s_{i_2} \cdots \geq s_{i_\ell}$ and $s_{i_\ell} - s_{i_{\ell+1}} \geq \tau$; $\tau > 0$ is a threshold parameter that we discuss later. See Fig. 4 for an overview of our LSTM-based model and the entire pipeline.

To test our technique, we applied it to a much more expressive version of the Flash Fill DSL [4] that includes operators over rich data types such as numbers and dates. For training and testing our technique, we collected 375 benchmarks from real-world customer scenarios. Each benchmark consists of a set of input strings and their corresponding outputs. We selected 300 benchmarks for training and remaining 75 for testing.

For each training benchmark, we generated top 1000 programs using existing top-down enumerative approach and logged relevant information for our grammar enumeration. For example, when we want to expand certain grammar

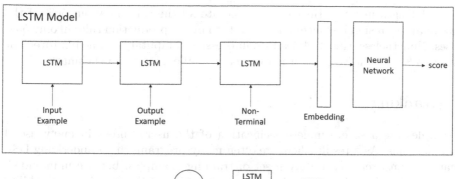

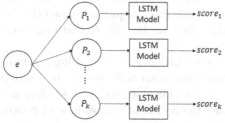

Fig. 4. LSTM-based model for computing score for the candidate set of production rules $P_1, \ldots, P_k$ during the grammar expansion process. The top figure shows details of the ML model used to compute the score for a candidate production rule when placed in the context of the given input-output examples.

symbol (say expr in Fig. 3) with the goal of mapping given inputs to required outputs, we log all the relevant production rules P_i, $\forall i$ (i.e., rules in Line 1 of Fig. 3). We also log the score s_i of the top program that is generated by applying production rule P_i. That is, each training instance is (ψ, P_i, s_i) for a given node with input-output examples ψ. We use standard DNN tools to train the model for grammar enumeration. That is, whenever we need to decide on which production rule to select for expansion, we compute score for each possible rule P_i and select the rules whose scores are higher than the remaining rules by a margin of τ.

Threshold τ is an interesting knob that helps decide between exploration vs exploitation. That is, smaller τ implies that we trust our ML model completely and select the best choice presented by the model. On the other hand, larger τ forces system to be more conservative and use ML model sparingly, i.e., only when it is highly confident. For example, on the 75 test benchmarks, setting $\tau = 0$ i.e. selecting ML model's predicted production rule for every grammar expansion decision, we select the correct production rule in 92% of the instances. Unfortunately, selecting a wrong production rule 8% of the times might lead to synthesis of a relatively poor program or in worst case, no program. However, by increasing τ to 0.1, we can increase chances of selection of a correct production rule to 99%. Although in this case, for nearly 50% instances the ML model does not differentiate between production rules, i.e., the predicted scores are all within

$\tau = 0.1$ length interval. Hence, we enumerate all the rules in about 50% of the grammar expansion instances and are able to prune production rules in only 50% cases. Nonetheless, this itself leads to impressive computation time improvement of up to 8x over naïve exploration for many challenging test benchmarks.

5 Ranking

Examples are a severe under-specification of the user's intent in many useful task domains. As a result, there are often many programs in an underlying DSL that are consistent with a given set of training examples, but are unintended, i.e., they would produce an undesired output on some other test input. Usability concerns further necessitate that we are able to learn an intended program from as few examples as possible.

PBE systems address this challenge by leveraging a ranking scheme to select between different programs consistent with the examples provided by the user. Ideally, we want to bias the ranking of programs so that *natural* programs are ranked higher. We capture the notion of *naturalness* of programs by performing training on real-world datasets.

The ranking can either be performed in a phase subsequent to the one that identifies the many programs that are consistent with the examples [21], or it can be in-built as part of the search process [22,23]. Furthermore, the ranking can be a function of the program structure or additional test inputs.

5.1 Ranking Based on Program Structure

A basic ranking scheme can be specified by defining a preference order over program expressions based on their features. Two general principles that are useful across various domains are: prefer small expressions (inspired by the classic notion of Kolmogorov complexity) and prefer expressions with fewer constants (to force generalization). For specific DSLs, more specific preferences or features can be defined based on the operators that occur in the DSL.

5.2 Ranking Based on Test Inputs

The likelihood of a program being the intended one not only depends on the structure of that program, but also on features of the input data on which that program will be executed and the output data produced by executing that program. In some PBE settings, the synthesizer often has access to some additional test inputs on which the intended program is supposed to be executed. Singh showed how to leverage these additional test inputs to guess a reduction in the search space with the goal to speed up synthesis and rank programs better [24]. Ellis and Gulwani observed that the additional test inputs can be used to re-rank programs based on how similar are the outputs produced by those programs on the test inputs to the outputs in the training/example inputs provided by the user [25].

For instance, consider the task of extracting years from input strings of the kind shown in the table below.

Input	Output
Missing page numbers, 1993	1993
64–67, 1995	1995

The program $P1$: "Extract the last number" can perform the intended task. However, if the user provides only the first example, another reasonable program that can be synthesized is $P2$: "Extract the first number". There is no clear way to rank $P1$ higher than $P2$ from just examining their structure. However, the output produced by $P1$ (on the various test inputs), namely $\{1993, 1995, \ldots, \}$ is a more meaningful set (of 4 digit numbers that are likely years) than the one produced by $P2$, namely (which manifests greater variability). The meaningfulness or similarity of the generated output can be captured via various features such as IsYear, numeric deviation, IsPersonName, and number of characters.

5.3 ML-based Ranking Function

Typically, *natural* or intended programs tend to have subtle properties that cannot be captured by just one feature or by an arbitrary combination of the multiple features identified above; empirical results presented in Fig. 5 confirm this hypothesis where the accuracy of the shortest-program-based ranker or a random ranker is poor. Hence, we need to learn a ranking function that appropriately combines the features in order to produce the intended natural programs. In fact, learning rankers over programs/sub-expressions represents an exciting domain where insights from ML and PL can have an interesting and impactful interplay.

Below, we present one such case study where we learn a ranking function that ranks sub-expressions and programs during the search process itself. We learn the ranking function using training data that is extracted from diverse real-world customer scenarios. However learning such a ranking function that can be used to rank sub-expressions during the search process itself poses certain unique challenges. For example, we need to rank various non-homogeneous sub-expressions during each step of the search process but the feedback about our ranking decisions is provided only after synthesis of the final program. Moreover, the ranking function captures the intended program only if the final program is correct, hence, a series of "correct" ranking decisions over various sub-expressions may be nullified by one incorrect ranking decision.

To solve the above set of problems, we implement a simple program-embedding-based approach. Consider a program P that is composed of expressions $\{e_1, \ldots, e_m\}$. Now, using the previously mentioned classes of features, we embed each of our sub-expression in a d-dimensional vector space. Formally, $\phi(e_i) \in \mathbb{R}^d$ is a d-dimensional embedding of sub-expression e_i and the program P itself is represented as a weighted combination of these sub-expressions:

$\phi(P) = \sum_i w_i \phi(e_i)$, where $w_i \geq 0$ are positive weights that are also learned depending on the type of sub-expression e_i. That is, $\phi(P)$ is a d-dimensional vector representation of program P.

We now pose the ranking problem as: find $\theta \in \mathbb{R}^d$ s.t. $\sum_j \theta_j \phi(P_a)_j \geq \sum_j \theta_j \phi(P_b)_j$ where P_a is a "correct" program, i.e., it produces desired output on training datasets and P_b is an "incorrect" program. θ_j and $\phi(P)_j$ represents the j-th coordinate of θ and $\phi(P)$ respectively.

For learning θ as well as weights w_i, we use training benchmarks where each benchmark consists of a set of inputs and their corresponding outputs. For each benchmark, we synthesize 1000 programs using the first input-output pair in that benchmark, treating it as an example input-output pair. We categorize a synthesized program as "correct" if it generates correct output on all the other benchmark inputs, and "incorrect" otherwise. We then embed each sub-expression and the program in d-dimensional space using hand-crafted features. Our features reflect certain key properties of the programs, e.g., length of the program etc. We then use straightforward block-coordinate descent based methods to learn θ, w_i's in an iterative fashion.

Empirical Results: Similar to search experiments described in Sect. 4.3, we learn our ranking function using a collection of important benchmarks from real-world customer scenarios. We select about 75 benchmarks for training and test our system on remaining 300 benchmarks. We evaluate performance of our ranker using precision@k metric, which is the fraction of test benchmarks in which at least one "correct" program lies in the top-k programs (as ranked by our ranker). We also compute precision@k for different specification sizes, i.e., for different number of input-output examples being supplied.

The tables in Fig. 5 compare accuracy (measured in precision@k) of our method with two baselines: (a) random ranker, which at each node selects a random sub-expression, (b) shortest program, which selects programs with the smallest number of operators. Note that with 1 input-output example, our method is 50% more accurate than the two baselines. Naturally with 4 examples, baselines' performance also improves as there are very few programs that satisfy 4 examples, i.e., with 4 input-output examples searching for "any" consistent program is enough. However, as mentioned earlier, in many settings providing even 4 examples is going to burden the user significantly and hence renders

No. I/O	Random	Shortest	ML-Ranker
1	14.2%	2.4%	69.2%
2	53.7%	77.5%	91.4%
3	77.0%	88.0%	96.5%
4	86.6%	94.4%	98.6%

No. I/O	Random	Shortest	ML-Ranker
1	19.1%	9.3%	70.6%
2	57.1%	74.0%	88.1%
3	77.3%	86.8%	94.8%
4	86.8%	92.8%	97.8%

Fig. 5. Ranking: Left table compares precision@1 accuracy for various methods when supplied different number of input-output example pairs while right table compares precision@5 accuracy. Our ML-ranker provides significantly higher accuracy and estimates correct program for 69% test benchmarks using just one input-output example.

the solution impractical. Moreover, with bigger and more powerful grammars, even 4 examples might lead to several thousands of consistent programs, thus necessitating a data driven ranker of the sub-expressions/programs.

6   Interactivity

While use of ranking in the synthesis methodology attempts to avoid selecting an unintended program, it cannot always succeed. Hence, it is important to design appropriate user interaction models for the PBE paradigm that can provide the equivalent of debugging experience in standard programming environments. There are two important goals for a user interaction model that is associated with a PBE technology [26]. First, it should provide transparency to the user about the synthesized program(s). Second, it should guide the user in resolving ambiguities in the provided specification.

In order to facilitate transparency, the synthesized program can be displayed to the user. In that context, it would be useful to have readability as an additional criterion during synthesis. The program can also be paraphrased in natural language, especially to facilitate understanding by non-programmers.

In order to resolve ambiguities, we can present multiple synthesized programs to the user and ask the user to pick between those. More interestingly, we can also leverage availability of other test input data on which the synthesized program is expected to be executed. This can be done in few different ways. A set of representative test inputs can be obtained by clustering the test inputs and picking a representative element from each cluster [27]. The user can then check the results of the synthesized program on those representative inputs. Alternatively, clustering can also be performed on the outputs produced by the synthesized program. Yet, another approach can be to leverage *distinguishing inputs* [28]. The idea here is to synthesize multiple programs that are consistent with the examples provided by the user but differ on some test inputs. The PBE system can then ask the user to provide the intended output on one or more of these distinguishing inputs. The choice for the distinguishing input to be presented to the user can be based on its expected potential to distinguish between most of those synthesized programs.

There are many heuristic decisions in the above-mentioned interaction models that can ideally be learned using ML techniques such as what makes a program more readable, or which set of programs to present to the user, or how to cluster the input or output columns. Below, we discuss one such investigation related to clustering of strings in a column.

6.1   Clustering of Strings

We propose an agglomerative-hierarchical-clustering-based method for clustering a collection of strings. Intuitively, we want to cluster strings such that each cluster can be represented by a specific but natural description. For example, given strings $\{1990, 1995, 210\text{BC}, 450\text{BC}\}$, we want to find the two clusters that can be described by the regular expressions Digit^4 and $\text{Digit}^3 \cdot \text{BC}$.

To partition a given set of strings into such natural clusters, we learn regular expressions as cluster descriptions, using program synthesis over a DSL that describes regular expressions [27]. Our clustering algorithm first randomly samples a few strings and then generates candidate regular expressions by synthesizing regular expressions that describe various pairs of strings. We define a measure to compute the cost of describing a string using a candidate regular expression. Using this cost measure, we apply standard complete-linkage agglomerative hierarchical clustering to obtain compact clusters with low cost of describing the contained strings with a regular expression.

For example, given strings from a dataset containing postal codes such as: $\{99518, 61021\text{-}9150, 2645, \text{K0K 2C0}, 61604\text{-}5004, \text{S7K7K9},...\}$, our system identifies clusters described by regular expressions such as:

- Digit^5
- Digit^4
- $\text{UpperCase} \cdot \text{Digit} \cdot \text{UpperCase} \cdot \text{Space} \cdot \text{Digit} \cdot \text{UpperCase} \cdot \text{Digit}$
- $61\text{Digit}^3 - \text{Digit}^4$
- S7K7K9

Note that these regular expressions not only capture the key clusters such as Digit^5 etc., but they also expose certain anomalies such as S7K7K9. We evaluated our system over real-world datasets, and used a Normalized Mutual Information (NMI) metric, which is a standard clustering metric, to measure the accuracy of our system in its ability to identify the expected clusters.

We observe that, given enough computation time, our system is able to achieve nearly optimal NMI of ≈ 1.0. Moreover, by using appropriate sampling and synthesizing regular expressions, we can speed up the computation by a factor of 2 despite recovering clusters with over 0.95 NMI. We refer the interested readers to [27] for more details.

7   Future Directions

Applications: General-purpose programmable robots may be a common household entity in a few decades from now. Each household will have its own unique geography for the robot to navigate and a unique set of chores for the robot to perform. Example-based training would be an effective means for personalizing robots for a household.

Multi-model intent specification: While this article has focused on leveraging examples as specification of intent, certain classes of tasks are best described using natural language such as spreadsheet queries [29] and smartphone scripts [30]. The next generation of programming experience shall be built around multi-modal specifications that are natural and easy for the user to provide. The new paradigm shall allow the user to express intent using combination of various means [31] such as examples, demonstrations, natural language, keywords, and sketches [32].

Predictive Synthesis: For some task domains, it is often possible to predict the user's intent without any input-output examples, i.e., from input-only examples. For instance, extracting tables from web pages or log files, or splitting a column into multiple columns [18]. While providing examples is already much more convenient than authoring one-off scripts, having the system guess the intent without any examples can power novel user experiences.

Adaptive Synthesis: Another interesting future direction is to build systems that learn user preferences based on past user interactions across different program synthesis sessions. For instance, the underlying ranking can be dynamically updated. This can pave the way for personalization and learning across users within an organization or within the cloud.

PL meets ML: While PL has democratized access to machine implementations of precise ideas, ML has democratized access to discovering heuristics to deal with fuzzy and noisy situations. The new AI revolution requires frameworks that can facilitate creation of AI-infused software and applications. Synergies between PL and ML can help lay the foundation for construction of such frameworks [33–36]. For instance, language features can be developed that allow the developer to express non-determinism with some default resolution strategies that can then automatically become smarter with usage. As opposed to traditional AI-based domains such as vision, text, bioinformation, such self-improving systems present entirely different data formats and pose unique challenges that foreshadow an interesting full-fledged research area with opportunities to impact how we program and think about interacting with computer systems in general.

8 Conclusion

PBE is set to revolutionize the programming experience for both developers and end users. It can provide a 10–100x productivity increase for developers in some task domains, and also enable computer users, 99% of whom are non-programmers, to create small scripts to automate repetitive tasks. In fact, several studies show that data scientists spend 80% time wrangling data while developers spend up to 40% time refactoring code in a typical application migration scenario. Hence, data wrangling and code refactoring seem to be two killer applications for PBE today where PBE-based systems stand to significantly improve productivity of data scientists as well as developers.

Building a usable and practical PBE system is challenging and can leverage insights from both PL (for symbolic reasoning) and ML (for heuristics). A key challenge in PBE is to search for programs that are consistent with the examples provided by the user. On the symbolic reasoning side, our search methodology in PBE leverages two key ideas: restrict the search to a domain-specific language specified as a grammar, and perform a goal-directed top-down search that leverages inverse semantics of operators to decompose a goal into a choice of multiple sub-goals. However, this search can be made even more tractable by learning tactics to prefer certain choices over others during both grammar enumeration and sub-goal selection.

Another key challenge in PBE is to understand the user's intent in the face of ambiguity that is inherent in example-based specifications, and furthermore, to understand it from as few examples as possible. For this, we leverage use of a ranking function with the goal of the search now being to pick the highest ranked program that is consistent with the examples provided by the user. The ranker is a function of various symbolic features of a program such as size, number of constants, and use of a certain combination of operators. It is also a function of the outputs generated by the program (non-null or not, same type as the example outputs or not) and more generally the execution traces of the program on new test inputs. While various PL concepts go into defining the features of a ranking function, ML-based techniques combine these features so that performance of the ranker is good over real-world customer scenarios.

A third challenge relates to debuggability: provide transparency to the user about the synthesized program and help the user to refine the specification in an interactive loop. We have investigated user interaction models that leverage concepts from both PL and ML including active learning based on synthesis of multiple top-ranked programs, clustering of inputs and outputs to identify discrepancies, and navigation through a large program set represented succinctly as a grammar.

All the above-mentioned directions highlight opportunities to design novel techniques that carefully combine symbolic reasoning and declarative insights with novel ML models to solve the various technical challenges associated with a PBE system. We believe that the ongoing AI revolution shall further drive novel synergies between PL and ML to facilitate creation of intelligent software in general. PBE systems, and more generally program synthesis systems that relate to real-time intent understanding, are a great case study for investigating ideas in this space.

Acknowledgments. We thank Nagarajan Natarajan, Naren Datha, Danny Simmons, Abhishek Mohta, Alex Polozov, and Daniel Perelman for their participation in the ongoing unpublished work that we have described in this article related to using ML techniques for search and ranking. We thank the entire PROSE team (https://microsoft.github.io/prose/team/) that has been developing and productizing the PBE technology inside many Microsoft products while also inspiring relevant research problem definitions. We thank Sriram Rajamani, Rishabh Singh, and Joseph Sirosh for stimulating discussions related to the topics discussed in this article.

References

1. Gulwani, S., Polozov, O., Singh, R.: Program synthesis. Found. Trends Program. Lang. **4**(1–2), 1–119 (2017)
2. Gulwani, S.: Programming by examples - and its applications in data wrangling. In: Dependable Software Systems Engineering, pp. 137–158 (2016)
3. Le, V., Gulwani, S.: FlashExtract: a framework for data extraction by examples. In: PLDI, pp. 542–553 (2014)

4. Gulwani, S.: Automating string processing in spreadsheets using input-output examples. In: POPL, pp. 317–330 (2011)
5. Singh, R., Gulwani, S.: Learning semantic string transformations from examples. PVLDB 5(8), 740–751 (2012)
6. Singh, R., Gulwani, S.: Synthesizing number transformations from input-output examples. In: CAV, pp. 634–651 (2012)
7. Singh, R., Gulwani, S.: Transforming spreadsheet data types using examples. In: Proceedings of the 43rd Annual ACM SIGPLAN-SIGACT Symposium on Principles of Programming Languages, POPL 2016, St. Petersburg, FL, USA, January 20–22, 2016, pp. 343–356 (2016)
8. Barowy, D.W., Gulwani, S., Hart, T., Zorn, B.G.: FlashRelate: extracting relational data from semi-structured spreadsheets using examples. In: Proceedings of the 36th ACM SIGPLAN Conference on Programming Language Design and Implementation, Portland, OR, USA, June 15–17, 2015, pp. 218–228 (2015)
9. Harris, W.R., Gulwani, S.: Spreadsheet table transformations from examples. In: PLDI, pp. 317–328 (2011)
10. Raza, M., Gulwani, S., Milic-Frayling, N.: Programming by example using least general generalizations. In: AAAI, pp. 283–290 (2014)
11. Rolim, R., Soares, G., D'Antoni, L., Polozov, O., Gulwani, S., Gheyi, R., Suzuki, R., Hartmann, B.: Learning syntactic program transformations from examples. In: Proceedings of the 39th International Conference on Software Engineering, ICSE 2017, Buenos Aires, Argentina, May 20–28, 2017, pp. 404–415 (2017)
12. Graves, A., Wayne, G., Reynolds, M., Harley, T., Danihelka, I., Grabska-Barwinska, A., Colmenarejo, S.G., Grefenstette, E., Ramalho, T., Agapiou, J., Badia, A.P., Hermann, K.M., Zwols, Y., Ostrovski, G., Cain, A., King, H., Summerfield, C., Blunsom, P., Kavukcuoglu, K., Hassabis, D.: Hybrid computing using a neural network with dynamic external memory. Nature 538(7626), 471–476 (2016)
13. Joulin, A., Mikolov, T.: Inferring algorithmic patterns with stack-augmented recurrent nets. In: NIPS, pp. 190–198 (2015)
14. Neelakantan, A., Le, Q.V., Sutskever, I.: Neural programmer: inducing latent programs with gradient descent. CoRR abs/1511.04834 (2015)
15. Alur, R., Bodík, R., Dallal, E., Fisman, D., Garg, P., Juniwal, G., Kress-Gazit, H., Madhusudan, P., Martin, M.M.K., Raghothaman, M., Saha, S., Seshia, S.A., Singh, R., Solar-Lezama, A., Torlak, E., Udupa, A.: Syntax-guided synthesis. In: Dependable Software Systems Engineering, pp. 1–25 (2015)
16. Gulwani, S., Harris, W.R., Singh, R.: Spreadsheet data manipulation using examples. Commun. ACM 55(8), 97–105 (2012)
17. Alur, R., Radhakrishna, A., Udupa, A.: Scaling enumerative program synthesis via divide and conquer. In: TACAS, pp. 319–336 (2017)
18. Raza, M., Gulwani, S.: Automated data extraction using predictive program synthesis. In: AAAI, pp. 882–890 (2017)
19. Devlin, J., Uesato, J., Bhupatiraju, S., Singh, R., Mohamed, A., Kohli, P.: Robustfill: neural program learning under noisy I/O. In: ICML (2017)
20. Hochreiter, S., Schmidhuber, J.: Long short-term memory. Neural Comput. 9(8), 1735–1780 (1997)
21. Singh, R., Gulwani, S.: Predicting a correct program in programming by example. In: Kroening, D., Păsăreanu, C.S. (eds.) CAV 2015. LNCS, vol. 9206, pp. 398–414. Springer, Cham (2015). https://doi.org/10.1007/978-3-319-21690-4_23

22. Menon, A.K., Tamuz, O., Gulwani, S., Lampson, B.W., Kalai, A.: A machine learning framework for programming by example. In: Proceedings of the 30th International Conference on Machine Learning, ICML 2013, Atlanta, GA, USA, 16–21 June 2013, pp. 187–195 (2013)
23. Balog, M., Gaunt, A.L., Brockschmidt, M., Nowozin, S., Tarlow, D.: Deepcoder: learning to write programs. In: ICLR (2017)
24. Singh, R.: Blinkfill: semi-supervised programming by example for syntactic string transformations. PVLDB 9(10), 816–827 (2016)
25. Ellis, K., Gulwani, S.: Learning to learn programs from examples: going beyond program structure. In: IJCAI, pp. 1638–1645 (2017)
26. Mayer, M., Soares, G., Grechkin, M., Le, V., Marron, M., Polozov, O., Singh, R., Zorn, B.G., Gulwani, S.: User interaction models for disambiguation in programming by example. In: UIST, pp. 291–301 (2015)
27. Padhi, S., Jain, P., Perelman, D., Polozov, O., Gulwani, S., Millstein, T.: Flashprofile: interactive synthesis of syntactic profiles. arXiv preprint arXiv:1709.05725 (2017)
28. Jha, S., Gulwani, S., Seshia, S.A., Tiwari, A.: Oracle-guided component-based program synthesis. In: ICSE, pp. 215–224 (2010)
29. Gulwani, S., Marron, M.: Nlyze: interactive programming by natural language for spreadsheet data analysis and manipulation. In: SIGMOD, pp. 803–814 (2014)
30. Le, V., Gulwani, S., Su, Z.: Smartsynth: synthesizing smartphone automation scripts from natural language. In: The 11th Annual International Conference on Mobile Systems, Applications, and Services (MobiSys), pp. 193–206 (2013)
31. Raza, M., Gulwani, S., Milic-Frayling, N.: Compositional program synthesis from natural language and examples. In: IJCAI, pp. 792–800 (2015)
32. Solar-Lezama, A.: Program Synthesis by Sketching. Ph.D. thesis, University of California, Berkeley (2008)
33. Simpkins, C.: Integrating reinforcement learning into a programming language. In: Proceedings of the Twenty-Fourth AAAI Conference on Artificial Intelligence, AAAI 2010, Atlanta, Georgia, USA, July 11–15, 2010 (2010)
34. Bielik, P., Raychev, V., Vechev, M.T.: Programming with "big code": Lessons, techniques and applications. In: 1st Summit on Advances in Programming Languages, SNAPL 2015, May 3–6, 2015, Asilomar, California, USA, pp. 41–50 (2015)
35. Feser, J.K., Brockschmidt, M., Gaunt, A.L., Tarlow, D.: Neural functional programming. CoRR abs/1611.01988 (2016)
36. Singh, R., Kohli, P.: AP: artificial programming. In: 2nd Summit on Advances in Programming Languages, SNAPL 2017, May 7–10, 2017, Asilomar, CA, USA, pp. 16:1–16:12 (2017)

Synthesizing SystemC Code from Delay Hybrid CSP

Gaogao Yan[1,2], Li Jiao[1], Shuling Wang[1(✉)], and Naijun Zhan[1,2(✉)]

[1] State Key Laboratory of Computer Science, Institute of Software,
Chinese Academy of Sciences, Beijing, China
{yangg,ljiao,wangsl,znj}@ios.ac.cn
[2] University of Chinese Academy of Sciences, Beijing, China

Abstract. Delay is omnipresent in modern control systems, which can prompt oscillations and may cause deterioration of control performance, invalidate both stability and safety properties. This implies that safety or stability certificates obtained on idealized, delay-free models of systems prone to delayed coupling may be erratic, and further the incorrectness of the executable code generated from these models. However, automated methods for system verification and code generation that ought to address models of system dynamics reflecting delays have not been paid enough attention yet in the computer science community. In our previous work, on one hand, we investigated the verification of delay dynamical and hybrid systems; on the other hand, we also addressed how to synthesize SystemC code from a verified hybrid system modelled by Hybrid CSP (HCSP) without delay. In this paper, we give a first attempt to synthesize SystemC code from a verified delay hybrid system modelled by Delay HCSP (dHCSP), which is an extension of HCSP by replacing ordinary differential equations (ODEs) with delay differential equations (DDEs). We implement a tool to support the automatic translation from dHCSP to SystemC.

Keywords: Delay dynamical systems · Approximate bisimulation · Code generation · Delay hybrid CSP · SystemC

1 Introduction

Model-Driven Design (MDD) is considered as an effective way of developing reliable complex embedded systems (ESs), and has been successfully applied in industry [17,20], therefore drawn increasing attentions recently. A challenging problem in MDD is to transform a verified abstract model at high-level step by step to more concrete models at lower levels, and to executable code at the end. To make sure that the final code generated in MDD is correct and reliable,

This work is partially supported by "973 Program" under grant No. 2014CB340701, by NSFC under grants 61625206, 61732001 and 91418204, by CDZ project CAP (GZ 1023), and by the CAS/SAFEA International Partnership Program for Creative Research Teams.

B.-Y.E. Chang (Ed.): APLAS 2017, LNCS 10695, pp. 21–41, 2017.
https://doi.org/10.1007/978-3-319-71237-6_2

the transformation process must be guaranteed to preserve consistency between observational behaviors of the models at different levels in a rigorous way. However, this is difficult, due to the inherent complexity of most ESs, especially for hybrid systems, which contain complicated behaviour, like continuous and discrete dynamics, and the complex interactions between them, time-delay, and so on, while code only contains discrete actions. Obviously, the exact equivalence between them can never be achieved, due to the unavoidable error of discretization of continuous dynamics of hybrid systems.

As an effective way for analyzing hybrid systems and their discretization, approximate bisimulation [14] can address the above problem. Instead of requiring observational behaviors of two systems to be exactly identical, it allows errors but requires the distance between two systems remains bounded by some precisions. In our previous work [24], we used Hybrid CSP (HCSP), an extension of CSP by introducing ordinary differential equations (ODEs) for modelling continuous evolutions and interrupts for modelling interaction between continuous and discrete dynamics, as the modelling language for hybrid systems; and then, we extended the notion of approximate bisimulation to general hybrid systems modelled as HCSP processes; lastly, we presented an algorithm to discretize an HCSP process (a control model) by a discrete HCSP process (an algorithm model), and proved that they are approximately bisimilar if the original HCSP process satisfies the globally asymptotical stability (GAS) condition. Here the GAS condition requires the ODEs starting from any initial state can always infinitely approach to its equilibrium point as time proceeds [8]. Recently, in [26], we further considered how to discretize an HCSP process without GAS, and refine the discretized HCSP process to SystemC code, which is approximately bisimilar to the original HCSP process in a given bounded time.

On the other hand, in practice, delay is omnipresent in modern control systems. For instance, in a distributed real-time control system, control commands may depend on communication with sensors and actuators over a communication network introducing latency. This implies that safety or stability certificates obtained on idealized, delay-free models of systems prone to delayed coupling may be erratic, and further the incorrectness of the code generated from these models. However, automated methods for system verification and code generation that ought to address models of system dynamics reflecting delays have not been paid enough attention yet in the computer science community.

Zou et al. proposed in [28] a safe enclosure method to automatic stability analysis and verification of delay differential equations by using interval-based Taylor over-approximation to enclose a set of functions by a parametric Taylor series with parameters in interval form. Prajna et al. extended the barrier certificate method for ODEs to the polynomial time-delay differential equations setting, in which the safety verification problem is formulated as a problem of solving sum-of-square programs [23]. Huang et al. presents a technique for simulation based time-bounded invariant verification of nonlinear networked dynamical systems with delayed interconnections by computing bounds on the sensitivity of trajectories (or solutions) to changes in initial states and inputs of the system [18]. A similar simulation method integrating error analysis of the numeric solving and the sensitivity-related state bloating algorithms was proposed in [11] to obtain safe enclosures of time-bounded reach sets for systems modelled by DDEs.

However, in the literature, there is few work on how to refine a verified ES model with delay to executable code in MDD. In this paper, we address this issue, and the main contributions can be summarized as follows:

- First of all, we extend HCSP by allowing delay, called Delay HCSP (*d*HCSP), which is achieved by replacing ODEs with DDEs in HCSP. Obviously, HCSP is a proper subset of *d*HCSP as all ODEs can be seen as specific DDEs in which time delay is zero. Then, we propose the notion of *approximately bisimilar* over *d*HCSP processes.
- In [11], the authors presented an approach to discretizing a DDE by a sequence of states corresponding to discrete time-stamps and meanwhile the error bound that defines the distance from the trajectory is computed automatically on-the-fly. As a result, by adjusting step size of the discretization, the given precision can be guaranteed. Inspired by their work, we consider how to discretize a *d*HCSP process *S* such that the discretized *d*HCSP process is approximately bisimilar to *S*. This is done by defining a set of rules and proving that any *d*HCSP process *S* and its discretization are approximately bisimilar within bounded time with respect to the given precision.
- Finally, we present a set of code generation rules from discrete *d*HCSP to executable SystemC code and prove the equivalence between them.

We implement a prototypical tool to automatically transform a *d*HCSP process to SystemC code and provide some case studies to illustrate the above approach. Due to space limitation, the proofs of theorems in this paper are available in [25].

1.1 Related Work

Generating reliable code from control models is a dream of embedded engineering but difficult. For some popular models such as Esterel [10], Statecharts [16], and Lustre [15], code generation is supported. However, they do not take continuous behavior into consideration. Code generation is also supported in some commercial tools such as Simulink [2], Rational Rose [1], and TargetLink [3], but the correctness between the model and the code generated from it is not formally guaranteed, as they mainly focus on the numerical errors. The same issue exists in SHIFT [12], a modelling language for hybrid automata. Generating code from a special hybrid model, CHARON [5], was studied in [6,7,19]. Particularly, in order to ensure the correctness between a CHARON model and its generated code, a formal criteria *faithful implementation* is proposed in [7], but it can only guarantee the code model is under-approximate to the original hybrid model. The main difference between the above works and ours lies in that the delayed dynamics is considered for the code generation from hybrid models in our work.

For the discretization of DDEs, we can refer to some existing works which focus on the verification of systems containing delayed differential dynamics. In [28], a method for analyzing the stability and safety of a special class of DDEs was proposed, which cannot deal with the mixed ODE-DDE form. In [22], the authors proposed a method for constructing a symbolic model from an incrementally input-to-state stable (δ-ISS) nonlinear time-delay system, and moreover proved the symbolic model and the original model are approximately bisimilar. After that, they proved the same result for the incrementally input-delay-to-state stable (δ-IDSS) nonlinear time-delay system with unknown and time-varying delays in [21]. Unfortunately, the δ-ISS and δ-IDSS condition are difficult to check in practice. A simulation-based method is proposed in [18] for computing an over-approximate reachable set of a time-delayed nonlinear networked dynamical system. Within this approach, a significant function (i.e., the IS discrepancy function), used for bounding the distance between two trajectories, is difficult to find for general dynamical systems. In [11], a further extension of [18] that can handle any kind of DDEs with constant time delays is introduced, which can be appropriately used for the discretization of DDEs in dHCSP. But no work is available on how to generate executable code from a verified model with delay.

The rest of this paper is organized as: Some preliminary notions on DDEs and SystemC are introduced in Sect. 2. Section 3 extends HCSP to dHCSP and defines the approximate bisimulation on dHCSP. In Sect. 4, the discretization of dHCSP processes is presented and the correctness of the discretization is proved. The translation from discrete dHCSP to SystemC code is presented in Sect. 5. In Sect. 6, a case study is provided to illustrate our approach. Section 7 concludes the paper and discusses the future work.

2   Preliminaries

In this section, we introduce some preliminary knowledge that will be used later.

2.1   Delay Dynamical Systems

For a vector $\mathbf{x} \in \mathbb{R}^n$, $\|\mathbf{x}\|$ denotes its L^2 norm, i.e., $\|\mathbf{x}\| = \sqrt{x_1^2 + x_2^2 + ... + x_n^2}$. Given a vector $\mathbf{x} \in \mathbb{R}^n$ and $\epsilon \in \mathbb{R}_0^+$, $N(\mathbf{x}, \epsilon)$ is defined as the ϵ-neighbourhood of $\mathbf{x}$, i.e., $N(\mathbf{x}, \epsilon) = \{\mathbf{y} \in \mathbb{R}^n \mid \|\mathbf{x} - \mathbf{y}\| \le \epsilon\}$. Then, for a set $S \subseteq \mathbb{R}^n$, $N(S, \epsilon)$ is defined as $N(S, \epsilon) = \bigcup_{\mathbf{x} \in S}\{\mathbf{y} \in \mathbb{R}^n \mid \|\mathbf{x} - \mathbf{y}\| \le \epsilon\}$, and $conv(S)$ is denoted as the convex hull of S. If S is compact, $dia(S) = sup_{\mathbf{x}, \mathbf{x}' \in S}\|\mathbf{x} - \mathbf{x}'\|$ denotes its diameter.

In this paper, we consider delay dynamical systems governed by the form:

$$\begin{cases} \dot{\mathbf{x}}(t) = \mathbf{f}(\mathbf{x}(t), \mathbf{x}(t - r_1), ..., \mathbf{x}(t - r_k)), \ t \in [0, \infty) \\ \mathbf{x}(t) = \mathbf{g}(t), \qquad\qquad\qquad\qquad\quad t \in [-r_k, 0] \end{cases} \tag{1}$$

where $\mathbf{x} \in \mathbb{R}^n$ is the state, $\dot{\mathbf{x}}(t)$ denotes the derivative of $\mathbf{x}$ with respect to t, and $\mathbf{x}(t) = \mathbf{g}(t)$ is the *initial condition*, where $\mathbf{g}$ is assumed to be $C^0[-r_k, 0]$. Without loss of generality, we assume the delay terms are ordered as $r_k > ... > r_1 > 0$.

A function $X(\cdot) : [-r_k, \nu) \rightarrow \mathbb{R}^n$ is said to be a *trajectory* (solution) of (1) on $[-r_k, \nu)$, if $X(t) = \mathbf{g}(t)$ for all $t \in [-r_k, 0]$ and $\dot{X}(t) = \mathbf{f}(X(t), X(t - r_1), ..., X(t - r_k))$ for all $t \in [0, \nu)$. In order to ensure the existence and uniqueness of the maximal trajectory from a continuous initial condition $\mathbf{g}(t)$, we assume $\mathbf{f}$ is continuous for all arguments, and moreover $\mathbf{f}$ is continuously differentiable in the first argument (i.e., $\mathbf{x}(t)$). Then, we write $X(t, \mathbf{g}(t_0))$ with $t_0 \in [-r_k, 0]$ to denote the point reached at time t from the initial state $\mathbf{g}(t_0)$, which should be uniquely determined. Moreover, if $\mathbf{f}$ is Lipschitz, i.e., there exists a constant $L > 0$ s.t. $\|\mathbf{f}(\mathbf{x}) - \mathbf{f}(\mathbf{y})\| \leq L \|\mathbf{x} - \mathbf{y}\|$ holds for all $\mathbf{x}, \mathbf{y}$, we can conclude $X(\cdot)$ is unique over $[-r_k, \infty)$. Please refer to [9] for the theories of *delay differential equations*.

2.2   SystemC

SystemC is a system-level modelling language supporting both system architecture and software development. It provides a uniform platform for the modelling of complex embedded systems. Essentially it is a set of C++ classes and macros. According to the naming convention of SystemC, most identifiers are prefixed with *SC_* or *sc_*, such as *SC_THREAD*, *SC_METHOD*, *sc_inout*, *sc_signal*, *sc_event*, etc.

Modules, denoted by *SC_MODULE*, are the basic blocks of a SystemC model. A model usually contains several modules, within which sub-designs, constructors, processes, ports, channels, events and other elements may be included. Each module is defined as a class. The constructor of a module is denoted as *SC_CTOR()*, in which some initialization operations carry out. Processes are member functions of the module, describing the actual functionality, and multiple processes execute concurrently in nature. A process has a list of sensitive events, by whose notifications its execution is controlled. Two major types of processes, *SC_METHOD* and *SC_THREAD*, are supported in SystemC. Generally, an *SC_METHOD* can be invoked multiple times, whereas an *SC_THREAD* can only be invoked once.

Ports in SystemC are components using for communicating with each other between modules. They are divided into three kinds by the data direction, i.e., *sc_in*, *sc_out* and *sc_inout* ports. Only ports with the same data type can be connected (via channels). *Channels* are used for connecting different sub-designs, based on which the communication is realized (by calling corresponding methods in channels, i.e., *read()* and *write()*). Channels are declared by $sc\_signal\langle\rangle$. Another important element using for synchronization is *event*, which has no value and no duration. Once an event occurs, the processes waiting for it will be resumed. Generally, an event can be notified immediately, one delta-cycle (defined in the execution phase below) later, or some constant time later.

The simulation of a SystemC model starts from the entrance of a method named *sc_main()*, in which three phases are generally involved: elaboration, execution and post-processing. During the elaboration and the post-processing phase, some initialization and result processing are carried out, respectively. We mainly illustrate the execution phase in the next.

The execution of SystemC models is event-based and it can be divided into four steps: (1) Initialization, executing all concurrent processes in an unspecified order until they are completed or suspended by a *wait()*; (2) Evaluation, running all the processes that are ready in an unspecified order until there are no more ready process; (3) Updating, copying the value of containers (e.g., channels) to the current location, then after that, if any event occurs, go back to step 2. Here, the cycle from evaluation to updating and then go back to evaluation is known as the delta-cycle; (4) Time advancing, if no more processes get ready currently, time advances to the nearest point where some processes will be ready. If no such point exists or the time is greater than a given time bound, the execution will terminate. Otherwise, go back to Step 2.

3   Delay Hybrid CSP (*d*HCSP)

In this section, we first extend HCSP with delay, and then discuss the notion of approximate bisimulation over *d*HCSP processes by extending the corresponding notion of HCSP defined in [24].

3.1   Syntax of *d*HCSP

*d*HCSP is an extension of HCSP by introducing DDEs to model continuous evolution with delay behavior. The syntax of *d*HCSP is given below:

$$P ::= \text{skip} \mid x := e \mid \text{wait } d \mid ch?x \mid ch!e \mid P;Q \mid B \to P \mid$$
$$P \sqcap Q \mid P^* \mid [\!]_{i \in I}(io_i \to Q_i) \mid \langle F(\dot{\mathbf{s}}(t), \mathbf{s}(t), \mathbf{s}(t - r_1), ..., \mathbf{s}(t - r_k)) = 0 \& B \rangle \mid$$
$$\langle F(\dot{\mathbf{s}}(t), \mathbf{s}(t), \mathbf{s}(t - r_1), ..., \mathbf{s}(t - r_k)) = 0 \& B \rangle \trianglerighteq [\!]_{i \in I}(io_i \to Q_i)$$
$$S ::= P_1 \| P_2 \| ... \| P_n \text{ for some } n \geq 1$$

where $x, \mathbf{s}$ stand for variables and vectors of variables, respectively, B and e are Boolean and arithmetic expressions, d is a non-negative real constant, ch is a channel name, io_i stands for a communication event (i.e., either $ch_i?x$ or $ch_i!e$ for some x, e), $k \geq 0$ is an index and for each r_i, $r_i \in \mathbb{R}_0^+$, P, Q, P_i, Q_i are sequential process terms, and S stands for a *d*HCSP process term, that may be parallel. The informal meaning of the individual constructors is as follows:

- skip, $x := e$, wait d, $ch?x$, $ch!e$, $P;Q$, $[\!]_{i \in I}(io_i \to Q_i)$, $B \to P$, $P \sqcap Q$ and P^* are defined the same as in HCSP.
- $\langle F(\dot{\mathbf{s}}(t), \mathbf{s}(t), \mathbf{s}(t - r_1), ..., \mathbf{s}(t - r_k)) = 0 \& B \rangle$ is the time-delay continuous evolution statement. It forces the vector $\mathbf{s}$ of real variables to obey the DDE F as long as B, which defines the domain of $\mathbf{s}$, holds, and terminates when B turns false. Without loss of generality, we assume that the set of B is open, thus the escaping point will be at the boundary of B. The special case when $k = 0$ corresponds to an ODE that models continuous evolution without delay. The communication interrupt $\langle F(\dot{\mathbf{s}}(t), \mathbf{s}(t), \mathbf{s}(t - r_1), ..., \mathbf{s}(t - r_k)) = 0 \& B \rangle \trianglerighteq$ $[\!]_{i \in I}(io_i \to Q_i)$ behaves like $\langle F(\dot{\mathbf{s}}(t), \mathbf{s}(t), \mathbf{s}(t - r_1), ..., \mathbf{s}(t - r_k)) = 0 \& B \rangle$, except that the continuous evolution is preempted as soon as one of the communications io_i takes place, which is followed by the respective Q_i. These two statements are the essential extensions of *d*HCSP from HCSP.

– For $n \geq 1$, $P_1 \| P_2 \| \ldots \| P_n$ builds a system in which n concurrent processes run independently and communicate with each other along the common channels connecting them.

To better understand dHCSP, we introduce delay behavior to the water tank system considered in [4, 24].

Example 1. The system is a parallel composition of two components *Watertank* and *Controller*, modelled by *WTS* as follows:

$$WTS \stackrel{\text{def}}{=} Watertank \| Controller$$

$$Watertank \stackrel{\text{def}}{=} v := v_0; d := d_0; (v = 1 \rightarrow$$
$$\langle \dot{d}(t) = Q_{max} - \pi s^2 \sqrt{g(d(t) + d(t-r))} \rangle \unrhd (wl!d \rightarrow cv?v);$$
$$v = 0 \rightarrow \langle \dot{d}(t) = -\pi s^2 \sqrt{g(d(t) + d(t-r))} \rangle \unrhd (wl!d \rightarrow cv?v)^*$$

$$Controller \stackrel{\text{def}}{=} y := v_0; x := d_0; (\text{wait } p; wl?x;$$
$$x \geq ub \rightarrow y := 0; x \leq lb \rightarrow y := 1; cv!y)^*$$

where Q_{max}, π, s and g are system parameters, the control variable v can take two values, 1 or 0, which indicate the watering valve on the top of the tank is open or closed, respectively, d is the water level of the *Watertank* and its dynamics depends on the value of v. For each case, the evolution of d follows a DDE that is governed by both the current state and the past state r time ago. The time delay r accounts for time involved in communication between the watertank and the controller.

The system is initialized by an initial state, i.e., v_0 and d_0 for the controller variable and water level, respectively. wl and cv are channels connecting *Watertank* and *Controller* for transferring information (water level and control variable respectively) between them. In the *Controller*, the control variable y is updated with a period of p, and its value is decided by the water level read from the *Watertank* (x in *Controller*). If $x \geq ub$ holds, where ub is an upper bound, y is set to 0 (valve closed), else if $x \leq lb$ holds, where lb is a lower bound, y is set to 1 (valve open), otherwise, y keeps unchanged. Basically, starting from the initial state, *Watertank* and *Controller* run independently for p time, then *Watertank* sends the current water level to *Controller*, according to which the value of the control variable is updated and then sent back to *Watertank*, after that, a new period repeats. The goal of the system is to maintain the water level within a desired scope.

3.2 Semantics of dHCSP

In order to define an operational semantics of dHCSP, we use non-negative reals $\mathbb{R}^+$ to model time, and introduce a global clock now to record the time in the execution of a process. Different from ODE, the solution of a DDE at a given time is not a single value, but a time function. Thus, to interpret a process S, we first define a state ρ as the following mapping:

$$\rho : (Var(S) \rightarrow (Intv \rightarrow \mathbb{R}^n)) \cup (\{now\} \rightarrow \mathbb{R}^+)$$

where $Var(S)$ represents the set of state variables of S, and $Intv$ is a timed interval. The semantics of each state variable with respect to a state is defined as a mapping from a timed interval to the value set. We denote by $\mathcal{D}$ the set of such states. In addition, we introduce a flow H as a mapping from a timed interval to a state set, i.e. $H : Intv \to \mathcal{D}$ called $flow$, to represent the continuous flow of process S over the timed interval $Intv$.

A structural operational semantics of dHCSP is defined by a set of transition rules. Each transition rule has the form of $(P, \rho) \xrightarrow{\alpha} (P', \rho', H)$, where P and P' are dHCSP processes, α is an event, ρ, ρ' are states, H is a $flow$. It expresses that, starting from initial state ρ, by performing event α, P evolves into P', ends in state ρ', and produces the execution flow H. The label α represents events, which can be a discrete non-communication event, e.g. skip, assignment, or the evaluation of Boolean expressions, uniformly denoted by τ, or an external communication event $ch!c$ or $ch?c$, or an internal communication $ch.c$, or a time delay d, where $c \in \mathbb{R}, d \in \mathbb{R}^+$. When both $ch!c$ and $ch?c$ occur, a communication $ch.c$ occurs.

Before defining the semantics, we introduce an abbreviation for manipulating states. Given a state ρ, $d \in \mathbb{R}^+$, and a set of variables V, $\rho[V \Downarrow_d]$ means the clock takes progress for d time units, and the values of the variables in V at time $\rho(now)+d$ is defined as a constant function over timed interval $[\rho(now), \rho(now)+d]$. Precisely, for any t in the domain,

$$\rho[V \Downarrow_d](x)(t) \stackrel{\text{def}}{=} \begin{cases} \rho(x)(t) & \text{if } x \notin V \\ \rho(x)(\rho(now)) & \text{otherwise} \end{cases}$$

For space of limitation, we only present the transition rules for the time-delayed continuous evolution statement here, the rules for other constructors can be defined similarly to the ones in HCSP, see [27]. The first rule represents that the DDE evolves for d time units, while B always preserves true throughout the extended interval.

$$\frac{\begin{array}{c} \text{Assume } X : [0, \infty) \to ([-r, \infty) \to \mathbb{R}^{d(\mathbf{s})}) \text{ is the solution of } \langle F(\dot{\mathbf{s}}(t), ..., \mathbf{s}(t - r_k))=0 \& B \rangle \\ \text{with initial value } \mathbf{s}(t) = H(t)(\mathbf{s})(t) \text{ for } t \in [\rho(now) - r, \rho(now)] \text{ and} \\ \forall d > 0. \forall t \in [0, d), \llbracket B \rrbracket_L^{\rho[now \mapsto now+t, \mathbf{s} \mapsto X_t]} = \mathbf{True} \end{array}}{(\langle F(\dot{\mathbf{s}}(t), ..., \mathbf{s}(t - r_k))=0 \& B \rangle, \rho) \xrightarrow{d} \left(\begin{array}{c} \langle F(\dot{\mathbf{s}}(t), ..., \mathbf{s}(t - r_k))=0 \& B \rangle, \\ \rho[V \backslash \{\mathbf{s}\} \Downarrow_d][now \mapsto now+d, \mathbf{s} \mapsto X_d], H_d^{\rho, \mathbf{s}, X} \end{array} \right)}$$

where H is the initial history before executing the DDE (recording the past state of $\mathbf{s}$); and for any t, X_t is defined as a function over timed interval $[\rho(now), \rho(now)+t]$ such that $X_t(a) = X(t)(a-\rho(now))$ for each a in the domain; and the produced flow $H_d^{\rho, \mathbf{s}, X}$ is defined as: $\forall t \in [\rho(now), \rho(now)+d]. H_d^{\rho, \mathbf{s}, X}(t) = \rho[now \mapsto t, \mathbf{s} \mapsto X_{t-\rho(now)}]$.

The second rule represents that, when the negation $\neg B$ is true at the initial state, the DDE terminates.

$$\frac{\llbracket \neg B \rrbracket_L^{\rho} = \mathbf{True}}{(\langle F(\dot{\mathbf{s}}(t), ..., \mathbf{s}(t - r_k))=0 \& B \rangle, \rho) \xrightarrow{\tau} (\epsilon, \rho)}$$

3.3 Approximate Bisimulation on dHCSP

First of all, as a convention, we use $\xrightarrow{\alpha}$ to denote the τ transition closure of transition α, i.e., there is a sequence of τ actions before and/or after α. Given a state ρ defined over interval $[t_1, t_2]$, for each $t \in [t_1, t_2]$, we define $\rho \downarrow_t$ of type $Var(S) \cup \{now\} \to Val$ to restrict the value of each variable to the result of the corresponding function at time t:

$$\rho \downarrow_t (x) = \begin{cases} \rho(x)(t) & \text{for all } x \in Var(S) \\ \rho(x) & \text{for } x = now \end{cases}$$

With this function, we can reduce the operations manipulating a state with function values to the ones manipulating states with point values. Meanwhile, we assume $(S, \rho) \xrightarrow{0} (S, \rho)$ always holds for any process S and state ρ.

Definition 1 (Approximate bisimulation). *Suppose $\mathcal{B}$ is a symmetric binary relation on* $\mathrm{d}HCSP$ *processes such that S_1 and S_2 share the same set of state variables for $(S_1, S_2) \in \mathcal{B}$, and d is the metric of L^2 norm, and $h \in \mathbb{R}^+$ and $\varepsilon \in \mathbb{R}^+$ are the given time and value precision, respectively. Then, we say $\mathcal{B}$ is an approximately bisimulation w.r.t. h and ε, denoted by $\mathcal{B}_{h,\varepsilon}$, if for any $(S_1, S_2) \in \mathcal{B}_{h,\varepsilon}$, and (ρ_1, ρ_2) with $d(\rho_1 \downarrow_{\rho_1(now)}, \rho_2 \downarrow_{\rho_2(now)}) \leq \varepsilon$, the following conditions are satisfied:*

1. *if $(S_1, \rho_1) \xrightarrow{\alpha} (S_1', \rho_1')$ and $\alpha \notin \mathbb{R}^+$, then there exists (S_2', ρ_2') such that $(S_2, \rho_2) \xrightarrow{\alpha} (S_2', \rho_2')$, $(S_1', S_2') \in \mathcal{B}_{h,\varepsilon}$ and $d(\rho_1' \downarrow_{\rho_1'(now)}, \rho_2' \downarrow_{\rho_2'(now)}) \leq \varepsilon$, or there exist (S_2^*, ρ_2^*), (S_2', ρ_2') and $0 < t \leq h$ such that $(S_2, \rho_2) \xrightarrow{t} (S_2^*, \rho_2^*, H_2^*)$, $(S_2^*, \rho_2^*) \xrightarrow{\alpha} (S_2', \rho_2')$, $(S_1, S_2^*) \in \mathcal{B}_{h,\varepsilon}$, $d(\rho_1 \downarrow_{\rho_1(now)}, \rho_2^* \downarrow_{\rho_2^*(now)}) \leq \varepsilon$; $(S_1', S_2') \in \mathcal{B}_{h,\varepsilon}$ and $d(\rho_1' \downarrow_{\rho_1'(now)}, \rho_2' \downarrow_{\rho_2'(now)}) \leq \varepsilon$.*

2. *if $(S_1, \rho_1) \xrightarrow{t} (S_1', \rho_1', H_1)$ for some $t > 0$, then there exist (S_2', ρ_2') and $t' \geq 0$ such that $|t - t'| \leq h$, $(S_2, \rho_2) \xrightarrow{t'} (S_2', \rho_2', H_2)$, $(S_1', S_2') \in \mathcal{B}_{h,\varepsilon}$, and for any $o \in [\rho_1(now), \rho_1(now) + \min(t, t')]$, $d(\rho_1' \downarrow_o, \rho_2' \downarrow_o) \leq \varepsilon$, and $d(\rho_1' \downarrow_{\rho_1'(now)}, \rho_2' \downarrow_{\rho_2'(now)}) \leq \varepsilon$.*

Definition 2. *Two* $\mathrm{d}HCSP$ *processes S_1 and S_2 are approximately bisimilar with respect to precision h and ε, denoted by $S_1 \cong_{h,\varepsilon} S_2$, if there exists an (h, ε)-approximate bisimulation relation $\mathcal{B}_{h,\varepsilon}$ s.t. $(S_1, S_2) \in \mathcal{B}_{h,\varepsilon}$.*

Theorem 1. *Given two* $\mathrm{d}HCSP$ *processes, it is decidable whether they are approximately bisimilar on $[0, T]$ for a given $T \in \mathbb{R}^+$.*

4 Discretization of dHCSP

The process on generating code from dHCSP is similar to that from HCSP [24], consisting of two phases: (1) discretization of the dHCSP model; (2) code generation from the discretized dHCSP model to SystemC.

Benefiting from its compositionality, dHCSP can be discretized by defining rules for all the constructors, in which the discretization of delay continuous dynamics (i.e., DDE) is the most critical. Let S be a dHCSP process, $T \in \mathbb{R}^+$ be a time bound, h and ε be the given precisions for time and value, respectively. Our goal is to construct a discrete dHCSP process $D_{h,\varepsilon}(S)$ from S, s.t. S is (h, ε)-approximately bisimilar to $D_{h,\varepsilon}(S)$ on $[0,T]$, i.e., $S \cong_{h,\varepsilon} D_{h,\varepsilon}(S)$ on $[0,T]$. To achieve this, we firstly introduce a simulation-based method (inspired by [11]) for discretizing a single DDE and then extend it for multiple DDEs to be executed in sequence; afterwards, we present the discretization of dHCSP in bounded time.

4.1 Discretization of DDE (DDEs) in Bounded Time

To solve DDEs is much more difficult than to solve ODEs, as DDEs are history dependent, therefore, non-Markovian, in contrast, ODEs are history independent and Markovian. So, in most cases, explicit solutions to DDEs are impossible, therefore, DDEs are normally solved by using approximation based techniques [9]. In [11], the authors propose a novel method for safety verification of delayed differential dynamics, in which a validated simulator for a DDE is presented. The simulator produces a sequence of discrete states for approximating the trajectory of a DDE and meanwhile calculates the corresponding local error bounds. Based on this work, we can obtain a validated discretization of a DDE w.r.t. the given precisions h and ε. Furthermore, we can easily extend the simulator to deal with systems containing multiple DDEs in sequence.

Next we first consider the discretization of a DDE within bounded time $T_d \in \mathbb{R}^+$, for some $T_d \leq T$. The purpose is to find a discrete step size h s.t. the DDE and its discretization are (h, ξ)-approximately bisimilar within $[0, T_d]$, for a given precision ξ that is less than the global error ε. For simplifying the notations, we consider a special case of DDE in which only one delay term, $r > 0$, exists, as in

$$\begin{cases} \dot{\mathbf{x}}(t) = \mathbf{f}(\mathbf{x}(t), \mathbf{x}(t-r)), \ t \in [0, \infty) \\ \mathbf{x}(t) = \mathbf{g}(t), \qquad\qquad t \in [-r, 0] \end{cases} \tag{2}$$

where we use $\mathbf{f}(\mathbf{x}, \mathbf{x}_r)$ to denote the dynamics, $\mathbf{x}$ for current state and $\mathbf{x}_r$ for the past state at $t-r$. In fact, the method for this special case can be easily extended to the general case as in (1), by recording the past states between $t - r_k$ and t, the detailed discussion can be found in [11].

For a DDE $\mathbf{f}(\mathbf{x}, \mathbf{x}_r)$ with initial condition $\mathbf{g}(t)$ which is continuous on $[-r, 0]$, delay term r, step size h, and time bound T_d, the validated simulator in [11] can produce three *lists* (denoted as $[\![\cdot]\!]$) with the same length, namely, (1) $\mathbf{t} = [\![t_{-m}, ..., t_0, t_1, ..., t_n]\!]$, storing a sequence of time stamps on which the approximations are computed ($t_{-m}, ..., t_0$ for the time before 0, i.e., $[-r, 0]$, with $m = r/h$), satisfying $t_{-m}, ..., t_{-1} < 0 = t_0 < t_1 < ... < t_n = T_d$ and $t_i - t_{i-1} = h$ for all $i \in [-m+1, n]$, (2) $\mathbf{y} = [\![\mathbf{x}_{-m}, ..., \mathbf{x}_0, \mathbf{x}_1, ..., \mathbf{x}_n]\!]$, recording a sequence of approximate states of $\mathbf{x}$ starting from $\mathbf{x}_{-m}$, corresponding to time stamps in $\mathbf{t}$, (3) $\mathbf{d} = [\![d_{-m}, ..., d_0, d_1, ..., d_n]\!]$, recording the corresponding sequence of local error bounds. The implementation of the simulator is based on the well-known *forward Euler method*, i.e., $\mathbf{x} := \mathbf{x} + h\mathbf{f}(\mathbf{x}, \mathbf{x}_r)$. In addition, we usually require the delay term r be an integral multiple of the step size h, i.e., $m \in \mathbb{N}^+$, in order to ensure the past state $\mathbf{x}_r$ could be found in $\mathbf{y}$.

A remarkable property of the simulator

$$X(t, \mathbf{g}(0)) \in conv(N(\mathbf{x}_i, d_i) \cup N(\mathbf{x}_{i+1}, d_{i+1}))$$

holds for each $t \in [t_i, t_{i+1}]$ with $i = 0, 1, ..., n - 1$, where $X(\cdot)$ is the trajectory of $\dot{\mathbf{x}} = \mathbf{f}(\mathbf{x}, \mathbf{x}_r)$, and $N(\mathbf{x}_i, d_i)$ is the d_i-neighbourhood of $\mathbf{x}_i$ ($\mathbf{x}_i$ and d_i are elements of $\mathbf{y}$ and $\mathbf{d}$, respectively). Based on this fact, we can use $\mathbf{x}_{i+1}$ as the approximation of $X(t, \mathbf{g}(0))$ for all $t \in [t_i, t_{i+1}]$ for any $i \in [0, n-1]$, s.t. the DDE (2) and the sequence $[\![\mathbf{x}_0, \mathbf{x}_1, ..., \mathbf{x}_n]\!]$ are (h, ξ)-approximately bisimilar on $[0, T_d]$, if the diameter of every $conv(N(\mathbf{x}_i, d_i) \cup N(\mathbf{x}_{i+1}, d_{i+1}))$ is less than the precision ξ, i.e., $dia(conv(N(\mathbf{x}_i, d_i) \cup N(\mathbf{x}_{i+1}, d_{i+1}))) < \xi$ for all $i \in [0, n-1]$.

Theorem 2 (Approximation of a DDE). *Let Γ be a DDE as in (2), and $\mathbf{f}$ in (2) is continuously differentiable on $[0, T_d]$, and $\mathbf{x}_0 \in \mathbb{R}^n$ with $\|\mathbf{x}_0 - \mathbf{g}(0)\| \leq d_0$. Then for any precision $\xi > 0$ and $0 < d_0 < \xi$, there exists a step size $h > 0$ such that Γ and*

$$\mathbf{x} := \mathbf{x}_0; (wait\ h; \mathbf{x} := \mathbf{x} + h\mathbf{f}(\mathbf{x}, \mathbf{x}_r))^{\frac{T_d}{h}};$$

are (h, ξ)-approximately bisimilar on $[0, T_d]$.

Based on the simulation algorithm given in [11], we design a method for automatically computing a step size h s.t. the DDE as in (2) and its discretization are (h, ξ)-approximately bisimilar on $[0, T_d]$, as presented in Algorithms 1 and 2.

Algorithm 1. ComStepsize_oneDDE: computing the step size h for the one DDE

Input: The dynamics $\mathbf{f}(\mathbf{x}, \mathbf{x}_r)$, initial state $\mathbf{x}_0$, delay term r, precision ξ, and time bound T_d;

1: $h = r; v = true; \mathbf{t} = [\![-h, 0]\!]; \mathbf{y} = [\![\mathbf{x}_0, \mathbf{x}_0]\!]; \mathbf{d} = [\![0, 0]\!];$
2: **while** *true* **do**
3:    $CheckStepsize(\mathbf{f}(\mathbf{x}, \mathbf{x}_r), r, h, \xi, [0, T_d], \mathbf{t}, \mathbf{y}, \mathbf{d}, v);$
4:    **if** $v = false$ **then**
5:       $h = h/2; v = true;$
6:       $\mathbf{t} = [\![-h, 0]\!];$
7:    **else**
8:       break;
9:    **end if**
10: **end while**
11: **return** h;

Algorithm 1 is designed for computing a valid step size h for a given DDE. It first initializes the value of h to r and Boolean variable v, which indicates whether the current h is a valid step size, to *true*, and the lists for simulating the DDE, i.e., $\mathbf{t}, \mathbf{y}$, and $\mathbf{d}$ (line 1). Here, we assume the initial condition is a constant function, i.e., $\mathbf{x}_t = \mathbf{x}_0$, on $[-r, 0]$, therefore, states before time 0 are represented as one state at $-h$. Then, it iteratively checks whether the current value of h can make Theorem 2 hold, by calling the function *CheckStepsize* that is defined in Algorithm 2 (lines 2–10). If current h is not valid (v is set to *false* for this case), h is set to a smaller value, i.e., $h/2$, and v is reset to *true*, and $\mathbf{t}$ is reinitialized according to the new h (lines 4–6). Otherwise, a valid h is found, then the while loop exits (lines 7–9). The termination of the algorithm can be guaranteed by Theorem 2, thus a valid h can always be found and returned (line 11).

Algorithm 2. CheckStepsize: checking whether the step size h is valid for precision ξ

Input: The dynamics $\mathbf{f}(\mathbf{x}, \mathbf{x}_r)$, delay term r, step size h, precision ξ, time span $[T_1, T_2]$, boolean variable v, and simulation history $\langle \mathbf{t}, \mathbf{y}, \mathbf{d} \rangle$ before T_1;

1:   $n = length(\mathbf{t}); \ m = r/h$;
2: **while** $\mathbf{t}(n) < T_2$ **do**
3:     $\mathbf{t}(n+1) = \mathbf{t}(n) + h$;
4:     $\mathbf{y}(n+1) = \mathbf{y}(n) + \mathbf{f}(\mathbf{y}(n), \mathbf{y}(n-m)) * h$;
5:     $\mathbf{e}(n) = $ **Find** minimum e s.t.

$$\begin{cases} \|\mathbf{f}(\mathbf{x} + t * \mathbf{f}, \mathbf{x}_r + t * \mathbf{g}) - \mathbf{f}(\mathbf{y}(n), \mathbf{y}(n-m))\| \le e - \sigma, for \\ \forall t \in [0, h] \\ \forall \mathbf{x} \in N(\mathbf{y}(n), \mathbf{d}(n)) \\ \forall \mathbf{x}_r \in N(\mathbf{y}(n-m), \mathbf{d}(n-m)) \\ \forall \mathbf{f} \in N(\mathbf{f}(\mathbf{y}(n), \mathbf{y}(n-m)), e) \\ \forall \mathbf{g} \in N(\mathbf{f}(\mathbf{y}(n-m), \mathbf{y}(n-2m)), \mathbf{e}(n-m)); \end{cases}$$

6:     $\mathbf{d}(n+1) = \mathbf{d}(n) + h * \mathbf{e}(n)$;
7:     **if** $\max(\mathbf{y}(n)+\mathbf{d}(n), \mathbf{y}(n+1)+\mathbf{d}(n+1)) - \min(\mathbf{y}(n)-\mathbf{d}(n), \mathbf{y}(n+1)-\mathbf{d}(n+1)) > \xi$ **then**
8:       $v = $ *false*;
9:       break;
10:    **else**
11:       $\mathbf{t} = [\![\mathbf{t}, \mathbf{t}(n+1)]\!]; \ \mathbf{y} = [\![\mathbf{y}, \mathbf{y}(n+1)]\!]; \ \mathbf{d} = [\![\mathbf{d}, \mathbf{d}(n+1)]\!]$;
12:       $n = n + 1$;
13:    **end if**
14: **end while**
15: return $\langle v, \mathbf{t}, \mathbf{y}, \mathbf{d} \rangle$;

Algorithm 2 implements function *CheckStepsize*, which is slightly different from the simulation algorithm given in [11]. The history of $\langle \mathbf{t}, \mathbf{y}, \mathbf{d} \rangle$ is added to the inputs, for simulating multiple DDEs in sequence. At the beginning, the variable n that stores the last recent simulation step is initialized as the length of current $\mathbf{t}$, and an offset m is set to r/h thus $\mathbf{y}(n-m)$, i.e., the $(n-m)$th element of list $\mathbf{y}$, locates the delayed approximation at time $\mathbf{t}(n) - r$ (line 1). When current time (i.e., $\mathbf{t}(n)$) is less than the end of the time span (i.e., T_2), the lists $\mathbf{t}$, $\mathbf{y}$ and $\mathbf{d}$ are iteratively updated by adding new elements, until T_2 is reached (lines 2–14). In each iteration, firstly, the time stamp is added by the step size h and the approximate state at this time is computed by the *forward Euler method* (line 4), and then the local error bound $\mathbf{d}(n+1)$ is derived based on the local error slope $\mathbf{e}(n)$ (line 6), which is reduced to a constrained optimization problem (line 5) that can be solved by some solvers in Matlab or by some SMT solvers like iSAT [13] which can return a validated result, please refer to [11] for the details. After these values are computed, whether the diameter of the convex hull of the two adjacent approximate points at the time stamps $\mathbf{t}(n)$ and $\mathbf{t}(n+1)$ by taking their local error bounds into account is greater than the given error ξ is checked (lines 7–13). If the diameter is greater than ξ, the while loop is broken and v is set to *false* (lines 8–9), which means h will be reset to $h/2$ in Algorithm 1. Otherwise, h is valid for this simulation step and the new values of $\mathbf{t}$, $\mathbf{y}$ and $\mathbf{d}$ are added into the corresponding lists (lines 10–12), then a new iteration restarts until T_2 is reached. At last, the new values of v, $\mathbf{t}$, $\mathbf{y}$ and $\mathbf{d}$ are returned (line 15).

A dHCSP may contain multiple DDEs, especially for those to be executed in sequence in which the initial states of following DDEs may depend on the flows of previous DDEs. In order to handle such cases, we present Algorithm 3 for computing the global step size that meets the required precision ξ within bounded time T_d. Suppose a sequence of DDEs $\mathbf{f}_1(\mathbf{x}, \mathbf{x}_r), \mathbf{f}_2(\mathbf{x}, \mathbf{x}_r), \cdots, \mathbf{f}_k(\mathbf{x}, \mathbf{x}_r)$ is to be executed in sequence. For simplicity, assume all DDEs share the same delay term r, and the execution sequence of the DDEs is decided by a scheduler (*Schedule* in line 6). At the beginning, h and v are initialized as the delay term r and *true* respectively (line 1). Then, before the current time (i.e., $\mathbf{t}(end)$) reaches the end of the time span (i.e., T_d), a while loop is executed to check whether h satisfies the precision ξ, in which *ComStepsize_oneDDE* and *CheckStepsize* are called (lines 2–13). In each iteration, the three lists $\mathbf{t}$, $\mathbf{y}$ and $\mathbf{d}$ are initialised as before (line 3), then the valid h for the first DDE $\mathbf{f}_1(\mathbf{x}, \mathbf{x}_r)$ is computed by calling *ComStepsize_oneDDE* (line 4), where t_1 denotes the length of the execution time of $\mathbf{f}_1(\mathbf{x}, \mathbf{x}_r)$. Afterwards, for the following DDEs, an inner while loop to check whether the calculated h is within the error bound ξ is executed (lines 5–12). Thereof, which DDE should be executed is determined by *Schedule* (one DDE may be executed for multiple times), and the corresponding span of execution time is represented as $[t_{i-1}, t_i]$ for the i-th DDE (lines 6–7). If h is not valid for some DDE, i.e., $v = $ *false* (line 8), depending on the return value of *CheckStepsize* function, a new smaller h (i.e., $h/2$) is chosen and v is reset to *true*, then the inner *while* loop is broken (lines 8–11) and a new iteration restarts from time 0 with the new h (line 3); Otherwise, a valid h is found (line 13). Since we can always find small enough step size to make all DDEs meet the precision within $[0, T_d]$ by Theorem 2, Algorithm 3 is ensured to terminate (line 14).

Algorithm 3. ComStepsize_multiDDEs: computing the step size h for multiple DDEs

---

Input: A sequence of dynamics $\mathbf{f}_1(\mathbf{x}, \mathbf{x}_r), \mathbf{f}_2(\mathbf{x}, \mathbf{x}_r), ..., \mathbf{f}_k(\mathbf{x}, \mathbf{x}_r)$, initial state $\mathbf{x}_0$, delay term r, precision ξ, and time bound T_d (assume running from $\mathbf{f}_1(\mathbf{x}, \mathbf{x}_r)$);
1: $h = r$; $v = true$;
2: **while** $\mathbf{t}(end) < T_d$ **do**
3:     $\mathbf{t} = [\![-h, 0]\!]$; $\mathbf{y} = [\![\mathbf{x}_0, \mathbf{x}_0]\!]$; $\mathbf{d} = [\![0, 0]\!]$;
4:     $h = ComStepsize\_oneDDE(\mathbf{f}_1(\mathbf{x}, \mathbf{x}_r), \mathbf{x}_0, r, \xi, t_1)$;
5:     **while** $\mathbf{t}(end) < T_d$ **do**
6:        $i = Schedule(\mathbf{f}_1(\mathbf{x}, \mathbf{x}_r), \mathbf{f}_2(\mathbf{x}, \mathbf{x}_r), ..., \mathbf{f}_k(\mathbf{x}, \mathbf{x}_r))$;
7:        $CheckStepsize(\mathbf{f}_i(\mathbf{x}, \mathbf{x}_r), r, h, \xi, [t_{i-1}, t_i], \mathbf{t}, \mathbf{y}, \mathbf{d}, v)$;
8:        **if** $v = false$ **then**
9:           $h = h/2$; $v = true$;
10:           break;
11:        **end if**
12:     **end while**
13: **end while**
14: **return** h;

4.2   Discretization of dHCSP in Bounded Time

Now we can define the set of rules to discretize a given dHCSP process S and obtain a discrete dHCSP process $D_{h,\varepsilon}(S)$ such that they are (h, ε)-approximately bisimilar on $[0, T]$, for given h, ε and T. The rule for the discretization of DDE is given below, and other rules are the same as the ones for HCSP presented in [24].

$$\frac{\langle \dot{\mathbf{x}} = \mathbf{f}(\mathbf{x}, \mathbf{x}_r) \& B \rangle}{(N(B, \varepsilon) \wedge N'(B, \varepsilon) \rightarrow (\text{wait } h; \mathbf{x} := \mathbf{x} + h\mathbf{f}(\mathbf{x}, \mathbf{x}_r)))^{\frac{T}{h}};}$$
$$N(B, \varepsilon) \wedge N'(B, \varepsilon) \rightarrow \textbf{stop}$$

For a Boolean expression B, $N(B, \varepsilon)$ is defined as its ε-neighbourhood. For instance, $N(B, \varepsilon) = \{x | x > 2 - \varepsilon\}$ for $B = \{x | x > 2\}$. Then, $\langle \dot{\mathbf{x}} = \mathbf{f}(\mathbf{x}, \mathbf{x}_r) \& B \rangle$ is discretized as follows: first, execute a sequence of assignments (T/h times) to $\mathbf{x}$ according to *Euler method*, i.e., $\mathbf{x} := \mathbf{x} + h\mathbf{f}(\mathbf{x}, \mathbf{x}_r)$, whenever $N(B, \varepsilon) \wedge N'(B, \varepsilon)$ holds, where $N'(B, \varepsilon) = N(B, \varepsilon)[\mathbf{x} \mapsto \mathbf{x} + h\mathbf{f}(\mathbf{x}, \mathbf{x}_r)]$, i.e., the value of $N(B, \varepsilon)$ at the next discretized step; then, if both $N(B, \varepsilon)$ and $N'(B, \varepsilon)$ still hold, but the time has already reached the upper bound T, the process behaves like **stop**, which indicates that the behavior after T will not be concerned.

4.3   Correctness of the Discretization

In order to ensure $D_{h,\varepsilon}(S)$ defined in Sect. 4.2 is approximately bisimilar to S, we need to put some extra conditions on S, i.e., requiring it to be robustly safe. The condition is similar to that in [24]. We define the $(-\epsilon)$-neighbourhood like the ϵ-neighbourhood, i.e., for a set $\phi \subseteq \mathbb{R}^n$ and $\epsilon \geq 0$, $N(\phi, -\epsilon) = \{\mathbf{x} | \mathbf{x} \in \phi \wedge \forall \mathbf{y} \in \neg\phi. \|\mathbf{x} - \mathbf{y}\| > \epsilon\}$. Intuitively, $\mathbf{x} \in N(\phi, -\epsilon)$ means $\mathbf{x}$ is inside ϕ and moreover the distance between it and the boundary of ϕ is greater than ϵ. To distinguish the states of process S from those of dynamical systems, we use ρ (ρ_0 for initial state) to denote the states of S here. Below, the notion of a robustly safe system is given.

Definition 3 ((δ, ϵ)-**robustly safe**). *Let $\delta > 0$ and $\epsilon > 0$ be the given time and value precisions, respectively. A dHCSP process S is (δ, ϵ)-robustly safe with respect to a given initial state ρ_0, if the following two conditions hold:*

- *for every continuous evolution $\langle \dot{\mathbf{x}} = \mathbf{f}(\mathbf{x}, \mathbf{x}_r)\&B \rangle$ occurring in S, when S executes up to $\langle \dot{\mathbf{x}} = \mathbf{f}(\mathbf{x}, \mathbf{x}_r)\&B \rangle$ at time t with state ρ, if $\rho(B) = false$, and there exists $\hat{t} > t$ with $\hat{t} - t < \delta$ and $\mathbf{d}(\rho, \rho_0[\mathbf{x} \mapsto X(\hat{t}, \rho_0(\mathbf{x}))]) < \epsilon$, then $\rho \in N(\neg B, -\epsilon)$;*
- *for every alternative process $B \to P$ occurring in S, if B depends on continuous variables of S, then when S executes up to $B \to P$ at state ρ, $\rho \in N(B, -\epsilon)$ or $\rho \in N(\neg B, -\epsilon)$.*

Intuitively, the (δ, ϵ)-robustly safe condition ensures the difference, between the violation time of the same Boolean condition B in S and $D_{h,\varepsilon}(S)$, is bounded. As a result, we can choose appropriate values for δ, ϵ, h and ε s.t. S and $D_{h,\varepsilon}(S)$ can be guaranteed to have the same control flows, and furthermore the distance between their "jump" time (the moment when Boolean condition associated with them becomes false) can be bounded by h. Finally the "approximation" between the behavior of S and $D_{h,\varepsilon}(S)$ can be guaranteed. The range of both δ and ϵ can be estimated by simulation.

Based on the above facts, we have the main theorem as below.

Theorem 3 (Correctness). *Let S be a dHCSP process and ρ_0 the initial state at time 0. Assume S is (δ, ϵ)-robustly safe with respect to ρ_0. Let $0 < \varepsilon < \epsilon$ be a precision and $T \in \mathbb{R}^+$ a time bound. If for any DDE $\dot{\mathbf{x}} = \mathbf{f}(\mathbf{x}, \mathbf{x}_r)$ occurring in S, $\mathbf{f}$ is continuously differentiable on $[0, T]$, and there exists h satisfying $h < \delta < 2h$ if $\delta > 0$ such that Theorem 2 holds for all $\mathbf{f}$ in S, then $S \cong_{h,\varepsilon} D_{h,\varepsilon}(S)$ on $[0, T]$.*

Notice that for a given precision ε, there may not exist an h satisfying the conditions in Theorem 3. It happens when the DDE fails to leave far enough away from the boundary of its domain B in a limited time. However, for the special case that $\delta = 0$, we can always find a sufficiently small h such that $S \cong_{h,\varepsilon} D_{h,\varepsilon}(S)$ on $[0, T]$.

5   From Discretized dHCSP to SystemC

For a dHCSP process S, its discretization $D_{h,\varepsilon}(S)$ is a model without continuous dynamics and therefore can be implemented with an algorithm model. In this section, we illustrate the procedure for automatically generating a piece of SystemC code, denoted as $SC(D_{h,\varepsilon}(S))$, from a discretized dHCSP process $D_{h,\varepsilon}(S)$, and moreover ensure they are "equivalent", i.e., bisimilar. As a result,

Table 1. Part of rules for code generation of dHCSP

$x := e$	$\rightarrow$	$x = e; wait(SC\_ZERO\_TIME);$
wait d	$\rightarrow$	$wait(d, SC\_TU);$
$D_{h,\varepsilon}(P); D_{h,\varepsilon}(Q)$	$\rightarrow$	$SC(D_{h,\varepsilon}(P)); SC(D_{h,\varepsilon}(Q));$
$B \rightarrow D_{h,\varepsilon}(P)$	$\rightarrow$	$if(B)\{SC(D_{h,\varepsilon}(P));\}$
$D_{h,\varepsilon}(P) \sqcap D_{h,\varepsilon}(Q)$	$\rightarrow$	$if(rand()\%2)\{SC(D_{h,\varepsilon}(P));\} \, else\{SC(D_{h,\varepsilon}(Q));\}$
$(D_{h,\varepsilon}(P))^*$	$\rightarrow$	$while(i <= num(P^*))\{ SC(D_{h,\varepsilon}(P)); i++;\}$

for a given precision ε and time bound T, if there exists h such that Theorem 3 holds, i.e., $S \cong_{h,\varepsilon} D_{h,\varepsilon}(S)$ on $[0, T]$, we can conclude that the generated SystemC code $SC(D_{h,\varepsilon}(S))$ and the original dHCSP process S are (h, ε)-approximately bisimilar on $[0, T]$.

Based on its semantics, a dHCSP model that contains multiple parallel processes is mapped into an SC_MODULE in SystemC, and each parallel component is implemented as a thread, e.g., $D_{h,\varepsilon}(P_1) \| D_{h,\varepsilon}(P_2)$ is mapped into two concurrent threads, $SC\_THREAD(SC(D_{h,\varepsilon}(P_1)))$ and $SC\_THREAD(SC(D_{h,\varepsilon}(P_2)))$, respectively. For each sequential process, i.e., $D_{h,\varepsilon}(P_i)$, we define the corresponding rule for transforming it into a piece of SystemC code, according to the type of $D_{h,\varepsilon}(P_i)$.

In Table 1, parts of generation rules are shown for different types of the sequential process $D_{h,\varepsilon}(P_i)$. For $x := e$, it is mapped into an equivalent assignment statement (i.e., $x = e$), followed by a statement $wait(SC\_ZERO\_TIME)$ for making the update valid. For wait d, it is straightforward mapped into a statement $wait(d, SC\_TU)$, where SC_TU is the time unit of d, such as SC_SEC (second), SC_MS (millisecond), SC_US (microsecond), etc. The sequential composition and alternative statements are defined inductively. Nondeterminism is implemented as an *if-else* statement, in which $rand()\%2$ returns 0 or 1 randomly. A *while* statement is used for implementing the repetition constructor, where $num(P^*)$ returns the upper bound of the repeat times for P.

In order to represent the communication statement, additional channels in SystemC (i.e., sc_signal) and events (i.e., sc_event) are introduced to ensure the synchronization between the input side and output side. Consider the discretized input statement, i.e., $ch? := 1; ch?x; ch? := 0$, Boolean variable $ch?$ is represented as an sc_signal (i.e., ch_r) with Boolean type, and moreover additional sc_event (i.e., ch_r_done) is imported to represent the completion of the action that reads values from channel ch. As a result, the SystemC code generated from it is defined as: first, Boolean signal ch_r is initialized as 1, which means channel ch is ready for reading (lines 2–3); then, the reading process waits for the writing of the same channel from another process until it has done (lines 4–6); after that, it gets the latest value from the channel and assigns it to variable x (lines 7–8); at last, it informs the termination of its reading to other processes and resets ch_r to 0 (lines 9–11). Here, there are two sub-phases within the second phase (lines 4–6): first, deciding whether the corresponding writing side is ready (line 4), if not (i.e., $ch\_w = 0$), the reading side keep waiting until the writing side gets ready, i.e., $ch\_w = 1$ (line 5); afterwards, the reading side will wait for another event which indicates that the writing side has written a new value into the channel ch (line 6), for ensuring the synchronization.

```
1   // code for input statement
2   ch_r=1;
3   wait(SC_ZERO_TIME);
4   if(!ch_w)
5       wait(ch_w.posedge_event());
6   wait(ch_w_done);
7   x=ch.read();
8   wait(SC_ZERO_TIME);
9   ch_r_done.notify();
10  ch_r=0;
11  wait(SC_ZERO_TIME);
```

The discretized continuous statement is mapped into two sequential parts in SystemC. For the first part, i.e., $(N(B,\varepsilon) \land N'(B,\varepsilon)) \to$ (wait $h; \mathbf{x} := \mathbf{x} + h\mathbf{f}(\mathbf{x}, \mathbf{x}_r)))^{\frac{T}{h}}$, a **for** loop block is generated (lines 2–8), in which a sequence of *if* statements, corresponding to Boolean condition $(N(B,\varepsilon) \land N'(B,\varepsilon))$, are executed (lines 3–7). Within every conditional statement, a **wait** statement and an assignment statement (based on *Euler method*) are sequentially performed (lines 4–6). Here, $N(B,e)$, $N\_p(B,e)$ and $f(x,x\_r)$ are helper functions (implemented by individual functions) that are generated from $N(B,\varepsilon)$, $N'(B,\varepsilon)$ ($e = \varepsilon$ here) and $\mathbf{f}(\mathbf{x}, \mathbf{x}_r)$, respectively. For the second part, i.e., $N(B,\varepsilon) \land N'(B,\varepsilon) \to$ **stop**, it is mapped into a **return** statement guarded by a condition that is identical with that in line 3 (lines 9–10).

```
1   // code for delayed continuous statement
2   for(int i=0;i<T/h;i++){
3       if(N(B,e)&&N_p(B,e)){
4           wait(h,SC_TU);
5           x=x+h*f(x,x_r);
6           wait(SC_ZERO_TIME);
7       }
8   }
9   if(N(B,e)&&N_p(B,e)){
10      return;
11  }
```

For space limitation, the rest of the code generation rules can be found in [25]. Thus now, for a given discretized dHCSP process $D_{h,\varepsilon}(S)$, we can generate its corresponding SystemC implementation $SC(D_{h,\varepsilon}(S))$. Furthermore, their "equivalence" can be guaranteed by the following theorem.

Theorem 4. *For a dHCSP process S, $D_{h,\varepsilon}(S)$ and $SC(D_{h,\varepsilon}(S))$ are bisimilar.*

6 Case Study

In this section, we illustrate how to generate SystemC code from dHCSP through the example of water tank in Exmaple 1. As discussed above, for a given dHCSP process, the procedure of code generation is divided into two steps: (1) compute the value of step size h that can ensure the original dHCSP process and its discretization are approximately bisimilar with respect to the given precisions; (2) generate SystemC code from the discretized dHCSP process. We have implemented a tool that can generate code from both HCSP and dHCSP processes[1].

Continue to consider Exmaple 1. For given h, ε and T, by using the discretized rules, a discretization system $WTS_{h,\varepsilon}$ is obtained as follows:

$$WTS_{h,\varepsilon} \overset{\text{def}}{=} Watertank_{h,\varepsilon} \| Controller_{h,\varepsilon}$$

$$
\begin{aligned}
Watertank_{h,\varepsilon} \overset{\text{def}}{=}\ & v := v_0; d := d_0; (v = 1 \rightarrow (wl! := 1; (wl! \wedge \neg wl? \rightarrow \\
& (wait\ h; d(t+h) = d(t) + h(Q_{max} - \pi s^2 \sqrt{g(d(t) + d(t-r))})))^{\frac{T}{h}}; \\
& wl! \wedge wl? \rightarrow (wl!d; wl! := 0; cv? := 1; cv?v; \\
& cv? := 0); wl! \wedge \neg wl? \rightarrow \mathbf{stop}); \\
& v = 0 \rightarrow (wl! := 1; (wl! \wedge \neg wl? \rightarrow (wait\ h; \\
& d(t+h) = d(t) + h(-\pi s^2 \sqrt{g(d(t) + d(t-r))})))^{\frac{T}{h}}; \\
& wl! \wedge wl? \rightarrow (wl!d; wl! := 0; cv? := 1; cv?v; \\
& cv? := 0); wl! \wedge \neg wl? \rightarrow \mathbf{stop}))^*
\end{aligned}
$$

$$
\begin{aligned}
Controller_{h,\varepsilon} \overset{\text{def}}{=}\ & y := v_0; x := d_0; (wait\ p; wl! := 1; wl?x; \\
& wl? := 0; x \geq ub \rightarrow y := 0; x \leq lb \rightarrow y := 1; \\
& cv! := 1; cv!y; cv! := 0)^*
\end{aligned}
$$

Given $Q_{max} = 2.0$, $\pi = 3.14$, $s = 0.18$, $g = 9.8$, $p = 1$, $r = 0.1$, $lb = 4.1$, $ub=5.9$, $v_0 = 1$ and $d_0 = 4.5$, we first build an instance of WTS (the Watertank_delay.hcsp file). Then, according to the simulation result, we can estimate that the valid scope of δ and ϵ for WTS is $\delta = 0$ and $\epsilon \leq 0.217$, respectively. By Theorem 3, we can infer that a discretized time step h must exist s.t. WTS and $WTS_{h,\varepsilon}$ are (h, ε)-approximately bisimilar, with $\varepsilon \leq \epsilon$. For given values of ε and time bound T, e.g., $\varepsilon = 0.2$ and $T = 10$, we obtain $h = 0.025$ (by Algorithm 3 in Sect. 4.1) s.t. Theorem 3 holds, i.e., $WTS \cong_{h,\varepsilon} D_{h,\varepsilon}(WTS)$ on $[0, 10]$. After that, we can automatically generate SystemC code equivalent to $D_{h,\varepsilon}(WTS)$ (by calling HCSP2SystemC.jar).

The comparison of the results, i.e., the curves of the water level (d in the figure), which are acquired from the simulation of the original dHCSP model and the generated SystemC code respectively is shown in Fig. 1. The result on the whole time interval $[0, 10]$ is illustrated in Fig. 1(a), and the specific details around two vital points, i.e., 5 and 8, are shown in Fig. 1 (b) and (c), respectively.

---

[1] The tool and all examples for HCSP and dHCSP can be found at https://github.com/HCSP-CodeGeneration/HCSP2SystemC.

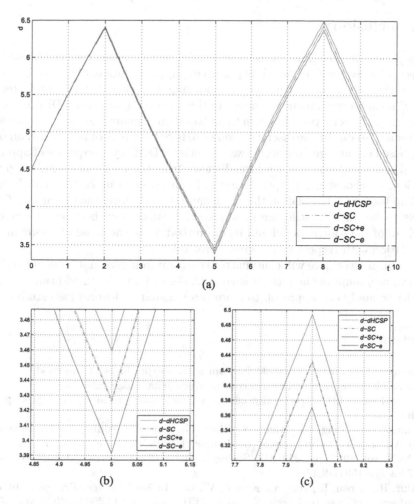

Fig. 1. The dHCSP model *vs.* the SystemC code of WTS (Color figure online).(a) The result on [0,10]; (b) Zoom in on the result around 5; (c) Zoom in on the result around 8.

In the figures, the simulation result (by calling the DDE solver $dde23$ in Matlab) is represented by green solid (i.e., d-d$HCSP$), and the result obtained by running the generated SystemC code is represented by blue dashed (i.e., d-SC). The upper bound (lower bound) of the SystemC result, by adding (subtracting) the local error bounds computed in Algorithm 3, is represented by red solid (dark red solid), i.e., d-SC+e (d-SC-e). As Fig. 1 shows, the results of simulation and SystemC code both always fall into the interval determined by the upper and lower error bounds, which indicates the correctness of the discretization. Moreover, the distance between the state of the simulation and the state of SystemC code is less than the required precision (i.e., $\varepsilon = 0.2$), in every interval of h length.

7 Conclusion

In this paper, we present an automatic translation from abstract dHCSP models to executable SystemC code, while preserving approximate equivalence between them within given precisions. As a modelling language for hybrid systems, dHCSP includes continuous dynamics in the form of DDEs and ODEs, discrete dynamics, and interactions between them based on communication, parallel composition and so on. In the discretization of dHCSP within bounded time, on one hand, based on our previous work, we discretize a DDE by a sequence of approximate discrete states and control the distance from the trajectory within a given precision, by choosing a proper discretized time step to make the error bound less than the precision; and on the other hand, by requiring the original dHCSP models to be robustly safe, we guarantee the consistency between the execution flows of the source model and its discretization in the sense of approximate bisimulation with respect to the given error tolerance.

As a future work, we will continue to transform from SystemC code into other practical programming languages, such as C, C++, java, etc. In addition, we also consider to apply our approach to more complicated real-world case studies.

References

1. Rational Rose. http://www-03.ibm.com/software/products/en/rosemod
2. Simulink. https://cn.mathworks.com/products/simulink.html
3. TargetLink. https://www.dspace.com/en/inc/home/products/sw/pcgs/targetli.cfm
4. Ahmad, E., Dong, Y., Wang, S., Zhan, N., Zou, L.: Adding formal meanings to AADL with hybrid annex. In: Lanese, I., Madelaine, E. (eds.) FACS 2014. LNCS, vol. 8997, pp. 228–247. Springer, Cham (2015). https://doi.org/10.1007/978-3-319-15317-9_15
5. Alur, R., Grosu, R., Hur, Y., Kumar, V., Lee, I.: Modular specification of hybrid systems in charon. In: Lynch, N., Krogh, B.H. (eds.) HSCC 2000. LNCS, vol. 1790, pp. 6–19. Springer, Heidelberg (2000). https://doi.org/10.1007/3-540-46430-1_5
6. Alur, R., Ivancic, F., Kim, J., Lee, I., Sokolsky, O.: Generating embedded software from hierarchical hybrid models. In: LCTES 2003, pp. 171–182 (2003)
7. Anand, M., Fischmeister, S., Hur, Y., Kim, J., Lee, I.: Generating reliable code from hybrid-systems models. IEEE Trans. Comput. 59(9), 1281–1294 (2010)
8. Angeli, D., et al.: A Lyapunov approach to incremental stability properties. IEEE Trans. Autom. Control 47(3), 410–421 (2002)
9. Bellen, A., Zennaro, M.: Numerical Methods for Delay Differential Equations. Oxford University Press, Oxford (2013)
10. Berry, G.: The foundations of esterel. In: Proof, Language, and Interaction, Essays in Honour of Robin Milner, pp. 425–454 (2000)
11. Chen, M., Fränzle, M., Li, Y., Mosaad, P.N., Zhan, N.: Validated simulation-based verification of delayed differential dynamics. In: Fitzgerald, J., Heitmeyer, C., Gnesi, S., Philippou, A. (eds.) FM 2016. LNCS, vol. 9995, pp. 137–154. Springer, Cham (2016). https://doi.org/10.1007/978-3-319-48989-6_9

12. Deshpande, A., Göllü, A., Varaiya, P.: SHIFT: a formalism and a programming language for dynamic networks of hybrid automata. In: Antsaklis, P., Kohn, W., Nerode, A., Sastry, S. (eds.) HS 1996. LNCS, vol. 1273, pp. 113–133. Springer, Heidelberg (1997). https://doi.org/10.1007/BFb0031558
13. Fränzle, M., Herde, C., Ratschan, S., Schubert, T., Teige, T.: Efficient solving of large non-linear arithmetic constraint systems with complex Boolean structure. J. Satisf. Boolean Model. Comput. 1, 209–236 (2007)
14. Girard, A., Pappas, G.: Approximation metrics for discrete and continuous systems. IEEE Trans. Autom. Control 52(5), 782–798 (2007)
15. Halbwachs, N., Caspi, P., Raymond, P., Pilaud, D.: The synchronous dataflow programming language lustre. In: Proceedings of the IEEE, pp. 1305–1320 (1991)
16. Harel, D.: Statecharts: a visual formalism for complex systems. Sci. Comput. Program. 8(3), 231–274 (1987)
17. Henzinger, T.A., Sifakis, J.: The embedded systems design challenge. In: Misra, J., Nipkow, T., Sekerinski, E. (eds.) FM 2006. LNCS, vol. 4085, pp. 1–15. Springer, Heidelberg (2006). https://doi.org/10.1007/11813040_1
18. Huang, Z., Fan, C., Mitra, S.: Bounded invariant verification for time-delayed nonlinear networked dynamical systems. Nonlinear Anal. Hybrid Syst. 23, 211–229 (2017)
19. Hur, Y., Kim, J., Lee, I., Choi, J.-Y.: Sound code generation from communicating hybrid models. In: Alur, R., Pappas, G.J. (eds.) HSCC 2004. LNCS, vol. 2993, pp. 432–447. Springer, Heidelberg (2004). https://doi.org/10.1007/978-3-540-24743-2_29
20. Lee, E.: What's ahead for embedded software? Computer 33(9), 18–26 (2000)
21. Pola, G., Pepe, P., Di Benedetto, M.: Symbolic models for nonlinear time-varying time-delay systems via alternating approximate bisimulation. Int. J. Robust Nonlinear Control 25(14), 2328–2347 (2015)
22. Pola, G., Pepe, P., Di Benedetto, M., Tabuada, P.: Symbolic models for nonlinear time-delay systems using approximate bisimulations. Syst. Control Lett. 59(6), 365–373 (2010)
23. Prajna, S., Jadbabaie, A.: Methods for safety verification of time-delay systems. In: CDC 2005, pp. 4348–4353 (2005)
24. Yan, G., Jiao, L., Li, Y., Wang, S., Zhan, N.: Approximate bisimulation and discretization of hybrid CSP. In: Fitzgerald, J., Heitmeyer, C., Gnesi, S., Philippou, A. (eds.) FM 2016. LNCS, vol. 9995, pp. 702–720. Springer, Cham (2016). https://doi.org/10.1007/978-3-319-48989-6_43
25. Yan, G., Jiao, L., Wang, S., Zhan, N.: Synthesizing SystemC code from delay hybrid CSP (full version). https://www.dropbox.com/s/rxbrib49bx1yv60/APLAS2017-FULL.pdf?dl=0
26. Yan, G., Jiao, L., Wang, L., Wang, S., Zhan, N.: Automatically generating SystemC code from HCSP formal models (Submitted)
27. Zhan, N., Wang, S., Zhao, H.: Formal Verification of Simulink/Stateflow Diagrams: A Deductive Way. Springer, New York (2016)
28. Zou, L., Fränzle, M., Zhan, N., Mosaad, P.N.: Automatic verification of stability and safety for delay differential equations. In: Kroening, D., Păsăreanu, C.S. (eds.) CAV 2015. LNCS, vol. 9207, pp. 338–355. Springer, Cham (2015). https://doi.org/10.1007/978-3-319-21668-3_20

Security

Taming Message-Passing Communication in Compositional Reasoning About Confidentiality

Ximeng Li$^{(\boxtimes)}$, Heiko Mantel$^{(\boxtimes)}$, and Markus Tasch$^{(\boxtimes)}$

Department of Computer Science, TU-Darmstadt, Darmstadt, Germany
{li,mantel,tasch}@mais.informatik.tu-darmstadt.de

Abstract. We propose a solution for verifying the information-flow security of distributed programs in a compositional manner. Our focus is on the treatment of message passing in such a verification, and our goal is to boost the precision of modular reasoning using rely-guarantee-style reasoning. Enabling a more precise treatment of message passing required the identification of novel concepts that capture assumptions about how a process's environment interacts. Our technical contributions include a process-local security condition that allows one to exploit such assumptions when analyzing individual processes, a security type system that is sensitive in the content as well as in the availability of messages, and a soundness proof for our security type system. Our results complement existing solutions for rely-guarantee-style reasoning about information-flow security that focused on multi-threading and shared memory.

1 Introduction

Information-flow security aims at end-to-end security guarantees for IT systems. Noninterference [9] is a formally defined property that requires a system's publicly observable output to not depend on secrets. Multiple variants of noninterference exist and can be used to capture that system runs do not reveal information about secrets [17]. The formal verification of a noninterference-like property provides a high level of assurance, but can be non-trivial.

Compositional reasoning can be applied to reduce the conceptual complexity of a formal verification of information-flow security [21]. In compositional reasoning, one infers the security of a complex system from the security of its individual components based on a compositionality theorem. The local security of an individual system component can, again, be expressed using a noninterference-like property. To ensure soundness of compositional reasoning, the locally verified security properties might be more restrictive than the globally desired security guarantees. Hence, a key question in compositional reasoning is how to benefit from the reduction of conceptual complexity without loosing too much precision.

One can increase the precision of modular reasoning by exploiting assumptions in the local verification of a component, i.e., by rely-guarantee reasoning [13]. While being established in other areas, sound solutions for rely-guarantee-style reasoning about information-flow security appeared relatively late [19]. Moreover,

© Springer International Publishing AG 2017
B.-Y.E. Chang (Ed.): APLAS 2017, LNCS 10695, pp. 45–66, 2017.
https://doi.org/10.1007/978-3-319-71237-6_3

their focus was on systems with shared-memory communication [3,18,19,22]. This article is complementary in this respect. We develop a solution for rely-guarantee-style reasoning for systems with message-passing communication.

The problem of verifying information-flow security for systems with message passing in a modular fashion has been addressed before, e.g., in [7,25]. There are two main reasons why message passing received special attention. Firstly, the fact that a message is present or not might communicate information that needs to be protected. Hence, it does not suffice to protect just the confidentiality of a message's content [25]. Secondly, messages are usually buffered until they have been received. Hence, when a message is received, it is deleted from a buffer [27]. That is, receive commands differ from read commands in that they block if no message is present and in that they alter a system's state when a message is received. Such peculiarities of message passing must be taken into account.

A solution for rely-guarantee-style reasoning about information-flow security for systems with remote procedure calls was proposed in [10]. This constitutes a step towards supporting message-passing communication, but it is limited to systems with unbufferred communication and with a hierarchical communication structure. In this article, we aim for a general solution that, in particular, addresses buffered message-passing communication and that is suitable for the flexible interaction patterns commonly used in distributed systems. Ultimately, the goal is to support both fundamental principles of communication (i.e., message passing and shared memory [27]). The solution for message passing presented here is compatible with the solution for shared memory in [19].

The main technical contributions of this article are:

(A) a sound, yet precise solution for modular reasoning about distributed system security at the semantic level, via a novel process-local security condition
(B) a sound, fine-grained security analysis that provides the basis for automating the verification of the process-local security condition.

More concretely, our process-local security condition, called local security, captures the intuition that an individual process of a distributed system does not leak secrets under explicit assumptions about the process's interface. The ability to exploit assumptions increases the precision of local reasoning about security. Local security is compositional in allowing one to conclude the security of the overall distributed system from the local security of all processes. This compositionality lifts the precision gain in local reasoning to the global level.

Our analysis for local security is realized as a security type system [28]. This security type system exploits the assumptions explicitly made in a program to perform fine-grained type checking of the program. Typing constraints are relaxed for a receive command when an assumption indicates the non-blockage of the receive. Furthermore, the type system is content-sensitive and availability-sensitive: it deals with programs where the confidentiality of the content and presence of messages may vary over the same communication channel.

We evaluate our approach at examples with communication patterns taken from real-world distributed systems. All processes in the examples are typable, and the systems are proven secure using the compositionality of local security.

2   Motivation and Approach at a Glance

We illustrate that without making assumptions about message passing, the local information-flow analysis of processes is overly restrictive. For three simplistic example programs, we provide environments in which the programs cause information leakage and environments in which the programs behave securely. That is, these programs must be classified as insecure unless one is able to characterize the environments in which the respective program behaves securely.

We propose a language for specifying assumptions about a component's environment. We explain how one can apply this language to capture environments in which our three example programs behave securely. The identification of assumptions that are suitable for this purpose was a key step in our research project. By exploiting the assumptions in a compositional verification of information-flow security, one can increase the precision of the overall analysis substantially.

Consider the following three example programs:

$$content = \text{recv}(\underline{enc}, x); \text{send}(\underline{pub}, x)$$
$$presence_1 = \text{recv}(\underline{pri}, x); \text{send}(\underline{pub}, 1)$$
$$presence_2 = \text{if } h > 0 \text{ then recv}(\underline{pri}, x) \text{ else skip fi}; \text{send}(\underline{pub}, 1)$$

where x is a *local variable* (i.e., it cannot be accessed by other processes), h is a *high local variable* (i.e., it might contain a secret), $\underline{pri}$ is a *private channel* (i.e., its content cannot be seen by attackers), $\underline{enc}$ is an *encrypted channel* (i.e., the existence of messages might be visible to attackers, but not the messages' content), and $\underline{pub}$ is a *public channel* (i.e., its content might be visible to attackers).

That is, *content* awaits a message via an encrypted channel and forwards this message over a public channel. The program $presence_1$ awaits a message from a private channel, and then outputs 1 to a public channel. If its then-branch is taken, $presence_2$ awaits a message from a private channel and subsequently outputs 1 to a public channel. Otherwise, $presence_2$ just outputs 1 to the public channel. Note that which branch is chosen depends on potentially secret information. There is a danger of information leakage for each of these programs, but there are also environments in which the programs behave securely.

Example 1. If an environment sends a secret over the encrypted channel $\underline{enc}$ then *content* causes information leakage because it forwards the secret to the public channel $\underline{pub}$, whose content might be visible to attackers.In contrast, if the environment provides a public message over $\underline{enc}$ (e.g., a username over HTTPS) then *content* forwards a public value to $\underline{pub}$, i.e., no secrets are leaked.

If an environment only sends a message over $\underline{pri}$ if some secret value is positive then $presence_1$ leaks information: The attacker sees 1 on $\underline{pub}$ only if the secret is positive. Otherwise, $\underline{pri}$ blocks at the receive command and the send command is never reached. However, if secrets do not influence whether the environment sends messages on $\underline{pri}$ then $presence_1$ does not cause information leakage.

If an environment does not send any messages over $\underline{pri}$ then $presence_2$ causes information leakage: The attacker sees 1 on $\underline{pub}$ only if the value of h is negative or zero. If the value of h is positive, then $presence_2$ blocks at the receive command and the send command is never reached. In contrast, if the environment definitely sends some message over $\underline{pri}$ before the command $\mathsf{recv}(\underline{pri}, x)$ is reached then the program $presence_2$ does not cause any information leakage.   ◇

Our Solution at a Glance. The program $content$ does not leak secrets in environments that provide a public message on $\underline{enc}$ as explained in Example 1. We explicate that we expect the next available message to have public content by annotating the receive command in $content$ with $\mathbb{L}^\bullet$, which results in:

$$\{\mathbb{L}^\bullet\}\,\mathsf{recv}(\underline{enc}, x); \mathsf{send}(\underline{pub}, x)$$

The annotation $\mathbb{L}^\bullet$ indicates that the program shall only be run in environments that guarantee a public message to be received. This assumption can then be exploited to make the local security analysis more permissive.

For explicating that $presence_1$ and $presence_2$ shall only run in environments that provide messages on $\underline{pri}$ before the programs try to receive, we employ NE:

$$\{NE\}\,\mathsf{recv}(\underline{pri}, x); \mathsf{send}(\underline{pub}, 1)$$
$$\text{if } h > 0 \text{ then } {}^{\{NE\}}\mathsf{recv}(\underline{pri}, x) \text{ else skip fi}; \mathsf{send}(\underline{pub}, 1)$$

We introduce $\mathbb{L}^\circ$ to capture that the availability of messages does not depend on secrets. This assumption is weaker than the one captured by NE. Since $presence_1$ does not leak secrets in environments satisfying $\mathbb{L}^\circ$, we can use it instead of NE:

$$\{\mathbb{L}^\circ\}\,\mathsf{recv}(\underline{pri}, x); \mathsf{send}(\underline{pub}, 1)$$

In summary, we propose the following language of assumptions:

$$asm:: = \mathbb{L}^\bullet \mid NE \mid \mathbb{L}^\circ$$

These assumptions can be used to constrain the environments in which a program may be run. We will show how to exploit the assumptions in modular reasoning about information-flow security, both at a semantic level (Sect. 5) and at a syntactic level (Sect. 6). Note that our annotations are helpful hints for the security analysis, but they do not alter a program's behavior in any way.

3   Model of Computation

We consider distributed systems whose processes have a local memory and communicate using message passing both with each other and with the environment. We model the communication lines used for message passing by a set of *channels* Ch. We use $ECh \subseteq Ch$ to denote the set of *external channels*, i.e. the system's interface to its environment. We use $ICh = Ch \setminus ECh$ to denote the set of *internal channels*, i.e. the channels that cannot be accessed by the system's environment.

Snapshots. We model each snapshot of a single process by a pair $\langle prog; mem \rangle$ consisting of a control state $prog$ and a memory state mem. The *control state* $prog$ equals the program that remains to be executed by the process. We denote the set of all programs by $Prog$ and leave this set underspecified. The *memory state* mem is a function of type $Mem = Var \to Val$, where Var is a set of *program variables* and Val is a set of *values*. We call pairs $\langle prog; mem \rangle$ *process configurations* and use $PCnf$ to denote the set of all process configurations.

We model each snapshot of a distributed system by a pair $\langle pcnfl; \sigma \rangle$ consisting of a list of process configurations $pcnfl \in PCnf^*$ and a channel state σ. The list $pcnfl$ models the local state of each process. The *channel state* σ is a function of type $\Sigma = Ch \to Val^*$ that models, by a FIFO queue, which messages have been sent, but not yet received on each communication line.

We call pairs $\langle pcnfl; \sigma \rangle$ *global configurations* and use $GCnf$ to denote the set of all global configurations.

We use *local configurations* to capture the local view of individual processes during a run. Formally, a local configuration $lcnf$ is a pair $\langle pcnf; \sigma \rangle$ where $pcnf \in PCnf$ and $\sigma \in \Sigma$. In a global configuration $\langle [pcnf_1, \ldots, pcnf_i, \ldots, pcnf_n]; \sigma \rangle$, the local configuration of process i is $\langle pcnf_i; \sigma \rangle$.

Runs. We model runs of distributed systems by *traces*, i.e. finite lists of global configurations, and use $Tr = GCnf^*$ to denote the set of all traces. Appending a global configuration to the end of a trace captures either the effect of a computation step by the distributed system or of an interaction with its environment.

We model system environments by functions of type $\varXi = Tr \to (ECh \to Val^*)$, which we call *strategies*. The function $\xi(tr)$ defines which inputs the environment modeled by ξ provides and which outputs it consumes on each external communication line after the run modeled by tr. That is, $\xi(tr)(ch)$ equals the content of $ch \in ECh$ after the environment's interaction subsequent to tr.

We use the judgment $tr \to_\xi tr'$ to capture that the trace tr' might result by one computation or communication step after the trace tr under the strategy ξ. The calculus for this judgment consists of the following two rules.

$$\frac{\langle pcnfl; \sigma \rangle = last(tr) \qquad \sigma' = \xi(tr)}{tr \to_\xi tr \cdot \langle pcnfl; \sigma[ECh \mapsto \sigma'(ECh)] \rangle} \qquad \frac{\langle [\ldots, pcnf_i, \ldots]; \sigma \rangle = last(tr) \qquad \langle pcnf_i; \sigma \rangle \to \langle pcnf'_i; \sigma' \rangle}{tr \to_\xi tr \cdot \langle [\ldots, pcnf'_i, \ldots]; \sigma' \rangle}$$

The first rule captures how the environment interacts with the system using external communication lines. The expression $\sigma[ECh \mapsto \sigma'(ECh)]$ in the conclusion of this rule denotes the pointwise update of the function σ such that each $ch \in ECh$ is mapped to $\sigma'(ch)$ and each $ch \in ICh$ to $\sigma(ch)$. Note that one communication step might update multiple channels.

The second rule captures how the system itself performs a step. The choice of the acting process is non-deterministic, which reflects a distributed system without global scheduler. The judgment $\langle pcnf_i; \sigma \rangle \to \langle pcnf'_i; \sigma' \rangle$ (second premise of the rule) captures how the chosen process updates its own configuration and the channel state. We will introduce a calculus for this judgment later.

We model the possible runs of a distributed system by a set of traces. We define this set by $traces_\xi(gcnf) = \{tr' \in Tr \mid [gcnf] \, (\rightarrow_\xi)^* \, tr'\}$, where $gcnf \in GCnf$ is an initial configuration and $(\rightarrow_\xi)^*$ the reflexive transitive closure of $\rightarrow_\xi$.

We view a *distributed program* as a list of programs, use $\|$ to indicate that the programs in the list are executed by concurrently running processes, and define the set of all distributed programs by $DProg = Prog^*$. Given a distributed program $dprog = [prog_1 \| \cdots \| prog_n]$, we define its possible traces under ξ by

$$traces_\xi(dprog) = traces_\xi(\langle[\langle prog_1; mem_{\text{init}}\rangle, \ldots, \langle prog_n; mem_{\text{init}}\rangle]; \sigma_{\text{init}}\rangle)$$

The initial memory mem_{init} maps all variables to the designated initial value v_{init}, and the initial channel state σ_{init} maps all channels to the empty list ϵ.

Programming Language. We consider a simple while-language extended with message-passing commands to make things concrete. The syntax is defined by

$$prog::\,= \mathsf{recv}(ch, x) \mid \mathsf{if\text{-}recv}(ch, x, x_\mathrm{b}) \mid \mathsf{send}(ch, e) \mid \mathsf{skip} \mid x := e \mid$$
$$prog_1; prog_2 \mid \mathsf{if}\ e\ \mathsf{then}\ prog_1\ \mathsf{else}\ prog_2\ \mathsf{fi} \mid \mathsf{while}\ e\ \mathsf{do}\ prog\ \mathsf{od} \mid \mathsf{stop}$$

Derivability of the judgment $\langle pcnf; \sigma \rangle \rightarrow \langle pcnf'; \sigma' \rangle$ is defined by a structural operational semantics of the programming language, where rules for most commands are straightforward (and, hence, omitted here to save space).

The command skip terminates without effects. An assignment $x := e$ stores the value of the expression e in x. Sequential composition $prog_1; prog_2$, conditional branching $\mathsf{if}\ e\ \mathsf{then}\ prog_1\ \mathsf{else}\ prog_2\ \mathsf{fi}$, and loops $\mathsf{while}\ e\ \mathsf{do}\ prog\ \mathsf{od}$ have the usual semantics. The symbol stop is used to signal that the process has terminated, and it is not part of the surface syntax used for writing programs.

The blocking receive $\mathsf{recv}(ch, x)$ removes the first message from the message queue $\sigma(ch)$ and stores it in x (first rule on the right). If no message is available on

$$\frac{\sigma(ch) = v \cdot \gamma \qquad mem' = mem[x \mapsto v] \qquad \sigma' = \sigma[ch \mapsto \gamma]}{\langle\langle\mathsf{recv}(ch, x); mem\rangle; \sigma\rangle \rightarrow \langle\langle\mathsf{stop}; mem'\rangle; \sigma'\rangle}$$

$$\frac{[\![e]\!]_{mem} = v \qquad \sigma' = \sigma[ch \mapsto \sigma(ch) \cdot v]}{\langle\langle\mathsf{send}(ch, e); mem\rangle; \sigma\rangle \rightarrow \langle\langle\mathsf{stop}; mem\rangle; \sigma'\rangle}$$

ch, then the execution blocks until a message becomes available. The non-blocking receive $\mathsf{if\text{-}recv}(ch, x, x_\mathrm{b})$ uses the variable x_b to record whether a receive was successful ($x_\mathrm{b} = tt$) or not ($x_\mathrm{b} = ff$). If no message could be received, then the program run continues with x unchanged. The send command appends the value of e to $\sigma(ch)$ (second rule above).

Relations Between Channel States. If two channel states agree on the availability of messages on some channel, then executing a receive command on this channel either succeeds or blocks in both channel states. For each $ch \in Ch$, we introduce an equivalence relation $\overset{ch}{=}_\# \subseteq \Sigma \times \Sigma$ to characterize agreement in this respect. That is, we define $\overset{ch}{=}_\#$ by $\sigma_1 \overset{ch}{=}_\# \sigma_2$ iff $|\sigma_1(ch)| > 0 \Leftrightarrow |\sigma_2(ch)| > 0$.

For each $ch \in Ch$, we define a second equivalence relation $\overset{ch}{=}_1$ on channel states in which ch is non-empty by $\sigma_1 \overset{ch}{=}_1 \sigma_2$ iff $first(\sigma_1(ch)) = first(\sigma_2(ch))$. We lift $\overset{ch}{=}_1$ to arbitrary channel states by defining channel states with $|\sigma(ch)| = 0$ to be related to all channel states. That is, $\overset{ch}{=}_1 \subseteq \Sigma \times \Sigma$ is defined by $\sigma_1 \overset{ch}{=}_1 \sigma_2$ iff $(|\sigma_1(ch)| > 0 \land |\sigma_2(ch)| > 0) \Rightarrow first(\sigma_1(ch)) = first(\sigma_2(ch))$. Note that $\overset{ch}{=}_1$ is intransitive and, hence, not an equivalence relation (on arbitrary channel states).

We will use $\overset{ch}{=}_{\#}$ and $\overset{ch}{=}_1$ in our definition of local security in Sect. 5.2.

Remark 1. Note that an alternative way of lifting $\overset{ch}{=}_1$ to arbitrary channel states is to require a channel state σ with $|\sigma(ch)| = 0$ to be related to no other channel state. This alternative would impose the restriction that the lifted $\overset{ch}{=}_1$ is included in $\overset{ch}{=}_{\#}$. With our design choice, this restriction is not imposed, and the relations $\overset{ch}{=}_{\#}$ and $\overset{ch}{=}_1$ are kept more independent of each other.

4   Attacker Model and Baseline Security

In information-flow security, one considers an attacker who has access to parts of a system's interface and who knows how the system operates in principle (e.g., by knowing a program's code). The attacker combines the observations that he makes during a system run with his knowledge of the system logic to infer additional information. A system has secure information flow if such an attacker is unable to obtain any secrets (i.e., by his observations and by his inference).

Observation Model. As described in Sect. 3, we consider distributed systems and use the set of external channels ECh to model a system's interface. We assume that an attacker's observations are limited by access control and encryption. That is, some channels are private (messages on these channels are inaccessible), some are encrypted (the content of messages on theses channels is protected), and the remaining ones are public (the messages on these channels are unprotected). In line with Sect. 2, we model the three kinds of external channels by partitioning the set ECh into three subsets: the public channels $PubCh$, the encrypted channels $EncCh$, and the private channels $PriCh$.

If a message is transmitted over a channel, then the attacker observes the whole message – if the channel is public, its presence – if the channel is encrypted, and nothing – if the channel is private. Formally, we use a value $v \in Val$ to capture the observation of a message's content on a public channel, and use the special symbol $\odot$ to capture the observation of a message's presence on an encrypted channel. We use a sequence of values (resp. $\odot$) to capture the observation on a public (resp. encrypted) channel. Finally, we use the special symbol $\oslash$ to indicate the absence of an observation. That is, the set of possible observations by the attacker is $Obs = Val^* \cup \{\odot\}^* \cup \{\oslash\}$.

We define the function $ob : (ECh \times \Sigma) \rightarrow Obs$ to retrieve the observation on an external channel from a channel state.

$$ob(ch, \sigma) \triangleq \begin{cases} \oslash & \text{if } ch \in PriCh \\ \odot^{|\sigma(ch)|} & \text{if } ch \in EncCh \\ \sigma(ch) & \text{if } ch \in PubCh \end{cases}$$

Attacker's Knowledge. We call two channel states distinguishable if the attacker's observations of them differ. Complementarily, we define two channel states to be *indistinguishable* for the attacker by $\sigma_1 \simeq_\Sigma \sigma_2$ iff $\forall ch \in ECh$: $ob(ch, \sigma_1) = ob(ch, \sigma_2)$. We call traces distinguishable if the corresponding channel states in the traces are distinguishable. Complementarily, we define two traces to be *indistinguishable* for the attacker by $tr_1 \simeq_{Tr} tr_2$ iff $\overline{ob}(tr_1) = \overline{ob}(tr_2)$ where $\overline{ob}([\langle pcnfl_1; \sigma_1 \rangle, ..., \langle pcnfl_n; \sigma_n \rangle]) \triangleq [\lambda ch : ECh. ob(ch, \sigma_1), ..., \lambda ch : ECh. ob(ch, \sigma_n)]$.

The attacker's ability to distinguish different traces allows him to infer possible environments in which the system is run. More concretely, he only deems environments that are compatible with his observations possible. We capture which environments the attacker deems possible for his observations by a set of strategies and call this set the *attacker's knowledge*. We define the attacker's knowledge for each observation by the function $\mathcal{K} : (DProg \times (ECh \rightarrow Obs)^*) \rightarrow 2^\Xi$.

$$\mathcal{K}(dprog, otr) \triangleq \{\xi \in \Xi \mid \exists tr \in traces_\xi(dprog) : \overline{ob}(tr) = otr\}$$

Knowledge-Based Security. The attacker tries to infer information about secrets coming from the environment. That is, he tries to exclude environments with the same observable interaction but different unobservable interaction. We capture that two environments differ only in their unobservable interaction by the indistinguishability relation $\simeq_\Xi$ on strategies.

$$\xi_1 \simeq_\Xi \xi_2 \triangleq \forall tr_1, tr_2 : tr_1 \simeq_{Tr} tr_2 \Rightarrow \forall ch \in ECh : ob(ch, \xi_1(tr_1)) = ob(ch, \xi_2(tr_2))$$

Based on this notion of indistinguishability on strategies, we define a distributed program to be *knowledge-based secure* (in the spirit of [4]):

Definition 1 (Knowledge-based Security). *A distributed program dprog is knowledge-based secure, denoted by KBSec(dprog), if for all $\xi \in \Xi$ and $tr \in traces_\xi(dprog)$, we have $\mathcal{K}(dprog, \overline{ob}(tr)) \supseteq \{\xi' \in \Xi \mid \xi' \simeq_\Xi \xi\}$.*

That is, a distributed program *dprog* is secure if the attacker is not able to use an observation $\overline{ob}(tr)$ made when *dprog* is run under a strategy ξ to exclude any strategy ξ' indistinguishable to ξ. Hence, the attacker is unable to exclude environments with the same observable interaction but different unobservable interaction. Thus, the attacker is unable to obtain secrets coming from the environment – *dprog* has secure information flow.

5   Compositional Reasoning About Noninterference

It is non-trivial to monolithically verify noninterference for complex systems. Our goal is to simplify such a verification by providing better support for modular reasoning. We define a notion of local security for individual processes that is a variant of noninterference (i.e., it requires the observable behavior of a process to not depend on secrets). Local security is compositional in the sense that security of a system (as defined in Sect. 4) follows from local security of all processes.

Technically, we define local security using a notion of bisimilarity on process configurations. We define a program to satisfy local security if all pairings of the program with two low-indistinguishable memories (e.g., [19,25]) are bisimilar. In the definition of this bisimilarity, we universally quantify over pairs of channel states that are indistinguishable for the attacker (as in [7,25]). Unlike in prior work, we restrict the universal quantification of pairs of channel states further based on assumptions. This exploitation of assumptions is the key to achieving substantially better precision in a modular security analysis.

5.1 Annotated Programs

Recall our set $Asm = \{NE, \mathbb{L}^\bullet, \mathbb{L}^\circ\}$ of assumptions from Sect. 2. In order to exploit these assumptions in local reasoning, they need to be extractable from programs with annotations. We use the function $asm\text{-}of : Prog \to 2^{AsmCh}$ to extract which assumptions are made over which channels, from annotated programs. Here, $AsmCh$ is the set $Asm \times Ch$ of pairs of assumptions and channels.

For concrete examples, we augment our language from Sect. 3 with annotations over receive commands (abusing $prog$ for programs in this new language):

$$prog ::= p \mid {}^{as}\mathsf{recv}(ch, x) \mid {}^{as}\mathsf{if\text{-}recv}(ch, x, x_\mathsf{b})$$
$$p \in Prog \setminus \{\mathsf{recv}(ch,x), \mathsf{if\text{-}recv}(ch,x,x_\mathsf{b})\}, \ as \subseteq Asm$$

For this language, we define the function $asm\text{-}of$ by $asm\text{-}of({}^{as}\mathsf{recv}(ch,x)) = asm\text{-}of({}^{as}\mathsf{if\text{-}recv}(ch,x,x_\mathsf{b})) = as \times \{ch\}$, $asm\text{-}of(prog_1; prog_2) = asm\text{-}of\ (prog_1)$, and $asm\text{-}of(prog) = \emptyset$ otherwise.

5.2 Process-Local Security Condition

We use the security lattice $(\{\mathbb{L}, \mathbb{H}\}, \sqsubseteq, \sqcup, \sqcap)$ with $\mathbb{L} \sqsubseteq \mathbb{H}$ to express security policies for the variables local to an individual process. For a variable, the security level $\mathbb{H}$ (high) indicates that it may contain (or depend on) secrets, and the security level $\mathbb{L}$ indicates that it must not. We use the environment $lev : Var \to Lev$ to record the security level of each variable.

As usual, we define the *low-equivalence relation* $=_\mathbb{L}$ to capture agreement of memory states on low variables as follows.

Definition 2. $mem_1 =_\mathbb{L} mem_2 \triangleq \forall x \in Var : lev(x) = \mathbb{L} \Rightarrow mem_1(x) = mem_2(x)$

Hence, low-equivalent memory states can differ only in high variables.

For each $acs \in 2^{AsmCh}$, we define a relation $\stackrel{acs}{=\!=} \subseteq \Sigma \times \Sigma$ using the relations $\stackrel{ch}{=}_\#$ and $\stackrel{ch}{=}_1$, which are defined in Sect. 3.

Definition 3. $\sigma_1 \stackrel{acs}{=\!=} \sigma_2 \triangleq \forall asm \in Asm : \forall ch \in ICh : (asm, ch) \in acs \Rightarrow$
$$(asm = \mathbb{L}^\circ \Rightarrow \sigma_1 \stackrel{ch}{=}_\# \sigma_2) \wedge (asm = \mathbb{L}^\bullet \Rightarrow \sigma_1 \stackrel{ch}{=}_1 \sigma_2)$$

The relation $\overset{acs}{=\!=\!=}$ captures a similarity of channel states. If $\sigma_1 \overset{acs}{=\!=\!=} \sigma_2$ and $(\mathbb{L}^\circ, ch) \in acs$, then the two channel states agree wrt. the availability of messages on the channel ch. If $\sigma_1 \overset{acs}{=\!=\!=} \sigma_2$, $(\mathbb{L}^\bullet, ch) \in acs$, and both $\sigma_1(ch)$ and $\sigma_2(ch)$ are non-empty, then the first message available on ch is the same in σ_1 and σ_2. Note that Definition 3 imposes these restrictions only for internal channels.

Recall from Sect. 4 that the relation $\simeq_\Sigma$ captures an agreement of channel states wrt. the attacker's observations on external channels. We use $\simeq_\Sigma$ in combination with $\overset{acs}{=\!=\!=}$ in our definition of local security.

We say that a channel state σ satisfies an assumption (NE, ch) if $|\sigma(ch)| > 0$. We introduce a relation $\ltimes^{NE} \subseteq \Sigma \times 2^{AsmCh}$ to capture that all assumptions of the form (NE, ch) in a set of assumptions are satisfied.

Definition 4. $\sigma \ltimes^{NE} acs \triangleq \forall ch \in Ch : (NE, ch) \in acs \Rightarrow |\sigma(ch)| > 0$

Our notion of local security builds on a notion of assumption-aware bisimilarity, that characterizes process configurations with similar observable data and behavior, despite potential differences in secrets.

Definition 5. *A symmetric relation R on process configurations is an* assumption-aware bisimulation, *if $pcnf_1 \, R \, pcnf_2$, $pcnf_1 = \langle prog_1; mem_1 \rangle$, $pcnf_2 = \langle prog_2; mem_2 \rangle$, $acs_1 = asm\text{-}of(prog_1)$, and $acs_2 = asm\text{-}of(prog_2)$, imply $mem_1 =_L mem_2$, $prog_1 = \mathsf{stop} \Leftrightarrow prog_2 = \mathsf{stop}$, and*

$$\left(\begin{array}{l} \langle pcnf_1; \sigma_1 \rangle \rightarrow \langle pcnf_1'; \sigma_1' \rangle \wedge \\ \sigma_1 \simeq_\Sigma \sigma_2 \wedge \sigma_1 \overset{acs_1 \cup acs_2}{=\!=\!=\!=\!=\!=} \sigma_2 \wedge \\ \sigma_1 \ltimes^{NE} acs_1 \wedge \sigma_2 \ltimes^{NE} acs_2 \end{array} \right) \Rightarrow \left(\begin{array}{l} \exists pcnf_2', \sigma_2' : \\ \langle pcnf_2; \sigma_2 \rangle \rightarrow \langle pcnf_2'; \sigma_2' \rangle \wedge \\ \sigma_1' \simeq_\Sigma \sigma_2' \wedge pcnf_1' \, R \, pcnf_2' \end{array} \right)$$

We call two process configurations assumption-aware bisimilar *if there is an assumption-aware bisimulation in which they are related.*

If two process configurations are assumption-aware bisimilar, then differences between their memories can only exist in high variables. In addition, if one process is unable to take a step, then the other process is not able to either. Furthermore, after each lockstep taken by the respective processes under assumptions, differences in secrets over the channels and in the variables are not propagated to the low variables or to the observations that can be made by the attacker. It follows that no observable differences can result from differences in secrets after an arbitrary number of locksteps taken under assumptions. Note that channel states in the beginning of each lockstep are limited to ones that differ only in the channels over which $\mathbb{L}^\circ$ and $\mathbb{L}^\bullet$ are not used, and ones where the availability of messages agrees with the use of NE. By limiting the potential channel states, the potential environments of the program is more precisely characterized. Also note that the preservation of $\sigma_1 \overset{acs_1 \cup acs_2}{=\!=\!=\!=\!=\!=} \sigma_2$ by each lockstep is not required. We explain why compositional reasoning using local security is sound in Sect. 5.5.

We define the relation $\approx$ to be the union of all assumption-aware bisimulations. It is easy to see that $\approx$ is again an assumption-aware bisimulation. Based on $\approx$, we define an indistinguishability relation on programs, and our notion of local security by classifying a program as secure if it is indistinguishable to itself.

Definition 6. *We say two programs $prog_1$ and $prog_2$ are* indistinguishable, *denoted by $prog_1 \sim prog_2$, if $mem_1 =_\mathbb{L} mem_2 \Rightarrow \langle prog_1; mem_1 \rangle \approx \langle prog_2; mem_2 \rangle$.*

Definition 7 (Local Security). *A program prog is* locally secure, *denoted by $LSec(prog)$, if $prog \sim prog$.*

Local security allows one to reason about a program in a restricted class of environments meeting explicit assumptions. This fine-grained treatment of environments provides formal underpinnings for the intuitive security of programs (e.g., ones in Sects. 2 and 6.3) that are deemed leaky by existing security properties (e.g., [5, 24, 25]) for message-passing communication or interaction.

Remark 2. Note that the local security of a program is preserved when a private external channel is turned into an internal channel, or vice versa, in case no assumption out of $\mathbb{L}^\bullet$ and $\mathbb{L}^\circ$ is made over the channel.

Remark 3. Note also that the local security of a program is not affected by using the assumptions $\mathbb{L}^\bullet$ and $\mathbb{L}^\circ$ over external channels. Technically, this is because of Definitions 5, 6, and 7. That is, our definitions reflect a conservative approach to reasoning about open systems. In fact, we do not expect $\mathbb{L}^\bullet$ and $\mathbb{L}^\circ$ to be used over external channels.

5.3   Compositional Reasoning About Information-Flow Security

Our notion of local security allows one to decompose the verification of knowledge-based security for distributed programs into the verification of processes.

Theorem 1 (Soundness of Compositional Reasoning). *For a distributed program $dprog = \|_i prog_i$, if $LSec(prog_i)$ holds for all i, and dprog ensures a sound use of assumptions, then we have $KBSec(dprog)$.*

This theorem requires that a distributed program ensures a sound use of assumptions. Intuitively, "sound use of assumptions" means that assumptions are met by the actual environment of the component program inside the distributed program. We will precisely define this notion in Sect. 5.4.

Since local security needs to be verified for less complex systems (i.e., processes), Theorem 1 reduces the conceptual complexity of verifying the security of distributed programs considerably. Since assumptions can be exploited when verifying local security, compositional reasoning based on Theorem 1 is also less restrictive than in existing work on systems with message passing (e.g., [7, 8, 25]).

5.4   Instrumented Semantics and Sound Use of Assumptions

We define the notion that a distributed program ensures a sound use of assumptions through an instrumentation of the semantics of our programming language.

We use *instrumentation states* to over-approximate the dependency of message content and presence on secrets over internal channels. Instrumentation states are from the set $InSt = \{\mu \in ICh \rightarrow (Lev^* \times Lev) \mid \mu(ch) = (llst, \mathbb{H}) \Rightarrow \exists n : llst = \mathbb{H}^n\}$. An instrumentation state maps each internal channel to a pair $(llst, \ell)$. Here $llst$ is a list of security levels, each for a message over the channel, while ℓ is the security level for the overall presence of messages over the channel. The level $\mathbb{H}$ (confidential) indicates that message content or presence might depend on secrets, while the level $\mathbb{L}$ (public) indicates that message content or presence must not depend on secrets. In case $\ell = \mathbb{H}$, all levels in $llst$ are $\mathbb{H}$, which reflects that presence cannot be more confidential than content (e.g., [24, 25]).

We use the relation $\models$ between $\Sigma \times InSt$ and $AsmCh$ to say that an assumption for a channel holds in a channel state and an instrumentation state.

Definition 8. *The relation $\models$ is defined by*

$$(\sigma, \mu) \models (NE, ch) \text{ iff } |\sigma(ch)| > 0$$
$$(\sigma, \mu) \models (\mathbb{L}^\bullet, ch) \text{ iff } ch \in ICh \wedge \mu(ch) = (\ell \cdot llst, \ell') \Rightarrow \ell = \mathbb{L}$$
$$(\sigma, \mu) \models (\mathbb{L}^\circ, ch) \text{ iff } ch \in ICh \wedge \mu(ch) = (llst, \ell') \Rightarrow \ell' = \mathbb{L}$$

That is, the assumption NE on a channel ch holds if some message is available over ch. The assumption $\mathbb{L}^\bullet$ on an internal channel ch holds if the next message over ch is public. The assumption $\mathbb{L}^\circ$ on an internal channel ch holds if the presence of messages over ch is public. We lift $\models$ to sets of assumptions by $(\sigma, \mu) \models acs$ iff $\forall ac \in acs : (\sigma, \mu) \models ac$.

We use *rich traces* to explicate the update of instrumentation states in an execution of a distributed program. A rich trace rtr is a sequence of configurations of the form $\langle pcnfl; \sigma; \mu \rangle$, extending a global configuration $\langle pcnfl; \sigma \rangle$ with the instrumentation state μ. We use the expression $rtraces_\xi(dprog)$ to represent the set of possible rich traces of $dprog$ under the strategy ξ. We define $rtraces_\xi(dprog)$ based on an *instrumented semantics* (omitted here to save space), analogously to defining $traces_\xi(dprog)$ based on the basic semantics of our language in Sect. 3.

With the help of instrumentation states and rich traces, we precisely define "sound use of assumptions" as appearing in Theorem 1.

Definition 9. *The distributed program $dprog$ ensures a sound use of assumptions, if $rtr \cdot \langle [\langle prog_1; mem_1 \rangle, \dots, \langle prog_n; mem_n \rangle]; \sigma; \mu \rangle \in rtraces_\xi(dprog)$ implies $\forall j \in \{1, \dots, n\} : (\sigma, \mu) \models asm\text{-}of(prog_j)$.*

This definition characterizes the sound use of assumptions as a property over individual rich traces – as a safety property [15] rather than a hyperproperty [6].

Remark 4. How to verify the sound use of assumptions for information-flow security has been shown in [18]. The adaptation of the techniques in [18] to verify the sound use of NE and $\mathbb{L}^\circ$ is straightforward. For verifying the sound use of $\mathbb{L}^\bullet$, communication topology analyses [20] that approximate the correspondences between inputs and outputs can be built upon. If with each $\mathbb{L}^\bullet$ at a receive, the corresponding send comes with a public expression, then the use of $\mathbb{L}^\bullet$ is sound.

5.5 Soundness of Compositional Reasoning

We sketch our proof of Theorem 1. To begin with, we define a notion of low projection, on messages and message queues. A low projection reveals message content and presence without actual dependency on secrets according to the security levels tracked in the instrumentation states.

Definition 10. *We define the function* $\lfloor \cdot \rfloor_\ell : Val \rightarrow Val \cup \{\odot\}$ *for the low projection of a message under* $\ell \in Lev$, *by* $\lfloor v \rfloor_{\mathrm{L}} = v$ *and* $\lfloor v \rfloor_{\mathrm{H}} = \odot$.

The low projection of a message reveals the content or the mere existence ($\odot$) of the message depending on whether the content is public or confidential.

Definition 11. *We define the partial function* $\lfloor \cdot \rfloor_{(llst,\ell)} : Val^* \rightharpoonup (Val \cup \{\odot\})^* \cup \{\odot\}$ *for the low projection of a message queue under* $llst \in Lev^*$ *and* $\ell \in Lev$, *by* $\lfloor \epsilon \rfloor_{(\epsilon,\mathrm{L})} = \epsilon$, $\lfloor vlst \cdot v \rfloor_{(llst \cdot \ell,\mathrm{L})} = \lfloor vlst \rfloor_{(llst,\mathrm{L})} \cdot \lfloor v \rfloor_\ell$, *and* $\lfloor vlst \rfloor_{(llst,\mathrm{H})} = \odot$.

The low projection of a message queue reveals the content or existence of the individual messages, or the mere existence of the queue ($\odot$), depending on whether the overall message presence is public or confidential.

The following result bridges equality of low projections of message queues in given channel and instrumentation states, and low-equivalence of the channel states under assumptions that hold in the channel and instrumentation states.

Proposition 1. *If* $\forall ch \in ICh : \lfloor \sigma_1(ch) \rfloor_{\mu_1(ch)} = \lfloor \sigma_2(ch) \rfloor_{\mu_2(ch)}$, $(\sigma_1, \mu_1) \models acs_1$, *and* $(\sigma_2, \mu_2) \models acs_2$, *then* $\sigma_1 \xrightarrow{acs_1 \cup acs_2} \sigma_2$.

The essence of this proposition is: If message content or presence does not actually depend on secrets over an internal channel, then it is safe to reason under the assumption that message content or presence is public.

For a given distributed program $dprog = \|_i prog_i$, if we could show that for an arbitrary strategy ξ giving rise to a trace tr, each strategy ξ' indistinguishable to ξ gives rise to a trace tr' with the same observation to that of tr, then $KBSec(dprog)$ would follow immediately.

Since $LSec(prog_i)$ holds for each program $prog_i$ by the hypotheses of Theorem 1, and $mem_{\text{init}} =_{\mathrm{L}} mem_{\text{init}}$ holds, there exists an assumption-aware bisimulation relating each process configuration $\langle prog_i; mem_{\text{init}} \rangle$ to itself. We show the existence of tr' by simulating each step in tr taken by the program $prog_i$ in the assumption-aware bisimulation for $prog_i$. As a key part of establishing this single-step simulation, we establish the condition $\sigma_1 \xrightarrow{acs_1 \cup acs_2} \sigma_2$ in the corresponding assumption-aware bisimulation using Proposition 1. Among the hypotheses of this proposition, we obtain $(\sigma_1, \mu_1) \models acs_1$ and $(\sigma_2, \mu_2) \models acs_2$ by the hypothesis of Theorem 1 that $dprog$ ensures a sound use of assumptions. We establish $\forall ch \in ICh : \lfloor \sigma_1(ch) \rfloor_{\mu_1(ch)} = \lfloor \sigma_2(ch) \rfloor_{\mu_2(ch)}$ as a property enforced by our instrumented semantics. For space reasons, we omit the details of the proof.

6   Security Type System and Evaluation

In information-flow security, it is often not straightforward to verify a system by directly applying the security definition. In our case, it is not straightforward to verify the local security of a program by constructing an assumption-aware bisimulation (although this is possible). Security type systems [28] are an effective technique for the verification of noninterference properties [26]. Local security (cf. Sect. 5) not only permits compositional reasoning about global security (cf. Sect. 4), but also admits sound verification using security type systems. We devise a sound security type system for local security, and evaluate our type system using more practical examples than in Sect. 2.

6.1   Judgment and Typing Rules

Our security type system establishes the judgment $lev \vdash prog$, which says that the program $prog$ is well-typed given the environment $lev : Var \to Lev$.

$$\frac{NE \notin as \Rightarrow lev^\circ(ch, as) = \mathbb{L}}{lev^\circ(ch, as) \sqcup lev^\bullet(ch, as) \sqsubseteq lev(x)}{lev \vdash {}^{as}\mathsf{recv}(ch, x)}$$

$$\frac{NE \notin as \Rightarrow lev^\circ(ch, as) \sqsubseteq lev(x_b)}{lev^\circ(ch, as) \sqcup lev^\bullet(ch, as) \sqsubseteq lev(x)}{lev \vdash {}^{as}\mathsf{if\text{-}recv}(ch, x, x_b)}$$

$$\frac{lev\langle e \rangle \sqsubseteq lev^\bullet(ch, \emptyset)}{lev \vdash \mathsf{send}(ch, e)} \quad \frac{lev\langle e \rangle \sqsubseteq lev(x)}{lev \vdash x := e} \quad \frac{}{lev \vdash \mathsf{skip}} \quad \frac{lev \vdash prog_1 \quad lev \vdash prog_2}{lev \vdash prog_1; prog_2}$$

$$\frac{lev \vdash prog_1 \quad lev \vdash prog_2 \quad lev\langle e \rangle = \mathbb{H} \Rightarrow prog_1 \sim prog_2}{lev \vdash \mathsf{if}\ e\ \mathsf{then}\ prog_1\ \mathsf{else}\ prog_2\ \mathsf{fi}} \quad \frac{lev\langle e \rangle = \mathbb{L} \quad lev \vdash prog}{lev \vdash \mathsf{while}\ e\ \mathsf{do}\ prog\ \mathsf{od}}$$

$$lev^\bullet(ch, as) = \begin{cases} \mathbb{L} & \text{if } ch \in ICh \land \mathbb{L}^\bullet \in as \\ & \lor ch \in PubCh \\ \mathbb{H} & \text{otherwise} \end{cases} \quad lev^\circ(ch, as) = \begin{cases} \mathbb{L} & \text{if } ch \in ICh \land \mathbb{L}^\circ \in as \lor \\ & ch \in PubCh \lor ch \in EncCh \\ \mathbb{H} & \text{otherwise} \end{cases}$$

Fig. 1. The security type system

The typing rules are presented in Fig. 1. They are formulated with the auxiliary functions $lev^\bullet$ and lev° of type $(Ch \times 2^{Asm}) \to Lev$. The function $lev^\bullet$ gives the content levels of channels according to the protection of external channels, and to the potential assumption $\mathbb{L}^\bullet$ for internal channels. The function lev° gives the presence levels of channels according to the protection of external channels, and to the potential assumption $\mathbb{L}^\circ$ for internal channels.

The first premise of the rule for ${}^{as}\mathsf{recv}(ch, x)$ says that without the assumption NE, message presence over ch is required to be public. The first premise of the rule for ${}^{as}\mathsf{if\text{-}recv}(ch, x, x_b)$ says that without NE, message presence over ch is required to be no more confidential than the flag variable x_b. The intuition for these two premises is: If the receiving channel is non-empty, the blocking receive cannot block, and the non-blocking receive always completes with x_b set to true;

hence no information leakage occurs via blocking or via x_b. The second premise in each of the receive rules says that the receiving variable x is more confidential than the presence and content of messages over the receiving channel ch. This premise reflects that the value of x after the receive could reflect both the presence and the content of messages over ch at the receive. The premise allows relaxing the typing constraint on x with the use of $\mathbb{L}^{\bullet}$ and $\mathbb{L}^{\circ}$ that signals temporarily public message content and presence over an internal receiving channel. For $\mathsf{send}(ch, e)$, the only premise is concerned with message content. This is because a send never blocks, and hence does not leak information via blockage. For a conditional, in case the guard is confidential, the branches are required to be indistinguishable, since which branch is executed might be affected by secrets. Note that the indistinguishability of the branches is a semantic condition. In an implementation of the rule for conditionals, one would not directly check this indistinguishability, but would rather check a syntactic approximation of it. In an addendum of this paper, we present a type system for local security, where syntactic approximation is employed via the notion of low slices (e.g., [18]).[1] For a loop, the typing rule requires the looping condition to be public, for ensuring progress-sensitive security. The remaining rules in Fig. 1 are straightforward.

Our security type system is novel in exploiting assumptions to enable permissive type-checking. The assumption NE makes type-checking permissive by providing the information that a receive cannot block. In addition, the assumptions $\mathbb{L}^{\bullet}$ and $\mathbb{L}^{\circ}$ make type-checking permissive by enabling content-sensitivity (varying content confidentiality over one single channel) and availability-sensitivity (varying presence confidentiality over one single channel).

Our security type system is syntax-directed, i.e., the choice of an applicable typing rule is deterministic for each given program. Hence, the implementation of our security type system (with the syntactic approximation) is straightforward.

Remark 5. Note that the type system in Fig. 1 is not flow-sensitive [12]. Flow-sensitivity could be added by allowing separate typing environments for variables at different program points as in [12]. This extension would, however, unnecessarily complicate our technical exposition.

6.2   Soundness

Our type system is sound: The typability of a given program implies that the program is secure in the sense of Definition 7.

Theorem 2 (Soundness). *If lev ⊢ prog, then LSec(prog).*

This theorem permits sound reasoning about local security at a syntactic level, exploiting assumptions at receive commands as described by our type system.

---

[1] The addendum can be found at http://www.mais.informatik.tu-darmstadt.de/ WebBibPHP/papers/2017/LiMantelTasch-addendum-APLAS2017.pdf.

The following corollary says that the security of a distributed program can be verified by locally typing its constituent programs under suitable assumptions, and globally verifying the sound use of these assumptions. This corollary immediately follows from Theorems 1 and 2.

Corollary 1. *For a distributed program* $dprog = \|_i prog_i$, *if* $lev \vdash prog_i$ *for all* i, *and* $dprog$ *ensures a sound use of assumptions, then* $KBSec(dprog)$.

This corollary replaces the semantic condition of local security in Theorem 1 with the syntactic condition of typability. It provides a path to automated security analysis for distributed programs that enjoys both modularity and precision.

6.3 Examples of Typable Programs

All example programs in Sect. 2 are typable with suitable use of assumptions. We further evaluate our security type system using two additional examples that more closely reflect communication patterns identifiable in real-world applications. In both examples, we preclude the possibility for the attacker to directly obtain information via wiretapping. Correspondingly, we model some of the communication lines as internal channels represented by int_1 and int_2.

Example: Authentication. Consider the distributed program *auth* in Fig. 2. It captures an authentication scenario where the server process executes the program on the right, and the client process executes the program on the left.

```
send(int₁, uid);                    {L•,L°}recv(int₁, id);
{L•,L°}recv(int₂, x);               if find(id, uids) then
if x == "pass" then                     send(int₂, "pass");
    recv(enc, pwd);                     {L°}recv(int₁, pw);
    send(int₁, pwd)                     send(pub, id)
else                                else
    skip                                send(int₂, "id")
fi                                  fi
```

Fig. 2. Authentication system $auth = [auth\text{-}cl \parallel auth\text{-}srv]$

The server receives the user's ID over the channel int_1. If the ID exists in the database, it requests the user's password. If it then receives a password, it forwards the ID over the channel pub to a logging process that maintains a log in the environment. The log needs to be analyzable by parties not entitled to know the passwords, for e.g., detecting and tracing potential brute-force attacks.

The client sends the user's ID over the channel int_1 to the server. If it then receives a password request, the client receives the user's secret password over the channel enc, and forwards it over int_1. Otherwise, it terminates.

Annotation. The authentication server receives both the public user ID and the secret password over the channel int_1. The assumption $\mathbb{L}^\bullet$ at $\mathsf{recv}(int_1, id)$ in the server program captures that the user ID provided by the environment (the client) is expected to be public. On the other hand, the default invisibility of int_1 is in line with the password to be received at $\mathsf{recv}(int_1, pw)$ being confidential.

Typability. Supposing $lev(id) = lev(uids) = lev(uid) = lev(x) = \mathbb{L}$ and $lev(pw) = lev(pwd) = \mathbb{H}$, we explain how the server program *auth-srv* is type checked. For $^{\{\mathbb{L}^\bullet, \mathbb{L}^\circ\}}\mathsf{recv}(int_1, id)$, since $NE \notin \{\mathbb{L}^\bullet, \mathbb{L}^\circ\}$, the first premise of the receive rule requires $lev^\circ(int_1, \{\mathbb{L}^\bullet, \mathbb{L}^\circ\}) = \mathbb{L}$, which holds. The second premise of the receive rule is also satisfied since $lev^\circ(int_1, \{\mathbb{L}^\bullet, \mathbb{L}^\circ\}) \sqcup lev^\bullet(int_1, \{\mathbb{L}^\bullet, \mathbb{L}^\circ\}) = \mathbb{L}$, which allows id to be public. For $^{\{\mathbb{L}^\circ\}}\mathsf{recv}(int_1, pw)$, since $lev^\circ(int_1, \{\mathbb{L}^\circ\}) = \mathbb{L}$, the first premise of the receive rule is satisfied. Since $lev(pw) = \mathbb{H}$, the second premise is also satisfied. Without going into further details, we claim that both *auth-srv* and *auth-cl* are typable.

Sound Use of Assumptions. Using our instrumented semantics, we can verify that *auth* ensures a sound use of assumptions. Intuitively, the use of $\mathbb{L}^\circ$ is sound because neither *auth-cl* nor *auth-srv* contains high branches or loops that might cause sending to an internal channel in a secret-dependent fashion. The use of $\mathbb{L}^\bullet$ is sound because the only secret message is sent at $\mathsf{send}(int_1, pwd)$. This message cannot be received at any receive command annotated with $\mathbb{L}^\bullet$.

Knowledge-based Security. Corollary 1 allows us to conclude $KBSec(auth)$.

Remark 6 (An ill-typed variant). Note that if the assumption $\mathbb{L}^\bullet$ in the receive command $^{\{\mathbb{L}^\bullet, \mathbb{L}^\circ\}}\mathsf{recv}(int_1, id)$ had been missing, this command would have been ill-typed. In this situation, the message to be received over int_1 is expected to be confidential, which conflicts with the receiving variable id being public.

Example: Auction. Consider the distributed program *auct* in Fig. 3. It captures a single-bid sealed auction where a bidder is allowed to blindly submit a sole bid for an auction. The server process handling the auction executes the program on the right, and the client process executes the program on the left.

The server waits for the bidder's registration over int_1 (for simplicity represented abstractly by "reg"). Afterwards, it forwards the registration over *pub* to a publicly accessible bulletin board. Then it sends the minimal bid (i.e., the price below which the item cannot be sold) to the bidder over int_2. If it receives a bid over int_1, it forwards this bid over *pri* to the process determining the outcome of the auction. Otherwise, it terminates.

The client's behavior depends on a secret threshold for placing a bid. The client receives this threshold *thres* over *enc*. Afterwards, it registers for the auction over int_1. If the minimal bid received over int_2 does not exceed the threshold *thres*, the client computes and sends a bid over int_1. Otherwise, it terminates.

```
recv(enc, thres);                    {L•,L°}recv(int₁, bdr);
send(int₁, "reg");                   send(pub, bdr);
{L•,L°}recv(int₂, min);              send(int₂, minBid);
if min ≤ thres then                  if-recv(int₁, bid, b);
    send(int₁, calc                  if b then
         (min, thres))                   send(pri, bid)
else                                 else
    skip                                 skip
fi                                   fi
```

Fig. 3. Auction System $auct = [auct\text{-}cl \parallel auct\text{-}srv]$

Annotation. Over the channel int_1, the auction server receives both a registration whose presence is public, and a bid whose presence is confidential (to keep the threshold a secret). The assumption $\mathbb{L}^\circ$ at ${}^{\{L^\bullet,L^\circ\}}\mathsf{recv}(int_1, bdr)$ in the server program captures that the presence of a registration coming from the environment (the client) is expected to be public. On the other hand, the default invisibility of int_1 is in line with the presence of a bid being confidential.

Typability. Supposing $lev(bdr) = lev(minBid) = lev(min) = \mathbb{L}$ and $lev(bid) = lev(b) = lev(thres) = \mathbb{H}$, we explain how the server program $auct\text{-}srv$ is type checked. The typing derivation of ${}^{\{L^\bullet,L^\circ\}}\mathsf{recv}(int_1, bdr)$ is analogous to the typing derivation of ${}^{\{L^\bullet,L^\circ\}}\mathsf{recv}(int_1, id)$ in the authentication example. For the command if-recv(int_1, bid, b), since $NE \not\subseteq \emptyset$, the first premise of the rule for nonblocking receive requires $lev^\circ(int_1, \emptyset) \sqsubseteq lev(b)$. This constraint is satisfied since $lev(b) = \mathbb{H}$. The second premise is also satisfied since $lev(bid) = \mathbb{H}$. Because $lev(b) = \mathbb{H}$, send(pri, bid) and skip are required to be indistinguishable by the rule for conditional branching. Their indistinguishability can be established by constructing a suitable assumption-aware bisimulation. Without going into further details, we claim that both $auct\text{-}srv$ and $auct\text{-}cl$ are typable.

Sound Use of Assumptions. Using our instrumented semantics, we can verify that $auct$ ensures a sound use of assumptions. Below, we provide the intuition for the sound use of $\mathbb{L}^\circ$. The only possibility for message presence to become dependent on secrets over an internal channel is via the send command over int_1 in the high branching on $min \leq thres$. However, the only receive over int_1 with the assumption $\mathbb{L}^\circ$ is always executed before this high branching is entered.

Knowledge-based Security. Corollary 1 allows us to conclude $KBSec(auct)$.

Remark 7 (An ill-typed variant). Note that if the assumption $\mathbb{L}^\circ$ in the receive command ${}^{\{L^\bullet,L^\circ\}}\mathsf{recv}(int_1, bdr)$ had been missing, this command would have been ill-typed. In this situation, the presence of a message over int_1 is expected to be confidential, which conflicts with the receiving variable bdr being public.

7 Related Work

Rely-Guarantee-style Reasoning for Information-Flow Security. The first development on rely-guarantee-style reasoning for information-flow security is [19]. It permits exploiting *no-read* and *no-write* assumptions on shared variables to achieve modular yet permissive security verification for shared-memory concurrent programs. The verification of the sound use of assumptions is addressed using Dynamic Pushdown Networks in [18].

The exploitation of assumptions for shared-memory concurrent programs has been developed further. In [3], a hybrid security monitor is proposed, while in [22], a static verification of value-sensitive security policies is proposed.

In [10], service-based systems with unidirectional invocation of services are addressed. While components communicate via calls and responses of services, the services of a component communicate via shared memory. Rely-guarantee-style reasoning is employed for the inter-component invocation of services.

Securing Communication in Distributed Systems. There are several approaches to statically securing communication in distributed systems. In [25], modular reasoning without exploiting assumptions is proposed. In [7], explicit treatment of cryptography is introduced and a property similar in spirit to that of [25] is enforced. In [1], "fast simulations" are proposed to guarantee termination-insensitive security under observational determinism [29], and the flow constraints needed to secure a system are thereby relaxed. No modular reasoning is supported in [1]. The closest development to rely-guarantee-style reasoning about message-passing communication (as in this article) might be [10]. In [10], the communication pattern is highly restricted: Communication is only used to model argument-passing and result-retrieval for remote procedure calls.

Security Type Systems. Security type systems (see, e.g., [26]) are a prominent class of techniques for the static verification of information-flow security. We only discuss closely related developments in the literature.

For message content, value-sensitive flow policies (e.g., [2,16]) and first class information-flow labels (e.g., [30]) in principle enable the treatment of channels with varying content confidentiality. Value-sensitive policies require the code to contain variables that regulate the security policies. First-class labels require built-in language support. Moreover, the actual transmission of the labels could lead to increased attack surface as well as performance overhead.

For message presence, the type systems of [5,11,14] enforce security properties concerned with the *permanent* blockage of input caused by secrets. To relax typing constraints wrt. message presence, linear types are used in [11], and a deadlock detection mechanism is used in [14]. In comparison, we enforce a stronger security property sensitive to the extent that public communication can be delayed, and relax typing constraints wrt. message presence by exploiting assumptions. The type system of [25] rejects all blocking inputs over high presence channels. A coarse-grained way of adjusting presence levels to make the analysis succeed is implicitly provided. The type system of [24] allows high presence input to be followed by low assignment, but not low output. Thus, the relaxation of presence constraints in our type system and that of [24] is incomparable. No additional precision via availability-sensitivity is provided in [24, 25].

8 Conclusion

Our aim has been to resolve the imprecision problem in the modular reasoning about information-flow security for distributed systems, in the presence of message-passing communication. Our solution consists of a process-local security condition that soundly modularizes global security for distributed programs, and a security type system that soundly enforces the process-local condition. By exploiting assumptions about the interface of each process, our solution enables the relaxation of information-flow constraints concerned with the blockage of communication, and allows the treatment of channels that are content-sensitive and availability-sensitive at both the semantic level and the syntactic level.

Our development is performed for a simplified language. The adaption of our approach to real-world languages such as C and Java requires the treatment of features such as procedure calls and heaps. These features have been considered in existing type-based analyses of information-flow security (e.g., [23]), and we expect the treatment to be orthogonal to our treatment of communication.Furthermore, our use of assumptions is non-intrusive, the annotation of assumptions does not introduce changes to the underlying programming language. This non-intrusiveness facilitates the adaption of our approach to a realistic language.

A potential direction for future work is type inference. For our security type system, the inference of security levels for variables is straightforward – it can be performed in the same manner as for sequential languages. On the other hand, the inference of assumption annotations on receive commands is a separate research problem that we plan to address in the future.

Acknowledgments. The authors thank the anonymous reviewers for their helpful comments. This work was supported partially by the DFG under project RSCP (MA 3326/4-2/3) in the priority program RS3 (SPP 1496), and partially by the German Federal Ministry of Education and Research (BMBF) as well as by the Hessen State Ministry for Higher Education, Research and the Arts (HMWK) within CRISP.

References

1. Alpízar, R., Smith, G.: Secure information flow for distributed systems. In: Degano, P., Guttman, J.D. (eds.) FAST 2009. LNCS, vol. 5983, pp. 126–140. Springer, Heidelberg (2010). https://doi.org/10.1007/978-3-642-12459-4_10
2. Amtoft, T., Hatcliff, J., Rodríguez, E., Robby, H.J., Greve, D.: Specification and checking of software contracts for conditional information flow. In: Cuellar, J., Maibaum, T., Sere, K. (eds.) FM 2008. LNCS, vol. 5014, pp. 229–245. Springer, Heidelberg (2008). https://doi.org/10.1007/978-3-540-68237-0

3. Askarov, A., Chong, S., Mantel, H.: Hybrid monitors for concurrent noninterference. In: CSF 2015, pp. 137–151 (2015)
4. Askarov, A., Sabelfeld, A.: Gradual release: unifying declassification, encryption and key release policies. In: S&P 2007, pp. 207–221 (2007)
5. Capecchi, S., Castellani, I., Dezani-Ciancaglini, M., Rezk, T.: Session types for access and information flow control. In: Gastin, P., Laroussinie, F. (eds.) CONCUR 2010. LNCS, vol. 6269, pp. 237–252. Springer, Heidelberg (2010). https://doi.org/10.1007/978-3-642-15375-4_17
6. Clarkson, M.R., Schneider, F.B.: Hyperproperties. J. Comput. Secur. **18**(6), 1157–1210 (2010)
7. Focardi, R., Centenaro, M.: Information flow security of multi-threaded distributed programs. In: PLAS 2008, pp. 113–124 (2008)
8. Focardi, R., Gorrieri, R.: Classification of security properties (part I: information flow). In: Focardi, R., Gorrieri, R. (eds.) FOSAD 2000. LNCS, vol. 2171, pp. 331–396. Springer, Heidelberg (2001). https://doi.org/10.1007/3-540-45608-2_6
9. Goguen, J.A., Meseguer, J.: Security policies and security models. In: S&P 1982. IEEE Computer Society (1982)
10. Greiner, S., Grahl, D.: Non-interference with what-declassification in component-based systems. In: CSF 2016, pp. 253–267 (2016)
11. Honda, K., Vasconcelos, V., Yoshida, N.: Secure information flow as typed process behaviour. In: Smolka, G. (ed.) ESOP 2000. LNCS, vol. 1782, pp. 180–199. Springer, Heidelberg (2000). https://doi.org/10.1007/3-540-46425-5_12
12. Hunt, S., Sands, D.: On flow-sensitive security types. In: POPL 2006, pp. 79–90 (2006)
13. Jones, C.B.: Development methods for computer programs including a notion of interference. Oxford University Computing Laboratory (1981)
14. Kobayashi, N.: Type-based information flow analysis for the pi-calculus. Acta Inf. **42**(4–5), 291–347 (2005)
15. Lamport, L.: Proving the correctness of multiprocess programs. IEEE Trans. Softw. Eng. **3**(2), 125–143 (1977)
16. Li, X., Nielson, F., Nielson, H.R., Feng, X.: Disjunctive information flow for communicating processes. In: Ganty, P., Loreti, M. (eds.) TGC 2015. LNCS, vol. 9533, pp. 95–111. Springer, Cham (2016). https://doi.org/10.1007/978-3-319-28766-9_7
17. Mantel, H.: Information flow and noninterference. In: van Tilborg, H.C.A., Jajodia, S. (eds.) Encyclopedia of Cryptography and Security, 2nd edn, pp. 605–607. Springer, New York (2011)
18. Mantel, H., Müller-Olm, M., Perner, M., Wenner, A.: Using dynamic pushdown networks to automate a modular information-flow analysis. In: LOPSTR 2015 (2015)
19. Mantel, H., Sands, D., Sudbrock, H.: Assumptions and guarantees for compositional noninterference. In: CSF 2011, pp. 218–232 (2011)
20. Martel, M., Gengler, M.: Communication topology analysis for concurrent programs. In: Havelund, K., Penix, J., Visser, W. (eds.) SPIN 2000. LNCS, vol. 1885, pp. 265–286. Springer, Heidelberg (2000). https://doi.org/10.1007/10722468_16
21. McCullough, D.: A hookup theorem for multilevel security. IEEE Trans. Softw. Eng. **16**(6), 563–568 (1990)
22. Murray, T.C., Sison, R., Pierzchalski, E., Rizkallah, C.: Compositional verification and refinement of concurrent value-dependent noninterference. In: CSF 2016 (2016)
23. Myers, A.C., Liskov, B.: A decentralized model for information flow control. In: SOSP 1997, pp. 129–142 (1997)

66   X. Li et al.

24. Rafnsson, W., Hedin, D., Sabelfeld, A.: Securing interactive programs. In: CSF 2012, pp. 293–307 (2012)
25. Sabelfeld, A., Mantel, H.: Securing communication in a concurrent language. In: SAS 2002, pp. 376–394 (2002)
26. Sabelfeld, A., Myers, A.C.: Language-based information-flow security. IEEE J. Sel. Areas Commun. **21**(1), 5–19 (2003)
27. Tanenbaum, A.S., van Steen, M.: Distributed Systems - Principles and Paradigms, 2nd edn. Prentice-Hall Inc., Upper Saddle River (2007)
28. Volpano, D.M., Irvine, C.E., Smith, G.: A sound type system for secure flow analysis. J. Comput. Secur. **4**(2/3), 167–188 (1996)
29. Zdancewic, S., Myers, A.C.: Observational determinism for concurrent program security. In: CSFW 2003, pp. 29–43 (2003)
30. Zheng, L., Myers, A.C.: Dynamic security labels and static information flow control. Int. J. Inf. Sec. **6**(2–3), 67–84 (2007)

Capabilities for Java: Secure Access to Resources

Ian J. Hayes, Xi Wu[✉], and Larissa A. Meinicke

School of ITEE, The University of Queensland, Brisbane 4072, Australia
Ian.Hayes@itee.uq.edu.au, {xi.wu,l.meinicke}@uq.edu.au

Abstract. This paper explores adding capabilities to Java with the objective of tightening security management for access to resources both within the Java Class Library and Java applications. Code can only access resources if it is given explicit capabilities, allowing replacement of the use of doPrivileged blocks. Capabilities provide restricted access to their implementing object – like an interface – but when a capability is created, it has a more restrictive dynamic type than its implementing object, and hence access to the full facilities of the implementing object (e.g. via down casting) are precluded. We used the Annotation Processing Tool to track the declaration and use of capabilities.

1 Introduction

The programming language Java is widely used in a variety of domains, ranging from embedded devices to e-commerce. Security issues raised by Java are drawing a growing interest, from both industry and academia. Security flaws within the Java Class Library are the most critical because they expose vulnerabilities for any application. Securing the Java Class Library is a challenging task because Java-SE consists of around 500 packages and over a million lines of code.

This section reviews the important features of Java security and explores some security issues raised by Java including an example of trusted method chaining. Then we informally introduce our contributions to address these issues.

1.1 Java Security

Basic knowledge of the Java security architecture is assumed but a brief review of the important features is provided here. Authentication and encryption facilities are assumed to be the same as currently provided and are not of concern here.

Security Manager. Security in Java is controlled by a security manager that provides facilities for checking that access to a resource is allowed by the current access control context. Code within the Java Class Library has unrestricted access to resources. It is responsible for checking that access to a resource is allowed by calling the method checkPermission of SecurityManager before accessing a resource on behalf of a user. There are two ways of accessing a resource:

direct access to a resource, such as a file, (possibly using native methods to access the resource on the runtime platform), and

© Springer International Publishing AG 2017
B.-Y.E. Chang (Ed.): APLAS 2017, LNCS 10695, pp. 67–84, 2017.
https://doi.org/10.1007/978-3-319-71237-6_4

indirect access to a resource via other classes that (directly or indirectly) provide access to the resource.

A class directly accessing a resource is responsible for checking permissions, while a class accessing a resource indirectly may either check permissions itself or rely on the classes it calls to perform the checks.

Normally, a permission check traverses the runtime stack and only succeeds if all methods in the call chain have the required permission. The permissions of a method in the call chain are determined by the permissions assigned to its class by its class loader. As well as requiring a user making a call that accesses resources to have permission to do so, any intermediate methods in the call chain must also have permission. The requirement for intermediate methods to have the required permissions handles a user calling untrusted code, perhaps inadvertently. For example, a user has the required permissions to access a resource R but calls an untrusted method that does not have permission to access R; if the untrusted method tries to access R, it will fail even though the user has the required permissions, because the permission checking requires all methods on the call stack to have the required permission.

Privileged Blocks. A class providing facilities to users may have more permissions than a user, e.g. if the class is part of the Java Class Library. As well as accessing resources on behalf of the user (for which the above full stack traversal is appropriate), the class may require access to its own internal resources, which need to be accessible to the class but not the user. To access its internal resources, the class makes use of the doPrivileged method of AccessController to run code with its own privileges without checking the privileges of methods higher in its call chain. The effect of doPrivileged is to truncate the stack traversal used for checking permissions at the caller of the doPrivileged method.

1.2 Java Security Issues

This section explores security issues in Java [4], while Sect. 1.3 overviews the possible advantages of using capabilities to control access to resources within Java.

doPrivileged. Code run within a doPrivileged block can run with fewer restrictions and hence any such code could be the focus of a possible security exploit. Because code in the Java Class Library is usually granted unrestricted privileges, any security flaws in its use of doPrivileged are of particular concern [17].

Caller-sensitive methods. Caller sensitive methods have similar issues to the use of doPrivileged, except they depend on the privileges of the class loader of the caller rather than the privileges of the caller [2].

Subclassing privileged classes. One insidious form of attack is via subclassing (non-final) classes in the Java Class Library and overriding existing methods with rogue code. For example, a class may write to a file with a given name, where a check is made that the user has permission to write that file when the class instance is allocated. The class may have a getFileName method that returns the file's name. If getFileName is not final, it may be overridden by a rogue method that returns the name of a file that the user does not have permission to write. If the privileged class inadvertently calls the overridden method, the rogue method may return a different file name that the user does not have permission to write but, because the original file name was checked, no further checking is done before the (wrong) file is written by the privileged class library method. To operate securely the privileged class must use its local copy of the file name rather than using the (overridable) getFileName method. Some classes currently supplying capability-like objects, such as FileOutputStream discussed later, are not final and hence they are potentially subject to unprivileged subclasses overriding methods with rogue methods that may be unintentionally called in privileged mode.

Privileged access escape. Privileged access escape occurs when access to a privileged object escapes to unauthorised domains. This can happen when access to objects used internally in the implementation of privileged classes are made accessible to unauthorised users. Obvious candidates are current capability-like objects like FileOutputStream (see Sect. 2).

Trusted method chaining. Some issues mentioned above can be demonstrated via an example abstracted from Java trusted method chaining [11], in which it is possible to use methods inherited from a superclass to implement interface methods. In Listing 1, if unprivileged code tries to directly call m in SS, any permission checks within sensitiveMethod will fail because the unprivileged call is part of the call stack that is checked. However, method oMethod in class O invokes j.m in privileged mode, where j is an instance of an interface J. Class NS extends SS and hence implements method m of interface J with method m of SS which includes a call to a security-sensitive method sensitiveMethod. To exploit the vulnerability, an instance of NS is passed to oMethod, which then calls the sensitive code in privileged mode. One possible solution based on capabilities is given in the end of Sect. 3.

1.3   Contributions

This paper examines how capabilities can be incorporated into Java in order to provide more secure access to resources, with the aim of preventing security flaws. The focus is on security issues in the Java Class Library, but the ideas apply more widely to applications needing to securely handle user-sourced operations. The Annotation Processing Tool has been used to track the declaration and use of capabilities.

The philosophy behind capabilities is that code can only access a resource if it is given an explicit capability to do so. In an object-oriented context, a capability can be thought of as an object with a restricted interface. It provides a set of operations that can be invoked. These operations are more general than simple read/write access control permissions because they encapsulate what one can do with a resource. Access to the resource is only allowed via the methods of the interface and no other access is permitted. Any permission checking is done

Listing 1. An example of Java trusted method chaining

```
// Defined in the Java Class Library
public interface J {  void m();  }
// Class using interface J
public class O {
    public oMethod (J j){
        // Runs j.m in privileged mode
        doPrivileged( public void run(){ j.m(); } );
    }
}
// Class not using J but defines m which is part of J
public class SS {
    void m(){
        //Call a Security-Sensitive Method
        sensitiveMethod();
    }
}
/******************************************************
 * Defined in some untrusted code
 * The implementation of m is inherited from SS
 ******************************************************/
public class NS extends SS implements J {

    // Exploiting the vulnerability
    ...
    J  j = new NS();
    p = new O();
    p.oMethod(j);
    ...
}
```

when a capability is created. After that, access to the resource via the methods of the capability normally requires no further permission checking. In summary, the advantages of the capability can be outlined as follows:

– Capabilities make the specification of security requirements more explicit, which allows a more straightforward security analysis.
– Capabilities curtail the unnecessary use of doPrivileged blocks and caller-sensitive methods. It is proposed to restrict privileges to packages to a given set of capabilities and only these capabilities are open to exploit by flawed code.
– Capabilities restrict the interface provided by objects to only allow access to the methods in the interface of the capability and no other aspects of the implementing object. Classes implementing capabilities are not directly accessible to users and hence cannot be overridden.

– Capabilities provide a focus for checking that unauthorised access is not provided via the escape of capabilities in a security scheme based on them.

Proper use of capabilities requires discipline in order to ensure that only the capabilities required by a component are passed to it, in the same way that Java policy files require disciplined use to ensure only the necessary permissions are given to code. Capabilities are vulnerable to privilege escape if a capability is incorrectly passed to untrusted code, in the same way that a FileOutputStream can be improperly passed to untrusted code.

Organization. A review of the use of existing classes and interfaces as capabilities is given in Sect. 2 and Sect. 3 gives details of a capability scheme for Java that mitigates the effects of the security issues. Section 4 presents semantics of capabilities based on a translation from programs with capabilities to the standard Java programs. An overview of implementing capabilities using Annotation Processing Tool (APT) is given in Sect. 5. A discussion of the related work is given in Sect. 6 before Sect. 7 concludes the paper and points out the future directions.

2   Classes and Interfaces as Capabilities

The class FileOutputStream in the Java Class Library is like a capability to write a file in the sense that the check of write access permission to the file is done in the constructor for FileOutputStream and a SecurityException exception is thrown if permission is not granted. No further checks are made on write operations. This has the advantage of not performing the (expensive) permission check on every write operation, although a check on each write would be potentially more secure. Class FileInputStream is similar but the interface it provides has different methods (read rather than write methods). FileInputStream and FileOutputStream provide different capabilities for accessing a file.

FileOutputStream and FileInputStream are classes that inherit (indirectly) from Object. Hence as well as the methods explicitly provided for accessing files, they provide the methods provided by Object, such as getClass and toString, which provide attackers access to information beyond the basic functionality expected for writing/reading a file.

An interface is the closest thing to a capability in Java, in that the methods declared in an interface provide a restricted view of the implementing class. However, in Java a variable declared to have an interface type is an object and inherits all the attributes of Object, including methods like getClass and toString. Furthermore, it can be cast down to the implementing class type thus providing access to methods of the implementation that are not part of the interface. Such access to the underlying implementation object provides the potential for security vulnerabilities. Tightening access to such interfaces via a capability mechanism is explored in Sect. 3.

Listing 2. Capability interfaces for input and output streams

```
capability CloseCap { // Implicitly extends NullCap
    void close();
}
capability InCap extends CloseCap {
    int read();
    int read(byte[] b);
    int read(byte[] b, int off, int len);
    long skip(long n);
}
capability OutCap extends CloseCap {
    void write(int b);
    void write(byte[] b);
    void write(byte[] b, int off, int len);
    void flush();
}
capability InOutCap extends InCap, OutCap {
    // Only the methods from InCap and OutCap.
    // Note that InCap and OutCap share method close.
}
```

3   Capabilities for Java

The syntax used here for a capability is the same as an interface, except that the keyword **capability** is used. The main difference between capabilities and interfaces is that capabilities implicitly inherit from the empty capability Null-Cap, rather than the root of the class hierarchy Object, and hence they do not inherit the methods of Object (see Sect. 3.4). Variables of the capability type are restricted to access only the methods of the interface of the capability. For example, separate capability interfaces for input and output access to a stream are given in Listing 2, as well as a combined capability for both input and output.

3.1   Securing Capabilities

Instances of capabilities act like restricted interfaces that only provide the methods listed in the capability. Unlike instances of interfaces, instances of capabilities restrict access to the object implementing the capability and hence

- if an instance of a capability or the class implementing the capability is "wrapped" with an explicit capability type, then it may not be cast down to a type which is below this explicit capability type,
- methods inherited from class Object are disallowed unless explicitly included in the capability's interface,

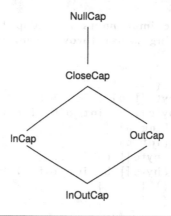

Fig. 1. Lattice of capabilities for the example in Listing 2

- reflection on capabilities must only expose the interface of the capability and no details of the implementing object, and
- either serialisation of capabilities is disallowed or deserialisation has to re-establish capabilities afresh.

Note that, while Java allows a variable of an interface type to be cast down, with some exceptions (see Sect. 3.3), this is generally considered to be poor style because it breaks the abstraction that the interface was introduced to represent. Hence it can be argued that capabilities enforce better style.

The capability NullCap is defined as having no methods at all. It is the top of the capability lattice (instead of Object, which is the top of the class lattice). The lattice for the capabilities declared in Listing 2 is given in Fig. 1.

Classes implementing a capability treat it the same as the equivalent interface. Because they control access to resources, the implementing classes are private to the system. Only their capability interface becomes publicly accessible. For example, RandomAccessFile in Listing 3 implements InOutCap from Listing 2 and hence InCap, OutCap and CloseCap. It provides the methods to read and write a file. Note that neither the class nor its constructor are public and hence instantiation of the class is restricted to trusted code. Trusted code with access to class RandomAccessFile may create an instance of a RandomAccessFile and wrap it as an InOutCap capability as follows.

```
InOutCap inOut =
        capability (InOutCap) new RandomAccessFile(name);
```

The additional keyword capability is added to indicate that inOut should be treated as having dynamic type InOutCap rather than RandomAccessFile.

Listing 3. Implementation of file stream capabilities

```
class RandomAccessFile implements InOutCap {
 RandomAccessFile(String name) throws FileNotFoundException {
      // Open the file
    }
    public int read() { ... }
    public int read(byte[] b) { ... }
    public int read(byte[] b, int off, int len) { ... }
    public long skip(long n) { ... }
    public void write(int b) { ... }
    public void write(byte[] b) { ... }
    public void write(byte[] b, int off, int len) { ... }
    public void flush() { ... }
    public void close() { ... } // Shared by InCap and OutCap
}
```

3.2   Generating Capabilities

Capabilities provide access to resources but capabilities themselves need to be created and managed. Access to a capability manager is itself a form of (meta)capability. A capability manager provides methods whereby capabilities (such as an output stream on a file) can be requested and the manager is responsible for checking the user/process has the necessary permissions to grant the capability. The methods that generate capabilities are the components that need to be carefully checked for vulnerabilities. A process without access to a capability manager can only access the capabilities explicitly passed to it.

Listing 4. Capability manager for file access

```
capability FileAccessCap {
    InCap requestInCap(String name)
        throws FileNotFoundException, SecurityException;
    OutCap requestOutCap(String name)
        throws FileNotFoundException, SecurityException;
    InOutCap requestInOutCap(String name)
        throws FileNotFoundException, SecurityException;
}
```

Capability managers can be specialised for particular resources, for example, the capability for a file access manager includes the ability to generate capabilities to read/write files as input/output streams (see Listing 4). Capability managers can be devised for specialised purposes, such as providing access to files in a particular directory.

While RandomAccessFile implements InOutCap, it does not provide a way to generate such a capability. That is the role of class RandomAccessFileManager in Listing 5. It implements FileAccessCap and hence provides the ability to create capabilities to access files. It is responsible for performing the appropriate security access checks to ensure the generated capabilities are permitted. The version given here makes use of the existing security manager to check permissions in the usual manner. It is assumed that RandomAccessFileManager is in the same package as RandomAccessFile and hence has access to its (non-public) constructor. RandomAccessFileManager and its constructor are public so that instances of the manager can be created but a more restrictive version would only allow instances to be constructed via another capability.

Listing 5. Implementation of a file access capability manager

```
public class RandomAccessFileManager implements FileAccessCap {
    public RandomAccessFileManager() { }
    /* Factory method for InCap */
    public InCap requestInCap(String name)
        throws SecurityException , FileNotFoundException {
        SecurityManager sm = System.getSecurityManager();
        if( sm != null ) {
            sm.checkPermission(new FilePermission(name,"read"));
        }
        return capability (InCap) new RandomAccessFile(name);
    }
    public OutCap requestOutCap(String name)
        throws SecurityException , FileNotFoundException {
        ... similar to requestInCap ... }
    public InOutCap requestInOutCap(String name)
        throws SecurityException , FileNotFoundException {
        ... similar to requestInCap ... }
}
```

A capability can be created from an implementing object by wrapping the object up with the type of the capability. For example, the method requestInCap in Listing 5 constructs a new RandomAccessFile object, which is then wrapped with the type of InCap in its return statement. The effect is to give the explicit dynamic type InCap to the new object, which means that it can no longer be treated as a normal object of type RandomAccessFile (e.g. one can no longer cast it back down to RandomAccessFile). In Java, if B is a subclass of A, then casting an expression of type B to be of type A is redundant, for example, the cast "(A)" in the following is redundant.

```
A p = (A) new B();
```

At compile time p is treated as having static type A but at run time it has dynamic type B. However, for capabilities it is important that the run time type is restricted to the interface of the capability and not the type of the class implementing the capability. Hence in the example in Listing 5, the wrapping of the reference as a capability of type InCap is essential. The explicit wrapping ensures that the dynamic type of the object returned by the method is InCap and that it cannot be cast down to any strict subtype of InCap.

An InOutCap extends both InCap and OutCap and hence can be restricted to either of these capabilities, for example, the following downgrades the InOutCap capability inOut to an InCap capability in by wrapping it as an InCap.

Listing 6. Downgrading a capability by casting up

```
FileAccessCap  fileAccess  =  new  RandomAccessFileManager ();
...
InOutCap  inOut  =  fileAccess . requestInOutCap ( fileName );
...
InCap  in  =  capability  ( InCap )  inOut ;
```

The capabilities inOut and in share their implementing object and hence provide two views on the one resource. Note that inOut is wrapped with the explicit dynamic type InCap when it is assigned to in, and thus one cannot retrieve the InOutCap capability from it because one cannot cast its type down to a type below InCap.

Revisiting the security issues in Java trusted method chaining in Sect. 1.2, one can see that it is no longer possible for application code to extend privileged classes. Because classes implementing capabilities are not directly accessible to users and hence cannot be overridden, Java trusted method chaining and other forms of subclassing privileged class attacks are no longer possible for classes implementing capabilities. Specifically, we consider the example shown in Listing 1. The class *SS*, which invokes the security-sensitive method *sensitiveMethod*(), is hidden as a class inside a package that publicly provides the capability *SSCap*, implemented by *SS*, and its capability manager. This means that other classes (e.g. class *NS* defined in some untrusted code) outside the package can only use the capability *SSCap* rather than extending the class *SS*. That is, classes implementing capabilities are not directly accessible to users and hence cannot be overridden.

3.3 Heterogeneous Data Structures

If a capability of dynamic type InOutCap is assigned to a variable x of type NullCap *without* wrapping, the dynamic type of x remains as InOutCap and it may be cast back down to InOutCap (or any of its super types). This allows one to construct heterogeneous lists of capabilities as in Listing 7. In this example, variable in, of dynamic type InCap, is added as the first element of a list of NullCap and inOut, of dynamic type InOutCap, is added as the second element. Both elements of the list retain their respective dynamic types. When the first element is retrieved it can be cast back down to InCap but not InOutCap, while the second element can be cast back down to either InCap or its dynamic type InOutCap.

Listing 7. Example of a heterogeneous list

```
// Declare instances of capabilities
InOutCap inOut = fileAccess.requestInOutCap(fileName);
// Wrapping up to InCap
InCap in = capability (InCap) inOut;
...
List <NullCap> L = new ArrayList<NullCap>();
// Different capability instances are added
L.add(in);
L.add(inOut);
...
InCap in2 = (InCap) L.get(0);// Allowed
InOutCap inOut2 = (InOutCap) L.get(1);// Allowed

// Casting down to InOutCap which is below InCap
InOutCap wrong = (InOutCap) L.get(0);  // Disallowed
```

3.4   Methods of Class Object

The preferred approach from a security perspective is to not allow capabilities to be treated as being of subtypes of Object and hence they do not supply any of the methods from Object. However, any methods of Object may be explicitly included in a capability's interface, thus giving access to that method. If the methods inherited from Object are supported, restrictions need to be placed on these methods. Below each of these methods is considered individually.

clone it is tempting not to support cloning but, if supported, it must return a capability equivalent to the one being cloned (and not expose the underlying object).

equals could be restricted to reference equality, otherwise it must compare capabilities for equality in a manner that does not depend on information in the implementing object that is not accessible through the capability's interface.

finalize allows desirable activities, such as closing a file, to take place when the object is deallocated but finalization is an issue for the object implementing the interface and does not have to be made available via the capability's interface.

getClass should not expose the class of the implementing object but only the capability's interface, i.e. a restricted view on the object; the capability type acts like a (final) class with just the members of its interface.

hashCode needs to be consistent with equals in the sense that it returns the same value if called on equal capabilities.

notify, notifyAll, wait these methods are unlikely to raise security concerns.

toString the method of the implementing object must not expose privileged information of the implementation object that is not accessible through the interface of the capability.

4   Semantics of Capabilities

The semantics of capabilities can be given by a translation from a source program using capabilities to a target standard Java program, augmented with some additional classes. The null capability is represented by an interface NullCap, which has no methods, and a class CapNullCap that overrides all the methods of class Object with methods that throw an UnsupportedOperationException.

Listing 8. Translated capability NullCap

```java
interface NullCap {
    //no methods
}

class CapNullCap implements NullCap {
    CapNullCap() {
        super();
    }

    // All methods supported by Object are overridden
    public String toString() {
        throw new UnsupportedOperationException();
    }
    ...
}
```

Each capability C declared in the source program is translated into the corresponding target interface C plus an additional corresponding class with a fresh name, CapC, not used in the source program. Listing 9 gives a source capability C and Listing 10 gives the corresponding translated target form.

Listing 9. Source capability C

```java
capability C {
    T1 m1( A1 arg1 );
    T2 m2( A2 arg2 );
}
```

The interface in the target matches the capability in the source, except that it uses the keyword **interface** rather than **capability**. The additional class CapC implements C. It has a private field impl holding the implementation object of the capability and a constructor that takes an implementation object (of type C) and saves it in impl. For each method m declared in the source capability C, a corresponding method m is declared within CapC that simply calls the method m of the implementing object impl. Because CapC extends CapNullCap, all methods of class Object, except those provided by the capability, will throw an exception if called.

Listing 10. Translated capability C

```
interface C {
    T1 m1( A1 arg1 );
    T2 m2( A2 arg2 );
}

class CapC extends CapNullCap implements C {
    private C impl;

    CapC( C impl ) {
        super();
        this.impl = impl;
    }
    /* Each method of the capability calls the corresponding
       implementation method */
    public T1 m1( A1 arg1 ) { return impl.m1( arg1 ); }
    public T2 m2( A2 arg2 ) { return impl.m2( arg2 ); }
    /* All methods supported by Object, except those
       explicitly declared in the capability are inherited
       from CapNullCap and hence throw an exception if called.
    */
}
```

The other construct that needs to be translated is the wrapping of a capability. Assuming that an object d is of a class that implements the interface C, the source capability is wrapped as follows.

```
C c = capability (C) d;
```

That is translated to a call on the constructor of CapC with the implementation object d as a parameter, as follows.

```
C c = new CapC( d );
```

The object c has dynamic type CapC, which only allows calls on the methods declared in the source capability C, and these calls are translated into calls on the implementing object.

This translation scheme also supports wrapping an existing wrapped capability C to a super-type capability B. In this case the implementing object is of type CapC. Calls on a super type B capability method m call the corresponding method m of the generated class CapB, which in turn calls the corresponding method m of the generated class CapC, which in turn calls the corresponding method m of the implementing object.

The translation scheme given here provides a semantics for capabilities in terms of standard Java programs. While it can be used as a prototype for exploring capabilities, a more direct implementation within the Java compiler and run time can provide a more efficient implementation of capabilities as discussed in the next section.

```
Listing 11. File streams program with annotation
@capability
interface CloseCap { ... }
@capability
interface InCap extends CloseCap { ... }
@capability
interface OutCap extends CloseCap { ... }
@capability
interface InOutCap extends InCap, OutCap { ... }
```

5   Implementation of Capabilities

At run time, a capability has to be distinguished from a normal object reference because once an object or an instance of a capability is wrapped as a more restrictive capability type, it cannot be cast down to a type below its explicit capability type. A capability can be represented by a pair consisting of:

- a reference to the object implementing the capability, and
- a dispatch table matching the interface of the capability for the type of the implementing object.

The dispatch table can be determined (once) when the capability is created (the "wrapping" steps in Listings 5 and 6) and hence provides efficient access to the methods of the capability object. At compile time, we can modify the Java compiler to add a new keyword **capability** or use an annotation **@capability** on an interface. As a first step for implementing capabilities, here we use the Annotation Processing Tool (APT) to track the use of capabilities, while the run-time checking or adding a new keyword in Java compiler will be left as a further step of our implementation in the future work to capture more features of capabilities.

APT is a built-in tool of the Java compiler and it is used for scanning and processing annotations at compile time. APIs available in the packages javax.lang.model and javax.annotation.processing, details of which can be found in [1,10], can be used to process annotations. The example about the file input and output streams, given in Listing 2 using the new keyword **capability** is allowed as an input file and we transform it into a program, replacing the new keyword **capability** with an annotation **@capability** and a Java standard keyword **interface**, as an output file. Other parts of the input file are kept unchanged and the transformed program with annotations is illustrated in Listing 11.

If an instance of capabilities is wrapped with an explicit capability type (i.e., the dynamic type of this instance), it cannot be cast down to a type which is below its explicit dynamic type. In order to track the declaration and use of capabilities, an annotation processor CapabilityProcessor extended from Abstract-Processor is given so that all the interfaces annotated with **@capability** are added in a set of capabilities. Then we construct the Abstract Syntax Tree (AST)

```
$ cd processor
$ javac Capability.java CapabilityCheck.java CapabilityProcessor.java
CapabilityScanner.java
$ cd ..
$ java processor/CapabilityCheck

All Annotated Interface are :
processor.FileAccessCap, processor.Closeable, processor.OutCap, processor.InOutCap,
processor.InCap

processor.InCap is a Capability
processor.InOutCap is a Capability

warning: "(InOutCap) in" is a down cast from processor.InCap to processor.InOutCap
```

Fig. 2. Tracking the declaration and use of capabilities via annotation

of the whole program, and use CapabilityScanner, extended from TreePathScan-
ner, to visit TypeCastTree nodes of the AST for further type cast checking, which
is achieved by overriding the method visitTypeCast(TypeCastTree, Void). If it is
a down casting of a capability, the down casting will be reported as a warning;
otherwise, the check will be passed. Note that, (1) the down casting checking
is achieved by the method isSubType of a Types object, and (2) we focus on
conducting such a checking if the casted type is in the set of capabilities.

The implementation code is written in Java language and it is able to run on
the machine which installs Java SE Development Kit 8 (JDK 8). We successfully
ran it under the MACOS X 10.11.6 operating system and regarding the case of
file input and output stream, the result given by CapabilityProcessor is given in
Fig. 2.

6   Related Work

The object-capability model is a language-level security model, supporting by
secure programming languages such as E [14], Joe-E (a security-oriented subset of
Java) [12,13] and Caja (based on JavaScript) [5,15]. In these models, a capability
is regarded as an unforgeable reference, which can be sent by messages between
different objects. When one object creates another one, it needs to supply the
capabilities it has to the newly created object as its initial capabilities, thus
the capability generation in object capabilities is based on the owner creation.
Whereas, the capabilities in our paper can be regarded as an object with a
strictly restricted interface, and resources can only be accessed via the methods
of the interface. If an object or an instance of a capability is wrapped with
an explicit capability type, it cannot be cast back down to a type below the
explicit capability type; otherwise, casting between instances of capabilities can
be treated as the same as the one in the standard Java language. Moreover, with
the intention of improving access control security, we try to provide relatively
lightweight modifications to Java, thus we do not impose as many language
restrictions as Joe-E. However, the explicit identification of capabilities provides

a focus for checking privileged access escape and also encapsulates what one can do with a resource.

Deny capabilities are proposed in [3], which describe what other aliases are denied by the existence of a reference. Based on deny properties, the authors provide a basis for uniqueness and immutability, introducing a new form of write uniqueness and guaranteeing atomic behaviours. Similar work is also done in [7], which presents a new approach to isolation and uniqueness in an existing, widely-used language, Scala. Hermann *et al.* [8] propose a capability inference mechanism for libraries written in Java, trying to determine which resources are actually used by the various Java Class Library methods (or by other libraries using the Java Class Library). All these three works can be regarded as a complementary to the capability mechanism presented here.

A secure shell, Shill, is proposed by Moore *et al.* [16], which is in contrast to the object-capability languages and the capability mechanism presented in this paper. Instead of focusing on general programming and using capability-based design patterns, it targets a particular domain, shell scripting, and uses contracts to manage capabilities.

Method handle lookup (java.lang.invoke.MethodHandle [6,9]) provides a capability for a single method. The permission checking on the ability to call the method is done when the method handle is created and calls can be effected without any further permission checking. Using this, one can build up a set of method handles to give access to an object. To call the method one needs to use invoke on the handle. By comparison, capabilities provide a handle on an interface to an object rather than just a single method and hence a single capability can be passed to methods needing access to its resources, rather than needing to pass a set of method handles. Calls on the methods of the capability are direct, rather than via invoke and hence the use of a method of a capability appears to the user to be just like a standard method call in Java. This allows compile-time checking that the call is valid, which is an important consideration for effective use of capabilities in user applications.

Project Jigsaw [18] adds modules to Java as a way of grouping classes and restricting access. A module [19] may explicitly import and export classes and interfaces, and such exports can be restricted to an explicit list of other modules. If a module exports an interface I, but not its implementing class C, then another module importing the interface I is not able to access implementing class C, except via the methods provided by I, and hence cannot, for example, cast a reference to an interface I down to the implementing class type C. This allows a restricted form of a capability to be provided via the module mechanism. What it doesn't allow is a hierarchy of capabilities, within which capabilities may only be cast up and not down.

7   Conclusions and Future Work

Providing capabilities for Java has the long-term goal of improving the security of both the Java Class Library and Java applications. For simple applications it is sufficient to explicitly give a set of capabilities to the application to allow it access to just the resources provided by those capabilities. More sophisticated applications will require a capability manager to generate capabilities, such as FileAccessCap in Listing 4. Capability managers are responsible for checking that the calling code has the required permissions for the supplied capability.

Classes in the Java Class Library typically have unfettered access to system resources through the use of caller-sensitive methods and doPrivileged blocks, including for example, the ability to change or remove the security manager. Utilising capabilities internally within the Java Class Library has the prospect of reducing (and hopefully eliminating) the need to use doPrivileged blocks by replacing the use of doPrivileged by access via capabilities supplied to the class to allow it to perform just those privileged operations it needs.

Supporting capabilities in the Java language provides the ability to restrict access to just the interface of the capability and avoid security exploits that make use of subclassing of classes in the Java Class Library thus eliminating a particularly subtle form of exploit that is difficult to detect. The main difference to interfaces is that references to capabilities may not be cast down to their implementing object if they are wrapping up with an explicit capability type.

Conceptually, adding capabilities to Java is quite straightforward. Two extensions are required:

- capability interfaces need to be distinguished from normal interfaces because they inherit from NullCap, rather than Object, and
- the mechanism for wrapping capabilities needs to be supported in the language and at run time.

Because capabilities provide access to restricted resources they should not be passed to untrusted code that does not have the required permissions for the given capability. Furthermore, the analysis of applications or libraries for secure use of resources is facilitated by explicitly recognising that certain objects are capabilities. The capabilities become the focus of analysis of the flow of information in the application.

Acknowledgements. The research presented here is supported by Australian Research Linkage Grant LP140100700 in collaboration with Oracle Labs Australia. We would like to thank Cristina Cifuentes, Paddy Krishnan, Yi Lu, Raghavendra K.R. and John Rose for feedback on the ideas presented here. The paper has benefited from insightful feedback from the reviewers.

References

1. Getting Started with the Annotation Processing Tool, apt. https://docs.oracle.com/javase/7/docs/technotes/guides/apt/GettingStarted.html
2. Cifuentes, C., Gross, A., Keynes, N.: Understanding caller-sensitive method vulnerabilities: a class of access control vulnerabilities in the Java platform. In: Proceedings of the 4th ACM SIGPLAN International Workshop on State Of the Art in Program Analysis, SOAP@PLDI 2015, pp. 7–12. ACM (2015)

3. Clebsch, S., Drossopoulou, S., Blessing, S., McNeil, A.: Deny capabilities for safe, fast actors. In: Proceedings of the 5th International Workshop on Programming Based on Actors, Agents, and Decentralized Control, AGERE! 2015, pp. 1–12. ACM (2015)
4. Gong, L., Ellison, G., Dageforde, M.: Inside Java 2 Platform Security: Architecture, API Design, and Implementation, 2nd edn. Addison Wesley (2003)
5. Google Caja Team: Google-Caja: A Source-to-Source Translator for Securing JavaScript-Based Web. http://code.google.com/p/google-caja/
6. Gosling, J., Joy, B., Steele, G., Bracha, G., Buckley, A.: The Java Language Specification: Java SE 8 Edition, 13 February 2015. https://docs.oracle.com/javase/specs/jls/se8/html/index.html
7. Haller, P., Loiko, A.: LaCaSa: lightweight affinity and object capabilities in scala. In: Proceedings of the ACM SIGPLAN International Conference on Object-Oriented Programming, Systems, Languages, and Applications, OOPSLA 2016, Part of SPLASH 2016, pp. 272–291. ACM (2016)
8. Hermann, B., Reif, M., Eichberg, M., Mezini, M.: Getting to know you: towards a capability model for Java. In: Proceedings of the 10th Joint Meeting on Foundations of Software Engineering, ESEC/FSE 2015, pp. 758–769. ACM (2015)
9. Java Platform, Standard Edition 8: API Specification. http://docs.oracle.com/javase/8/docs/api/. Accessed 20 May 2015
10. The Java Programming Language Compiler, javac. https://docs.oracle.com/javase/8/docs/technotes/guides/javac/index.html
11. Koivu, S.: Java Trusted Method Chaining (CVE-2010-0840/ZDI-10-056), 08 April 2010. http://slightlyrandombrokenthoughts.blogspot.com.au/2010/04/java-trusted-method-chaining-cve-2010.html
12. Mettler, A., Wagner, D.: The Joe-E language specification, Version 1.0. Technical report EECS-2008-91, University of California, Berkeley, August 2008
13. Mettler, A., Wagner, D., Close, T.: Joe-E: a security-oriented subset of Java. In: Proceedings of the Symposium on Network and Distributed System Security, NDSS 2010. The Internet Society (2010)
14. Miller, M.S.: Robust composition: towards a unified approach to access control and concurrency control. Ph.D. thesis, Johns Hopkins University (2006)
15. Miller, M.S., Samuel, M., Laurie, B., Awad, I., Stay, M.: Caja: safe active content in sanitized JavaScript, 15 January 2008. http://google-caja.googlecode.com/files/caja-spec-2008-01-15.pdf
16. Moore, S., Dimoulas, C., King, D., Chong, S.: SHILL: a secure shell scripting language. In: Proceedings of the 11th USENIX Symposium on Operating Systems Design and Implementation, OSDI 2014, pp. 183–199. USENIX Association (2014)
17. Pistoia, M., Flynn, R.J., Koved, L., Sreedhar, V.C.: Interprocedural analysis for privileged code placement and tainted variable detection. In: Black, A.P. (ed.) ECOOP 2005. LNCS, vol. 3586, pp. 362–386. Springer, Heidelberg (2005). https://doi.org/10.1007/11531142_16
18. Reinhold, M.: Project Jigsaw: Goals and Requirements, 02 July 2014. http://openjdk.java.net/projects/jigsaw/goals-reqs/03
19. Reinhold, M.: The State of the Module System, 08 March 2016. http://openjdk.java.net/projects/jigsaw/spec/sotms/

Enforcing Programming Guidelines with Region Types and Effects

Serdar Erbatur[1], Martin Hofmann[1], and Eugen Zălinescu[2(✉)]

[1] Ludwig-Maximilians-Universität, Munich, Bavaria, Germany
{serdar.erbatur,hofmann}@ifi.lmu.edu
[2] Institut Für Informatik, Technische Universität München, Munich, Germany
eugen.zalinescu@in.tum.de

Abstract. We present in this paper a new type and effect system for Java which can be used to ensure adherence to guidelines for secure web programming. The system is based on the region and effect system by Beringer, Grabowski, and Hofmann. It improves upon it by being parametrized over an arbitrary guideline supplied in the form of a finite monoid or automaton and a type annotation or mockup code for external methods. Furthermore, we add a powerful type inference based on precise interprocedural analysis and provide an implementation in the Soot framework which has been tested on a number of benchmarks including large parts of the Stanford SecuriBench.

1 Introduction

We present in this paper a new type and effect system for Java which can be used to ensure adherence to guidelines for secure web programming such as proper sanitization of externally supplied strings or appropriate authorization prior to access to sensitive data. Unlike its precursors, the system can be freely configured and in this way it can guarantee adherence to a whole host of such guidelines.

The type system is based on the region and effect systems given in [6, 13] but improves upon and extends them in a number of ways. First, our system is parametrized by an arbitrary monoid abstracting both string values and sequences of events such as writing certain strings to files or invoking certain framework methods.

Second, in [6] heuristic context information was used in two places: first, in order to index several types for one and the same method and thus to provide a limited amount of polymorphism and secondly in order to determine regions for newly allocated objects. As a side effect this provided for the first time a rigorous type-theoretic underpinning for context-sensitive and points-to analyses. The system presented here keeps heuristic, user-dependent context information for the points-to part, i.e. to determine regions for newly allocated objects, but uses precise and fully automatic interprocedural analysis for method typings.

This research is funded by the German Research Foundation (DFG) under research grant 250888164 (GuideForce).

B.-Y.E. Chang (Ed.): APLAS 2017, LNCS 10695, pp. 85–104, 2017.
https://doi.org/10.1007/978-3-319-71237-6_5

Third, we have implemented an automatic type inference for the system using the Soot framework [20]. This makes our analysis applicable to actual Java source code via Soot's builtin translation into control-flow graphs which are sufficiently close to the academic language Featherweight Java [17] extended with updates and strings (FJEUS) on which our type system and its theoretical analysis are based. This allowed us to test the type system on a number of interesting benchmarks including those from the SecuriBench and thus to practically demonstrate the assertion already made in [6] that region-based type and effect systems achieve the same accuracy as state-of-the-art context-sensitive pointer and points-to analyses [8,9,21,22].

Being formulated as a type system, our analysis enjoys a very clear semantic foundation in the form of a declarative type system which consists of fairly simple and natural rules and is sound with respect to a standard operational semantics. From there we move in three steps to the actual implementation of type inference. Each step is again sound with respect to the previous one. These steps are first a semi-declarative type system in which regions for newly allocated objects are selected deterministically as a function of program point and a context abstraction chosen by the user. At this point we may lose some precision but not soundness because the context abstraction might have been ill-chosen (this also happens in the case of classical points-to analysis). We then give an algorithmic type system whose rules are syntax-directed and can be read as a logic program. This latter system is sound *and* complete with respect to the semi-declarative system. The last step, finally, is the actual implementation using Soot which replaces the logic program implicit in the algorithmic type system with an actual fixpoint iteration both over control flow graphs (intraprocedural part) and over method call graphs (interprocedural part). Again, the algorithm underlying the implementation is sound and complete with respect to the algorithmic type system. We thus have semantic soundness of all stages and we can clearly delineate where precision is lost: first, we have the declarative type system which formalizes a certain degree of abstraction, e.g., by treating conditionals as nondeterministic choice (path-insensitivity) and by presupposing a finite set of regions. Second, we have the passage from the declarative to the semi-declarative system. All other stages are precision-preserving.

Before we start let us illustrate the approach with two simple examples.

Example 1. Consider the following small Java program to be subjected to taintedness analysis. User input (as obtained by getString) is assumed to be tainted and should not be given to putString as input without preprocessing.

```
class C {                          class D {
  main() {                           public String s;
    D f1 = new D(getString());       public D(String s) {
    D f2 = new D("test");              this.s = s; }}
    putString(f2.s); }}
```

To ensure this, our type system will refine String into two types: String@user containing "tainted" strings and String@ok which contains untainted strings such as literals from the program text or results from trusted sanitization functions. We also refine the class D using two *regions* into the refined class types D@red and D@green. For each of these we then have refined field and method typings: the s field of D@red objects is typed String@user and so is the parameter of their constructor. The class D@green uses String@ok instead. If there are more fields and methods that we want to differentiate we might need more regions than just two. With these typings in place, we can then see that the program is correct as follows: the variable f1 gets type D@red whereas f2 gets type D@green. Thus, f2.s has type String@ok and the external method call is permitted. We notice that if we had allowed only one region rather than two, i.e. without regions, we would be forced to give field would s the type String@user in view of the assignment to f1. We thus see how the regions provide object sensitivity. If, on the other hand, we had erroneously written putString(f1.s) then, since f1.s has type String@user a type error would have resulted no matter how many regions we use.

Consider now another example in which we need to take into account method effects, type casting, and library methods for which source code is not available.

Example 2. Consider the following method.

```
void doGet(HttpServletRequest req, HttpServletResponse resp) throws IOException {
  String s1 = req.getParameter("name");
  LinkedList<String> list = new LinkedList<String>();
  list.addLast(s1);
  String s2 = (String) list.getLast();
  PrintWriter writer = resp.getWriter();
  writer.println(s2); /* BAD */ }
```

In the last line, a possibly tainted string is written unsanitized.

We use two conceptually different ways to handle external methods whose code is not part of the program being analyzed but comes from some ambient framework or library: (1) builtin methods (like getString) that always take and return strings and are given semantically; (2) external methods (like addLast) that take and return values other than strings and are defined with mockup code.

For the builtin methods we provide their semantic behavior and typing by hand also taking into account tags representing taintedness, the action of sanitization functions, or similar. We also specify event traces produced by them. To this end, we assume an alphabet to represent tags and event traces, and use finite automata and monoids to obtain a finite abstraction of the event traces produced by the program. This eventually allows us to ensure that the set of traces produced by a program will be accepted by a given policy automaton.

Defined external methods are altogether different. We use mockup code to represent their implementation, so as to obtain a model of the part of the ambient framework that is relevant to the analysis. Mockup code is thus analyzed along with the user code. For the given example, we use the following mockup code for linked lists, where we want to impose the abstraction that all their entries are treated the same, e.g., if one entry is tainted then all entries count as tainted.

```
class LinkedList {
   Object o;                                  boolean addLast(Object e) { o = e; return true; }
   LinkedList(Object e) { o = e; }            Object getLast(int index) { return o; } ... }
```

The following mockup code implements the classes HttpServletRequest, etc. and their relevant methods in terms of the builtin methods getString and putString.

```
class HttpServletRequest { String getParameter(String s) { return getString(); } }
class HttpServletResponse { PrintWriter getWriter() { return new PrintWriter(); } }
class PrintWriter { void println(String s) { return putString(s); } }
```

An alternative to mockup code which we had also explored consists of ascribing refined types to library methods which then have to be justified manually. However, we found that the expressive power of mockup code is no less than that of arbitrary types and often intuitively clearer. This may be compared to the possibility of approximating stateful behavior of an unknown component with a state machine or alternatively (that would correspond to the use of manually justified types) with a temporal logic formula.

Lastly, to handle casts in general we extended FJEUS in [6] with appropriate semantics and refined type system. Regarding the application scope, we must add that our scope is not limited to guidelines for strings. Currently we are able to formalize guidelines that represent safety properties and further plan to extend our approach to liveness and fairness properties.

We stress that our type inference algorithm automatically finds and checks all field and method typings. There is no need for the user to fill in these typings. All a user needs to provide is:

- the policy or guideline to be checked;
- typings or mockup code for external framework methods;
- a context abstraction (usually taken from a few standard ones);
- the set of regions to be used (or their number).

Many details, examples, and proofs that have been omitted for space reasons can be found in the long version of this paper, available on the authors' websites.

2   Formalizing Programming Guidelines

In order to formalize a given guideline to be enforced we select a finite alphabet Σ to represent string *tags*, i.e. annotations that denote some extra information about strings, like taintedness, input kind etc. This same alphabet is also used to represent *events* generated during the program execution, like writing to a file or the invocation of external methods. One could use different alphabets for tags and events but for simplicity we chose not to do so.

We also assume an infinite set *Str* of *string literals*, and a function lit2word : $Str \rightarrow \Sigma^*$ that specifies the tag word $w \in \Sigma^*$ for a given string literal.

The operational semantics is then instrumented so that string literals are always paired with their tag words in Σ^* and evaluation of an expression always results in an event trace also represented as a finite word over Σ.

Next, we require a finite monoid Mon and a homomorphism $[-] : \Sigma^* \to Mon$ providing a finite abstraction of string tags and event traces. We let $Eff :=$ $\mathcal{P}(Mon)$ and use this abbreviation when referring to event trace abstractions, in contrast to string tag abstractions. We single out a subset $\mathsf{Allowed} \subseteq Mon$ consisting of the event traces that are allowed under the guideline to be formalized.

Then, we need to specify a collection of builtin methods such as $\mathsf{getString}$ and $\mathsf{putString}$ all of which are static and only take string parameters and return a string. We use fn to range over these builtin methods.

For each n-ary builtin method fn we assume given a function

$$sem(fn) : (Str \times \Sigma^*)^n \to \mathcal{P}(Str \times \Sigma^* \times \Sigma^*).$$

The intuition is that when $(t, w, w') \in sem(fn)((t_1, w_1), \ldots, (t_n, w_n))$ then this means that the invocation of the builtin method fn on string arguments $t_1, \ldots, t_n$ tagged as $w_1, \ldots, w_n$ can yield result string t tagged as w and leave the event trace w'. The nondeterminism, i.e. the fact that $sem(fn)$ returns a set of results allows us for instance to represent user input, incoming requests, or file contents.

Furthermore, we must specify a "typing" in the form of a function

$$M(fn) : Mon^n \to \mathcal{P}(Mon) \times Eff$$

such that whenever $t_1, \ldots, t_n \in Str$ and $w_1, \ldots, w_n \in \Sigma^*$ and $(t, w, w') \in sem(fn)((t_1, w_1), \ldots, (t_n, w_n))$, it holds that $[w] \in U$ and $[w'] \in U'$, where $(U, U') = M(fn)([w_1], \ldots, [w_n])$.

In summary, the formalization of a guideline thus comprises:

- tag and event alphabet, finite monoid,[1] allowed subset, and homomorphism,
- semantic functions and typings for builtin methods,
- mockup code for other framework components.

Example 3. Consider the program in Example 1. We set $\Sigma = \{\mathsf{user}, \mathsf{ok}\}$, $Mon = \{\mathsf{T}, \mathsf{U}\}$ (T, U standing for "tainted"/"untainted") with $\mathsf{UU} = \mathsf{U}$ and $\mathsf{UT} = \mathsf{TU} = \mathsf{TT} = \mathsf{T}$. Also, $[\mathsf{user}] = \mathsf{T}$, $[\mathsf{ok}] = \mathsf{U}$, and $\mathsf{Allowed} = \{\mathsf{U}\}$. The semantic function $sem(\mathsf{getString})$ returns nondeterministically a triple of the form $(t, \langle\mathsf{user}\rangle, \varepsilon)$ with t a string, ε the empty trace, and $\langle-\rangle$ denoting sequences. The semantic function $sem(\mathsf{putString})(t, w)$ returns the triple $(""", \varepsilon, \langle[w]\rangle)$, with empty strings representing void. The typing of $\mathsf{getString}$ is $M(\mathsf{getString})() = (\{[\mathsf{user}]\}, \{[\varepsilon]\}) = (\{\mathsf{T}\}, \{\mathsf{U}\})$. (Note that U is the monoid's neutral element). The typing of $\mathsf{putString}$ is $M(\mathsf{putString})(u) = (\{\mathsf{U}\}, \{u\})$, for any $u \in Mon$.

---

[1] Alternatively, the monoid can be generated automatically from the policy automaton (or its complement).

3   Featherweight Java with Updates, Casts, and Strings

FJEUCS is a formalized and downsized object-oriented language that captures those aspects of Java that are interesting for our analysis: objects with imperative field updates, and strings. The language is an extension of FJEUS [13] with casts, which itself extends FJEU [15] with strings, which itself extends Featherweight Java [17] with side effects on a heap.

3.1   Syntax

The following table summarizes the (infinite) abstract identifier sets in FJEUCS, the meta-variables we use to range over them, and the syntax of expressions. Notice that we only allow variables in various places, e.g., field access so as to simplify the metatheory. By using let-bindings, the effect of nested expressions can be restored (let normal form).

variables: $x, y \in Var$ fields: $f \in Fld$ string literals: $str \in Str$
classes: $C, D \in Cls$ methods: $m \in Mtd$ builtin methods: $fn \in Fn$

$$Expr \ni e :: = x \mid \text{let } x = e_1 \text{ in } e_2 \mid \text{if } x_1 = x_2 \text{ then } e_1 \text{ else } e_2 \mid \text{null} \mid \text{new } C$$
$$\mid (C)\, e \mid x.f \mid x_1.f := x_2 \mid x.m(\bar{y}) \mid fn(\bar{y}) \mid "str" \mid x_1 + x_2$$

We assume that Cls contains three distinguished elements, namely Object, String, and NullType.[2] In new C expressions, we require that $C \neq$ String and $C \neq$ NullType. Also, in $(C)\, e$ expressions, $C \neq$ NullType.

An FJEUCS program over the fixed set of builtin methods is defined by the following relations and functions.

subclass relation: $\prec \in \mathcal{P}^{fin}(Cls \times Cls)$
field list: $fields \in Cls \to \mathcal{P}^{fin}(Fld)$
method list: $methods \in Cls \to \mathcal{P}^{fin}(Mtd)$
method table: $mtable \in Cls \times Mtd \rightharpoonup Expr$
FJEUCS program: $P = (\prec, fields, methods, mtable)$

FJEUCS is a language with nominal subtyping: $D \prec C$ means D is an immediate subclass of C. The relation is well-formed if, when restricted to $Cls \setminus \{\text{NullType}\}$ it is a tree successor relation with root Object; thus, multiple inheritance is not allowed. We write $\preceq$ for the reflexive and transitive closure of $\prec$. We also require NullType $\preceq C$ for all $C \in Cls$ and that String is neither a subclass nor a superclass of any proper class (other than NullType, Object, String).

The functions $fields$ and $methods$ describe for each class C which fields and method objects of that class have. The functions are well-formed if for all classes C and D such that $D \preceq C$, $fields(C) \subseteq fields(D)$ and $methods(C) \subseteq methods(D)$, i.e. classes inherit fields and methods from their superclasses. For $C \in \{\text{NullType}, \text{String}\}$ we require that $fields(C) = methods(C) = \emptyset$. A method

---

[2] In Java, the NullType is the type of the expression null, see https://docs.oracle.com/javase/specs/jls/se7/html/jls-4.html#jls-4.1.

table *mtable* gives for each class and each method identifier its implementation, i.e. the FJEUCS expression that forms the method's body.

A method table is well-formed if the entry $mtable(C, m)$ is defined for all $m \in methods(C)$. An implementation may be overridden in subclasses for the same number of formal parameters. For simplicity, we do not include overloading. We assume that the formal argument variables of a method m are named x_1^m, x_2^m, etc., besides the implicit and reserved variable *this*. Only these variables may occur freely in the body of m. The number of arguments of m is denoted $ar(m)$.

A class table (F_0, M_0) models FJEUCS standard type system, where types are simply classes. The *field typing* $F_0 : (Cls \times Fld) \rightharpoonup Cls$ assigns to each class C and each field $f \in fields(C)$ the class of the field, which is required to be invariant with respect to subclasses of C. The *method typing* $M_0 : (Cls \times Mtd) \rightharpoonup Cls^* \times Cls$ assigns to each class C and each method $m \in methods(C)$ a *method type*, which specifies the classes of the formal argument variables and of the result value.

We make explicit the notion of program point by annotating expressions with *expression labels* $i \in Pos$: we write $[e]^i$ for FJEUCS expressions, where e is defined as before. An FJEUCS program is well-formed if each expression label i appears at most once in it. In the following, we only consider well-formed programs, and simply write e instead $[e]^i$ if the expression label i is not important.

3.2 Semantics

A state consists of a store (variable environment or stack) and a heap (memory). Stores map variables to values, while heaps map locations to objects. The only kinds of values in FJEUCS are object locations and *null*. We distinguish two kinds of objects: *ordinary objects* contain a class identifier and a valuation of the fields, while *string objects* are immutable character sequences tagged with a word over the alphabet Σ. The following table summarizes this state model.

locations: $l \in Loc$	stores: $s \in Var \rightharpoonup Val$
values: $v \in Val = Loc \uplus \{null\}$	heaps: $h \in Loc \rightharpoonup Obj \uplus SObj$
string objects: $\quad SObj = Str \times \Sigma^*$	objects: $\quad Obj = Cls \times (Fld \rightharpoonup Val)$

The FJEUCS semantics is defined as a big-step relation $(s, h) \vdash e \Downarrow v, h' \ \& \ w$, which means that, in store s and heap h, the expression e evaluates to the value v and modifies the heap to h', generating the event trace $w \in \Sigma^*$. The operational semantics rules can be found in the long version of the paper.

4 Region-Based Type and Effect Systems

4.1 Refined Types, Effects, and Type System Parameters

Refined Types. We assume a finite set *Reg* of *regions*, with $Mon \subseteq Reg$. We refine the standard object types by annotating objects with sets of regions:

$$Typ \ni \tau, \sigma ::= C_R \qquad \text{where } C \in Cls, R \subseteq Reg$$

such that if $C = \texttt{String}$ then $R \subseteq Mon$.

A value typed with C_R, with $R \cap Mon = \emptyset$, intuitively means that it is a location pointing to an ordinary object of class C (or a subclass of C), and this location is abstracted to a region $r \in R$, but no other region. A value typed with $\mathtt{String}_U$ (or $\mathtt{Object}_U$ with $U \subseteq Mon$) intuitively means that it is a location that refers to a string object that is tagged with a word w such that $[w] \in U$. We use subsets of Reg rather than single elements to account for joining branches of conditionals (including the conditionals implicit in dynamic dispatch).

Since region sets are an over-approximation of the possible locations where a non-string object resides, and string annotations are an over-approximation of the tags, we define a subtyping relation $<:$ based on set inclusion:

$$\frac{C \preceq D \qquad R \subseteq S}{C_R <: D_S}$$

The subtyping relation is extended to type sequences as expected: $\bar{\sigma} <: \bar{\tau}$ iff $|\bar{\sigma}| = |\bar{\tau}|$ and $\sigma_i <: \tau_i$, for all $i \in \{1, \dots, |\bar{\sigma}|\}$.

If R is a singleton we call refined types C_R *atomic (refined) types* and denote the set of atomic types by $ATyp$. We often write C_r instead of $C_{\{r\}}$. For a refined type C_R, let $\mathrm{atoms}(C_R) := \{C_r \mid r \in R\}$. For a sequence $\bar{\tau} = (\tau_1, \dots \tau_k)$ of refined types, let $\mathrm{atoms}(\bar{\tau}) := \{(\sigma_1, \dots, \sigma_k) \mid \sigma_i \in \mathrm{atoms}(\tau_i), \text{ for each } i \text{ with } 1 \leq i \leq k\}$.

Type and Effect Lattice. We lift the subtyping relation to include effects as well. We define the partial order $\sqsubseteq$ on $\mathcal{L} := Typ \times \mathit{Eff}$ by $(C_R, U) \sqsubseteq (C'_{R'}, U')$ if and only if $C_R <: C'_{R'}$ and $U \subseteq U'$, for any $C, C' \in Cls$, $R, R' \subseteq Reg$, and $U, U' \subseteq Mon$. Given two refined types C_R and D_S, we define their *join* as $C_R \sqcup D_S = E_{R \cup S}$ where E is the smallest (wrt $\preceq$) common superclass[3] of C and D. Given two elements $\ell, \ell' \in \mathcal{L}$ with $\ell = (C_R, U)$ and $\ell' = (C'_{R'}, U')$, we define their *join*, denoted $\ell \sqcup \ell'$, by $(C_R \sqcup C'_{R'}, U \cup U')$. Thus $(Typ, \sqcup)$ and $(\mathcal{L}, \sqcup)$ are join-/upper-semilattices. Given $T = \{\tau_1, \dots, \tau_n\} \subseteq Typ$ for some $n \geq 0$, we denote by $\sqcup T$ the type $\tau_1 \sqcup \tau_2 \sqcup \cdots \sqcup \tau_n$, where by convention $\sqcup T = \mathtt{Object}_{Reg}$ when $T = \emptyset$. For $L \subseteq \mathcal{L}$, the notation $\sqcup L$ is defined similarly.

Parameters of the Type and Effect System. The following table summarizes the parameters of our system: a set of regions, a set of contexts, a context transfer function, and an object abstraction function. We explain them here briefly.

Regions (finite):	$r, s, t \in Reg$
Contexts (finite):	$z \in Ctx$
Context transfer function:	$\phi \in Ctx \times Cls \times Reg \times Mtd \times Pos \to Ctx$
Object abstraction function:	$\psi \in Ctx \times Pos \to Reg$

Regions are already defined in Sect. 4.1. They represent abstract memory locations. Each region stands for zero or more concrete locations. Different

---

[3] Note that such a class always exists, as $C \preceq \mathtt{Object}$, for any $C \in Cls$.

regions represent disjoint sets of concrete locations, hence they partition or color the memory. Two pointers to different regions can therefore never alias. Thus the type system serves also as a unifying calculus for pointer analysis.

Let us assume that we have the *call graph* of a program. A method m is then represented by a node in this graph, and a *context* corresponds to a possible path that leads to the node. The *finite* set Ctx abstracts these paths. For example, it can be chosen to consists of all locations in the program code or the latter together with, say, the last 3 method calls on the stack (3CFA). The meaning of these contexts is given by the functions ϕ and ψ which we explain next. The *context transfer function* ϕ represents the edges in the abstract call graph. It selects a context for the callee based on the caller's context, the class of the receiver object, its region, the method name, and the call site. An *object abstraction function* ψ assigns a region for a new object, given the allocation site and the current method context. Notice that Ctx is an arbitrary finite set and ϕ, ψ are arbitrary functions. Their choice does not affect soundness but of course accuracy of the analysis. In [29] a similar factorization of ϕ and ψ for callee contexts and object allocation names is presented.

4.2 Declarative Type System

As said earlier, the declarative type and effect system is general in the sense that it produces method typings without considering contexts. The method typings along with effects are computed with regard to only method signatures and the associated region information. In addition, new objects are assigned arbitrary regions in a context-insensitive manner.

The typing judgment takes the form $\Gamma \vdash_d e : \tau \,\&\, U$, where e is an expression, the *variable context (store typing)* $\Gamma : Var \rightharpoonup Typ$ maps variables (at least those in e) to types, τ is a type, and U is an element of *Eff*. The meaning is that, if the values of the variables comply with Γ and the evaluation of e terminates successfully, then the result complies with τ, and the event trace generated during this evaluation belongs to one of the equivalence classes in U. In particular, if $U \subseteq$ Allowed then e adheres to the guideline. It suffices to perform this latter check for an entry point such as (the body of) a main method.

From a theoretical point of view, the declarative type system forms the basis of our analysis. Once we prove its soundness w.r.t. operational semantics, the soundness of the semi-declarative and algorithmic systems follows directly.

Class Tables. A declarative class table (T_d, F, M_d) fixes a set of $T_d \subseteq ATyp$ of relevant atomic refined types and models FJEUCS's class member types declaratively. The set T_d is required to be closed under "supertyping", that is, for any $C_r \in T_d$ and $D \in Cls$ with $C \prec D$, we have that $D_r \in T_d$. One can often assume that the set T_d of relevant types contains all types, i.e. $T_d = ATyp$. However, when we take $T_d \subsetneq ATyp$, by having $C \prec D$, $C_r \notin T$, and $D_r \in T$, there is an implicit promise that an object with type D_r is never an object of type C_r that has just been upcast.

The *field typing* $F : (Fld \times ATyp) \rightharpoonup Typ$ assigns to each class C, region r, and field $f \in fields(C)$ the type $F(f, C_r)$ of the field. The type is required to be invariant with respect to subclasses of C. More formally, a field typing F is *well-formed* if $F(f, D_r) = F(f, C_r)$, for all classes C, subclasses $D \preceq C$, regions r with $D_r \in T_d$, and fields $f \in fields(C)$. For simplicity, in contrast to [6], we do not use covariant get-types and contravariant set-types for fields.

The *declarative method typing* $M_d : (Mtd \times ATyp) \rightharpoonup \mathcal{P}(Typ^* \times Typ \times Eff)$ assigns to each class C, region r, and method $m \in methods(C)$, a set $M_d(m, C_r)$ of tuples $(\bar{\sigma}, \tau, U)$, where $\bar{\sigma}$ is a sequence of atomic refined types for the methods' arguments, τ is the refined type of the result value, and U are the possible effects of the method. Every overriding method should be contravariant in the argument types, covariant in the result class, and have a smaller effect set. Formally, M_d is *well-formed* if for all classes C, subclasses $C' \preceq C$, regions r with $C'_r \in T_d$, and methods $m \in methods(C)$, it holds that

$$\forall(\bar{\sigma}, \tau, U) \in M_d(m, C_r). \; \exists(\bar{\sigma}', \tau', U') \in M_d(m, C'_r). \; (\bar{\sigma}', \tau', U') \sqsubseteq_m (\bar{\sigma}, \tau, U)$$

where we lift the partial order $\sqsubseteq$ to $Typ^* \times Typ \times Eff$ using $(\bar{\sigma}', \tau', U') \sqsubseteq_m (\bar{\sigma}, \tau, U)$ iff $\bar{\sigma} <: \bar{\sigma}'$ and $(\tau', U') \sqsubseteq (\tau, U)$.

Finally, all types occurring in the field and methods typings are relevant. Formally, $C_r \in T_d$, for any C_r occurring in the domain of F or M_d, and for any $C_r \in atoms(C_R)$ with C_R occurring in the image of F or M_d.

Type System. For space reasons, we only present three of the type rules, given in Fig. 1. The complete rules are given in the long version. In the rule TD-NEW, we choose an arbitrary region as the abstract location of the object allocated by this expression, as long as the respective type is relevant. For method calls, TD-INVOKE requires that for all regions $r \in R$ where the receiver object x may reside, there exists an entry in M_d for the called method and its class such that the resulting type and effect is suitable for the given argument types and the expected result type and effect. In the rule TD-BUILTIN we obtain the refined type of the string returned by a call to the builtin method *fn*, by calling

$$\text{TD-NEW} \; \frac{C_r \in T_d}{\Gamma \vdash_d \mathbf{new}\, C : C_{\{r\}} \; \& \; \{[\varepsilon]\}}$$

$$\text{TD-INVOKE} \; \frac{\text{for all } r \in R, \text{ there is } (\bar{\sigma}', \tau', U') \in M_d(m, C_r)}{\text{such that } (\bar{\sigma}', \tau', U') \sqsubseteq_m (\bar{\sigma}, \tau, U)}{\Gamma, x : C_R, \bar{y} : \bar{\sigma} \vdash_d x.m(\bar{y}) : \tau \; \& \; U}$$

$$\text{TD-BUILTIN} \; \frac{ar(fn) = n \quad \Gamma(x_1) = \mathtt{String}_{U_1}, \ldots, \Gamma(x_n) = \mathtt{String}_{U_n}}{M(fn)(u_1, \ldots, u_n) \sqsubseteq (U, U'), \text{ for all } u_1 \in U_1, \ldots, u_n \in U_n}{\Gamma \vdash_d fn(x_1, \ldots, x_n) : \mathtt{String}_U \; \& \; U'}$$

Fig. 1. Selected rules of the declarative type system.

the builtin method typing $M(fn)$ on the tag abstractions of fn's arguments. Note that also denote by $\sqsubseteq$ the partial order over $\mathcal{P}(Mon) \times Eff$ defined by: $(R', U') \sqsubseteq (R, U)$ iff $R' \subseteq R$ and $U' \subseteq U$.

An FJEUCS program $P = (\prec, fields, methods, mtable)$ is *well-typed* with respect to the class table $(T_{\mathsf{d}}, F, M_{\mathsf{d}})$ if for all classes C, regions r, methods $m \in methods(C)$, and tuples $(\bar{\sigma}, \tau, U) \in M_{\mathsf{d}}(m, C_r)$, the judgment $\Gamma \vdash_{\mathsf{d}} mtable(C, m) : \tau \,\&\, U$ can be derived with $\Gamma = [this \mapsto C_r] \cup [x_i^m \mapsto \sigma_i]_{i \in \{1,\ldots,ar(m)\}}$.

Type System Soundness. We state next the guarantees provided by the type system, namely that if $\Gamma \vdash_{\mathsf{d}} e : \tau \,\&\, U$ can be derived and $U \subseteq$ Allowed, then any event trace of the expression e is allowed by the guideline. See the long version for a more general statement of the soundness theorem and its proof.

Theorem 1 (Soundness). *Let P be a well-typed program and e an expression with no free variables. If $\Gamma \vdash_{\mathsf{d}} e : \tau \,\&\, U$ and $(s, h) \vdash e \Downarrow v, h' \,\&\, w$, for some τ, U, v, h', and w, and with Γ, s, and h the empty mappings, then $[w] \in U$.*

4.3 Semi-declarative Type System

As already mentioned we rely on heuristic context information in order to infer regions for newly created objects. That is to say, we use the user-provided function ψ in order to select a region for the newly created object based on the position of the statement (expression label) and the current context which is an abstraction of the call stack. Clearly, the use of such arbitrary user-provided decision functions incurs an unavoidable loss of precision. The semi-declarative type system which we now present precisely quantifies this loss of precision. It is still declarative in the sense that types for methods and classes can be arbitrary (sets of simple types), but it is algorithmic in that regions for newly created objects are assigned using the function ψ. It also uses the equally user-provided function ϕ to manage the context abstractions. The semi-declarative system is therefore sound (Theorem 2) with respect to the declarative one and thus also with respect to the operational semantics via Theorem 1.

Further down, in Sect. 4.4 we will then give an algorithmic type system which can be understood as a type inference algorithm presented as a logic program. This algorithmic type system will be shown sound (Theorem 3) *and* complete (Theorem 4) w.r.t. the semi-declarative system.

Class Tables. We define next semi-declarative class tables $(T_{\mathsf{s}}, F, M_{\mathsf{s}})$. The set of allowed refined types is parametrized by a context, that is, T_{s} is a function from Ctx to $ATyp$. Each set $T_{\mathsf{s}}(z)$ is closed under supertyping as in the declarative case. The field typing F is as in the fully declarative case. The *semi-declarative method typing* $M_{\mathsf{s}} : (Mtd \times Ctx \times ATyp) \to \mathcal{P}(Typ^* \times Typ \times Eff)$ assigns to each class C, region r, context z, and method $m \in methods(C)$ a set $M_{\mathsf{s}}(m, z, C_r)$ of tuples $(\bar{\sigma}, \tau, U)$ as in the fully declarative case. As before, overriding methods have to satisfy the following condition: for any context z, atomic refined typed $C'_r \in T_s(z)$, class C with $C' \preceq C$, and method $m \in \textit{methods}(C)$, it holds that

$$\forall (\bar{\sigma}, \tau, U) \in M_s(m, z, C_r). \exists (\bar{\sigma}', \tau', U') \in M_s(m, z, C'_r). (\bar{\sigma}', \tau', U') \sqsubseteq_m (\bar{\sigma}, \tau, U).$$

Typing Rules. The parametric typing judgment takes the form $\Gamma; z \vdash_s e : \tau \& U$, where Γ, e, τ, and U are as for the declarative typing judgment $\Gamma \vdash_d e : \tau \& U$, while $z \in \textit{Ctx}$ is a context. The judgment has the same meaning as before, with the addition that it is relative to the context z. The derivation rules are the same as for the declarative system, with the addition of the context z in each judgment, except for the two rules given next. In the rule TS-NEW, we choose the region specified by ψ as the abstract location of the object allocated by this expression. For method calls, TS-INVOKE requires that for all regions $r \in R$ where the receiver object x may reside, the method typing in the context selected by ϕ is suitable for the given argument types and the expected result type and effect.

$$\text{TS-NEW} \quad \frac{r = \psi(z, i) \qquad C_r \in T_s(z)}{\Gamma; z \vdash_s [\text{new } C]^i : C_r \& \{[\varepsilon]\}}$$

$$\text{TS-INVOKE} \quad \frac{\begin{array}{c} \text{for all } r \in R, \text{ there is } (\bar{\sigma}', \tau', U') \in M_s(m, z', C_r) \\ \text{such that } (\bar{\sigma}', \tau', U') \sqsubseteq_m (\bar{\sigma}, \tau, U), \text{ where } z' = \phi(z, C, r, m, i) \end{array}}{\Gamma, x : C_R, \bar{y} : \bar{\sigma}; z \vdash_s [x.m(\bar{y})]^i : \tau \& U}$$

A program $P = (\prec, \textit{fields}, \textit{methods}, \textit{mtable})$ is *well-typed* w.r.t. the class table (T_s, F, M_s) if for all classes C, contexts z, regions r, methods $m \in \textit{methods}(C)$, and tuples $(\bar{\sigma}, \tau, U) \in M_s(m, z, C_r)$, the judgment $\Gamma; z \vdash_s \textit{mtable}(C, m) : \tau \& U$ can be derived with $\Gamma = [\textit{this} \mapsto C_r] \cup [x_i^m \mapsto \sigma_i]_{i \in \{1, \ldots, \textit{ar}(m)\}}$.

Soundness of the semi-declarative type system follows directly from the soundness of declarative type system. That is, since the rules of semi-declarative system are obtained by adding context information to the rules of the declarative system, the soundness result from the previous subsection carries over here.

Theorem 2 (Soundness). *If an FJEUCS program is well-typed with respect to a semi-declarative class table (T_s, F, M_s), then it is well-typed with respect to the corresponding declarative class table (T_d, F, M_d), where $T_d := \bigcup_{z \in \textit{Ctx}} T_s(z)$ and $M_d(m, C_r) := \bigcup_{z \in \textit{Ctx}} M_s(m, z, C_r)$.*

Regarding the announced lack of completeness with respect to the declarative system, consider e.g. the case where ψ returns one and the same region irrespective of context and position. In this case, two newly created objects:

```
StringBuffer x = new StringBuffer();
StringBuffer y = new StringBuffer();
```

will be sent to the same region and, e.g., writing an unsanitized string into x followed by outputting y would be overcautiously considered an error. More interesting examples would involve a single allocation statement called several times in different contexts. No matter how fine the abstraction function is chosen, we can always find a situation where two different allocations are sent to the same region because the two contexts are identified by the context abstraction.

4.4 Algorithmic Type System

The algorithmic type system is the one we use in our analysis. It returns the most precise typings and is complete with respect to the semi-declarative system.

Class Tables. We defined next algorithmic class tables (T_a, F, M_a). The sets $T_a(z)$ of relevant refined types per context z, and the field typing F are as in the semi-declarative case. The *algorithmic method typing* $M_a : (Mtd \times Ctx \times ATyp \times ATyp^*) \rightharpoonup Typ \times Eff$ assigns to each class C, region r, context z, and method $m \in methods(C)$, and sequence $\bar{\sigma}$ of atomic refined types for the methods' arguments (i.e. $|\bar{\sigma}| = ar(m)$), a type and effect value $M_a(m, z, C_r, \bar{\sigma})$, which specifies the refined type of the result value, as well as the possible effects of the method. Also, as for the other type systems, we require that for any context z, atomic refined type $C'_r \in T_a(z)$, class C with $C' \preceq C$, region r, and method $m \in methods(C)$, and atomic type sequences $\bar{\sigma} <: \bar{\sigma}'$ with $|\bar{\sigma}| = ar(m)$, it holds that $M_a(m, z, C'_r, \bar{\sigma}') \sqsubseteq M_a(m, z, C_r, \bar{\sigma})$.

Typing Rules. The algorithmic typing judgment $\Gamma; z \vdash_a e : \tau \& U$ takes the same form and has the same meaning as the semi-declarative typing judgment. The rules, given in the long version of the paper, are in essence more specialized versions of the ones in the semi-declarative system. For instance, in the rule TA-INVOKE we take the join of all types which are computed with respect to all regions in which the object x may reside and all contexts returned by ϕ.

$$\text{TA-INVOKE} \quad \frac{(\tau, U) = \bigsqcup \{M_a(m, z', C_r, \bar{\sigma}) \mid r \in R, z' = \phi(z, C, r, m, i)\}}{\Gamma, x : C_R, \bar{y} : \bar{\sigma}; z \vdash_a [x.m(\bar{y})]^i : \tau \& U}$$

An FJEUCS program $P = (\prec, fields, methods, mtable)$ is *well-typed* with respect to the class table (T_a, F, M_a) if for all classes C, contexts z, regions r, methods $m \in methods(C)$, and sequence $\bar{\sigma}$ of argument types such that $(m, z, C_r, \bar{\sigma}) \in dom(M_a)$, the judgment $\Gamma; z \vdash_a mtable(C, m) : \tau \& U$ can be derived with $\Gamma = [this \mapsto C_r] \cup [x_i^m \mapsto \sigma_i]_{i \in \{1, \dots, ar(m)\}}$, where $M_a(m, z, C_r, \bar{\sigma}) = (\tau, U)$.

Theorem 3 (Soundness). *If an FJEUCS program P is well-typed with respect to algorithmic class table (T_a, F, M_a), then it is well-typed with respect to the corresponding semi-declarative class table (T_a, F, M_s), where*

$$M_s(m, z, C_r) := \{(\bar{\sigma}, \tau, U) \mid (m, z, C_r, \bar{\sigma}) \in dom(M_a), M_a(m, z, C_r, \bar{\sigma}) = (\tau, U)\}.$$

Soundness of algorithmic type system is inherited from the soundness of semi-declarative system. Next, we state the completeness of the algorithmic system with respect to the semi-declarative system

Theorem 4 (Completeness). *Let P be a program and (T_s, F, M_s) a semi-declarative class table. If P is well-typed w.r.t. (T_s, F, M_s) then there is an algorithmic method typing M_a such that the following conditions hold:*

- *P is well-typed w.r.t. (T_s, F, M_a),*
- *"M_a has better types than M_s," that is, for each $(m, z, C_r) \in \mathrm{dom}(M_s)$, each $(\bar{\sigma}, \tau, U) \in M_s(m, z, C_r)$, and each $\bar{\sigma}_a \in atoms(\bar{\sigma})$, there is a $(\tau', U') \in M_a(m, z, C_r, \bar{\sigma}_a)$ such that $(\tau', U') \sqsubseteq (\tau, U)$.*

The desired algorithmic typing M_a is constructed as the least fix-point of the operator that computes the most precise types of method bodies under an assumed method typing. If we had not introduced ψ to resolve the nondeterminism in the rule TD-NEW, we would obtain a typing like $\mathcal{P}(Typ \times Eff)$ rather than $(Typ \times Eff)$ for the algorithmic types, but then it would not be clear how to compare "best" typings by iteration as we do. For one thing, the cardinality of $\mathcal{P}(Typ \times Eff)$ is exponentially larger than that of $(Typ \times Eff)$. More importantly there is no obvious ordering on $\mathcal{P}(Typ \times Eff)$ to represent improvement. It seems that the automatic inference of regions without using contexts is a computationally harder problem with a disjunctive flavor requiring for instance SAT-solving but not doable by plain fix-point iteration.

Type Inference Algorithm. From the algorithmic type system, a type inference algorithm can easily be constructed by reading the rules as a functional program. The long version of the paper presents a more general type inference algorithm that infers an algorithmic class table for a given program P, provided the standard Java types of the program's methods and fields are also given in form of a class table (F_0, M_0). As output it returns an algorithmic class table (T_a, F, M_a) such that P is well-typed with respect to it. Thus the algorithm can be readily used to check whether an expression e follows a guideline.

5   Experimental Evaluation

5.1   Implementation

We have implemented a variant of the type inference algorithm from Sect. 4.4 which applies to actual Java programs rather than FJEUCS.[4] We describe next the main ingredients of the implementation, see the long version for more details. Most importantly, we phrase our analysis as a dataflow problem; it is well-known that type inference can be formulated as a dataflow problem, see e.g. [23]. We thus distinguish between intraprocedural analysis and interprocedural analysis.

Our implementation is built on top of the Soot framework [20,30]. We benefit from Soot in two ways. First, we use it to transform Java code into Jimple code (a model for Java bytecode), which represents the source language of our analysis. Second, we use Soot's generic intraprocedural dataflow analysis (extending the

---

[4] The implementation is available for download from one of the authors' homepage.

ForwardFlowAnalysis class) to implement our intraprocedural analysis. The interprocedural analysis is implemented through a standard fix-point iteration using summary tables. Namely, each iteration starts with a summary table, returns a new table, and the two tables are compared; if there is a difference the old one is replaced with the new one and the next iteration starts with the latter. It is clear that the new table extends the old one at each iteration so that a fix-point is reached and hence the analysis terminates [25].

5.2 Experiments

We tested and evaluated our tool on the Stanford Securibench Micro benchmark.[5] Among the 12 categories of test cases provided by the benchmark, we have analyzed all of them, excluding the one on reflection. Table 1 lists the results obtained. The table also contains a row for the additional examples we considered, which include the ones appearing in the long version of the paper. The 't' and 'w' columns denote respectively the number of tests in the category, and how many of those run as expected. Whenever the result is not as expected, the reason is mentioned in the "comments" column, as follows:

(1) Detection of the problem in the test case requires path-sensitivity, while our analysis is path-insensitive.
(2) Field updates are conservatively treated as weak updates, which sometimes leads to false positives.
(3) We believe this test case was wrongly marked as violating by the benchmark.
(4) We do not yet support two-dimensional arrays and concurrent features.

Each test case is analyzed in at most a few seconds (on a standard desktop computer, with a 2.8 GHz Intel Core i7 CPU), except for one case which required 14 s.

We have also successfully analyzed (in 0.3 s) an application from the Stanford Securibench benchmark,[6] namely blueblog.

Table 1. Results on the SecuriBench Micro benchmark and on additional examples.

Test category	w/t	Comments	Test category	w/t	Comments
Aliasing	5/6	(3)	Inter	14/14	
Arrays	8/10	(4): matrices	Pred	7/9	(1)
Basic	42/42		Sanitizers	6/6	
Collections	14/14		Sessions	3/3	
DataStructures	6/6		StrongUpdates	3/5	(2), (4): synchronize
Factories	3/3		Our examples	24/25	(1)

---

[5] https://suif.stanford.edu/~livshits/work/securibench-micro/.
[6] https://suif.stanford.edu/~livshits/work/securibench/.

6   Related Work

We present a review of recent work in the literature that is relevant to our work. Static analysis has a long history as a research area, which has also been subject to interest from industry. Among many books and surveys available in the literature, we refer to [23] for fundamentals and to [7] for an application-oriented reference. In [7] authors give a detailed explanation of static analysis as part of code review, explain secure programming guidelines and provide exercises with the Fortify code analyzer [3]. Other commercial static analysis tools that help with secure web programming in particular include CheckMarx [1], AppScan [4], and Coverity [2]. These tools check source code against vulnerabilities for various languages including C and Java, and provide compliance with guidelines offered by institutions such as OWASP, MISRA, SANS, and Mitre CWE at different levels. Although this fact is expressed in their data sheets, the question of how the commercial tools formalize the guidelines differs from one tool to another and the common practice in general is to hardwire a given guideline into the tool. One of our partially reached goals is to formalize guidelines so that they are specified separately from the source code of our tool and are open to independent review.

Skalka et al. develop a type and effect inference system to enforce trace-based safety properties for higher-order [28] and object-oriented [26,27] languages. They represent event traces of programs as effects and compute a set of constraints which are later fed into off-the-shelf model-checking tools. Thus combining type inference and model checking, Skalka et al. are able to analyze programs with respect to trace properties, in particular flow-sensitive security properties such as access control and resource usage policies. The difference to our approach is that types do not contain the full information about the possible traces but only a finite abstraction which is just fine enough to decide compliance with a given policy. In this way, one may expect more succinct types, more efficient inference, and better interaction with the user. Another difference is that our approach is entirely based on type systems and abstract interpretation and as such does not rely on external model-checking software. This might make it easier to integrate our approach with certification. One can also argue that our approach is more in line with classical type and effect systems where types do not contain programs either but rather succinct abstractions akin to our effects. Our work performs string analysis by reducing the problem to a type inference analysis, wherein to track strings types are extended with regions.

Closer to the present work is the Java(X) system [10,11]. It uses ML-style type inference based on parametrically polymorphic (refined!) types rather than full polymorphism as we do (polymorphic in the sense that a method type is an arbitrary set of simple, refined types). Also the system does not have region-based tracking of aliasing. On the other hand, Java(X) supports *type state* [12], i.e. the ability of changing the type of an object or a variable through a modifying action. For this to be sound it is clear that the resource in question must be referenced by a unique pointer and a linear typing discipline is used in loc.cit. to ensure this. We think that type state is essentially orthogonal to our approach and could be added if needed. So far, we felt that for the purpose of enforcing guidelines for secure web programming type state is not so relevant.

7 Conclusion

We have developed a type-based analysis to check Java[7] programs against secure programming guidelines. The analysis is sound, albeit incomplete: if the analysis reports "success", then this means the given program follows the guideline, if it reports "failure" the program may or may not follow the guideline.

Our system is based on the region-based type system in [6] and extends it in several directions. First, we enhanced the refined type system in [6] with an effect mechanism to track event traces, following [13]. Second, we parametrized the system over arbitrary guidelines using (a) syntactic monoids to abstract traces and string values, (b) external static methods given by their semantics, and (c) using mockup code to represent library components. Third, we provide a more precise polymorphism for method typings via a precise interprocedural analysis (implemented based on our algorithmic type and effect system) while the system in [6] mainly uses contexts to index refined types and gives only a limited amount of polymorphism requiring user intervention. In [6] contexts provided a novel rigorous type-theoretic foundation for context-sensitive and points-to analyses. We still use contexts to determine regions for newly allocated objects. Fourth, we provide a clear semantic foundation for our analysis and obtain the implementation of type inference in three steps, namely via declarative, semi-declarative, and algorithmic type systems. We establish correctness of our system by proving that each type system is sound with respect to its precursor and that the algorithmic system is also complete w.r.t. the semi-declarative system. Finally, we implemented our system allowing us to analyze actual Java code. We rely on the Soot Framework and analyze on the level of Soot intermediate code (i.e. Jimple) which gives us a variety of language features such as various loop and branching constructs, as well as a limited amount of exception handling for free. While our implementation is for now a prototype, it has allowed us to check a significant part of the SecuriBench Micro benchmark and also a medium-size application.

It is possible to extend our work in several ways. The obvious direction is to formalize more guidelines taken, e.g., from the OWASP or SANS portals to secure web programming. This will further validate our approach to formalization through the described mix of automata, monoids, and modelling of framework code. It will also motivate various extensions to our type-based analysis which we will tackle as needed. We describe here the most important ones.

Reflection. While unconstrained use of reflection would seem to preclude any kind of meaningful static analysis it appears that the use of reflection in actual applications is rather restricted. Being able, for example, to integrate into our analysis

---

[7] As usual, the formal description of our analysis is in terms of an idealized language, FJEUCS. The implementation takes genuine Java programs. However, it does not support certain features such as concurrency and reflection, which we discuss below.

the contents of XML-manifests and similar data which is usually processed via reflection would carry a long way.

Path sensitivity. If needed, a limited amount of path sensitivity can be obtained by introducing a class of booleans with subclasses representing true and false. One could then use refined typings for certain predicates which depending on the *refined* types of their parameters ensure that the result is true or false.

More general automata. Some guidelines may require us to look beyond regular properties. This may require having to use richer specification formalisms, like automata over infinite alphabets [18], to capture authorization per resource rather than per resource kind. Also, we might want to analyze infinitary program properties, e.g. liveness and fairness properties of infinite program traces. To this end it should be possible to replace our finite state machines with Büchi automata, and accordingly, our monoids with so-called ω-semigroups. We have successfully carried out initial investigations along those lines [14,16].

Concurrency and higher-order. Other possibilities for extension are concurrency and higher-order functions, i.e. anonymous methods, inner classes, and similar. We believe that ideas from higher-order model checking in type-theoretic form [19] could be fruitful there and initial investigations have confirmed this.

IFDS. Another interesting extension would be to harness the approach to interprocedural analysis IFDS [24] for our type inference which has been integrated with Soot in the form of the Heros plugin. While this would not extend expressivity or accuracy of our approach the increased efficiency might increase its range. As we see it, the gist of IFDS is on the one hand the restriction of function summaries to atoms using distributivity and on the other a clever management of updates to summaries so that repeated recomputation during fixpoint iteration can be reduced to a minimum. Our approach already incorporates the first aspect because types of callees and method parameters are always atomic. We think that this is the reason why our approach works surprisingly well. Nevertheless, we hope that some more efficiency could be squeezed out of the second ingredient and it would be particularly interesting to use Heros as a kind of solver to which we can offload the computation of the final method table.

Certification. While we have not actually fleshed this out, it is clear that the type-theoretic formulation of our analysis lends itself particularly well to independent certification. Indeed, we could write a type checker (which would involve no fixpoint iteration and similar algorithmic techniques at all) for the declarative system and then have the algorithmic type inference generate a derivation in the former system to be checked. This might be much easier than verifying the implementation of the inference engine. Similarly, our soundness proof can be formalized in a theorem prover and declarative typing derivations can then be used to generate formal proofs of correctness; see e.g. the Mobius project [5].

References

1. Checkmarx. https://www.checkmarx.com
2. Coverity. http://www.coverity.com
3. Fortify. https://software.microfocus.com/en-us/software/sca
4. IBM AppScan. http://www.ibm.com/software/products/en/appscan-source
5. Barthe, G., et al.: MOBIUS: mobility, ubiquity, security. In: Montanari, U., Sannella, D., Bruni, R. (eds.) TGC 2006. LNCS, vol. 4661, pp. 10–29. Springer, Heidelberg (2007). https://doi.org/10.1007/978-3-540-75336-0_2
6. Beringer, L., Grabowski, R., Hofmann, M.: Verifying pointer and string analyses with region type systems. Comput. Lang. Syst. Struct. **39**(2), 49–65 (2013)
7. Chess, B., West, J.: Secure Programming with Static Analysis, 1st edn. Addison-Wesley Professional, Erewhon (2007)
8. Christensen, A.S., Møller, A., Schwartzbach, M.I.: Precise analysis of string expressions. In: Cousot, R. (ed.) SAS 2003. LNCS, vol. 2694, pp. 1–18. Springer, Heidelberg (2003). https://doi.org/10.1007/3-540-44898-5_1
9. Crégut, P., Alvarado, C.: Improving the security of downloadable Java applications with static analysis. ENTCS **141**(1), 129–144 (2005)
10. Degen, M.: JAVA(X) a type-based program analysis framework. Ph.D. thesis, Universität Freiburg, June 2011
11. Degen, M., Thiemann, P., Wehr, S.: Tracking linear and affine resources with JAVA(X). In: Ernst, E. (ed.) ECOOP 2007. LNCS, vol. 4609, pp. 550–574. Springer, Heidelberg (2007). https://doi.org/10.1007/978-3-540-73589-2_26
12. DeLine, R., Fähndrich, M.: Typestates for objects. In: Odersky, M. (ed.) ECOOP 2004. LNCS, vol. 3086, pp. 465–490. Springer, Heidelberg (2004). https://doi.org/10.1007/978-3-540-24851-4_21
13. Grabowski, R., Hofmann, M., Li, K.: Type-based enforcement of secure programming guidelines — code injection prevention at SAP. In: Barthe, G., Datta, A., Etalle, S. (eds.) FAST 2011. LNCS, vol. 7140, pp. 182–197. Springer, Heidelberg (2012). https://doi.org/10.1007/978-3-642-29420-4_12
14. Hofmann, M., Chen, W.: Abstract interpretation from Büchi automata. In: CSL-LICS, pp. 51:1–51:10 (2014)
15. Hofmann, M., Jost, S.: Type-based amortised heap-space analysis. In: Sestoft, P. (ed.) ESOP 2006. LNCS, vol. 3924, pp. 22–37. Springer, Heidelberg (2006). https://doi.org/10.1007/11693024_3
16. Hofmann, M., Ledent, J.: A cartesian-closed category for higher-order model checking. In: LICS, pp. 1–12 (2017)
17. Igarashi, A., Pierce, B.C., Wadler, P.: Featherweight Java: a minimal core calculus for Java and GJ. ACM Trans. Program. Lang. Syst. **23**(3), 396–450 (2001)
18. Kaminski, M., Francez, N.: Finite-memory automata. Theoret. Comput. Sci. **134**(2), 329–363 (1994)
19. Kobayashi, N., Ong, C.L.: A type system equivalent to the modal mu-calculus model checking of higher-order recursion schemes. In: LICS, pp. 179–188. IEEE Computer Society (2009)
20. Lam, P., Bodden, E., Lhoták, O., Hendren, L.: The Soot framework for Java program analysis: a retrospective. In: CETUS (2011)
21. Lenherr, T.: Taxonomy and applications of alias analysis. Master's thesis, ETH Zürich (2008)
22. Lhoták, O.: Program analysis using binary decision diagrams. Ph.D. thesis, McGill University, January 2006

23. Nielson, F., Nielson, H.R., Hankin, C.: Principles of Program Analysis. Springer, Heidelberg (1999)
24. Reps, T.W., Horwitz, S., Sagiv, S.: Precise interprocedural dataflow analysis via graph reachability. In: POPL, pp. 49–61. ACM Press (1995)
25. Sharir, M., Pnueli, A.: Two approaches to interprocedural data flow analysis. In: Muchnick, S.S., Jones, N.D. (eds.) Program Flow Analysis - Theory and Applications, pp. 189–233. Prentice-Hall, Englewood Cliffs (1981)
26. Skalka, C.: Types and trace effects for object orientation. High.-Order Symbolic Comput. **21**(3), 239–282 (2008)
27. Skalka, C., Smith, S.F., Horn, D.V.: A type and effect system for flexible abstract interpretation of Java. ENTCS **131**, 111–124 (2005)
28. Skalka, C., Smith, S.F., Horn, D.V.: Types and trace effects of higher order programs. J. Funct. Program. **18**(2), 179–249 (2008)
29. Smaragdakis, Y., Bravenboer, M., Lhoták, O.: Pick your contexts well: understanding object-sensitivity. In: POPL, pp. 17–30 (2011)
30. Vallée-Rai, R., Co, P., Gagnon, E., Hendren, L.J., Lam, P., Sundaresan, V.: Soot - a Java bytecode optimization framework. In: CASCON, IBM (1999)

Automatically Generating Secure Wrappers for SGX Enclaves from Separation Logic Specifications

Neline van Ginkel[✉], Raoul Strackx[✉], and Frank Piessens[✉]

imec-DistriNet, KU Leuven, Leuven, Belgium
{neline.vanginkel,raoul.strackx,frank.piessens}@cs.kuleuven.be

Abstract. Intel Software Guard Extensions (SGX) is a recent technology from Intel that makes it possible to execute security-critical parts of an application in a so-called SGX enclave, an isolated area of the system that is shielded from all other software (including the OS and/or hypervisor). SGX was designed with the objective of making it relatively straightforward to take a single module of an existing C application, and put that module in an enclave. The SGX SDK includes tooling to semi-automatically generate wrappers for an enclaved C module. The wrapped enclave can then easily be linked to the legacy application that uses the module.

However, when the enclaved module and the surrounding application share a part of the heap and exchange pointers (a very common case in C programs), the generation of these wrappers requires programmer annotations and is error-prone – it is easy to introduce security vulnerabilities or program crashes.

This paper proposes a separation logic based language for specifying the interface of the enclaved C module, and shows how such an interface specification can be used to automatically generate secure wrappers that avoid these vulnerabilities and crashes.

1 Introduction

One of the classic security principles says that the *trusted computing base (TCB)* should be as small as possible, where the TCB is the collection of hardware and software that should remain uncompromised and work reliably for security to be guaranteed.

Intel Software Guard Extensions (Intel SGX) [1,13] is a promising new technology that makes it possible to execute application code in a so-called *enclave*, an isolated area of the execution platform that is shielded from all other software on that platform, including the OS, hypervisor or other system software. Hence, Intel SGX makes it possible to significantly reduce the TCB of software applications by running security-critical parts of these applications in enclaves.

SGX was designed with the objective of making it easy to convert existing applications to SGX. An enclave is conceptually similar to a dynamically loaded library: it runs in user mode – not kernel mode – and shares its virtual memory

© Springer International Publishing AG 2017
B.-Y.E. Chang (Ed.): APLAS 2017, LNCS 10695, pp. 105–123, 2017.
https://doi.org/10.1007/978-3-319-71237-6_6

address space with the application that uses the enclave. The main difference is that some security restrictions apply: the processor hardware enforces memory access control and restricts how an application can enter the enclave.

The SGX Software Development Kit (SGX SDK) [7] provides tool support to create enclaves. To support the objective of making it easy to convert existing applications, the SDK includes tools to semi-automatically convert legacy C modules to enclaves. The underlying idea is the following: to port an existing application to SGX, the developer identifies and separates the most security-critical module(s), for instance the authentication module of a web server. That module is then processed by the SDK tools to generate an enclave that offers the same API to the remainder of the application as the original module. The legacy web server can now link to the enclaved authentication module and get the additional benefit that authentication code and data is much better protected. SGX also supports remote provisioning of enclaves, in order to prevent the application from reading secrets at load-time.

Unfortunately, the tooling provided by the SGX SDK is quite ad-hoc and limited. When the enclaved module and the surrounding application share a part of the heap and exchange pointers (a very common case in C programs), the tools require ad-hoc programmer annotations that are error-prone. This makes it easy to introduce security vulnerabilities or unexpected program crashes.

The main contribution of this paper is that it proposes a principled approach to semi-automatically convert C modules to enclaves. The key observation underlying our approach is that a separation logic interface specification of the enclaved module contains exactly the information needed to generate appropriate wrapper code. More specifically, our contributions are:

- We propose an approach to generate wrapper code for an enclaved module from a separation logic specification of that module.
- We implement this approach for a significant subset of the logic supported by the VeriFast C program verification tool [8].
- We evaluate performance, security and precision of the approach, both by performing micro-benchmarks, and by a macro-benchmark in which we apply our approach to enclave an authentication module of the Apache web server.

2 Background

2.1 Intel Software Guard Extensions

Basic operation. We explain Intel SGX by discussing a use case that is relevant for this paper. Consider a large application (like a web browser or web server) that contains a security-critical module that manages security sensitive data (like a password manager for the browser, or an authentication module for the web server). If the large application, or the underlying OS, has a security vulnerability (e.g. a memory safety vulnerability), an attacker can compromise the application and steal the sensitive data: a modern OS protects data only at the granularity of

```
// enclave1.c -- enclave code        // enclave1.edl -- enclave definition
static int pin;                       enclave {
static int secret;                      trusted {
                                          public int get_secret();
int get_secret() {                      }
  int nb = read_pin();                  untrusted {
  if (nb == pin) return secret;           int read_pin();
  else return 0;                        }
}                                     }
```

Fig. 1. Pin module in SGX

a process, and processes are not protected from the OS. This is a serious concern, as evidenced by the recent wave of memory scanning malware attacks [6].

Intel SGX is designed to help mitigate this concern. Consider a very simplified example of a password manager module in the left side of Fig. 1.

This module manages one secret integer that can only be retrieved when the correct PIN is provided by the user, but as discussed above a buggy or malicious context (rest of the application or OS) can easily read or modify the secret. Recall that the `static` keyword in this C program means that the variable is a global variable only visible in its containing compilation unit (file). We use such `static` modifiers throughout this paper to indicate module state that remains confidential and protected from tampering.

Intel SGX [1,13] introduces the notion of an *enclave*, essentially an access-controlled segment of a virtual memory address space that can contain both code and data. In addition, an enclave has one or more *entry points*, addresses pointing into the code part of the enclave. In Intel SGX the following memory access control model is enforced *in hardware* by the processor:

- When the Instruction Pointer (IP) points outside of the enclave, access to memory in the enclave is prohibited.
- When the IP points inside the enclave, data memory of that specific enclave can be read and written, and code memory can be executed. Data memory of the untrusted context also remains accessible.
- One way for the IP to enter an enclave is by performing an *ecall* (enclave call) to call one of the designated entry points. The IP leaves the enclave again on return from the ecall, or when the code in the enclave performs an *ocall*, i.e. calls a function in the context. Returning from an ocall is another way to reenter the enclave. The call to `read_pin()` in Fig. 1 is an example of such an ocall. Jumping directly into the enclave is prevented.

This access control model makes it possible for modules to guard access to their private state. We can load our example module in an enclave and make sure all its state (in this case its call-stack, and the `pin` and `secret` variables) is also in the enclave. If we give the enclave a single entry point to call the `get_secret()` function, then the variables `pin`, and `secret` can only be accessed by the `get_secret()` function. Because of the memory access control, they can no longer be "scraped" from memory by malicious code in one of the other modules, or by malware in the kernel.

Initializing enclaves. An interesting question is how enclaves can be initialized with secret data under an attacker model where OS and surrounding application are untrusted. Such initialization can be done with the help of a trusted server from which the enclave can retrieve a previously saved state. Such a server should use the attestation and cryptographic features of SGX to ensure secure saving and restoring of state. Alternatively, state can be saved and restored locally, but in this case it is tricky to ensure security against replay of older saved states, a problem known as *state continuity*. Several proposals on how to handle this problem have appeared in the literature [17,21,22]. For lack of space, we do not describe the initialization of enclaves (and the saving/restoring of state) here. The enclave examples we use in the paper have their initial secret data as `static` module global variables (as in the `pin` and `secret` variables in our earlier example). The specificities of initialization, and how to save/restore secret data are orthogonal to the results in this paper.

Intel SGX SDK. The Intel SGX Software Development Kit (SGX SDK) [7] provides tool support for this use case of enclaves. It offers tools and libraries to create enclaves. For our purpose, it suffices to discuss the `sgx_edger8r` tool.

The `sgx_edger8r` tool requires the developer to provide an interface description of the module that needs to be enclaved in the form of an Enclave Description Language (EDL) file. The interface description is divided in two parts: a list of trusted functions inside the enclave, that can be called from the untrusted context, and a list of functions that reside in the untrusted context, but can be called by functions in the enclave. The right side of Fig. 1 shows the EDL file for our example module. Using this EDL file the `sgx_edger8r` tool automatically generates two types of glue code: a *trusted wrapper* that wraps the original module and executes inside the enclave, and an *untrusted wrapper* that wraps the enclave and runs as part of the context. For the simple example module, the wrappers serve no security purpose, but just handle the mechanics of entering and exiting the enclave.

But now consider the example in Fig. 2, where the function `get_secret()` uses an output parameter. If the PIN is correct, the secret is written to the memory pointed to by `s_out`, otherwise 0 is written. If the context is buggy or malicious, it might pass in an invalid pointer, or a pointer pointing into enclave memory. If the module does not check the pointer before using it, the program might crash, or overwrite data in the enclave itself, such as the pin.

For instance, if the attacker passes a pointer to `pin` as parameter, and then enters an invalid PIN, the variable `pin` will be changed to 0. On the next invocation of `get_secret` the attacker provides a pointer to context memory and will get the secret by entering the PIN 0. In a larger example the attacker would be able to overwrite other security-critical data. Checking context-provided pointers is thus of vital importance for ensuring the security of an enclave.

```
// enclave2.c                    // enclave2.edl
static int pin;                  enclave {
static int secret;                 trusted {
int get_secret(int *s_out) {         public int get_secret([out] int *s_out);
  int nb = read_pin();             }
  if (nb == pin) {                 untrusted {
    *s_out = secret;                 int read_pin();
    return 1;                      }
  } else {                       }
    *s_out = 0;                  // simplified wrapper code for get_secret
    return 0;                    int sgx_get_secret(int *s_out) {
  }                                CHECK_POINTER(s_out, sizeof(*s_out));
}                                  int *local_s_out = malloc(sizeof(*s_out));
                                   int ret = get_secret(local_s_out);
// untrusted.c                    memcpy(s_out, local_s_out, sizeof(*s_out));
// -- untrusted context           return ret;
int read_pin();                  }
```

Fig. 2. Pin module in SGX, with output parameter.

The trusted wrapper that sgx_edger8r generates includes defensive checks to avoid these attacks against the enclave, but this requires additional annotations in the EDL file. We discuss the annotations for the trusted functions; similar annotations exist for the untrusted functions. For each parameter with a non-basic type, such as pointers and arrays, an additional annotation describes how the parameter needs to be handled: the specification [in] means the memory pointed to needs to be copied into the enclave before execution, the specification [out] means the parameter is an out-parameter and memory pointed to needs to be copied to the untrusted context after the function has executed. The annotation [user_check] means that the memory pointed to does not need to be copied in or out by the generated wrapper, but will be handled manually by the developer instead. The sgx_edger8r tool will also enforce that each annotated pointer points to memory outside the enclave. The size or count annotation defines the amount of memory that will be copied, starting from the pointer provided. Alternatively, the size_func annotation allows the user to calculate a custom size. Finally, the string annotation describes a C-string where the size is determined through the built-in strlen function.

The right side of Fig. 2 shows the EDL file for our second example, with an [out] annotation on the parameter of get_secret(). It also shows (a simplified version of) the trusted wrapper code generated by sgx_edger8r.

In Fig. 3, the function get_secret() has a character array as input. The developer needs to annotate this parameter as [string, in], a string that is given as input. In this case sgx_edger8r generates a wrapper function that checks the pointer, determines the length of the string, copies the string to freshly allocated memory within the enclave, adds a null byte at the end of the string, and provides the wrapped function with a pointer to this copy.

```
// enclave3.c                    // enclave3.edl
static char *pass;               enclave {
static int secret;                 trusted {
                                     public int get_secret([string,in] char *p);
int get_secret(char *p) {          }
  if (!strcmp(pass, p)) {        }
    return secret;               // simplified wrapper code for get_secret
  } else {                       int sgx_get_secret(char *p) {
    return 0;                      int len = strlen(p);
  }                                CHECK_POINTER(p, len);
}                                  char *local_p = malloc(len + 1);
                                   memcpy(local_p, p, len);
                                   local_pass[len] = '\0';
                                   int ret = get_secret(local_p);
                                   return ret;
                                 }
```

Fig. 3. Password module in SGX, with a string as input.

```
// enclave4.c                    // enclave4.edl
struct cred {                    enclave {
  char *user;                      trusted {
  char *pass;                        public int get_secret([in] struct cred *c);
};                                 }
                                 }
static char *pass;               // simplified wrapper code for get_secret
static int secret;               int sgx_get_secret(struct cred *c) {
                                   CHECK_POINTER(c, sizeof(*c));
int get_secret(struct cred *c) {   struc cred *local_c = malloc(sizeof(*c));
  if (!strcmp(c->pass, pass))      memcpy(local_c, c, sizeof(*c));
    return secret;                 int ret = get_secret(local_c);
  else return 0;                   return ret;
}                                }
```

Fig. 4. Password module in SGX, with a structure as input.

In the previous examples, sgx_edger8r is able to generate correct wrappers, as long as the developer provides the correct annotations. But other more complex cases can not be handled by the tool. In Fig. 4 we see another version of the password module, this time with a structure as input. Since the software module requires access to the struct, we annotate it with [in], but the resulting wrapper code is not sufficient. The wrapper code copies in the struct itself, but not the strings pointed to by the fields in the struct. If the developer does not take care of these issues manually, this can cause the program to misbehave. First, if the module returns a struct with one or more pointers, a pointer might accidentally be pointing into enclave memory, and the context would not be allowed to access this data and hence could crash. This is an example of a case where a good program that was working well before enclaving the module now fails with a crash. Second, if the module has a struct as parameter (as is the case for this example module) the context would be able to pass unchecked pointers into the enclave, for example a pointer to the password stored in the enclave, thus making it possible for the context to tamper with enclave data or to leak it. This is an example of a security vulnerability: a compromised or malicious context can circumvent the access control offered by SGX.

In summary, the existing tools in the SGX SDK can automatically generate secure wrappers for simple cases, but require the developer to manually handle more complex cases.

2.2 Separation Logic

Separation logic [16,19] is an extension of Hoare logic that supports specifying and verifying imperative programs that dynamically allocate memory and pass pointers to that memory around. Let us consider a simple imperative programming language that has integer values and pointers, where for simplicity we assume that pointers are themselves positive integers (addresses). For such programs, the program state (s, h) at a given point of execution consists of a *store* s (a finite partial function from variables to integers) and a *heap* h (a finite partial mapping from addresses to integers).

The syntax of our variant of separation logic is:

$$e ::= n \mid x \mid e + e \mid e - e$$
$$b ::= \texttt{true} \mid \texttt{false} \mid e == e \mid e < e \mid !b$$
$$a ::= b \mid b ? a : a \mid e \texttt{ |-> } e \mid a * a \mid \exists x.a$$

The semantics of integer expressions e and boolean expressions b given a store s providing values for the variables x occurring in these expressions is completely standard and obvious. Let us write $[e]_s$ (or $[b]_s$) for the evaluation of e (or b) under a store s.

Separation logic assertions a specify program states. The semantics of assertions defines what program states (s, h) satisfy an assertion.

A program state (s, h) satisfies b if b evaluates to true in the store s. The assertion $b ? a_1 : a_2$ is an if-then-else expression, i.e. a program state (s, h) satisfies it if $[b]_s$ is true and (s, h) satisfies a_1, or $[b]_s$ is false and (s, h) satisfies a_2.

The more interesting assertions are the *spatial* assertions: (s, h) satisfies e_1 |-> e_2 (read as: e_1 points to e_2) if $[e_1]_s$ is a positive integer, and the heap h is the one-element heap that maps address $[e_1]_s$ on $[e_2]_s$, i.e. it is a finite partial function that is only defined on $[e_1]_s$.

The state (s, h) satisfies $a_1 * a_2$ if the heap h can be partitioned in two disjoint subheaps h_1 and h_2 such that (s, h_1) satisfies a_1 and (s, h_2) satisfies a_2. The operator $*$ is called the *separating conjunction*.

Finally, existential quantification can introduce new *logical variables*, in addition to program variables, just like in standard Hoare logic. A state (s, h) satisfies $\exists x.a$ if there exists an integer v, such that (s', h) satisfies a, where s' is the store s extended with a mapping of x on v.

We will make use of standard *predicate definitions* to define more complex assertions, and we will freely use standard data types like lists to inductively define predicates. For instance, if we write [] for the empty list, and $h : t$ for construction of a list with head h and tail t, then:

$$string(s, []) = \quad s \ |\text{->} \ 0$$
$$string(s, c : tl) = \quad s \ |\text{->} \ c \quad * \quad string(s + 1, tl)$$

inductively defines an indexed family of predicates $string(s, l)$ (indexed by the list l) that say that program variable s points to a null-terminated string specified by l as the list of ASCII values of its characters.

Like Hoare logic, separation logic can be used as a program logic to specify the behavior of programs using Hoare triples $\{P\}c\{Q\}$. Such a triple states that if one starts program c in a program state that satisfies assertion P (the pre-condition), then c will not fault, and if it terminates it will terminate in a program state that satisfies the assertion Q (the post-condition). Separation logic verifiers like the VeriFast tool [8] can verify the validity of such triples.

The hallmark of separation logic is its support for *local reasoning*: the specification of a piece of code also defines what parts of the heap the code could access (the so-called *footprint* of the code). The points-to assertions that are part of the pre-condition explicitly say what addresses in the heap the code could potentially access. It is exactly this property of separation logic that makes the logic so useful for the problem we consider in this paper.

This brief summary should suffice to understand our use of separation logic in this paper, but the reader is encouraged to look at other papers [9,16,19,23] for a more extensive and rigorous description of separation logic and for examples.

Since our implementation uses the variant of separation logic implemented by the VeriFast tool [8], we make use of two kinds of syntactic sugar supported by VeriFast: First, we use the notation $?x$ for introducing an existentially quantified logical variable. So $s \ |\text{->} \ ?x$ is syntactic sugar for $\exists x.s \ |\text{->} \ x$. Second, we use VeriFast's notation $e\text{->}\texttt{field}$ for indexing into a struct pointed to by e. This can be seen as syntactic sugar for $e + o$ where o is the (statically determined) offset of the field in memory.

3   Problem Statement

When a C module has an interface that accepts and returns pointers (possibly as part of an array or struct), enclaving that module is non-trivial. Code within the enclave should not naively dereference pointers it received from the context (as this is a potential security vulnerability) and it should not return pointers to memory within the enclave to the context (as this leads to a program crash on dereferencing the pointer because of memory access control).

To avoid such issues, trusted wrapper code can use a combination of defensive checks, in-copying and out-copying such that (1) the program keeps working as it did before enclaving the module (a property we call *precision*) and (2) a malicious context can not tamper with or steal sensitive data stored within the enclave (a property we call *security*). We have seen that the sgx_edger8r tool offers limited and ad-hoc support for automating the generation of such trusted wrappers based on a very basic specification of the enclaved module.

The objective of this paper is to come up with a more principled and general approach to generate trusted wrappers that are precise, secure and efficient. We propose the Enhanced Enclave Description Language (EEDL), an alternative to Intel's EDL, based on a variant of separation logic. Our module specification language specifies what parts of the heap the module considers to be private to (i.e., owned by) the module, and it specifies for each ecall and ocall how ownership of parts of the heap is transferred between context and module. From such a specification, we automatically generate trusted wrappers that:

- on entry to the enclave (on an ecall or return from an ocall) copy in all heap memory that the enclave might need to access – and at the same time check conditions specified in the interface on that in-copied data
- on exit of the enclave (on an ocall or return from an ecall) copy out all heap memory currently inside the enclave that might need to be accessed by the context

4   Proposed Approach

Figure 5 gives a high-level overview of our approach. The enclave is the segment of process memory in the blue box. We reserve virtual address space for a *shadow heap* inside the enclave, and define a bijective pointer translation between context heap and shadow heap. We choose to simply translate pointer p on the context heap to $p + \Delta$ on the shadow heap.

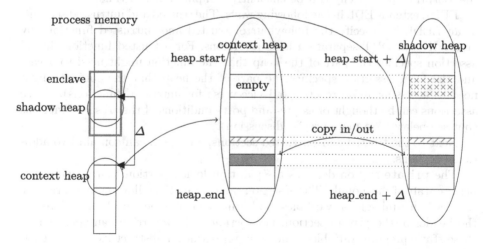

Fig. 5. Overview of our approach.

The wrapped code within the enclave always operates on the shadow heap using translated pointers and never reads/writes the context heap. The trusted wrappers we generate take care of copying data between the two heaps and translating pointers as required.

Besides shared data, we also consider heap-allocated data that is private to the enclave. Data objects that are "captured" by the enclave (made part of the enclave's private state) are not copied out again. Such objects are marked as allocated on both heaps, but the context heap will not contain the actual data (marked as *empty* on Fig. 5).

At first sight, having two heaps seems expensive in terms of memory use, but as memory pages that remain empty in the context or shadow heap do not have to be backed by physical memory, memory consumption of this approach remains limited.

The trusted wrappers we generate will ensure that (1) heap objects will be copied between the two heaps when required by the enclave's interface specification, (2) pointers are translated on copying between the heaps, and (3) all data passed into the enclave complies with the specification of the enclave interface.

4.1   The Enhanced Enclave Description Language (EEDL)

To realize this approach, we need an enclave interface specification that specifies the initial private state of the module, as well as what needs to be copied in/out on module entry/exit. Our EEDL is based on separation logic as reviewed in Sect. 2.2. Separation logic's ability to specify the *footprint* of code, i.e. the parts of the heap that will be accessed by that code is exactly what we need in our setting. We restrict assertions in EEDL to the *precise* assertions of VeriFast's program logic [2]. Precise assertions have the property that their validity and the footprint they specify can be efficiently computed at run time.

EEDL extends EDL in the following ways. The trusted and untrusted sections in an EEDL file specify the behaviour of trusted and untrusted functions by giving IN and OUT separation logic assertions. For a trusted function the IN assertion specifies the part of the heap that the function might need to access and the OUT assertion specifies the part of the heap that the context might need to access again on return (and vice-versa for untrusted functions). These assertions can be thought of as pre- and post-conditions of the trusted functions (but see below for a more precise discussion).

Next to the trusted and untrusted sections, an EEDL can contain two additional sections.

The **private** section declares a separation logic assertion that specifies the private state of the module. The assertion can contain the following free variables: the static module global variables, and a number of logic variables declared in the header of the private section. For instance, the assertion can specify how these static program variables concretely represent an abstract list l (where l is a logic variable).

Finally, the **predicates** section inductively defines zero or more separation logic predicates that can be used further in the EEDL file.

Figure 6 shows the EEDL specifications for the examples in Figs. 2 and 3. It includes the (very simple) specification of the private state of these examples.

```
// enclave2.eedl                  // enclave3.eedl
enclave {                         enclave {
  private (p,s) {                   predicates {
    pin == p * secret == s            string(sp,[]) = sp |-> 0
  }                                   string(sp,c:tl) = sp |-> c * string(sp+1,tl)
  trusted {                         }
    int get_secret( int *out );     private (p,s) {
      IN: out |-> _                   string(pass, p) * secret == s;
      OUT: out |-> _                }
  }                                 trusted {
  untrusted {                         int get_secret( char *pass );
    int read_pin();                     IN: string(pass,_)
  }                                     OUT: string(pass,_)
}                                   }
                                    untrusted {
                                      int read_pin();
                                    }
                                  }
```

Fig. 6. The EEDL-specification for Figs. 2 and 3

It also shows the definition of a simple `string(sp,s)` predicate that says that the program variable `sp` (of type `char *`) points to a null-terminated sequence of bytes that represent the (abstract) string s. This predicate is used in the specification of `get_secret()` of Example 3.

Formally, the EEDL file specifies the behaviour of the trusted functions in the module in the following way. Let us assume for simplicity that the private section declares one logic variable m, and that the module has one static variable s. We define the predicate $P(s, m) = a$ where a is the assertion declared in the private section. Then a trusted function has to satisfy the separation logic contract with pre-condition $P(s, ?m) * IN$ and post-condition $P(s, ?m') * OUT$, i.e. it can expect to have access to some well-formed module private state and whatever is specified in its IN assertion, and it should ensure as postcondition a well-formed private state and its OUT assertion.

Dually, the untrusted section specifies the contracts that the module expects to hold of the untrusted functions, where for these untrusted functions the P predicate should be considered abstract [16], i.e. the untrusted functions do not know the predicate definition, and hence all they can do is use that assertion to call one of the trusted functions.

4.2   Extended Example

We use the example in Fig. 7 to demonstrate our approach. The enclave maintains a linked list of credentials and the program context registers one additional pair of credentials. The EEDL specification is shown in Fig. 8.

As discussed before, we do not describe initialization of the enclave. Initialization should make sure that the enclave private state satisfies the private assertion of the EEDL specification, in this case that `creds` points to a (potentially empty) linked list of credentials.

```
1   // main.c
2   struct cred_t {
3     char *user, *pass;
4     };
5   int main() {
6     // sgx enclave initialisation
7
8     char *username = malloc(101);
9     scanf("%100s", username);
10    char *password = malloc(101);
11    scanf("%100s", password);
12    struct cred_t *c = malloc(sizeof(*c));
13    c->user = username;
14    c->pass = password;
15
16    reg_user(c);
17    free(c);
18  }


20  //enclave.h
21  struct cred {
22    char *user, *pass;
23    struct cred *next;
24  };
25
26  static struct cred *creds;
27
28  void reg_user(struct cred_t *cred);
```

```
30  // enclave.c
31  struct cred *create(char *u, char *p) {
32    struct cred *new =
33      malloc(sizeof(struct cred));
34    if (new == 0) abort();
35    new->user = u;
36    new->pass = p;
37    new->next = 0;
38    return new;
39  }
40
41  void reg_user(struct cred_t *cred) {
42    struct cred *old = creds;
43    struct cred *new =
44      create(cred->user, cred->pass);
45    if (old == 0) {
46      creds = new;
47    } else {
48      while (old->next != 0)
49        old = old->next;
50      old->next = new;
51    }
52  }
```

Fig. 7. The extended example: an unverified context interacting with a trusted password database enclave

```
// extended-example.eedl
enclave {
  predicates {
    credslist(lp,[]) = lp == 0
    credslist(lp,(u,p):tl) = string(lp->user ,u) * string(lp->pass,p) *
        credslist(lp->next,tl)
  }
  private (l) {
    credslist(creds, l)
  }
  trusted {
    void reg_user(struct cred_t *c);
    IN: c!=0 * c->user |-> ?u * c->pass |-> ?p * string(u, _) * string(p, _)
    OUT: c->user |-> _ * c->pass |-> _
  }
}
```

Fig. 8. EEDL for the extended example

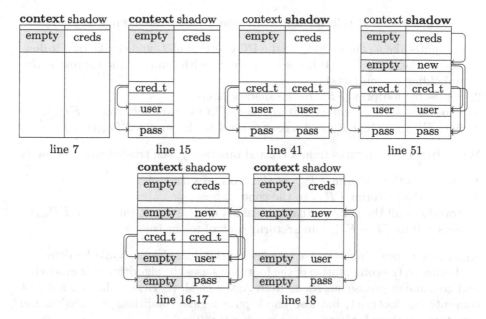

Fig. 9. Context and shadow heaps during execution. the **active** heap is shown in bold

Before discussing how to generate the wrapper functions, we first show their intended behaviour graphically.

In Fig. 9 we see how context and shadow heap evolve as execution progresses. After initialization (line 7 in `main()`), the initial private state is loaded in the shadow heap and the corresponding segment of the context heap is allocated but contains dummy data (marked *empty* in Fig. 9). Then, `main()` performs three allocations on the context heap (line 15). On entering the enclave with the `reg_user()` call, the wrappers check that the c parameter is not null and copy in the struct as well as the two strings it points to (as specified in the IN assertion). Note that all pointers are translated to point into the shadow heap (line 41). Then enclave code runs and extends the credential list, thus capturing the **user** and **pass** strings in the private state (line 51). Hence, on leaving the enclave, the wrappers only copy out the struct (line 16–17). Finally main deallocates the struct (line 18). If `main()` terminates, the enclave should persist its private state such that it can be initialized again correctly in the next run, but as mentioned before we do not discuss the details of initialization/persistence.

4.3   Generating Trusted Wrappers

Generalizing from the example, we see that the functionality of the trusted wrappers is as follows. The wrapper maintains as state the current footprint FP of the module (as a set of addresses). After initialization, FP contains a footprint corresponding to the private assertion.

When the context calls a trusted function f, the trusted wrapper for f:

1. computes the footprint FP_{in} of the IN assertion of f, and checks that it does not overlap with FP. (If it does, terminate with error, as the context is not upholding its contracts)
2. copies the footprint FP_{in} to the shadow heap.
3. translates all the pointers that are passed in (as parameters or in FP_{in}).
4. Sets FP to $FP \cup FP_{in}$ and passes control to the wrapped function f.

When the enclave returns from a trusted function f, the trusted wrapper for f:

1. computes the footprint FP_{out} of the OUT assertion of f.
2. copies the footprint FP_{out} to the context heap.
3. translates all the pointers that are passed out (as result value or in FP_{out}).
4. Sets FP to $FP - FP_{out}$ and returns control to the context.

Again, on an ocall from enclave to context, the dual checks should be done.

Formally, the computation of the footprints uses the algorithms for producing and consuming precise assertions from Agten et al. [2] Hence, they do not just compute the footprint, but also check pure logical conditions specified in the assertions, such as for instance the check `c != 0` in Fig. 8.

5   Implementation and Evaluation

We implemented a prototype of our approach as a source-to-source compiler written in OCaml, using VeriFast syntax [8] for specifying enclave interfaces directly inside the C files (no separate EEDL file). In this Section, we evaluate performance, and we discuss the implications of the tool on the security and precision of enclaved C modules.

Prototype limitations. In the current prototype, the shadow stack and heap are not dynamically allocated, but are statically allocated variables of a predefined size in the data section of the enclave. In order to support dynamic allocation, enclaves should be dynamically resizable, a feature that will only appear in Intel SGX 2. [1] When this feature arrives, the stack and heap can be located at the beginning respectively the end of an enclave's virtual address space, and be expanded whenever memory outside the currently allocated area is encountered.

5.1   Micro Benchmarks

We used the prototype to compare our approach with the wrappers generated by `sgx_edger8r`. The benchmarks were executed on a Dell laptop with an Intel Core i5-7200U with Linux kernel 4.10.5. Each benchmark executed 100 times and we report the median timings after removing outliers. Table 1 shows the results of our benchmarks.

Table 1. Micro benchmarks of our approach.

operation	time(ms) sgx_edger8r	time(ms) our prototype
dummy call	0.003	0.003
get_secret(int *) (Fig. 2)	0.006	0.008
get_secret(char *) (Fig. 3, len(pass)=10)	0.004	0.009
get_secret(char *) (Fig. 3, len(pass)=100)	0.004	0.027
get_secret(char *) (Fig. 3, len(pass)=1,000)	0.005	0.198

When a dummy function without arguments or return value is called, neither tool adds security checks and both complete the enclave call in 0.003 ms. Checking a pin code read from an ocall (see Fig. 2) doubles the number of enclave boundary crosses. In that example sgx_edger8r only temporarily allocates a memory region within the enclave and copies the secret out after the final call. In our approach we have an additional set-up cost for bookkeeping currently owned memory, making our approach slightly more expensive.

Finally we measured the impact of the size of the provided password on example 3 (see Fig. 3). In the sgx_edger8r tool this takes 0.004 to 0.005 ms for passwords ranging from 10 to 1,000 characters. In our approach overhead increases linearly with the password size up to 0.198 ms for a 1,000 character password. This is due to the way we generate the copying code: we perform one function call per character that is copied in. Obviously significant optimizations are possible there.

5.2   Macro Benchmarks

We performed a macro benchmark to provide evidence that even the straightforward and expensive implementation in our prototype has negligible overhead in larger applications. We added an authentication module to an Apache 2.4.25 server running Wordpress 4.7.3. We sent 1024 requests with a maximum concurrency of 4 requests. The sgx_edger8r had a throughput of 26.81 requests/sec, while our implementation had a throughput of 26.87 request/sec, which is equal within the margin of error, making both implementations comparable in performance.

5.3   Security and Precision

Security. Our approach provides strong assurance for interesting security properties. First, it protects the integrity of the state of the enclaved module in the following sense: if the module is verified to satisfy its EEDL contract, then any assertion about the module state that can be verified in separation logic is guaranteed to hold at runtime. This property follows from Agten et al.'s theorem [2] about the algorithms for computing the footprint and checking separation logic assertions. While Agten et al. use a different mechanism for footprint integrity protection, their proof does not depend on the specifics of that mechanism – it just assumes a mechanism to "snapshot" the footprint and ensure that at a later time the footprint is still equal to the snapshot. In our approach, this is achieved by means of the in/out copying of the footprint.

Second, and in contrast to Agten et al.'s work, our approach also provides substantial confidentiality protection. By keeping module private state only in the shadow heap, Intel SGX provides strong hardware-enforced access control to that state. Formalizing the exact confidentiality guarantees is future work, but we hope to be able to show that a malicious context can not observe more of the module's state than a verified C context. In other words, the module leaks no more information than what it leaks to specification-compliant clients.

Precision. An important advantage of our approach over sgx_edger8r is that we guarantee the property that for a well-behaved context our wrappers do not impact the execution of the program (beyond an increase in execution time and memory use). More formally: Let P be a program, and let M be a module of P. If M can be verified to satisfy the trusted function specifications, and if the untrusted functions implemented in P satisfy the untrusted function specifications, then P has the same executions whether it is executed with M enclaved and wrapped or not.

The informal argument for precision is that the enclaved M executes exactly the same code as M but on a "shifted" heap. If untrusted functions satisfy their contracts, they never read or write M's footprint and hence can not observe this shifting. The in/out copying by the trusted wrappers ensures that content of all heap addresses in the footprint is the same in the shifted heap. Since a verified M can not observe absolute pointer values, and only accesses memory within its footprint, it operates exactly the same on the shifted heap.

6   Related Work

While our implementation targets Intel SGX, there is a whole line of related research that proposes similar protection mechanisms, collectively known as *protected module architectures*. Early designs such as Flicker [12] and TrustVisor [11] required in- and output arguments to be marshalled explicitly by the developer. Modules were not able to directly access the untrusted context. More recent architectures [4,14,15] are more closely related to SGX and require strong input checking. Our approach can be ported to these architectures with minimal effort.

Writing defensive interfaces is known to be a hard problem. The same security vulnerabilities that may arise when SGX enclave writers do not insert proper input checks exist in other scenarios as well. For instance, Kermerlis et al. [10] showed that a kernel that fails to properly filter pointers to user space, may be tricked to jump to shellcode in user space. To avoid such exploits both x86 and ARM added hardware modifications to avoid that user space code can be directly accessed (smap) or executed (smap, PXN) from kernel mode. Our approach could avoid the same vulnerabilities on platforms without explicit hardware support.

Generating defensive checks from interface specifications is closely related to contract checking as studied extensively in higher-order languages. A recent account is given by Dimoulas et al. [5], but this line of work focuses on checking contracts on the boundaries between components in a safe language.

Most closely related to our work, Agten et al. [2] show how runtime checks can guarantee integrity checks on enclaved execution on the Sancus [14] platform. Our approach is based on their algorithm for checking separation logic assertions and computing their footprint, but in contrast to their work, we use a shadow heap which enables us to also provide confidentiality guarantees. Our use of a shadow heap is also secure in the presence of a multi-threaded context, whereas Agten et al.'s heap integrity checks are not.

Defensive checks at the boundaries of protected modules have also been used in the context of compiling Java-like languages to protected module architectures [3,18].

Finally, Sinha et al. [20] propose a complementary approach to verify that compiled enclaves keep specific data confidential. In contrast, we propose a way to automatically generate C code to help developers keep data confidential.

7   Conclusion and Future Work

In this paper we discussed how the Intel SGX sgx_edger8r tool can be used to generate wrappers for enclave boundary functions. These wrappers copy data according to the annotations described in an EDL file. We have shown the limitations of the annotations supported by sgx_edger8r. These limitations imply that complex data types, such as structs with pointers, need additional care, to ensure secure enclaves.

We have shown that separation logic specifications can be used to accurately describe such data types. Moreover, these specifications can not only describe the parameters of SGX enclave functions accurate enough to copy the data needed by the enclave, but can also describe as much additional constraints as the developer requires.

We have shown how separation logic specifications can automatically be translated to secure wrappers. We also evaluated performance and have shown that in larger applications, the performance of the generated wrappers is comparable to those generated by sgx_edger8r.

In future work, we plan to investigate special cases of our approach that can be implemented even more efficiently, such as the case where the private state maintained by the enclave never captures or releases memory on the context heap. For that case, enclave state can be on a separate private heap, and there is no longer a need for a shadow heap, or the bookkeeping related to the enclave footprint. Another special case to investigate is the case where the contents of memory do not need to be copied in or out, since the content is never used.

Acknowledgments. Raoul Strackx holds a Postdoctoral mandate from the Research Foundation - Flanders (FWO). This research is partially funded by project grants from the Research Fund KU Leuven, and from the Research Foundation - Flanders (FWO).

References

1. Intel© software guard extensions programming reference. https://software.intel. com/sites/default/files/managed/48/88/329298-002.pdf. Accessed 31 May 2016
2. Agten, P., Jacobs, B., Piessens, F.: Sound modular verification of C code executing in an unverified context. In: POPL 2015 (2015)
3. Agten, P., Strackx, R., Jacobs, B., Piessens, F.: Secure compilation to modern processors. In: CSF 2012 (2012)
4. Brasser, F., El Mahjoub, B., Sadeghi, A.R., Wachsmann, C., Koeberl, P.: Tytan: Tiny trust anchor for tiny devices. In: DAC 2015 (2015)
5. Dimoulas, C., New, M.S., Findler, R.B., Felleisen, M.: Oh lord, please don't let contracts be misunderstood (functional pearl). In: ICFP 2016 (2016)
6. Huq, N.: PoS RAM scraper malware: Past, present, and future. Technical report, Trend Micro (2015)
7. Intel: Intel Software Guard Extensions Developer Guide (2017). https://software. intel.com/en-us/node/703016
8. Jacobs, B., Smans, J., Philippaerts, P., Vogels, F., Penninckx, W., Piessens, F.: Verifast: A powerful, sound, predictable, fast verifier for C and Java. In: Bobaru, M., Havelund, K., Holzmann, G.J., Joshi, R. (eds.) NFM 2011. LNCS, vol. 6617, pp. 41–55. Springer, Heidelberg (2011). https://doi.org/10.1007/978-3-642-20398-5_4
9. Jacobs, B., Smans, J., Piessens, F.: A quick tour of the verifast program verifier. In: Ueda, K. (ed.) APLAS 2010. LNCS, vol. 6461, pp. 304–311. Springer, Heidelberg (2010). https://doi.org/10.1007/978-3-642-17164-2_21
10. Kemerlis, V.P., Polychronakis, M., Keromytis, A.D.: ret2dir: Rethinking kernel isolation. In: USENIX Security (2014)
11. McCune, J.M., Li, Y., Qu, N., Zhou, Z., Datta, A., Gligor, V., Perrig, A.: TrustVisor: Efficient TCB reduction and attestation. In: S&P 2010 (2010)
12. McCune, J.M., Parno, B., Perrig, A., Reiter, M.K., Isozaki, H.: Flicker: An execution infrastructure for TCB minimization. In: EuroSys 2008 (2008)
13. McKeen, F., Alexandrovich, I., Berenzon, A., Rozas, C.V., Shafi, H., Shanbhogue, V., Savagaonkar, U.R.: Innovative instructions and software model for isolated execution. In: HASP 2013 (2013)
14. Noorman, J., Agten, P., Daniels, W., Strackx, R., Van Herrewege, A., Huygens, C., Preneel, B., Verbauwhede, I., Piessens, F.: Sancus: Low-cost trustworthy extensible networked devices with a zero-software trusted computing base. In: 22nd USENIX Security symposium, pp. 479–494. USENIX Association (2013)
15. Noorman, J., Bulck, J.V., Mühlberg, J.T., Piessens, F., Maene, P., Preneel, B., Verbauwhede, I., Götzfried, J., Müller, T., Freiling, F.: Sancus 2.0: A low-cost security architecture for IoT devices. ACM Trans. Priv. Secur. 20(3) (2017)
16. Parkinson, M., Bierman, G.: Separation logic and abstraction. In: POPL 2005 (2005)
17. Parno, B., Lorch, J.R., Douceur, J.R., Mickens, J., McCune, J.M.: Memoir: Practical state continuity for protected modules. In: Proceedings of the 2011 IEEE Symposium on Security and Privacy, pp. 379–394. IEEE Computer Society (2011)
18. Patrignani, M., Agten, P., Strackx, R., Jacobs, B., Clarke, D., Piessens, F.: Secure compilation to protected module architectures. In: TOPLAS 2014 (2014)
19. Reynolds, J.C.: Separation logic: A logic for shared mutable data structures. In: LICS 2002 (2002)
20. Sinha, R., Rajamani, S., Seshia, S., Vaswani, K.: Moat: Verifying confidentiality of enclave programs. In: CCS 2015 (2015)

21. Strackx, R., Jacobs, B., Piessens, F.: Ice: a passive, high-speed, state-continuity scheme. In: Proceedings of the 30th Annual Computer Security Applications Conference (ACSAC 2014), pp. 106–115. ACM (2014)
22. Strackx, R., Piessens, F.: Ariadne: A minimal approach to state continuity. In: Proceedings of the 25th USENIX Security Symposium, pp. 875–892. USENIX Association (2016)
23. Vogels, F., Jacobs, B., Piessens, F.: Featherweight verifast. Logical Methods Comput. Sci. **11**(3), 1–57 (2015)

Heap and Equivalence Reasoning

Black-Box Equivalence Checking Across Compiler Optimizations

Manjeet Dahiya$^{(\boxtimes)}$ and Sorav Bansal

Indian Institute of Technology Delhi, New Delhi, India
{dahiya,sbansal}@cse.iitd.ac.in

Abstract. Equivalence checking is an important building block for program synthesis and verification. For a synthesis tool to compete with modern compilers, its equivalence checker should be able to verify the transformations produced by these compilers. We find that the transformations produced by compilers are much varied and the presence of undefined behaviour allows them to produce even more aggressive optimizations. Previous work on equivalence checking has been done in the context of translation validation, where either a pass-by-pass based approach was employed or a set of handpicked optimizations were proven. These settings are not suitable for a synthesis tool where a *black-box* approach is required.

This paper presents the design and implementation of an equivalence checker which can perform black-box checking across almost all the composed transformations produced by modern compilers. We evaluate the checker by testing it across unoptimized and optimized binaries of SPEC benchmarks generated by `gcc`, `clang`, `icc` and `ccomp`. The tool has overall success rates of 76% and 72% for O2 and O3 optimizations respectively, for this first of its kind experiment.

1 Introduction

Equivalence checking is an important building block for program synthesis and verification. For a target sequence, the synthesis tool generates many possible optimized sequences and discharges the correctness check to the equivalence checker. The checker returns a proof of equivalence or it fails. Because the problem is undecidable in general, incorrect failures are inevitable, i.e., the equivalence checker can't be both sound and complete. In the setting of program synthesis and superoptimization, the checker must produce sound results: an incorrect equivalence failure (incompleteness) would result in a potentially missed optimization; on the other hand, a false positive (unsoundness) produces incorrect translation by the synthesis tool. Akin to compilers, a synthesis tool does not have test cases or traces given to it, requiring that the underlying equivalence checker be static. Another important difference from previous work on translation validation is that the equivalence checker is not aware of the exact nature of transformations performed. The transformation is a *black-box* to the checker, and the checker should be able to verify multiple composed transformations without knowing about the actual transformations or their sequence.

© Springer International Publishing AG 2017
B.-Y.E. Chang (Ed.): APLAS 2017, LNCS 10695, pp. 127–147, 2017.
https://doi.org/10.1007/978-3-319-71237-6_7

Previous work on equivalence checking has been performed in the context of translation validation. The goal of translation validation is to verify the correctness of a translation. This prior work has largely employed a pass-by-pass based approach [14,26] where each pass is verified separately by the equivalence checker, and/or worked with a set of handpicked transformations [14,26,37]. A pass-by-pass approach simplifies the verification process by dividing a big step into smaller and simpler steps, and the result is obtained by composing the results of individual steps. While this meets the objective of translation validation, these are unsuitable settings for a synthesis tool, where the nature and sequence of transformations are unknown. Note that an equivalence checker of a synthesis tool can be used for translation validation, while the converse is not true. In other words, the requirements on equivalence checking are stronger for synthesis than for translation validation. We also find that the underlying algorithms of previous techniques are not robust with respect to the transformations produced by modern compilers, e.g., Necula's TVI [26] fails when a simple if-block is replaced by a conditional move instruction (cmov). A detailed comparison with previous work is available in Sect. 6.

For a synthesis tool to compete with modern compilers, its equivalence checker should be able to verify the optimizations produced by these compilers. We find that the transformations produced by these compilers are much varied and presence of language level *undefined behaviour* allows them to produce even more aggressive optimizations. We present the design and implementation of an equivalence checker which meets the requirements of a synthesis tool and can verify the transformations produced by modern compilers. Our contributions towards this goal are:

- A new algorithm to determine the proof of equivalence across programs. The algorithm is robust with respect to modern compiler transformations and in a black-box manner, can handle almost all composed transformations performed by the modern compilers.
- New insights in equivalence checking, the most important being handling of language level undefined behaviour based optimizations. Previous work had disabled these optimizations, yet we find that these optimizations are very commonly used in compilers. For example, our equivalence checking success rates increase by 15%–52%, through modeling some important classes of undefined behaviour. To our knowledge, we are the first to handle undefined behaviour in equivalence checking for programs containing loops.
- Comprehensive experiments: we evaluate our implementation across blackbox optimizations produced by modern compilers gcc, clang, icc (Intel's C Compiler), and ccomp (CompCert). Our tool can automatically generate proofs of equivalence, across O2/O3 compiler transformations, for 74% of the functions in C programs belonging to the SPEC benchmark suite across all four compilers. These results are comparable (and, in some cases, better) to the success rates achieved by previous translation validation tools which operated in much more restricted settings. This is a first of its kind experimental

setup for evaluating an equivalence checker. We have also successfully tested a preliminary superoptimizer supporting loops, with our equivalence checker.

2   Simulation Relation as the Basis of Equivalence

Two programs are equivalent if for all equal inputs, the two programs have identical observables. We compute equivalence for C programs at function granularity. The inputs in case of C functions are the formal arguments and memory (minus stack) at function entry and the observables are the return values and memory (minus stack) at exit. Two functions are equivalent if for same arguments and memory (minus stack), the functions return identical return values and memory state (minus stack).

A simulation relation is a structure to establish equivalence between two programs. It has been used extensively in previous work on translation validation [14,26,28,32,41]. A simulation relation is a witness of the equivalence between two programs, and is represented as a table with two columns: Location and Relations. Location is a pair (L_1, L_2) of PC (program counter) in the two programs and relations are predicates (P) in terms of the variables at these respective PCs. The predicates P represent the invariants that hold across the two programs, when they are at the corresponding locations $L1$ and $L2$ respectively. A row $((L_1, L_2), P)$ of the simulation relation encodes that the relation P holds whenever the two programs are at L_1 and L_2 respectively. For a valid simulation relation, predicates at each location should be inductively provable from predicates at the predecessor locations. Further, the predicates at the entry location (pair of entry points of the two programs) must be provable using the input equivalence condition (base case). If the equivalence of the required observables is provable at the exit location (pair of exits of two programs) using the simulation relation predicates, we can conclude that the programs are equivalent.

Figure 3a shows a simulation relation between the programs in Fig. 2a and b. It has three rows, one each for entry (b0, b0'), exit (b4, b3') and loop-node (b1, b1'). The predicates at entry and exit represent the equivalence of inputs (formal arguments and memory) and outputs (memory state (minus stack)) respectively. The predicates at the loop-node are required for the inductive proof of correctness of the simulation relation. The predicates represent the invariants which hold across the two programs, e.g., the predicate $i_A = i_B$ at loop-node represents that the "i" variables of the two programs, at b1 and b1' are equal. Init represents the input equivalence conditions and Pre represents the preconditions which can be assumed to be true for the programs; we model undefined behaviour through such preconditions. The only observable of this function is memory without the stack, as the function return type is void. The given simulation relation is valid and the predicates at the exit row can prove equivalence of observables, i.e., $M_A =_\Delta M_B$.

This simulation relation based technique can only prove equivalence across bi-similar transformations, e.g., it can not prove equivalence across the loop

```
int g[144]; int sum=0;
void sum_positive(int n) {
  int *ptr = g;
  for(int i = 0; i < n;
      i++, ptr++) {
    if (*ptr > 0)
      sum = sum + *ptr;
  }
}
```

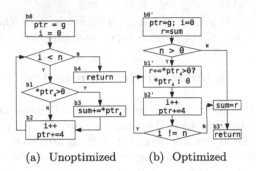

(a) Unoptimized   (b) Optimized

Fig. 1. An example function accessing global variables g and sum. Undefined behaviour if n > 144 (our algorithm would capture this as preconditions).

Fig. 2. Abstracted versions of unoptimized and optimized implementations of the program in Fig. 1. The ternary operator a?b:c represents the cmov assembly instruction.

tiling transformation. Fortunately, most compiler transformations preserve bisimilarity. Further, our notion of equivalence does not model constructs like non termination, exceptions, interrupts and concurrency.

In contrast with checking the correctness of a simulation relation, constructing the same is harder, and is in fact undecidable. The goal of our equivalence checking algorithm (Sect. 4.3) is to try and construct a valid simulation relation which can prove the equivalence. Before going into the details of the algorithm, we show its working for the example program of Fig. 1.

3   An Illustrative Example

Figure 2a, b show the abstracted, unoptimized (A) and optimized (B) versions, of the program in Fig. 1. The optimized program has been compiled by gcc using -O3 flag. While the programs are in x86 assembly, we have abstracted them into C like syntax and flow charts for readability and exposition. The program has undergone multiple optimizations like (1) loop inversion, (2) condition inequality $(i < n)$ to condition disequality $(i \neq n)$ conversion, (3) usage of conditional move instruction (cmov) to get rid of a branch, and (4) register allocation (sum is written only once outside the loop). The last optimization is interesting, as it assumes that ptr cannot alias with the pointer sum. Notice that n is unknown and in general it is possible for ptr $\in [g, g + 4*n)$ to overlap with sum. And hence, as such, the register allocation of global variable is not correct across the loop. However, compilers commonly apply such transformations by relying on aliasing based undefined behaviour assumptions. C specifies that an access beyond the size of a variable is undefined behaviour. In this example, the semantics restrict the value of ptr to lie within $[g, g + 4*144)$ and thus the compiler is free to assume that ptr cannot alias with sum.

In our knowledge, no previous work can handle this transformation. All of the previous work fail in proving this transformation correct, either due to one or multiple optimizations (from the above four). There are three broad improvements we make over previous work: (1) A robust algorithm for finding the correlation of program points. Our algorithm is the first to be demonstrated to work across black-box compiler transformations. (2) We present a systematic guess and check based inference of predicates without assumptions on the transformations performed. Our careful engineering of the guessing heuristics to balance efficiency and robustness is a novel contribution, and we evaluate it through experiments. Previous translation validation approaches, which can make more assumptions on the nature of transformations, did not need such a robust predicate inference procedure. (3) We model C level undefined behaviour conditions. Previous work on translation validation disabled transformations which exploit undefined behaviour.

Our goal is to first model the undefined behaviour (preconditions) and infer the simulation relation. Among all types of C undefined behaviour, aliasing based undefined behaviour is perhaps the most commonly exploited by compilers for optimization. In Fig. 1, the assumption that `ptr` and `sum` cannot alias with each other is an example of aliasing based undefined behaviour. To model such behaviour, we first need to reconstruct aliasing information from the compiled code. The details on our alias analysis algorithm and generation of the related undefined behaviour assumptions are available in [4]. In Fig. 1, alias analysis determines that `ptr` may alias with global variable g, and as per C semantics, `ptr` must always point within the region of g. This is represented by preconditions: (`ptr≥g`) and (`ptr<g+144*4`). These preconditions are then used as assumptions while discharging proof obligations at the time of determining the correlation, and during the final simulation relation proof.

We now discuss how our algorithm computes a valid simulation relation; a simulation relation is represented using a *joint transfer function graph* (JTFG) (Sect. 4.2) which is constructed incrementally at each step. A JTFG represents a correlation across nodes and edges of the two programs. A JTFG node represents two PC values, one belonging to the first program and the other to the second program. Similarly, a JTFG edge represents one control flow edge in the first program and its correlated edge in the second program. Further, we assume that for two edges to be correlated in a JTFG, they should have equivalent *edge condition*, i.e., if one program makes a certain control transfer (follows an edge), the other program will make a corresponding control transfer along the respective correlated edge in the JTFG, and vice-versa. The individual edges of an edge of a JTFG could be composite: a composite edge (Sect. 4.2) between two nodes is formed by composing a sequence of edges (into a *path*), or by combining a disjunction of multiple paths (an example of a composite edge involving a disjunction of multiple paths is available in the following discussion).

Determining the correlation across program points and control transfers, is one of the trickiest problems during the construction of a simulation relation. Our algorithm proceeds as follows. We first fix the program points (PCs) and

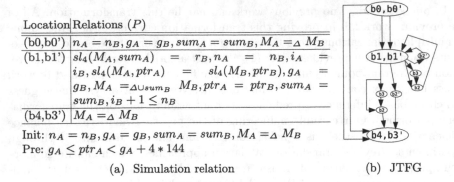

Location	Relations (P)
(b0,b0')	$n_A = n_B, g_A = g_B, sum_A = sum_B, M_A =_\Delta M_B$
(b1,b1')	$sl_4(M_A, sum_A) = r_B, n_A = n_B, i_A = i_B, sl_4(M_A, ptr_A) = sl_4(M_B, ptr_B), g_A = g_B, M_A =_{\Delta \cup sum_B} M_B, ptr_A = ptr_B, sum_A = sum_B, i_B + 1 \le n_B$
(b4,b3')	$M_A =_\Delta M_B$

Init: $n_A = n_B, g_A = g_B, sum_A = sum_B, M_A =_\Delta M_B$
Pre: $g_A \le ptr_A < g_A + 4 * 144$

(a) Simulation relation   (b) JTFG

Fig. 3. Simulation relation (JTFG) for the TFGs in Fig. 5. Table shows the predicates at each node and graph shows the correlation of edges and nodes of the two TFGs. Init is the initial conditions representing equivalence of inputs. Pre is the preconditions (undefined behaviour). $=_\Delta$ represents equivalent arrays except Δ; Δ represents the stack region. Operator sl_4 is a shorthand of *select* of size 4. The edges of the two programs between (b1,b1') to (b4,b3') and (b1,b1') are composite edges made up of the individual edges in between.

composite edges in one program (say $Prog_B$) and try to find the respective correlated program points and composite edges in the other program ($Prog_A$). For sound reasoning of loops, we ensure that a correlation exists for at least one node in a loop, for all the loops. We pick the entry, exit and loop heads in $Prog_B$, as the *interesting* PCs that need to be correlated with PCs in $Prog_A$. In our example, we pick (b0', b1', b3') in $Prog_B$. Thus, $Prog_B$ can be represented as the three picked nodes, and a set of composite edges, $edges_B$ =(b0'-b1', b1'-b2'-b1', b1'-b2'-b3', b0'-b3'). We now try and find the correlated composite edges in $Prog_A$ for each composite edge in $Prog_B$. When all the composite edges of $Prog_B$ get correlated, we obtain a candidate correlation between the two programs.

Running our algorithm on the example, we initialize the JTFG with its entry node (b0, b0'). We pick an $edge_B$ from $edges_B$ (sorted in DFS order) and find the list of composite edges in $Prog_A$ (up to some fixed length) which can be correlated with $edge_B$. For edge (b0'-b1') of $Prog_B$ we get (b0-b1, b0-b4, b0-b1-b2, b0-b1-b3, b0-b1-b3-b2, b0-b1-b2||b0-b1-b3-b2)[1] as the list of potential composite edges in $Prog_A$, up to unroll factor 1 (unrolling the loop once). The last edge involves a disjunction of two paths. The conditions of these edges are $(0 < n_A, 0 \ge n_A, 0 < n_A \wedge *ptr_4 \le 0, 0 < n_A \wedge *ptr_4 > 0, 0 < n_A \wedge *ptr_4 > 0, 0 < n_A)$ respectively. And the condition of the current $edge_B$ is $0 < n_B$. However, the edge conditions of the two programs cannot be compared because there is no relation between n_A and n_B. Before comparing the conditions across these two programs, we need to find predicates which relate the variables of the two programs at (b0, b0'). In this example, we require the predicate $n_A = n_B$ at

---

[1] a-b-c is sequential composition of edges a-b and b-c. a-b-c||a-d-c is parallel composition of edges a-b-c and a-d-c.

(b0, b0') (we later discuss how to obtain such predicates). Predicate $n_A = n_B$ proves that the conditions of (b0-b1) and (b0'-b1') are equal, implying that the correlation is correct. We then try to correlate the next composite edge of $Prog_B$ until all the composite edges are correlated and a simulation relation (JTFG) is found which can prove the required equivalence. At each step, it is possible for multiple composite edges in $Prog_A$ to have the required edge condition for correlation, while only one (or a few of the choices) may yield a provable simulation relation. To handle this, our algorithm backtracks to explore the remaining choices for correlated edges (discussed later).

At each step of the algorithm, a partial JTFG gets constructed. For future correlation we need to infer the predicates at the nodes of the currently constructed partial JTFG. We use a guess-and-check strategy to infer these predicates. This is similar to previous work on invariant inference (Houdini [8]), except that we are inferring these invariants/predicates on the JTFG, while previous work used this strategy for inferring invariants of an individual program. This guess-and-check procedure is formalized in Sect. 4.3.

The constructed JTFG may be incorrect on several counts. For example, it is possible that the predicates inferred at intermediate steps are stronger than what is eventually provable, and hence we infer an incorrect correlation. An incorrect correlation would mean that we will fail to successfully correlate in future steps of the algorithm, or will finish with a simulation relation that cannot prove observable equivalence. To handle either of these cases of incorrect correlation, our algorithm backtracks to try other potential composite edges for correlation, unwinding the decisions at each step. In theory, the algorithm is exponential in the number of edges to be correlated, but in practice, backtracking is rare, especially if the candidate edges for correlation are heuristically prioritized. Our simple heuristic to minimize backtracking is to explore the composite edges in the order of increasing depth, up to a given maximum limit controlled by unroll factor (μ). This heuristic is based on the assumption that a majority of the compiler transformations do not perform unrolling, and can thus be proven at smaller depths. If the algorithm succeeds in finding a JTFG that proves observable equivalence at the exit node, we have successfully computed a provable simulation relation, and hence completed the equivalence proof.

4   Formalization and Algorithm

4.1   Abstracting Programs as Transfer Function Graph

We need an abstract program representation as a logical framework for reasoning about semantics and equivalence. This abstraction is called the transfer function graph (TFG). A TFG is a graph with nodes and edges. Nodes represent locations in the program, e.g., program counter (PC). Edges encode the effect of the instruction and the condition under which the edge is taken. The state of the program consists of bitvectors and a byte-addressable array, representing registers and memory respectively.

$$\mathbb{T} \qquad ::= ([\varepsilon], [\varepsilon], [\varepsilon], \mathbb{G}([node], [edge]))$$
$$node \qquad ::= pc(int) \mid exit(int)$$
$$edge \qquad ::= (node, node, edgecond, \tau)$$
$$edgecond ::= state \rightarrow \varepsilon$$
$$\tau \qquad ::= state \rightarrow state$$
$$state \qquad ::= [(string, \varepsilon)]$$
$$\varepsilon \qquad ::= var(string) \mid nryop(\varepsilon, \varepsilon) \mid select(\varepsilon, \varepsilon, int) \mid store(\varepsilon, \varepsilon, int, \varepsilon) \mid uif([\varepsilon])$$

Fig. 4. Transfer function graph ($\mathbb{T}$).

A simplified TFG grammar is presented in Fig. 4. The TFG $\mathbb{T}$ consists of preconditions, inputs, outputs and a graph $\mathbb{G}$ with nodes and edges. A node is named either by its PC location ($pc(int)$), or by an exit location ($exit(int)$); a TFG could have multiple exits. An edge is a four-tuple with from-node and to-node (first two fields), its edge condition *edgecond* (third field) represented as a function from state to expression, and its transfer function τ (fourth field). An expression ε could be a boolean, bitvector, byte-addressable array, or an uninterpreted function. Expressions are similar to standard SMT expressions, with a few modifications for better analysis and optimization (e.g., unlike SMT, `select` and `store` operators have an additional third integer argument representing the number of bytes being read/written). An edge is taken when its *edgecond* holds. An edge's transfer function represents the effect of taking that edge on the program state, as a function of the state at the from-node. A state is represented as a set of (string, ε) tuples, where the string names the state element (e.g., register name). Apart from registers and memory, the state also includes an "IO" element indicating I/O activity, that in our setting, could occur only due to a function call (inside the callee)[2]. A procedure's TFG will have an entry node, and a single return (exit) node.

The C function calls in programs are modeled as uninterpreted functions (`uif`) in TFGs. The `uif` inputs include the callee function's ID, signature and the IO element value. `uif` modifies the state as per function signature. All "outputs" of the function call (memory, return values, and IO) are modified through `uif`. Figure 5 shows the TFGs of unoptimized and optimized versions of our running example program.

4.2 Joint Transfer Function Graph

A joint transfer function graph (JTFG) is a subgraph of the cartesian product of the two TFGs. Additionally, each JTFG node has predicates (second column of simulation relation) representing the invariants across the two programs. Intuitively, a JTFG represents a correlation between two programs: it correlates the move (edge) taken by one program with the move taken by the other program,

---

[2] In the programs we consider, the only method to perform I/O is through function calls (that may internally invoke system calls).

Edge	condition	$\tau(ptr, i, n, M) =$
b0-b1	$n > 0$	$(g, 0, n, M)$
b0-b4	$n \leq 0$	$(g, 0, n, M)$
b1-b2	$sl_4(M, ptr) \leq 0$	(ptr, i, n, M)
b1-b3	$sl_4(M, ptr) > 0$	(ptr, i, n, M)
b3-b2	$true$	$let\ v = sl_4(M, ptr) + sl_4(M, sum)$ $(ptr, i, n, st_4(M, sum, v))$
b2-b1	$i + 1 < n$	$(ptr + 4, i + 1, n, M)$
b2-b4	$i + 1 \geq n$	$(ptr + 4, i + 1, n, M)$

Edge	condition	$\tau(ptr, i, r, n, M) =$
b0'-b1'	$n > 0$	$(g, 0, sl_4(M, sum), n, M)$
b1'-b2'-b1'	$i + 1 \neq n$	$let\ u = sl_4(M, ptr)$ $(ptr + 4, i + 1, r + (u > 0?u : 0), n, M)$
b1'-b2'-b3'	$i + 1 = n$	$let\ u = sl_4(M, ptr)$ $let\ v = r + (u > 0?u : 0)$ $(ptr + 4, i + 1, v, n, st_4(M, sum, v))$
b0'-b3'	$n \leq 0$	$(g, 0, sl_4(M, sum), n, M)$

Fig. 5. TFGs of the unoptimized (top) and optimized programs, represented as a table of edges. The 'condition' column represents the edge condition, and τ represents the transfer function. Operators sl_4 and st_4 are shorthands of *select* and *store* of size 4. *sum* and g represent the addresses of globals sum and g[] respectively.

and vice-versa. Formally, a JTFG (J_{AB}) between TFG_A and TFG_B is defined as:

$$TFG_A = (N_A, E_A), TFG_B = (N_B, E_B), J_{AB} = (N_{AB}, E_{AB})$$

$$N_{AB} = \{n_{AB} | n_{AB} \in (N_A \times N_B) \wedge (\bigvee_{e \in outedges_{n_{AB}}} edgecond_e)\}$$

$$E_{AB} = \{(e_{u_A \rightarrow v_A}, e_{u_B \rightarrow v_B}) | \{(u_A, u_B), (v_A, v_B)\} \in N_{AB} \wedge$$
$$edgecond_{e_{u_A \rightarrow v_A}} = edgecond_{e_{u_B \rightarrow v_B}}\}$$

Here N_A and E_A represent the nodes and edges of TFG_A respectively and $e_{u_A \rightarrow v_A}$ is an edge in TFG_A from node u to node v. The condition on n_{AB} (in N_{AB}'s definition) stipulates that the disjunction of all the outgoing edges of a JTFG node should be **true**. The two individual edges ($e_{u_A \rightarrow v_A}$ and $e_{u_B \rightarrow v_B}$) in an edge of JTFG should have equivalent edge conditions. The individual edge (e.g., $e_{u_A \rightarrow v_A}$) within a JTFG edge could be a composite edge. Recall that a composite edge between two nodes may be formed by composing multiple paths between these two nodes into one. The transfer function of the composite edge is determined by composing the transfer functions of the constituent edges, predicated with their respective edge conditions. We use the **ite** (if-then-else) operator to implement predication. Figure 3b shows a JTFG for the programs in Fig. 5.

Function *Correlate(TFG$_A$, TFG$_B$)*
| jtfg ← InitializeJTFG(EntryPC$_A$, EntryPC$_B$)
| edges$_B$ ← DfsGetEdges(TFG$_B$)
| proofSuccess = CorrelateEdges(jtfg, edges$_B$, μ)

Function *CorrelateEdges(jtfg, edges$_B$, μ)*
| **if** *edges$_B$ is empty* **then**
| | **return** ExitAndIOConditionsProvable(jtfg)
| **end**
| edge$_B$ ← RemoveFirst(edges$_B$)
| fromPC$_B$ ← GetFromPC(edge$_B$)
| fromPC$_A$ ← FindCorrelatedFirstPC(jtfg, fromPC$_B$)
| cedges$_A$ ← GetCEdgesTillUnroll(TFG$_A$,fromPC$_A$,μ)
| **foreach** *cedge$_A$ in cedges$_A$* **do**
| | AddEdge(jtfg, cedge$_A$, edge$_B$)
| | PredicatesGuessAndCheck(jtfg)
| | **if** *IsEqualEdgeConditions(jtfg)* $\wedge$ *CorrelateEdges(jtfg, edges$_B$, μ)* **then**
| | | **return** true
| | **else**
| | | RemoveEdge(jtfg, cedge$_A$, edge$_B$)
| | **end**
| **end**
| **return** false

Function *IsEqualEdgeConditions(jtfg)*
| **foreach** *e in edges(jtfg)* **do**
| | rel ← GetSimRelationPredicates(e$_{fromPC}$)
| | **if** $\neg$ *(rel $\implies$ (e$_{FirstEdgeCond}$ $\iff$ e$_{SecondEdgeCond}$))* **then**
| | | **return** false
| | **end**
| **end**
| **return** true

Algorithm 1. Determining correlation. μ is the unroll factor.

4.3 Algorithm for Determining the Simulation Relation

Our correlation algorithm works across black-box compiler transformations, which is the primary difference between our work and previous work. Algorithm 1 presents the pseudo code of our algorithm. Function `Correlate()` is the top-level function which takes the TFGs of the two programs, and returns either a provable JTFG or a proof failure. The JTFG (`jtfg`) is initialized with its entry node, which is the pair of entry nodes of the two TFGs. Then, we get the edges (*edges$_B$*) of TFG_B in depth-first-search order by calling `DfsGetEdges()`. And finally, the initialized `jtfg`, *edges$_B$*, and μ are passed as inputs to the `CorrelateEdges()` function, which attempts to correlate each edge in *Prog$_B$* with a composite edge in *Prog$_A$*.

`CorrelateEdges()` consumes one edge from *edges$_B$* at a time, and then recursively calls itself on the remaining *edges$_B$*. In every call, it first checks whether all $edges_B$ have been correlated (i.e., the jtfg is complete and correct). If it is so, it tries proving the observables, through ExitAndIOConditionsProvable(), and returns the status of this call. However, if there are still some edges left for correlation (i.e., jtfg is not complete), we pick an edge ($edge_B$) from $edges_B$ and try to find its respective candidate composite edge for correlation in TFG_A. Because we are correlating the edges in DFS order, the from-node of $edge_B$ (say fromPC$_B$) would have already been correlated with a node in TFG_A (say fromPC$_A$). We next compute the composite edges originating at fromPC$_A$ in TFG_A, to identify candidates for correlation with $edge_B$. The function GetCEdgesTillUnroll() returns the list of all composite edges ($cedges_A$) which start at fromPC$_A$ with a maximum unrolling of loops bounded by μ (unroll factor). $cedges_A$ represents the potential candidates for correlation with $edge_B$. The unroll factor μ allows our algorithm to capture transformations involving loop unrolling and software pipelining.

We check every $cedge_A$ in $cedges_A$ for potential correlation in the foreach loop in CorrelateEdges(). This is done by adding the edge ($cedge_A$, $edge_B$) to the JTFG and checking whether their edge conditions are equivalent; before computing this equivalence however, we need to infer the predicates on this partial JTFG through PredicatesGuessAndCheck() (discussed next). These inferred predicates are required to relate the variables at already correlated program points across the two programs. If the edge conditions are proven equivalent (IsEqualEdgeConditions()) we proceed to correlate (recursive call to CorrelateEdges()) the remaining edges in $edges_B$. If the conditions are not equal or the recursive call returns false (no future correlation found) the added edge is removed (RemoveEdge()) from jtfg and another $cedge_A$ is tried. If none of the composite edges can be correlated, the algorithm backtracks, i.e., the current call to CorrelateEdges() returns false.

Predicates guess-and-check is an important building block of our algorithm and it is one of the elements that lend robustness to our algorithm. Previous work has relied on inferring a relatively small set of syntactically generated predicates (e.g., [26, 32]) which are usually weaker, and do not suffice for black-box compiler transformations. Like Houdini [8], we guess several predicates generated through a grammar, and run a fixed point procedure to retain only the provable predicates. The guessing grammar needs to be general enough to capture the required predicates, but cannot be too large, for efficiency.

Guess: At every node of the JTFG, we guess predicates generated from a set $\mathbb{G} = \{\star_A \oplus \star_B, M_A =_{\star_A \cup \star_B} M_B\}$, where operator $\oplus \in \{<, >, =, \leq, \geq\}$. $\star_A$ and $\star_B$ represent the program values (represented as symbolic expressions) appearing in TFG_A and TFG_B respectively (including preconditions) and $M_A =_X M_B$ represents equal memory states except the region X. The guesses are formed through a cartesian product of values in TFG_A and TFG_B using the patterns in $\mathbb{G}$. This grammar for guessing predicates has been designed to work well with the transformations produced by modern compilers, while keeping the proof obligation discharge times tractable.

Check: Our checking procedure is a fixed point computation which eliminates the unprovable predicates at each step, until only provable predicates remain. At each step, we try and prove the predicates across a JTFG edge, i.e., prove the predicates at the head of the edge, using the predicates at the tail of the edge, and the edge's condition and transfer function. Further, the preconditions (*Pre*) determined through our model of language level undefined behaviour are used as assumptions during this proof attempt. The predicates at the entry node of JTFG are checked using the initial conditions across the two programs, represented by `Init`. `Init` consists of predicates representing input equivalence (C function arguments and input memory state). At each step, the following condition is checked for every edge:

$$\bigvee_{(X \to Y) \in edges} (Pre \wedge edgecond_{X \to Y}) \Rightarrow (preds_X \Rightarrow pred_Y)$$

Here $preds_X$ represents the conjunction of all the (current) guessed predicates at node X and $pred_Y$ represents a guessed predicate at node Y. $edgecond_{X \to Y}$ is the edge condition for the edge (X→Y). If this check fails for some guessed predicate $pred_Y$ at some node Y, we remove that predicate, and repeat.

Undefined behaviour assumptions. Most undefined behaviour modeling is straightforward. Aliasing based undefined behaviour requires a detailed alias analysis, however. For every memory access, our alias analysis algorithm determines the variables with which the memory address *may* alias. If an address a may alias with only one variable v, we emit preconditions encoding that a must belong to the region allocated to v. If an address may alias with multiple variables (or could point within the heap), then the corresponding preconditions involve a disjunction over all the respective regions. Additional precondition clauses are generated to encode that these regions allocated to different variables (and heap) may not overlap with each other. These aliasing based undefined behaviour assumptions are critical for achieving reasonable success rates for black-box equivalence checking across compiler transformations (Sect. 5).

We have tested the algorithm and its implementation across transformations like loop inversion, loop peeling, loop unrolling, loop splitting, loop invariant code hoisting, induction variable optimizations, inter-loop strength reduction, SIMD vectorization, and software pipelining. On the other hand, it does not support loop reordering transformations that are not simulation preserving, such as tiling and interchange. Also, if the transformations involve a reduction in the number of loops (e.g., replacing a loop-based computation with a closed form expression), the algorithm, in its current form, may fail to construct the proof.

5   Implementation and Evaluation

We compile multiple C programs by multiple compilers at different optimization levels, for x86, to generate unoptimized (-O0) and optimized (-O2 and -O3) binary executables. We then harvest functions from these executable files and reconstruct C-level information, necessary for modeling undefined behaviour assumptions and for performing equivalence checks. Once the functions are harvested and C-level information is reconstructed, we perform the equivalence checks between the functions from unoptimized (O0) and optimized (O2/O3) executables.

The high level C program information necessary for performing the equivalence checking and modeling undefined behaviour are global variables and their scope/type attributes, local stack, function declarations and function calls, and program logic (function body). We reconstruct the language level semantics from ELF executables by using certain (standard) ELF headers. We rely on the debug headers (-g), symbol table and relocation table (-fdata-sections --emit-relocs) for getting the required high level information. Debug headers contain information about the functions and their signatures. Symbol table provides the global variable name, address, size and binding attributes. The relocation headers allows precise renaming of addresses appearing in code, to respective global variable identifiers with appropriate offsets, ensuring that the different placement of globals in different executables are abstracted away. None of these flags affect the quality of generated code. All these flags (or equivalent) are available in gcc, clang, icc and ccomp. Our reconstruction procedures are identical for both O0 and O2/O3 executables. The difference is that while the reconstructed information from O0 is used for obtaining the high level C program specification, the reconstructed information from O2/O3 is used only to help with proof construction.

Table 1. Benchmarks characteristics. Fun, UN and Loop columns represent the total number of functions, the number of functions containing unsupported opcodes, and the number of functions with at least one loop, resp. SLOC is determined through the sloccount tool. ALOC is based on gcc-O0 compilation. Globals represent the number of global variables in the executable.

Bench	Fun	UN	Loop	SLOC	ALOC	Globals
mcf	26	2	21	1494	3676	43
bzip2	74	2	30	3236	9371	100
ctests	101	0	63	1408	4499	53
crafty	106	5	56	12939	72355	517
gzip	106	1	66	5615	14350	212
sjeng	142	3	68	10544	38829	312
twolf	191	17	140	17822	84295	348
vpr	272	69	155	11301	44981	153
parser	323	2	240	7763	30998	223
gap	854	0	466	35759	177511	330
vortex	922	5	116	49232	167947	815
perlbmk	1070	65	271	72189	175852	561

Several optimizations were necessary to achieve reasonable results for equivalence across assembly programs. We have developed custom simplification procedures over expression trees to reduce expression size, for efficient pattern matching (e.g., for `select` and `store`) and efficient discharge of proof obligations. We use Z3 [5] and Yices [6] SMT solvers running in parallel for discharging proof obligations over our custom-simplified expressions, and use the result of solver which finishes first. We also employ caching of SMT query results to improve performance.

The programs that were compiled and checked, are listed in Table 1 along with their characteristics. `ctests` is a program taken from the CompCert testsuite and involves a variety of different C features and behaviour; the other programs are taken from the SPEC CPU2000 integer benchmarks. The SPEC benchmark programs do not include `gcc` and `eon` because their ELF executables files are very big, and our tool to harvest instruction sequences from executable files does not support such large ELF files. We also include an integer program from the SPEC CPU2006 integer benchmarks: `sjeng`. `sjeng` is one of the few C benchmarks in SPEC CPU2006 that is not already present in CPU2000, *and* has a low fraction of floating point operations. We avoid programs with significant floating-point operations, as our semantic models for x86 floating point instructions are incomplete. While compiling these programs, we disabled inlining, type based strict aliasing based assumptions, and signed integer strict overflow assumptions: our tool cannot handle interprocedural optimizations and does not model type based and signed integer overflow undefined behaviour assumptions.

A total of 4% of the functions contain unsupported (usually floating-point) opcodes (Table 1), and we plot results only for the functions which contain only supported opcodes. Figure 6 plots the success rates as a function of the number of assembly instructions in a function, and Fig. 8 plots the success rates for each benchmark-compiler-optimization pair. There were 26007 function-pairs tested

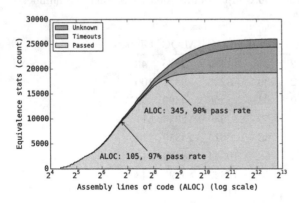

Bench	% change
gzip-gcc2	26
gzip-clang2	15
bzip2-gcc2	44
bzip2-clang2	42
mcf-gcc2	52
mcf-clang2	46
parser-gcc2	43
parser-clang2	19

Fig. 6. Cumulative success rate (pass/fail) vs. ALOC.

Fig. 7. The effect of modeling aliasing based undefined behaviour assumptions. The % change represents the difference between the success rates with and without modeling these undefined behaviour assumptions.

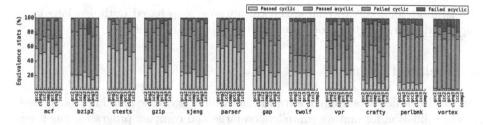

Fig. 8. Equivalence statistics. Functions with at least one loop are called "cyclic". The bar corresponding to a compiler (e.g., `clang`) represents the results across O0/O2 and O0/O3 transformations for that compiler (e.g., for `clang2` and `clang3` resp.). The average success rate across 26007 equivalence tests on these benchmarks, is 76% for O2 and 72% for O3 (dashed blue and red lines resp.). The missing bars for `ccomp` are due to compilation failures for those benchmarks.

across all benchmarks and compiler/optimization pairs. The timeout value used was five hours. Overall, our tool is able to generate sound equivalence proofs across almost all transformations across multiple compilers for 76% of the tested function-pairs for O2 optimization level, and 72% of the tested function-pairs for O3 optimization level. The success rates are much higher for smaller functions, as seen in Fig. 6. The mean and median values for runtimes for passing equivalence tests are 313 s and 8.5 s respectively. 5% of the passing tests take over 1000 s to generate the result. Failures are dominated by timeouts (5 h), inflating the mean and median runtimes for all (failing + passing) equivalence tests to 3962 s and 22 s respectively. The largest function for which equivalence was computed successfully has 4754 ALOC; the most complex function for which equivalence was computed successfully has 31 composite edges in its TFG_B.

Modeling undefined behaviour conditions is crucial for robustness. Figure 7 shows the impact of modeling aliasing based undefined behaviour. If we do not model these undefined behaviour assumptions, the success rates decrease by 15%–52% for these programs.

Our experiments led to the discovery of one bug in GCC-4.1.0 [9] and two bugs in ICC-16.0.3 (one of them is confirmed, and the second involves confusion on the semantics of an ICC flag) [11,12]. Each bug entails equivalence failures across multiple functions.

Finally, we have used our tool inside a 32-bit x86 brute-force superoptimizer that supports a rudimentary form of loops: it allows enumeration of straight-line instruction sequences potentially containing the x86 string instructions `scas`, `stos`, and `cmps` (the equivalent of `memchr`, `memset`, and `memcmp` functions, resp.); each of these instructions is modeled as a TFG containing a cycle. Through supporting these instructions, optimized implementations for common routines like initializing an array, and comparing elements of two arrays, get synthesized automatically, that are 1.04–12x faster than compiled code generated by any of the four compilers we discussed (across O2 and O3). In general, we expect the support for loops to enable general-purpose loop-based optimizations in a superoptimizer, and this work is an initial step towards this goal.

6 Related Work

One of the earliest examples of a translation validator can be found in [30]. Translation validation for mature compilers on large and complex programs, has been reported in at least two previous works: Translation validation infrastructure (TVI) [26] for GCC, and Value-graph translation validation [34,38] for LLVM.

TVI demonstrated the validation of the gcc-2.91 compiler and the Linux-2.2 kernel, across five IR passes in GCC, namely branch optimization, common-subexpression elimination (CSE), loop unrolling and inversion, register allocation, and instruction scheduling. In TVI, validation is performed across each IR pass, i.e., first the input IR is validated against the output of the first pass, then the output of the first pass is validated against the output of the second pass, and so on. The TVI paper reports around 87% validation success rates. Necula's algorithm does not support loop unrolling, and that was reported as the primary cause for validation failures. There are several issues with TVI when applied to end-to-end (black-box and composed transformations) equivalence checking. First, this pass-based approach is not possible in a synthesis/super-optimizer setting. Second, TVI's heuristics for branch and memory-access correlations at basic-block granularity are syntactic, and fail for a large number of compiler transformations. Third, TVI relies on weakest-precondition based inference of simulation relation predicates, which is both expensive and less robust than our guessing procedure. For end-to-end checks, the substituted expressions generated by weakest-precondition become large and unwieldy, resulting in SMT solver timeouts. Further, guessing based on only weakest preconditions is often inadequate. Finally, TVI was tested across five compiler passes, and did not address several transformations, including those relying on undefined behaviour.

Value-graph translation validation for LLVM has been performed previously in two independent efforts [34,38]. The value-graph based technique works by adding all known equality-preserving transformations for a program, to a *value graph*, until it saturates. Equivalence checking now involves checking if the graphs are isomorphic. In the work by Tristan et al. [38], validation is performed across a known set of transformations, namely, dead-code elimination, global value numbering, sparse-condition constant propagation, loop-invariant code motion, loop deletion, loop unswitching, and dead-store elimination. Stepp et al. [34] support all these transformations, and additionally enable partial-redundancy elimination, constant propagation, and basic block placement. While these tools capture several important transformations, they also omit many, e.g., loop inversion and unrolling, branch optimization, common-subexpression elimination, and instruction scheduling, to name a few. Some of these omitted transformations (e.g., loop inversion) enable more aggressive transformations, and so by omitting one of those, a chain of important transformation passes gets omitted. Also, none of these transformations rely on language-level undefined behaviour. For example, the transformations do not include the ones that could reorder accesses to global variables (e.g., by register-allocating them). Both papers report roughly 60–90% success rates for LLVM IR across the transformations they support. Compared head-to-head, this is comparable to our success rates, albeit in a much more restricted setting. A value-graph approach is limited by the vocabulary of transformations that are supported by the translation validator, and thus seems less general than constraint-based approaches like TVI and ours. Also, the number of possible translations for passes like register allocation and instruction scheduling is likely to grow exponentially in a value-graph approach. At least with the current evidence, it seems unlikely that the value-graph based translation validation approach would yield good results for end-to-end black-box equivalence checking.

Data-driven equivalence checking (DDEC) [32] is an effort perhaps closest to our goals of checking equivalence on x86 assembly programs. However, DDEC takes a radically different approach of relying on the availability of execution traces for high-coverage tests, an assumption that is not always practical in a general compiler optimization setting. DDEC was tested on a smaller set of examples (around 18) of x86 assembly code generated using GCC and CompCert, and all DDEC test examples are a part of our ctests benchmark. Compared head-to-head with DDEC, our algorithm is static (does not rely on execution traces), supports a richer set of constructs (stack/memory/global accesses, function calls, undefined behaviour), is more robust (tested on a much larger set of programs, and across a richer set of transformations), and more efficient (when compared head-to-head on the same programs). While DDEC can infer linear equalities through execution traces, it cannot handle several other types of non-linear invariants (e.g., inequalities) often required to prove equivalence across modern compiler transformations. Recent work on loop superoptimization for Google Native Client [3] extends DDEC by supporting inequality-based invariants; the evaluation however is limited to a small selection of test cases, and hence does not address several scalability and modeling issues that we tackle in our equivalence checker. For example, the authors do not model undefined behaviour, which we find is critical for black-box equivalence checking across real programs.

The *Correlate* module of parameterized program equivalence checking (PEC) [14] computes simulation based equivalence for optimization patterns represented as parameterized programs containing *meta-variables*. In contrast, we are interested in equivalence checking across black-box transformations involving low level syntax, as is typical in synthesis and superoptimization settings: our correlation algorithm with guessing procedures have been evaluated for this use case. In PEC's setting, the presence of meta-variables usually provides an easier correspondence between the two programs, greatly simplifying the correlation procedure; the relations (predicates relating variables in two programs) across meta-variables are also easier to determine in this setting.

Previous work on regression verification [7,35] determines equivalence across structurally similar programs, i.e., programs that are closely related, with similar control structure and only a small (programmer introduced) delta between the two programs. In our setting, the programs being compared are significantly different because of transformations due to multiple composed compiler optimizations. While our equivalence checker can correctly compute equivalence across all the examples presented in regression verification [7,35], the converse is not true.

There are more approaches to translation validation and equivalence checking (e.g., [13,22,24,29,41,44]), and most have been evaluated on a variety of relatively smaller examples. To our knowledge, previous work has not dealt with compiler transformations in as much generality, as our work. Our work also overlaps with previous work on verified compilation [21,42,43], compiler testing tools [17,18,40], undefined behaviour detection [39], and domain specific languages for coding and verifying compiler optimizations [19,20].

In terms of the correlation algorithm, our approach is perhaps closest to CoVaC [41], in that we both construct the JTFG incrementally, and rely on an invariant generation procedure, while determining the correlations. There are important differences however. CoVaC relies on an oracular procedure called *InvGen*; we show a concrete implementation of `PredicatesGuessAndCheck()`. Further, we differ significantly in our method to identify the correlations. CoVaC relies on correlating *types* of operations (e.g., memory reads and writes are different types), which is similar to TVI's syntactic memory correlations, and is less general than our semantic treatment of memory. Also, CoVaC relies on the *satisfiability* of the conjunction of edge conditions (viz. *branch alignment*) in the two TFGs, which is unlikely to work across several common transformations that alter the branch structure. CoVaC was tested on smaller examples across a handful of transformations. In contrast, our correlation method based on *equality* of condition of composite edges is more general, and we demonstrate this through experiments. Further, backtracking and careful engineering of guessing heuristics are important novel features of our procedure.

Most previous translation validation work (except DDEC) has been applied to IR. There has also been significant prior work on assembly level verification, through equivalence checking. SymDiff [10,15,16] is an effort towards verifying compilers and regression verification, and works on assembly code. However, the support for loops in SymDiff is quite limited — they handle loops by unrolling them twice. Thus, while SymDiff is good for checking partial equivalence, and to catch errors across program versions and translations, generation of sound equivalence proofs for programs with loops is not supported.

Alive [23] verifies *acyclic* peephole optimization patterns of the `InstCombine` pass of LLVM and models undefined behaviour involving undefined values, poison values and arithmetic overflow. While Alive computes equivalence across acyclic programs, we are interested in simulation based equivalence for programs with loops.

Program synthesis and superoptimization techniques [1,2,25,27,31,33,36] rely on an equivalence checker (verifier) for correctness. The capabilities of a synthesis based optimizer are directly dependent on the capabilities of its underlying equivalence checker. We hope that our work on black-box equivalence checking informs future work in program synthesis and superoptimization.

References

1. Bansal, S., Aiken, A.: Automatic generation of peephole superoptimizers. In: Proceedings of the 12th International Conference on Architectural Support for Programming Languages and Operating Systems, ASPLOS XII, pp. 394–403. ACM (2006)
2. Bansal, S., Aiken, A.: Binary translation using peephole superoptimizers. In: Proceedings of the 8th USENIX Conference on Operating Systems Design and Implementation, OSDI 2008, pp. 177–192. USENIX Association (2008)
3. Churchill, B., Sharma, R., Bastien, J., Aiken, A.: Sound loop superoptimization for Google native client. In: Proceedings of the Twenty-Second International Conference on Architectural Support for Programming Languages and Operating Systems, ASPLOS 2017, pp. 313–326. ACM (2017)
4. Dahiya, M., Bansal, S.: Modeling undefined behaviour semantics for checking equivalence across compiler optimizations. In: Hardware and Software: Verification and Testing - 13th International Haifa Verification Conference, HVC 2017 (2017)
5. De Moura, L., Bjørner, N.: Z3: an efficient SMT solver. In: Proceedings of the Theory and Practice of Software, 14th International Conference on Tools and Algorithms for the Construction and Analysis of Systems, TACAS 2008/ETAPS 2008, pp. 337–340 (2008)
6. Dutertre, B.: Yices 2.2. In: Biere, A., Bloem, R. (eds.) CAV 2014. LNCS, vol. 8559, pp. 737–744. Springer, Cham (2014). https://doi.org/10.1007/978-3-319-08867-9_49
7. Felsing, D., Grebing, S., Klebanov, V., Rümmer, P., Ulbrich, M.: Automating regression verification. In: Proceedings of the 29th ACM/IEEE International Conference on Automated Software Engineering, ASE 2014, pp. 349–360. ACM (2014)
8. Flanagan, C., Leino, K.R.M.: Houdini, an annotation assistant for ESC/Java. In: Oliveira, J.N., Zave, P. (eds.) FME 2001. LNCS, vol. 2021, pp. 500–517. Springer, Heidelberg (2001). https://doi.org/10.1007/3-540-45251-6_29
9. GCC Bugzilla - Bug 68480. https://gcc.gnu.org/bugzilla/show_bug.cgi?id=68480
10. Hawblitzel, C., Lahiri, S.K., Pawar, K., Hashmi, H., Gokbulut, S., Fernando, L., Detlefs, D., Wadsworth, S.: Will you still compile me tomorrow? Static cross-version compiler validation. In: Proceedings of the 2013 9th Joint Meeting on Foundations of Software Engineering, ESEC/FSE 2013, pp. 191–201. ACM (2013)
11. ICC developer forums discussion: icc-16.0.3 not respecting fno-strict-overflow flag? https://software.intel.com/en-us/forums/intel-c-compiler/topic/702516
12. ICC developer forums discussion: icc-16.0.3 not respecting no-ansi-alias flag? https://software.intel.com/en-us/forums/intel-c-compiler/topic/702187
13. Kanade, A., Sanyal, A., Khedker, U.P.: Validation of GCC optimizers through trace generation. Softw. Pract. Exper. **39**(6), 611–639 (2009)
14. Kundu, S., Tatlock, Z., Lerner, S.: Proving optimizations correct using parameterized program equivalence. In: Proceedings of the 2009 ACM SIGPLAN Conference on Programming Language Design and Implementation, PLDI 2009, pp. 327–337. ACM (2009)

15. Lahiri, S.K., Hawblitzel, C., Kawaguchi, M., Rebêlo, H.: SYMDIFF: a language-agnostic semantic diff tool for imperative programs. In: Madhusudan, P., Seshia, S.A. (eds.) CAV 2012. LNCS, vol. 7358, pp. 712–717. Springer, Heidelberg (2012). https://doi.org/10.1007/978-3-642-31424-7_54

16. Lahiri, S.K., Sinha, R., Hawblitzel, C.: Automatic rootcausing for program equivalence failures in binaries. In: Kroening, D., Păsăreanu, C.S. (eds.) CAV 2015. LNCS, vol. 9206, pp. 362–379. Springer, Cham (2015). https://doi.org/10.1007/978-3-319-21690-4_21

17. Le, V., Afshari, M., Su, Z.: Compiler validation via equivalence modulo inputs. In: Proceedings of the 35th ACM SIGPLAN Conference on Programming Language Design and Implementation, PLDI 2014, pp. 216–226. ACM (2014)

18. Le, V., Sun, C., Su, Z.: Finding deep compiler bugs via guided stochastic program mutation. In: Proceedings of the 2015 ACM SIGPLAN International Conference on Object-Oriented Programming, Systems, Languages, and Applications, OOPSLA 2015, pp. 386–399. ACM (2015)

19. Lerner, S., Millstein, T., Chambers, C.: Automatically proving the correctness of compiler optimizations. In: Proceedings of the ACM SIGPLAN 2003 Conference on Programming Language Design and Implementation, PLDI 2003, pp. 220–231. ACM (2003)

20. Lerner, S., Millstein, T., Rice, E., Chambers, C.: Automated soundness proofs for dataflow analyses and transformations via local rules. In: Proceedings of the 32nd ACM SIGPLAN-SIGACT Symposium on Principles of Programming Languages, POPL 2005, pp. 364–377. ACM (2005)

21. Leroy, X.: Formal certification of a compiler back-end, or: programming a compiler with a proof assistant. In: 33rd ACM Symposium on Principles of Programming Languages, pp. 42–54. ACM Press (2006)

22. Leung, A., Bounov, D., Lerner, S.: C-to-verilog translation validation. In: Formal Methods and Models for Codesign (MEMOCODE), pp. 42–47 (2015)

23. Lopes, N.P., Menendez, D., Nagarakatte, S., Regehr, J.: Provably correct peephole optimizations with alive. In: Proceedings of the 36th ACM SIGPLAN Conference on Programming Language Design and Implementation, PLDI 2015, pp. 22–32. ACM (2015)

24. Lopes, N.P., Monteiro, J.: Automatic equivalence checking of programs with uninterpreted functions and integer arithmetic. Int. J. Softw. Tools Technol. Transf. 18(4), 359–374 (2016)

25. Massalin, H.: Superoptimizer: a look at the smallest program. In: Proceedings of the Second International Conference on Architectual Support for Programming Languages and Operating Systems, ASPLOS II, pp. 122–126. IEEE Computer Society Press (1987)

26. Necula, G.C.: Translation validation for an optimizing compiler. In: Proceedings of the ACM SIGPLAN 2000 Conference on Programming Language Design and Implementation, PLDI 2000, pp. 83–94. ACM (2000)

27. Phothilimthana, P.M., Thakur, A., Bodik, R., Dhurjati, D.: Scaling up superoptimization. In: Proceedings of the Twenty-First International Conference on Architectural Support for Programming Languages and Operating Systems, ASPLOS 2016, pp. 297–310. ACM (2016)

28. Pnueli, A., Siegel, M., Singerman, E.: Translation validation. In: Steffen, B. (ed.) TACAS 1998. LNCS, vol. 1384, pp. 151–166. Springer, Heidelberg (1998). https://doi.org/10.1007/BFb0054170

29. Poetzsch-Heffter, A., Gawkowski, M.: Towards proof generating compilers. Electron. Notes Theor. Comput. Sci. 132(1), 37–51 (2005)

30. Samet, H.: Proving the correctness of heuristically optimized code. Commun. ACM **21**(7), 570–582 (1978)
31. Schkufza, E., Sharma, R., Aiken, A.: Stochastic superoptimization. In: Proceedings of the Eighteenth International Conference on Architectural Support for Programming Languages and Operating Systems, ASPLOS 2013, pp. 305–316. ACM (2013)
32. Sharma, R., Schkufza, E., Churchill, B., Aiken, A.: Data-driven equivalence checking. In: Proceedings of the 2013 ACM SIGPLAN International Conference on Object Oriented Programming Systems Languages and Applications, OOPSLA 2013, pp. 391–406. ACM (2013)
33. Sharma, R., Schkufza, E., Churchill, B., Aiken, A.: Conditionally correct superoptimization. In: Proceedings of the 2015 ACM SIGPLAN International Conference on Object-Oriented Programming, Systems, Languages, and Applications, OOPSLA 2015, pp. 147–162. ACM (2015)
34. Stepp, M., Tate, R., Lerner, S.: Equality-based translation validator for LLVM. In: Gopalakrishnan, G., Qadeer, S. (eds.) CAV 2011. LNCS, vol. 6806, pp. 737–742. Springer, Heidelberg (2011). https://doi.org/10.1007/978-3-642-22110-1_59
35. Strichman, O., Godlin, B.: Regression verification - a practical way to verify programs. In: Meyer, B., Woodcock, J. (eds.) VSTTE 2005. LNCS, vol. 4171, pp. 496–501. Springer, Heidelberg (2008). https://doi.org/10.1007/978-3-540-69149-5_54
36. Tate, R., Stepp, M., Lerner, S.: Generating compiler optimizations from proofs. In: Proceedings of the 37th Annual ACM SIGPLAN-SIGACT Symposium on Principles of Programming Languages, POPL 2010, pp. 389–402. ACM (2010)
37. Tate, R., Stepp, M., Tatlock, Z., Lerner, S.: Equality saturation: a new approach to optimization. In: Proceedings of the 36th Annual ACM SIGPLAN-SIGACT symposium on Principles of Programming Languages, POPL 2009, pp. 264–276. ACM (2009)
38. Tristan, J.B., Govereau, P., Morrisett, G.: Evaluating value-graph translation validation for LLVM. In: Proceedings of the 32nd ACM SIGPLAN Conference on Programming Language Design and Implementation, PLDI 2011, pp. 295–305. ACM (2011)
39. Wang, X., Zeldovich, N., Kaashoek, M.F., Solar-Lezama, A.: Towards optimization-safe systems: analyzing the impact of undefined behavior. In: Proceedings of the Twenty-Fourth ACM Symposium on Operating Systems Principles, SOSP 2013 (2013)
40. Yang, X., Chen, Y., Eide, E., Regehr, J.: Finding and understanding bugs in C compilers. In: Proceedings of the 32nd ACM SIGPLAN Conference on Programming Language Design and Implementation, PLDI 2011, pp. 283–294. ACM (2011)
41. Zaks, A., Pnueli, A.: CoVaC: compiler validation by program analysis of the cross-product. In: Cuellar, J., Maibaum, T., Sere, K. (eds.) FM 2008. LNCS, vol. 5014, pp. 35–51. Springer, Heidelberg (2008). https://doi.org/10.1007/978-3-540-68237-0_5
42. Zhao, J., Nagarakatte, S., Martin, M.M., Zdancewic, S.: Formalizing the LLVM intermediate representation for verified program transformations. In: Proceedings of the 39th Annual ACM SIGPLAN-SIGACT Symposium on Principles of Programming Languages, POPL 2012, pp. 427–440. ACM (2012)
43. Zhao, J., Nagarakatte, S., Martin, M.M., Zdancewic, S.: Formal verification of SSA-based optimizations for LLVM. In: Proceedings of the 34th ACM SIGPLAN Conference on Programming Language Design and Implementation, PLDI 2013, pp. 175–186. ACM (2013)
44. Zuck, L., Pnueli, A., Fang, Y., Goldberg, B.: Voc: a methodology for the translation validation of optimizing compilers. J. Univ. Comput. Sci. **9**(3), 223–247 (2003)

Weakly Sensitive Analysis for Unbounded Iteration over JavaScript Objects

Yoonseok Ko[1](✉), Xavier Rival[2], and Sukyoung Ryu[1](✉)

[1] School of Computing, KAIST, Daejeon, South Korea
mir597@kaist.ac.kr , sryu@cs.kaist.ac.kr
[2] DIENS, École Normale Supérieure, CNRS, PSL Research University and INRIA,
Paris, France

Abstract. JavaScript framework libraries like jQuery are widely used, but complicate program analyses. Indeed, they encode clean high-level constructions such as class inheritance via dynamic object copies and transformations that are harder to reason about. One common pattern used in them consists of loops that copy or transform part or all of the fields of an object. Such loops are challenging to analyze precisely, due to weak updates and as unrolling techniques do not always apply. In this paper, we observe that precise field correspondence relations are required for client analyses (e.g., for call-graph construction), and propose abstractions of objects and program executions that allow to reason separately about the effect of distinct iterations without resorting to full unrolling. We formalize and implement an analysis based on this technique. We assess the performance and precision on the computation of call-graph information on examples from jQuery tutorials.

1 Introduction

As JavaScript became popular, JavaScript libraries such as jQuery were also widely adopted. Among others, these libraries implement high-level programming constructions like module systems or class inheritance. While framework libraries are prevalent and contribute to making programs modular and reusable, they also make it more difficult to statically compute semantic properties of JavaScript programs such as type information and call graphs. This is due to the conversion of static high-level constructions into JavaScript dynamic constructions like objects [8]. Abundant works have been carried out so as to compute static information for type checking [14], optimization [11], program understanding [10], and security auditing [20]. However, they are not yet able to analyze JavaScript framework libraries precisely due to the highly dynamic features.

One of the problematic dynamic features is the read/write access to object fields the names of which are computed at runtime. In JavaScript, an object has a set of fields, each of which consists of a name and a value pair, and the field lookup and update operations take the value of an expression as an index that designates the field to read or write. JavaScript framework libraries exploit

B.-Y.E. Chang (Ed.): APLAS 2017, LNCS 10695, pp. 148–168, 2017.
https://doi.org/10.1007/978-3-319-71237-6_8

this facility to build an object from another object by copying all fields one by one (shallow copy) or by computing fields defined by the source object (e.g., to simulate accessor methods). To reason over such *field copy or transformation* patterns (for short, FCT patterns), analysis tools need to resolve precisely the fields of objects, the relations among them, and how they encode the higher-level programming constructs. This is considerably harder than the resolution of classes in a direct Java-like implementation.

As an example, we consider the jQuery implementation of class-inheritance based on the field copies of the fields of an object, as shown in Fig. 1. To achieve that, the function fix copies the fields of oE designated as the elements of an array copy into an array e. This copy of the fields of object oE takes place in the loop at lines 3–7. More generally, an FCT pattern boils down to an assignment of the form o1[$f(v)$] = g(o2[v]), where v is a variable, o1 and o2 are two objects, f is a function over field names and g is a function over values. We call the variable v the *key variable* of the FCT pattern. In Fig. 1, the statements at lines 5 and 6 define an FCT pattern e[p] = oE[p] with the key variable p, where f and g both are the identity function.

```
1  function fix( e ) {
2      i = copy.length;
3      while ( i-- ) {
4          p = copy[ i ];
5          t = oE[ p ];
6          e[ p ] = t;
7      }  // oE.x ⋈ e.x, oE.y ⋈ e.y
8  }
9  var oE = {x: f1, y: f2}, o = {};
10 fix( o );
11 o.x();
```

Fig. 1. A simplified excerpt from jQuery 1.7.2 and an example use case

When fields that get copied store closures, the static resolution of function calls requires to identify precise field relations. This is the case of the call at line 11, in the code of Fig. 1. Therefore, the computation of a call-graph for this code requires a precise analysis of the effect of the FCT pattern at lines 5 and 6. Indeed, to determine the function called at line 11, we need to observe that the value of the field x in the object e is a copy of the value in the field x of the object oE. We note oE.x ⋈ e.x for this *field correspondence relation*. A basic points-to analysis that applies no sensitivity technique on the loop (such as loop unrolling) will fail to establish this field correspondence relation, hence will not allow to determine to compute call-graph. Indeed, it would consider that at line 11, o.x() may call not only f1 (that is actually called when executing the program), but also the spurious callee f2.

In this paper, we design a static analysis for the inference of precise field correspondence relations in programs that define FCT patterns. The inference of precise field correspondence relations is especially difficult when it takes place in loops (as in Fig. 1, line 3), due to the possibly unbounded number of replicated fields. This complicates significantly the analysis of meta-programming framework libraries like jQuery. To achieve this, we observe that, while some loops can be analyzed using existing sensitivity techniques, others require a more sophisticated abstraction of the structure of objects, which can describe field correspondence relations over unbounded collections of fields. A first application of our analysis is the static computation of precise call-graph information, but it would also apply to other analyses, that also require tracking values propagated in FCT patterns. We make the following contributions:

– in Sect. 2, we categorize loops that perform field copies and transformations to two sorts, and characterize the techniques adapted for each of them;
– in Sect. 3, we construct a new analysis to infer precise field correspondence relations for programs that perform field copies and transformations;
– in Sect. 4, we evaluate our analysis on micro-benchmarks and real code.

2   Background

In this section, we study the categories of loops that contain FCT patterns, and discuss to what extent existing techniques can cope with them. Based on this discussion, we emphasize the need for different semantic abstraction techniques, to deal with cases that cannot be handled well.

Categories of loops with FCT patterns. A very common static analysis technique for loops proceeds by full or partial unrolling. Thus, we seek for categories of loops containing FCT patterns into two groups, depending on whether loop unrolling will allow to resolve impacted fields precisely. For instance, let us consider a loop the body of which contains an FCT pattern $o1[f(v)] = g(o2[v])$. Then, field correspondence relations are parameterized by the value of the key variable v. Thus, to infer such relations precisely, we need a precise characterization of the range of values of v. When v is the loop index, and the number of iterations is fixed to a known number N, we can simply unroll the loop fully N times.

```
1  for (var v in o1) {
2      o2[v] = o1[v];
3  }
```

```
1  var i = arr.length;
2  while ( i-- ) {
3      v = arr[i];
4      o2[v] = o1[v];
5  }
```

(a)   (b)

Fig. 2. Examples of loops with FCT patterns

JavaScript features both `for-in` and `while` loops, and we need to consider both kinds. Figure 2(a) displays a full FCT pattern based on a `for-in` loop: all fields of o1 are copied into o2. Figure 2(b) shows a partial FCT pattern that is based on a **while** loop: the loop selects only fields that belong to **arr**. In both cases, to compute a precise field correspondence relation, we need to identify precisely the impacted fields and the relation between source and target objects.

When all iterations can be fully enumerated (e.g., by loop unrolling), it is possible to achieve this. In the case of the program in Fig. 2(a), this is the case when the names and values of the fields of the object o1 are known exactly from the pre-condition. We call such an instance a "concrete" **for-in** loop (which we abbreviate as CF). By contrast, when the set of fields is not known statically in the pre-condition, simple loop unrolling will not be sufficient to resolve fields precisely. We call such a case "abstract" **for-in** loop (or, for short, AF). The same distinction can be made for the **while** loop of Fig. 2(b): when the pre-condition guarantees a fixed and known set of elements for the array **arr**, unrolling can make the analysis fully precise, and we call this configuration a "concrete" general loop (CG); otherwise, we call it "abstract" (AG).

We now briefly discuss the consequences of the imprecision that can follow from AF and AG loops, where no loop unrolling technique will prevent the weak updates in the analysis of FCT patterns in the loop body. Essentially, relations between field names and field values will be lost, as values of the key variable v range over a set that is statically undetermined. To illustrate this, we consider the case of Fig. 2(b), and assume that the object o1 has two fields named x and y, respectively storing closures fx and fy as values. Due to weak updates, the analysis of the partial copy loop will produce spurious field correspondence relations such as (o1.x ⋈ o2.y). As a consequence, the control flow analysis of a subsequent statement o2.y() would produce a spurious call edge to fx. Thus, call-graph information would be much less precise.

Analysis applied of loops with FCT patterns. When a loop that contains an FCT pattern can be categorized as CG or CF, unrolling is possible, and will allow strong updates. Thus, the above imprecision is eliminated. This technique is used in the state-of-the-art JavaScript analyzers such as TAJS [1] and SAFE$_{LSA}$ [16]. Since many of the loops in simple JavaScript programs are categorized as CG or CF, the dynamic unrolling approach has been successful to infer precise field correspondence relations so far. On the other hand, these sensitivity and unrolling based techniques cannot cope precisely with AF and AG loops. We note that the categorization of a loop as CF or AF (resp., as CG or AG) depends on the pre-condition of the loop, thus the computation of a more precise pre-condition may allow to reduce the analysis of an "abstract" loop to that of a "concrete" one. However, this is not always feasible. In particular, when the set of inputs of a program is infinite, and causes the pre-condition to include states with objects that may have an unbounded number of fields, this is not doable.

In the rest of the paper, we devise a new abstraction that can handle more precisely FCT patterns to compute more accurate field correspondence relations. The key idea is to let the analysis of one iteration of a loop with an FCT pattern o1[$f(v)$] = g(o2[v]) describe a set of concrete iterations with the same value of the key variable. Since iteration orders do not matter for inferring the relations, one can abstract a set of non-consecutive iterations to an abstract iteration.

3 Composite Abstraction

We provide a high-level description of a composite abstraction to compute a precise over-approximation of field correspondence relations over FCT patterns.

3.1 Overview

We overview our approach with the analysis of an AG loop following the terminology of Sect. 2. We consider the program of Fig. 2(b) assuming that the array arr is unknown and that o1 has two fields with names x and y. This program carries out a partial copy of fields of o1 into object o2 depending on the contents of the array arr. Under this pre-condition, the loop is indeed AG, since the fields to be copied are not known statically. The variable v is key here, as it stores the value of the indices of the fields to consider.

Even though arr is unknown, the program may copy only the fields in o1: the field x is either absent from o1 or copied into o2, and the same for the field y (for short, we call the field designated by the name v "the field v" and use this terminology throughout the paper). Therefore, the field correspondence relation at the end of the execution of the loop may be any subset of $\{(\mathtt{o1.x} \bowtie \mathtt{o2.x}), (\mathtt{o1.y} \bowtie \mathtt{o2.y})\}$.

Abstraction. We first study the predicates that the analysis needs to manipulate, and the abstraction that they define. In general, we let *abstract addresses* used in the analysis be marked with a hat symbol, as in $\hat{a}$. Since the set of addresses that occur in a program execution is not known statically and is unbounded, the analysis needs to manipulate *summary* abstract addresses that may denote several concrete addresses. The analysis of a write into a summary address needs to account for the effect of a modification to any address it describes, thus it will result in a *weak update* [3]. On the other hand, a write into a *non-summary* address can be handled with a more precise *strong update*.

We need to tie to abstract addresses abstractions of sets of concrete objects that may not have exactly the same set of fields. Therefore, we let abstract objects collect *abstract fields* that may occur in the concrete objects they describe with an annotation that says whether the field must appear: "!" (resp., "?") designates a field that *must* (resp., *may*) exist. We also let abstract objects map fields that *must not* exist to undefined (or for short, $\hat{\odot}$).

In Fig. 3, the abstract states ⓐ, ⓑ, and ⓒ show invariants at each program point in the first iteration over the loop. The state ⓐ shows an initial abstract state, where o1, o2, and arr point to abstract objects at addresses $\hat{a}_1$, $\hat{a}_2$, and $\hat{a}_3$, respectively, which are non-summary abstract addresses. The object o1 has two abstract fields $\hat{x}$ and $\hat{y}$, and their values are $\hat{v}_1$ and $\hat{v}_2$. The field names $\hat{x}$ and $\hat{y}$ are non-summary abstract values which respectively denote the strings

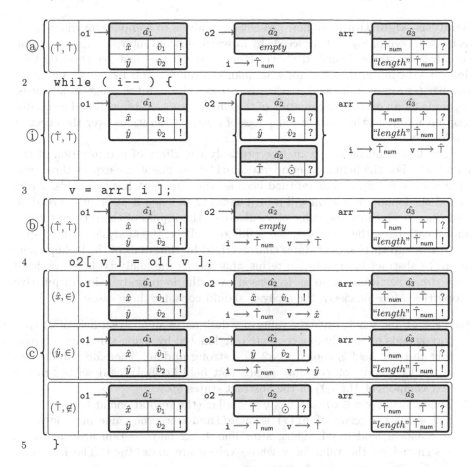

Fig. 3. Invariants for the program of Fig. 2(b): loop invariant at ⓘ and abstract states in the first iteration for all the other points.

"x" and "y", and the values $\hat{v}_1$ and $\hat{v}_2$ are the values of the variables v1 and v2. The fields of o1 are annotated with !, as we know that the fields of o1 is exactly $\{x, y\}$. The array arr has a definitely existing field "length" and its value is an unknown number. The other abstract field $(\hat{\top}_{\text{num}}, \hat{\top}, ?)$ expresses that the array has 0 or many elements, with unknown value. In the initial state, the object o2 is empty, and the value of i is an unknown number $\hat{\top}_{\text{num}}$.

The state ⓘ designates both the loop invariant and the post-condition of the program. We observe that the fields of o2 are annotated with a question mark, which means they may or may not appear. We note that it captures the intended field correspondence relations (o1.x ⋈ o2.x) and (o1.y ⋈ o2.y): if o2 has a field x, the value of that field is the same as o1.x (and the same for y).

Analysis Algorithm. We now present an analysis to compute invariants such as those shown in Fig. 3. It proceeds by forward abstract interpretation [4], using the abstract states described above. It starts with the abstract state ⓑ that describes the initial states: v stores an unknown value $\hat{\top}$ and i stores an unknown number (as arr is unknown). It then progresses through the program forwards, accounts for an over-approximation of the effect of each statement, and computes loop invariants as the limit of sequences of abstract iterations over the effect of the loop body.

The first challenge is to analyze precisely the effect of one iteration of the loop body. For the field lookup operation o1[v] at line 4, we expect three possible results: $\hat{v}_1$, $\hat{v}_2$, and undefined because the object o1 has two fields, $\hat{x}$ and $\hat{y}$, and the lookup operation will return undefined when it attempts to read an undefined field. Since the value of v subsumes the inputs of those three results, and in each case, the loop body has a different effect, the analysis needs to split the states into three sets of states characterized by the result of the lookup operation. In abstract interpretation terms, this means the analysis should perform some *trace partitioning*, so as to reason over the loop body using disjunctive properties. More precisely, the analysis should consider three cases:

1. If v ∈ o1 and v is $\hat{x}$, since the value of v designates an abstract field of o1 that corresponds to exactly *one* concrete cell denoted by a non-summary address, this abstract field is copied to o2 as a strong update. Therefore, at the end of the loop body, o2 contains an abstract field $(\hat{x}, \hat{v}_1, !)$, as described in the first component $\{(\hat{x}, \in)\}$ of the abstract states ⓒ.
2. The case where v ∈ o1 and v is $\hat{y}$ is similar (the second one at ⓒ).
3. If v ∉ o1, the result of o1[v] is undefined since the value of v does not designate a field in o1. Thus, after line 4, o2 may contain abstract fields designated by the value of v whose values are undefined. The last state $(\hat{\top}, \notin)$ of ⓒ corresponds to this case.

This partitioning operation turns one abstract state into a disjunction of several abstract states that cover the initial abstract state. In our implementation, this partitioning is carried out into two stages: first, the analysis discriminates executions depending on whether v is the name of a field of o1; second, when v is the name of a field of o1, the analysis produces a disjunction over the abstract fields of o1.

The second challenge is to compute precise approximations for unions of sets of states, as *abstract joins* (merging of partitions and control flow paths) and *widening* (union of abstract iterates to let the analysis of loops converge).

First, we observe that joining partitioned abstract states early would cause a precision loss, so that the analysis needs to delay their join. Indeed, let us assume that the analysis joins the results that correspond to the three sets of states at the end of the loop body at line 5. Then, the resulting abstract object would become the one in Fig. 4, and the third field $(\hat{\top}, \{\hat{v}_1, \hat{v}_2, \hat{\circ}\}, ?)$ means that the value of any field in the object is either $\hat{v}_1$, $\hat{v}_2$, or $\hat{\circ}$; this abstraction fails to capture the precise field correspondence relation. Thus, instead of joining all the analysis results at the end of the loop body, our analysis maintains two abstract objects for the object pointed by o2 as described in ⓘ.

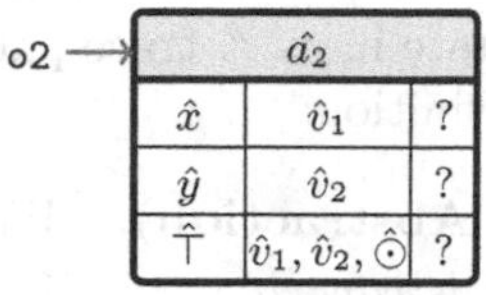

Fig. 4. The join of all the results at the end of the loop body in Fig. 3.

However, in order to avoid overly large sets of disjuncts caused by delayed joins, the analysis also requires an efficient join algorithm, able to merge abstract states that are similar enough so that the imprecision shown in Fig. 4 can be avoided. To do this, we rely on a join condition that states when abstract objects are "close enough" to be joined without a significant precision loss. Essentially, our analysis does not join objects with possibly overlapping abstract fields, the values of which are not similar. For example, at ©, the abstract objects o2 $(\hat{x}, \in)$ and $(\hat{y}, \in)$ satisfy the join condition and are joined. On the contrary, at the same point, the abstract object $(\hat{\top}, \notin)$ is not joined with any other.

To ensure the convergence of abstract iterates, a widening operation over abstract objects is necessary. The widening algorithm is based on a similar principle as the join algorithm, but instead of merging two abstract objects, the analysis applies widening to them. Since the widening algorithm also relies on a join condition, it also does not lose the field correspondence relation. For example, at the loop head after the second iteration, the analysis applies widening to the state from the first iteration ⓐ and the state from the second iteration ⓘ. The widening finds two matchings for o2 in ⓐ and ⓘ: the empty object in ⓐ with each of the objects in ⓘ. Because each field does not need widening, the result of widening for those two matchings are the same as the one in o2 in ⓘ.

In the rest of the section, we formalize our composite abstraction to reason over FCT patterns and to infer precise field correspondence relations. It consists of two layers. The partitioning abstraction (Sect. 3.2) allows case splits, and the object abstraction (Sect. 3.3) describes accurate properties over fields, so as to disambiguate the field correspondence relations even after abstract joins.

3.2 Trace Partitioning Abstraction

A partitioning abstraction splits a set of traces based on a specific trace abstraction so as to reason more accurately on smaller sets of executions. We first set up a general partitioning framework, then define two instances with two trace abstractions that provide the two stages of partitioning we used in Sect. 3.1.

First, we fix a few notations. A concrete *program state* $s \in \mathbb{S}$ is a pair made of a *control state* (program counter at a given time) $c \in \mathbb{C}$ and a *memory state*

$m \in \mathbb{M}$, thus $\mathbb{S} = \mathbb{C} \times \mathbb{M}$. We write $c \approx c'$ to denote that the syntactic program points of two control states c and c' are the same. A trace σ is a finite sequence $\langle s_0, ..., s_n \rangle$ where $s_0, ..., s_n \in \mathbb{S}$. We write $\mathbb{S}^\star$ for the set of traces, and let our concrete domain be $(\mathbb{D}, \sqsubseteq) = (\mathcal{P}(\mathbb{S}^\star), \subseteq)$. Also, if σ is a trace, we write $\sigma_{\downarrow M}$ for the memory state of the last state in σ. A trace partitioning abstraction will be an instance of the following definition:

Definition 1 (Partitioning Abstraction). *We let $\mathbb{D}_T^\sharp$ and $\gamma_T : \mathbb{D}_T^\sharp \to \mathbb{D}$ define a trace abstraction that is covering (i.e., $\mathbb{D} = \cup \{\gamma_T(t^\sharp) \mid t^\sharp \in \mathbb{D}_T^\sharp\}$) and we assume that $\mathbb{D}_M^\sharp$ and $\gamma_M : \mathbb{D}_M^\sharp \to \mathcal{P}(\mathbb{M})$ defines a store abstraction. Then, the partitioning abstraction parameterized by these two abstractions is defined by the domain $\mathbb{D}^\sharp = \mathbb{D}_T^\sharp \to \mathbb{D}_M^\sharp$ and the concretization function γ defined by:*

$$\gamma : \mathbb{D}^\sharp \longrightarrow \mathbb{D}$$
$$\hat{X} \longmapsto \{\sigma \in \mathbb{S}^\star \mid \forall t^\sharp \in \mathbb{D}_T^\sharp, \ \sigma \in \gamma_T(t^\sharp) \Rightarrow \sigma_{\downarrow M} \in \gamma_M(\hat{X}(t^\sharp))\}.$$

Trace abstraction by field existence. The first instance of partitioning abstraction that we need abstracts traces depending on the existence or absence of a field in an object. It is based on the following trace abstraction:

Definition 2 (Abstract Trace by Field Existence). *The trace abstraction $\mathbb{D}_{fe}^\sharp$ is defined by the following abstract elements and abstraction relations:*

- *a quadruple $(c, \mathbf{x}, \mathbf{y}, p)$, where $c \in \mathbb{C}$, $\mathbf{x}$ is a variable, $\mathbf{y}$ is a variable (pointing to an object) and $p \in \{\in, \notin\}$, denotes all the traces that went through the control state c with a memory state such that the membership of the field the name of which is the value of $\mathbf{x}$ in the object $\mathbf{y}$ is characterized by p;*
- *$\hat{\top}$ abstracts any trace.*

For example, an abstract trace $(c, \mathbf{x}, \mathbf{y}, \in)$ denotes a set of traces such that an object $\mathbf{y}$ has a field designated by the value of the variable $\mathbf{x}$ at a given control state c. The first two states $(\hat{x}, \in)$ and $(\hat{y}, \in)$ of ⓒ in Fig. 3 are the states partitioned by the abstract trace $(c, \mathbf{v}, \mathbf{o1}, \in)$.

Trace abstraction by variable value. The second instance of partitioning abstraction required by our analysis discriminates traces based on the value of a variable at a specific control point, and is parameterized by a value abstraction $\mathbb{V}_{val}^\sharp$:

Definition 3 (Abstract Trace by Variable Value). *The trace abstraction $\mathbb{D}_{vv}^\sharp$ is defined by the following abstract element and abstraction relations:*

- *a triple $(c, \mathbf{x}, \hat{v})$, where $c \in \mathbb{C}$, $\mathbf{x}$ is a program variable, and $\hat{v}$ is an abstract value $\hat{v} \in \mathbb{V}_{val}^\sharp$, describes the traces that visited c with a memory state such that the value of $\mathbf{x}$ can be described by $\hat{v}$;*
- *$\hat{\top}$ abstracts any trace.*

In Fig. 3, the abstract state $(\hat{x}, \in)$ at ⓒ denotes the partitioned states by the abstract trace $(c, \mathbf{v}, \hat{x})$.

Combination of trace abstractions. Trace abstractions can be combined into a reduced product abstraction, which defines the two-stage partitioning abstraction discussed in Sect. 3.1:

Definition 4 (Combination of Abstract Traces). *An abstract trace characterized by a combination of two abstract traces is a reduced product [5] of their trace abstractions.*

Our analysis uses product $\mathbb{D}_T^\sharp \stackrel{\mathrm{def}}{=} \mathbb{D}_{\mathrm{fe}}^\sharp \times \mathbb{D}_{\mathrm{vv}}^\sharp$. For example, the three states at point ⓒ in Fig. 3 correspond to the partitions defined by $((c, \mathsf{v}, \mathsf{o1}, \in), (c, \mathsf{v}, \hat{x}))$, $((c, \mathsf{v}, \mathsf{o1}, \in), (c, \mathsf{v}, \hat{y}))$, and $((c, \mathsf{v}, \mathsf{o1}, \notin), (c, \mathsf{v}, \hat{\top}))$.

$$
\begin{aligned}
\gamma_{\mathbb{O}^\sharp} : \quad & \mathbb{O}^\sharp \longrightarrow \mathcal{P}(\mathbb{O}) \\
& l \longmapsto \{o \in \mathbb{O} \mid o \in \gamma_l(l) \wedge \mathsf{Dom}(o) \subseteq \mathsf{Dom}_l^\sharp(\mathsf{l})\} \\[4pt]
\gamma_l : \quad & p \longmapsto \gamma_p(p) \\
& l_0 \wedge l_1 \longmapsto \gamma_l(l_0) \cap \gamma_l(l_1) \\
& l_0 \vee l_1 \longmapsto \gamma_l(l_0) \cup \gamma_l(l_1) \\[4pt]
\gamma_p : \quad & \epsilon \longmapsto \mathbb{O} \\
& (\hat{s} \mapsto !, \hat{v}) \longmapsto \{o \in \mathbb{O} \mid \forall s \in \gamma_{\mathrm{str}}(\hat{s}),\ o(s) \in \gamma_{\mathrm{val}}(\hat{v})\} \\
& (\hat{s} \mapsto ?, \hat{v}) \longmapsto \{o \in \mathbb{O} \mid \forall s \in \gamma_{\mathrm{str}}(\hat{s}),\ s \in \mathsf{Dom}(o) \Rightarrow o(s) \in \gamma_{\mathrm{val}}(\hat{v})\} \\[4pt]
\mathsf{Dom}_l^\sharp : \quad & p \longmapsto \mathsf{Dom}_p^\sharp(p) \qquad\qquad\qquad\quad \mathsf{Dom}_p^\sharp : \qquad \epsilon \longmapsto \emptyset \\
& l_0 \wedge l_1 \longmapsto \mathsf{Dom}_l^\sharp(l_0) \cup \mathsf{Dom}_l^\sharp(l_1) \qquad\quad (\hat{s} \mapsto E, \hat{v}) \longmapsto \gamma_{\mathrm{str}}(\hat{s}) \\
& l_0 \vee l_1 \longmapsto \mathsf{Dom}_l^\sharp(l_0) \cup \mathsf{Dom}_l^\sharp(l_1)
\end{aligned}
$$

Fig. 5. Concretization of abstract objects

3.3 Object Abstraction

The object abstraction forms the second layer of our composite abstraction, and describes the fields of JavaScript objects. A JavaScript object consists of a (non-fixed) set of mutable fields, and the main operations on the objects are field lookup, field update, and field deletion. A concrete object is a map $o \in \mathbb{O} = \mathbb{V}_{\mathrm{str}} \to_{\mathrm{fin}} \mathbb{V}_{\mathrm{val}}$, where $\mathbb{V}_{\mathrm{str}}$ stands for the set of string values and $\mathbb{V}_{\mathrm{val}}$ stands for the set of values. We write $\mathsf{Dom}(o)$ for the set of fields of an object o.

To accurately handle absent fields, our object abstraction can track cases where a field is definitely absent. Similarly, to handle lookup of definitely existing fields precisely, the object abstraction annotates such fields with the predicate "!". Fields that may or may not exist are annotated with the predicate "?": the lookup of such fields may return a value or the value **undefined**. In the following, we assume an abstraction for values defined by the domain $\mathbb{V}_{\mathrm{val}}^\sharp$ and the concretization function $\gamma_{\mathrm{val}} : \mathbb{V}_{\mathrm{val}}^\sharp \to \mathcal{P}(\mathbb{V}_{\mathrm{val}})$, and an abstraction for string values defined by the finite height domain $\mathbb{V}_{\mathrm{str}}^\sharp$ and the concretization function $\gamma_{\mathrm{str}} : \mathbb{V}_{\mathrm{str}}^\sharp \to \mathcal{P}(\mathbb{V}_{\mathrm{str}})$.

Definition 5 (Abstract Object). *An* abstract object $\hat{o} \in \mathbb{O}^\sharp$ *is a logical formula described by the following grammar:*

$$\hat{o} ::= l \qquad\qquad l ::= p \mid l \wedge l \mid l \vee l \qquad \hat{s} \in \mathbb{V}^\sharp_{str}$$
$$p ::= \epsilon \mid (\hat{s} \mapsto E, \hat{v}) \qquad E ::= ! \mid ? \qquad\qquad \hat{v} \in \mathbb{V}^\sharp_{val}$$

The concretization of $\gamma_{\mathbb{O}^\sharp}(\hat{o})$ of an abstract object $\hat{o}$ is defined in Fig. 5.

An abstract field p is either ϵ, which represents an object with unknown fields, or $(\hat{s} \mapsto E, \hat{v})$, which represents any object such that the membership of fields the names of which are represented by $\hat{s}$ is described by E and the values of the corresponding fields (if any) by $\hat{v}$. Note that E may be ! (must exist) or ? (may exist). A logical formula l describes a set of objects, either as an abstract field p, or as a union or intersection of sets of objects. A conjunction of abstract fields represents a set of concrete open objects. A disjunction $l_0 \vee l_1$ represents two abstract objects l_0 and l_1 as for the object o2 in the abstract state at point ① in Fig. 3. Because the objects represented by an abstract field p may have an unbounded number of fields, the concretization of abstract objects $\gamma_{\mathbb{O}^\sharp}$ bounds the set of fields with $\mathsf{Dom}(o) \subseteq \mathsf{Dom}^\sharp_l(l)$. The auxiliary function $\mathsf{Dom}^\sharp_l(l)$ represents a set of fields that are defined in a given logical formula l, which denotes that a field is definitely absent if the field is not defined in l. For example, the concretization of an abstract field $\gamma_p(\hat{x} \mapsto !, \hat{v})$ represents a set of objects, where the values of the fields designated by the abstract string $\hat{x}$ are represented by the abstract value $\hat{v}$ and the other fields are unknown, whereas the abstract object concretization $\gamma_{\mathbb{O}^\sharp}(\hat{x} \mapsto !, \hat{v})$ represents a set of objects all fields of which are abstracted by $\hat{x}$ (i.e., any field not described by $\hat{v}$ is absent). The conjunction and disjunction are conventional.

Then, the object box notation used in Fig. 3 is interpreted as follows:

$\hat{x}$	$\hat{v}_1$	?
$\hat{y}$	$\hat{v}_2$	?

$\hat{\top}$	$\hat{\odot}$	?

is equivalent to

$$\begin{array}{c}((\hat{x} \mapsto ?, \hat{v}_1) \wedge (\hat{y} \mapsto ?, \hat{v}_2)) \\ \vee \\ (\hat{\top} \mapsto ?, \hat{\odot}).\end{array}$$

3.4 Analysis Algorithms

We now study the analysis algorithms to infer invariants such as those shown in Fig. 3. These rely on the trace partitioning abstraction defined in Sect. 3.2 and on the object abstraction defined in Sect. 3.3. We focus on the introduction of partitions and on the join algorithm to achieve precise analysis of the FCT patterns.

Partitioning Algorithm. As we have shown in Sect. 3.1, the analysis needs to create partitions dynamically. We first discuss the analysis of loops classified as AF, and consider the case of AG loops afterwards.

For-in loops. We desugar the `for-in` loop in Fig. 2(a) with high-level `iterInit`, `iterHasNext`, `iterNext`, and `merge` instructions as shown in Fig. 6(a). The semantics of the `for-in` statement is as follows: it iterates over the fields of a given object `o1`, and lets the index variable `v` range over their names. To mimic this behavior, the instruction `v = iterInit(o1)` generates the list of the fields of the object `o1`; `iterHasNext(t)` checks whether there exists a field that has not been visited yet, and `iterNext(o1, t)` returns the next field to visit. Since the order a `for-in` loop uses to visit fields is undefined in the language semantics [9], we simply assume a non-deterministic order of fields. We add the `merge(v)` pseudo-instruction at the end of each loop to denote the end of the FCT pattern with the key variable `v`. In order to reason over distinct fields separately, the analysis performs dynamic partitioning during the analysis of the `v = iterNext(o1, t)` instruction, and generates partitions for each possible field name. Because the analysis needs to analyze field names in each partition precisely so that it can analyze the field lookup instruction at line 4 precisely, it collects a set of field names in the given object `o1`, and generates partitions for each field name in the set. In Fig. 7(a), we illustrate such a case. At the end of the loop body, the partitions are merged by the `merge` instruction as shown in Fig. 7(c).

```
var v, t = iterInit(o1);          var i = arr.length;
while (iterHasNext(t)) {          while ( i-- ) {
    v = iterNext(o1, t);              v = arr[i];
    o2[v] = o1[v];                    o2[v] = o1[v];
    merge(v);                         merge(v);
}                                 }
          (a)                               (b)
```

Fig. 6. Desugared version of `for-in` and `while` loops shown in Fig. 2.

General loops. We first perform a simple syntactic pre-analysis, which finds variables that are used as index variables in field lookup and update instructions in the loop body, in order to identify key variables of the FCT pattern. The pre-analysis adds the `merge(x)` instruction at the end of the loop when it identifies `x` as the key variable of an FCT pattern. We consider the `while` loop in Fig. 2(b), and we show the result of the pre-analysis in Fig. 6(b). In this instance, `v` is identified as a key variable as it appears for both a field lookup and a field update in the loop body. On the contrary, the variable `i` is not a key variable because it is only used for field lookup.

Based on the result of this pre-analysis, the analysis creates partitions when it encounters a field lookup indexed by a key variable. It essentially creates one partition per possible (defined or undefined) abstract value produced as the result of the lookup operation. For example, Fig. 7(b) shows that for such cases when the field lookup may return either the field $\{(\hat{q}, \hat{v}_1)\}$ or the field $\{(\hat{w}, \hat{v}_2)\}$,

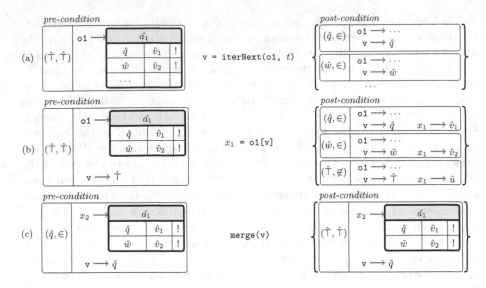

Fig. 7. Example cases for (a) the `iterNext` instruction, (b) the field lookup instruction with the key variable v, and (c) the `merge` instruction by the key variable v with the first post-state of both of (a) and (b).

or the **undefined** value $\{\hat{\odot}\}$ (if the field is absent in the object). The variable x_1 is temporarily created to hold the result of the lookup. Each generated partition corresponds to a field correspondence relation. Similarly for the **for-in** loop case, the partitions are merged at the end of the loop body.

Soundness of partitioning algorithm. The partitioning algorithm is sound since (1) the generated partitions for the `iterNext` instruction subsumes all possible iterations in a given **for-in** loop, and (2) the abstract lookup operation returns a disjunction of cases that subsume the result of the concrete lookup operation.

Join and Widening Algorithms. We now discuss the join and widening that allow to merge abstract partitions at `merge` pseudo instructions and to analyze loops. For instance, in Fig. 3, the analysis computes the object o2 at point ⓘ by joining the three objects o2 of ⓒ.

To simplify the algorithms, we make sure that each abstract object is in "disjunctive normal form", which means that its logical formula is a disjunction of "conjunctive abstract objects" that consist of a conjunction of abstract fields or of the empty abstract field ϵ. The join algorithm takes two abstract objects in this form and computes an over-approximation of all the concrete objects they represent. For two such abstract objects o0 and o1, the join algorithm searches for a matching of the conjunctive abstract objects in o0 and o1, that can be merged without too significant a precision loss, as characterized by a *join condition* that we discuss below. When c0 and c1 satisfy this condition and can be joined, they are replaced with a new conjunctive abstract object, where each abstract field approximates abstract fields of c0 and c1.

We now make this join condition used to decide which conjunctive objects to join. Let us consider the join of a pair of abstract fields. When the name of one of these fields subsumes the name of the other but is not equal to it, their names and values are merged and the result fails to capture an optimal field correspondence relation. For example, the result of joining two abstract fields $(\hat{x}, !, \hat{v}_1)$ and $(\hat{\top}, ?, \hat{v}_2)$ is $(\hat{\top}, ?, \{\hat{v}_1, \hat{v}_2\})$ because the name $\hat{\top}$ subsumes the name of the other field $\hat{x}$. Thus, we avoid joining abstract objects containing such pairs of abstract fields as characterized by the definition below:

Definition 6 (Join Condition). *Two sets of abstract fields $\hat{P}_1$ and $\hat{P}_2$ are correlated if and only if $\forall \hat{s}_1 \in N(\hat{P}_1)$, $\forall \hat{s}_2 \in N(\hat{P}_2)$, $\gamma_{\mathrm{str}}(\hat{s}_1) \cap \gamma_{\mathrm{str}}(\hat{s}_2) \neq \emptyset$ where $N(\hat{P})$ (resp., $V(\hat{P})$) denotes the names (resp., values) of the fields in $\hat{P}$.*

Two abstract objects $\hat{o}_1$ and $\hat{o}_2$ satisfy the join condition if and only if, for all the correlated abstract fields $\hat{P}_1$ and $\hat{P}_2$ in $\hat{o}_1$ and $\hat{o}_2$, one of the following conditions holds:

- *$\hat{N}_1 = \hat{N}_2$*
- *$\hat{N}_1 \subseteq \hat{N}_2 \wedge \hat{V}_1 \sqsubseteq \hat{V}_2$, or, symmetrically $\hat{N}_2 \subseteq \hat{N}_1 \wedge \hat{V}_2 \sqsubseteq \hat{V}_1$*
- *$\hat{N}_1 \cap \hat{N}_2 \neq \emptyset \wedge \hat{V}_1 = \hat{V}_2$*

where $\hat{N}_1 = \{\gamma_{\mathrm{str}}(\hat{s}) \mid \hat{s} \in N(\hat{P}_1)\}$, $\hat{N}_2 = \{\gamma_{\mathrm{str}}(\hat{s}) \mid \hat{s} \in N(\hat{P}_2)\}$, $\hat{V}_1 = \cup V(\hat{P}_1)$, and $\hat{V}_2 = \cup V(\hat{P}_2)$.

For example, the object o2 in the third disjunct at Ⓒ does not satisfy the join condition with the object o2 in either of the other two disjuncts at that point. On the other hand, the abstract objects corresponding to o2 in the first two disjuncts at Ⓒ satisfy this condition, and will be joined together.

Join soundness. The abstract join algorithm is sound. It returns a conservative over-approximation of its inputs when the join condition holds; otherwise, it returns their disjunction, the result of which also over-approximates them.

Widening and termination. The analysis of a loop proceeds by computation of a sequence of abstract iterates. To ensure its convergence, we use a widening operator [4], that is, an operator that computes an over-approximation of union and ensures termination. Since the height of the baseline string abstraction is finite, the second join condition ($\hat{N}_1 \subseteq \hat{N}_2$ or $\hat{N}_2 \subseteq \hat{N}_1$) can be satisfied for at most finitely many iterations. This entails that any sequence of abstract joins is ultimately stationary, which ensures the termination of the analysis of loops.

Analysis Termination and Soundness. The analysis terminates and computes a sound over-approximation for the set of concrete program behaviors. Thus, it computes a conservative approximation of the call-graph of an input program.

4   Evaluation

This section seeks for an experimental validation that the composite abstraction is necessary and useful for the computation of precise call-graph information.

Analysis implementation and experimentation settings. We implemented the analyzer CompAbs, based on our new composite abstraction. CompAbs was built on top of the open-source JavaScript analysis framework SAFE [15]. CompAbs is fully context sensitive except for recursive calls, which are unrolled at most j times, where j is a parameter of the analysis. Dynamic unrolling of loops is also bounded by a parameter k. Moreover, CompAbs abstracts strings based on creation-site, and on a reduced product of a string constant domain and a prefix string domain. We used different parameters for different experiments. We performed all the experiments on a Linux machine with 4.0 GHz Intel Core i7-6700K CPU and 32 GB Memory.

Analysis of micro benchmarks with different loop patterns. The goal of this experiment is to observe the current status of the state-of-the-art JavaScript static analyzers TAJS and SAFE$_{LSA}$ for each category of loops introduced in Sect. 2.

We ran TAJS, SAFE$_{LSA}$, and CompAbs on a number of small diagnostic benchmarks, each of which consists of a loop containing an FCT pattern. We manually wrote the test cases to assess whether an analysis can precisely infer a field correspondence relation or not for each category of loops. The benchmarks do not use DOM-related features. They are set up so that each loop is being classified in the same category in all of three analyzers TAJS, SAFE$_{LSA}$, and CompAbs. At the end of each loop, we attempt to verify the precise field correspondence relation by equality check between fields (o.x $\neq$ o.y). Since we compare the analysis result on small benchmarks, CompAbs used $j = 0$ and $k = 0$ as parameters, which leads to merging all recursive calls and no dynamic unrolling.

The inset table summarizes the result of the micro benchmarks whether each analyzer can precisely infer the field correspondence relation or not. The first column shows the FCT pattern category of each single loop program. The remaining

Subject	TAJS	SAFE$_{LSA}$	CompAbs
CF	✓	✓	✓
CG	✓	✓	✓
AF	✗	✗	✓
AG	✗	✗	✓

columns report whether each analysis successfully infers the precise field correspondence relation or not. TAJS and SAFE$_{LSA}$ fail to infer precise field correspondence relations in the case of "abstract" loops (AF or AG), which is consistent with our observation that such loops cannot be addressed by using only the unrolling techniques implemented in these tools.

This confirms that the existing analyzers fail to infer precise field correspondence relations for loops with an FCT pattern, which are classified as "abstract".

Analysis of jQuery tutorials. The goal of this experiment is to compare our approach with the existing analyzers using jQuery tutorial benchmarks. We measured the number of programs that have "abstract" loops to assess the necessity of our approach. We also measured the number of programs that can be analyzed in a given time limit to assess the scalability, and measured the number of spurious call edges in the result to assess the precision. To evaluate the analysis of FCT patterns in framework libraries, we use the jQuery benchmarks from the experiments of TAJS [1]. They used 71 programs chosen from the jQuery tutorial[1] that performs simple operations using jQuery 1.10.0. In order to minimize the effects of DOM modeling on the analysis results, our experiments use jQuery 1.4.4 that supports all the features required for the benchmarks while using fewer DOM-related features than jQuery 1.10.0. We faithfully implemented DOM models based on a Chrome browser to support the semantics of DOM-related code in our benchmarks. We do not abstract the DOM tree in the initial state, and abstract a set of dynamically generated DOM elements to an abstract DOM element depending on its allocation site. The programs are about 7430 lines of code including jQuery.

First, to investigate the necessity of our work, we measured how many programs have "abstract" loops during analysis. In order to compute a precise precondition to reduce the analysis of an "abstract" loop to that of a "concrete" one, CompAbs used $j = 2$ and $k = 30$ as parameters, which leads to unrolling recursive calls twice and bounding dynamic unrolling depth to 30 (when it can be applied). We chose the parameters by experiments. Among 71 benchmarks, we observed that 27 programs have at least one abstract loop. Thus, about 38% of the benchmarks need to handle abstract loops, which may require our technique.

Table 1. Scalability and precision for call graphs compared to existing analyzers.

	Success	SE	SC	Cov (%)
CompAbs	68/71	0.03	14.9	99.8
TAJS	2/71	6.00	132.8	77.3
SAFE$_{LSA}$	0/71	45.96	51.1	81.7

Second, to compare the analysis scalability, we measured the number of programs the analysis of which terminates in less than 4 h by CompAbs, TAJS, and SAFE$_{LSA}$. The second column in Table 1 summarizes the scalability measurements; out of 71 benchmarks, CompAbs finished analysis of 68 programs among these within 4 h; TAJS finished analysis of 2 programs among these; and SAFE$_{LSA}$ did not finish analysis of any of these 71 programs. CompAbs finished analysis of each of 64 programs within 6 min, and it took 27 s on average (minimum, median, and maximum are 5, 9, and 315 s, respectively) for each program. Among the 7 other programs, CompAbs analyzed each of 4 programs within 4 h, and analyzed each of the rest of 3 programs within 2.1 days. Our manual investigation revealed that two reasons caused the analysis performance overhead: (1) a large number of recursive call cycles, and (2) long call chains. The large number of recursive

---

[1] http://www.jquery-tutorial.net/.

call cycles is a common problem in static analysis, and the techniques to mitigate the complexity are beyond the scope of this paper. Also, since CompAbs is fully context sensitive, longer call chains make the analysis take more time. On the other hand, TAJS finished analysis of 2 programs within 7 min. However TAJS did not complete the analysis of any of the 69 other programs within 4 h. SAFE$_{LSA}$ did not finish analysis of any of these 71 programs within 4 h.

At last, to assess the analysis precision, we measured the number of spurious call edges in analysis results. We identify spurious call edges in the analysis result of a program by using dynamic call graphs constructed by real execution of the instrumented program in a Chrome browser. Since the benchmarks are simple and we ran them several times trying to cover all the possible execution flows, we assume that the dynamic call graphs contain a complete set of call edges. Then, in the analysis results, if a call site has more than one call edge that do not appear in the dynamic call graphs, we consider them spurious call edges.

We found spurious call edges from eight subjects (39, 40, 44, 47, 50, 53, 69, and 71) out of 71. We manually investigated them, and observed that dynamic call graphs for five subjects (40, 44, 50, 53, 71) were incomplete because Chrome browser had an HTML parsing problem. We confirmed that the spurious call edges from the five subjects disappeared after we revised the HTML documents to bypass the parsing problem. We found that each of the remaining 3 subjects had one callsite with spurious call edges, all of which are due to imprecise DOM modeling or infeasible execution flows. Because our DOM modeling does not consider the precise semantics of browser layout engines, the analysis cannot precisely analyze several DOM-related functions such as querySelectorAll or getComputedStyle. Imprecise analysis results of such function calls affect the analysis results of execution flows, which may cause spurious call edges.

The third to the fifth columns of Table 1 summarize the precision measurements of 71 benchmarks; SE denotes the number of spurious call edges on average, and SC denotes the number of spurious call sites on average; Cov denotes the coverage ratio of actual call sites. Since we measured the number of spurious call edges from an incomplete analysis result when an analyzer does not finish analyzing a program in 4 h, the average coverage ratio is not 100%, and the actual number of spurious call edges may be larger than the one in the table. We use the revised HTML documents to bypass the browser parsing problem.

CompAbs outperforms TAJS and SAFE$_{LSA}$ in analysis time and precision. TAJS and SAFE$_{LSA}$ lose their precision and scalability when they analyze "abstract" loops. TAJS used a modified jQuery library by manually removing abstract field names that can cause "abstract" loops in their evaluation [1]. Since we do not use the modification in our benchmarks, the scalability of TAJS got worse than what they presented in their evaluation. Since the approach of SAFE$_{LSA}$ to handle loops is similar to TAJS, SAFE$_{LSA}$ has the same issue.

We also checked the soundness of CompAbs using dynamic call graphs. We confirmed that static call graphs of 70 out of 71 programs subsumed their corresponding dynamic call graphs. Because the subject (4) used eval that constructs code dynamically, static call graphs could not cover dynamically constructed call edges, for which CompAbs reports possible unsoundness warnings.

Comparison with an unsound approach. The goal of this experiment is to compare the results of a sound approach and an unsound one. We first evaluate CompAbs, which computes over-approximation of call graphs, and the practical unsound JavaScript call graph analyzer [10] by two metrics: the scalability and precision. We write ACG to denote the practical unsound call graph analyzer[2]. The experiment also uses the 71 jQuery benchmarks.

Table 2. Scalability and precision for call graphs compared to dynamic call graphs.

	Time			SE	SC	Prec (%)	Cov (%)
	Avg	Med	Max				
CompAbs	5687 s	10 s	2.1 days	0.03	14.9	99.995	99.97
ACG	<1 s	<1 s	<1 s	85.37	1061.5	65.148	84.39

Table 2 summarizes the scalability and precision. The second to the forth columns show the average, the median, and the worst case analysis time, respectively. The remaining columns show the analysis precision; SE, SC, and Cov are as in Table 1, and Prec denotes the percentage of "true" call edges among all call edges, which is computed as $\frac{|D \cap S|}{|S|}$ where D is the set of call edges of a given call site in the dynamic call graph and S is the set of call edges determined by the analysis.

The analysis time of ACG is dramatically faster than CompAbs because it does not consider dynamic field lookup and update instructions, does not keep more than one abstract object, and does not reason about any non-functional values. On the other hand, since ACG does not compute over-approximation, the analysis cannot capture 15.61% of actual call-sites. In addition, while CompAbs identifies exactly what is missing in the branch coverage, ACG does not show what is missing, which is unsound. CompAbs computes more precise call graphs than that of ACG. Since CompAbs precisely tracks the program flows, it produces fewer spurious call sites and fewer spurious call edges.

Thus, ACG is more appropriate than CompAbs in supporting tools such as the "Jump to Declaration" feature in Integrated Development Environment (IDE). Since ACG does not require the full source code of a target program to analyze, it is applicable to incomplete source code which is under development. In the case of IDE usage, the increased scalability can compensate the low precision of the analysis and the unsoundness. While CompAbs supports call edges only in reachable code, ACG also supports call edges in dead code. In this case, the low precision of the number of spurious call sites is rather an advantage.

---

[2] https://github.com/xiemaisi/acg.js

On the other hand, CompAbs is more appropriate than ACG in verifying semantic properties of JavaScript programs such as private information leakage. Since a verification tool requires zero false negatives, formalizing the analysis as abstract interpretation to compute over-approximations of program behaviors as in CompAbs is appropriate in this purpose. Also, the high-precision of CompAbs will be useful in reducing the number of false alarms in a verification tool. Verification tools do not need to provide instant feedback to developers, and we believe that the importance of verification compensates analysis time overhead.

5   Related Work

SAFE [15] is an analysis framework for JavaScript web applications, which supports DOM modeling [17] and web API misuse detection [2], among others. It is based on abstract interpretation, and supports various analysis sensitivities including k-CFA, parameter sensitivity, object sensitivity, and loop-sensitive analysis (LSA) [16]. While its aggressively unrolling LSA works well for programs using simple loops with bounded iterations, we showed that it does not scale for complex loops with unbounded numbers of iterations or imprecise pre-conditions.

TAJS [1,14] is an open-source static analyzer for JavaScript, which supports DOM modeling [13]. It uses a simple object abstraction, which can be represented by a limited form of conjunctions, without disjunctions. While the object abstraction is clearly designed and highly tuned for their own string abstraction, it does not support various string abstractions for a field name abstraction. In addition, as we described in Sect. 2, it may lose precision when it disambiguates field correspondence relations after joining the states from loop iterations.

HOO [6] computes a very different abstraction of JavaScript objects, which captures abstract forms of field relations. Indeed, HOO lets symbolic set variables denote unbounded size sets of fields of JavaScript objects to express logical facts on these sets, using specific set abstract domains [7]. For instance, it can express that two objects have exactly the same set of fields, or that the fields of a first object are included into the fields of a second object. Such program invariants are useful to reason over libraries that may be used in a general and unknown context, or in order to implement a modular verifier. By contrast, this approach is less adequate to compute precise information about the result of long and complex initialization routines like the codes our analysis targets.

WALA [12] supports static analysis of JavaScript programs. It performs a conventional propagation-based pointer analysis with techniques that can handle some of the FCT patterns [18,19].

ACG [10] is a field-based, intentionally unsound call graph analysis. The analysis ignores dynamic field lookup and update instructions, does not track non-functional values, and does not distinguish JavaScript objects since it abstracts all concrete objects into a single abstract object. Thus, ACG achieves a practical level of scalability and precision. Since ACG does not compute an over-approximation of program behaviors, the analysis is not appropriate to verify safety properties in a program. On the other hand, it is useful to support development tools.

6   Conclusion

We presented a composite abstraction that can capture precise field correspondence relations by local reasoning about loop iterations. The composite abstraction consists of two layers of abstractions: the partitioning abstraction that summarizes loop iterations in an iteration order independent way, and the object abstraction that accurately captures field correspondence relation of JavaScript objects. While most existing JavaScript analyses unroll loops aggressively, which does not scale for loops that cannot be unrolled, our analysis can infer field correspondence relations precisely even for loops which cannot be unrolled. The results of experiments based on a prototype implementation show that the analysis can avoid a large number of spurious callees caused by the precision loss of the field correspondence relation in jQuery examples.

Acknowledgment. The research leading to these results has received funding from Korea Ministry of Education, Science and Technology (MEST)/National Research Foundation of Korea (NRF) (Grants NRF-2017R1A2B3012020 and NRF-2014R1A2A2A01003235), Samsung Electronics, and the European Research Council under the EU FP 7, grant Agreement 278673, Project MemCAD.

References

1. Andreasen, E., Møller, A.: Determinacy in static analysis for jQuery. In: OOPLSA (2014)
2. Bae, S., Cho, H., Lim, I., Ryu, S.: SAFE$_{WAPI}$: web API misuse detector for web applications. In: ESEC/FSE (2014)
3. Balakrishnan, G., Reps, T.: Recency-abstraction for heap-allocated storage. In: Yi, K. (ed.) SAS 2006. LNCS, vol. 4134, pp. 221–239. Springer, Heidelberg (2006). https://doi.org/10.1007/11823230_15
4. Cousot, P., Cousot, R.: Abstract interpretation: a unified lattice model for static analysis of programs by construction or approximation of fixpoints. In: POPL (1977)
5. Cousot, P., Cousot, R.: Systematic design of program analysis frameworks. In: POPL (1979)
6. Cox, A., Chang, B.-Y.E., Rival, X.: Automatic analysis of open objects in dynamic language programs. In: Müller-Olm, M., Seidl, H. (eds.) SAS 2014. LNCS, vol. 8723, pp. 134–150. Springer, Cham (2014). https://doi.org/10.1007/978-3-319-10936-7_9
7. Cox, A., Chang, B.-Y.E., Sankaranarayanan, S.: QUIC graphs: relational invariant generation for containers. In: Castagna, G. (ed.) ECOOP 2013. LNCS, vol. 7920, pp. 401–425. Springer, Heidelberg (2013). https://doi.org/10.1007/978-3-642-39038-8_17
8. Eshkevari, L., Mazinanian, D., Rostami, S., Tsantalis, N.: JSDeodorant: class-awareness for JavaScript programs. In: ICSE (2017)
9. European Association for Standardizing Information and Communication Systems (ECMA): ECMA-262: ECMAScript Language Specification. Edition 5.1 (2011)
10. Feldthaus, A., Schäfer, M., Sridharan, M., Dolby, J., Tip, F.: Efficient construction of approximate call graphs for JavaScript IDE services. In: ICSE (2013)

11. Hackett, B., Guo, S.: Fast and precise hybrid type inference for JavaScript. In: PLDI, New York, NY, USA (2012)
12. IBM Research: T.J. Watson Libraries for Analysis (WALA). http://wala.sf.net
13. Jensen, S.H., Madsen, M., Møller, A.: Modeling the HTML DOM and browser API in static analysis of JavaScript web applications. In: ESEC/FSE (2011)
14. Jensen, S.H., Møller, A., Thiemann, P.: Type analysis for JavaScript. In: Palsberg, J., Su, Z. (eds.) SAS 2009. LNCS, vol. 5673, pp. 238–255. Springer, Heidelberg (2009). https://doi.org/10.1007/978-3-642-03237-0_17
15. Lee, H., Won, S., Jin, J., Cho, J., Ryu, S.: SAFE: formal specification and implementation of a scalable analysis framework for ECMAScript. In: FOOL (2012)
16. Park, C., Ryu, S.: Scalable and precise static analysis of JavaScript applications via loop-sensitivity. In: ECOOP (2015)
17. Park, C., Won, S., Jin, J., Ryu, S.: Static analysis of JavaScript web applications in the wild via practical DOM modeling. In: ASE (2015)
18. Schäfer, M., Sridharan, M., Dolby, J., Tip, F.: Dynamic determinacy analysis. In: PLDI (2013)
19. Sridharan, M., Dolby, J., Chandra, S., Schäfer, M., Tip, F.: Correlation tracking for points-to analysis of JavaScript. In: Noble, J. (ed.) ECOOP 2012. LNCS, vol. 7313, pp. 435–458. Springer, Heidelberg (2012). https://doi.org/10.1007/978-3-642-31057-7_20
20. Wei, S., Ryder, B.G.: Practical blended taint analysis for JavaScript. In: ISSTA (2013)

Decision Procedure for Entailment of Symbolic Heaps with Arrays

Daisuke Kimura[1]([✉]) and Makoto Tatsuta[2]

[1] Toho University, Chiba, Japan
kmr@is.sci.toho-u.ac.jp
[2] National Institute of Informatics, Tokyo, Japan
tatsuta@nii.ac.jp

Abstract. This paper gives a decision procedure for the validity of entailment of symbolic heaps in separation logic with Presburger arithmetic and arrays. The correctness of the decision procedure is proved under the condition that sizes of arrays in the succedent are not existentially bound. This condition is independent of the condition proposed by the CADE-2017 paper by Brotherston et al., namely, one of them does not imply the other. For improving efficiency of the decision procedure, some techniques are also presented. The main idea of the decision procedure is a novel translation of an entailment of symbolic heaps into a formula in Presburger arithmetic, and to combine it with an external SMT solver. This paper also gives experimental results by an implementation, which shows that the decision procedure works efficiently enough to use.

1 Introduction

Separation logic can be used to verify/analyze heap-manipulating imperative programs with pointers, and mainly it is successful for verify/analyze memory safety [3]. The aim of our paper is also memory safety. The advantage of separation logic is modularity by the frame rule, by which we can independently verify/analyze each function that may manipulate heaps [9]. The study in this paper goes along this line.

The final goal of our research is to develop a fully-automated program verifier of pointer programs based on separation logic. For this, this paper introduces a formal system of symbolic heap fragment of separation logic with arrays, shows decidability of its entailment problem, then gives an implementation (called **SLar**) of our decision procedure, and finally discusses its improvement for efficiency.

Symbolic heaps are formulas of separation logic in a simple form $\exists \vec{x}(\Pi \land \Sigma)$. The pure part Π describes properties of between terms (denoted by t, u), which represent memory addresses and values. The spatial part Σ is a separating conjunction of the empty predicate emp, the points-to predicate $t \mapsto u$, and the array predicate $\mathrm{Arr}(t, u)$. It represents some shape of heaps: emp means the

© Springer International Publishing AG 2017
B.-Y.E. Chang (Ed.): APLAS 2017, LNCS 10695, pp. 169–189, 2017.
https://doi.org/10.1007/978-3-319-71237-6_9

empty heap, $t \mapsto u$ means the single heap that uses only one address t and the value at t is u, $\mathrm{Arr}(t, u)$ means the heap that contains only an array starting from t ending at u, a separating conjunction $\Sigma_1 * \Sigma_2$ means a heap which can be split into two disjoint sub-heaps that are represented by Σ_1 and Σ_2.

In order to achieve our final goal, it is necessary to develop a solver for the entailment problem. An *entailment* has the form $\phi \vdash \phi_1, \ldots, \phi_k$, where ϕ and ϕ_i are symbolic heaps. It is said to be valid when $\phi \to \bigvee_i \phi_i$ is valid with respect to the usual heap model. The *entailment problem* is the validity checking problem of given entailments.

In the literature, many researches for verification of pointer programs based on symbolic-heap systems have been done. In particular symbolic-heap systems with inductive predicates have been studied intensively [1–3, 6, 10–14, 20]. Berdine et al. [2, 3] introduced the symbolic-heap system with hard-coded list and tree predicates, and showed decidability of its entailment problem. Iosif et al. [13, 14] considered the system with general inductive predicates, and showed its decidability under the bounded tree-width condition. Tatsuta and Kimura [20] introduced the system with general monadic inductive predicates.

Array is one of the primitive data structures of pointer programs. It is an important issue of verifying pointer programs to ensure that there is no buffer overflow. So we need to consider the array structure as primitive. However, as far as we know, there are two researches about symbolic-heap systems that have arrays as primitive [7, 8]. Calcagno et al. [8] studied shape analysis based on symbolic-heap system in the presence of pointer arithmetic. Brotherston et al. [7] investigated several problems about a symbolic-heap system with arrays.

When we extend separation logic with arrays, it may be different from previous array logics in the points that (1) it is specialized for memory safety, and (2) it can scale up by modularity. Bradley et al. [5], Bouajjani et al. [4], and Lahiri and Qadeer [16] discussed logics for arrays but their systems are essentially different from separation logic. We cannot apply their techniques to our case. Piskac et al. [17] proposed a separation logic system with list segments, and it can be combined with various SMT solvers, including array logics. However, if we combine it with array logics, the arrays are external and the resulting system does not describe the arrays by spatial formulas with separating conjunction. So their techniques cannot solve our case.

In [7], they proposed a decision procedure for the entailment problem by giving an equivalent condition to existence of a counter-model for a given entailment, then checking a Presburger formula that expresses the condition. In order to do this, they imposed the restriction that the second argument of a points-to predicate in the succedent of an entailment is not existentially bound.

Our motivating example is $\mathrm{Arr}(x, x) \vdash x \mapsto 0, \exists y (y > 0 \wedge x \mapsto y)$, which means that if the heap consists of the array from x to x, then the heap consists of a single cell at address x with content 0, or the heap consists of a single cell at address x with content y for some $y > 0$. Since it is trivially true and simple, we expect an entailment checker could decide it. So far there was no decision procedure of a class of entailments which contains this example, since it does not satisfy the restriction of [7].

The current paper shows decidability of the entailment problem under a condition: the sizes of arrays in the succedent of the given entailment do not contain any existential variables. It means that the shape of heaps represented by the succedent is completely determined by the antecedent. We need this condition for proving correctness of our decision procedure. Our result decides an independent class of entailments (including our motivating example) to the class decided by [6]. That is, our class neither contains the class of [6] nor is contained by it.

The basic idea of our decision procedure is a novel translation of a given entailment into an equivalent formula in Presburger arithmetic. The key idea used in the translation is the notion of "*sorted*" symbolic heaps. Any heap represented by a sorted symbolic heap has addresses arranged in the order of the spatial part of the symbolic heap. If we assume the both sides of given entailment are sorted, the entailment is valid if no contradiction is found in comparing spatial parts on both sides starting from left to right.

We also propose two ideas for improving the performance of our decision procedure. The performance heavily depends on the size (number of the separating conjunction symbol $*$) of a given entailment. Consider a single conclusion entailment $\phi_1 \vdash \phi_2$. Let n and m be numbers of the separating conjunction in ϕ_1 and ϕ_2, respectively. Then this entailment will be decomposed into $n!$ sorted entailments with $m!$ disjunctions on the right-hand side. So it is quite important to reduce the number of $*$ as much as possible at an early stage of the procedure.

This paper also presents our entailment checker **SLar**, which is an implementation of our decision procedure. **SLar** first (1) optimizes a given entailment according to the improvement idea mentioned above, (2) decomposes the resulting entailment into some sorted entailments, then (3) translates the decomposed entailments into the corresponding Presburger formulas, and finally (4) checks their validity by invoking an external SMT solver **Z3** [21]. The original entailment is answered valid if and only-if all of the decomposed sorted entailments are valid. The improvement techniques made our system run in a second in most cases of experiments, and made our system 200 times faster in some cases.

We introduce our system of separation logic with arrays in Sect. 2. Section 3 defines the decision procedure of the entailment problem of the system. The correctness of the decision procedure is shown in Sect. 4. Two improvement ideas of the decision procedure are discussed in Sect. 5. Section 6 discusses the entailment checker **SLar** based on this decision algorithm, and evaluates its performance with experimental data. Section 7 concludes. Detailed proofs are given in [15].

2 Separation Logic with Arrays

This section defines the syntax and semantics of our separation logic with arrays. We first give the separation logic with arrays **G** in an ordinary style. Then we define the symbolic-heap system **SLAR** as a fragment of **G**.

2.1 Syntax of System of Separation Logic with Arrays

We have first-order variables $x, y, z, \ldots \in$ Vars and constants $0, 1, 2, \ldots$. The syntax of $\mathbf{G}$ is defined as follows:

Terms $t :: = x \mid 0 \mid 1 \mid 2 \mid \ldots \mid t + t$.
Formulas $\varphi :: = t = t \mid \varphi \wedge \varphi \mid \neg \varphi \mid \exists x \varphi \mid \mathrm{emp} \mid t \mapsto t \mid \mathrm{Arr}(t,t) \mid \varphi * \varphi$.

An atomic formula of the form $t \mapsto u$ or $\mathrm{Arr}(t, u)$ is called a points-to atomic formula or an array atomic formula, respectively. The truth of each formula is interpreted under a state of variables and a heap: emp is true when the heap is empty; $t \mapsto u$ is true when the heap only has a single memory cell of address t that contains the value u; $\mathrm{Arr}(t, u)$ is true when the heap only has an array of index from t to u; a separating conjunction $\varphi_1 * \varphi_2$ is true when the heap is split into two disjoint sub-heaps, φ_1 is true under one, and φ_2 is true under the other. The formal definition of these interpretation is given in the next subsection.

The set of free variables (denoted by $\mathrm{FV}(\varphi)$) of φ is defined as usual. We also define $\mathrm{FV}(\overrightarrow{\varphi})$ as the union of $\mathrm{FV}(\varphi)$, where $\varphi \in \overrightarrow{\varphi}$.

We sometimes use the symbol σ to denote emp, $t \mapsto u$, or $\mathrm{Arr}(t, u)$.

We use abbreviations $\varphi_1 \vee \varphi_2$, $\varphi_1 \to \varphi_2$, and $\forall x \varphi$ defined in a usual way. We also write $t \neq u$, $t \leq u$, $t < u$, and true as abbreviations of $\neg(t = u)$, $\exists x.(u = t + x)$, $t + 1 \leq u$, and $0 = 0$, respectively.

A formula is said to be *pure* if it is a formula of Presburger arithmetic.

2.2 Semantics of System of Separation Logic with Arrays

Let N be the set of natural numbers. We define the following semantic domains:

$\mathrm{Val} =_{\mathrm{def}} N$, $\quad$ $\mathrm{Loc} =_{\mathrm{def}} N \setminus \{0\}$, $\quad$ $\mathrm{Stores} =_{\mathrm{def}} \mathrm{Vars} \to \mathrm{Val}$, $\quad$ $\mathrm{Heaps} =_{\mathrm{def}}$ $\mathrm{Loc} \to_{\mathrm{fin}} \mathrm{Val}$.

Loc means addresses of heaps. 0 means Null. An element s in Stores is called a *store* that means a valuation of variables. An element h in Heap is called a *heap*. The domain of h (denoted by $\mathrm{Dom}(h)$) means the memory addresses which are currently used. $h(n)$ means the value at the address n if it is defined. We sometimes use notation $h_1 + h_2$ for the disjoint union of h_1 and h_2, that is, it is defined when $\mathrm{Dom}(h_1)$ and $\mathrm{Dom}(h_2)$ are disjoint sets, and $(h_1 + h_2)(n)$ is $h_i(n)$ if $n \in \mathrm{Dom}(h_i)$ for $i = 1, 2$. A pair (s, h) is called a *heap model*.

The interpretation $s(t)$ of a term t by s is defined by extending the definition of s by $s(n) = n$ for each constant n, and $s(t + u) = s(t) + s(u)$.

The interpretation $s, h \models \varphi$ of φ under the heap model (s, h) is defined inductively as follows:

$s, h \models t = u$ iff $s(t) = s(u)$,
$s, h \models \varphi_1 \wedge \varphi_2$ iff $s, h \models \varphi_1$ and $s, h \models \varphi_2$,
$s, h \models \neg \varphi$ iff $s, h \not\models \varphi$,
$s, h \models \exists x \varphi$ iff $s[x := a], h \models \varphi$ for some $a \in \mathrm{Val}$,
$s, h \models \mathrm{emp}$ iff $\mathrm{Dom}(h) = \emptyset$,
$s, h \models t \mapsto u$ iff $\mathrm{Dom}(h) = \{s(t)\}$ and $h(s(t)) = s(u)$,

$s, h \models \mathrm{Arr}(t, u)$ iff $\mathrm{Dom}(h) = \{x \in N \mid s(t) \le x \le s(u)\}$ and $s(t) \le s(u)$,
$s, h \models \varphi_1 * \varphi_2$ iff $s, h_1 \models \varphi_1$, $s, h_2 \models \varphi_2$, and $h = h_1 + h_2$ for some h_1, h_2.

We sometimes write $s \models \varphi$ if $s, h \models \varphi$ holds for any h. This notation is mainly used for pure formulas, since their interpretation do not depend on the heap-part of heap models. We also write $\models \varphi$ if $s, h \models \varphi$ holds for any s and h.

The notation $\varphi \models \psi$ is an abbreviation of $\models \varphi \to \psi$, that is, $s, h \models \varphi$ implies $s, h \models \psi$ for any s and h.

Let I be a finite set. In this paper we implicitly assume a linear order on I (this order will be used in the definition of the translation P given in the next section). Then we sometimes write $\{\phi_i \mid i \in I\}$ for $\bigvee\{\phi_i \mid i \in I\}$, that is, disjunction $\bigvee_{i \in I} \phi_i$ of formulas ϕ_i $(i \in I)$ under the order of I. We sometimes abbreviate $\{\phi_i \mid i \in I\}$ by $\{\phi_i\}_{i \in I}$. It may be further abbreviated by $\overrightarrow{\phi}$ when I is not important.

2.3 Symbolic-Heap System with Arrays

The symbolic-heap system **SLAR** is defined as a fragment of **G**. The syntax of **SLAR** is given as follows. Terms of **SLAR** are the same as the terms of **G**. Formulas of **SLAR** (called *symbolic heaps*) have the following form:

$$\phi :: = \exists \overrightarrow{x} (\Pi \wedge \Sigma)$$

where Π is a pure formula of **G** and Σ is the spatial part defined by

$$\Sigma :: = \mathrm{emp} \mid t \mapsto t \mid \mathrm{Arr}(t, t) \mid \Sigma * \Sigma.$$

We sometimes write $\exists \overrightarrow{x} \Sigma$ as an abbreviation of $\exists \overrightarrow{x} (\mathrm{true} \wedge \Sigma)$. We use notations Π_ϕ and Σ_ϕ that mean the pure part and the spatial part of ϕ, respectively.

In this paper, we consider *entailments* of **SLAR** that have the form:

$$\phi \vdash \{\phi_i \mid i \in I\} \qquad (I \text{ is a finite set})$$

The symbolic heap on the left-hand side is called the antecedent of the entailment. The symbolic heaps on the right-hand side are called the succedents of the entailment. As we noted before, the right-hand side $\{\phi_i \mid i \in I\}$ of an entailment means the disjunction of the symbolic heaps ϕ_i $(i \in I)$.

An entailment $\phi \vdash \{\phi_i \mid i \in I\}$ is said to be *valid* if $\phi \models \{\phi_i \mid i \in I\}$ holds.

A formula of the form $\Pi \wedge \Sigma$ is called a *QF symbolic heap* (denoted by φ). Note that existential quantifiers may appear in the pure part of a QF symbolic heap. We can easily see that $\exists \overrightarrow{x} \varphi \models \overrightarrow{\phi}$ is equivalent to $\varphi \models \overrightarrow{\phi}$. So we often assume that the left-hand sides of entailments are QF symbolic heaps.

We call entailments of the form $\varphi \vdash \{\varphi_i \mid i \in I\}$ *QF entailments*.

2.4 Analysis/Verification of Memory Safety

We intend to use our entailment checker for a part of our analysis/verification system for memory safety. We briefly explain it for motivating our entailment checker.

The target programming language is essentially the same as that in [18] except we extend the allocation command for allocating more than one cells. We define our programming language in programming language C style.

Expressions $e:: = x \mid 0 \mid 1 \mid 2 \ldots \mid e + e$.
Boolean expressions $b:: = e == e \mid e < e \mid b\&\&b \mid b\|b \mid !b$.
Programs $P:: = x = e; \mid$ if $(b)\{P\}$ else $\{P\}; \mid$ while $(b)\{P\}; \mid P\ P \mid$
$\quad x = \mathtt{malloc}(y); \mid x = *y; \mid *x = y; \mid$ free$(x);$.

$x = \mathtt{malloc}(y);$ allocates y cells and set x to the pointer to the first cell. Note that this operation may fail if there is not enough free memory.

Our assertion language is a disjunction of symbolic heaps, namely,
Assertions $A:: = \phi_1 \vee \cdots \vee \phi_n$.

In the same way as [18], we use a triple $\{A\}\,P\,\{B\}$ that means that if the assertion A holds at the initial state and the program P is executed, then (1) if P terminates then the assertion B holds at the resulting state, and (2) P does not cause any memory errors.

As inference rules for triples, we have ordinary inference rules for Hoare triples including the consequence rule, as well as the following rules for memory operations. We write $\mathrm{Arr2}(x,y)$ for $\exists z(\mathrm{Arr}(x,z) \wedge x + y = z + 1)$. $\mathrm{Arr2}(x,y)$ means the memory block at address x of size y. We sometimes write a formula that is not a disjunction of symbolic heaps for an equivalent assertion obtained by ordinary logical equivalence rules. We also write $x \mapsto \_$ for $\exists z(x \mapsto z)$ where z is fresh.

$\{A\}\, \mathtt{x} = \mathtt{malloc(y)}; \{\exists x'(A[x := x'] \wedge (x = \mathrm{nil} \vee \mathrm{Arr2}(x, y[x := x'])))\}$,
$\{A * y \mapsto t\}\, \mathtt{x} = \mathtt{*y}; \{\exists x'(A[x := x'] * y \mapsto t[x := x'] \wedge x = t[x := x'])\}$ (x' fresh),
$\{A * x \mapsto \_)\}\, \mathtt{*x} = \mathtt{y}; \{A * x \mapsto y\}$,
$\{A * x \mapsto \_)\}\, \mathtt{free(x)}; \{A\}$.

In order to prove memory safety of a program P under a precondition A, it is sufficient to show that $\{A\}P\{\mathrm{true}\}$ is provable.

By separation logic with arrays, we can show a triple $\{A\}\, \mathtt{x} = \mathtt{malloc(y)};$ $\{A \wedge x = \mathrm{nil} \vee A * \mathrm{Arr2}(x, y) \wedge x \neq \mathrm{nil}\}$ but it is impossible without arrays since y in $\mathtt{malloc}(y)$ is a variable. With separation logic with arrays, we can also show $\{\mathrm{Arr}(p, p + 3)\}\, \mathtt{*p} = \mathtt{5}; \{p \mapsto 5 * \mathrm{Arr}(p + 1, p + 3)\}$.

For the consequence rule

$$\frac{\{A'\}\,\mathrm{P}\,\{B'\}}{\{A\}\,\mathrm{P}\,\{B\}} \qquad (\text{if } A \to A', B' \to B)$$

we have to check the side condition $A \to A'$. Let A be $\phi_1 \vee \ldots \vee \phi_n$ and A' be $\phi'_1 \vee \ldots \vee \phi'_m$. Then we will use our entailment checker to decide $\phi_i \vdash \phi'_1, \ldots, \phi'_m$ for all $1 \leq i \leq n$.

2.5   Other Systems of Symbolic Heaps with Arrays

We will impose the following restrictions for correctness of our entailment decision procedure: For a given entailment, if any array atomic formula in the succedent has the form $\mathrm{Arr}(t, t + u)$ such that the term u does not contain any existential variables.

Other known systems of symbolic heaps with arrays are only the system given in Brotherston et al. [7]. They gave an independent condition for decidability of the entailment problem of the same symbolic-heap system. Their condition disallows existential variables in u for each points-to predicate $t \mapsto u$ in the succedent of an entailment. In order to clarify the difference between our condition and their condition, we consider the following entailments:

(i) $\mathrm{Arr}(x, x) \vdash x \mapsto 0, \exists y (y > 0 \land x \mapsto y)$
(ii) $\mathrm{Arr}(1, 5) \vdash \exists y, y' (\mathrm{Arr}(y, y + 1) * \mathrm{Arr}(y', y' + 2))$
(iii) $\mathrm{Arr}(1, 5) \vdash \exists y (\mathrm{Arr}(1, 1 + y) * \mathrm{Arr}(2 + y, 5))$
(iv) $\mathrm{Arr}(1, 5) \vdash \exists y, y' (\mathrm{Arr}(1, 1 + y) * 2 + y \mapsto y' * \mathrm{Arr}(3 + y, 5))$

The entailment (i) can be decided by our decision procedure, but it cannot be decided by their procedure. The entailment (ii) is decided by both theirs and ours. The entailment (iii) is decided by theirs, but it does not satisfy our condition. The entailment (iv) is decided by neither theirs nor ours.

Our system and the system in [7] have the same purpose, namely, analysis/verification of memory safety. Basically their target programming language and assertion language are the same as ours given in this section. These entailment checkers are essentially used for deciding the side condition of the consequence rule. As explained above, ours and theirs have different restrictions for decidability. Hence the class of programs is the same for ours and theirs, but some triples can be proved only by ours and other triples can be proved only by theirs, according to the shape of assertions. We explain them by example.

The triple

$$\{p \mapsto \_\} \, \mathrm{y} = \mathrm{x} + 2; *\mathrm{p} = \mathrm{y}; \mathrm{x} = 2; \mathrm{y} = 3; \{\exists x' y' (y' = x' + 1 \land p \mapsto y')\}$$

is true and provable in our system, but it is not provable in their system, since it is proved by the assignment statement rule and the consequence rule with the side condition $\exists x' y' y'' (y' = x' + 2 \land x = 2 \land y = 3 \land p \mapsto y') \vdash \exists x' y' (y' = x' + 1 \land p \mapsto y')$, and this entailment is out of their system. On the other hand, the following triple, which is slightly different from but very similar to it,

$$\{p \mapsto \_\} \, \mathrm{y} = 1; *\mathrm{p} = \mathrm{y}; \mathrm{x} = 2; \mathrm{y} = 3; \{\exists y' (y' = 1 \land p \mapsto y')\}$$

is true and provable in both of our and their systems.

The triple $\{\mathrm{emp}\} \, \mathrm{y} = \mathrm{x} + 2; \mathrm{p} = \mathtt{malloc}(\mathrm{y}); \mathrm{x} = 2; \mathrm{y} = 3;$
$\quad \{\exists x' y' (y' = x' + 1 \land (p = \mathrm{nil} \lor \mathrm{Arr2}(p, y')))\}$

is true and provable in their system, but it is not provable in our system, since it is proved by the assignment statement rule and the consequence rule with the side condition $\exists x' y' y'' p' (y' = x' + 2 \land x = 2 \land y = 3 \land (p = \mathrm{nil} \lor \mathrm{Arr2}(p, y'))) \vdash \exists x' y' (y' = x' + 1 \land (p = \mathrm{nil} \lor \mathrm{Arr2}(p, y')))$, and this entailment is out of our system. On the other hand, the following triple, which is slightly different from but very similar to it, {emp} y = 1; p = malloc(y); x = 2; y = 3; $\{\exists x'y'(y' = 1 \land (p = \text{nil} \lor \text{Arr2}(p, y')))\}$

is true and provable in both of our and their systems.

All these kinds of triples are necessary for program verification in the real world, and in this sense both our system and their system have advantage and disadvantage. We can use both systems together to prove a single triple, by using one of them to check each necessary side condition, depending on the shape of the side condition.

Note that our and their restrictions are not determined by a program syntax and they depend on a context of an assignment statement. It is because both our and their restrictions are involved in existential variables, which are $\exists x'$ introduced by the assignment statement x:=e;, and a program syntax cannot decide where x' appears in a current assertion.

3   Decision Procedure

3.1   Sorted Entailments

This subsection describes our key idea, namely *sorted* symbolic heaps. The addresses of heaps represented by a sorted symbolic heap must be sorted, that is, their order can be determined by the order of the spatial part of the sorted symbolic heap.

We sometimes regard Σ as a list of emp, $t \mapsto u$, and $\text{Arr}(t, u)$. We also regard the symbol $*$ written like $t \mapsto u * \Sigma$ as the list constructor. By abuse of notation, we write emp in order to represent the empty list.

A symbolic heap ϕ is called *sorted* at (s, h) if s, h satisfies ϕ and the addresses of the heap h are arranged in the order of the spatial part of ϕ.

In order to express this notion, we introduce pure formulas $t < \Sigma$ and $\text{Sorted}(\Sigma)$, which mean the first address expressed by Σ is greater than t, and Σ is sorted, respectively. They are inductively defined as follows:

$t < \text{emp} =_{\text{def}} \text{true}, \qquad t < (\text{emp} * \Sigma_1) =_{\text{def}} t < \Sigma_1,$
$t < (t_1 \mapsto u_1 * \Sigma_1) =_{\text{def}} t < t_1, \qquad t < (\text{Arr}(t_1, u_1) * \Sigma_1) =_{\text{def}} t < t_1,$
$\text{Sorted}'(\text{emp}) =_{\text{def}} \text{true},$
$\text{Sorted}'(\text{emp} * \Sigma_1) =_{\text{def}} \text{Sorted}'(\Sigma_1),$
$\text{Sorted}'(t \mapsto u * \Sigma_1) =_{\text{def}} t < \Sigma_1 \land \text{Sorted}'(\Sigma_1),$
$\text{Sorted}'(\text{Arr}(t, u) * \Sigma_1) =_{\text{def}} t \leq u \land u < \Sigma_1 \land \text{Sorted}'(\Sigma_1),$
$\text{Sorted}(\Sigma) =_{\text{def}} 0 < \Sigma \land \text{Sorted}'(\Sigma).$

The formula $\text{Sorted}(\Sigma) \land \Sigma$ is sometimes abbreviated by $\widetilde{\Sigma}$ or $\Sigma^{\sim}$. We also write $\widetilde{\phi}$ (or $\phi^{\sim}$) for the symbolic heap which is obtained from ϕ by replacing Π_ϕ by $\Pi_\phi \land \text{Sorted}(\Sigma_\phi)$.

We claim that ϕ is a sorted symbolic heap at (s, h) iff $\widetilde{\phi}$ is true in (s, h).

We define $\text{Perm}(\Sigma)$ as the set of permutations of Σ with respect to $*$. A symbolic heap ϕ' is called a permutation of ϕ if $\Sigma_{\phi'} \in \text{Perm}(\Sigma_\phi)$ and the other parts of ϕ and ϕ' are same. We write $\text{Perm}(\phi)$ for the set of permutations of ϕ.

Note that $s, h \models \phi$ iff $s, h \models \widetilde{\phi'}$ for some $\phi' \in \text{Perm}(\phi)$.

An entailment is said to be sorted if all of its antecedent and succedents have the form $\widetilde{\phi}$. We claim that checking validity of entailments can be reduced to checking validity of sorted entailments. The formal statement of this property will be given later (see Lemma 1).

The basic idea of our decision procedure is as follows: (1) A given entailment is decomposed into sorted entailments according to Lemma 1; (2) the decomposed sorted entailments are translated into Presburger formulas by the translation P given in the next subsection; (3) the translated formulas are decided by the decision procedure of Presburger arithmetic.

3.2   Translation P

We define the translation P from QF entailments into Presburger formulas. We note that the resulting formula may contain new fresh variables (denoted by z).

For saving space, we use some auxiliary notations. Let $\{t_j\}_{j \in J}$ be a set of terms indexed by a finite set J. We write $u = t_J$ for $\bigwedge_{j \in J} u = t_j$. We also write $u < t_J$ for $\bigwedge_{j \in J} u < t_j$.

The definition of $P(\Pi, \Sigma, S)$ is given as listed in Fig. 1, where S is a finite set $\{(\Pi_i, \Sigma_i)\}_{i \in I}$. We assume that pattern-matching is done from top to bottom.

In order to describe the procedure P, we temporarily extend terms to include $u - t$ where u, t are terms. In the result of P, which is a Presburger arithmetic formula, we eliminate these extended terms by replacing $t' + (u - t) = t''$ and $t' + (u - t) < t''$ by $t' + u = t'' + t$ and $t' + u < t'' + t$, respectively.

The $=_{\mathrm{def}}$ steps terminate since $(|\Sigma| + \sum_{i \in I} |\Sigma_i|, |S|)$ decreases where $|\Sigma|$ is the number of $*$ in Σ and $|S|$ is the number of elements in S. Note that this measure does not decrease for some $=_{\mathrm{def}}$, but the left-hand sides of the definition are mutually exclusive and hence combination of $=_{\mathrm{def}}$ eventually decreases the measure. For example, $(\mapsto\mapsto)$ will eventually come after $(\mathbf{Arr}\mapsto)$.

The formula $P(\Pi, \Sigma, \{(\Pi_i, \Sigma_i)\}_{i \in I})$ means that the QF entailment $\Pi \wedge \widetilde{\Sigma} \vdash \{\Pi_i \wedge \widetilde{\Sigma}\}_{i \in I}$ is valid (in fact, we can show their equivalence by induction on the definition of P). From this intuition, we sometimes call Σ the left spatial formula, and also call $\{\Sigma_i\}_{i \in I}$ the right spatial formulas. We call the left-most position of a spatial formula the head position. The atomic formula appears at the head position is called the head atom.

We will explain the meaning of each clause in Fig. 1.

The clauses (**EmpL**) and (**EmpR**) just remove emp at the head position.

The clause (**EmpNEmp**) handles the case where the left spatial formula is emp. A pair (Π', Σ') in the third argument of P is removed if Σ' is not emp, since $\Pi' \wedge \Sigma'$ cannot be satisfied by the empty heap.

The clause (**EmpEmp**) handles the case where the left formula and all the right spatial formulas are emp. This case P returns a Presburger formula which is equivalent to the corresponding entailment is valid.

The clause (**NEmpEmp**) handles the case where the left spatial formula is not emp and a pair (Π', emp) appears in the third argument of P. We remove the pair since $\Pi' \wedge \mathrm{emp}$ cannot be satisfied by any non-empty heap. For example, $P(\mathrm{true}, x \mapsto 0 * y \mapsto 0, \{(\mathrm{true}, \mathrm{emp})\})$ becomes $P(\mathrm{true}, x \mapsto 0 * y \mapsto 0, \emptyset)$.

$$P(\Pi, \mathrm{emp} * \Sigma, S) \qquad\qquad =_{\mathrm{def}} P(\Pi, \Sigma, S) \qquad\qquad\qquad\qquad\qquad \textbf{(EmpL)}$$

$$P(\Pi, \Sigma, \{(\Pi', \mathrm{emp} * \Sigma')\} \cup S) =_{\mathrm{def}} P(\Pi, \Sigma, \{(\Pi', \Sigma')\} \cup S) \qquad\qquad\quad \textbf{(EmpR)}$$

$$P(\Pi, \mathrm{emp}, \{(\Pi', \Sigma')\} \cup S) \quad\ =_{\mathrm{def}} P(\Pi, \mathrm{emp}, S), \quad \text{where } \Sigma' \not\equiv \mathrm{emp} \ \ \textbf{(EmpNEmp)}$$

$$P(\Pi, \mathrm{emp}, \{(\Pi_i, \mathrm{emp})\}_{i \in I}) \quad =_{\mathrm{def}} \Pi \to \bigvee_{i \in I} \Pi_i \qquad\qquad\qquad\qquad \textbf{(EmpEmp)}$$

$$P(\Pi, \Sigma, \{(\Pi', \mathrm{emp})\} \cup S) \quad =_{\mathrm{def}} P(\Pi, \Sigma, S), \qquad \text{where } \Sigma \not\equiv \mathrm{emp} \ \ \textbf{(NEmpEmp)}$$

$$P(\Pi, \Sigma, \emptyset) \qquad\qquad\qquad =_{\mathrm{def}} \neg(\Pi \wedge \mathrm{Sorted}(\Sigma)) \qquad\qquad\qquad \textbf{(empty)}$$

$$P(\Pi, t \mapsto u * \Sigma, \{(\Pi_i, t_i \mapsto u_i * \Sigma_i)\}_{i \in I}) \qquad\qquad\qquad\qquad\qquad\qquad (\mapsto\mapsto)$$
$$=_{\mathrm{def}} P(\Pi \wedge t < \Sigma, \Sigma, \{(\Pi_i \wedge t = t_i \wedge u = u_i \wedge t_i < \Sigma_i, \Sigma_i)\}_{i \in I})$$

$$P(\Pi, t \mapsto u * \Sigma, \{(\Pi_i, \mathrm{Arr}(t_i, t_i') * \Sigma_i)\} \cup S) \qquad\qquad\qquad\qquad\qquad (\mapsto\mathbf{Arr})$$
$$=_{\mathrm{def}} P(\Pi \wedge t_i' = t_i, t \mapsto u * \Sigma, \{(\Pi_i, t_i \mapsto u * \Sigma_i)\} \cup S)$$
$$\wedge\ P(\Pi \wedge t_i' > t_i, t \mapsto u * \Sigma, \{(\Pi_i, t_i \mapsto u * \mathrm{Arr}(t_i + 1, t_i') * \Sigma_i)\} \cup S)$$
$$\wedge\ P(\Pi \wedge t_i' < t_i, t \mapsto u * \Sigma, S)$$

$$P(\Pi, \mathrm{Arr}(t, t') * \Sigma, S) \qquad\qquad\qquad\qquad\qquad\qquad\qquad\qquad\qquad (\mathbf{Arr}\mapsto)$$
$$=_{\mathrm{def}} P(\Pi \wedge t' > t, t \mapsto z * \mathrm{Arr}(t + 1, t') * \Sigma, S)$$
$$\wedge\ P(\Pi \wedge t' = t, t \mapsto z' * \Sigma, S), \quad \text{where } (\Pi'', t'' \mapsto u'' * \Sigma'') \in S \text{ and } z, z' \text{ are fresh}$$

$$P(\Pi, \mathrm{Arr}(t, t') * \Sigma, \{(\Pi_i, \mathrm{Arr}(t_i, t_i') * \Sigma_i)\}_{i \in I}) \qquad\qquad\qquad\qquad (\mathbf{ArrArr})$$
$$=_{\mathrm{def}} \bigwedge_{I' \subseteq I} P \left(\begin{array}{l} \Pi \wedge m = m_{I'} \wedge m < m_{I \setminus I'} \wedge t \le t' \wedge t' < \Sigma, \Sigma, \\ \{(\Pi_i \wedge t_i + m < \Sigma_i, \Sigma_i)\}_{i \in I'} \cup \{(\Pi_i, \mathrm{Arr}(t_i + m + 1, t_i') * \Sigma_i)\}_{i \in I \setminus I'} \end{array} \right)$$
$$\wedge \bigwedge_{\emptyset \ne I' \subseteq I} P \left(\begin{array}{l} \Pi \wedge m' < m \wedge m' = m_{I'} \wedge m' < m_{I \setminus I'}, \mathrm{Arr}(t + m' + 1, t') * \Sigma, \\ \{(\Pi_i \wedge t_i + m' < \Sigma_i, \Sigma_i)\}_{i \in I'} \cup \{(\Pi_i, \mathrm{Arr}(t_i + m' + 1, t_i') * \Sigma_i)\}_{i \in I \setminus I'} \end{array} \right),$$

where m, m_i, and m' are abbreviations of $t' - t$, $t_i' - t_i$, and $m_{\min I'}$, respectively.

Fig. 1. The translation P

The clause **(empty)** handles the case where the third argument of P is empty. This case P returns a Presburger formula which is equivalent to that the left symbolic heap $\Pi \wedge \Sigma$ is not satisfiable. For example, $P(\mathrm{true}, x \mapsto 0 * y \mapsto 0, \emptyset)$ returns $\neg(\mathrm{true} \wedge x < y)$.

The clause $(\mapsto\mapsto)$ handles the case where all the head atoms of Σ and $\{\Sigma_i\}_{i \in I}$ are the points-to predicate. This case we remove all of them and put equalities on the right pure parts. By this rule the measure is strictly reduced. For example, $P(3 < 4, 3 \mapsto 10 * 4 \mapsto 11, \{(\mathrm{true}, 3 \mapsto 10 * \mathrm{Arr}(4, 4))\})$ becomes

$$P(3 < 4 \wedge 3 < 4, 4 \mapsto 11, \{(\mathrm{true} \wedge 3 = 3 \wedge 4 = 4 \wedge 3 < 4, \mathrm{Arr}(4, 4))\})$$

This can be simplified to $P(3 < 4, 4 \mapsto 11, \{(3 = 3 \wedge 4 = 4 \wedge 3 < 4, \mathrm{Arr}(4, 4))\})$, since $3 < 4 \wedge 3 < 4$ is logically equivalent to $3 < 4$ and $\mathrm{true} \wedge 3 = 3$ is logically equivalent to $3 = 3$. In the following examples, we implicitly use similar simplifications.

The clause $(\mapsto\mathbf{Arr})$ handles the case where the head atom of the left spatial formula is the points-to predicate and some right spatial formula Σ_i has the array predicate as its head atom. Then we split the array atomic formula into the points-to and the rest. We have three subcases according to the length of the head array. The first case is when the length of the array is 1: We replace the head array by a points-to atomic formula. The second case is when the length of the head array is greater than 1: We split the head array into the points-to predicate and the rest array. The last case is when the length of the head array is less than 1: We just remove (Π_i, Σ_i), since the array predicate is false. We note that this rule can be applied repeatedly until all head arrays of the right spatial formulas are unfolded, since the left spatial formula is unchanged. Then the measure is eventually reduced by applying $(\mapsto\mapsto)$. For example, $P(\text{true}, 4 \mapsto 11, \{(3 = 3 \land 10 = 10, \text{Arr}(4, 4))\})$ becomes

$$P(3 < 4 \land 4 = 4, 4 \mapsto 11, \{(3 = 3 \land 10 = 10, 4 \mapsto 11)\})$$
$$\land P(3 < 4 \land 4 < 4, 4 \mapsto 11, \{(3 = 3 \land 10 = 10, 4 \mapsto 11 * \text{Arr}(5, 4))\})$$
$$\land P(3 < 4 \land 4 > 4, 4 \mapsto 11, \emptyset).$$

The clause $(\textbf{Arr}\mapsto)$ handles the case where the head atom of the left spatial formula is array and there is a right spatial formula whose head atom is the points-to predicate. We have two subcases according to the length of the head array. The first case is when the length of the array is 1: The array is unfolded and it is replaced by a points-to atomic formula with a fresh variable z. The second case is the case where the length of the array is greater than 1: The array is split into the points-to predicate (with a fresh variable z') and the rest array. We note that the left head atom becomes a points-to atomic formula after applying this rule. Hence the measure is eventually reduced, since $(\mapsto\mapsto)$ or $(\mapsto\textbf{Arr})$ will be applied next. For example, $P(\text{true}, \text{Arr}(x, x), \{(\text{true}, x \mapsto 10)\})$ becomes

$$P(x > x, x \mapsto z * \text{Arr}(x + 1, x), \{(\text{true}, x \mapsto 10)\})$$
$$\land P(x = x, x \mapsto z', \{(\text{true}, x \mapsto 10)\}).$$

The last clause $(\textbf{ArrArr})$ handles the case where all the head atoms in the left and right spatial formulas are arrays. We first find the head arrays with the shortest length among the head arrays. Next we split each longer array into two arrays so that the first part has the same size to the shortest array. Then we remove the first parts. The shortest arrays are also removed. In this operation we have two subcases: The first case is when the array of the left spatial formula has the shortest size and disappears by the operation. The second case is when the array of the left spatial formula has a longer size, it is split into two arrays, and the second part remains. We note that the measure is strictly reduced, since at least one shortest array is removed. For example, $P(\text{true}, \text{Arr}(3, 5), \{(\text{true}, \text{Arr}(3, 3) * \text{Arr}(4, 5))\})$ becomes

$$P(2 < 0 \land 3 \leq 5, \text{emp}, \{(\text{true}, \text{Arr}(6, 3) * \text{Arr}(4, 5))\})$$
$$\land P(2 = 0 \land 3 \leq 5, \text{emp}, \{(\text{true} \land 3 < 4, \text{Arr}(4, 5))\})$$
$$\land P(0 < 2 \land 0 = 0, \text{Arr}(4, 5), \{(\text{true}, \text{Arr}(4, 5))\}).$$

Note that the sizes of $\text{Arr}(3, 5)$ and $\text{Arr}(3, 3)$ are 3 and 1 respectively, and we have three cases for $2 < 0$, $2 = 0$, and $0 < 2$, by comparing them (actually comparing (them - 1)).

Example. The sorted entailment $(3 \mapsto 10 * 4 \mapsto 11)^{\sim} \vdash \mathrm{Arr}(3, 4)^{\sim}$ is translated by computing $P(\mathrm{true}, 3 \mapsto 10 * 4 \mapsto 11, \{(\mathrm{true}, \mathrm{Arr}(3, 4))\})$. We will see its calculation step by step. It first becomes

$$P(3 = 4, 3 \mapsto 10 * 4 \mapsto 11, \{(\mathrm{true}, 3 \mapsto 10)\})$$
$$\wedge P(3 < 4, 3 \mapsto 10 * 4 \mapsto 11, \{(\mathrm{true}, 3 \mapsto 10 * \mathrm{Arr}(4, 4))\})$$
$$\wedge P(3 > 4, 3 \mapsto 10 * 4 \mapsto 11, \emptyset)$$

by ($\mapsto$Arr). The first conjunct becomes $P(3 = 4 \wedge 3 < 4, 4 \mapsto 11, \{(3 = 3 \wedge 10 = 10, \mathrm{emp})\})$ by ($\mapsto\mapsto$), then it becomes $\neg(3 = 4 \wedge 3 < 4)$ by (NEmpEmp) and (empty). The third conjunct becomes $\neg(3 > 4 \wedge 3 < 4)$ by (empty). The second conjunct becomes $P(3 < 4, 4 \mapsto 11, \{(3 = 3 \wedge 10 = 10, \mathrm{Arr}(4, 4))\})$ by ($\mapsto\mapsto$), then it becomes

$$P(3 < 4 \wedge 4 = 4, 4 \mapsto 11, \{(3 = 3 \wedge 10 = 10, 4 \mapsto 11)\})$$
$$\wedge P(3 < 4 \wedge 4 < 4, 4 \mapsto 11, \{(3 = 3 \wedge 10 = 10, 4 \mapsto 11 * \mathrm{Arr}(5, 4))\})$$
$$\wedge P(3 < 4 \wedge 4 > 4, 4 \mapsto 11, \emptyset)$$

by ($\mapsto$Arr). Hence we have

$$P(3 < 4 \wedge 4 = 4, \mathrm{emp}, \{(3 = 3 \wedge 10 = 10 \wedge 4 = 4 \wedge 11 = 11, \mathrm{emp})\})$$
$$\wedge P(3 < 4 \wedge 4 < 4, \mathrm{emp}, \{(3 = 3 \wedge 10 = 10 \wedge 4 = 4 \wedge 11 = 11, \mathrm{Arr}(5, 4))\})$$
$$\wedge \neg(3 < 4 \wedge 4 > 4)$$

by ($\mapsto\mapsto$) and (empty). We note that the second one becomes $P(3 < 4 \wedge 4 < 4, \mathrm{emp}, \emptyset\})$ by (EmpNEmp). Thus we obtain

$$(3 < 4 \wedge 4 = 4) \to (3 = 3 \wedge 10 = 10 \wedge 4 = 4 \wedge 11 = 11)$$
$$\wedge \neg(3 < 4 \wedge 4 < 4) \wedge \neg(3 < 4 \wedge 4 > 4)$$

by (EmpEmp) and (empty). Finally we obtain $\neg(3 = 4 \wedge 3 < 4) \wedge (3 < 4 \wedge 4 = 4) \to (3 = 3 \wedge 10 = 10 \wedge 4 = 4 \wedge 11 = 11) \wedge \neg(3 < 4 \wedge 4 < 4) \wedge \neg(3 > 4 \wedge 3 < 4)$.

In our decision procedure the produced Presburger formula will be checked by an external SMT solver.

3.3   Decidability

The aim of P is to give an equivalent formula of Presburger arithmetic to a given entailment. The correctness property of P is stated as follows.

Theorem 1 (Correctness of Translation P). *If any array atomic formula in Σ_i has the form $\mathrm{Arr}(t, t + u)$ such that the term u does not contain $\overrightarrow{y}$, then*

$$\Pi \wedge \widetilde{\Sigma} \models \{\exists \overrightarrow{y_i}(\Pi_i \wedge \widetilde{\Sigma_i})\}_{i \in I} \quad iff \quad \models \forall \overrightarrow{z} \exists \overrightarrow{y} \, P(\Pi, \Sigma, \{(\Pi_i, \Sigma_i)\}_{i \in I})$$

where $\overrightarrow{y}$ is a sequence of $\overrightarrow{y_i}$ ($i \in I$), and $\overrightarrow{z}$ is $\mathrm{FV}(P(\Pi, \Sigma, \{(\Pi_i, \Sigma_i)\}_{i \in I})) \setminus \mathrm{FV}(\Pi, \Sigma, \{\Pi_i\}_{i \in I}, \{\Sigma_i\}_{i \in I})$.

We note that $\overrightarrow{z}$ are the fresh variables introduced in the unfolding of $P(\Pi, \Sigma, \{(\Pi_i, \Sigma_i)\}_{i \in I})$.

The proof of this theorem will be given in the next section.

The correctness property is shown with the condition described in the theorem. This condition avoids a complicated situation for $\overrightarrow{y}$ and $\overrightarrow{z}$, such that some variables in $\overrightarrow{y}$ depend on $\overrightarrow{z}$, and some determine $\overrightarrow{z}$. For example, if we consider $\mathrm{Arr}(1,5) \vdash \exists y_1 y_2 (\mathrm{Arr}(1,y_1) * y_1 + 1 \mapsto y_2 * \mathrm{Arr}(y_1 + 2, 5))$, we will have $y_1 + 1 \mapsto z$ during the unfolding of $P(\mathrm{true}, \mathrm{Arr}(1,5), \{(\mathrm{true}, \mathrm{Arr}(1,y_1) * y_1 + 1 \mapsto y_2 * \mathrm{Arr}(y_1 + 2, 5))\})$. Then finally we have $z = y_2$ after some logical simplification. This fact means that y_2 depends on z, and moreover z is indirectly determined by y_1. The latter case occurs when sizes of array depend on $\overrightarrow{y}$. We need to exclude this situation.

Finally we have the decidability result for the entailment problem of **SLAR** under the condition from the above theorem and the property of sorted entailments (stated in Lemma 1).

Corollary 1 (Decidability of Validity Checking of Entailments). *Validity checking of entailments $\Pi \wedge \Sigma \vdash \{\exists \overrightarrow{y_i}(\Pi_i \wedge \Sigma_i)\}_{i \in I}$ of **SLAR** is decidable, if any array atomic formula in Σ_i has the form $\mathrm{Arr}(t, t + u)$ such that the term u does not contain $\overrightarrow{y_i}$.*

Example. Our motivating example $\mathrm{Arr}(x,x) \vdash x \mapsto 0, \exists y(y > 0 \wedge x \mapsto y)$ satisfies the condition, and its validity is checked in the following way.

- It is decomposed into several sorted entailments: in this case, it produces the same entailment.
- Compute $P(\mathrm{true}, \mathrm{Arr}(x,x), S_1)$, where S_1 is $\{(\mathrm{true}, x \mapsto 0), (y > 0, x \mapsto y)\}$. It becomes $P(x < x, x \mapsto z * \mathrm{Arr}(x + 1, x), S_1) \wedge P(x = x, x \mapsto z, S_1)$ by ($\mathrm{Arr}\mapsto$). Then it becomes
  $$P(x < x \wedge x < x + 1, \mathrm{Arr}(x + 1, x), S_2) \wedge P(x = x \wedge x < x + 1, \mathrm{emp}, S_2),$$
  where S_2 is $\{(x = x \wedge z = 0, \mathrm{emp}), (y > 0 \wedge x = x \wedge z = y, \mathrm{emp})\}$. The former conjunct becomes $P(x = x \wedge x < x + 1, \mathrm{Arr}(x + 1, x), \emptyset)$ by (NEmpEmp), then, by (empty), it becomes $\neg(x = x \wedge x < x + 1 \wedge x + 1 \leq x)$, which is equivalent to $\neg(x < x + 1 \wedge x + 1 \leq x)$. The latter conjunct becomes $x = x \wedge x < x + 1 \rightarrow (x = x \wedge z = 0) \vee (y > 0 \wedge x = x \wedge z = y)$, which is equivalent to $x < x + 1 \rightarrow z = 0 \vee (y > 0 \wedge z = y)$,
- Check validity of the formula $\forall x z \exists y P(\mathrm{true}, \mathrm{Arr}(x,x), S_1)$, which is equivalent to $\forall x z \exists y(\neg(x < x + 1 \wedge x + 1 \leq x) \wedge (z = 0 \vee (y > 0 \wedge z = y)))$. Finally the procedure answers "valid", since the produced Presburger formula is valid.

Remark 1. Our result can be extend to the class of entailments which are semantically equivalent to entailments that satisfy the condition. For example, the entailment $\mathrm{Arr}(1, 10) \vdash \mathrm{Arr}(1, x) * \mathrm{Arr}(x + 1, 10)$ does not satisfy the condition because the occurrences of the array atomic formulas on the succedent are not in the form required by the condition. However it can be decided, since it is equivalent to the following entailment which satisfy the condition:

$$x = 1 + z \wedge x + w = 9 \wedge \mathrm{Arr}(1, 10) \vdash \mathrm{Arr}(1, 1 + z) * \mathrm{Arr}(z + 2, (z + 2) + w).$$

In other words, our procedure can decide an entailment that the lengths of the array predicate on the succedent do not depend on the existential variables.

4   Correctness of Decision Procedure

This section shows correctness of our decision procedure. We first show the basic property of sorted entailments.

Lemma 1. $s \models \varphi \to \bigvee_{i \in I} \phi_i$ *is equivalent to*
$s \models \widetilde{\varphi'} \to \bigvee \{ \widetilde{\phi'} \mid i \in I, \phi' \in \mathrm{Perm}(\phi_i) \}$ *for all* $\varphi' \in \mathrm{Perm}(\varphi)$

Proof. We first show the left-to-right part. Assume the left-hand side of the claim. Fix $\varphi' \in \mathrm{Perm}(\varphi)$ and suppose $s, h \models \widetilde{\varphi'}$. Then we have $s, h \models \varphi$. By the assumption, $s, h \models \phi_i$ for some $i \in I$. Hence we have $s, h \models \bigvee \{ \widetilde{\phi'} \mid i \in I, \phi' \in \mathrm{Perm}(\phi_i) \}$. Next we show the right-to-left part. Assume the right-hand side and $s, h \models \varphi$. We have $s, h \models \widetilde{\varphi'}$ for some $\varphi' \in \mathrm{Perm}(\varphi)$. By the assumption, $s, h \models \widetilde{\phi'}$ for some $\phi' \in \mathrm{Perm}(\phi_i)$. Thus we have $s, h \models \phi_i$ for some $i \in I$.   □

This lemma shows that validity checking problem of a given entailment can be reduced to that of several sorted entailments.

4.1   Correctness of Translation

This subsection shows correctness of the translation P. The main difficulty for showing correctness is how to handle the new variables (denoted by z) that are introduced during the unfolding P. In order to do this, we temporarily extend our language with new terms, denoted by $[t]$. A term $[t]$ means the value at the address t, that is, it is interpreted to $h(s(t))$ under (s, h). We will use this notation instead of z, since z must appear in the form $t \mapsto z$ during unfolding P, and this t is unique for z. Notice that both s and h are necessary for interpreting a formula of the extended language even if it is a pure formula.

In this extended language, we temporarily introduce a variant P' of P so that we use $[t]$ instead of z, which is defined in the same way as P except

$$P'(\Pi, \mathrm{Arr}(t, t') * \Sigma, S) =_{\mathrm{def}} P'(\Pi \wedge t' = t, t \mapsto [t] * \Sigma, S)$$
$$\wedge \, P'(\Pi \wedge t' > t, t \mapsto [t] * \mathrm{Arr}(t+1, t') * \Sigma, S),$$

when $(\Pi'', t'' \mapsto u'' * \Sigma'') \in S$. Note that P' never introduces any new variables.

We will introduce some notations. Let S be $\{ (\Pi, \Sigma) \}_{i \in I}$. Then we write $\widetilde{S}$ for $\{ \Pi_i \wedge \widetilde{\Sigma_i} \}_{i \in I}$. We write $\mathrm{Dom}(s, \Sigma)$ for the set of addresses used by Σ under s, that is, it is inductively defined as follows: $\mathrm{Dom}(s, \mathrm{emp}) = \emptyset$, $\mathrm{Dom}(s, \mathrm{emp} * \Sigma_1) = \mathrm{Dom}(s, \Sigma_1)$, $\mathrm{Dom}(s, t \mapsto u * \Sigma_1) = \{ s(t) \} \cup \mathrm{Dom}(s, \Sigma_1)$, and $\mathrm{Dom}(s, \mathrm{Arr}(t, u) * \Sigma_1) = \{ s(t), \ldots, s(u) \} \cup \mathrm{Dom}(s, \Sigma_1)$ if $s(t) \leq s(u)$.

The next lemma clarifies the connections between entailments, P, and P'.

Lemma 2. (1) *Assume* $s, h \models \hat{\Pi} \wedge \hat{\Sigma}$. *Suppose* $P'(\Pi, \Sigma, S)$ *appears in the unfolding of* $P'(\hat{\Pi}, \hat{\Sigma}, \hat{S})$. *Then*
$$s, h|_{\mathrm{Dom}(s, \Sigma)} \models P'(\Pi, \Sigma, S) \text{ iff } s, h|_{\mathrm{Dom}(s, \Sigma)} \models \Pi \wedge \mathrm{Sorted}(\Sigma) \to \bigvee \widetilde{S}.$$

(2) $\forall sh(s, h \models \Pi \wedge \widetilde{\Sigma} \rightarrow s, h \models \exists \overrightarrow{y} P'(\Pi, \Sigma, S))$ iff $\Pi \wedge \widetilde{\Sigma} \models \exists \overrightarrow{y} \bigvee \widetilde{S}$.

(3) $\models \neg(\Pi \wedge \mathrm{Sorted}(\Sigma)) \rightarrow P(\Pi, \Sigma, S)$.

(4) $\forall sh(s, h \models \Pi \wedge \widetilde{\Sigma} \rightarrow s, h \models \forall \overrightarrow{z} \exists \overrightarrow{y} P(\Pi, \Sigma, S))$ iff $\models \forall \overrightarrow{z} \exists \overrightarrow{y} P(\Pi, \Sigma, S)$.

Proof. The claim (1) is shown by induction on the steps $=_{\mathrm{def}}$. The claim (2) can be obtained by using (1). The claim (3) is proved by induction on the steps of $=_{\mathrm{def}}$. The claim (4) is shown by using (3). □

Recall that our condition requires that lengths of arrays on the succedent does not depend on existential variables. We note that, under our condition, each t that appears as $t \mapsto u$ or $\mathrm{Arr}(t, t')$ in the second argument of P' during the unfolding of P' does not contain any existential variables. By this fact, we can see that each term $[t]$ does not contain existential variables, since it first appears as $t \mapsto [t]$ in the second argument of P' during the unfolding of P'.

Proof of Theorem 1. Let S be $\{(\Pi_i, \Sigma_i)\}_{i \in I}$. Then the left-hand side is equivalent to $\Pi \wedge \widetilde{\Sigma} \models \exists \overrightarrow{y} \bigvee \widetilde{S}$. Moreover, by Lemma 2 (2), it is equivalent to

$$\forall sh(s, h \models \Pi \wedge \widetilde{\Sigma} \rightarrow s, h \models \exists \overrightarrow{y} P'(\Pi, \Sigma, S)) \tag{a}$$

By Lemma 2 (4), the right-hand side is equivalent to

$$\forall sh \forall \overrightarrow{z}(s, h \models \Pi \wedge \widetilde{\Sigma} \rightarrow s \models \exists \overrightarrow{y} P(\Pi, \Sigma, S)). \tag{b}$$

Now we will show the equivalence of (a) and (b). Here we assume $[t_1], \ldots, [t_n]$ appear in $P'(\Pi, \Sigma, S)$ and $s \models t_1 < \ldots < t_n$, we let $\overrightarrow{z} = z_1, \ldots, z_n$. Notice that each $[t_j]$ does not contain any existential variable because of the condition. So we can obtain $P'(\Pi, \Sigma, S) = P(\Pi, \Sigma, S)[\overrightarrow{z} := [\overrightarrow{t}]]$. Hence (a) is obtained from (b) by taking z_i to be $[t_i]$ for $1 \leq i \leq n$.

We show the inverse direction. Assume (a). Fix s, h, and $\overrightarrow{a}$ for $\overrightarrow{z}$. Let s' be $s[\overrightarrow{z} := \overrightarrow{a}]$. Let h' be $h[s(\overrightarrow{t}) := \overrightarrow{a}]$. Then by (a), we have

$$s, h' \models \Pi \wedge \widetilde{\Sigma} \rightarrow s, h' \models \exists \overrightarrow{y} P'(\Pi, \Sigma, S).$$

We claim that $s, h' \models \exists \overrightarrow{y}.P'(\Pi, \Sigma, S)$ is equivalent to $s' \models \exists \overrightarrow{y}.P(\Pi, \Sigma, S)$. We also claim that $s, h' \models \Pi \wedge \widetilde{\Sigma}$ is equivalent to $s, h \models \Pi \wedge \widetilde{\Sigma}$, since each t_i appears as an address of an array predicate in Σ. Therefore we have (b). □

5 Improvement of Decision Procedure

Our decision procedure is not efficient because of the decomposition. The given unsorted entailment is decomposed into some sorted entailments with very large number of succedents. Recall that $|\Sigma|$ is the number of $*$ in Σ. Then an unsorted entailment $\Pi \wedge \Sigma \vdash \{\exists \overrightarrow{y_i}(\Pi_i \wedge \Sigma_i)\}_{i \in I}$ is decomposed into $|\Sigma|!$ -sorted entailments with $\sum_{i \in I} |\Sigma_i|!$ -succedents.

We currently adapt the following two ideas to improve this situation.

(U) Elimination of redundancy by using unsatisfiability checking. We can easily observe that sorted entailments after decomposition often contain many redundant parts. For example, let σ_1, σ_2 and σ_3 be $1 \mapsto 10$, $2 \mapsto 20$ and $3 \mapsto 30$, respectively. An unsorted entailment $\sigma_2 * \sigma_1 \vdash \sigma_1 * \sigma_2, \sigma_3$ is decomposed into the following sorted entailments (after some simplification)

$$2 < 1 \wedge \sigma_2 * \sigma_1 \vdash 1 < 2 \wedge \sigma_1 * \sigma_2, \, 2 < 1 \wedge \sigma_2 * \sigma_1, \, \sigma_3$$
$$1 < 2 \wedge \sigma_1 * \sigma_2 \vdash 1 < 2 \wedge \sigma_1 * \sigma_2, \, 2 < 1 \wedge \sigma_2 * \sigma_1, \, \sigma_3$$

The first entailment is trivially valid, since its antecedent is unsatisfiable. So we can skip checking this entailment. The last two succedents of the second entailment are redundant, since they never satisfied with the antecedent. So we can drop them. More formally, we apply the following reduction rule:

$$\varphi \vdash \overrightarrow{\phi_1}, \phi, \overrightarrow{\phi_2} \text{ is reduced to } \varphi \vdash \overrightarrow{\phi_1}, \overrightarrow{\phi_2} \text{ if } \varphi \wedge \phi \text{ is unsatisfiable.}$$

(F) Frame elimination by using the invertible frame rule. Our second improvement is to reduce the number of separating conjunctions in the given unsorted entailment (before the decomposition process). This improvement is effective since reducing the number of separating conjunctions reduces the number of the succedents after decomposition.

In order to reduce separating conjunctions, we use the frame rule: $\Pi \wedge \Sigma \vdash \Pi' \wedge \Sigma'$ implies $\Pi \wedge \sigma * \Sigma \vdash \Pi' \wedge \sigma * \Sigma'$, where σ is $t \mapsto u$ or $\mathrm{Arr}(t, u)$. However the frame rule of this form is not invertible, that is, the inverse direction of the implication does not generally hold. In our setting, since we have inequalities, we can define $\mathrm{Disj}(\sigma, \Sigma)$ as a pure formula, which means the memory cells used by σ and Σ are disjoint. Hence we have the following **invertible frame rule**:

$$\Pi \wedge \sigma * \Sigma \vdash \{\exists \overrightarrow{y_i}(\Pi_i \wedge \sigma * \Sigma_i)\}_{i \in I} \iff \Pi \wedge \mathrm{Disj}(\sigma, \Sigma) \wedge \Sigma \vdash \{\exists \overrightarrow{y_i}(\Pi_i \wedge \Sigma_i)\}_{i \in I}$$

We consider this invertible frame rule as a rewriting rule from the left-hand side to the right-hand side. By applying this rewriting rule as much as possible, the given entailment can be rewritten to entailments with a smaller number of $*$.

This procedure has a great effect on efficiency improvement of our decision procedure, since reducing the number of $*$ highly contributes to reduce the sizes and the number of sorted entailments that are generated by the decomposition.

6   Implementation and Experiments

This section explains our tool **SLar**, which is the implementation of our decision procedure.

6.1   Entailment Checker SLar

The behavior of **SLar** is based on the decision procedure discussed in the previous sections. It consists of the following three parts:

(1) The optimizing part, which reduces the size of a given entailment by the invertible frame rule (**F**). It also checks satisfiability of the antecedent of the entailment. **SLar** immediately answers "valid" if the antecedent is unsatisfiable.

(2) The decomposing part, which decomposes the reduced entailment into several sorted entailments, that is, the given unsorted entailment $\varphi \vdash \{\phi_i\}_{i \in I}$ is decomposed into sorted entailments $\widetilde{\varphi'} \vdash \{\widetilde{\phi'} \mid i \in I, \phi' \in Perm(\phi_i)\}$, where $\varphi' \in Perm(\varphi)$. The correctness of this part is guaranteed by Lemma 1. After decomposition, redundant parts are reduced by the unsatisfiability checking (**U**).

(3) The translating part, which translates sorted entailments into Presburger formulas according to the translation P given in the Sect. 3. The theoretical correctness of this part is guaranteed by Theorem 1.

(4) The checking part, in which the SMT-solver **Z3** [21] is invoked to check validity of the generated Presburger formula.

The current version of **SLar** is written in about 3900 lines of OCaml codes (360 lines for the decomposing part and some optimization, 1900 lines for the translating part, and 1200 lines for the checking part).

The improvements **U** and **F** mentioned above are optional, that is, **SLar** has options which changes its behavior with (or without) them.

6.2   Experiments and Evaluation

This subsection reports on the performance of **SLar**. As far as we know, there is no suitable benchmark of entailments with arrays. So we automatically generated 120 entailments by using our analyzer of the C language. Each entailment has a single conclusion and is of small size (there are 1 or 2 separating conjunctions on each side). We call this set of entailments Base. 40 out of 120 are entailments with only the points-to predicate (called the group Pto). Another 40 are entailments with only arrays (called the group Array). The rest 40 entailments contain both the points-to and array predicates (called the group Mix). In each case, half of the entailments are valid.

Then we automatically produced the following sets of entailments from Base. All experimental files can be found in the web[1].

- SingleFrame-n ($n = 2, 3$): A set of single-conclusion entailments produced by putting a frame of size n to the entailments of Base. The frames are chosen to keeping the grouping, that is, frames of the points-to predicate are used for Pto, frames of arrays are used for Array, and random frames are used for Mix;

- SingleNFrame-n ($n = 2, 3$): A set of single-conclusion entailments produced by putting different spatial predicates of length n to each side of the entailments of Base. The spatial predicates are chosen to keeping the grouping;

---

[1] https://github.com/DaisukeKimura/slar.

- Multi: A set of multi-conclusion entailments with at most 3 disjuncts. They are produced by adding extra conclusions to the entailments of Base.

In order to evaluate the effect of our improvement discussed in the previous subsection, we provided the options that change whether **SLar** uses the unsatisfiability checking (U) and the invertible frame rule (F).

For each categories Base, SingleFrame-n, SingleNFrame-n and Multi, we executed our tool with (or without) the options of U and F, and recorded its execution time (with timeout 300 s). Our PC environment is MacOS X machine with Intel Core i5 3.1 GHz processor and 8 GB memory.

The results summarized in the tables of Fig. 2, where $U + F$ means that the both options of the invertible frame rule and of the unsatisfiability checking are turned on. U and F means that only corresponding option is used. None means that none of them are used. Each table shows the number of entailments (out of 120) whose solved time satisfy the time condition displayed on the top of the table. For example, the table of Base shows that 111 entailments are solved in less than 0.1 s by using both options ($U + F$).

Base					time out
	< 0.1s	< 1s	< 10s	< 300s	(300s)
$U + F$	111	120	120	120	0
U	103	120	120	120	0
F	106	120	120	120	0
None	82	116	120	120	0

Multi					time out
	< 0.1s	< 1s	< 10s	< 300s	(300s)
$U + F$	57	108	120	120	0
U	45	106	120	120	0
F	24	101	115	120	0
None	23	101	111	118	2

SingleFrame-2					time out
	< 0.1s	< 1s	< 10s	< 300s	(300s)
$U + F$	101	118	120	120	0
U	78	119	120	120	0
F	97	116	120	120	0
None	31	68	88	120	0

SingleFrame-3					time out
	< 0.1s	< 1s	< 10s	< 300s	(300s)
$U + F$	81	107	118	120	0
U	37	95	120	120	0
F	80	105	116	119	1
None	14	66	84	106	14

SingleNFrame-2					time out
	< 0.1s	< 1s	< 10s	< 300s	(300s)
$U + F$	79	119	120	120	0
U	71	119	120	120	0
F	81	117	120	120	0
None	31	80	111	119	1

SingleNFrame-3					time out
	< 0.1s	< 1s	< 10s	< 300s	(300s)
$U + F$	34	102	119	120	0
U	33	87	118	120	0
F	39	97	117	120	0
None	14	64	99	116	4

Fig. 2. Experimental results

For Base, almost the entailments (111 out of 120) are answered within 0.1 s if both options are used. The rest 9 entailments are solved within 0.2 s. All are answered within 2.1 s without the acceleration options. Comparing $U + F$ and None, our tool becomes up to 15 times, average 4 times faster.

The categories SingleFrame-n ($n = 2, 3$) show the effect of using the invertible frame rule, because entailments of these categories are in the form for which the invertible frame rule can be applied. In SingleFrame-3, the cases of $U + F$ are about 10 times faster on average than that of **U** (without the invertible frame rule). Sometimes the tool becomes more than 200 times faster!

The categories SingleNFrame-n ($n = 2, 3$) are intended to limit use of the invertible frame rule. In the case of **U** + **F** of SingleNFrame-3, almost entailments (102 out of 120) are solved within 1 s.

Checking the category Multi is mainly accelerated by the unsatisfiability checking. This is because unsatisfiable disjuncts of the succedent are eliminated in early stage of the decision procedure. The cases of **U** + **F** are about 8 times faster on average than that of **F** (without the unsatisfiability checking).

In the case of **U** + **F** of each category, the average time of the group Pto is less than 0.3 s, the average time of Array is less than 0.6 s, the average time of Mix is less than 0.7 s. The average time about invalid entailments is faster than that of valid entailments. It is because that our procedure immediately answers "invalid" when it finds an invalid decomposed entailment.

From the results of Base, our tool works very quickly for small entailments (the number of separating conjunctions on each side is less than or equal to 2). However, as we expected, it becomes slower for entailments with greater sizes. Hence it is quite important to reduce the sizes of entailments. The results of SingleFrame-3 and SingleNFrame-3 shows that the invertible frame rule greatly contributes for reducing sizes and improving efficiency. The effect of our improvement remarkably appears when sizes of entailments are large. In this experiment the effect worked well in the case of SingleNFrame-3 (Fig. 3).

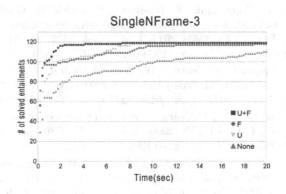

Fig. 3. Experimental result of SingleNFrame-3

7   Conclusion and Future Work

In this paper we investigated the separation logic with arrays, and showed decidability of its entailment problem under the size condition. We also implemented our decision procedure that checks validity of entailments. The performance of our algorithm deeply depends on the number of separating conjunctions. So it is quite important to reduce their number. From the results of the experiments, we are convinced that the invertible frame rule and the undecidability checking work well and contribute for improving the entailment checking tool.

Currently we have put a condition for proving correctness of the decision procedure. However our tool also seems to work well for entailments that are out of the condition. So we conjecture that correctness of the decision procedure also can be shown without the condition.

Our algorithm is still inefficient since the performance of our tool slows sharply as the number of separating conjunction increases. One possible way is to split the given entailment into some smaller entailments, that is, split $\Pi_1 \wedge \Sigma_1 * \Sigma_1' \vdash \Pi_2 \wedge \Sigma_2 * \Sigma_2'$ into $\Pi_1 \wedge \Sigma_1 \vdash \Pi_2 \wedge \Sigma_2$ and $\Pi_1 \wedge \Sigma_1' \vdash \Pi_2 \wedge \Sigma_2'$. Of course the difficult point of this approach is to find the correct splitting point. However the memory model of the C language can be considered as the set of pairs of the form (p, n), where p is an identifier that indicates a domain and n is an offset integer [19]. If we carefully translate C codes into formulas of separation logic without losing the information of domains, it would be reasonable to choose a boundary of two different domains as a splitting point.

Acknowledgments. We would like to thank Prof. Xiaokang Qiu and the anonymous referees for valuable comments.

References

1. Antonopoulos, T., Gorogiannis, N., Haase, C., Kanovich, M., Ouaknine, J.: Foundations for decision problems in separation logic with general inductive predicates. In: Muscholl, A. (ed.) FoSSaCS 2014. LNCS, vol. 8412, pp. 411–425. Springer, Heidelberg (2014). https://doi.org/10.1007/978-3-642-54830-7_27

2. Berdine, J., Calcagno, C., O'Hearn, P.W.: A decidable fragment of separation logic. In: Lodaya, K., Mahajan, M. (eds.) FSTTCS 2004. LNCS, vol. 3328, pp. 97–109. Springer, Heidelberg (2004). https://doi.org/10.1007/978-3-540-30538-5_9

3. Berdine, J., Calcagno, C., O'Hearn, P.: Symbolic execution with separation logic. In: Yi, K. (ed.) APLAS 2005. LNCS, vol. 3780, pp. 52–68. Springer, Heidelberg (2005). https://doi.org/10.1007/11575467_5

4. Bouajjani, A., Drăgoi, C., Enea, C., Sighireanu, M.: A logic-based framework for reasoning about composite data structures. In: Bravetti, M., Zavattaro, G. (eds.) CONCUR 2009. LNCS, vol. 5710, pp. 178–195. Springer, Heidelberg (2009). https://doi.org/10.1007/978-3-642-04081-8_13

5. Bradley, A.R., Manna, Z., Sipma, H.B.: What's decidable about arrays? In: Emerson, E.A., Namjoshi, K.S. (eds.) VMCAI 2006. LNCS, vol. 3855, pp. 427–442. Springer, Heidelberg (2005). https://doi.org/10.1007/11609773_28

6. Brotherston, J., Fuhs, C., Gorogiannis, N., Navarro Pérez, J.A.: A decision procedure for satisfiability in separation logic with inductive predicates. In: Proceedings of CSL-LICS, Article No. 25 (2014)

7. Brotherston, J., Gorogiannis, N., Kanovich, M.: Biabduction (and related problems) in array separation logic. In: de Moura, L. (ed.) CADE 2017. LNCS (LNAI), vol. 10395, pp. 472–490. Springer, Cham (2017). https://doi.org/10.1007/978-3-319-63046-5_29

8. Calcagno, C., Distefano, D., O'Hearn, P.W., Yang, H.: Beyond reachability: shape abstraction in the presence of pointer arithmetic. In: Yi, K. (ed.) SAS 2006. LNCS, vol. 4134, pp. 182–203. Springer, Heidelberg (2006). https://doi.org/10.1007/11823230_13

9. Calcagno, C., Distefano, D., O'Hearn, P.W., Yang, H.: Compositional shape analysis by means of bi-abduction. J. ACM **58**(6), 1–66 (2011)

10. Cook, B., Haase, C., Ouaknine, J., Parkinson, M., Worrell, J.: Tractable reasoning in a fragment of separation logic. In: Katoen, J.-P., König, B. (eds.) CONCUR 2011. LNCS, vol. 6901, pp. 235–249. Springer, Heidelberg (2011). https://doi.org/10.1007/978-3-642-23217-6_16

11. Enea, C., Saveluc, V., Sighireanu, M.: Compositional invariant checking for overlaid and nested linked lists. In: Felleisen, M., Gardner, P. (eds.) ESOP 2013. LNCS, vol. 7792, pp. 129–148. Springer, Heidelberg (2013). https://doi.org/10.1007/978-3-642-37036-6_9

12. Enea, C., Lengál, O., Sighireanu, M., Vojnar, T.: Compositional entailment checking for a fragment of separation logic. In: Garrigue, J. (ed.) APLAS 2014. LNCS, vol. 8858, pp. 314–333. Springer, Cham (2014). https://doi.org/10.1007/978-3-319-12736-1_17

13. Iosif, R., Rogalewicz, A., Simacek, J.: The tree width of separation logic with recursive definitions. In: Bonacina, M.P. (ed.) CADE 2013. LNCS (LNAI), vol. 7898, pp. 21–38. Springer, Heidelberg (2013). https://doi.org/10.1007/978-3-642-38574-2_2

14. Iosif, R., Rogalewicz, A., Vojnar, T.: Deciding entailments in inductive separation logic with tree automata. In: Cassez, F., Raskin, J.-F. (eds.) ATVA 2014. LNCS, vol. 8837, pp. 201–218. Springer, Cham (2014). https://doi.org/10.1007/978-3-319-11936-6_15

15. Kimura, D., Tatsuta, M.: Decision procedure for entailment of symbolic heaps with arrays (2017). An extended version https://arxiv.org/abs/1708.06696

16. Lahiri, S., Qadeer, S.: Back to the future: revisiting precise program verification using SMT solvers. In: Proceedings of POPL 2008, pp. 171–182 (2008)

17. Piskac, R., Wies, T., Zufferey, D.: Automating separation logic using SMT. In: Sharygina, N., Veith, H. (eds.) CAV 2013. LNCS, vol. 8044, pp. 773–789. Springer, Heidelberg (2013). https://doi.org/10.1007/978-3-642-39799-8_54

18. Reynolds, J.C.: Separation logic: a logic for shared mutable data structures. In: Proceedings of Seventeenth Annual IEEE Symposium on Logic in Computer Science (LICS2002), pp. 55–74 (2002)

19. Sekiguchi, T.: A practical pointer analysis for C language. Comput. Softw. **21**(6), 456–471 (2004)

20. Tatsuta, M., Kimura, D.: Separation logic with monadic inductive definitions and implicit existentials. In: Feng, X., Park, S. (eds.) APLAS 2015. LNCS, vol. 9458, pp. 69–89. Springer, Cham (2015). https://doi.org/10.1007/978-3-319-26529-2_5

21. de Moura, L., Bjørner, N.: Z3: an efficient SMT solver. In: Ramakrishnan, C.R., Rehof, J. (eds.) TACAS 2008. LNCS, vol. 4963, pp. 337–340. Springer, Heidelberg (2008). https://doi.org/10.1007/978-3-540-78800-3_24

Bringing Order to the Separation Logic Jungle

Qinxiang Cao$^{(\boxtimes)}$, Santiago Cuellar, and Andrew W. Appel

Princeton University, Princeton, NJ, USA
{qinxiang,scuellar,appel}@princeton.edu

Abstract. Research results from so-called "classical" separation logics are not easily ported to so-called "intuitionistic" separation logics, and vice versa. Basic questions like, "Can the frame rule be proved independently of whether the programming language is garbage-collected?" "Can amortized resource analysis be ported from one separation logic to another?" should be straightforward. But they are not. Proofs done in a particular separation logic are difficult to generalize. We argue that this limitation is caused by incompatible semantics. For example, emp sometimes holds everywhere and sometimes only on units.

In this paper, we introduce a unifying semantics and build a framework that allows to reason parametrically over all separation logics. Many separation algebras in the literature are accompanied, explicitly or implicitly, by a preorder. Our key insight is to axiomatize the interaction between the join relation and the preorder. We prove every separation logic to be sound and complete with respect to this unifying semantics. Further, our framework enables us to generalize the sound0.ness proofs for the frame rule and CSL. It also reveals a new world of meaningful intermediate separation logics between "intuitionistic" and "classical".

Keywords: Separation logic · Order · Separation algebra

1 Introduction

Separation logic, introduced at the turn of the millennium by Reynolds [32], has led to tremendous progress in modular verification in a multitude of applications: for reasoning about multiple languages, including those with C-like (malloc/free) or Java-like (garbage-collected) memory model; for reasoning about concurrency; for amortized resource analysis; or for static automated bug analysis. Unfortunately, many of those instances disagree on the definitions of separation logic itself. In 2010, Parkinson [27] warned us about this indiscriminate proliferation of separation logics.

The problem with this proliferation of logics is that each logic requires a new soundness proof.

— *The Next 700 Separation Logics*

© Springer International Publishing AG 2017
B.-Y.E. Chang (Ed.): APLAS 2017, LNCS 10695, pp. 190–211, 2017.
https://doi.org/10.1007/978-3-319-71237-6_10

Seven years later, separation logics are still tailored for particular uses, which makes them incompatible and hard to extend; they have different proof rules, they use custom underlying models and impose conflicting semantics.

The best example of the divide originates from the conventional wisdom [1,5,18,28] that "intuitionistic separation logics are for garbage-collected languages, classical separation logics are for malloc/free languages." We think that intuitionistic vs. classical is not the right way to look at it; the problem with the nomenclature is twofold.

First, it creates a false dichotomy. The literature has almost exclusively dealt with these two flavors of logic, while ignoring a large variety of intermediate logics. For example, it is known that the elimination rule of separating conjunction ($\vdash \varphi * \psi \rightarrow \varphi$) is incompatible with the law of excluded middle [19] but, as we show in this paper, it is compatible with some weaker forms. The resulting intermediate separation logics are rich and meaningful but have largely been neglected. In fact, we found separation logic instances that admitted intermediate rules unbeknownst to the authors [1,11,17].

Second, the naming convention creates two seemingly incompatible bodies of work. Since authors choose one or the other framework, results are often hard to extend and different works are hard to compare. For instance, the soundness of the *frame rule* given the *frame property* [19] has to be prZZoved anew for every different semantic model. Similarly, the soundness of concurrent separation logic proved by Brookes [7] does not naturally extend to garbage-collected languages. Other works that are hard to extend include the discussion of *preciseness* and the conjunction rule [16,26], and recent advances in logics for concurrency [22].

The main difficulty in unifying the two worlds is that authors use different and sometimes incompatible semantics. For instance, one side enforces that emp holds only on units, while for the other side it is simply equal to True. In fact, even within each side there are several conflicting semantics.

Ideally, the semantics of the separating operators would be given by the intuitive definitions

$$m \vDash \varphi * \psi \triangleq \text{exists } m_1 m_2 \text{ s.t. } \oplus (m_1, m_2, m) \text{ and } m_1 \vDash \varphi \text{ and } m_2 \vDash \psi \quad (4.1)$$

$$m \vDash \varphi \ast\!\!-\!\!\ast \psi \triangleq \text{for any } m_1 m_2, \text{ if } \oplus (m, m_1, m_2), m_1 \vDash \varphi \text{ implies } m_2 \vDash \psi \quad (4.2)$$

where $\oplus$ is a join operation on the underlying model, called a *separation algebra* [10]. Unfortunately, when the objects of interest are not just simple heaplets— when step-indexing [6,17] or topology [31, Sect. 3] or amortized analysis [4] or buffer flushing [11] is involved—authors have had to define more intricate semantics; the simple semantics is (apparently) unsound. We explain this in Sect. 5.3. Not only are these "messier" semantic definitions inconvenient, they cause non-portability of results.

In this paper we show that all of those semantics are in fact instances of a *flat semantics* over the generalized *ordered separation algebras*. An ordered separation algebra is just a separation algebra together with a preorder $\leq$.

Ordered separation algebras are not a new idea. In fact, the heap model defined by Reynolds in his first paper on separation logic [32] is ordered by heap extension. Similarly, the monotonic state of Pilkiewicz and Pottier [29] and the amortized resource of Atkey [4] are also ordered. Furthermore, Pym *et al.* [31], Galmiche *et al.* [15] and Jensen [20] have used ordered separation algebras explicitly as their semantic model. Despite this common trend, orders have been used to define different semantics, tailored to specific models, and no unification had yet been discovered.

Contributions. We argue that all models of separation logic are ordered separation algebras (Sect. 5.1) and we show that all semantics in the literature, to the best of our knowledge, can be formulated as instances of our *flat semantics* (Theorem 3). Our unification holds for the "classical" side, the "intuitionistic" side and all separation logics in between.

By this unifying semantics, we establish a correspondence between all different separation logics and classes of ordered separation algebras. We prove that any separation logic is sound and complete w.r.t. flat semantics in its corresponding class of models (Sect. 6).

We generalize two theoretical applications of separation logics (Sect. 7). We show that the frame rule (given frame property) and CSL are sound parametrically on different separation logic semantics.

All the definitions, propositions, lemmas and theorems in this paper have been formalized in Coq. We will often omit uninteresting proofs, but a curious reader can find them in our publicly available development.

2 Related Work

Authors use both "separation logic" and "bunched logic" to describe a propositional logic extended with separating connectives ($*$ and $-\!*$). Usually, "bunched logics" (or bunched implication, BI) [25] are used when the semantics are defined over abstract relational Kripke models while "separation logics" [32] are used when the semantics are defined over some specific memory model. This distinction is not absolute. Calcagno *et al.* [10] first studied separation logic over abstract models, i.e. separation algebras. In this paper, we always use the name "separation logic". What the bunched logic literatures call BI is, in our terminology, the proof theory IP + SL; what they call Boolean BI (BBI) we characterize as IP + SL + EM. Some authors also use "separation logic" to describe Hoare logics whose assertion languages contain $*$ and $-\!*$. In this paper, we call them Hoare separation logics.

Ishtiaq and O'Hearn [19] showed a modal translation $(\cdot)^\circ$ that embeds separation logic without excluded middle [32] into their logic with excluded middle. The translation preserves validity; i.e. $s, h \models^{Reynolds} P \Leftrightarrow s, h \models^{Ishtiaq} P^\circ$. The translation is enough to show the soundness of both logics with respect to their model, but not for other models. Of particular interest, they show the *frame rule* is sound w.r.t. operational semantics with the *frame property*. We extend the soundness of the frame rule, parametrically on different semantic models.

Galmiche and Larchey-Wendling [14] prove the completeness of classical separation logics (BBI). Our soundness and completeness proof generalizes their result to nonclassical logics.

Pym, O'Hearn and Yang [31] derive a Kripke semantic model for separation logics (called PDM) from topology semantics and prove its soundness and completeness. It is later used by other authors as a unifying semantic model. This semantics is equivalent to downwards semantics in this paper. Their model cannot cover step indexed models [6,17] and some variants of FSCQ's semantic model [11], which are instances of upwards semantics in this paper.

Jensen [20] has a thorough review of separation logics and separation algebras. The chapter is expositional, but he explicitly imposes an order on each separation algebra. Our presentation of separation logic semantics is closely related to his. In particular, his Propositions 3.6 and 3.7 correspond to our Definitions 13.1 (upwards semantics) and 13.2 (downwards semantics), of which he writes:

> The conditions of neither Proposition 3.6 nor Proposition 3.7 generalise the conditions of the other, so perhaps a unifying theorem is still waiting to be discovered.

Our Theorem 3 is exactly that theorem.

It is well known that separation logic is a kind of binary modal logic [31]. Some authors have proposed different semantics of intuitionistic (unary) modal logic—Simpson [33] showed that the main disagreement among them is a choice between requiring the frame to satisfy a closure property and building the monotonicity property into the semantic definition of modalities. Our discussion of upwards semantics, downwards semantics and flat semantics for separation logic is similar to that discussion in Simpson's thesis about modal logic. But we go further in this paper, we show a unifying solution of all these semantics.

3   Taxonomy of Separation Logic

In this section, we formally define the scope of separation logics based on their proof systems. In turn, this allows us to group the separation logics to provide parametric proofs of soundness and completeness in Sect. 6. This classification will hopefully dispel the unfortunate nomenclature (classical vs. intuitionistic) that has been prevalent.

We take the syntax below to be the assertion language of separation logic.

Definition 1 (Separation logic syntax). *For a given set of atomic assertions Σ, we use $\mathcal{L}(\Sigma)$ to represent the smallest language with all following assertions:*

$$\varphi ::= p(\in \Sigma) \mid \varphi_1 \wedge \varphi_2 \mid \varphi_1 \vee \varphi_2 \mid \varphi_1 \to \varphi_2 \mid \varphi_1 * \varphi_2 \mid \varphi_1 \mathbin{-\!\!*} \varphi_2 \mid \bot \mid \mathsf{emp}$$

As usual, we use the following connectives as abbreviations: $\varphi_1 \leftrightarrow \varphi_2 \triangleq (\varphi_1 \to \varphi_2) \wedge (\varphi_2 \to \varphi_1)$, $\neg\varphi \triangleq \varphi \to \bot$, $\top \triangleq \bot \to \bot$.

We will define separation logics based on a Hilbert-style proof system; that is a set of axioms and proof rules. Intuitionistic propositional logic is defined by the rules IP in Fig. 1. EM, GD and WEM in Fig. 2 are optional axioms for propositional logic. A logic with EM is classical, while the weaker axioms GD and WEM give rise to intermediate logics. Many other similar axioms give rise to more intermediate logics; we omit them here for the sake of space.

$$\frac{\vdash \varphi \quad \vdash \varphi \to \psi}{\vdash \psi} \text{ (MP)} \qquad \frac{\vdash \varphi \to \psi \to \varphi \wedge \psi}{(\wedge \text{I})} \qquad \frac{\vdash \varphi \wedge \psi \to \psi}{(\wedge \text{E}_2)} \qquad \frac{\vdash \psi \to \varphi \vee \psi}{(\vee \text{I}_2)}$$

$$\frac{\vdash \varphi \to (\psi \to \varphi)}{(\to_1)} \qquad \frac{\vdash \varphi \wedge \psi \to \varphi}{(\wedge \text{E}_1)} \qquad \frac{\vdash \varphi \to \varphi \vee \psi}{(\vee \text{I}_1)} \qquad \frac{\vdash \bot \to \varphi \; (\bot \text{E})}{}$$

$$\frac{\vdash (\varphi \to \psi \to \chi) \to (\varphi \to \psi) \to (\varphi \to \chi)}{(\to_2)} \qquad \frac{\vdash (\varphi \to \chi) \to (\psi \to \chi) \to (\varphi \vee \psi \to \chi)}{(\vee \text{E})}$$

Fig. 1. Axioms and rules of intuitionistic propositional logic (IP)

$$\vdash \neg\varphi \vee \neg\neg\varphi \qquad \text{(WEM)} \qquad\qquad \vdash \varphi * \psi \to \varphi \qquad (*\text{E})$$

$$\vdash \varphi \to \psi \vee \psi \to \varphi \qquad \text{(GD)} \qquad\qquad \vdash \mathsf{emp} \wedge (\varphi * \psi) \to \varphi \qquad (\text{eE})$$

$$\vdash \varphi \vee \neg\varphi \qquad \text{(EM)} \qquad\qquad \vdash \mathsf{emp} \wedge \varphi \to \varphi * \varphi \; (\text{eDUP})$$

Fig. 2. Optional axioms for propositional logic

Fig. 3. Optional axioms for separating connectives

The axioms and rules for minimum separation logic (SL) are in Fig. 4: commutativity, associativity, adjoint property of the separating operators, monotonicity of separation over implication and the fact the emp is a separation unit. The double line in *ADJ implies the derivation works both ways. The axioms *E, eE and eDUP in Fig. 3 are optional: *E is the elimination rule of the separating conjunction; eE enforces that every empty piece to be non-splittable; and eDUP says all empty pieces are duplicable.

Even with the axioms and proof rules in minimum separation logic (IP + SL), many useful properties can be derived. For example, all of the following assertions are provable in any separation logic: $\vdash (\varphi \!-\!\!*\psi) * \varphi \to \psi$, $\vdash (\varphi \vee \psi) * \chi \leftrightarrow (\varphi * \chi \vee \psi * \chi)$, $\vdash (\varphi \wedge \psi) * \chi \to (\varphi * \chi \wedge \psi * \chi)$.

To dispel the unfortunate nomenclature, we call a separation logic with EM *classical*, those with *E *garbage-collected* and those with eE and eDUP *malloc/free*.

$$\frac{}{\vdash \varphi * \psi \to \psi * \varphi}\ (*\text{COMM}) \qquad \frac{\vdash \varphi * \psi \to \chi}{\vdash \varphi \to \psi \text{-}* \chi}\ (*\text{ADJ}) \qquad \frac{}{\vdash \varphi * \text{emp} \leftrightarrow \varphi}\ (\text{EMP})$$

$$\frac{}{\vdash (\varphi * \psi) * \chi \to \varphi * (\psi * \chi)}\ (*\text{ASSOC}) \qquad \frac{\vdash \varphi_1 \to \psi_1 \quad \vdash \varphi_2 \to \psi_2}{\vdash \varphi_1 * \varphi_2 \to \psi_1 * \psi_2}\ (*\text{MONO})$$

Fig. 4. Axioms and rules for separating connectives (SL)

Degenerate separation logic. Reynolds [32] and Ishtiaq and O'Hearn [19] informally postulated that EM and $*$E are "incompatible". It turns out that if a separation logic Γ is classical and garbage-collected, its separating connectives collapses, i.e. for any φ and ψ: $\vdash^\Gamma \varphi * \psi \leftrightarrow \varphi \wedge \psi$ and $\vdash^\Gamma (\varphi \text{-}* \psi) \leftrightarrow (\varphi \to \psi)$.

Brotherston and Kanovich [8] prove that a separation logic collapses if it is malloc/free and garbage-collected at the same time. They also show that a classical and garbage-collected separation logic is malloc/free.

4 Background

4.1 Separation Algebra

The semantics of all separation logics are built on structures (e.g., heaps, histories, amortized resources) that share common properties such as associativity and commutativity.

Definition 2 (Commutativity). *For a set M, the relation $\oplus \subseteq M \times M \times M$ is commutative iff for all m_1, m_2, and m: $\oplus(m_1, m_2, m)$ implies $\oplus(m_2, m_1, m)$.*

Definition 3 (Associativity). *For a set M, the relation $\oplus \subseteq M \times M \times M$ is associative iff for all m_x m_y m_z m_{xy} and m_{xyz}, if $\oplus(m_x, m_y, m_{xy})$ and $\oplus(m_{xy}, m_z, m_{xyz})$, there exists m_{yz} such that $\oplus(m_y, m_z, m_{yz})$ and $\oplus(m_x, m_{yz}, m_{xyz})$.*

Calcagno, O'Hearn and Yang [10] first called such structures $(M, \oplus)$ *separation algebras* and proposed them to be also cancellative, functional (i.e. $\oplus(a, b, c)$ and $\oplus(a, b, c')$ implies $c = c'$) and with a unit. Since then, the definition has been revisited several times [12,13,16,30]. We follow Brotherston and Villard [9] in that the $\oplus$ relation is neither functional nor cancellative. We depart from them in that we require no units, so we only require a separation algebra to be commutative and associative.

Using the algebras, Calcagno, O'Hearn and Yang define the semantics of separation logic as in Definition 4. This is the most widely used and intuitive definition. Foreshadowing the stronger Definition (12), we will call them *weak semantics.*

Definition 4 (Weak Semantics.)

$$m \vDash \varphi * \psi \triangleq exists \ m_1 m_2 \ s.t. \ \oplus (m_1, m_2, m) \ and \ m_1 \vDash \varphi \ and \ m_2 \vDash \psi \quad (4.1)$$

$$m \vDash \varphi \text{-\!*} \psi \triangleq for \ any \ m_1 m_2, \ if \ \oplus (m, m_1, m_2), \ m_1 \vDash \varphi \ then \ m_2 \vDash \psi \quad (4.2)$$

4.2 Kripke Semantics for Intuitionistic Logic

The Kripke semantics [23] for the propositional language is defined on Kripke models.

Definition 5 (Kripke model). *For an intuitionistic logic with atomic proposition set Σ, a* Kripke model *is a tuple $(M, \leq, J)$ in which*

1. *$\leq$ is a preorder on M*
2. *$J \in M \rightarrow \mathcal{P}(\Sigma)$ is an interpretations of atomic propositions and is monotonic, i.e., for any $m, n \in M$, if $m \leq n$ then $J(m) \subseteq J(n)$.*

We also call such tuple $(M, \leq)$ a Kripke structure.

Definition 6 (Kripke Semantics). *Given a Kripke model $(M, \leq, J)$, the satisfaction relation $(\cdot \ \vDash_{(M, \leq, J)} \ \cdot)$ is defined as follows (when the Kripke model is unambiguous from the context, we will omit it for conciseness)*

$m \vDash p \triangleq \ p \in J(m)$ $m \vDash \varphi \vee \psi \triangleq \ m \vDash \varphi \ or \ m \vDash \psi$

$m \vDash \bot \triangleq \quad never$ $m \vDash \varphi \rightarrow \psi \triangleq \quad for \ any \ m_0, \ if \ m \leq m_0$

$m \vDash \varphi \wedge \psi \triangleq \ m \vDash \varphi \ and \ m \vDash \psi$ $then \ m_0 \vDash \varphi \ implies \ m_0 \vDash \psi$

Intuitionistic propositional logic is sound and complete w.r.t. this semantics. Moreover, Kripke semantics is a unifying solution of intuitionistic and classical propositional logics: the identity relation is a trivial order and classical logic is sound and complete w.r.t. Kripke semantics in all models with a discrete order.

5 Model and Semantics

In this section, we introduce a framework to define *flat semantics* on *ordered separation algebras* which unifies all different semantics of separation logic (we know of) in the literature.

We introduce *ordered separation algebras*, define properties that they and their elements may have (*increasing, unital, upwards-closed, downwards-closed*). We show examples from the literature of algebras with and without these properties. We show ways of constructing downwards-closed upwards-closed algebras. We demonstrate examples from the literature of different semantics of separation logic and we show that they are all equivalent to instances of *flat semantics*.

5.1 Ordered Separation Algebras

Using a Kripke semantics is a motivation to impose an order over separation algebras and in fact this is a very common practice (implicitly or explicitly). For example, the heap model defined by Reynolds in his first paper of separation logic [32] is ordered by heap extension, and the resources of a monotonically increasing counter [21,29] are ordered by the order of natural numbers.

More interesting examples are those that impose an execution order. For instance, states that are step indexed [2] will be ordered by the index, which decreases with execution. In the same vein, Pottier [30] has an *active execution order*[1] for elements of his algebra. The separation algebra by Jung *et al.* [6] is ordered both by heap extension and step index.

Since the identity relation is also a preorder, it is not overly restrictive to require separation algebras to be ordered—any separation algebra is trivially ordered by the discrete order. With that in mind we define *ordered separation algebra* as a more expressive way to view separation algebras.

Definition 7 (Ordered separation algebra). *An ordered separation algebra is a tuple* $(M, \leq, \oplus)$, *where* M *is the carrier set,* $\leq$ *is a preorder on* M *and* $\oplus \subseteq M \times M \times M$ *is a three-place relation that is commutative and associative.*

Just like in Dockins et al. [13], OSA form an algebra closed under cartesian product, disjoint sum and exponentiation.

If the order is irrelevant or can be inferred by context we will simply call it a *separation algebra*. Also, we call a tuple $(M, \leq, \oplus, J)$ an extended Kripke model if $(M, \leq, \oplus)$ is an OSA and $(M, \leq, J)$ is a Kripke model.

The most obvious example of OSAs are heaps $\mathcal{H}_V : \mathsf{adr} \rightharpoonup V$, which are most commonly discrete (i.e. ordered by $\Delta_2 \triangleq \{(h, h) \mid h \in \mathcal{H}_V\}$) or ordered by heap extension (i.e. $\sqsubseteq_{\mathcal{H}_V} \triangleq \{(h_1, h_2) \mid \mathsf{dom}\, h_1 \subseteq \mathsf{dom}\, h_2 \text{ and } \forall x \in \mathsf{dom}\, h_1, h_1(x) = h_2(x)\}$). Many other resources are OSAs, such as ordered monoids, which are used for amortized resource analysis [4].

5.2 Increasing Elements and Algebras

Definition 7 imposes almost no constraints on $\leq$ other than being a preorder. Particularly, there is no relation between $\oplus$ and $\leq$. We do this in order to be as general as possible and we will revisit this goal in Sect. 5.3. However, it is worth spelling out an intuitive and important connection between the two relations. In heaps with heap-extension order, joining two heaps always results in a larger heap. We capture this property in the following definitions.

Definition 8 (Increasing element and algebra). *For a separation algebra* $(M, \leq, \oplus)$, *an* increasing *element* $e \in M$ *is one such that for all* $m, n \in M$, *if* $\oplus(e, m, n)$ *then* $m \leq n$. *Similarly, a separation algebra is* increasing *if all its elements are increasing.*

---

[1] Pottier also adds a *passive execution order* which constitutes what he calls a *monotonic separation algebra*. The idea is similar but goes in a different direction, aiming for a type system and not a separation logic.

The increasing OSAs also form an algebra closed under cartesian product, disjoint sum and exponentiation. The intuition towards *increasing* will be made clear throughout the paper; it is used for the semantics of emp (Sect. 5.5) and it is key for defining separation logics for garbage-collected languages (Theorem 5).

5.3   Extending Kripke Semantics

It is a fundamental property of Kripke semantics that the denotations of all assertions are monotonic, not just those of atomic assertions. More precisely,

Definition 9 (Monotonic denotation). *An assertion φ has monotonic denotation in a Kripke model $(M, \leq)$ w.r.t. a semantics $(\cdot \vDash \cdot)$ iff for any $n, m \in M$,*

$$\text{If } n \leq m \text{ then } n \vDash \varphi \text{ implies } m \vDash \varphi \tag{1}$$

This property is critical in proving soundness of intuitionistic logic and any of its extensions (e.g. intuitionistic first order logic or intuitionistic modal logic).

Therefore, in extending Kripke semantics with separating connectives, property (1) must be preserved. To do so, if separating conjunction is defined as in (4.1), then the separation algebra must be *upwards-closed*:

Definition 10 (Upwards-closed separation algebra (UCSA)). *An OSA $(M, \leq, \oplus)$ is upwards-closed if the join relation is upwards-closed with respect to the order. In other words, for all m_1, m_2, m and n, If $\oplus(m_1, m_2, m)$ and $m \leq n$, then there exist n_1 and n_2 s.t. $\oplus(n_1, n_2, n)$ and $m_1 \leq n_1$ and $m_2 \leq n_2$.*

Similarly, if separating implication is defined as in (4.2), then we must require our separation algebra to be *downwards-closed*:

Definition 11 (Downwards-closed separation algebra (DCSA)). *An OSA $(M, \leq, \oplus)$ is downwards-closed if the join relation is downwards-closed w.r.t. the order. In other words, for all m_1, m_2, m, n_1 and n_2 : If $\oplus (m_1, m_2, m), n_1 \leq m_1$ and $n_2 \leq m_2$ then there exists n s.t. $\oplus (n_1, n_2, n)$ and $n \leq m$.*

Theorem 1 (Weak semantics monotonicity). *For any assertions φ and ψ with monotonic denotation,*

1. *the weak denotation of $\varphi * \psi$ (4.1) is monotonic in any UCSA*
2. *the weak denotation of $\varphi -\!\!* \psi$ (4.2) is monotonic in any DCSA*

Here, these two definitions are justified by Theorem 1. Moreover, a separation algebra with a discrete order is UCSA and DCSA. Also UCSA and DCSA are closed under cartesian product, disjoint sum and exponentiation.

Unfortunately, many separation algebras don't satisfy requirements 10 and 11. For instance, the following example describes a heap where short is two bytes long. It is motivated by the treatment of multibyte locks in VST [1, pp. 366–7].

Example 1 (Typed Heaps). Let a typed heap be $\mathcal{H}_\mathcal{T} : \mathbb{N} \rightharpoonup \{\mathsf{char}, \mathsf{short}_1, \mathsf{short}_2\}$, such that $H(n) = \mathsf{short}_1$ iff $H(n+1) = \mathsf{short}_2$. Define $\oplus$ as the typical heap addition (i.e. disjoint map union) and define the order as follows

$$H_1 \sqsubseteq_{\mathcal{H}_\mathcal{T}} H_2 \triangleq \forall n \in \mathsf{dom}\ H_1,\ n \in \mathsf{dom}\ H_2 \text{ and } H_1(n) = H_2(n) \text{ or } H_1(n) = \mathsf{char}$$

Then $(\mathcal{H}_\mathcal{T}, \sqsubseteq_{\mathcal{H}_\mathcal{T}}, \oplus)$ is an OSA which is DCSA but not UCSA.

In order to be as inclusive as possible, it is desirable to avoid requirements 10 and 11. With that goal, stronger semantics of $*$ and $-\!\!*$ have been proposed [17,31] to be monotonic by design. Theorem 2 justifies the choice.

Definition 12 (Strong semantics).

$$m \vDash \varphi * \psi \triangleq \exists\ m_0,\ m_1,\ m_2 \text{ s.t. } m_0 \leq m, \oplus(m_1, m_2, m_0) \qquad (12.1)$$
$$\text{and } m_1 \vDash \varphi \text{ and } m_2 \vDash \psi$$

$$m \vDash \varphi -\!\!* \psi \triangleq \text{ for any } m_0,\ m_1,\ m_2 \text{ if } m \leq m_0, \oplus(m_0, m_1, m_2) \qquad (12.2)$$
$$\text{then } m_1 \vDash \varphi \text{ implies } m_2 \vDash \psi$$

Theorem 2 (Strong semantics monotonicity). *For any assertion φ and ψ, if their denotations are both monotonic, then*

1. *strong semantics of separating conjunction (12.1) ensures the denotation of $\varphi * \psi$ to be monotonic*
2. *strong semantics of separating implication (12.2) ensures the denotation of $\varphi -\!\!* \psi$ to be monotonic.*

Alas, it is not always possible to use both strong semantics (12.1) and (12.2). These definitions enforce monotonicity, but might break other proof rules. As we show with the following example, separation logic becomes unsound w.r.t such strong semantics in the OSAs that are closed in neither direction.

Example 2 Consider the following separation algebra:

- Let M be $\{\bot, a_1, a_2, b_1, b_2, \top\}$.
- Let $\oplus$ be $\{(a_1, a_1, a_2), (b_1, b_1, b_2)\}$.
- Let $\leq$ be $\{(\bot, a_1), (a_2, b_1), (b_2, \top)\} \cup \{(s, s) | s \in M\}$.

On this model, $*$ASSOC is unsound w.r.t. the semantics of $*$ and $-\!\!*$ defined by (12.1) and (12.2).

Consequently, one must accept at least one restriction (i.e. upwards-closed or downwards-closed) over OSAs. There are only three viable semantics, each paired with a family of OSAs:

Definition 13 (Separation Logic semantics). *Over the propositional connectives (i.e. $\wedge$, $\vee$, $\rightarrow$, $\bot$), the semantics of separation logic is defined by Definition 6. The semantics of the separating connectives is then defined as follows*

1. *In* upwards semantics $(\cdot \vDash^{\Uparrow} \cdot)$, *which is defined on upwards closed OSAs, the conjunction is weak and implication strong (i.e. 4.1 and 12.2);*
2. *In* downwards semantics $(\cdot \vDash^{\Downarrow} \cdot)$, *which is defined on downwards closed OSAs, the conjunction is strong and implication weak (i.e. 12.1 and 4.2).*
3. *In* flat semantics $(\cdot \vDash^{=} \cdot)$, *which is defined on OSAs closed in two directions, both separating connectives are weak (i.e. 4.1 and 4.2).*

Lemma 1. *If a separation algebra is upwards-closed, the weak semantics of* $*$ *on it is equivalent to the strong semantics. If a separation algebra is downwards-closed, the weak semantics of* $-\!\!*$ *on it is equivalent to the strong semantics.*

Corollary 1. *For separation algebras with discrete order, upwards semantics, downwards semantics and flat semantics are equivalent.*

A *flat semantics* is by far the most common and intuitive; it is used whenever the algebra is discrete, as suggested by Corollary 1, and was used in Reynolds's original logic [32]. But in many applications, there is no natural flat semantics since the underlying model is not closed in both ways. The *upwards* semantics is used by Dockins *et al.* [13]. The *downwards* semantics appears in [15,24,31].

To the best of our knowledge, all semantics are covered by Definition 13, although in some cases it is not immediately obvious [4–6]. The followings are typical examples.

Example 3 (Step-indexed heap). Consider a heap (unordered) separation algebra $(\mathcal{H}, \oplus_{\mathcal{H}})$, the following is a semantics of separation logic defined on $\mathbb{N} \times \mathcal{H}$:

$$(i, h) \vDash \varphi * \psi \triangleq \exists\, h_1 h_2 \text{ s.t. } \oplus_{\mathcal{H}} (h_1, h_2, h) \text{ and } (i, h_1) \vDash \varphi \text{ and } (i, h_2) \vDash \psi$$

$$(i, h) \vDash \varphi -\!\!* \psi \triangleq \text{ for any } j, h_1 \text{ and } h_2$$
$$\text{if } i \geq_{\mathbb{N}} j \text{ and } \oplus (h, h_1, h_2) \text{ then } (j, h_1) \vDash \varphi \text{ implies } (j, h_2) \vDash \psi$$

Such models are used to define mixvariant recursive predicates [3] inside heaps.

In fact, this semantics on step indexed heap is just an upwards semantics on a product algebra, as formalized in Proposition 1. It seems like a hybrid semantics: upwards for the indices (in the inverted order of naturals) and flat for the heap. But since the monotonic heap is upwards-closed, by Lemma 1, such hybrid semantics is equivalent to an upwards semantics.

Proposition 1. *The semantics defined in Example 3 is equivalent to upwards semantics on the cartesian product of the index algebra (i.e.* $\mathbb{N}, \geq_{\mathbb{N}}, \Delta_3$*) and the heap (i.e.* $\mathcal{H}, \sqsubseteq_{\mathcal{H}}, \oplus_{\mathcal{H}}$*). Here,* $\Delta_3 \triangleq \{(n, n, n)|n \in \mathbb{N}\}$.

The following example is first used in FSCQ [11] to reason about a file system in which the hardware may crush. This separation logic is so powerful that its developer has verified a crush-recovery program even if a crush may happen again in the recovery process. In their separation logic, an assertion is required to be invariant w.r.t. buffer flushing, i.e. if an assertion is true before flushing then it should be true after flushing.

Example 4 (Heap with write buffer). Let V^+ be the set of non-empty lists of V. Such a nonempty list of values can represent one storage location with a write buffer. We call $l' \in V^+$ a flushing result of $l \in V^+$ if l' is a suffix of l, i.e. exists l'' such that $l = l''l'$. A heap with write buffer is an OSA $(\mathcal{B}, \oplus_{\mathcal{B}}, \leq_{\mathcal{B}})$: $\mathcal{B} \triangleq$ adr $\rightharpoonup V^+$, $\oplus_{\mathcal{B}}$ is heap-join relation and $\leq_{\mathcal{B}} \triangleq \{(b_1, b_2) \mid$ dom $b_1 =$ dom b_2 and $\forall x \in$ dom $b_1. \exists l. b_1(x) = l \ b_2(x)\}$.

This OSA is upwards closed and downwards closed, and the separational logic defined by FSCQ is actually the flat semantics on it. The following variants of it show the flexibility of our framework.

Example 5 (More refined buffer flushing). (1) $\preccurlyeq_{\mathcal{B}} \triangleq \{(b_1, b_2) \in \leq_{\mathcal{B}} \mid \forall x \in$ dom b_1. either $b_1(x) = b_2(x)$ or $b_2(x)$ is a singleton list$\}$. This denies any partial flushing on every single location. (2) $\sqsubseteq_{\mathcal{B}} \triangleq \{(b_1, b_2) \in \leq_{\mathcal{B}} \mid$ either $\forall x \in$ dom $b_1. b_1(x) = b_2(x)$ or $\forall x \in$ dom $b_1. b_2(x)$ is a singleton list$\}$. This denies any partial flushing on the whole heap.

The OSA defined by the first variant is still closed in both directions. However, the second variant is only upwards closed. Thus, only upwards semantics can be defined on it.

5.4 Semantic Equivalence

For now, we have defined upwards semantics on upwards closed OSAs, downwards semantics on downwards closed OSAs, and have defined flat semantics on OSAs closed in both directions.

In this subsection, we show that they are all equivalent to instances of each other. This is not to say that we can define flat semantics on OSAs with only one closed property. Instead, we demonstrate a practical way of converting an upwards closed *or* downwards closed OSA into an upwards closed *and* downwards closed OSA. We show an equivalence between the flat semantics on the new OSA and the upwards or downwards semantics on the original OSA.

As our first step, we define the following two model transformations:

Definition 14 (Upwards closure and downwards closure). *Given a separation algebra* $(M, \leq, \oplus)$*, its upwards closure is the triple* $(M, \leq, \oplus^{\Uparrow})$ *where* $\oplus^{\Uparrow}(m_1, m_2, m)$ *iff there is* m' *such that* $m' \leq m$ *and* $\oplus(m_1, m_2, m')$.

Given a separation algebra $(M, \leq, \oplus)$*, its downwards closure is the triple* $(M, \leq, \oplus^{\Downarrow})$ *where* $\oplus^{\Downarrow}(m_1, m_2, m)$ *iff there are* m_1' *and* m_2' *such that* $m_1 \leq m_1'$, $m_2 \leq m_2'$ *and* $\oplus(m_1', m_2', m)$.

For example, the downwards closure of index algebra (*i.e.* $\mathbb{N}, \geq_{\mathbb{N}}, \Delta_3$) is the *minimum algebra* $(\mathbb{N}, \leq_{\mathbb{N}}, \oplus_{\min})$, with $\oplus_{\min} \triangleq \{(x, y, z) \mid z \leq_{\mathbb{N}} x$ and $z \leq_{\mathbb{N}} y\}$.

Lemma 2. *Given an ordered separation algebra* $(M, \leq, \oplus)$*: If* $(M, \leq, \oplus)$ *is upwards closed,* $(M, \leq, \oplus^{\Downarrow})$ *is a downwards closed and upwards closed ordered separation algebra. If* $(M, \leq, \oplus)$ *is downwards closed,* $(M, \leq, \oplus^{\Uparrow})$ *is a downwards closed and upwards closed ordered separation algebra.*

At this point, you might think that any OSA can be made downwards- and upwards-closed by taking both of its closures. Unfortunately, such a two-sided closure might not be an ordered separation algebra at all!

Proposition 2. Let $(M, \leq, \oplus^{\Downarrow\Uparrow})$ be the upwards closure of the downwards closure of Example 2. Then $(M, \leq, \oplus^{\Downarrow\Uparrow})$ is not associative.

When the algebra is upwards- or downwards-closed the closure is upwards- and downwards-closed. Then, we can use the flat semantics on closures, which happens to be equivalent with a stronger semantics over the original algebra:

Theorem 3. Given an extended Kripke model $\mathcal{M} = (M, \leq, \oplus, J)$

1. if it is downwards closed, then the flat semantics on $\mathcal{M}^{\Uparrow}$ is equivalent to the downwards semantics on $\mathcal{M}$, i.e. for any φ and m, $m \vDash^{=}_{\mathcal{M}^{\Uparrow}} \varphi$ iff $m \vDash^{\Downarrow}_{\mathcal{M}} \varphi$
2. if it is upwards closed, then the flat semantics on $\mathcal{M}^{\Downarrow}$ is equivalent to the upwards semantics on $\mathcal{M}$, i.e. for any φ and m, $m \vDash^{=}_{\mathcal{M}^{\Downarrow}} \varphi$ iff $m \vDash^{\Uparrow}_{\mathcal{M}} \varphi$

Here, $\mathcal{M}^{\Uparrow} \triangleq (M, \leq, \oplus^{\Uparrow}, J)$ and $\mathcal{M}^{\Downarrow} \triangleq (M, \leq, \oplus^{\Downarrow}, J)$.

Recall that flat semantics are direct instances of upwards semantics and downwards semantics: the theorem follows as a corollary of Lemma 1.

Theorem 4. Given an extended Kripke model $\mathcal{M} = (M, \leq, \oplus, J)$ with downwards closed and upwards closed separation algebra, for any φ and m: (1) $m \vDash^{=}_{\mathcal{M}} \varphi$ iff $m \vDash^{\Uparrow}_{\mathcal{M}} \varphi$ (2) $m \vDash^{=}_{\mathcal{M}} \varphi$ iff $m \vDash^{\Downarrow}_{\mathcal{M}} \varphi$

Thus, in summary, flat semantics is a direct instance of upwards semantics and downwards semantics (Theorem 4). Upwards semantics and downwards semantics are instances of flat semantics via the closures (Theorem 3).

As far as we know, the idea of our model transformation and the semantic preservation is completely novel. However, we consider Atkey's separation logic for amortized resource analysis [4] a precursor worth mentioning. To use separation logic for amortized resource analysis, Atkey used the cartesian product of a discrete heap and a *consumable* resource (which is just an ordered monoid). The author wanted to use the usual and simpler flat semantics, but this is impossible because ordered monoids are not necessarily upwards-closed. To solve the problem, he defined an unusual separation algebra that is equivalent to the product of a discrete heap and the closure of the resource.

Example 6 (Resource-bounds). Suppose $(\mathcal{R}, \oplus_{\mathcal{R}}, \leq_{\mathcal{R}})$ is an ordered commutative monoid (for any $r_1 \leq_{\mathcal{R}} r_1'$ and $r_2 \leq_{\mathcal{R}} r_2'$, $r_1 \oplus_{\mathcal{R}} r_2 \leq_{\mathcal{R}} r_1' \oplus_{\mathcal{R}} r_2'$), and $(\mathcal{H}, \oplus_{\mathcal{H}})$ is an unordered heap. The following OSA on the product type, $(\mathcal{R} \times \mathcal{H}, \oplus_{\mathcal{R} \times \mathcal{H}}, \leq_{\mathcal{R} \times \mathcal{H}})$, is upwards closed and downwards closed.

$$\leq_{\mathcal{R} \times \mathcal{H}} \triangleq \{(i, h), (j, h) \mid i \leq_{\mathcal{R}} j\}$$
$$\oplus_{\mathcal{R} \times \mathcal{H}} \triangleq \{(i_1, h_1), (i_2, h_2), (i_3, h_3) \mid \oplus_{\mathcal{H}} (h_1, h_2, h_3) \text{ and } i_1 \oplus_{\mathcal{R}} i_2 \leq_{\mathcal{R}} i_3\}$$

This OSA is equivalent with $(\mathcal{R}, \oplus_{\mathcal{R}}, \leq_{\mathcal{R}})^{\Uparrow} \times (\mathcal{H}, =, \oplus_{\mathcal{H}})$.

5.5 Semantics of emp

Garbage-collect separation logic and malloc/free separation logic disagree on the semantics of emp. In a malloc/free separation logic,

$$m \models \mathsf{emp} \quad \triangleq \quad m \text{ is a unit} \qquad (\mathrm{Emp}_1)$$

and for a garbage-collected separation logic, emp just means True, i.e.

$$m \models \mathsf{emp} \quad \triangleq \quad \text{always} \qquad (\mathrm{Emp}_2)$$

We propose the following unification of the semantics of emp:

Definition 15 (Semantics of emp). *For a separation algebra* $(M, \leq, \oplus)$ *and* $m \in M$, $m \models \mathsf{emp}$ *iff* m *is increasing*

Definition 15 will not be sound if the set of increasing elements is not monotonic. To solve that, just like we did in Sect. 5.3, we can define a stronger semantics to ensure soundness. This stronger semantics is an instance of Definition 15 via the downwards closure, just like in Theorem 3. Nevertheless, we know of no practical application of such semantics, we omit the discussion here. In what follows we just assume that the increasing set is monotonic.

Lemma 3. *If the algebra is downwards-closed, the increasing set is monotonic.*

For increasing algebras, all elements are increasing, so the semantics of emp is equivalent to (Emp_2). For algebras with discrete order, as stated in the lemma below, only units are increasing, so the semantics of emp is equivalent to (Emp_1)

Lemma 4. *In a separation algebra with discrete order, an element is increasing iff it is a unit.*

Finally, we define a *unital separation algebra* as one in which each element has a "increasing part".

Definition 16 (Residue). *In a separation algebra* $(M, \leq, \oplus)$, *we say* m *is a* residue *of* n *if there exists* n' *such that* $\oplus(m, n', n)$ *and* $n \leq n'$.

Definition 17 (Unital separation algebras). *A separation algebra is* unital *if all elements have an increasing residue. For antisymmetric orders this is equivalent to: all elements have a identity element.*

Unital OSAs are closed under product, sum and exponentiation.

6 Parametric Soundness and Completeness

It is known that different propositional logics are sound and complete with respect to their corresponding class of Kripke models. Intuitionistic logic is sound and complete w.r.t. Kripke semantics in all models [23]; Classical logic is sound and complete w.r.t. Kripke semantics in the Kripke models with a discrete order.

In this section, we determine corresponding classes of extended Kripke models for each separation logic, as defined in Sect. 3, based on the framework for separation algebras developed in Sect. 5. We then proceed to prove soundness and completeness for each separation logic w.r.t the flat semantics in it's corresponding class of models. According to the equivalence theorem proved in Sect. 5.4, separation logics are then also proven sound and complete w.r.t. upwards semantics and downwards semantics.

Definition 18. *An order $\leq$ is* nonbranching *iff for any m, n and n', with $m \leq n$ and $m \leq n'$ then $n \leq n'$ or $n' \leq n$.*

An order $\leq$ always-joins *iff for any m, n and n', if $m \leq n$ and $m \leq n'$ then exists n'' s.t. $n \leq n''$ and $n' \leq n''$.*

Definition 19. *An OSA has its* increasing elements self-joining *iff for any m, if it is increasing then $\oplus(m, m, m)$.*

An OSA has normal increasing elements *iff for any n_1, n_2 and m, if $n_1 \oplus n_2 = mm$ is increasing then $n_1 \leq m$. In other words, an increasing element can only be split into smaller pieces.*

Definition 20 (Corresponding class of extended Kripke models). *Given a separation logic Γ, its* corresponding class of extended Kripke models *are the set of models which (1) are upwards-closed (2) are downwards-closed (3) are unital (4) satisfies the canonical properties of all optional axioms in Γ, as listed in this table:*

Optional axiom	Canonical property
EM $\in \Gamma$	Discrete order
GD $\in \Gamma$	Nonbranching order
WEM $\in \Gamma$	Always-joining order
$*$E $\in \Gamma$	Increasing
eDUP $\in \Gamma$	Increasing elements self-joining
eE $\in \Gamma$	Have normal increasing elements

Theorem 5 (Parametric soundness and completeness). *A separation logic Γ is sound and complete w.r.t. the flat semantics in Γ's corresponding class of models.*

Here, soundness and completeness are defined in the usual way. The soundness proof is trivial. We establish completeness by a Henkin-style proof. An interesting thing here is that the canonical model (constructed by derivable-closed disjunction-witnessed consistent sets of assertions) is upwards closed and downwards closed. This in some sense justifies our unifying solution. We put a detailed proof in an online appendix.

Remark. The correspondences between GD and nonbranching order, and between WEM and always-joining order, are standard results in propositional logics. But we find separation logic instances that admitted these intermediate rules unbeknownst to the authors For example, the step-indexed model of VST [1] has a nonbranching order so its separation logic should have GD. The order used in FSCQ [11] is always-joining so its separation logic should have WEM.

7   Applications of the Unifying Semantics

In the past 15 years, separation logic has been prolific tool for modular program verification. However, until now, most research was only applicable to one specific semantic model. For example, Ishtiaq and O'Hearn [19] showed that the frame rule is sound as long as the operational semantics has the frame property, but their conclusion was only demonstrated for unordered separation algebras (in our framework, separation algebra with discrete order). So, their work does not directly benefit separation-logic-based verification tools such as VST [1] and Iris [22], since their semantics are based on step-indexed models. Similarly, the soundness of CSL [7] was only established on unordered separation algebra.

We have already shown one example of how to generalize results about separation logic. The soundness proof of IP + SL, in Sect. 6, holds for all semantics of separation logic (because they are instances of the flat semantics). In this sections, we will further shows that the two soundness results mentioned above—frame rule and CSL— can be generalized to any ordered separation algebra with flat semantics, and thus for all separation logics.

7.1   Frame Rule

The frame is a fundamental rule for modular reasoning in separation logic.

$$\frac{\{\varphi\}\ c\ \{\psi\}}{\{\varphi * \xi\}\ c\ \{\psi * \xi\}}\ \text{(FRAME)}$$

Ishtiaq and O'Hearn [19] showed that the frame rule is sound with their "classical" separation logic, as long as the operational semantics has, what the called, *the frame property*. Here, we generalize the definition of frame property for all OSAs, and show that the soundness of frame rule still holds.

Definition 21 (Small-step semantics). *A small-step semantics of a programming language is a tuple* $(M, \mathbf{cmd}, \rightsquigarrow)$ *in which* M *represents program states,* $\mathbf{cmd}$ *represents program commands and* $\rightsquigarrow$ *is a binary relation between* $(M \times \mathbf{cmd})$ *and* $(M \times \mathbf{cmd} + \{\mathbf{Err}, \mathbf{NT}\})$. *Here,* $\mathbf{Err}$ *and* $\mathbf{NT}$ *means error state and nonterminating state respectively.*

We write $\rightsquigarrow^*$ *to mean the transitive reflexive closure of* $\rightsquigarrow$

Definition 22 (Accessibility from small-step semantics). *Given a small-step semantics* $(M, \mathbf{cmd}, \rightsquigarrow)$, *we define accessibility as a binary relation between* M *and* $M + \{\mathbf{Err}, \mathbf{NT}\}$:

1. $m \xrightarrow{c} m'$ *iff* $(m, c) \rightsquigarrow^* (m', \mathrm{skip})$
2. $m \xrightarrow{c} \mathbf{Err}$ *iff* $(m, c) \rightsquigarrow^* \mathbf{Err}$
3. $m \xrightarrow{c} \mathbf{NT}$ *iff* $(m, c) \rightsquigarrow^* \mathbf{NT}$ *or there exist infinite sequences* $\{m_k\}$ *and* $\{c_k\}$ *(for* $k \in \mathbb{N}$) *such that* $(m, c) \rightsquigarrow (m_0, c_0)$ *and* $(m_k, c_k) \rightsquigarrow (m_{k+1}, c_{k+1})$.

Definition 23 (Frame property). *An accessibility relation* $(\cdot \xrightarrow{c} \cdot)$ *satisfies frame property w.r.t. an ordered separation algebra* $(M, \leq, \oplus)$ *if for all* $m, m_f, n, n' \in M$ *and any command* c,

1. *if* $\oplus(m, m_f, n)$ *and* $n \xrightarrow{c} \mathbf{Err}$, *then* $m \xrightarrow{c} \mathbf{Err}$
2. *if* $\oplus(m, m_f, n)$ *and* $n \xrightarrow{c} \mathbf{NT}$, *then* $m \xrightarrow{c} \mathbf{NT}$
3. *if* $\oplus(m, m_f, n)$, $n \xrightarrow{c} n'$ *and executing* c *terminates normally from* m, *then there exists* $m'_f, m' \in M$ *s.t.* $m \xrightarrow{c} m'$, $\oplus(m', m'_f, n')$ *and* $m_f \leq m'_f$

Definition 24 (Validity of Hoare triple). *Given a small-step semantics, a Hoare triple* $\{\varphi\}\, c\, \{\psi\}$ *is valid if and only if for any* $m \in M$, *if* $m \models^= \varphi$ *then* (1) $m \not\xrightarrow{c} \mathbf{Err}$ (2) *for any* n, *if* $m \xrightarrow{c} n$ *then* $n \models^= \psi$.

Theorem 6 (Soundness of frame rule). *If the operational semantics satisfies the frame property w.r.t. an ordered separation algebra* $(M, \leq, \oplus)$ *which is upwards closed and downwards closed, then the frame rule is sound, i.e. if* $\{\varphi\}\, c\, \{\psi\}$ *is valid then* $\{\varphi * \chi\}\, c\, \{\psi * \chi\}$ *is valid.*

7.2 Concurrent Separation Logic

Concurrent separation logic is an extension of separation Hoare logic to reason about concurrent programs. Brookes [7] proved CSL to be sound for unordered heap models; in particular, he required cancellativity of the algebra. But separation logics with ghost resources [22] don't have cancellative algebras: the ghosts don't naturally cancel. Is CSL with ghost resources sound? As we show, the Brookes's soundness proof of CSL can be generalized to any models of ordered separation algebra, even without cancellativity.

Brookes defines the behavior of his imperative programming language (with concurrent primitives) via trace semantics.

Definition 25 (Trace semantics). *A trace semantics of a programming language is defined by a program state set M, a set R of resource identifiers, a command denotation function $[\![\,\cdot\,]\!]$ and a enable relation $\cdot \leadsto_a \cdot$. Specifically, for any program c, its denotation $[\![c]\!]$ is a set of traces; every trace is a finite or infinite list of actions. For any action a, $\cdot \leadsto_a \cdot$ is a relation between $\mathcal{P}(R) \times M$ and $\mathcal{P}(R) \times M + \{\mathbf{Err}\}$.*

In all actions, two kinds are special: $\mathrm{rel}(r)$ and $\mathrm{acq}(r)$ which means releasing and acquiring a resource r respectively. All other actions are nonresource actions. Actions' behavior satisfies the following properties:

$(A, m) \leadsto_{\mathrm{rel}(r)} (B, n)$ iff $r \notin B$, $A = B \cup \{r\}$ and $m = n$

$(A, m) \leadsto_{\mathrm{acq}(r)} (B, n)$ iff $r \notin A$, $B = A \cup \{r\}$ and $m = n$

$(A, m) \not\leadsto_{\mathrm{rel}(r)} \mathbf{Err}$ and $(A, m) \not\leadsto_{\mathrm{acq}(r)} \mathbf{Err}$

If a is a nonresource action and $(A, m) \leadsto_a (B, n)$ then $A = B$

If a is a nonresource action, $\cdot \leadsto_a \cdot$ satisfies a frame property like Definition 23.

From a trace semantics, we can define the validity of guarded Hoare triples following Brookes's method.

Definition 26 (Thread-local enable relation). *Suppose Γ is a partial function from resource identifiers to their resource invariants and the program state is the underlying set of an upwards closed and downwards closde OSA, $\mathcal{M} = (M, \leq, \oplus)$, then the thread-local enable relation $\cdot \leadsto_{a,\Gamma} \cdot$ is defined as follows:*

1. *$(A, m) \leadsto_{\mathrm{rel}(r),\Gamma} (B, n)$ iff $r \notin B$, $A = B \cup \{r\}$ and exists f such that $f \vDash^= \Gamma(r)$ and $\oplus(m, f, n)$*
2. *$(A, m) \not\leadsto_{\mathrm{rel}(r),\Gamma} \mathbf{Err}$*
3. *$(A, m) \leadsto_{\mathrm{acq}(r),\Gamma} (B, n)$ iff $r \notin A$, $B = A \cup \{r\}$ and n is the greatest element in $\{n \mid \text{exists } f \text{ such that } f \vDash^= \Gamma(r) \text{ and } \oplus(n, f, m)\}$*
4. *$(A, m) \leadsto_{\mathrm{acq}(r),\Gamma} \mathbf{Err}$ iff $r \notin A$ and there is no n and f such that $f \vDash^= \Gamma(r)$ and $\oplus(n, f, m)$*
5. *If a is a nonresource action, $\cdot \leadsto_{a,\Gamma} \cdot$ is the same as $\cdot \leadsto_a \cdot$.*

Definition 27 (Accessibility from trace semantics). *For any invariant mapping Γ, any trace t, $\alpha \in \mathcal{P}(R) \times M$ and $\beta \in \mathcal{P}(R) \times M + \{\mathbf{Err}, \mathbf{NT}\}$, $\alpha \xrightarrow[\Gamma]{c} \beta$ iff exists $t \in [\![c]\!]$ such that $\alpha \leadsto^*_{t,\Gamma} \beta$. Here $\cdot \leadsto^*_{t,\Gamma} \cdot$ is defined by $\cdot \leadsto_{a,\Gamma} \cdot$ like Definition 22.*

We call $\cdot \xrightarrow[\Gamma]{c} \cdot$ the thread-local accessibility relation. Similarly, we define $\cdot \xrightarrow{c} \cdot$ from the (nonlocal) enable relation $\cdot \leadsto_a \cdot$. We omit the details here.

Definition 28 (Validity of guarded Hoare triple). *A guarded Hoare triple $\Gamma \vdash \{\varphi\}\, c\, \{\psi\}$ is valid if and only if for any $m \in M$, if $m \vDash^= \varphi$ then (1) $(\{\}, m) \not\xrightarrow[\Gamma]{c} \mathbf{Err}$ (2) for any n, if $(\{\}, m) \xrightarrow[\Gamma]{c} (\{\}, n)$ then $n \vDash^= \psi$.*

Brookes showed that if $\Gamma \vdash \{\varphi\} \, c \, \{\psi\}$ is valid and $m \vDash^= \varphi$ then (1) $(\{\}, m) \not\to$ **Err** (2) for any n, if $(\{\}, m) \xrightarrow{c} (\{\}, n)$ then $n \vDash^= \psi$. This means: although triples' validity is defined on a thread-local view, it ensures global safety.

Another preparation before presenting Hoare rules is defining the concept of *preciseness*. In heap model, an assertion φ is precise when inside any memory m there is at most one submemory m_1 which satisfies φ. The following is our generalization. It is reasonable since it is the original preciseness on any cancellative separation algebra with discrete order.

Definition 29 (Preciseness). *Given an upwards closed and downwards closed separation algebra* $(M, \leq, \oplus)$, *an assertion* φ *is precise iff for any* m, *if* $S \triangleq \{m_1 \mid exists \ m_2 \ such \ that \ \oplus (m_1, m_2, m), m_2 \vDash^= \varphi\}$ *is nonempty then* S *has a greatest element.*

We are now ready to state our generalized theorem for the soundness of CSL.

Theorem 7 (Soundness of CSL). *If all resource invariants are precise, then Hoare rules in CSL are sound w.r.t. flat semantics of separation logic. The following are the Hoare rules of concurrent primitives:*

1. *If* $\Gamma \vdash \{\varphi_1\}c_1\{\psi_1\}$ *and* $\Gamma \vdash \{\varphi_2\}c_2\{\psi_2\}$, *then* $\Gamma \vdash \{\varphi_1 * \varphi_2\} \, c_1 \| c_2 \, \{\psi_1 * \psi_2\}$
2. *If* $\Gamma \vdash \{\varphi * \xi\} \, c \, \{\psi * \xi\}$ *and* r *does not freely occur in* c, *then* $\Gamma; r : \xi \vdash \{\varphi\}$ *with* r *do* c $\{\psi\}$

Here, $[\![c_1 \| c_2]\!]$ *is the resource coherent interleaving of* $[\![c_1]\!]$ *and* $[\![c_2]\!]$, *and* $[\![$ *with* r *do* $c]\!]$ *is acquiring* r, *applying* $[\![c]\!]$ *and releasing* r.

The proof follows the same lines as Brookes's proof. We formalize it in Coq and omit it here.

8   Future Work

We are particularly excited to use the present work as a starting point to find a unifying framework of Hoare separation logic. There are many incompatible definitions for the semantics for Hoare triples [1,19,22] which make their different results incompatible. We believe the present work is the first step towards resolving this incompatibility, but there are many issues yet to be solved. For instance, the two examples in Sect. 7 have first order Hoare logics, but Hoare logics for programs with function calls are high ordered. Unifying such Hoare logics is more challenging. It will also be particularly challenging to unify the operational semantics for verifying concurrent programs. We believe this is the way to solve Parkinson's challenge for the next 700 separation logics.

Our hope is that the present work will be a fertile ground for generalizing many known results, as we did in Sect. 7. Of particular interest to us is whether *preciseness* is required in a Hoare logic with the conjunction rule [16,26]. A related conundrum is whether a separation algebra must be cancellative in order to have the conjunction rule. Both questions have been answered for classical, malloc/free logics, but are open in general.

9   Conclusion

We have clarified the terminology "classical vs. intuitionistic" and "malloc/free vs. garbage-collected" separation logic. They are two independent taxonomies.

We present flat semantics on upwards-closed and downwards-closed OSA as a unification for all different semantics of separation logics. All separation logics are proved sound and complete w.r.t. corresponding model classes. This unification is powerful enough to generalize related concepts like *frame property* and *preciseness* and to generalize theoretical applications of separation logic like the soundness of frame rule (given frame property) and the soundness of CSL.

All the definitions, propositions, lemmas and theorems in this paper have been formalized in Coq. We also put a detailed paper proof of two main theorems of this paper in an appendix: semantic equivalence theorem (Theorem 3) and completeness theorem (Theorem 5). Our Coq development and paper proofs are both accessible online[2].

Acknowledgment. This research was supported in part by NSF Grant CCF-1521602.

References

1. Appel, A.W., Dockins, R., Hobor, A., Beringer, L., Dodds, J., Stewart, G., Blazy, S., Leroy, X.: Program Logics for Certified Compilers, Cambridge (2014)
2. Appel, A.W., McAllester, D.A.: An indexed model of recursive types for foundational proof-carrying code. ACM Trans. Program. Lang. Syst. **23**(5), 657–683 (2001)
3. Appel, A.W., Melliès, P.-A., Richards, C.D., Vouillon, J.: A very modal model of a modern, major, general type system. In: Proceedings of the 34th ACM SIGPLAN-SIGACT Symposium on Principles of Programming Languages (2007)
4. Atkey, R.: Amortised resource analysis with separation logic. Logical Methods Comput. Sci. **7**(2) (2011)
5. Bengtson, J., Jensen, J.B., Sieczkowski, F., Birkedal, L.: Verifying object-oriented programs with higher-order separation logic in Coq. In: van Eekelen, M., Geuvers, H., Schmaltz, J., Wiedijk, F. (eds.) ITP 2011. LNCS, vol. 6898, pp. 22–38. Springer, Heidelberg (2011). https://doi.org/10.1007/978-3-642-22863-6_5
6. Birkedal, L., Reus, B., Schwinghammer, J., Støvring, K., Thamsborg, J., Yang, H.: Step-indexed Kripke models over recursive worlds. In: Proceedings of the 38th ACM SIGPLAN-SIGACT Symposium on Principles of Programming Languages (2011)
7. Brookes, S.: A semantics for concurrent separation logic. In: Gardner, P., Yoshida, N. (eds.) CONCUR 2004. LNCS, vol. 3170, pp. 16–34. Springer, Heidelberg (2004). https://doi.org/10.1007/978-3-540-28644-8_2
8. Brotherston, J., Kanovich, M.: Undecidability of propositional separation logic and its neighbours. In: 2010 25th Annual IEEE Symposium on Logic in Computer Science (LICS), pp. 130–139. IEEE (2010)

---

[2] Coq development: https://github.com/QinxiangCao/UnifySL. Appendix: http://www.cs.princeton.edu/~appel/papers/bringing-order-appendix.pdf.

9. Brotherston, J., Villard, J.: Parametric completeness for separation theories. In: The 41st Annual ACM SIGPLAN-SIGACT Symposium on Principles of Programming Languages (2014)

10. Calcagno, C., O'Hearn, P.W., Yang, H.: Local action and abstract separation logic. In: Proceedings of the 22nd Annual IEEE Symposium on Logic in Computer Science, LICS 2007, pp. 366–378, Washington, DC, USA. IEEE Computer Society (2007)

11. Chen, H., Ziegler, D., Chajed, T., Chlipala, A., Kaashoek, M.F., Zeldovich, N.: Using crash hoare logic for certifying the FSCQ file system. In: Miller, E.L., Hand, S. (eds.) Proceedings of the 25th Symposium on Operating Systems Principles, SOSP 2015, Monterey, CA, USA, 4–7 October 2015, pp. 18–37. ACM (2015)

12. Dinsdale-Young, T., Birkedal, L., Gardner, P., Parkinson, M.J., Yang, H.: Views: compositional reasoning for concurrent programs. In: The 40th Annual ACM SIGPLAN-SIGACT Symposium on Principles of Programming Languages (2013)

13. Dockins, R., Hobor, A., Appel, A.W.: A fresh look at separation algebras and share accounting. In: Hu, Z. (ed.) APLAS 2009. LNCS, vol. 5904, pp. 161–177. Springer, Heidelberg (2009). https://doi.org/10.1007/978-3-642-10672-9_13

14. Galmiche, D., Larchey-Wendling, D.: Expressivity properties of Boolean BI through relational models. In: Arun-Kumar, S., Garg, N. (eds.) FSTTCS 2006. LNCS, vol. 4337, pp. 357–368. Springer, Heidelberg (2006). https://doi.org/10.1007/11944836_33

15. Galmiche, D., Méry, D., Pym, D.J.: The semantics of BI and resource tableaux. Mathe. Struct. Comput. Sci. 15(6), 1033–1088 (2005)

16. Gotsman, A., Berdine, J., Cook, B.: Precision and the conjunction rule in concurrent separation logic. Electr. Notes Theor. Comput. Sci. 276, 171–190 (2011)

17. Hobor, A., Dockins, R., Appel, A.W.: A theory of indirection via approximation. In: Proceedings of the 37th ACM SIGPLAN-SIGACT Symposium on Principles of Programming Languages (2010)

18. Hur, C.-K., Dreyer, D., Vafeiadis, V.: Separation logic in the presence of garbage collection. In: Proceedings of the 26th Annual IEEE Symposium on Logic in Computer Science, LICS 2011, 21–24 June 2011, Toronto, Ontario, Canada, pp. 247–256 (2011)

19. Ishtiaq, S.S., O'Hearn, P.W.: BI as an assertion language for mutable data structures. In: Conference Record of POPL 2001: The 28th ACM SIGPLAN-SIGACT Symposium on Principles of Programming Languages (2001)

20. Jensen, J.B.: Techniques for model construction in separation logic. Ph.D. thesis, IT University of Copenhagen, March 2014

21. Jensen, J.B., Birkedal, L.: Fictional separation logic. In: Programming Languages and Systems - 21st European Symposium on Programming (2012)

22. Jung, R., Swasey, D., Sieczkowski, F., Svendsen, K., Turon, A., Birkedal, L., Dreyer, D.: Iris: Monoids and invariants as an orthogonal basis for concurrent reasoning. In: Proceedings of the 42nd Annual ACM SIGPLAN-SIGACT Symposium on Principles of Programming Languages (2015)

23. Kripke, S.A.: Semantical analysis of intuitionistic logic i. Studies Logic Found. Mathe. 50, 92–130 (1965)

24. Larchey-Wendling, D., Galmiche, D.: Exploring the relation between intuitionistic BI and boolean BI: an unexpected embedding. Mathe. Struct. Comput. Sci. 19(3), 435–500 (2009)

25. O'Hearn, P.W., Pym, D.J.: The logic of bunched implications. Bull. Symbolic Logic 5(2), 215–244 (1999)

26. O'Hearn, P.W., Yang, H., Reynolds, J.C.: Separation and information hiding. In: Proceedings of the 31st ACM SIGPLAN-SIGACT Symposium on Principles of Programming Languages, POPL 2004, Venice, Italy, 14–16 January 2004, pp. 268–280 (2004)

27. Parkinson, M.: The next 700 separation logics. In: Leavens, G.T., O'Hearn, P., Rajamani, S.K. (eds.) VSTTE 2010. LNCS, vol. 6217, pp. 169–182. Springer, Heidelberg (2010). https://doi.org/10.1007/978-3-642-15057-9_12

28. Parkinson, M.J., Summers, A.J.: The relationship between separation logic and implicit dynamic frames. In: Barthe, G. (ed.) ESOP 2011. LNCS, vol. 6602, pp. 439–458. Springer, Heidelberg (2011). https://doi.org/10.1007/978-3-642-19718-5_23

29. Pilkiewicz, A., Pottier, F.: The essence of monotonic state. In: Proceedings of TLDI 2011: 2011 ACM SIGPLAN International Workshop on Types in Languages Design and Implementation, pp. 73–86 (2011)

30. Pottier, F.: Syntactic soundness proof of a type-and-capability system with hidden state. J. Funct. Program. **23**(1), 38–144 (2013)

31. Pym, D.J., O'Hearn, P.W., Yang, H.: Possible worlds and resources: the semantics of BI. Theor. Comput. Sci. **315**(1), 257–305 (2004)

32. Reynolds, J.C.: Intuitionistic reasoning about shared mutable data structure. In: Millennial Perspectives in Computer Science, pp. 303–321. Palgrave (2000)

33. Simpson, A.K.: The proof theory and semantics of intuitionistic modal logic. Technical report, University of Edinburgh, College of Science and Engineering, School of Informatics (1994)

Concurrency and Verification

Programming and Proving with Classical Types

Cristina Matache$^{(\boxtimes)}$, Victor B.F. Gomes$^{(\boxtimes)}$, and Dominic P. Mulligan$^{(\boxtimes)}$

Computer Laboratory, University of Cambridge, Cambridge, UK
cris.matache@gmail.com, vb358@cam.ac.uk, dominic.p.mulligan@gmail.com

Abstract. The propositions-as-types correspondence is ordinarily presented as linking the metatheory of typed λ-calculi and the proof theory of intuitionistic logic. Griffin observed that this correspondence could be extended to classical logic through the use of *control operators*. This observation set off a flurry of further research, leading to the development of Parigot's $\lambda\mu$-calculus. In this work, we use the $\lambda\mu$-calculus as the foundation for a system of *proof terms* for classical first-order logic. In particular, we define an extended call-by-value $\lambda\mu$-calculus with a type system in correspondence with full classical logic. We extend the language with polymorphic types, add a host of data types in 'direct style', and prove several metatheoretical properties. All of our proofs and definitions are mechanised in Isabelle/HOL, and we automatically obtain an interpreter for a system of proof terms *cum* programming language—called μML—using Isabelle's code generation mechanism. Atop our proof terms, we build a prototype LCF-style interactive theorem prover—called μTP—for classical first-order logic, capable of synthesising μML programs from completed tactic-driven proofs. We present example closed μML programs with classical tautologies for types, including some inexpressible as closed programs in the original $\lambda\mu$-calculus, and some example tactic-driven μTP proofs of classical tautologies.

1 Introduction

Propositions are types; λ-terms encode derivations; β-reduction and proof normalisation coincide. These three points are the crux of the propositions-as-types correspondence—a product of mid-20th century mathematical logic—connecting the proof theory of intuitionistic propositional logic and the metatheory of the simply-typed λ-calculus. As the core ideas underpinning the correspondence gradually crystallised, logicians and computer scientists expanded the correspondence in new directions, providing a series of intellectual bridges between mainstream mathematical logic and theoretical computer science.

Yet, for the longest time, the connection between logic and computation exposed by the propositions-as-types correspondence was thought to be specific to intuitionistic logics. These logics stand in contrast to the classical logic typically used and understood by mainstream mathematicians. Indeed, prior to the early 1990 s any extension of the correspondence connecting typed λ-calculi with classical logic was by-and-large considered inconceivable: classical proofs

© Springer International Publishing AG 2017
B.-Y.E. Chang (Ed.): APLAS 2017, LNCS 10695, pp. 215–234, 2017.
https://doi.org/10.1007/978-3-319-71237-6_11

simply did not contain any 'computational content'. Many were therefore surprised when Griffin discovered that *control operators*—of the same family as the call/cc made infamous by the Scheme programming language—were the technology required to extend the propositions-as-types correspondence to classical logic [Gri90]. Classical proofs do contain 'computational content' after all.

Griffin's publication set off a flurry of further research into classical computation (see for example [Par92, Par93a, Par93b, BB94, dG94b, dG94a, RS94, dG95, BB95, Par97, BHS97, BBS97, dG98, Bie98, dG01, AH03, AHS04], amongst many others). Soon, refinements of his original idea were developed, most prominently in Parigot's $\lambda\mu$-calculus [Par92], which provided a smoother correspondence between classical logic and computation than Griffin's original presentation and now acts as a nexus for further research into classical computation. Griffin took Felleisen's $\mathcal{C}$ operator [FFKD87] as a primitive and assigned it the classical type $\neg\neg A \to A$, finding it neccessary to impose restrictions on the reduction relation of his calculus. Parigot observed that this latter requirement was a side effect of the single-conclusion Natural Deduction system Griffin used as the basis for his typing relation, and by using a deduction system with multiple conclusions instead, one could engineer a classically-typed calculus that enjoyed the usual confluence and preservation properties whilst imposing fewer *a priori* constraints on the reduction strategy. Expressions can be explicitly named with μ-variables to form *commands*. This, coupled with a new binding form, allows control flow to 'jump' in a similar spirit to exceptions and their handling mechanisms in mainstream programming languages.

In this work, we explore what a theorem-prover based on classical type theory may look like, and propose to using terms of the $\lambda\mu$-calculus as a serialisation, or *proof term*, mechanism for such a system. As a first step, we focus on classical (first-order) logic. In systems based on intuitionistic type-theory, e.g. Coq [HH14] and Matita [ARCT11], one is able to extract a proof term from a completed proof. Aside from their use in facilitating computation within the logic, these proof terms have a number of important purposes:

1. Proof terms are independently verifiable pieces of *evidence* that the respective theorem proving system correctly certified that a goal is indeed a theorem. Proof terms can be checked by an auditing tool, implemented independently of the system kernel, which is able to certify that the proof term in hand indeed represents a valid proof. Accordingly, proof terms in theorem proving systems such as Coq and Matita form an important component of the *trust story* for the respective systems, with this idea of an independent checking tool sometimes referred to as the *De Bruijn criterion* [BW05].

2. Proof terms may act as a bridge between independent theorem proving systems. Early versions of Matita maintained proof-term compatibility with contemporaneous versions of Coq. As a result, the Matita system was able to import theorems proved in Coq, and use and compute with them as ordinarily as if they had been proved within the Matita system itself.

3. Proof terms can facilitate proof transformations, and refactorings. By affecting program transformations at the level of proof terms, one automatically obtains a notion of proof transformation.
4. Proof terms are used to extract the 'computational content' of proofs, which has important applications in computer science (e.g. in extracting verified software from mechanised proofs), and in mathematical logic (e.g. in explorations of the Curry-Howard correspondence, and in realisability theory [Kri16]).

Given the existence of Parigot's $\lambda\mu$-calculus, including typed variants, we may expect to be able to use $\lambda\mu$-terms directly to serialise derivations. However, there are two snags: the issue of data types—which theorem proving systems must support in order to permit the verification of interesting programs—and the necessary use of open terms to encode classical tautologies in Parigot's calculus, a more subtle problem which will be explained below.

Addressing first the issue of data types, Parigot explored data type embeddings in his early papers on the $\lambda\mu$-calculus (see e.g. [Par92, Sect. 3.5]). In particular, in systems of typed λ-calculi based on intuitionistic logic, one typically observes a uniqueness (or canonicity) result when embedding data types into the language, a property inherited from intuitionistic Natural Deduction where theorems possess a unique cut-free proof. This property fails in the classical setting, as classical Natural Deduction does not possess a corresponding uniqueness property, and 'junk' numbers inhabit the usual type of Church-encoded natural numbers as a result. Instead, one can introduce 'selection functions' that pick out the unique intuitionistic inhabitant of a type from the sea of alternatives—a strategy Parigot followed. After Parigot, several others considered classical calculi extended with data. One popular approach has been to consider CPS translations of types—as in [Mur91, CP11, BU02]—as opposed to introducing data types and their operational semantics into a calculus in 'direct style', or imposing various conditions on the arguments of primitive recursive functions added to the calculus—as in [RS94]. Indeed, it is not until the work of Ong and Stewart working in a call-by-value setting [OS97], and later Geuvers et al. working in a call-by-name setting [GKM13], that calculi with data types and an operational semantics in 'direct style' are presented. In the latter work, the $\lambda\mu$-calculus is augmented with an encoding of the natural numbers, along with a primitive recursor for defining recursive functions over the naturals, in the style of Gödel's System T [Göd58] to obtain the $\lambda\mu^{\mathbf{T}}$-calculus. Doing this whilst maintaining desirable metatheoretical properties—such as preservation and normalisation— is a delicate process, and requires balancing a mostly call-by-name reduction strategy with the necessarily strict reduction needed to obtain the normal form property for natural number data.

So, rather than the $\lambda\mu$-calculus, we take the $\lambda\mu^{\mathbf{T}}$-calculus as our starting point for a system of proof terms—with a caveat. As Ariola and Herbelin [AH03] noted, and as we alluded to previously, the closed typeable terms of the $\lambda\mu$-calculus (and by extension, the $\lambda\mu^{\mathbf{T}}$-calculus) correspond to a restricted variant of classical logic: 'minimal classical logic'. This logic validates some familiar classical tautologies but not others: the Double Negation Elimination law cannot be captured as a closed, typed program in either calculus, and requires a term with free μ-variables, for example. As working with terms with free variables restricts program transformations and refactoring, this is undesirable from a programming and theorem-proving perspective. We therefore follow Ariola and Herbelin in presenting a calculus with a distinguished μ-constant (called 'top') that can be substituted but not bound by a μ-abstraction. Following our earlier exception analogy, this 'top' element corresponds to an uncatchable exception that bubbles up through a program before eventually *aborting* a program's execution. In this way, familiar classical tautologies and their derivations can be captured as closed programs in our language.

Our system of proof terms is therefore a combination of $\lambda\mu^{\mathbf{T}}$ and the terms of Ariola and Herbelin's calculus. Yet, we must proceed with caution! Adding classical constructs to programming languages and calculi has a fraught history: extending Standard ML with a `call/cc` combinator inadvertently made the language's type system unsound, for example [HL91]. This problem is especially acute as we propose to build a theorem proving system around our terms, and therefore must be sure that our typing system is sound, and reduction well-behaved. We therefore provide a mechanised proof of correctness of the soundness of our proof terms. In particular, our contributions in this work are as follows:

1. We provide an Isabelle/HOL [Gor91] implementation of Parigot's $\lambda\mu$-calculus, along with mechanised proofs of important metatheoretical results. As always, the treatment of name binding is delicate, especially in a calculus with two binding forms with very different runtime behaviour. We use De Bruijn indices [dB72] to handle α-equivalence for λ- and μ-bound variables. This contribution is not discussed in this paper any further, since the next contribution subsumes it. All results can be found in our public repository, mentioned below, and in the Archive of Formal Proofs [MGM17].
2. We extend the calculus above to obtain an explicitly-polymorphic call-by-value[1] variant of the $\lambda\mu$-calculus, *à la* System F [Gir71], mechanised in Isabelle/HOL, along with proofs of desired results. This adds yet another new variety of De Bruijn index for universally quantified type variables. This is presented in Sect. 2.
3. Extending further, we blend previous work on type systems for full classical logic and work extending Parigot's calculus with data to obtain a typed $\lambda\mu$-calculus with primitive datatypes and a type system corresponding to full first-order classical logic. We provide proofs of progress and type preservation for the reduction relation of this language. This is presented in Sect. 3.
4. Using our formalisation, we obtain an interpreter for a prototype call-by-value programming language, which we call μML, using Isabelle/HOL's code generation mechanism and a hand-written parser. We show a closed program

---

[1] Strictly speaking, our evaluation strategy is a call-by-weak-head-normal-form. A pure call-by-value $\lambda\mu$-calculus could get stuck when evaluating an application whose argument is a μ-abstraction, which is undesirable. We retain the terminology call-by-value since it gives a better intuition of the desired behaviour.

whose type is an instance of the Double Negation Elimination law, which is not typeable in the $\lambda\mu$-calculus. The progress and preservation theorems presented in Sect. 3 ensure that 'well-typed programs do not go wrong' at runtime, and that our proof terms are therefore well-behaved. This is presented in Sect. 4.

5. We have built a prototype LCF-style theorem prover called μTP for first-order classical logic around our proof terms. Our theorem prover is able to synthesise μML programs directly from complete tactic-driven proofs in the logic. This theorem prover, as well as example tactic-driven proofs and synthesised programs, is described in Sect. 5.

All of our proofs are mechanically checked and along with the source code of our LCF kernel are available from a public Bitbucket repository.[2]

2   A Polymorphic Call-by-Value $\lambda\mu$-Calculus

Fix three disjoint countably infinite sets of λ-*variables*, μ-*variables* and Λ-*variables* (type variables). We use x, y, z, and so on, to range over λ-variables; α, β, γ, and so on, to range over μ-variables; and a, b, c, and so on, to range over Λ-variables. We then mutually define *terms*, *commands* (or *named terms*) and *types* of the $\lambda\mu$-calculus with the following grammar:

$$s, t ::= x \mid \lambda x : \tau.t \mid ts \mid \Lambda a.t \mid t\tau \mid \mu\alpha : \tau.c$$
$$c ::= [\alpha]t$$
$$\sigma, \tau ::= a \mid \forall a.\tau \mid \sigma \to \tau$$

The variables x, α and a are said to be bound in the term $\lambda x : \tau.t$, $\mu\alpha : \tau.c$ and $\Lambda a.t$ respectively. As usual, we work modulo α-equivalence, and write $\mathtt{fv}(t)$, $\mathtt{fcv}(t)$ and $\mathtt{ftv}(t)$ for the set of *free* λ, μ and Λ-*variables* in a term t. These are defined recursively on the structure of t. We call a term t λ-*closed* whenever $\mathtt{fv}(t) = \{\}$, μ-*closed* whenever $\mathtt{fcv}(t) = \{\}$, Λ-*closed* whenever $\mathtt{fcv}(t) = \{\}$ and a term t is simply *closed* whenever it is λ-closed, μ-closed and Λ-closed.

The implementation of terms, commands, and types in Isabelle as HOL data types is straightforward—though terms and commands must be mutually recursively defined. To deal with α-equivalence, we use De Bruijn's nameless representation [dB72] wherein each bound variable is represented by a natural number, its index, that denotes the number of binders that must be traversed to arrive at the one that binds the given variable. Each free variable has an index that points into the top-level context, not enclosed in any abstractions. Under this scheme, if a free variable occurs under n abstractions, its index is at least n. For example, if the index of the free variable x is 3 in the top-level context, the λ-term $\lambda y.\lambda z.((z\ y)\ x)$ is represented in De Bruijn notation as $\lambda.\lambda.((0\ 1)\ 5)$.

---

[2] See: https://bitbucket.org/Cristina_Matache/prog-classical-types.

In the polymorphic $\lambda\mu$-calculus, there are three distinct binding forms, and therefore we have three disjoint sets of indices. Henceforth, a λ-abstraction is written as $\lambda : \tau.t$ where τ is a type annotation and the name of the bound variable is no longer specified. Similarly for μ-abstractions. Universal types and type variable abstractions are simply written as $\forall\tau$ and Λt, respectively.

Capture-avoiding substitution. The polymorphic $\lambda\mu$-calculus has four different substitution actions: a *logical substitution* used to implement ordinary β-reduction, a *structural substitution* used to handle substitution of μ-variables, and two substitutions for types, one into terms, and one into other types.

Write $\uparrow_\lambda^n (t)$ and $\uparrow_\mu^n (t)$ for the De Bruijn *lifting* (or *shifting*) functions for λ- and μ-variables, respectively. These increment the indices of all free λ-variables (respectively μ-variables) in term t that are greater or equal to the parameter n. An analogous pair of operations, the De Bruijn *dropping* (or *down-shifting*), written $\downarrow_\lambda^n (t)$ and $\downarrow_\mu^n (t)$, decrement indices that are strictly greater than n. Using the lifting functions, we define logical substitution recursively on the structure of terms, and write $t[x := s]$ for the term t with all free occurrences of x replaced by s in a capture-avoiding manner. We draw attention to two cases: λ and μ-abstractions. When a substitution is pushed under a λ-abstraction (respectively, a μ-abstraction), the indices of the free λ-variables in s are shifted by 1 so that they keep referring to the same variables as in the previous context:

$$(\lambda : \tau.t)[x := s] = \lambda : \tau.(t[x + 1 := \uparrow_\lambda^0 (s)])$$
$$(\mu : \tau.c)[x := s] = \mu : \tau.(c[x := \uparrow_\mu^0 (s)])$$

Note here that in the first clause above, the λ-variable x is pushed through a λ-abstraction, and must therefore be incremented, whilst in the second clause the λ-variable x is being pushed through a μ-abstraction, and therefore does not need to be incremented as there is no risk of capture.

We can also define de Bruijn lifting functions for free Λ-variables in terms, $\uparrow_\Lambda^n (t)$, and types, $\uparrow_\Lambda^n (\tau)$. Using these functions, define substitution of type τ for all free occurrences of type variable a in term t, $t[a := \tau]$, or in type σ, $\sigma[a := \tau]$. Two interesting cases in these definitions are for Λ-abstractions and $\forall$-types:

$$(\Lambda t)[a := \tau] = \Lambda(t[(a + 1) := \uparrow_\Lambda^0 (\tau)])$$
$$(\forall\sigma)[a := \tau] = \forall(\sigma[(a + 1) := \uparrow_\Lambda^0 (\tau)])$$

When substituting inside these binders, the index a and the indices of the free type variables in τ must be incremented.

Typing judgement. We implement *typing environments* as (total) functions from natural numbers to types, following the approach of Stefan Berghofer in his formalisation of the simply typed λ-calculus in the Isabelle/HOL library. An empty typing environment may be represented by an arbitrary function of the

$$\frac{\Gamma(x) = \tau}{\Gamma; \Delta \vdash x : \tau} \quad \frac{\Gamma\langle 0 : \sigma\rangle; \Delta \vdash t : \tau}{\Gamma; \Delta \vdash \lambda : \sigma.\ t : \sigma \to \tau} \quad \frac{\Gamma; \Delta \vdash t : \sigma \to \tau \quad \Gamma; \Delta \vdash s : \sigma}{\Gamma; \Delta \vdash t\ s : \tau}$$

$$\frac{\uparrow_\Lambda^0 (\Gamma); \uparrow_\Lambda^0 (\Delta) \vdash t : \tau}{\Gamma; \Delta \vdash \Lambda t : \forall \tau} \quad \frac{\Gamma; \Delta \vdash t : \forall \tau}{\Gamma; \Delta \vdash t\ \sigma : \tau[0 := \sigma]}$$

$$\frac{\Gamma; \Delta\langle 0 : \tau\rangle \vdash_C c}{\Gamma; \Delta \vdash \mu : \tau.\ c : \tau} \quad \frac{\Gamma; \Delta \vdash t : \tau \quad \Delta(\alpha) = \tau}{\Gamma; \Delta \vdash_C [\alpha]t}$$

Fig. 1. The rules for typing judgements in the polymorphic $\lambda\mu$-calculus.

correct type as it will never be queried when a typing judgement is valid. We split typing environments, dedicating one environment to λ-variables and another to μ-variables, and use Γ and Δ to range over the former and latter, respectively. Consequently, our typing judgement for terms is a four-part relation, $\Gamma; \Delta \vdash t : \sigma$, between two typing contexts, a term, and a type.

We write '$\Gamma; \Delta \vdash t : \sigma$', or say that '$\Gamma; \Delta \vdash t : \sigma$ is *derivable*', to assert that a complete derivation tree rooted at $\Gamma; \Delta \vdash t : \sigma$ and constructed using the rules presented in Fig. 1 exists. If $\Gamma; \Delta \vdash t : \sigma$, we say that t is *typeable* in Γ and Δ with type σ. We implement the typing judgement as a pair of mutually recursive inductive predicates in Isabelle—one for terms and one for commands. We write $\uparrow_\Lambda^n (\Gamma)$ and $\uparrow_\Lambda^n (\Delta)$ for the extension of the lifting operations to environments.

Note that care must be taken in the treatment of free variables in the implementation of our typing judgement. In particular, a free variable is represented by its top-level index, and this index must be incremented by 1 for each λ-binder above the variable. For example, consider the judgement $\Gamma, \Delta \vdash \lambda : \tau.(3\ 0) : \tau \to \delta$ which states that under the typing environments Γ and Δ the term $\lambda : \tau.(3\ 0)$ has type $\tau \to \delta$—the free variable 3 is actually represented by 2 in Γ, that is, $\Gamma\ 2 = \tau \to \delta$. To make sure that the typing environment is kept in a consistent state, the operation to add a new binding to the environment $\Gamma\langle 0 : \tau\rangle$ (respectively, $\Delta\langle 0 : \tau\rangle$) is a *shifting* operation. Here, the value of Γ at 0 is now τ, and all other variables that were previously in the environment are shifted up by one, and if 2 was associated with $\tau \to \delta$, 3 is instead associated with this type after shifting. This shifting operation is defined as:

$$\Gamma\langle i : a\rangle = \lambda j.\ \text{if}\ j < i\ \text{then}\ \Gamma j\ \text{else if}\ j = i\ \text{then}\ a\ \text{else}\ \Gamma(j-1).$$

and possesses the useful property $\Gamma\langle n : \tau\rangle\langle 0 : \delta\rangle = \Gamma\langle 0 : \delta\rangle\langle n+1 : \tau\rangle$. This equation is used extensively in our formalisation to rearrange typing contexts.

Important properties of the typing relation may be established by straightforward inductions on derivations in Isabelle. For example:

Theorem 1 (Unicity of typing). *A closed term has at most one type.*

It is also the case that the De Bruijn lifting functions preserve a term's typing:

Lemma 1. *If* $\Gamma; \Delta \vdash t : \tau$, *then*

1. $\Gamma\langle x : \delta\rangle; \Delta \vdash \ \uparrow_\lambda^x (t) : \tau$
2. $\Gamma; \Delta\langle\alpha : \delta\rangle \vdash \ \uparrow_\mu^\alpha (t) : \tau$
3. $\uparrow_\Lambda^a (\Gamma); \uparrow_\Lambda^a (\Delta) \vdash \ \uparrow_\Lambda^a (t) : \ \uparrow_\Lambda^a (\tau)$

As a corollary, we obtain a proof that logical substitution preserves a term's typing, which is established by induction on the derivation of $\Gamma\langle x : \delta\rangle; \Delta \vdash t : \tau$:

Lemma 2. *If* $\Gamma\langle x : \delta\rangle; \Delta \vdash t : \tau$ *and* $\Gamma; \Delta \vdash s : \delta$ *then* $\Gamma; \Delta \vdash t[x := s] : \tau$.

Similarly, type substitution preserves a term's typing:

Lemma 3. *If* $\uparrow_\Lambda^a (\Gamma); \uparrow_\Lambda^a (\Delta) \vdash t : \sigma$ *then* $\Gamma; \Delta \vdash t[a := \tau] : \sigma[a := \tau]$

Structural substitution. Defining structural substitution is more involved. We follow [GKM13] in defining a generalised version of Parigot's structural substitution with the help of *contexts*, and develop some associated machinery before defining substitution proper. This generalised version of structural substitution is particularly useful when considering extensions of the calculus, which we will discuss later in the paper. First, we define contexts with the following grammar:

$$E ::= \Box \mid E \, t \mid E \, \tau$$

Intuitively, a context is either a 'hole' in a term denoted by $\Box$, which can be filled by an associated *instantiation*, or a context applied to a fixed term—i.e. 'holes' are either at the top-level of a term, or on the left, in application position, applied to a series of fixed arguments. Note that contexts are linear, in the sense that only one hole appears in a context.

We write $E[t]$ for the term obtained by instantiating the hole in E with the term t. Naturally, we may wonder when instantiating the hole in a context is type-preserving. To assess this, we define a typing judgement for contexts $\Gamma; \Delta \vdash E : \delta \Leftarrow \tau$ which indicates that the term $E[t]$ has type δ whenever $\Gamma; \Delta \vdash t : \tau$. The definition of this relation is straightforward—and again is easily implemented in Isabelle as an inductive relation—so we elide the definition here. We can characterise the behaviour of this relation with the following lemma, which shows that the relation $\Gamma; \Delta \vdash E : \delta \Leftarrow \tau$ is correct:

Lemma 4. $\Gamma; \Delta \vdash E[t] : \delta$ *if and only if* $\Gamma; \Delta \vdash E : \delta \Leftarrow \tau$ *and* $\Gamma; \Delta \vdash t : \tau$ *for some type* τ.

The result follows by induction on the structure of E in one direction, and an induction on the derivation of $\Gamma; \Delta \vdash E : \delta \Leftarrow \tau$ in the other.

De Bruijn shifting operations can be lifted to contexts in the obvious way, commuting with the structure of contexts, lifting individual fixed terms and evaporating on holes. We write $\uparrow_\lambda^x (E)$, $\uparrow_\mu^\alpha (E)$ and $\uparrow_\Lambda^a (E)$ for the extensionof the shifting of a λ, a μ and a Λ-variable, respectively, to contexts. These operations preserve a context's typing, in the following sense:

Lemma 5. *1. If $\Gamma; \Delta \vdash E : \sigma \Leftarrow \rho$ then $\Gamma\langle x : \delta\rangle; \Delta \vdash \uparrow_\lambda^x (E) : \sigma \Leftarrow \rho$*
2. If $\Gamma; \Delta \vdash E : \sigma \Leftarrow \rho$ then $\Gamma; \Delta\langle \alpha : \delta\rangle \vdash \uparrow_\mu^\alpha (E) : \sigma \Leftarrow \rho$
3. If $\Gamma; \Delta \vdash E : \sigma \Leftarrow \rho$ then $\uparrow_\Lambda^\alpha (\Gamma); \uparrow_\Lambda^\alpha (\Delta) \vdash \uparrow_\Lambda^\alpha (E) : \uparrow_\Lambda^\alpha (\sigma) \Leftarrow \uparrow_\Lambda^\alpha (\rho)$

The proof is by induction on the derivation of $\Gamma; \Delta \vdash E : \sigma \Leftarrow \rho$, using Lemma 1.

With the extension of shifting to contexts, we may now define a generalised form of structural substitution. We write $t[\alpha := \beta E]$ for the substitution action which recursively replaces commands of the form $[\alpha]s$ in t by $[\beta]E[s[\alpha := \beta E]]$ whenever α is free. Figure 2 provides defining clauses for only the most complex cases. Here, the case split in the last equation is needed to ensure that typing will be preserved under structural substitution.

$$(\lambda : \tau.\ t)[\alpha := \beta E] = \lambda : \tau.\ (t[\alpha := \beta \uparrow_\lambda^0 (E))])$$

$$(\mu : \tau.\ c)[\alpha := \beta E] = \mu : \tau.\ (c[(\alpha + 1) := (\beta + 1) \uparrow_\mu^0 (E))])$$

$$(\Lambda t)[\alpha := \beta E] = \Lambda(t[\alpha := \beta \uparrow_\Lambda^0 (E))])$$

$$([\gamma]t)[\alpha := \beta E] = \begin{cases} [\beta](E[t[\alpha := \beta E]]) & \text{if } \gamma = \alpha, \\ [\gamma - 1](t[\alpha := \beta E]) & \text{if } \alpha < \gamma \leq \beta, \\ [\gamma + 1](t[\alpha := \beta E]) & \text{if } \beta \leq \gamma < \alpha, \\ [\gamma](t[\alpha := \beta E]) & \text{otherwise.} \end{cases}$$

Fig. 2. Structural substitution.

We now provide an informal explanation of the final clause in Fig. 2, but first we note that correctly defining this generalised structural substitution was not *a priori* obvious, and the correct definition only became apparent later in the formalisation, after experimentation with a proof of type preservation. As a result, our explanation focusses on the structural substitution applied to a typed term *in context*.

Consider a term t, such that $\Gamma; \Delta \vdash t : \tau$, and the substitution $t[\alpha := \beta E]$. After applying the substitution, the free variable α will be replaced in the typing environment by β, so first examine the case $\alpha < \gamma \leq \beta$. If α has been added to the typing environment using the environment update operation, γ *really* represents the variable $\gamma - 1$ shifted up by 1. However, if β is added instead, $\gamma - 1$ is not shifted up, hence the need to decrement γ by 1 when α is replaced by β. The case $\beta \leq \gamma < \alpha$ is similar, following the same logic.

Here, we observe that the generalised structural substitution defined above preserves a term's typing, as the following lemma demonstrates, which follows from an induction on the derivation of $\Gamma; \Delta\langle \alpha : \delta\rangle \vdash t : \tau$, using Lemma 5:

Lemma 6. *If $\Gamma; \Delta\langle \alpha : \delta\rangle \vdash t : \tau$ and $\Gamma; \Delta \vdash E : \sigma \Leftarrow \delta$ then $\Gamma; \Delta\langle \beta : \sigma\rangle \vdash t[\alpha := \beta \uparrow_\mu^\beta (E)] : \tau$.*

The reduction relation. The *values* in the $\lambda\mu$-calculus are λ-abstractions and type abstractions, i.e. $v ::= \lambda : \tau.t \mid \Lambda t$. In Sect. 3, we will add data to our language, and hence add more values. We use v, v', and so on, to range over values. We say that a term t is in *weak-head-normal form* when one of the following conditions are met: either t is a value, or there exists α and v such that $t = \mu : \tau.[\alpha]v$ with $\alpha \in \mathtt{fcv}(v)$ whenever $\alpha = 0$.

Use n, n', and so on, to range over weak-head-normal forms. Define a *call-by-value reduction relation* between terms using the following six core rules:

$$(\lambda : \tau.\ t)\ n \longrightarrow t[0 := n]$$

$$(\mu : \tau_1 \to \tau_2.\ n)\ n' \longrightarrow \mu : \tau_2.\ (n[0 := 0(\square\ \uparrow_\mu^0 (n')))$$

$$(\mu : \tau.\ [0]v) \longrightarrow\ \downarrow_\mu^0 (v)\quad \text{provided that } 0 \notin \mathtt{fcv}(v)$$

$$[\alpha](\mu : \tau.\ n) \longrightarrow\ \downarrow_\mu^\alpha (n[0 := \alpha\square])$$

$$(\Lambda n)\tau \longrightarrow n[0 := \tau]$$

$$(\mu : \forall\sigma.\ n)\tau \longrightarrow \mu : (\sigma[0 := \tau]).\ (n[0 := 0(\square\tau)])$$

We combine these rules with 5 congruence rules to implement a fully deterministic call-by-value reduction strategy. In Sect. 3 we will add pairs and primitive recursion combinators to the language, and will maintain the same left-to-right call-by-value strategy.

Intuitively, weak-head-normal forms are the subset of terms that cannot be reduced further by our reduction relation defined above, and would ordinarily be considered 'values' in any other context. Indeed, we have the property that, for any term t, if there exists an s such that $t \longrightarrow s$ then t is *not* in normal form. Instead, we reserve the term 'value' for a subset of the normal forms which correspond more closely to what one would ordinarily think of as values, i.e. data elements. In particular, once we add data to our language, values will be gradually expanded to include e.g. the boolean and natural number constants, whilst the definition of weak-head-normal forms will remain static. Note that the structure of normal forms is constrained: they may be values, or they may be a value preceded by a single μ-abstraction and name-part that are irreducible (i.e. they are 'almost' values).

Write $t \longrightarrow u$ to assert that t *reduces in one step* to u, according to the rules above. We write $\longrightarrow^*$ for the *reflexive-transitive closure* of the reduction relation $\longrightarrow$, and write $t \longrightarrow^* u$ to assert that t *reduces to* u.

The first rule—the *logical reduction* rule—is the familiar β-reduction rule of the λ-calculus, and needs no further comment. The second rule—the *structural reduction* rule—pushes a normal form n' under a μ-abstraction. In order to avoid the capture of free μ-variables in n, indices must be appropriately incremented. In the third rule—a form of *extensionality* for μ-abstractions, akin to η-contraction in the λ-calculus—a useless μ-abstraction is garbage collected, and the free μ-variables in the value v are adjusted accordingly when v is no longer under the μ-abstraction. Note that we use a value here, as the term $[0]v$ is a normal form. In the fourth rule—the *renaming* rule—the μ-variables greater than α in n also need to be decremented as the μ-abstration is stripped from the term. The fifth rule is the β-reduction rule for types. The final rule is analogous to the second.

We conclude this section with two important metatheoretical results: type preservation and progress, which together imply that well-typed $\lambda\mu$-terms, interpreted as programs, do not 'go wrong' at runtime. In particular, reduction does not change the type of terms, and well-typed closed terms may either reduce further, or are a normal form. Having proved that logical, structural, and type substitution all preserve typing (in Lemmas 2, 3, and 6 respectively) we establish that reduction in the $\lambda\mu$-calculus has the type preservation property:

Theorem 2 (Preservation). *If $\Gamma; \Delta \vdash t : \tau$ and $t \longrightarrow s$ then $\Gamma; \Delta \vdash s : \tau$.*

The result follows by induction on the derivation of $\Gamma; \Delta \vdash t : \tau$. Finally, we establish the progress property for the reduction relation. Note here that progress holds for λ-closed terms, and there need not be any restriction on the set of free μ-variables in the term being reduced:

Theorem 3 (Progress). *For λ-closed t if $\Gamma; \Delta \vdash t : \tau$ then either t is a normal form or there exists a λ-closed s such that $t \longrightarrow s$.*

3 Some Extensions

As mentioned in the introduction, Parigot's $\lambda\mu$-calculus has a number of limitations when considered as a prototype 'classical' programming language.

First, 'real' programming languages contain base data types and type constructors, and the addition of data types to the $\lambda\mu$-calculus has historically been a challenge. Second, closed typed terms do not correspond to 'full' classical logic [AH03], as typed closed terms inhabit the type of Peirce's Law, but not the law of Double Negation Elimination. Parigot overcame this issue by allowing non-closed terms under μ-variables. For instance, a derivation of the Double Negation Elimination law is encoded as the term $\lambda y.\mu\alpha.[\phi](y(\lambda x.\mu\delta.[\alpha]x))$ in the $\lambda\mu$-calculus, and we note here that the μ-variable ϕ is free, not appearing bound by any μ-abstraction. From a programming perspective, this is undesirable: two morally equivalent terms inhabiting a type will not necessarily be α-equivalent, and substituting a typed term into an arbitrary context may result in μ-variable capture, restricting or complicating the class of refactorings, optimisations, and other code transformations that one may safely apply to a program.

In this section, we consider a number of extensions to the $\lambda\mu$-calculus mechanisation presented in Sect. 2. In the first instance, we extend the $\lambda\mu$-calculus to make its type system isomorphic to 'full' classical logic, using a technique developed by Ariola and Herbelin. Then, we follow Geuvers et al. in adding a type of natural numbers in 'direct style' to the expanded calculus. Finally, expanding on this addition, we further add booleans, products, and tagged union types to the calculus, to obtain a language more closely aligned with mainstream functional programming languages.

Full classical types. In order to extend the correspondence between the types of closed $\lambda\mu$-calculus to 'full' classical logic, Ariola and Herbelin [AH03] extended the calculus with a falsity type, $\bot$, and a distinguished μ-constant, $\top$, which behaved as any other μ-variable when interacting with structural substitution but could not be bound in a μ-abstraction. A new typing rule for the type $\bot$ was added to the calculus, to obtain the $\lambda\mu_{\text{top}}$-calculus, which was shown to be isomorphic to classical natural deduction.

Another approach—followed previously by Ong and Stewart [OS97], Bierman [Bie98], and Py [Py98], who all noted the peculiarity of open $\lambda\mu$-terms inhabiting tautologies—was to collapse the syntactic category of commands into that of terms, so that any term could be bound by a μ-abstraction. In this work, we follow Ariola and Herbelin's method, since it appears to be more 'modular': we have an existing mechanisation of the $\lambda\mu$-calculus which can easily be extended with new typing rules and constants. The collapsing method, on the other hand, appears to be more disruptive, requiring large changes to the typing system and grammar of our calculus. Accordingly, we extend $\lambda\mu$ with a top μ-variable and a new type $\bot$. The grammar for commands and types now reads:

$$c ::= \ldots \mid [\top]t \qquad \tau ::= \ldots \mid \bot$$

Additionally, we extend our definition of normal form to include $\mu : \tau.\ [\top]v$, whenever v is a value. We use Isabelle's option type to extend the domain and range of the structural substitution function to support the $\top$ constant. For example, the renaming rule for $\top$ is $[\top](\mu : \tau.c) \longrightarrow \downarrow_{\mu}^{0} (c[\text{Some}0 := \text{None}\Box])$, where None denotes the $\top$ constant in the structural substitution.

In a well-typed term, the command $[\top]t$ is well-typed whenever t is of type $\bot$. We therefore extend our typing system with the following additional rule:

$$\frac{\Gamma;\Delta \vdash t : \bot}{\Gamma;\Delta \vdash_C [\top]t}$$

Note that $\top$ need not be added to the μ-context Δ in the rule's premiss.

We may now write μ-closed terms that are not typeable in the $\lambda\mu$-calculus. For example, a proof of the Double Negation Elimination law is encoded as the term $\lambda.\mu.[\top](0\ (\lambda.\mu.[1]0))$ (with type annotations omitted).

Adding the natural numbers. We follow [GKM13] and extend our calculus with the natural numbers in 'direct style'. The grammar of terms, types, values and contexts is extended with the following new syntactic categories:

$$r, s, t ::= \ldots \mid 0 \mid S\,t \mid \text{nrec} : \tau\,r\,s\,t$$
$$\tau ::= \ldots \mid \mathbb{N}$$
$$v ::= \ldots \mid 0 \mid S v$$
$$E ::= \ldots \mid S\,E \mid \text{nrec} : \tau\,r\,s\,E$$

Modulo changes to the definition of values, the definition of normal forms does not change. Here, the terms 0 and S denote zero and the successor functions, respectively, used to embed the unary natural numbers into the calculus, *à la* Gödel's System T. The term $\mathtt{nrec} : \tau\, r\, s\, t$ is a primitive recursion combinator, and reduces to r if t is zero, and to $s\, t(\mathtt{nrec} : \tau\, r\, s\, \underline{n})$ if t is S $\underline{n}$

$$c ::= \ldots \mid [\top]t \qquad \tau ::= \ldots \mid \bot$$

$$\frac{}{\Gamma;\Delta \vdash 0 : \mathsf{N}} \qquad \frac{\Gamma;\Delta \vdash t : \mathsf{N}}{\Gamma;\Delta \vdash \mathsf{S}\, t : \mathsf{N}}$$

$$\frac{\Gamma;\Delta \vdash r : \rho \qquad \Gamma;\Delta \vdash s : \mathsf{N} \to \rho \to \rho \qquad \Gamma;\Delta \vdash t : \mathsf{N}}{\Gamma;\Delta \vdash \mathtt{nrec} : \rho\, r\, s\, t : \rho}$$

$$\mathsf{S}(\mu : \delta.\, n) \longrightarrow \mu : \delta.\, n[0 := 0\ (\mathsf{S}\square)]$$

$$\mathtt{nrec} : \tau\, n\, n'\, 0 \longrightarrow n$$

$$\mathtt{nrec} : \tau\, n\, n'\, (\mathsf{S}\, \underline{m}) \longrightarrow n'\, \underline{n}\, (\mathtt{nrec} : \tau\, n\, n'\, \underline{m})$$

$$\mathtt{nrec} : \tau\, n\, n'\, (\mu : \delta.\, n'') \longrightarrow \mu : \tau.\, n''[0 := 0\ (\mathtt{nrec} : \tau\ \uparrow^0_\mu (n)\ \uparrow^0_\mu (n')\ \square)]$$

Fig. 3. Typing rules and reduction cases added for natural number data.

The typing rules and reduction relation are extended to handle these new cases, and the extensions are presented in Fig. 3. Here, we write $\underline{m}$ for m-fold applications of S to 0, and note that in the last reduction rule for $\mathtt{nrec}$, the index of μ-variables are incremented by 1 to avoid capture of free variables. Evaluation proceeds in a left-to-right direction when evaluating the $\mathtt{nrec}$ combinator, in line with our previously established convention.

Adding booleans, products, and tagged unions. We extend further, adding booleans, products and tagged unions. The grammar of terms, types and values are extended as follows, with contexts also extended in a similar fashion:

$$t, r, s ::= \ldots \mid \mathtt{true} \mid \mathtt{false} \mid \mathtt{if} : \tau\, t\ \mathtt{then}\ r\ \mathtt{else}\ s \mid \langle t, s \rangle : \tau \mid \pi_1 t \mid \pi_2 t \mid$$
$$\mathtt{inl} : \tau\, t \mid \mathtt{inr} : \tau\, t \mid \mathtt{case} : \tau\, t\ \mathtt{of}\ \mathtt{inl}\ x \Rightarrow s \mid \mathtt{inr}\ y \Rightarrow r$$
$$\sigma, \tau ::= \ldots \mid \mathtt{Bool} \mid \sigma \times \tau \mid \sigma + \tau$$
$$v, w ::= \ldots \mid \mathtt{true} \mid \mathtt{false} \mid \langle v, w \rangle : \tau \mid \mathtt{inl} : \tau\, v \mid \mathtt{inr} : \tau\, v$$

Modulo changes to the grammar of values, normal forms remain unchanged. Here, $\langle t, s \rangle : \tau$ denotes a *pairing* construction, and $\pi_1 t$ and $\pi_2 t$ the first and second *projection* functions of a pair, respectively. Note that type annotations are used liberally, for example in the if construct the whole expression has type τ. This is somewhat unusual as such a simple type system would never ordinarily require such heavy type annotation. However, the reduction behaviour of the calculus makes the annotations necessary, as they provide the type for the continuation variable when reducing a μ-abstraction, for example, in the rule:

$$\text{if} : \tau \ (\mu : \sigma.n) \text{ then } s \text{ else } r \longrightarrow \mu : \tau.(n[0 := 0 \ (\text{if} : \tau \ \Box \text{ then } \uparrow_\mu^0 (s) \text{ else } \uparrow_\mu^0 (r))]$$

It is straightforward to extend the De Bruijn shifting and substitution functions to cope with the new datatypes and type constructors. We note that when handling $\text{case} : \rho \ (\text{inl} : \sigma + \tau \ t) \text{ of } \text{inl } x \Rightarrow s \mid \text{inr } y \Rightarrow r$, the indices of free λ-variables in s and r need to be incremented, since we implicitly represent the bound variables x and y by the De Brujin index 0 inside s and r, respectively.

We include the additional typing and reduction rules for booleans, products and tagged unions. For every type constructor, we have introduction and elimination rules, along with a congruence rule for μ-abstractions. In this extended system, it is straightforward to prove type preservation and progress, with both results following by straightforward inductions.

Theorem 4 (Preservation). *If $\Gamma; \Delta \vdash t : \tau$ and $t \longrightarrow s$ then $\Gamma; \Delta \vdash s : \tau$.*

Theorem 5 (Progress). *For λ-closed t if $\Gamma; \Delta \vdash t : \tau$ then either t is a normal form or there exists a λ-closed s such that $t \longrightarrow s$.*

Further, we can characterise the syntactic form of closed values, based on their type, producing a form of inversion result:

Lemma 7. *If t is a λ-closed value and $\Gamma; \Delta \vdash t : \sigma$ then:*

1. *If $\sigma = \mathbb{N}$ then either $t = 0$ or there exists a value $\underline{n}$ such that $t = \text{S } \underline{n}$,*
2. *If $\sigma = \text{Bool}$ then either $t = \text{true}$ or $t = \text{false}$,*
3. *If $\sigma = \tau_1 + \tau_2$ then either $t = \text{inl} : \tau_1 \ s$ or $t = \text{inr} : \tau_2 \ u$ for values s and u,*
4. *If $\sigma = \tau_1 \times \tau_2$ then $t = \langle s, u \rangle : \tau_1 \times \tau_2$ for values s and u,*
5. *If $\sigma = \tau_1 \rightarrow \tau_2$ then $t = \lambda : \tau_1.s$ for some term s.*
6. *If $\sigma = \forall \tau$ then $t = \Lambda s$ for some term s.*

The result follows by a straightforward induction. At first glance, Lemma 7 may appear useless, as our progress and preservation theorems merely guarantee that evaluation of a λ-closed program either diverges or evaluation progresses to a normal form. Note however that normal forms are constrained to either be a value, or some irreducible μ-abstraction and name-part combination wrapping a value, i.e. 'almost a value'. In either case, Lemma 7 can be used to inspect the syntactic structure of the value based on its type.

4 μML

μML is a prototype implementation of a strict 'classical' programming language derived from the calculus presented in Sect. 3. The core of the interpreter is derived from our Isabelle mechanisation via code generation: the interpreter's type-checker and reduction mechanism is extracted and paired with a handwritten parser using the Menhir parser generator [PRG17] and a thin transformation of the Abstract Syntax Tree into a nameless form. An operational semantics is provided by a small-step evaluation function that is proved sound and complete with respect to our evaluation relation. We therefore have the following theorem:

Theorem 6 (Determinism). *The reduction relation of the polymorphic $\lambda\mu$-calculus extended with datatypes is deterministic.*

Finally, our progress and preservation theorems ensure that μML programs do not 'go wrong' at runtime.

Example: Double Negation Elimination. We present a closed μML program inhabiting a type corresponding to the law of Double Negation Elimination:

```
tabs(A) ->
  fun (x : (A -> bot) -> bot) ->
    bind (a : A) -> [abort]. (x (fun (y : A) ->
      bind (b : bot) -> [a]. y
    end end)) end end end
```

Here, the keywords bind and abort are μML's rendering of the μ-abstraction and the distinguished μ-constant, $\top$, respectively, of our underlying calculus, whilst [a].t introduces a command (with name a). The keywords tabs and forall introduce a Λ-abstraction and a universal type respectively. When passed the program above, μML type-checks it, and presents the type back to the user:

```
    ... : forall(A)(((A -> bot) -> bot) -> A)
```

That is, $\neg\neg A \to A$, as expected. We obtain the value fun (x : bot) -> x after supplying fun (f : (bot -> bot) -> bot) -> f (fun (x : bot) -> x) to this function, along with a type parameter, and evaluating, as expected.

Example: implication and product. We present a closed μML program inhabiting a type corresponding to an instance of the classical tautology $\neg(A \to \neg B) \to A \wedge B$:

```
tabs(A) -> tabs(B) ->
  fun (x : (A -> B -> bot) -> bot) ->
    bind (a : A * B) -> [abort]. (x (fun (y : A) ->
      fun (z : B) -> bind (b : bot) ->
        [a]. {y, z} : A * B
    end end end)) end end end end
```

Here, $\{y, z\} : \tau$ is μML's concrete syntax for explicitly-typed pairs. When passed the program above, μML type-checks it, and presents the type back to the user:

```
    ... : forall(A)(forall(B)(((A -> B -> bot) -> bot) -> A * B))
```

That is, $\neg(A \to \neg B) \to A \times B$, as expected.

5   Synthesis via Theorem-Proving: μTP

We now present a small, prototype interactive theorem prover based on classical first-order logic, called μTP, and built around our μML proof terms. In particular, this system is able to synthesise μML programs from proofs.

With μTP, we follow the LCF-approach [Mil79] and provide a compact system kernel, written in OCaml, which provides an abstract type of theorems, with smart constructors being the only means of constructing a valid inhabitant of this type. Each smart constructor implements a particular proof rule from our typing relation, mapping valid theorems to new valid theorems. As well as incrementally constructing a formula (i.e. a μML type), each forward proof step also incrementally builds a μML term. Outwith the kernel, we provide a mechanism for backwards-proof, via a system of *tactics*, and a notion of a *proof state*. We note that we need not construct a μML term at all during backwards proof, and therefore there is no need to introduce metavariables into our programs to denote missing pieces of program deriving from incomplete derivations. Rather, the only step that synthesises a μML program is the last collapsing of a completed backwards proof, upon calling qed, via a series of *valuation* functions that 'undo' each backwards proof step, wherein a complete μML program is produced.

```
conjecture (mk_all_t (mk_arrow_t (mk_arrow_t (mk_arrow_t
   (mk_var_t 0) mk_bot_t) mk_bot_t) (mk_var_t 0)));
  apply 0 all_intro_tac;        apply 0 imp_intro_tac;
  apply 0 mu_top_intro_tac;
  apply 0 (imp_elim_tac (mk_arrow_t (mk_var_t 0) mk_bot_t));
  apply 0 (assm_tac 0);         apply 0 imp_intro_tac;
  apply 0 (mu_label_intro_tac 1); apply 0 (assm_tac 0);
qed ();
```

Fig. 4. A μTP tactic-driven proof of the conjecture $\forall A.\ \neg\neg A \longrightarrow A$.

```
conjecture (mk_all_t (mk_all_t (mk_arrow_t (mk_arrow_t
   (mk_neg_t (mk_var_t 0)) (mk_var_t 1)) (mk_sum_t
   (mk_var_t 0) (mk_var_t 1)))));
  apply 0 all_intro_tac;        apply 0 all_intro_tac;
  apply 0 imp_intro_tac;        apply 0 mu_top_intro_tac;
  apply 0 (imp_elim_tac (mk_neg_t (mk_var_t 0)));
  apply 1 imp_intro_tac;        apply 1 (mu_label_intro_tac 1);
  apply 1 disj_left_intro_tac; apply 1 (assm_tac 0);
  apply 0 imp_intro_tac;        apply 0 (mu_label_intro_tac 1);
  apply 0 disj_right_intro_tac;
  apply 0 (imp_elim_tac (mk_neg_t (mk_var_t 0)));
  apply 1 (assm_tac 0);         apply 0 (assm_tac 1);
qed ();
```

Fig. 5. A μTP tactic-driven proof of the conjecture $\forall B.\forall A.(\neg B \longrightarrow A) \longrightarrow B \lor A$.

We have used μTP to prove several theorems in classical first-order logic, and have successfully extracted μML programs from their proofs, including both programs presented in Sect. 4. As didactic examples we provide μTP proof scripts for the classical theorems $\forall A. \neg\neg A \longrightarrow A$ and $\forall B. \forall A. (\neg B \longrightarrow A) \longrightarrow B \vee A$ in Fig. 4 and Fig. 5, respectively.[3] The Law of Excluded Middle can be easily derived as well, and indeed follows almost immediately from the second theorem. Neither of these two theorems are intuitionistically derivable.

Proof construction with μTP is interactive. The function conjecture takes a closed formula (type) as conjecture and sets up an initial proof state, which can be pretty-printed for inspection by the user. The function apply takes a goal number and a tactic to apply and either progresses the proof state using that tactic or fails. Finally, qed closes a proof, producing an element of type thm, raising an error if the proof is not yet complete. This qed step also typechecks the μML proof term by the proof to ensure that the correct program was synthesised.

The basic tactics provided by the μTP system invert each of the typing rules of the μML language. For example, all_intro_tac works backwards from a universally quantified goal, whilst imp_intro_tac works backwards from an implicational goal, introducing a new assumption. Two tactics—mu_top_intro_tac and mu_label_intro_tac—are the primitive means of affecting classical reasoning in μTP, corresponding to the two ways to introduce a μ-binder and command combination in the underlying μML proof term. Note that this direct reasoning with μ-binders is low-level, and only intended to 'bootstrap' the theorem proving system: once familiar classical reasoning principles such as the Law of Excluded Middle are established, the user need never have to resort to using either of these two tactics directly.

A μML proof term serialising a μTP proof can be obtained programmatically by the user after finishing a proof. For example the program

```
tabs (B) -> tabs (A) -> (fun (x : (B -> bot) -> A) ->
  (bind (a : B + A) -> ([abort]. ((fun (y : B -> bot) ->
  (bind (b : bot) -> ([a]. ((inr (x y) : B + A)))))
  (fun (z : B) -> (bind (c : bot) ->
    ([a]. ((inl z : B + A)))))))))))
```

is automatically extracted from the proof presented in Fig. 5. The fact that this program inhabits the correct type is easily established.

6   Conclusions

Proof terms for theorem-proving systems based on intuitionistic type-theory—such as Coq and Matita—serve both as a means of communication between systems, and as a means of independently auditing the reasoning steps taken during a mechanised proof. In this latter respect, proof terms form a crucial component of the *trust story* of a theorem proving system. In this work, we

---

[3] Note that formulae are currently manually constructed, due to the lack of a parser.

explore the use of proof term technology in theorem-proving systems based on classical, rather than intuitionistic, logic.

In particular, we have used the $\lambda\mu$-calculus as the foundation for a system of proof terms for classical first-order logic. For this to be effective, two extensions were considered: adding data types in 'direct style', and extending the calculus to a full correspondence with classical logic so that all classical tautologies can be serialised by closed proof terms. Accordingly, we designed μML—either a prototype classical programming language or a system of proof terms for classical logic—based on the call-by-value $\lambda\mu$-calculus extended with data types and a distinguished μ-constant, $\top$. All of our proofs have been mechanised in Isabelle/HOL to guard against any unsoundness in the μML type system, and an interpreter for μML was extracted from our Isabelle/HOL definitions.

Atop our system of proof terms, we have built a small prototype LCF-style interactive theorem proving system for classical logic, called μTP. The μTP user may automatically synthesise μML programs from completed tactic-driven μTP proofs. We have presented a number of example tactic-driven proofs of classically (but not intuitionistically) derivable theorems that we have proved in μTP as evidence of the utility of our approach.

Future work. The logic considered in this work—first-order logic—is expressive, but strictly less expressive than the higher-order logics typically used in established interactive theorem proving systems. We therefore aim to extend μML further, first to a classical variant of F_ω, and then to consider a classical Calculus of Constructions. Lastly, to make μTP usable as a 'realistic' theorem proving system suitable for formalising real mathematics, one would need features such as conversions, tacticals, and a global definition database. We leave these for future work.

Related work. There has been extensive prior work by the developers of Isabelle to retrofit the theorem prover with a system of proof terms, primarily by Berghofer [BN00, Ber03]. Following the standard argument in favour of the LCF design philosophy, one only needs to trust the Isabelle kernel implementation in order to trust any proof carried out in the system, and proof terms *as a source of trust* are strictly not needed. However, this argument breaks down when the system kernel is complex and hard to manually audit—as in the case of Isabelle. As we summarised in the Introduction, proof terms convey several other advantages, such as permitting communication between systems and facilitating proof transformation, making their retrofit an attractive prospect for users and developers of existing systems. We note here that there is a difference in philosophy between our work and that of Berghofer: we take as our starting point a system of proof terms and build a theorem prover around them; Berghofer takes an existing theorem prover and extracts a system of proof terms tailored to it.

Tangentially, the Open Theory format [KH12] is intended to facilitate communication of higher-order logic theorems and definitions between theorem proving systems in the wider HOL family (HOL4, HOL Light, ProofPower, and Isabelle). Here, the unit of communication is a sequence of primitive HOL inferences, rather than a proof term.

Acknowledgments. Gomes and Mulligan acknowledge funding from EPSRC grant EP/K008528 ('REMS: Rigorous Engineering for Mainstream Systems'). We thank the anonymous referees and Peter Sewell for their helpful comments.

References

[AH03] Ariola, Z.M., Herbelin, H.: Minimal classical logic and control operators. In: Baeten, J.C.M., Lenstra, J.K., Parrow, J., Woeginger, G.J. (eds.) ICALP 2003. LNCS, vol. 2719, pp. 871–885. Springer, Heidelberg (2003). https://doi.org/10.1007/3-540-45061-0_68

[AHS04] Ariola, Z.M., Herbelin, H., Sabry, A.: A type-theoretic foundation of continuations and prompts. In: ICFP (2004)

[ARCT11] Asperti, A., Ricciotti, W., Sacerdoti Coen, C., Tassi, E.: The matita interactive theorem prover. In: Bjørner, N., Sofronie-Stokkermans, V. (eds.) CADE 2011. LNCS (LNAI), vol. 6803, pp. 64–69. Springer, Heidelberg (2011). https://doi.org/10.1007/978-3-642-22438-6_7

[BB94] Barbanera, F., Berardi, S.: A symmetric lambda calculus for "classical" program extraction. In: TACS (1994)

[BB95] Barbanera, F., Berardi, S.: A strong normalization result for classical logic. Ann. Pure Appl. Log. **76**(2), 99–116 (1995)

[BBS97] Barbanera, F., Berardi, S., Schivalocchi, M.: "Classical" programming-with-proofs in $\lambda_{\mathsf{Sym}}^{\mathsf{PA}}$: an analysis of non-confluence. In: TACS (1997)

[Ber03] Berghofer, S.: Proofs, programs and executable specifications in higher order logic. Ph.D. thesis, Technical University Munich, Germany (2003)

[BHS97] Barthe, G., Hatcliff, J., Sørensen, M.H.: A notion of classical pure type system. Electron. Notes Theor. Comput. Sci. **6**, 4–59 (1997)

[Bie98] Bierman, G.M.: A computational interpretation of the $\lambda\mu$-calculus. In: Brim, L., Gruska, J., Zlatuška, J. (eds.) MFCS 1998. LNCS, vol. 1450, pp. 336–345. Springer, Heidelberg (1998). https://doi.org/10.1007/BFb0055783

[BN00] Berghofer, S., Nipkow, T.: Proof terms for simply typed higher order logic. In: Aagaard, M., Harrison, J. (eds.) TPHOLs 2000. LNCS, vol. 1869, pp. 38–52. Springer, Heidelberg (2000). https://doi.org/10.1007/3-540-44659-1_3

[BU02] Barthe, G., Uustalu, T.: CPS translating inductive and coinductive types. In: PEPM (2002)

[BW05] Barendregt, H., Wiedijk, F.: The challenge of computer mathematics. Philos. Trans. A **363**, 2005 (1835)

[CP11] Crolard, T., Polonowski, E.: A program logic for higher-order procedural variables and non-local jumps. CoRR, abs/1112.1554 (2011)

[dB72] de Bruijn, N.G.: Lambda calculus notation with nameless dummies, a tool for automatic formula manipulation, with application to the Church-Rosser theorem. Indagationes Mathematicae **75**(5), 381–392 (1972)

[dG94a] de Groote, P.: A CPS-translation of the lambda-μ-calculus. In: CAAP (1994)

[dG94b] Groote, P.: On the relation between the $\lambda\mu$-calculus and the syntactic theory of sequential control. In: Pfenning, F. (ed.) LPAR 1994. LNCS, vol. 822, pp. 31–43. Springer, Heidelberg (1994). https://doi.org/10.1007/3-540-58216-9_27

[dG95] Groote, P.: A simple calculus of exception handling. In: Dezani-Ciancaglini, M., Plotkin, G. (eds.) TLCA 1995. LNCS, vol. 902, pp. 201–215. Springer, Heidelberg (1995). https://doi.org/10.1007/BFb0014054

[dG98] de Groote, P.: An environment machine for the $\lambda\mu$-calculus. Math. Struct. Comput. Sci. **8**(6), 637–669 (1998)

[dG01] Groote, P.: Strong normalization of classical natural deduction with disjunction. In: Abramsky, S. (ed.) TLCA 2001. LNCS, vol. 2044, pp. 182–196. Springer, Heidelberg (2001). https://doi.org/10.1007/3-540-45413-6_17

[FFKD87] Felleisen, M., Friedman, D.P., Kohlbecker, E.E., Duba, B.F.: A syntactic theory of sequential control. Theor. Comput. Sci. **52**, 205–237 (1987)

[Gir71] Girard, J.-Y.: Une extension de l'interprétation de Gödel à l'analyse et son application à l'élimination des coupures dans l'analyse et la théorie des types. In: Proceedings of the Second Scandinavian Logic Symposium (1971)

[GKM13] Geuvers, H., Krebbers, R., McKinna, J.: The $\lambda\mu^{T}$-calculus. Ann. Pure Appl. Logic **164**(6), 676–701 (2013)

[Göd58] Gödel, K.: Über eine bisher noch nicht benützte erweiterung des finiten standpunktes. Dialectica **12**(3–4), 280–287 (1958)

[Gor91] Gordon, M.J.C.: Introduction to the HOL system. In: HOL (1991)

[Gri90] Griffin, T.: A formulae-as-types notion of control. In: POPL (1990)

[HH14] Huet, G.P., Herbelin, H.: 30 years of research and development around Coq. In: POPL (2014)

[HL91] Harper, B., Lillibridge, M.: ML with callcc is unsound (1991). https://www.seas.upenn.edu/sweirich/types/archive/1991/msg00034.html

[KH12] Kumar, R., Hurd, J.: Standalone tactics using opentheory. In: Beringer, L., Felty, A. (eds.) ITP 2012. LNCS, vol. 7406, pp. 405–411. Springer, Heidelberg (2012). https://doi.org/10.1007/978-3-642-32347-8_28

[Kri16] Krivine, J-L.: Bar recursion in classical realisability: dependent choice and continuum hypothesis. In: CSL pp. 25:1–25:11 (2016)

[MGM17] Matache, C., Gomes, V.B.F., Mulligan, D.P.: The $\lambda\mu$-calculus. Archive of Formal Proofs (2017)

[Mil79] Milner, R.: Lcf: a way of doing proofs with a machine. In: Bečvář, J. (ed.) MFCS 1979. LNCS, vol. 74, pp. 146–159. Springer, Heidelberg (1979). https://doi.org/10.1007/3-540-09526-8_11

[Mur91] Murthy, C.R.: An evaluation semantics for classical proofs. In: LICS (1991)

[OS97] Ong, C.-H.L., Stewart, C.A.: A Curry-Howard foundation for functional computation with control. In: POPL. ACM Press (1997)

[Par92] Parigot, M.: $\lambda\mu$-Calculus: an algorithmic interpretation of classical natural deduction. In: Voronkov, A. (ed.) LPAR 1992. LNCS, vol. 624, pp. 190–201. Springer, Heidelberg (1992). https://doi.org/10.1007/BFb0013061

[Par93a] Parigot, M.: Classical proofs as programs. In: Gottlob, G., Leitsch, A., Mundici, D. (eds.) KGC 1993. LNCS, vol. 713, pp. 263–276. Springer, Heidelberg (1993). https://doi.org/10.1007/BFb0022575

[Par93b] Parigot, M.: Strong normalization for second order classical natural deduction. In: LICS (1993)

[Par97] Parigot, M.: Proofs of strong normalisation for second order classical natural deduction. J. Symb. Log. **62**(4), 1461–1479 (1997)

[PRG17] Pottier, F., Régis-Gianas, Y.: The Menhir parser generator (2017)

[Py98] Py, W.: Confluence en $\lambda\mu$-calcul. Ph.D. thesis (1998)

[RS94] Rehof, J., Sørensen, M.H.: The λ_{Δ}-calculus. In: TACS (1994)

Static Analysis of Multithreaded Recursive Programs Communicating via Rendez-Vous

Adrien Pommellet[1]([✉]) and Tayssir Touili[2]([✉])

[1] LIPN and Universite Paris-Diderot, Paris, France
`pommellet@lipn.univ-paris13.fr`
[2] LIPN, CNRS, and Universite Paris 13, Paris, France
`tayssir.touili@lipn.univ-paris13.fr`

Abstract. We present in this paper a generic framework for the analysis of multi-threaded programs with recursive procedure calls, synchronisation by rendez-vous between parallel threads, and dynamic creation of new threads. To this end, we consider a model called *Synchronized Dynamic Pushdown Networks* (SDPNs) that can be seen as a network of pushdown processes executing synchronized transitions, spawning new pushdown processes, and performing internal pushdown actions. The reachability problem for this model is unfortunately undecidable. Therefore, we tackle this problem by introducing an abstraction framework based on Kleene algebras in order to compute an abstraction of the execution paths between two regular sets of configurations. We combine an automata theoretic saturation procedure with constraint solving in a finite domain. We then apply this framework to a Counter-Example Guided Abstraction Refinement (CEGAR) scheme, using multiple abstractions of increasing complexity and precision.

Keywords: Dynamic pushdown networks · Synchronization · Execution paths · Kleene abstractions

1 Introduction

The use of parallel programs has grown in popularity in the past fifteen years, but these remain nonetheless fickle and vulnerable to specific issues such as race conditions or deadlocks. Static analysis methods for this class of programs remain therefore more relevant than ever.

Pushdown Systems (PDSs) are a natural model for programs with sequential, recursive procedure calls, as shown by Esparza et al. in [6]. Thus, networks of pushdown systems can be used to model multithreaded programs, where each PDS in the network models a sequential component of the whole program. In this context, *Dynamic Pushdown Networks* (DPNs) were introduced by Bouajjani et al. in [4].

This work was partially funded by the FUI project FREENIVI.

B.-Y.E. Chang (Ed.): APLAS 2017, LNCS 10695, pp. 235–254, 2017.
https://doi.org/10.1007/978-3-319-71237-6_12

Intuitively, this class of automata consists of a network of pushdown systems running independently in parallel. Each member of a DPN can, after a transition, spawn a new PDS which is then introduced as a new member of the network. Thus, DPNs can be used to represent a network of threads where each thread can recursively call procedures, perform internal actions, or spawn a new thread.

However, this model cannot represent synchronization between threads or parallel components. In order to handle communication in multithreaded programs, Bouajjani et al. introduced in [2] *Communicating Pushdown Systems* (CPDSs), a model which consists of a tuple of pushdown systems synchronized by rendez-vous on execution paths. However, CPDSs have a constant number of processes and cannot therefore handle dynamic creation of new threads.

Hence, we introduce in this paper a more accurate model, namely, *Synchronized Dynamic Pushdown Networks* (SDPNs) that combines DPNs with CPDSs in order to handle dynamic thread creation and communication at the same time. A SDPN can be seen as a DPN where PDS processes can synchronize via rendez-vous by sending and receiving messages. In a SDPN, pushdown processes can apply internal actions labelled by a letter τ without synchronization, just like a DPN, but can also synchronize through channels. To do so, we represent each channel by a pair of letters, as an example a and $\bar{a}$, that can be used to label transitions. If one thread can execute an action labelled with a signal a, and another thread another action labelled with $\bar{a}$, then both threads can synchronize and execute their respective transitions simultaneously, in a single step labelled by τ.

We consider the reachability problem for SDPNs, that is, finding if a critical configuration can be reached from the set of starting configurations of the program. An equivalent problem is to compute the set $Paths(\mathcal{C}, \mathcal{C}')$ of execution paths leading from a configuration in $\mathcal{C}$ to a configuration in $\mathcal{C}'$ and check if it is empty. This problem unfortunately remains undecidable for synchronized systems, as proven by Ramalingam in [10].

Therefore, the set of execution paths $Paths(C, C')$ cannot be computed in an exact manner. To overcome this problem, we proceed as in [2]: our approach is based on the computation of an abstraction $\alpha(Paths(\mathcal{C}, \mathcal{C}'))$ of the execution paths language. To this aim, we propose techniques based on:

- the representation of regular sets of configurations of SDPNs with finite word automata;
- the use of these automata to determine a set of constraints whose least fixpoint characterizes the set of execution paths of the program; to compute this set of constraints, (1) we consider a relaxed semantics on SDPNs that allows partially synchronized runs, (2) we abstract sets of execution paths as functions in a Kleene algebra, instead of simple elements of the abstract domain, and (3) we use a shuffle product on abstract path expressions to represent the interleaving and potential synchronization of parallel executions;
- the resolution of this set of constraints in an abstract domain; we consider in particular the case where the abstract domain is finite; the set of constraints can then be solved using an iterative fixpoint computation.

Note that the main contribution of our approach w.r.t. to [2,12] is the introduction of functions to represent sets of abstracted path expressions and the use of a shuffle product to model the interleaving of threads. The abstraction framework as defined in these papers cannot be applied to SDPNs due to the presence of dynamic thread creation, hence, the need for functions and shuffling.

We can then apply this abstraction framework for the reachability problem to a Counter-Example Guided Abstraction Refinement (CEGAR) scheme inspired by the work of Chaki et al. in [5]. The idea is the following: (1) we do a reachability analysis of the program, using a finite domain abstraction of order n in our abstraction framework; if the target set of configurations is not reachable by the abstract paths, it is not reachable by actual execution paths either; otherwise, we obtain a counter-example; (2) we check if the counter-example can be matched to an actual execution of the program; (3) if it does, then we have shown that the target set of configurations is actually reachable; (4) otherwise, we refine our abstraction and use instead a finite domain abstraction of order $n+1$ in step (2). This CEGAR scheme is then used to prove that a Windows driver first presented in [9] can reach an erroneous configuration, using an abstraction of the original program. An updated version of this driver is then shown to be error-free.

Related Work. Wenner introduced in [13] a model of *Weighted Dynamic Pushdown Networks* (WDPNs), extending the work of Reps et al. on *Weighted Pushdown Systems* in [11] to DPNs. WDPNs share some similarities with our abstraction framework on SDPNs: each transition is labelled by a weight in a bounded idempotent semiring, these weights can be composed along execution paths, and the sum of the weights of all execution paths between two sets of configurations can be computed, provided that a simple extension of the original semiring to an abstract set of execution hedges can be found. WDPNs, however, do not feature simultaneous, synchronized actions between pushdown processes. Moreover, in order to be efficient, the extensions of the abstract domain have to be chosen on a case-by-case basis in order to label tree automata, whereas our framework works for every finite-domain abstraction and only uses finite state automata.

Multi-Stack Pushdown Systems (MPDSs) are pushdown systems with two or more stacks, and can be used to model synchronized parallel programs. Qadeer et al. introduced in [8] the notion of context, that is, a part of an execution path during which only one stack of the automaton can be modified. The reachability problem within a bounded number of context switches is decidable for MPDSs. However, MPDSs have a bounded number of stacks and, unlike SDPNs, cannot therefore handle the dynamic creation of new threads.

Bouajjani et al. introduced in [1] *Asynchronous Dynamic Pushdown Networks*, or ADPNs. This model extends DPNs by adding a global control state to the whole network as a mean of communication between processes; each pushdown process can then apply rules either by reading its own local state or the global state of the network. The reachability problem within a bounded number of context switches is decidable for ADPNs, where a context here stands for a part of an execution path during which transitions altering global variables are all executed by the same process. This is an underapproximation of the actual reachability problem for synchronized parallel programs, whereas we compute in this paper an overapproximation of the same problem. The former can be used to find errors in a program but, unlike the latter, does not allow one to check that a program is free from errors.

Extensions of the Kleene algebra framework of [2] were defined in [3,12] to compute abstractions of execution paths of multithreaded recursive programs communicating via rendez-vous. However, unlike SDPNs, the models considered in these articles cannot describe thread spawns, where the father of a new thread can resume its execution independently of its children.

Paper Outline. In Sect. 2 of this paper, we define *Synchronized Dynamic Pushdown Networks* (SDPNs). We study in Sect. 3 the reachability problem for this class of automata. We present in Sect. 4 an abstraction framework based on Kleene algebras that allows us to overapproximate the set of execution paths between two sets of configurations C and C' of a SDPN. In Sect. 5, we define structures to represent this abstraction. This framework relies on an algorithm computing the set of abstract paths leading to a set of configurations C of a SDPN, which is explained in Sect. 6. Finally, in Sect. 7, we present a CounterExample Guided Abstraction Refinement scheme that relies on our abstraction framework and apply it to a model of an actual program in Sect. 8.

2   Synchronized Dynamic Pushdown Networks

2.1   The Model and Its Semantics

Definition 1 (Synchronized Dynamic Pushdown Networks). *A Synchronized Dynamic Pushdown Network (SDPN) is a quadruplet $M = (Act, P, \Gamma, \Delta)$ where Act is a finite set of actions, P a finite set of control states, Γ a finite stack alphabet disjoint from P, and $\Delta \subseteq (P\Gamma \times Act \times P\Gamma^*) \cup (P\Gamma \times Act \times P\Gamma^*P\Gamma^*)$ a finite set of transition rules.*

If $(p\gamma, a, w) \in \Delta$, $p \in P$, $\gamma \in \Gamma$, $a \in Act$, and $w \in P\Gamma^* \cup P\Gamma^*P\Gamma^*$, we write that $p\gamma \xrightarrow{a} w \in \Delta$. There are two types of transition rules in a SDPN:

– rules of the form $p\gamma \xrightarrow{a} p'w$ in $P\Gamma \times Act \times P$ allow a pushdown process in the network to pop a symbol γ from its stack, push a word w, then move from state p to p'; these rules are standard pushdown rules and model a thread calling or ending procedures while moving through its control flow;
– rules of the form $p\gamma \xrightarrow{a} p''w'p'w$ in $P\Gamma \times Act \times P\Gamma^*P\Gamma^*$ allow a pushdown process in the network to pop a symbol γ from its stack, push a word w, move from state p to p', then spawn a new pushdown process in state p'' and with initial stack w'; these rules model dynamic creation of new threads.

We assume that the set Act contains a letter τ that represents internal or synchronized actions, and that other letters in $Lab = Act \setminus \{\tau\}$ model synchronization signals. Moreover, to each synchronization signal a in Lab, we can match an unique co-action $\bar{a} \in Lab$, such that $\bar{\bar{a}} = a$.

We introduce the set $Conf_M = (P\Gamma^*)^*$ of configurations of a SDPN M. A configuration $p_1 w_1 \ldots p_n w_n$ represents a network of n processes where the i-th process is in control point p_i and has stack content w_i.

The Strict Semantics. We will model synchronization between threads as a form of *communication by rendez-vous*: two pushdown processes can synchronize if one performs a transition labelled with a and the other, a transition labelled with $\bar{a}$. Intuitively, one thread sends a signal over a channel and the other thread waits for a signal to be received along the same channel.

To this end, we define a strict transition relation $--\!\!\rightarrow_M$ on configurations of M according to the following *strict semantics*:

(1) given a symbol $a \in Act$, two rules $p\gamma \xrightarrow{a} w_1$ and $p'\gamma' \xrightarrow{\bar{a}} w_1'$ in Δ, and two configurations $u = u_1 p\gamma u_2 p'\gamma' u_3$ and $v = u_1 w_1 u_2 w_1' u_3$ of M, we have $u --\!\!\rightarrow_M v$; two synchronized processes perform a simultaneous action;
(2) given a rule $p\gamma \xrightarrow{\tau} w_1$ in Δ and two configurations $u = u_1 p\gamma u_2$ and $v = u_1 w_1 u_2$ of M, we have $u --\!\!\rightarrow_M v$; a process performs an internal action.

We say that v is reachable from u w.r.t. the strict semantics if $u --\!\!\rightarrow_M^* v$, where $--\!\!\rightarrow_M^*$ stands for the transitive closure of $--\!\!\rightarrow_M$.

The strict semantics accurately models communication by rendez-vous. However, for technical matters, we also need to consider a relaxed semantics for SDPNs.

The Relaxed Semantics. The *relaxed semantics* on SDPNs allow partially synchronized executions on a SDPN: a process can perform a transition labelled with $a \in Lab$ even if it doesn't synchronize with a matching process executing a transition labelled with $\bar{a}$.

We therefore introduce a relaxed transition relation $\rightarrow_M$ labelled in Act on configurations of M:

(1) & (2) given two configurations u and v of M, $u --\!\!\rightarrow_M v$ if and only if $u \xrightarrow{\tau}_M v$; $\rightarrow_M$ features rules **(1)** and **(2)** of $--\!\!\rightarrow_M$;
(3) given a rule $p\gamma \xrightarrow{a} w_1$ in Δ, a word $w_1 \in (P\Gamma^*) \cup (P\Gamma^*)^2$, and two configurations $u = u_1 p\gamma u_2$ and $v = u_1 w_1 u_2$ of M, we have $u \xrightarrow{a}_M v$; a process performs an action but does not synchronize.

The restriction of the relaxed semantics to rules **(2)** and **(3)** yields the DPN semantics, as defined by Bouajjani et al. in [4].

For a given word $\sigma = a_1 \ldots a_n \in Act^*$ and two configurations c, c' of M, we write that $c \xrightarrow{\sigma}_M^* c'$ if there are n configurations $c_1, \ldots, c_n$ of M such that $c \xrightarrow{a_1}_M c_1 \xrightarrow{a_2}_M c_2 \ldots c_n \xrightarrow{a_n}_M c_n$ and $c_n = c'$. We then say that c' is reachable from c w.r.t. the relaxed semantics. For a given set of configurations C, we introduce $pre^*(M, C) = \{c' \mid \exists c \in C, \exists w \in \Gamma^*, c' \xrightarrow{w}_M^* c\}$.

For two subsets C and C' of $Conf_M$, we define the set $Paths_M(C, C') = \{\sigma \in Act^* \mid \exists c \in C, \exists c' \in C', c \xrightarrow{\sigma}_M^* c'\}$ of all execution paths from C to C', including paths with non-synchronized actions labelled in Lab.

2.2   From a Program to a SDPN Model

We can assume that the program is given by a *control flow graph*, whose nodes represent control points of threads or procedures and whose edges are labelled by statements. These statements can be variable assignments, procedure calls or returns, spawns of new threads, or communications between threads through unidirectional point-to point channels, where a thread sends a value x through a channel c and another thread waits for this value then assigns it to a variable y.

Without loss of generality, we assume that threads share no global variables and instead can only synchronize through channels. We distinguish local variables that belong to a single procedure from thread-local variables that can be accessed by any procedure called by a given instance of a thread. We also consider that both local and global variables may only take a finite number of values.

Given a control flow graph, we define a corresponding SDPN. The set of states P is the set of possible valuations of thread-local variables. The stack alphabet Γ is the set of all pairs (n, l) where n is a node of the flow graph and l is a valuation of the local variables of the current procedure.

Channels can be used to send and receive values. For each channel c and value x that can be sent through c, a label $(c!, x)$ and its co-action $(c?, x) = \overline{(c!, x)}$ belong to Act. The internal action τ belongs to Act as well.

For each statement s labelling an edge of the flow graph between nodes n_1 and n_2, we introduce the following transition rules in the corresponding SDPN, where g_1 and g_2 (resp. l_1 and l_2) are the valuations of thread-local (resp. procedure-local) variables before and after the execution of the statement:

- if s is an assignment, it is represented by rules of the form $g_1(n_1, l_1) \xrightarrow{\tau} g_2(n_2, l_2)$; assigning new values to variables in g_1 and l_1 results in new valuations g_2 and l_2;
- if s is a procedure call, rules of the form $g_1(n_1, l_1) \xrightarrow{\tau} g_2(f_0, l_0)(n_2, l_2)$ represent s, where f_0 is the starting node of the called procedure and l_0 the initial valuation of its local variables;
- if s is a procedure return, it is represented by rules of the form $g_1(n_1, l_1) \xrightarrow{\tau} g_2\varepsilon$; we simulate returns of values by introducing an additional thread-local variable and assigning the return value to it in the valuation g_2;
- if s is a thread spawn, rules of the form $g_1(n_1, l_1) \xrightarrow{\tau} g_0(n_0, l_0)g_2(n_2, l_2)$ represent s, where g_0 and l_0 are respectively the initial valuations of the thread-local and procedure-local variables of the new thread, and n_0 its starting node;
- if s is an assignment of a value x carried through a channel c to a variable y, it is represented by rules of the form $g_1(n_1, l_1) \xrightarrow{(c?, x)} g_2(n_2, l_2)$ where g_1 and g_2 (resp. l_1 and l_2) are such that assigning the value x to the variable y in g_1 (resp. l_1) results in the new valuations g_2 (resp. l_2);
- if s is an output through a channel c of the value x of a variable y, it is represented by rules of the form $g_1(n_1, l_1) \xrightarrow{(c!, x)} g_2(n_2, l_2)$ such that the variable y has value x in either g_1 or l_1.

Finally, we consider the starting configuration $g_{init}(n_{init}, l_{init})$ where g_{init} and l_{init} are respectively the initial valuations of the thread-local and procedure-local variables of the main thread, and n_{init} its starting node.

3   The Reachability Problem

As described previously in Sect. 2.2, we can model the behaviour of a real multi-threaded program with a SDPN. Many static analysis techniques rely on being able to determine whether a given critical state is reachable or not from the starting configuration of a program.

Since checking reachability in a real program amounts to checking reachability in its corresponding SDPN w.r.t to the strict semantics, we want to solve the following *reachability problem*: given a SDPN M and two sets of configuration C and C', is there a configuration in C' that is reachable from C w.r.t. the *strict* semantics?

It has unfortunately been proven by Ramalingam in [10] that, even if C and C' are regular, this problem is undecidable for synchronization-sensitive pushdown systems, hence, SDPNs. Therefore, we reduce this problem to an execution path analysis of SDPNs with *relaxed* semantics.

3.1   From the Strict to the Relaxed Semantics

It is easy to see that the following Theorem holds:

Theorem 1. *Let M be a SDPN and c, c' two configurations of M; $c \dashrightarrow_M^* c'$ if and only if $\exists n \geq 0$ such that $c \xrightarrow{\tau^n}_M^* c'$.*

Intuitively, an execution path w.r.t. the relaxed semantics of the form τ^n only uses internal actions or synchronized actions between two threads: a synchronization signal a is always paired with its co-action $\bar{a}$. Any configuration reachable using this path can be reached w.r.t. the strict semantics as well. Such a path is said to be *perfectly synchronized*.

Therefore, the reachability problem amounts to determining whether:

$$Paths_M(C, C') \cap \tau^* = \emptyset$$

that is, if there is an execution path from C to C' w.r.t. the relaxed semantics of the form τ^n. Obviously, we can't always compute $Paths_M(C, C')$. Our idea is therefore to compute an abstraction (over-approximation) of $Paths_M(C, C')$ and check the emptiness of its intersection with τ^*: if it is indeed empty, then C' can't be reached from C w.r.t. the strict semantics.

It is worth noting that a configuration $p_1' w_1' p_2' w_2'$ reachable from $p_1 w_1 p_2 w_2$ w.r.t. the strict semantics by synchronizing two rules $p_1 w_1 \xrightarrow{a} p_1' w_1'$ and $p_2 w_2 \xrightarrow{\bar{a}} p_2' w_2'$ using the synchronization rule (1) can obviously be reached w.r.t. the relaxed semantics by applying these two rules sequentially, using rule (3) twice, although the resulting path would obviously not be perfectly synchronized. Hence, the following Theorem holds:

Theorem 2. *Let M be a SDPN and c, c' two configurations of M; c' is reachable from c w. r. t. the relaxed SDPN semantics if and only if it is reachable w. r. t. the DPN semantics.*

It implies that, since we can compute $pre^*(M,C)$ w.r.t. the DPN semantics, we can compute it w.r.t. the relaxed SDPN semantics as well.

3.2   Representing Infinite Sets of Configurations

In order to compute an abstraction of $Paths_M(C,C')$ we need to be able to finitely represent infinite sets of configurations of a SDPN M. To do so, we introduce a class of finite automata called M-automata, as defined in [4]:

Definition 2 (M-automata). *Given a SDPN $M = (Act, P, \Gamma, \Delta)$, an M-automaton is a finite automaton $A = (\Sigma, S, \delta, s_{init}, F)$ such that:*

- *$\Sigma = P \cup \Gamma$ is the input alphabet;*
- *the set of states $S = S_C \cup S_S$ can be partitioned in two disjoint sets S_C and S_S;*
- *$\delta \subseteq S \times \Sigma \times S$ is the set of transitions;*
- *$\forall s \in S_C$ and $\forall p \in P$, there is at most a single state s_p such that $(s, p, s_p) \in \delta$; moreover, $s_p \in S_S$ and s is the only predecessor of s_p; transitions from states in S_C are always labelled with state symbols in P and go to dedicated states in S_S;*
- *states in S_C do not have exiting transitions labelled with letters in Γ;*
- *states in S_S do not have exiting transitions labelled in P; transitions labelled with letters in Γ always go to states in S_S;*
- *transitions from S_S to S_C are always labelled with ε; these are the only allowed ε-transitions in the M-automaton;*
- *$s_{init} \in S_C$ is the initial state;*
- *$F \subseteq S_C$ is the set of final states.*

An M-automaton is designed in such a manner that every path accepting a configuration $p_1 w_1 \ldots p_n w_n$ is a sequence of sub-paths $s_i \xrightarrow{p_i}_\delta s_p \xrightarrow{w_i}{}^*_\delta q \xrightarrow{\varepsilon}_\delta s_{i+1}$ where $s_i \in S_C$, $s_{i+1} \in S_C$ and every state in the path $s_p \xrightarrow{w_i}{}^*_\delta q$ is in S_S. Being a finite state automaton, an M-automaton accepts a regular language that is a subset of $Conf_M$. Any regular language in $(P\Gamma^*)^*$ can be accepted by an M-automaton.

M-automata were introduced so that one could compute the set of predecessors of a DPN, hence, of a SDPN as well, by applying a saturation procedure to an M-automaton accepting the set of starting configurations, as shown by Bouajjani et al. in [4].

4   An Abstraction Framework for Paths

Since we can't compute the exact set $Paths_M(C,C')$, we will over-approximate it. To do so, we will use the following mathematical framework, basing our technique on the approach presented by Bouajjani et al. in [2].

4.1   Abstractions and Galois Connections

Let $\mathcal{L} = (2^{Act^*}, \subseteq, \cup, \cap, \emptyset, Act^*)$ be the complete lattice of languages on Act.

Our abstraction of $\mathcal{L}$ requires a lattice $E = (D, \leq, \sqcup, \sqcap, \bot, \top)$, from now on called the *abstract lattice*, where D is a set called the abstract domain, as well as a pair of mappings (α, β) called a *Galois connection*, where $\alpha : 2^{Act^*} \to D$ and $\beta : D \to 2^{Act^*}$ are such that $\forall x \in 2^{Act^*}, \forall y \in D, \alpha(x) \leq y \Leftrightarrow x \subseteq \beta(y)$.

$\forall L \in \mathcal{L}$, given a Galois connection (α, β), we have $L \subseteq \beta(\alpha(L))$. Hence, the Galois connection can be used to overapproximate a language, such as the set of execution paths of a SDPN.

Moreover, it is easy to see that $\forall L_1, \forall L_2 \in \mathcal{L}, \alpha(L_1) \sqcap \alpha(L_2) = \bot$ if and only if $\beta(\alpha(L)) \cap \beta(\alpha(L)) = \emptyset$. We therefore only need to check if $\alpha(Paths_M(C, C')) \sqcap \alpha(\tau^*) = \bot$. From then on, $\alpha(Paths_M(C, C'))$ will be called the *abstraction* of $Paths_M(C, C')$, although technically $\beta(\alpha(Paths_M(C, C')))$ is the actual overapproximation.

4.2   Kleene Algebras

We want to define abstractions of $\mathcal{L}$ such that we can compute the abstract path language $\alpha(Paths_M(C', C))$, assuming the sets C' and C are regular. In order to do so, we consider a special class of abstractions, called *Kleene abstractions*.

An idempotent semiring is a structure $K = (A, \oplus, \odot, \bar{0}, \bar{1})$, where $\oplus$ is an associative, commutative, and idempotent ($a \oplus a = a$) operation, and $\odot$ is an associative operation. $\bar{0}$ and $\bar{1}$ are neutral elements for $\oplus$ and $\odot$ respectively, $\bar{0}$ is an annihilator for $\odot$ ($a \odot \bar{0} = \bar{0} \odot a = \bar{0}$) and $\odot$ distributes over $\oplus$.

K is an *Act-semiring* if it can be generated by $\bar{0}, \bar{1}$, and elements of the form $v_a \in A, \forall a \in Act$. A semiring is said to be closed if $\oplus$ can be extended to an operator over countably infinite sets while keeping the same properties as $\oplus$.

We define $a^0 = \bar{1}$, $a^{n+1} = a \odot a^n$ and $a^* = \bigoplus_{n \geq 0} a^n$. Adding the $*$ operation to an idempotent closed *Act*-semiring K transforms it into a *Kleene algebra*.

4.3   Kleene Abstractions

An abstract lattice $E = (D, \leq, \sqcup, \sqcap, \bot, \top)$ is said to be compatible with a Kleene algebra $K = (A, \oplus, \odot, \bar{0}, \bar{1})$ if $D = A$, $x \leq y \Leftrightarrow x \oplus y = y$, $\bot = \bar{0}$ and $\sqcup = \oplus$.

A *Kleene abstraction* is an abstraction such that the abstract lattice E is compatible with the Kleene algebra and the Galois connection $\alpha : 2^{Act^*} \to D$ and $\beta : D \to 2^{Act^*}$ is defined by:

$$\alpha(L) = \bigoplus_{a_1 \ldots a_n \in L} v_{a_1} \odot \ldots \odot v_{a_n}$$

$$\beta(x) = \left\{ a_1 \ldots a_n \in 2^{Act^*} \mid v_{a_1} \odot \ldots \odot v_{a_n} \leq x \right\}$$

Intuitively, a Kleene abstraction is such that the abstract operations $\oplus$, $\odot$, and $*$ can be matched to the union, the concatenation, and the Kleene closure of the languages of the lattice $\mathcal{L}$, $\overline{0}$ and $\overline{1}$ to the empty language and $\{\varepsilon\}$, v_a to the language $\{a\}$, the upper bound $\top \in K$ to Act^*, and the operation $\sqcap$ to the intersection of languages in the lattice $\mathcal{L}$.

In order to compute $\alpha(L)$ for a given language L, each word $a_1 \ldots a_n$ in L is matched to its abstraction $v_{a_1} \odot \ldots \odot v_{a_n}$, and we consider the sum of these abstractions.

We can check if $\alpha(Paths_M(C, C')) \sqcap \bigoplus_{n \geq 0} v_\tau^n = \bot$; if it is indeed the case, then $\beta(\alpha(Paths_M(C, C'))) \cap \tau^* = \emptyset$, and since $\beta(\alpha(Paths_M(C, C')))$ is an over-approximation $Paths_M(C, C')$, it follows that $Paths_M(C, C') \cap \tau^* = \emptyset$.

A *finite-chain* abstraction is an abstraction such that the lattice $(K, \oplus)$ has no infinite ascending chains. In this paper, we rely on a particular class of finite-chain abstractions, called *finite-domain* abstractions, whose abstract domain K is finite, such as the following examples:

Prefix Abstractions. Let n be an integer and $W(n) = \{w \in Act^* \mid |w| \leq n\}$ be the set of words of length smaller than n. We define the n-th order *prefix* abstraction α_n^{pref} as follows: the abstract lattice $A = 2^W$ is generated by the elements $v_a = \{a\}$, $a \in Act$; $\oplus = \cup$; $U \odot V = \{\text{pref}_n(uv) \mid u \in U, v \in V\}$ where $\text{pref}_n(w)$ stands for the prefix of w of length n (or lower if w is of length smaller than n); $\overline{0} = \emptyset$; and $\overline{1} = \{\varepsilon\}$. From there, we build an abstract lattice where $\top = W$, $\sqcap = \cap$, and $\leq = \subseteq$. This abstraction is accurate for the n-th first steps of a run, then approximates the other steps by Act^*.

We can apply a prefix abstraction of order 2 to the example shown in Fig. 1. For ease of representation, we show a control flow graph, although we could use the procedure outlined in Sect. 2.2 to compute an equivalent SDPN. We also consider without loss of generality that spawns, calls, and returns are silent ε-transitions.

We check that, starting from an initial set of configurations C with a single thread M in state m_0, the set C' where M is in state m_2 can't be reached w.r.t. the strict semantics. We have $\alpha_2^{pref}(Paths_M(C, C')) = \{b, b\tau, ba, b\overline{a}\}$, $\alpha_2^{pref}(\tau^*) = \{\varepsilon, \tau, \tau\tau\}$, and $\alpha_2^{pref}(Paths_M(C, C')) \cap \alpha_2^{pref}(\tau^*) = \emptyset$, hence, C' can't be reached from C w.r.t. the strict semantics. Intuitively, the transition labelled with b in thread M can't synchronize as there isn't any transition labelled with $\overline{b}$ in the whole program.

Suffix Abstractions. Let W be the set of words of length smaller than n. We define the n-th order *suffix* abstraction α_n^{suff} as follows: the abstract lattice $A = 2^W$ is generated by the elements $v_a = \{a\}$, $a \in Act$; $\oplus = \cup$; $U \odot V = \{\text{suff}_n(uv) \mid u \in U, v \in V\}$ where $\text{suff}_n(w)$ stands for the suffix of w of length n (or lower if w is of length smaller than n); $\overline{0} = \emptyset$; and $\overline{1} = \{\varepsilon\}$. From there, we build an abstract lattice where $\top = W$, $\sqcap = \cap$, and $\leq = \subseteq$. This abstraction is accurate for the n-th last steps of a run, then approximates the other steps by Act^*.

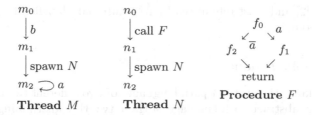

Fig. 1. Applying a second order prefix abstraction to an example

We apply a suffix abstraction of order 2 to the example shown in Fig. 2. We check that, starting from an initial set of configurations C with a single thread M in state m_0, the set C' where M is in state m_2 can't be reached w.r.t. the strict semantics. We have $\alpha_2^{suff}(Paths_M(C, C')) = \{b, ab, \bar{a}b, \tau b\}$, $\alpha_2^{suff}(\tau^*) = \{\varepsilon, \tau, \tau\tau\}$, and $\alpha_2^{suff}(Paths_M(C, C')) \cap \alpha_2^{suff}(\tau^*) = \emptyset$, hence, C' can't be reached from C w.r.t. the strict semantics. Intuitively, the transition labelled with b in thread M can't synchronize as there isn't any transition labelled with $\bar{b}$ in the whole program.

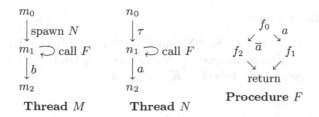

Fig. 2. Applying a second order suffix abstraction to an example

It is worth noting that the reachability problem in Fig. 2 can't be solved by a prefix abstraction, no matter its order. The reason is that $\forall n \geq 0$, there is an execution path $\tau^n b \in Paths_M(C, C')$, hence, $\tau^n \in \alpha_n^{pref}(Paths_M(C, C'))$. Intuitively, the two self-pointing loops of nodes m_1 and n_1 can synchronize.

Conversely, we can't use a suffix abstraction to solve the reachability problem in Fig. 1. The reason is that $\forall n \geq 0$, there is an execution path $b\tau^n \in Paths_M(C, C')$, hence, $\tau^n \in \alpha_n^{suff}(Paths_M(C, C'))$. Intuitively, the self-pointing loop of node m_2 can synchronize with the self-spawning loop in thread N.

Thus, these two abstractions (prefix and suffix) complement each other.

5 Representing Abstract Path Languages

We define structures to represent $\alpha(Paths_M(C, C'))$ and reduce their construction to a predecessor problem. To do so, we can't use the K multi-automata introduced in [2] and must rely instead on M-automata labelled by functions in the abstract domain.

5.1   The Shuffle Product

Assuming we know the abstract path languages of two different threads, we want to compute the abstract path language of these two threads running in parallel. Intuitively, this new language will be an interleaving of the two aforementioned sets, but can feature synchronized actions between the two threads as well.

To this end, we inductively define a shuffle operation $\sqcup\!\sqcup$ on abstract path expressions:

- $w \sqcup\!\sqcup \bar{1} = \bar{1} \sqcup\!\sqcup w = w$;
- if $b \neq \bar{a}$, then $(v_a \odot w_1) \sqcup\!\sqcup (v_b \odot w_2) = v_a \odot (w_1 \sqcup\!\sqcup (v_b \odot w_2)) \oplus v_b \odot ((v_a \odot w_1) \sqcup\!\sqcup w_2)$;
- $(v_a \odot w_1) \sqcup\!\sqcup (v_{\bar{a}} \odot w_2) = v_a \odot (w_1 \sqcup\!\sqcup (v_{\bar{a}} \odot w_2)) \oplus v_{\bar{a}} \odot ((v_a \odot w_1) \sqcup\!\sqcup w_2) \oplus v_\tau \odot (w_1 \sqcup\!\sqcup w_2)$; two synchronized actions a and $\bar{a}$ result in an internal action τ, hence, there is a component $v_\tau \odot (w_1 \sqcup\!\sqcup w_2)$ of the shuffle product where the two paths synchronize.

We can extend the operation $\sqcup\!\sqcup$ to sets of path expressions.

5.2 K-configurations

Let $M = (Act, P, \Gamma, \Delta)$ be a SDPN and $K = (A, \oplus, \odot, \bar{0}, \bar{1})$ a Kleene algebra corresponding to a Kleene abstraction. We define inductively the set Π_K of path expressions as the smallest subset of K such that:

- $\bar{1} \in \Pi_K$;
- if $\pi \in \Pi_K$, then $\forall a \in Act$, $v_a \odot \pi \in \Pi_K$.

For a given path expression π, we define its length $|\pi|$ as the number of occurrences of simple elements of the form v_a in π.

A K-configuration of M is a pair $(c, \pi) \in Conf_M \times \Pi_K$. We can extend the transition relation $\longrightarrow_M$ to K-configurations with the following semantics: $\forall a \in Act$, if $c \xrightarrow{a}_M c'$, then $\forall \pi \in \Pi_K$, $(c, v_a \odot \pi) \longrightarrow_{M,K} (c', \pi)$; $(c, v_a \odot \pi)$ is said to be an immediate K-predecessor of (c', π). The reachability relation $\leadsto_{M,K}$ is the reflexive transitive closure of $\longrightarrow_{M,K}$.

For a given set of configurations C, we introduce the set $pre_K^*(M, C)$ of K-configurations (c, π) such that $(c, \pi) \leadsto_{M,K} (c', \bar{1})$ for $c' \in C$:

$$pre_K^*(M, C) = \{(c', \pi) \mid c' \in pre^*(M, C), \pi \leq \alpha(Paths_M(\{c'\}, C))\}$$

As we will see later, the abstract path expression π is meant to be the abstraction of an actual execution path from c to c'.

5.3 (K, M)-Automata

We represent potentially infinite sets of K-configurations of a SDPN M with a class of labelled M-automata, called (K, M)-automata.

Definition 3. *Let $M = (Act, P, \Gamma, \Delta)$ be a SDPN, a (K, M)-automaton is a finite automaton $A = (\Sigma, S, \delta, s_{init}, F)$ where $\Sigma = P \cup \Gamma$ is the input alphabet, $S = S_C \cup S_S$ is a finite set of control states with $S_C \cap S_S = \emptyset$, $\delta \subseteq (S_C \times P \times S_S) \cup (S_S \times \Gamma \times K^K \times S_S) \cup (S_S \times \{\varepsilon\} \times S_C)$ a finite set of transition rules (where K^K is the set of functions from K to K), s_{init} an initial state, and F a set of final states.*

Moreover, A is such that, if we consider the projection δ_Σ of δ on $S \times \Sigma^* \times S$, ignoring labels in K^K, then $(\Sigma, S, \delta_\Sigma, s_i, F)$ is an M-automaton.

Intuitively, a (K, M)-automaton can be seen as an M-automaton whose transitions labelled by stack symbols in Γ have been given an additional label in K^K. We can consider a simple M-automaton as a (K, M)-automaton if we label each transition in $S_S \times \Gamma \times S_S$ with the identity function.

Before defining a proper transition relation of (K, M)-automata, we first explain the intuition behind the use of functions in K^K as labels.

The Need for Functions. The use of functions in K^K instead of simple abstract values in K as done in [2] is a novelty of this paper. Our intuition is that functions of the form $x \in K \longrightarrow f(x)$ where $f(x)$ is a monomial expression in $K[x]$ can be used to represent and compose sets of abstract paths. The variable x stands for parts of an execution path that can later be expanded by further transitions.

As an example, the set of abstract execution paths represented by the tree T_1 in Fig. 3 can be modelled by the function $f_1 : x \longrightarrow v_a \odot v_\tau \odot x \oplus v_{\overline{a}}$. If, from the node t_3 of the tree, it is possible to expand the abstract paths by either v_a or v_τ, as shown in Fig. 5, then a function representing this set of abstract paths can be computed by composing f_1 with the function $f_2 : x \longrightarrow v_a \odot x \oplus v_\tau \odot x$ representing the tree T_2 shown in Fig. 4.

Indeed, $f_1 \circ f_2(x) = v_a \odot v_\tau \odot v_a \odot x \oplus v_a \odot v_\tau \odot v_\tau \odot x \oplus v_{\overline{a}}$. When we no longer want to expand a set of execution paths, we can get rid of the variable x by considering the element of the abstract domain $f(\overline{1}) \in K$.

Had we instead represented T_1 and T_2 by two abstract values $v_a \odot v_\tau \oplus v_{\overline{a}}$ and $v_a \oplus v_\tau$ in K, as done in [2], the concatenation of these two values would have yielded $v_a \odot v_\tau \odot v_a \oplus v_a \odot v_\tau \odot v_\tau \oplus v_{\overline{a}} \odot v_\tau \oplus v_{\overline{a}} \odot v_a$. But $v_{\overline{a}} \odot v_\tau$ and $v_{\overline{a}} \odot v_a$ obviously should not belong to the abstraction of execution paths, hence, unlike [2], we need functions in K^K that can be composed and shuffled instead of simple abstract values in K.

The Transition Relation. Let A be a (K, M)-automaton. We define a simple transition relation $\longrightarrow_A$ according to the following semantics:

- if $(s, p, s') \in \delta \cap (S \times (P \cup \{\varepsilon\}) \times S)$, then $s \xrightarrow{p}_A s'$;

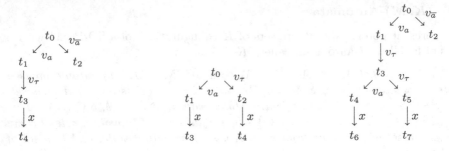

Fig. 3. Execution tree T_1 represented by f_1 **Fig. 4.** Execution tree T_2 represented by f_2 **Fig. 5.** Execution tree T_3 represented by $f_1 \circ f_2$

- if $(s, \gamma, e, s') \in \delta \cap (S_S \times \Gamma \times K^K \times S_S)$, then $s \xrightarrow{(\gamma,e)}_A s'$;
- if $s \xrightarrow{(w_1,e_1)}_A s_1$ and $s_1 \xrightarrow{(w_2,e_2)}_A s'$, then $s \xrightarrow{(w_1 w_2, e_1 \circ e_2)}_A s'$, where $\circ$ is the composition operation on functions.

We then extend this transition relation to a full path relation $\Longrightarrow_A \subseteq S \times \Sigma^* \times K^K \times S$:

- for each $s \in S_S$, $s \xrightarrow{(\varepsilon,Id)}_A s$, where Id stands for the identity function;
- if there is a sequence $s_0 \xrightarrow{(\gamma_1,e_1)}_A s_1 \dots s_{n-1} \xrightarrow{(\gamma_n,e_n)}_A s_n$ with $s_0, \dots, s_n \in S_S$, then $s_0 \xRightarrow{(w,e)}_A s_n$, where $w = \gamma_1 \dots \gamma_n$ and $e = e_1 \circ \dots \circ e_n$; this is a simple sequence of actions along a single thread;
- if there is a sequence $s \xrightarrow{p_1}_A s_{p_1} \xRightarrow{(w_1,e_1)}_A s'' \xrightarrow{\varepsilon}_A s' \xrightarrow{p_2}_A s'_{p_2} \xRightarrow{(w_2,e_2)}_A q$ such that $s, s'', q \in S_S$ and $s' \in S_C$, then $s_0 \xRightarrow{(w,e)}_A q$, where $w = p_1 w_1 p_2 w_2$ and $e : y \longrightarrow e_1(\bar{1}) \sqcup e_2(y)$; the automaton represents two parallel processes $p_1 w_1$ and $p_2 w_2$ whose abstract execution paths must be shuffled; moreover, since the first process will no longer be extended by further transitions of the automaton, we get rid of the variable x by considering $e_1(\bar{1})$ instead.

A path $s_0 \xRightarrow{(c,e)}_A s_n$ is said to be an execution of A if $s_0 = s_{init}$. It is then said to be accepting if $s_n \in F$. We then say that A accepts (c, π) for all $\pi \in \Pi_K$ such that $\pi \leq e(\bar{1})$. This way, accepting execution paths in (K, M)-automata can be used to represent whole sets of path expressions. We define the set $L_K(A)$ of all K-configurations of M accepted by A.

6   Computing the Abstraction

Let C and C' be two regular sets of configurations of a SDPN $M = (Act, P, \Gamma, \Delta)$. We want to check if $Paths_M(C, C') \cap \tau^* = \emptyset$. To that end, we compute an abstraction $\alpha(Paths_M(C, C'))$, where α is a *finite-domain* abstraction. To this aim, we will proceed as follows.

We first compute a (K, M)-automaton $A_{pre_K^*}$ accepting $pre_K^*(C')$. Our intuition is that, if $(c', \pi) \rightsquigarrow_{M,K} (c, \overline{1})$, then there is an execution path from c' to c w.r.t. the relaxed semantics whose abstraction is π. We can then restrict $A_{pre_K^*}$ to only accept K-configurations that are also in $C \times \Pi_K$ by computing the product automaton A' between $A_{pre_K^*}$ and an M-automaton accepting C.

We can then consider the following abstraction:

$$\alpha(Paths_M(C, C')) = \bigoplus \{\pi \mid (c, \pi) \in L_K(A')\}$$

Without loss of generality, we suppose that $\Delta \subseteq (P \times \Gamma \times Act \times P\Gamma P\Gamma) \cup (P \times \Gamma \times Act \times P\Gamma^{\leq 2})$: each transition rule of M can spawn at most one new process and push at most two stack symbols.

6.1   Computing $pre^*(M, C)$

Given a SDPN M and a regular set C of configurations of M accepted by an M-automaton A, we want to compute an M-automaton A_{pre^*} accepting $pre^*(M, C)$. Thanks to Theorem 2, we can apply the saturation procedure defined in [4] to A. Let us remind this procedure. Initially, $A_{pre^*} = A$, then we apply the following rules until saturation to A_{pre^*}:

(R_1) if $p\gamma \xrightarrow{a} p'w \in \Delta$ and $s \xrightarrow{p'w}{}^*_{A_{pre^*}} s'$ for $s \in S_S$, $s' \in S$, then add $s_p \xrightarrow{\gamma}{}^*_{A_{pre^*}} s'$;

(R_2) if $p\gamma \xrightarrow{a} p_1\gamma_1 p_2\gamma_2 \in \Delta$ and $s \xrightarrow{p_1\gamma_1 p_2\gamma_2}{}^*_{A_{pre^*}} s'$ for $s \in S_S$, $s' \in S$, then add $s_p \xrightarrow{\gamma}{}^*_{A_{pre^*}} s'$.

$\longrightarrow^*_{A_{pre^*}}$ stands for the transitive closure of the transition relation on the finite state automaton A_{pre^*}. The initial and final states remain the same.

Let us remind the intuition of these rules. We consider a subpath $s \xrightarrow{p'w}{}^*_{A_{pre^*}} s'$. By design of an M-automaton, s should be in S_C and there should be a path $s \xrightarrow{p'} s_{p'} \xrightarrow{w}{}^* s'$ in the automaton. If we apply the saturation rule (R_1), we add an edge $s_p \xrightarrow{p} s'$ to A_{pre^*} and create a subpath $s \xrightarrow{p\gamma}{}^* s'$ in the automaton. Therefore, if A_{pre^*} accepts a configuration $u_1 p'w'u_2$ with a path $s_{init} \xrightarrow{u_1}{}^* s_{p'} \xrightarrow{p'w}{}^* s' \xrightarrow{u_2}{}^* q_F$, $q_F \in F$, then it will accept its predecessor $u_1 p\gamma u_2$ as well with a path $s_{init} \xrightarrow{u_1}{}^* s_p \xrightarrow{p\gamma}{}^* s' \xrightarrow{u_2}{}^* q_F$. The role of ($R_2$) is similar.

Thus, when this saturation procedure ends, the M-automaton A_{pre^*} accepts the regular set $pre^*(M, C)$. Assuming the initial M-automaton A representing C is of constant size, the procedure terminates after a polynomial (in $|\Delta|$) number of steps.

6.2   From $pre^*(M,C)$ to $pre_K^*(M,C)$

Given a SDPN M and a regular set C of configurations of M accepted by an M-automaton A, we want to compute a (K,M)-automaton $A_{pre_K^*}$ accepting $pre_K^*(M,C)$. To this end, we will add new labels to the M-automaton A_{pre^*}. Our intuition is the following: $A_{pre_K^*}$ should be such that if we have $(c',\pi) \rightsquigarrow_{M,K} (c,\bar{1})$, $c \in C$, then c can be reached from c' by an execution path whose abstract representation in K is the path expression π.

In order to compute $A_{pre_K^*}$, we proceed as follows: we first accept configurations in C with the path expression $\bar{1}$, then, from there, set constraints on the labelling functions of transitions of A_{pre^*} depending on the relationship between edges introduced by the previous saturation procedure. This way, we build iteratively a set of constraints whose least fixpoint can abstract the set of execution paths from $pre^*(M,C)$ to C.

To this end, each transition t in A_{pre^*} labelled in Γ is given a second label $\lambda(t) \in K^K$. To do so, we compute a set of constraints whose smallest solution (according to the order $\leq$ of the Kleene algebra) will be the labels $\lambda(t)$. If $t = q_1 \xrightarrow{\gamma} q_2$, then we write $\lambda(t) = \lambda(q_1, \gamma, q_2)$.

The Constraints. Let x be the variable of functions in K^K. We now consider the following set of constraints on transitions of A_{pre^*} in $S_S \times \Gamma \times S_S$:

(Z_1) if t belongs both to A and A_{pre^*}, then for each $x \in K$:

$$x \leq \lambda(t)(x)$$

(Z_2) for each rule $p\gamma \xrightarrow{a} p'\gamma' \in \Delta$, for each $q \in Q$, for each $s \in S_c$:

$$v_a \odot \lambda(s_{p'}, \gamma', q) \leq \lambda(s_p, \gamma, q)$$

(Z_3) for each rule $p\gamma \xrightarrow{a} p'\varepsilon \in \Delta$, for each $s \in S_c$:

$$v_a \odot Id \leq \lambda(s_p, \gamma, s_{p'})$$

(Z_4) for each rule $p\gamma \xrightarrow{a} p'\gamma_1\gamma_2 \in \Delta$, for each $q \in Q$, for each $s \in S_c$:

$$\bigoplus_{q' \in Q} v_a \odot (\lambda(s_{p'}, \gamma_1, q') \circ \lambda(q', \gamma_2, q)) \leq \lambda(s_p, \gamma, q)$$

(Z_5) for each rule $p\gamma \xrightarrow{a} p_2\gamma_2 p_1\gamma_1 \in \Delta$, for each $q \in Q$, for each $s \in S_c$:

$$\bigoplus_{s'' \xrightarrow{\varepsilon}_{A_{pre^*}} s'} v_a \odot (\lambda(s_{p_2}, \gamma_2, s'')(\bar{1}) \sqcup \lambda(s'_{p_1}, \gamma_1, q)) \leq \lambda(s_p, \gamma, q)$$

We now explain intuitively the meaning of these constraints.

The Intuition. If c is a configuration of C, then $A_{pre_K^*}$ should accept $(c, \overline{1})$. This is expressed by constraint (Z_1).

Let $c' = p'\gamma'w \in pre^*(M, C)$. If $p\gamma \xrightarrow{a} p'\gamma' \in \Delta$ and $(c', \pi) \in pre_K^*(M, C)$, then $c = p\gamma w \in pre^*(M, C)$, $(c, v_a \odot \pi) \rightsquigarrow_{M,K} (c', \pi)$, and $(c, v_a \odot \pi) \in pre_K^*(M, C)$. Hence, if $A_{pre_K^*}$ accepts (c', π) and uses a transition $s_{p'} \xrightarrow{\gamma'} q$ while doing so, then it should accept $(c, v_a \odot \pi)$ as well using a transition $s_p \xrightarrow{\gamma} q$. This is expressed by constraint (Z_2).

Let $c' = p'w \in pre^*(M, C)$. If $p\gamma \xrightarrow{a} p'\varepsilon \in \Delta$ and $(c', \pi) \in pre_K^*(M, C)$, then $c = p\gamma w \in pre^*(M, C)$, $(c, v_a \odot \pi) \rightsquigarrow_{M,K} (c', \pi)$, and $(c, v_a \odot \pi) \in pre_K^*(M, C)$. Hence, if $A_{pre_K^*}$ accepts (c', π), then it should accept $(c, v_a \odot \pi)$ as well using a transition $s_p \xrightarrow{\gamma} s_p'$. This is expressed by constraint (Z_3).

Let $c' = p'\gamma_1\gamma_2 w \in pre^*(M, C)$. If $p\gamma \xrightarrow{a} p'\gamma_1\gamma_2 \in \Delta$ and also $(c', \pi) \in pre_K^*(M, C)$, then $c = p\gamma w \in pre^*(M, C)$, $(c, v_a \odot \pi) \rightsquigarrow_{M,K} (c', \pi)$, and $(c, v_a \odot \pi) \in pre_K^*(M, C)$. Hence, if $A_{pre_K^*}$ accepts (c', π) and uses two transition $s_{p'} \xrightarrow{\gamma_1} q'$ and $q' \xrightarrow{\gamma_2} q$ while doing so, then it should accept $(c, v_a \odot \pi)$ as well using a transition $s_p \xrightarrow{\gamma} q$. Moreover, there can be many possible intermediate states q' between s_p' and q such that $s_{p'} \xrightarrow{\gamma_1} q'$ and $q' \xrightarrow{\gamma_2} q$. In the automaton $A_{pre_K^*}$, the abstract path π should therefore be represented by the sum for all possible intermediate state q' of the concatenation of the two labelling functions $\lambda(s_{p'}, \gamma_1, q')$ and $\lambda(q', \gamma_2, q)$. This is expressed by constraint (Z_4).

Let $c' = p_2\gamma_2p_1\gamma_1 w \in pre^*(M, C)$. If $p\gamma \xrightarrow{a} p_2\gamma_2p_1\gamma_1 \in \Delta$ and $(c', \pi) \in pre_K^*(M, C)$, then $c = p\gamma w \in pre^*(M, C)$, $(c, v_a \odot \pi) \rightsquigarrow_{M,K} (c', \pi)$, and $(c, v_a \odot \pi) \in pre_K^*(M, C)$. The two processes $p_2\gamma_2$ and $p_1\gamma_1$ are interleaved, hence, their abstract execution paths must be shuffled: if π_1 is an execution path associated to $p_1\gamma_1$, and π_2, to $p_2\gamma_2$, then an abstract path $\pi' = \pi_2 \sqcup\!\sqcup \pi_1$ should be associated to $p_2\gamma_2p_1\gamma_1$. Moreover, if we consider a path $s_{p_2} \xrightarrow{\gamma_2} s'' \xrightarrow{\varepsilon} s' \xrightarrow{p_1} s_{p_1}' \xrightarrow{\gamma_1} q$ in the automaton $A_{pre_K^*}$, then no abstract path π_2 associated to $p_2\gamma_2$ can be extended further, and should therefore be represented by $(\lambda(s_{p_2}, \gamma_2, s')(\overline{1}))$. Again, we must also consider each possible intermediate state s'' in the previous path, hence, a sum of functions. This is expressed by constraint (Z_5).

Solving the Constraints. Since α is a finite-domain abstraction, the set K^K of functions in K is finite as well. Let $t_1, \ldots, t_m$ be an arbitrary numbering of the transitions of $A_{pre_K^*}$ labelled with functions in the abstract domain and let $k_1, \ldots, k_n$ be an enumeration of the elements of the finite domain K ($n = |K|$). The labelling constraints of Sect. 6.2 define a system of inequalities on $m*n$ variables $x_1, \ldots, x_{mn}$ such that its smallest solution is $t_1(k_1), \ldots, t_1(k_n)$, $t_2(k_1), \ldots, t_m(k_n)$. It is worth noting that we can replace two different inequalities $e_1(x) \leq t_i(x)$ and $e_2(x) \leq t_i(x)$ by a single inequality $e_1(x) \oplus e_2(x) \leq t_i(x)$. We therefore end up with a system of the form:

$$f_i(x_1, \ldots, x_{mn}) \leq x_i, \text{ for } i = 1, \ldots, mn$$

where the functions f_i are monomials in $K[x_1, \ldots, x_{mn}]$. Finding the least solution of this system of inequalities amounts to finding the least pre-fixpoint of the monotonic and continuous function:

$$F(x_1, \ldots, x_{mn}) = (f_1(x_1, \ldots, x_{mn}), \ldots, f_{mn}(x_1, \ldots, x_{mn}))$$

By Tarski's theorem, this fixpoint exists and is equal to $\bigoplus_{i \geq 0} F^i(\overline{0})$.

In a finite-domain, this iterative computation always terminates in a number of steps bounded by the length l of the longest ascending chain in K. There are mn functions f_i, each with a number of $\oplus$, $\odot$, and $\sqcup$ operations in $O(|\Delta||Q|)$. Moreover, we know that $m = O(|\Delta|^k)$ for an integer k. Each iteration step therefore features $O(|K||\Delta|^{k+1}|Q|)$ operations, and the whole procedure, $O(l|K||\Delta|^{k+1}|Q|)$ operations. For a prefix or suffix abstraction of order j, $|K| = |Act|^j$, hence, $O(l|Act|^j|\Delta|^{k+1}|Q|)$ operations

Once $A_{pre_K^*}$ is properly labelled, the following Theorem holds:

Theorem 3. *Let M be a SDPN and A an M-automaton accepting a regular set of configurations C. Then the (K, M)-automaton $A_{pre_K^*}$ accepts $pre_K^*(M, C)$.*

6.3   Finding the Abstraction

We can compute an automaton $A_{pre_K^*}$ that accepts the set $pre_K^*(M, C')$. We then want to find a (K, M)-automaton A' that accepts $pre_K^*(M, C') \cap C \times \Pi_K$.

To do so, we define the intersection $A' = (\Sigma, S', \delta', s'_{init}, F')$ of the automaton $A_{pre^*} = (\Sigma, S, \delta, s_{init}, F)$ with an M-automaton $A_1 = (\Sigma, S_1, \delta_1, s_{1,init}, F_1)$ accepting C, where $S' = S \times S_1$, $s'_{init} = (s_{init}, s_{1,init})$, $F = F \times F_1$, and $\delta = \{(q, q_1) \xrightarrow{a} (q', q'_1) \mid q \xrightarrow{a} q' \in \delta, q \xrightarrow{a} q' \in \delta_1\}$. Moreover, we label A' with abstract functions in such a manner that $\lambda((q, q_1), a, (q', q'_1)) = \lambda(q, a, q')$.

The (K, M)-automaton A' then obviously accepts $pre_K^*(M, C') \cap C \times \Pi_K$. Eventually, our abstraction is $\alpha(Paths_M(C, C')) = \bigoplus\{\pi \mid (c, \pi) \in L_K(A')\}$.

7   Using Our Framework in a CEGAR Scheme

Following the work of Chaki et al. in [5], we propose a semi-decision procedure that, in case of termination, answers exactly whether $Paths_M(C, C') \cap \tau^* = \emptyset$.

We first model a program as a SDPN M, as shown in Sect. 2.2, its starting configurations as a regular set C, and a set of critical configurations whose reachability we need to study as another regular set C'.

We then introduce the following Counter-Example Guided Abstraction Refinement (CEGAR) scheme based on the finite-domain abstraction framework detailed previously, starting from $n = 1$.

Abstraction: we compute abstractions $\alpha(Paths_M(C, C'))$ of the set of executions paths for $\alpha = \alpha_n^{pref}$ and $\alpha = \alpha_n^{suff}$;

Verification: for $\alpha = \alpha_n^{pref}$ and $\alpha = \alpha_n^{suff}$, we check if $\alpha(Paths_M(C, C')) \sqcap \alpha(\tau^*) = \perp$; if it is indeed true, then we conclude that C' can't be reached from C using only internal or synchronized actions;

Counter-Example Validation: if there is such a path, we then check if our abstraction introduced a spurious counter-example; this can be done in a finite number of steps by checking if this counter-example can be reached within the n-th first or last execution steps of the program, depending on which abstraction (prefix or suffix) provided us with a counter-example; if the counter-example is not spurious, then we conclude that C' is reachable from C w.r.t. the strict semantics;

Refinement: if the counter-example was spurious, we go back to the first step, but use this time finite-domain abstractions of order $n + 1$.

If this procedure ends, we can decide the reachability problem.

8 A Case Study

We use a CEGAR scheme to find an error in a Bluetooth driver for Windows NT. We consider here an abstracted version of a driver found in [9] that nonetheless keeps the erroneous trace, in a manner similar to [5,7]. We then fix the driver by changing one of its routines, then use the CEGAR scheme to prove that this new version of the driver is correct.

We model the network of processes in the driver as a SDPN. New requests for the driver are represented by thread spawns, and the driver's counter of active requests, by a counter on the stack, hence, a recursive process, making full use of our model's features.

We were able to discover the bug by applying our finite-domain abstraction in a CEGAR scheme: we start from abstractions of order 1 and increment the order until we deduce that the erroneous configuration is reachable using a prefix abstraction of size 12. We then correct one of the program's subroutines accordingly and apply our CEGAR scheme to prove it's now error-free.

Note that this bug was also discovered in [5,7,9]. However, our approach is more complete and precise than these works: [9] can only discover errors, whereas our scheme can also prove that the modified version of the driver is correct; [5] does not handle dynamic thread creation, and thus had to guess the number of threads for which the error arises; and [7] models thread creation as parallel calls (not as spawns), where the father process waits for its children to terminate in order to resume its execution.

References

1. Bouajjani, A., Esparza, J., Schwoon, S., Strejček, J.: Reachability analysis of multithreaded software with asynchronous communication. In: Sarukkai, S., Sen, S. (eds.) FSTTCS 2005. LNCS, vol. 3821, pp. 348–359. Springer, Heidelberg (2005). https://doi.org/10.1007/11590156_28
2. Bouajjani, A., Esparza, J., Touili, T.: A generic approach to the static analysis of concurrent programs with procedures. In: POPL 2003 (2003)
3. Bouajjani, A., Esparza, J., Touili, T.: Reachability analysis of synchronized pa systems. Electron. Notes Theor. Comput. Sci. **138**(3), 153–178 (2005)
4. Bouajjani, A., Müller-Olm, M., Touili, T.: Regular symbolic analysis of dynamic networks of pushdown systems. In: Abadi, M., de Alfaro, L. (eds.) CONCUR 2005. LNCS, vol. 3653, pp. 473–487. Springer, Heidelberg (2005). https://doi.org/10.1007/11539452_36
5. Chaki, S., Clarke, E., Kidd, N., Reps, T., Touili, T.: Verifying concurrent message-passing C programs with recursive calls. In: Hermanns, H., Palsberg, J. (eds.) TACAS 2006. LNCS, vol. 3920, pp. 334–349. Springer, Heidelberg (2006). https://doi.org/10.1007/11691372_22
6. Esparza, J., Hansel, D., Rossmanith, P., Schwoon, S.: Efficient algorithms for model checking pushdown systems. In: Emerson, E.A., Sistla, A.P. (eds.) CAV 2000. LNCS, vol. 1855, pp. 232–247. Springer, Heidelberg (2000). https://doi.org/10.1007/10722167_20
7. Patin, G., Sighireanu, M., Touili, T.: SPADE: verification of multithreaded dynamic and recursive programs. In: Damm, W., Hermanns, H. (eds.) CAV 2007. LNCS, vol. 4590, pp. 254–257. Springer, Heidelberg (2007). https://doi.org/10.1007/978-3-540-73368-3_28
8. Qadeer, S., Rehof, J.: Context-bounded model checking of concurrent software. In: Halbwachs, N., Zuck, L.D. (eds.) TACAS 2005. LNCS, vol. 3440, pp. 93–107. Springer, Heidelberg (2005). https://doi.org/10.1007/978-3-540-31980-1_7
9. Qadeer, S., Wu, D.: Kiss: keep it simple and sequential. In: PLDI 2004 (2004)
10. Ramalingam, G.: Context-sensitive synchronization-sensitive analysis is undecidable. ACM Trans. Program. Lang. Syst. **22**(2), 416–430 (2000)
11. Reps, T., Schwoon, S., Jha, S., Melski, D.: Weighted pushdown systems and their application to interprocedural dataflow analysis. Sci. Comput. Program. **58**(1), 206–263 (2005)
12. Touili, T.: Dealing with communication for dynamic multithreaded recursive programs. In: VISSAS 2005 (2005)
13. Wenner, A.: Weighted dynamic pushdown networks. In: Gordon, A.D. (ed.) ESOP 2010. LNCS, vol. 6012, pp. 590–609. Springer, Heidelberg (2010). https://doi.org/10.1007/978-3-642-11957-6_31

Verified Root-Balanced Trees

Tobias Nipkow$^{(\boxtimes)}$

Technische Universität München, Munich, Germany
http://www.in.tum.de/~nipkow

Abstract. Andersson introduced *general balanced trees*, search trees based on the design principle of partial rebuilding: perform update operations naively until the tree becomes too unbalanced, at which point a whole subtree is rebalanced. We define and analyze a functional version of general balanced trees which we call *root-balanced trees*. Using a lightweight model of execution time, amortized logarithmic complexity is verified in the theorem prover Isabelle. Experimental results show competitiveness of root-balanced with AVL and red-black trees.

1 Introduction

An old idea from the search tree literature is *partial rebuilding* [26]. Search trees are not rebalanced during every update operation but are allowed to degenerate before they are eventually rebalanced in a more drastic manner: a whole subtree is rebalanced to optimal height (in linear time). We build on the work of Andersson [2] who rebalances only if the height of the tree is no longer logarithmically bounded by the size of the tree. We call these trees *root-balanced*. We recast Andersson's ideas in a functional framework and verify their correctness in Isabelle: the *amortized* complexity is logarithmic. The main contributions are:

- The (as far as we know) first published executable formulation of root-balanced trees, imperative or functional. It is expressed in the functional language of the theorem prover Isabelle/HOL [23,24].
- A lightweight approach to modelling execution time of functional programs.
- The first formal verification of the amortized complexity of root-balanced trees. We develop the code by refinement and present the main definitions and theorems for the complexity proof. The full Isabelle definitions and proofs are found in the online Archive of Formal Proofs [22].
- Logarithm-free code. A direct implementation of Andersson's algorithms needs to compute logarithms. Because floating point computations are inexact this might lead to different behaviour and different actual complexity.
- The first published empirical evaluation of root-balanced trees. It shows that they are competitive with AVL and red-black trees.

Note that in a functional setting, amortized complexity reasoning is only valid if the data structure under consideration is used in a single-threaded manner, unless one employs lazy evaluation or memoization [25], which we do not.

T. Nipkow—Supported by DFG Koselleck grant NI 491/16-1.

© Springer International Publishing AG 2017
B.-Y.E. Chang (Ed.): APLAS 2017, LNCS 10695, pp. 255–272, 2017.
https://doi.org/10.1007/978-3-319-71237-6_13

We do not discuss the functional correctness proofs because they follow a method described elsewhere [21] and are automatic. The challenge is not correctness but amortized complexity.

2   Basics

Type variables are denoted by $'a$, $'b$, etc. The notation $t :: \tau$ means that term t has type τ. Type constructors follow postfix syntax, e.g. $'a\ set$ is the type of sets of elements of type $'a$.

The types nat, int and $real$ represent the sets $\mathbb{N}$, $\mathbb{Z}$ and $\mathbb{R}$. In this paper we often drop the coercion functions that are embeddings (like $real :: nat \to real$) but show $nat :: int \to nat$ because it maps the negative numbers to 0.

Lists over type $'a$, type $'a\ list$, come with the empty list [], the infix constructor "$\cdot$", the infix append operator @, hd (head), tl (tail), and the enumeration syntax $[x_1, \ldots, x_n]$.

Note that "=" on type $bool$ means "$\longleftrightarrow$".

2.1   Trees

datatype $'a\ tree = \langle\rangle \mid Node\ ('a\ tree)\ 'a\ ('a\ tree)$

We abbreviate $Node\ l\ a\ r$ by $\langle l, a, r\rangle$. The size ($|t|$) and height ($height\ t$) of a tree are defined as usual, starting with 0 for leaves. In addition we define $|t|_1 = |t| + 1$. Function $inorder$ is defined canonically. The minimal height is defined as follows:

$min\_height\ \langle\rangle = 0$
$min\_height\ \langle l, \_, r\rangle = min\ (min\_height\ l)\ (min\_height\ r) + 1$

We call a tree *balanced* iff its height and minimal height differ by at most 1:

$balanced\ t = (height\ t - min\_height\ t \leq 1)$

3   Balancing Trees

A number of imperative algorithms have been published that balance trees in linear time (e.g. [11,29]). We present a linear functional algorithm that first projects the tree to a list in linear time (using accumulation)

$inorder_2\ \langle\rangle\ xs = xs$
$inorder_2\ \langle l, x, r\rangle\ xs = inorder_2\ l\ (x \cdot inorder_2\ r\ xs)$

and builds the balanced tree from that:

$bal\ n\ xs =$
(if $n = 0$ then $(\langle\rangle, xs)$
else let $m = n\ div\ 2$;
      $(l, ys) = bal\ m\ xs$;
      $(r, y) = bal\ (n - 1 - m)\ (tl\ ys)$
   in $(\langle l, hd\ ys, r\rangle, y))$

$bal\_list\ n\ xs = (\text{let } (t,\ ys) = bal\ n\ xs \text{ in } t)$

$bal\_tree\ n\ t = bal\_list\ n\ (inorder_2\ t\ [])$

$balance\_tree\ t = bal\_tree\ |t|\ t$

This algorithm is most likely not new but we need it and its properties for rebalancing subtrees.

Lemma 1. *The order of elements is preserved and the result is balanced:*

$n \leq |t| \longrightarrow inorder\ (bal\_tree\ n\ t) = take\ n\ (inorder\ t)$
$balanced\ (bal\_tree\ n\ t)$

In order to avoid confusion with other notions of balancedness we refer to the above notion as *optimally balanced* in the text.

4 Time

There have been a number of proposals in the literature on how to model and analyze execution time of functional programs within functional programs or theorem provers (see Sect. 9). The key techniques are type systems and monads. We will also make use of a resource monad to accumulate execution time. The result is a lightweight approach to modelling and analyzing call-by-value execution time.

The basic principle of our approach is that the users define their programs in the monad and derive two separate functions from it, one that performs the computation and one that yields the time. Our time monad is based on

datatype $'a\ tm = TM\ 'a\ nat$

which combines a value with an internal clock:

$val\ (TM\ v\ n) = v$
$time\ (TM\ v\ n) = n$

The standard monadic combinators are

$s \ggeq f = (\text{case } s \text{ of}$
$\qquad\qquad TM\ u\ m \Rightarrow \text{case } f\ u \text{ of}$
$\qquad\qquad\qquad\qquad TM\ v\ n \Rightarrow TM\ v\ (m+n))$
$return\ v = TM\ v\ 0$

where $\ggeq$ (*bind*) adds the clocks of two computations and *return* is for free. Below we employ the usual do-notation instead of *bind*.

For simplicity our clock counts only function calls. In order to charge one clock tick for a function call we define the infix operator $=_1$ that does just that:

$lhs =_1 rhs$ abbreviates $lhs = (rhs \ggeq tick)$ where $tick\ v = TM\ v\ 1$.

That is, when defining a function f whose time we want to measure we need to write every defining equation $f\ p = t$ as $f\ p =_1 t$.

It is up to the users in how much detail they model the execution time, that is, how much of a computation they embed in the monad. In this paper we count all function calls (via the monad) except for constructors and functions on booleans and numbers. It would be easy to lift all of the latter functions into the monad as well, say with unit costs; this would merely lead to bigger constants in applications. This means that the concrete constants that appear in the time formulas we will prove are an underapproximation but could be made more precise if desired.

Let us look at an example, the monadic definition of function $inorder_2\_tm$:

$$inorder_2\_tm\ \langle\rangle\ xs =_1 return\ xs$$
$$inorder_2\_tm\ \langle l,\ x,\ r\rangle\ xs =_1 do\ \{$$
$$\quad rs \leftarrow inorder_2\_tm\ r\ xs;$$
$$\quad inorder_2\_tm\ l\ (x \cdot rs)$$
$$\}$$

From every monadic function f_tm we define the projections f and t_f on the value and the time. For $inorder_2\_tm$ these are

$$inorder_2\ t\ xs = val\ (inorder_2\_tm\ t\ xs)$$
$$t\_inorder_2\ t\ xs = time\ (inorder_2\_tm\ t\ xs)$$

From these definitions we prove (automatically, by simplification) recursion equations that follow the recursion of the monadic version:

$$inorder_2\ \langle\rangle\ xs = xs$$
$$inorder_2\ \langle l,\ x,\ r\rangle\ xs = (\mathsf{let}\ rs = inorder_2\ r\ xs\ \mathsf{in}\ inorder_2\ l\ (x \cdot rs))$$

$$t\_inorder_2\ \langle\rangle\ xs = 1$$
$$t\_inorder_2\ \langle l,\ x,\ r\rangle\ xs =$$
$$t\_inorder_2\ r\ xs + t\_inorder_2\ l\ (x \cdot inorder_2\ r\ xs) + 1$$

These, rather than the monadic versions, are used in the rest of the verification. For presentation reasons we sometimes expand lets if the let-bound variable occurs exactly once in the body, as in the definition of $inorder_2$ in Sect. 3.

For the running time function it is often possible to prove some non-recursive bound or even an exact value, for example

$$t\_inorder_2\ t\ xs = 2 * |t| + 1$$

The step from f_tm to f needs some attention because it must not change the running time in the process: f is the actual code, f_tm is only a means for describing the computation of the value and its time complexity simultaneously. For example, $f\_tm\ x = do\ \{\ y \leftarrow g\ x;\ return\ (h\ y\ y)\}$ should be transformed into $f\ x = (\mathsf{let}\ y = g\ x\ \mathsf{in}\ h\ y\ y)$, not into $f\ x = h\ (g\ x)\ (g\ x)$ because the latter evaluates $g\ x$ twice. Of course we cannot prove this because HOL functions are extensional and have no running time complexity. We can only argue that an intensional interpretation of the derived equation for f has the running time ascribed to it by the counter in the definition of f_tm. Our argument is that in the derivation of the equations for f we use only rewriting with the definitions of f_tm and f and with the following rules for pushing val inside and eliminating the clock.

$val \ (return \ x) = x$
$val \ (m \ggg f) = (\text{let } x = val \ m \text{ in } val \ (f \ x))$
$val \ (tick \ x) = x$
$val \ (\text{let } x = t \text{ in } f \ x) = (\text{let } x = t \text{ in } val \ (f \ x))$
$val \ (\text{if } c \text{ then } x \text{ else } y) = (\text{if } c \text{ then } val \ x \text{ else } val \ y)$

There are also obvious rules for case-expressions. All these rules do not change the running time of the intensional interpretation of the terms. The rules for val do not duplicate or erase parameters.

Outside of this section we do not show the original monadic definition of functions f_tm but only the derived equations for f; the definition of t_f is not shown either, it can be inferred from f.

Below we need the following results about the running times of the functions $size\_tree$ (normally shown as $|.|$) and bal_tree:

Lemma 2. $t\_size\_tree \ t = 2 * |t| + 1 and t\_bal\_tree \ |xs| \ xs = 4 * |xs| + 3$

Note that the soundness of our approach depends on the users observing data abstraction: monadic definitions must only use the monadic combinators $\ggg$ and $return$ (and $=_1$ or $tick$) but must not take monadic values apart, e.g. by pattern matching on TM. Alternatively one can write a tool that takes a normal function definition for f and generates the definition for t_f from it.

5   Root-Balanced Trees: Insertion

Root-balanced trees are (binary) search trees. To express that the elements in the trees must be ordered we employ Isabelle's type classes [19,32]. In the rest of the paper we assume that the type variable $'a$ in $'a \ tree$ is of class $linorder$, i.e., there are predicates $\leq$ and $<$ on $'a$ that form a linear order. Instead of using $\leq$ and $<$ directly we define a 3-way comparison function cmp:

datatype $cmp\_val = LT \mid EQ \mid GT$
$cmp \ x \ y = (\text{if } x < y \text{ then } LT \text{ else if } x = y \text{ then } EQ \text{ else } GT)$

Root-balanced trees should satisfy some minimal balance criterion at the root, something like $height \ t \leq c * \log_2 |t|$. We make this minimal balance criterion a parameter of our development: $bal_i :: nat \to nat \to bool$ where the subscript stands for "insertion". The two arguments of bal_i are the size and the height of the tree. The parameter bal_i is subject to two assumptions:

Assumption 1 (Monotonicity). $bal_i \ n \ h \wedge n \leq n' \wedge h' \leq h \longrightarrow bal_i \ n' \ h'$

Assumption 2. $bal_i \ |t| \ (height \ (balance\_tree \ t))$

Insertion works as follows. As for ordinary search trees, it searches for the element that is to be inserted. If that search ends up at a leaf, that leaf is replaced by a new singleton node. Then it checks if the new node has unbalanced the tree at the root (because it became too high). If so, then on the way back up it checks at every subtree if that is balanced, until it finds a subtree that is unbalanced and which then gets rebalanced. Thus the algorithm has to distinguish between unbalanced, balanced and unchanged trees (in case the element to be inserted was already in the tree):

datatype $'a \ up = Same \ | \ Bal \ ('a \ tree) \ | \ Unbal \ ('a \ tree)$

That is, if (a recursive call of) insertion returns *Same*, the tree remains unchanged; if it returns *Bal t*, the new subtree is t and no (more) rebalancing is necessary; if it returns *Unbal t*, the new subtree is t and some subtree higher up needs to be rebalanced because the root has become unbalanced.

5.1   A Naive Implementation

To reduce the complexity of the verification we start with a first inefficient implementation and show that it is functionally correct. A second efficient implementation will then be shown to be functionally equivalent and to have the desired complexity.

Function $ins :: nat \rightarrow nat \rightarrow 'a \rightarrow 'a \ tree \rightarrow 'a \ up$ inserts an element:

$ins \ n \ d \ x \ \langle\rangle =$
(if $bal_i \ (n+1) \ (d+1)$ then $Bal \ \langle\langle\rangle, \ x, \ \langle\rangle\rangle$ else $Unbal \ \langle\langle\rangle, \ x, \ \langle\rangle\rangle$)
$ins \ n \ d \ x \ \langle l, \ y, \ r\rangle = ($case $cmp \ x \ y$ of
$\qquad\qquad\qquad LT \Rightarrow up \ y \ r \ False \ (ins \ n \ (d+1) \ x \ l)$
$\qquad\qquad\quad | \ EQ \Rightarrow Same$
$\qquad\qquad\quad | \ GT \Rightarrow up \ y \ l \ True \ (ins \ n \ (d+1) \ x \ r))$

Parameter n is the size of the whole tree, parameter d the depth of the recursion, i.e. the distance from the root. Both parameters are needed in order to decide at the leaf level if the tree has become unbalanced because that information is needed on the way back up. Checking and rebalancing is performed by function *up* below, where *sib* is the sibling of the subtree inside u, *twist* indicates whether it is the left or right sibling and x is the contents of the node:

$up \ x \ sib \ twist \ u =$
(case u of
$\quad Same \Rightarrow Same$
$\ | \ Bal \ t \Rightarrow Bal \ (node \ twist \ t \ x \ sib)$
$\ | \ Unbal \ t \Rightarrow$
$\qquad$ let $t' = node \ twist \ t \ x \ sib;$
$\qquad\quad h' = height \ t';$
$\qquad\quad n' = |t'|$
$\qquad$ in if $bal_i \ n' \ h'$ then $Unbal \ t'$ else $Bal \ (balance\_tree \ t'))$

$node\ twist\ s\ x\ t = (\textsf{if}\ twist\ \textsf{then}\ \langle t,\ x,\ s\rangle\ \textsf{else}\ \langle s,\ x,\ t\rangle)$

Obviously ins increases the size by 1 (if the element is not there already); the height changes as follows:

$ins\ n\ d\ x\ t = Bal\ t' \longrightarrow height\ t' \leq height\ t + 1$
$ins\ n\ d\ x\ t = Unbal\ t' \longrightarrow height\ t \leq height\ t' \leq height\ t + 1$

In the first case the height may actually shrink due to rebalancing. The proof is by simultaneous induction and relies on Assumptions 1 and 2.

The return value $Unbal$ signals that the tree has become unbalanced at the root. Formally:

Lemma 3. $ins\ n\ d\ x\ t = Unbal\ t' \longrightarrow \neg\ bal_i\ (n + 1)\ (height\ t' + d)$

The proof is by induction and uses monotonicity of bal_i. An easy consequence:

Lemma 4. $ins\ n\ (d + 1)\ x\ l = Unbal\ l' \wedge bal_i\ n\ (height\ \langle l,\ y,\ r\rangle + d) \longrightarrow$
$height\ r < height\ l'$

There is a symmetric lemma for r instead of l. These two lemmas tell us that if insertion unbalances a balanced tree, then it climbs back up what has become the longest path in the tree.

The top-level insertion function is $insert$:

$insert\ x\ t = (\textsf{case}\ ins\ |t|\ 0\ x\ t\ \textsf{of}$
$\qquad\qquad Same \Rightarrow t$
$\qquad\quad |\ Bal\ t' \Rightarrow t')$

Note that the call of ins in $insert$ cannot return $Unbal$ because (by definition of up) this only happens if the tree is balanced, which contradicts Lemma 3:

Lemma 5. $|t| \leq n \longrightarrow ins\ n\ 0\ a\ t \neq Unbal\ t'$

Hence proofs about $insert$ do not need to consider case $Unbal$.

5.2 An Efficient Implementation

The above implementation computes the sizes and heights of subtrees explicitly and repeatedly as it goes back up the tree. We will now perform that computation incrementally. Of course one can store that information in each node but the beauty of this search tree is that only at the very root we need to store some extra information, the size of the tree. The incremental version of the algorithm works with a modified data type $'a\ up2$

datatype $'a\ up2 = Same_2 \mid Bal_2\ ('a\ tree) \mid Unbal_2\ ('a\ tree)\ nat\ nat$

where $Unbal_2\ t\ n\ h$ passes n and h, the size and height of t, back up the tree. The new version of function up is up_2:

up_2 x sib $twist$ u =
(case u of
    $Same_2$ $\Rightarrow$ $Same_2$
  | Bal_2 t $\Rightarrow$ Bal_2 ($node$ $twist$ t x sib)
  | $Unbal_2$ t n_1 h_1 $\Rightarrow$
      let n_2 = $|sib|$;
          h_2 = $height$ sib;
          t' = $node$ $twist$ t x sib;
          n' = $n_1 + n_2 + 1$;
          h' = max h_1 h_2 + 1
      in if bal_i n' h' then $Unbal_2$ t' n' h' else Bal_2 (bal_tree n' t'))

Note that instead of $balance\_tree$ we call bal_tree because that avoids the computation of the size of the tree that we have already. There are also corresponding new versions of ins and $insert$:

ins_2 n d x $\langle\rangle$ =
(if bal_i $(n + 1)$ $(d + 1)$ then Bal_2 $\langle\langle\rangle, x, \langle\rangle\rangle$ else $Unbal_2$ $\langle\langle\rangle, x, \langle\rangle\rangle$ 1 1)
ins_2 n d x $\langle l, y, r\rangle$ = (case cmp x y of
                    LT $\Rightarrow$ up_2 y r $False$ $(ins_2$ n $(d + 1)$ x $l)$
              | EQ $\Rightarrow$ $Same_2$
              | GT $\Rightarrow$ up_2 y l $True$ $(ins_2$ n $(d + 1)$ x $r))$

$insert_2$ x (t, n) = (case ins_2 n 0 x t of
            $Same_2$ $\Rightarrow$ (t, n)
           | Bal_2 t' $\Rightarrow$ $(t', n + 1))$

Note that the top-level function $insert_2$ operates on pairs (t, n) where $n = |t|$. The relationship between $ins/insert$ and $ins_2/insert_2$ is easy to state and prove:

$(ins_2$ n d x t = $Same_2)$ = $(ins$ n d x t = $Same)$
$(ins_2$ n d x t = Bal_2 $t')$ = $(ins$ n d x t = Bal $t')$
$(ins_2$ n d x t = $Unbal_2$ t' n' $h')$ =
$(ins$ n d x t = $Unbal$ t' $\wedge$ n' = $|t'|$ $\wedge$ h' = $height$ $t')$

$(insert_2$ x $(t, |t|)$ = $(t', n'))$ = $(t'$ = $insert$ x t $\wedge$ n' = $|t'|)$

Case $Unbal_2$ in up_2 is suboptimal because sib is traversed twice. But instead of introducing a combined size and height function it turns out we can simply drop the computation of $height$ sib. The reason is that, if initially balanced, the tree becomes unbalanced only if we have inserted a new node at the end of a longest path, which means that the height is determined by that path alone. This is what Lemma 4 expresses. The final version up_3 is obtained from up_2 by replacing the right-hand side of case $Unbal_2$ with the following expression:

let n_2 = $|sib|$;
    t' = $node$ $twist$ t x sib;
    n' = $n_1 + n_2 + 1$;
    h' = $h_1 + 1$
in if bal_i n' h' then $Unbal_2$ t' n' h' else Bal_2 (bal_tree n' t')

The corresponding insertion functions $ins_3/insert_3$ look like $ins_2/insert_2$ but call up_3/ins_3. Function $insert_3$ is the final implementation of insertion.

The relationship between level 2 and 3 requires that the tree is balanced and is more involved to prove:

$$bal_i \ n \ (height \ t + d) \longrightarrow ins_3 \ n \ d \ x \ t = ins_2 \ n \ d \ x \ t$$
$$bal_i \ n \ (height \ t) \longrightarrow insert_3 \ x \ (t, \ n) = insert_2 \ x \ (t, \ n)$$

The precondition is needed for using Lemma 4.

We will move silently between the three levels using the above equivalences.

5.3   Amortized Complexity

In the worst case, insertion can require a linear amount of work because the whole tree has to be rebalanced. We will show that each rebalancing must be preceded by a linear number of insertions without rebalancing over which the cost of the eventual rebalancing can be spread, increasing the cost of each insertion only by a constant. If bal_i is defined such that the height of balanced trees is logarithmic in the size, insertion has logarithmic amortized cost.

The core of the potential function argument by Andersson [2] is the *imbalance* of a node:

$$imbal \ \langle \rangle = 0$$
$$imbal \ \langle l, \ \_, \ r \rangle = nat \ |int \ |l| - int \ |r|| - 1$$

Thus $imbal \ \langle l, \ \_, \ r \rangle$ is the absolute value of the difference in size of l and r, minus 1. Because the subtraction of 1 is at type nat, it is cut off at 0. A consequence of subtracting 1 (which Andersson [1] does not do) will be that optimally balanced trees have potential 0.

The key property of $imbal$ is that insertion into a subtree can increase the imbalance of a node by at most 1: defining $\delta \ t \ s = real(imbal \ t) - real(imbal \ s)$ we obtain

Lemma 6. $ins \ n \ d \ x \ t = Bal \ t' \ \lor \ ins \ n \ d \ x \ t = Unbal \ t' \longrightarrow$
$\delta \ (node \ tw \ t' \ y \ s) \ (node \ tw \ t \ y \ s) \leq 1$

This follows by definition of $imbal$ from the fact that the height of t' can have increased by at most one.

Now we add another assumption about bal_i: when we climb back up the tree after an insertion and find an unbalanced node whose higher child (where we must have come from) is balanced, then the imbalance of the node is proportional to its size:

Assumption 3. $\neg \ bal_i \ |t| \ (height \ t) \ \land \ bal_i \ |hchild \ t| \ (height \ (hchild \ t) \ ) \ \land$
$t \neq \langle \rangle \longrightarrow |t|_1 \leq e * (imbal \ t + 1)$

where $hchild \ \langle l, \ _, \ r \rangle = $ (if $height \ l \leq height \ r$ then r else l) and e is some real number greater 0.

We define the actual potential function Φ as the sum of all imbalances in a tree, scaled by $6 * e$:

$\Phi \langle \rangle = 0$

$\Phi \langle l, x, r \rangle = 6 * e * imbal \langle l, x, r \rangle + \Phi l + \Phi r$

The factor 6 comes from the complexities of the size computations and the rebalancing. Both are linear, but with factors 2 and 4 (Lemma 2). These linear complexities need to be paid for by the potential.

Clearly $0 \le \Phi t$, as is required of a potential function. Moreover, the potential of a balanced tree is 0:

Lemma 7. $\Phi (balance\_tree\ t) = 0$

The main theorem expresses that the amortized complexity of $insert_3$ is linear in the height of the tree.

Theorem 1. $bal_i |t| (height\ t) \wedge insert_3\ a\ (t, |t|) = (t', n') \longrightarrow$
    $t\_insert_3\ a\ (t, |t|) + \Phi t' - \Phi t \le (6 * e + 2) * (height\ t + 1) + 1$

Now we plug that result into a framework for amortized analysis, and finally we show that for certain interpretations of bal_i and e, the height of the tree is logarithmic in the size.

Instantiating the Framework. We use an existing framework [20] for the analysis of the amortized complexity of data structures. It guarantees that, given certain key theorems, the data structure indeed has the claimed complexity. We instantiate the framework as follows: The state space consists of pairs (t, n). The initial state is $(\langle \rangle, 0)$. The invariant is $\lambda(t, n).\ n = |t| \wedge bal_i |t| (height\ t)$; the invariance proof relies on Asumptions 1 and 2. The potential function is $\lambda(t, n).\ \Phi t$. The amortized complexity of $insert_3\ x\ (t, n)$ is bounded from above by $(6 * e + 2) * (height\ t + 1) + 1$ (Theorem 1).

Logarithmic Height. So far the verification was parameterized by bal_i and e subject to some assumptions. Now we give a concrete instantiation that guarantees a logarithmic bound on the height. We follow Andersson [2] and define

$$bal_i\ n\ h\ =\ h \le \lceil c * \log_2 (n + 1) \rceil \qquad (1)$$

for some arbitrary $c > 1$.

We have to show that all assumptions are satisfied. Assumption 1 (Monotonicity) clearly holds. Assumption 2 is a consequence of the lemma $height\ (balance\_tree\ t) = nat\ \lceil \log_2 (|t| + 1) \rceil$. Assumption 3 follows by setting

$$e = 2^{1/c} / (2 - 2^{1/c}) \qquad (2)$$

Thus we know that (1) and (2) satisfy the above parameterized complexity analysis. Because we proved that bal_i is an invariant, we know that the height of the tree is bounded from above by $\lceil c * \log_2 |t|_1 \rceil$. Thus the amortized complexity of insertion is bounded from above by $(6 * e + 2) * (\lceil c * \log_2 |t|_1 \rceil + 1) + 1$.

6   Root-Balanced Trees: Deletion

The key idea is to perform standard deletions (no balancing) until enough deletions have occurred to pay for rebalancing at the *root*. This means that the data
structure needs to maintain a counter of the number of deletions; the counter
is reset when the root is rebalanced because of a deletion. Because balancing is
linear, any fixed fraction of the size of the tree will work. We parameterize the
whole development by that fraction, a constant $c_d > 0$. Thus the balance test
$bal_d :: nat \rightarrow nat \rightarrow bool$ to be used after each deletion is defined as

$$bal_d \; n \; dl = (dl < c_d * (n + 1))$$

where n is the number of nodes in the tree and dl the number of deletions that
have occurred since the last rebalancing after a deletion.

We extend the development of the previous section with a deletion function and a new top-level insertion function. Many of the existing functions and
lemmas are reused in the extended setting.

6.1   A Naive Implementation

The main supporting lemmas are proved about an implementation where the size
of the tree is not cached. That is rectified in a second step. The new top-level
insertion function $insert_d$ operates on a pair of a tree and the deletion counter.
We build upon function *ins* from Sect. 5.1.

$$insert_d \; x \; (t, \; dl) = (\text{case } ins \; (|t| + dl) \; 0 \; x \; t \text{ of}$$
$$Same \Rightarrow t$$
$$| \; Bal \; t' \Rightarrow t',$$
$$dl)$$

Why is the deletion counter added to the size? That way the sum stays invariant
under deletion and the invariant $bal_i \; (|t| + dl) \; (height \; t)$ for insertion will also
remain invariant under deletion.

Deletion works as for unbalanced trees. The deletion function *del* returns
$'a \; tree \; option$ to signal whether the element was in the tree or not:

datatype $'a \; option = None \; | \; Some \; 'a$

$del \; x \; \langle\rangle = None$
$del \; x \; \langle l, \; y, \; r \rangle =$
$(\text{case } cmp \; x \; y \text{ of}$
$\quad LT \Rightarrow up_d \; y \; r \; False \; (del \; x \; l)$
$\quad | \; EQ \Rightarrow \text{if } r = \langle\rangle \text{ then } Some \; l$
$\qquad\qquad \text{else let } (a', \; r') = del\_min \; r \text{ in } Some \; \langle l, \; a', \; r' \rangle$
$\quad | \; GT \Rightarrow up_d \; y \; l \; True \; (del \; x \; r))$

$del\_min \; \langle l, \; x, \; r \rangle =$
$(\text{if } l = \langle\rangle \text{ then } (x, \; r) \text{ else let } (y, \; l') = del\_min \; l \text{ in } (y, \; \langle l', \; x, \; r \rangle))$

$up_d\ x\ sib\ twist\ u = ($case u of
$\qquad\qquad None \Rightarrow None$
$\qquad\qquad |\ Some\ t \Rightarrow Some\ (node\ twist\ t\ x\ sib))$

The top-level deletion function rebalances the root if necessary and maintains the deletion counter:

$delete\ x\ (t,\ dl) =$
(case $del\ x\ t$ of
$\quad None \Rightarrow (t,\ dl)$
$\quad |\ Some\ t' \Rightarrow$ if $bal_d\ |t'|\ (dl + 1)$ then $(t',\ dl + 1)$ else $(balance\_tree\ t',\ 0))$

6.2   An Efficient Implementation

Just like before, we optimize insertion in two steps. First we cache the size n. That is, the data structure is now a triple $(t,\ n,\ dl)$. Thus $insert_d$ becomes

$insert_{d2}\ x\ (t,\ n,\ dl) = ($case $ins_2\ (n + dl)\ 0\ x\ t$ of
$\qquad\qquad Same_2 \Rightarrow (t,\ n,\ dl)$
$\qquad\qquad |\ Bal_2\ t' \Rightarrow (t',\ n + 1,\ dl))$

In another optimization step we call ins_3 instead of ins_2:

$insert_{d3}\ x\ (t,\ n,\ dl) = ($case $ins_3\ (n + dl)\ 0\ x\ t$ of
$\qquad\qquad Same_2 \Rightarrow (t,\ n,\ dl)$
$\qquad\qquad |\ Bal_2\ t' \Rightarrow (t',\ n + 1,\ dl))$

Function $delete$ is optimized in one step:

$delete_2\ x\ (t,\ n,\ dl) =$
(case $del\ x\ t$ of
$\quad None \Rightarrow (t,\ n,\ dl)$
$\quad |\ Some\ t' \Rightarrow$ let $n' = n - 1;$
$\qquad\qquad dl' = dl + 1$
$\qquad\qquad$ in if $bal_d\ n'\ dl'$ then $(t',\ n',\ dl')$ else $(bal\_tree\ n'\ t',\ n',\ 0))$

Functions $insert_{d3}$ and $delete_2$ are the final top level functions.

6.3   Amortized Complexity

The new potential function Φ_d is the sum of the previous potential function and an additive term that charges each deletion its share of the overall cost of rebalancing at the root:

$$\Phi_d\ (t,\ n,\ dl) = \Phi\ t + 4 * dl/c_d$$

The factor 4 is due to the cost of bal_tree (see Lemma 2).

The amortized complexity of insertion is the same as before:

Theorem 2. $insert_d\ a\ (t,\ dl) = (t',\ dl') \wedge bal_i\ (|t| + dl)\ (height\ t) \longrightarrow$
$t\_insert_{d3}\ a\ (t,\ |t|,\ dl) + \Phi\ t' - \Phi\ t \le (6 * e + 2) * (height\ t + 1) + 1$

Deletion is similar but its complexity also depends on c_d:

Theorem 3. $t\_delete_2\ x\ (t,\ |t|,\ dl) + \Phi_d\ (delete_2\ x\ (t,\ |t|,\ dl)) - \Phi_d\ (t,\ |t|,\ dl) \le (6 * e + 1) * height\ t + 4/c_d + 4$

Instantiating the Framework. Like in Sect. 5.3 we instantiate the generic amortized complexity framework: The state space consists of triples (t, n, dl). The initial state is $(\langle\rangle, 0, 0)$. The invariant is

$$\lambda(t, n, dl).\ n = |t| \wedge bal_i\ (|t| + dl)\ (height\ t) \wedge bal_d\ |t|\ dl$$

The potential function is Φ_d. The amortized complexity of $insert_{d3}\ x\ (t, n, dl)$ is bounded from above by $(6 * e + 2) * (height\ t + 1) + 1$ (Theorem 2). The amortized complexity of $delete_2\ x\ (t, n, dl)$ is bounded from above by $(6 * e + 1) * height\ t + 4/c_d + 4$ (Theorem 3).

Logarithmic Height. We interpret bal_i and e as in Definitions (1) and (2) above. However, the proof of logarithmic height in that section no longer works because the invariant $bal_i\ |t|\ (height\ t)$ has become $bal_i\ (|t| + dl)\ (height\ t)$. Following Andersson [2] we introduce another parameter $b > 0$, define

$$c_d = 2^{b/c} - 1 \tag{3}$$

and prove that the invariant implies $height\ t \leq \lceil b + \log_2 |t|_1 \rceil$. Overall, the amortized complexity is bounded by $(6 * e + 2) * (\lceil b + \log_2 |t|_1 \rceil + 1) + 1$ (for insertion) and $(6 * e + 1) * \lceil b + \log_2 |t|_1 \rceil + 4/c_d + 4$ (for deletion).

7 Avoiding Logarithms

The one remaining trouble spot is the logarithm in the computation of bal_i. Implementing it in floating point invalidates the complexity analysis because of rounding errors. As a result, trees may get rebalanced earlier or later than in the mathematical model, which could lead to a different complexity. This was not discussed by any of the previous analyses of this data structure.

We implement $bal_i\ n\ h$ by a table lookup. The idea is to construct a table $bal\_tab :: nat\ list$ such that $bal\_tab\ !\ h$ (where $xs\ !\ n$ is the n-th element of xs, starting with 0) is the least n such that $h \leq \lceil c * \log_2 (n + 1) \rceil$ and thus

$$bal_i\ n\ h = (bal\_tab\ !\ h \leq n)$$

That is, we have reduced a test involving the log function to a table lookup.

Of course tables are finite. Hence we can only guarantee partial correctness, up to some fixed value of h. But because h is logarithmic in the size of the tree, a small table suffices to hold enough values to cater for any tree that can be stored (for example) in the 64-bit address space.

The definition of bal_tab is straightforward: for a given c, set

$$bal\_tab\ !\ h = \lfloor 2^{(h - 1)/c} \rfloor \tag{4}$$

for $h = 0$ up to some maximum value. The difficulty is obtaining a verified table because the exponent $(h - 1)/c$ is in general not an integer. We solve this difficulty by result checking: we compute *bal_tab* externally (e.g. in some programming language), define *bal_tab* with the values obtained, and have Isabelle prove automatically that *bal_tab* is correct. We go through this process step by step.

First we fix some concrete c, compute *bal_tab* up to a sufficiently large size of the tree, and define *bal_tab* in Isabelle. For example, for $c = 3/2$ we have a table of 50 elements if we stop at 2^{33}:

$$bal\_tab = [0, 1, 1, 2, 4, 6, 10, 16, ..., 2705659852, 4294967296]$$

Then we verify the correctness of *bal_tab* in two steps. First we prove automatically that the values satisfy (4). This relies on a specialized proof method named *approximation* [15] based on interval arithmetic. It can prove propositions like $5 \leq x \leq 7 \longrightarrow \log_2 x \leq x - 21/10$, in particular if there are no free variables, e.g. $\log_2 5 \leq 3/2 * \log_2 3$. It proves in a few seconds that

Lemma 8. $\forall i < length\ bal\_tab.\ bal\_tab\ !\ i = \lfloor 2^{(i-1)/c} \rfloor$

By composition with some pre-proved generic lemmas the desired correctness proposition for our concrete *bal_tab* follows:

$$h < length\ bal\_tab \longrightarrow bal_i\ n\ h = (bal\_tab\ !\ h \leq n)$$

Finally note that although *bal_tab* is a list, it can be implemented as an immutable array.

8   Experimental Results

We have implemented root-balanced trees in Standard ML (with the help of Isabelle's code generator [5,12]) and compared their performance with those of two implementations of AVL and red-black trees [21]. To avoid floating point arithmetic, the tabulation approach from Sect. 7 was used. Keys are unbounded integers. The code was compiled with Poly/ML 5.6 [17] and executed under Linux on an Intel Core i7-2700K, 3.5 GHz fixed, and 16 GB RAM. We measured the total CPU time used, including garbage collection.

The table in Fig. 1 summarizes the results of our measurements. Each of the tests is executed with 10^5 elements in the tree. Each such test case was executed 100 times with each implementation to reduce statistical variations due to randomization and garbage collection.

Each test is executed with two versions of root-balanced trees: one where $c = c_d = 1.2$ and one where $c = c_d = 1.5$. They are called Root-Bal. 1.2 and Root-Bal. 1.5. In principle c and c_d are independent but we have identified them to reduce the number of versions to consider. The identification makes sense because in both cases a larger constant means lazier rebalancing.

We compare two kinds of workloads: uniformly distributed inputs ("Random") and decreasing inputs $n, \ldots, 1$ ("Sorted").

First we look at the upper part of the table with relative timing figures for insertion, deletion and search. The numbers are relative to Root-Bal. 1.5. For

	AVL	Red-Black	Root-Bal. 1.2	Root-Bal. 1.5
Insert Random	1.1	1.7	1.1	1
Insert Sorted	0.3	0.7	1.6	1
Delete Random	1.3	1.6	1.0	1
Delete Sorted	2.0	0.9	1.1	1
Search Random	0.9	1.1	1.0	1
Search Sorted	1.5	1.3	1.0	1
Path Length Random	0.8	0.9	0.9	1
Path Length Sorted	1.0	1.0	1.0	1

Fig. 1. Experimental results

example, Insert Random with red-black trees takes 1.7 times longer than with root-balanced trees where $c = c_d = 1.5$.

The insertion tests measure how long it takes to insert n elements into an initially empty tree, in random or in sorted order. In Insert Random, the two root-balanced trees beat AVL and red-black trees because root-balanced trees require less restructuring: randomly generated trees are already reasonably balanced. For sorted inputs, the trees get out of balance all the time and partial rebalancing becomes more costly than the local modifications in AVL and red-black trees. This is the only place where our choice of c's has a significant impact.

Deletion starts with the tree created by the corresponding insertion run and deletes all elements in random or sorted order. For random inputs, the performance of all four trees is almost the same. For sorted input, root-balanced trees beat AVL trees and are only slightly slower than red-black trees.

Searches start with the tree created by the corresponding insertion run; all elements in the tree are searched in random or sorted order. With random input there is very little difference between the four search trees. Search Sorted shows a noticeable slowdown for red-black and AVL trees. This could be a cache phenomenon because the nodes of red-black and AVL trees are larger.

Our measurements for insertion and deletion (roughly) confirm those by Galperin and Rivest [11], although they use weight-balanced rather than our height-balanced trees. The situation w.r.t. searches is more complicated. Their Fig. 4 shows that with random input, searching in root-balanced trees is 4 times faster than in red-black trees; they do not offer an explanation. In contrast, our data shows very little difference between the different kinds of search trees. Since all the trees we tested are binary search trees, the search time should only depend on their shape (ignoring cache issues, which favour the smaller root-balanced trees). If we search for all the elements in a tree (as we do in our Search tests), the search time should be proportional to the internal path length of the tree (the sum of the lengths of all paths from the root to a node). The last two lines in Fig. 1 show that the internal path lengths are relatively close together for Random and practically identical for Sorted. This confirms our measurements of search times and suggests that the discrepancy between root-balanced and other trees in Search Sorted is indeed due to cache behaviour.

9   Related Work

There is a rich literature on resource analysis and we can only mention the most relevant work. The problem of inferring cost functions for functional programs has been studied, for example, by Sands [28] and Vasconcelos and Hammond [30]. Early work on automatic complexity analysis includes Wegbreit's METRIC system [31] for LISP, Le Métayer's ACE system [16] for FP, and Benzinger's ACA [4] system for NUPRL. The recent work by Hoffmann et al. (e.g. [13,14]) is particularly impressive (although currently restricted to polynomials). Type systems are a popular framework for tracking resources [7,8,18]. The last two references follow the same monadic, dependently typed approach in different theorem provers. Our approach is similar but the running times are not tracked on the level of types but on the level of values. However, none of these papers makes an explicit connection to some cost model also formalized in the theorem prover. This is what sets Atkey's work [3] apart. He formalizes a separation logic that supports amortized resource analysis for an imperative language in Coq and proves the logic correct w.r.t. a semantics. Verified cost analyses for functional language have also been studied [9,10]. In summary one can say that there is a whole spectrum of approaches that differ in expressive power, in the complexity of the examples that have been dealt with, and in automation. Of the references above, only McCarthy et al. [18] has examples involving logarithms (instead of merely polynomials) and they are much simpler than root-balanced trees. Like this paper and our earlier work [21], the paper by Charguéraud and Pottier [6] is at the complex, interactive end: they verify the almost-linear amortized complexity of a Union-Find implementation in OCaml in Coq using a separation logic with time credits.

The idea of rebuilding whole substructures of a data structure, but only at intervals, goes back at least to Overmars and van Leeuwen [26,27] who called it *partial rebuilding* and applied it to weight-balanced trees. Partial rebuilding was again applied to weight-balanced trees by Galperin and Rivest [11] where the resulting data structure is called a *scapegoat tree*. We build on Andersson's work [1,2] who realized that one can apply partial rebuilding to trees balanced only at the root, which he called *trees of balanced height* [1] and later *general balanced trees* [2]. We call them *root-balanced* to emphasize the restriction of the balance criterion to the root. All these publications are high-level in that algorithms are described in words and the proofs are based on intuition rather than code. Our proofs roughly follow Andersson [2, Sect. 3] whose arguments are very high-level. In particular, he does not spell out the potential function. In Sect. 4 he performs a more precise analysis to obtain smaller constants, but now employing a potential function that can look into the future, an *ad hoc* concept. He argues informally that this concept is appropriate for the problem at hand. In contrast, we provide an explicit potential function of the standard kind. Andersson does not discuss the complications entailed by the logarithm in the balance test.

10   Conclusion

We have presented and verified a functional implementation of the general balanced trees by Andersson [2] in Isabelle. With the help of a lightweight monadic framework for modelling execution time we verified that insertion and deletion have amortized logarithmic complexity. We have also shown how to avoid computing with logarithms, which a direct implementation of Andersson's balance criterion would require. Finally we have presented experimental results showing that root-balanced trees are competitive with AVL and red-black trees.

Acknowledgement. Johannes Hölzl suggested the tabulation approach. Manuel Eberl ran the measurements. One of the referees suggested valuable improvements to the time monad.

References

1. Andersson, A.: Improving partial rebuilding by using simple balance criteria. In: Dehne, F., Sack, J.-R., Santoro, N. (eds.) WADS 1989. LNCS, vol. 382, pp. 393–402. Springer, Heidelberg (1989). https://doi.org/10.1007/3-540-51542-9_33
2. Andersson, A.: General balanced trees. J. Algorithms **30**(1), 1–18 (1999)
3. Atkey, R.: Amortised resource analysis with separation logic. Log. Methods Comput. Sci. **7**(2), 1–33 (2011)
4. Benzinger, R.: Automated higher-order complexity analysis. Theor. Comput. Sci. **318**(1–2), 79–103 (2004)
5. Berghofer, S., Nipkow, T.: Executing higher order logic. In: Callaghan, P., Luo, Z., McKinna, J., Pollack, R., Pollack, R. (eds.) TYPES 2000. LNCS, vol. 2277, pp. 24–40. Springer, Heidelberg (2002). https://doi.org/10.1007/3-540-45842-5_2
6. Charguéraud, A., Pottier, F.: Machine-checked verification of the correctness and amortized complexity of an efficient union-find implementation. In: Urban, C., Zhang, X. (eds.) ITP 2015. LNCS, vol. 9236, pp. 137–153. Springer, Cham (2015). https://doi.org/10.1007/978-3-319-22102-1_9
7. Crary, K., Weirich, S.: Resource bound certification. In: Proceedings of 27th Symposium on Principles of Programming Languages, POPL 2000, pp. 184–198. ACM (2000)
8. Danielsson, N.A.: Lightweight semiformal time complexity analysis for purely functional data structures. In: Proceedings of 35th Symposium on Principles of Programming Languages, POPL 2008, pp. 133–144. ACM (2008)
9. Danner, N., Licata, D.R., Ramyaa, R.: Denotational cost semantics for functional languages with inductive types. In: Proceedings of International Conference on Functional Programming, ICFP 2015, pp. 140–151. ACM (2015)
10. Danner, N., Paykin, J., Royer, J.: A static cost analysis for a higher-order language. In: Proceedings of Workshop Programming Languages Meets Program Verification, PLPV 2013, pp. 25–34. ACM (2013)
11. Galperin, I., Rivest, R.L.: Scapegoat trees. In: Ramachandran, V. (ed.) Proceedings of Fourth Annual ACM/SIGACT-SIAM Symposium on Discrete Algorithms, pp. 165–174 (1993)
12. Haftmann, F., Nipkow, T.: Code generation via higher-order rewrite systems. In: Blume, M., Kobayashi, N., Vidal, G. (eds.) FLOPS 2010. LNCS, vol. 6009, pp. 103–117. Springer, Heidelberg (2010). https://doi.org/10.1007/978-3-642-12251-4_9

13. Homann, J., Aehlig, K., Hofmann, M.: Multivariate amortized resource analysis. ACM Trans. Program. Lang. Syst. **34**(3), 14 (2012)
14. Hoffmann, J., Das, A., Weng, S.C.: Towards automatic resource bound analysis for OCaml. In: Proceedings of 44th Symposium on Principles of Programming Languages, POPL 2017, pp. 359–373. ACM (2017)
15. Hölzl, J.: Proving inequalities over reals with computation in Isabelle/HOL. In: Reis, G., Théry, L. (eds.) Programming Languages for Mechanized Mathematics Systems (ACM SIGSAM PLMMS 2009). pp. 38–45 (2009)
16. Le Métayer, D.: ACE: an automatic complexity evaluator. ACM Trans. Program. Lang. Syst. **10**(2), 248–266 (1988)
17. Matthews, D.: Poly/ML home page (2017). http://www.polyml.org/
18. McCarthy, J., Fetscher, B., New, M., Feltey, D., Findler, R.B.: A Coq library for internal verification of running-times. In: Kiselyov, O., King, A. (eds.) FLOPS 2016. LNCS, vol. 9613, pp. 144–162. Springer, Cham (2016). https://doi.org/10.1007/978-3-319-29604-3_10
19. Nipkow, T.: Order-sorted polymorphism in Isabelle. In: Huet, G., Plotkin, G. (eds.) Logical Environments, pp. 164–188 (1993)
20. Nipkow, T.: Amortized complexity verified. In: Urban, C., Zhang, X. (eds.) ITP 2015. LNCS, vol. 9236, pp. 310–324. Springer, Cham (2015). https://doi.org/10.1007/978-3-319-22102-1_21
21. Nipkow, T.: Automatic functional correctness proofs for functional search trees. In: Blanchette, J.C., Merz, S. (eds.) ITP 2016. LNCS, vol. 9807, pp. 307–322. Springer, Cham (2016). https://doi.org/10.1007/978-3-319-43144-4_19
22. Nipkow, T.: Root-balanced tree. Archive of Formal Proofs (2017). http://isa-afp.org/entries/Root_Balanced_Tree.html, Formal proof development
23. Nipkow, T., Klein, G.: Concrete Semantics with Isabelle/HOL. Springer, Heidelberg (2014). http://concrete-semantics.org
24. Nipkow, T., Wenzel, M., Paulson, L.C. (eds.): Isabelle/HOL. A Proof Assistant for Higher-Order Logic. LNCS, vol. 2283. Springer, Heidelberg (2002). https://doi.org/10.1007/3-540-45949-9
25. Okasaki, C.: Purely Functional Data Structures. Cambridge University Press, New York (1998)
26. Overmars, M.H.: The Design of Dynamic Data Structures. LNCS, vol. 156. Springer, Heidelberg (1983). https://doi.org/10.1007/BFb0014927
27. Overmars, M., van Leeuwen, J.: Dynamic multi-dimensional data structures based on quad- and k-d trees. Acta Informatica **17**, 267–285 (1982)
28. Sands, D.: Complexity analysis for a lazy higher-order language. In: Jones, N. (ed.) ESOP 1990. LNCS, vol. 432, pp. 361–376. Springer, Heidelberg (1990). https://doi.org/10.1007/3-540-52592-0_74
29. Stout, Q.F., Warren, B.L.: Tree rebalancing in optimal time and space. Commun. ACM **29**(9), 902–908 (1986)
30. Vasconcelos, P.B., Hammond, K.: Inferring cost equations for recursive, polymorphic and higher-order functional programs. In: Trinder, P., Michaelson, G.J., Peña, R. (eds.) IFL 2003. LNCS, vol. 3145, pp. 86–101. Springer, Heidelberg (2004). https://doi.org/10.1007/978-3-540-27861-0_6
31. Wegbreit, B.: Mechanical program analysis. Commun. ACM **18**(9), 528–539 (1975)
32. Wenzel, M.: Type classes and overloading in higher-order logic. In: Gunter, E.L., Felty, A. (eds.) TPHOLs 1997. LNCS, vol. 1275, pp. 307–322. Springer, Heidelberg (1997). https://doi.org/10.1007/BFb0028402

Safety and Liveness of MCS
Lock—Layer by Layer

Jieung Kim[✉], Vilhelm Sjöberg, Ronghui Gu, and Zhong Shao

Yale University, New Haven, USA
{jieung.kim,vilhelm.sjoberg,ronghui.gu,zhong.shao}@yale.edu

Abstract. The MCS Lock, a small but complex piece of low-level software, is a standard algorithm for providing inter-CPU locks with FIFO ordering guarantee and scalability. It is an interesting target for verification—short and subtle, involving both liveness and safety properties. We implemented and verified the MCS Lock algorithm as part of the CertiKOS kernel [8], showing that the C/assembly implementation *contextually refines* atomic specifications of the acquire and release lock methods. Our development follows the methodology of *certified concurrent abstraction layers* [7,9]. By splitting the proof into layers, we can modularize it into separate parts for the low-level machine model, data abstraction, and reasoning about concurrent interleavings. This separation of concerns makes the layered methodology suitable for verified programming in the large, and our MCS Lock can be composed with other shared objects in CertiKOS kernel.

1 Introduction

The MCS algorithm for scalable fair inter-CPU mutex locks makes for an interesting case study in program verification. Although the program is short, the proof is challenging. First, the implementation of a lock algorithm can not itself use locks, so it has to rely solely on atomic memory instructions and be robust against any possible interleavings between CPUs. This is the most challenging type of concurrency, so-called lock-free programming. Second, unlike algorithms which only promise mutual exclusion, the MCS algorithm also aims for fairness among CPUs. To check that it got it right, our correctness theorem needs to guarantee not only mutual exclusion (a safety property) but also bounded waiting time (a liveness property).

Previous work [19,22] has studied the correctness of the algorithm itself, but those verification efforts did not produce executable code, and did not explore how to integrate the proof of the algorithm into a larger system. We have created a fully verified implementation and added it as part of the CertiKOS kernel [8], which consists of 6500 lines of C and assembly implementation and 135K lines of Coq proofs.

In order to manage such a large verification effort, the CertiKOS team developed a methodology known as *certified (concurrent) abstraction layers*, as well

© Springer International Publishing AG 2017
B.-Y.E. Chang (Ed.): APLAS 2017, LNCS 10695, pp. 273–297, 2017.
https://doi.org/10.1007/978-3-319-71237-6_14

as a set of libraries and theorems to support it. Previous papers [7,9] described this framework, but many readers found them dense and hard to follow because they immediately present the formalism at its most abstract and general. This paper aims to be a complement: by zooming in on the implementation of one small part of the kernel (the MCS Lock module), we illustrate what it is like to *use* the framework, how to write specifications in the "layers" style, and what the corresponding proof obligations are. We hope this paper will be an easier entry point for understanding our verification framework.

As we will see, CertiKOS-style verification has several distinctive features which stem from the requirements of a large kernel. First, it is suitable for **dealing with low-level code**. To make the proofs tractable we mainly work at the C level (relying on the CompCert verified compiler [17]), but sometimes we need to go lower. For example the MCS algorithm needs to use atomic CPU instructions (*fetch-and-store* and *compare-and-swap*), so we need a way to mix C and assembly code. At the same time, C itself is too low-level to conveniently reason about, so we need **data abstraction** to hide the details about representation in memory.

Second, in order to handle large developments we need **separation of responsibilities**. In a small proof of an algorithm in isolation, you can state the specification as a single pre- and post-condition which specifies the shape and ownership of the data structure, the invariants (e.g. mutual exclusion), the liveness conditions, and even the behavior of the lock's client code (the critical section code). But such a proof is not modular and not re-usable. In our development, these are done as separate refinement steps, in separate modules with explicit interfaces, and can even be the responsibility of different software developers.

Finally, the layers approach is **general purpose**, in the sense that the same semantic framework can be used for proving all kinds of properties. The model of program execution exposed to the programmer is simple, mostly the same as for sequential code and with a notion of logs of events to model concurrency. Unlike working in a special-purpose program logic, we did not have to add any features to show a liveness property, because we can directly reason in Coq about **how long** an execution will take.

In the remaining parts of the paper, we first explain the C code that we will be verifying (Sect. 2). Then in the bulk of the paper, we explain our proof strategy by going through each abstraction layer in turn, concluding with the safety and starvation freedom properties (Sect. 4). Finally we explain how our proofs fit as a part of the larger CertiKOS development (Sect. 5) and discuss related and future work (Sect. 6). Our development makes several contributions:

- It provides a concrete example of CertiKOS-style verification; in particular we can see how to customize the machine model (Sect. 4.1) and how to split the verification effort into CPU-local reasoning (Sects. 3.1 and 4.2).
- We show a way to prove that an atomic specification refines a concurrent implementation, while still using downward rather than upward simulations.

The trick is to provide a *function* from low-level to high-level logs of events (Sects. 4.5 and 4.6).

– We propose a new way to specify the desired—atomic—behavior of the lock/unlock methods. To ensure liveness, the specification of the lock method itself includes a promise to later call unlock; we do this using a bounding counter (Sect. 4.5).

– And of course, we provide the first implementation of the MCS algorithm that has been both rigorously verified (with a mechanized proof) and at the same time realized (as part of a running kernel).

2   The MCS Algorithm

The MCS algorithm [21] is a list-based queuing lock, which provides a *fair* and *scalable* mutex mechanism for multi-CPU computers. Fairness means that CPUs that compete for the lock are guaranteed to receive it in the same order as they asked for it (FIFO order). With an unfair lock, CPUs that try to take the lock can get nondeterministically passed over (even a million times in a row [3]) creating unpredictable latency.

Fairness is also important to verification, because without it there is the possibility that one particular CPU is continuously passed over so it loops forever—this is infinitely improbable, but not impossible. So unless the lock guarantees fairness, there is no way to prove a termination-sensitive refinement between the implementation and a simple (terminating) specification. With a non-fair lock, we would have to settle for either an ugly specification that allowed non-termination, or for a weaker notion of correctness such as termination-insensitive refinement.

The data structure of an MCS Lock (Fig. 1) has one global field pointing to the last node of the queue structure, and per-CPU nodes forming each node in the queue. This is similar to an ordinary queue data structure. If the queue is empty, we set last to the value TOTAL_CPU, which acts as a null value (we could also have used e.g. −1). The queue is used to order the waiting CPUs, in order to ensure that lock acquisition is FIFO. The structs also include padding to take up a full cache lines and avoid false sharing. Each node is owned by one particular CPU (the array is indexed by CPU id). This is what makes the lock scalable: a CPU looping waiting for the lock will only read its own busy flag, so there is no cache-line bouncing. Simpler lock algorithms make all the CPUs read the same memory location, which does not scale past 10–40 CPUs [1].

Figure 1 shows the code for the acquire lock and release lock operations. The acquire lock function uses an atomic *fetch-and-store* expression to *fetch* the current last value and *store* its CPU-id as the last value of the lock in a single action (line 6). Then, if the previous last value was TOTAL_CPU, the CPU can directly acquire the lock and enter the critical section (line 7). If the previous last value was not TOTAL_CPU, it means that some other CPUs are in the critical section or in the queue waiting to enter it (line 9 to line 10). In this case, the current CPU will wait until the previous node in the queue sets the current CPU's busy flag as FREE during the lock release.

```
1  typedef struct _mcs_node{          6  typedef struct _mcs_lock{
2    uint next;                        7    uint last;
3    uint busy;                        8    uint _lock_padding[15];
4    uint _node_padding[14];           9    mcs_node ndpool[TOTAL_CPU];
5  }mcs_node;                         10  }mcs_lock;
```

```
1  void mcs_acquire(uint lk_id){      11  }
2    uint cpuid, prev;                12  void mcs_release(uint lk_id){
3    cpuid = get_CPU_ID();            13    uint cpuid, nid;
4    LK[lk_id].ndpool[cpuid].busy = BUSY;  14    cpuid = get_CPU_ID();
5    LK[lk_id].ndpool[cpuid].next =   15    if(CAS(&(LK[lk_id].last),cpuid,
       TOTAL_CPU;                             TOTAL_CPU) return;
6    prev = FAS(&(LK[lk_id].last),cpuid);  16    while (LK[lk_id].ndpool[cpuid].next==
7    if(prev == TOTAL_CPU) return;            TOTAL_CPU);
8    LK[lk_id].ndpool[prev].next = cpuid;  17    nid = LK[lk_id].ndpool[cpuid].next;
9    while(LK[lk_id].ndpool[cpuid].busy==  18    LK[lk_id].ndpool[nid].busy = FREE;
       BUSY);                         19    return;
10   return;                          20  }
```

Fig. 1. Data structure and the implementation of MCS Lock (in C).

Release lock also has two execution paths, based on the result of an atomic operation, *compare-and-swap* (line 15). The CAS operation succeeds, immediately releasing the lock, if the current CPU is the only one in the queue. If the CAS fails, this implies that some other CPU has already performed the *fetch-and-store* operation (line 6). Thus, the current CPU busy waits until that other CPU sets the next field (line 8), and then passes the lock to the head of the waiting queue by assigning busy.

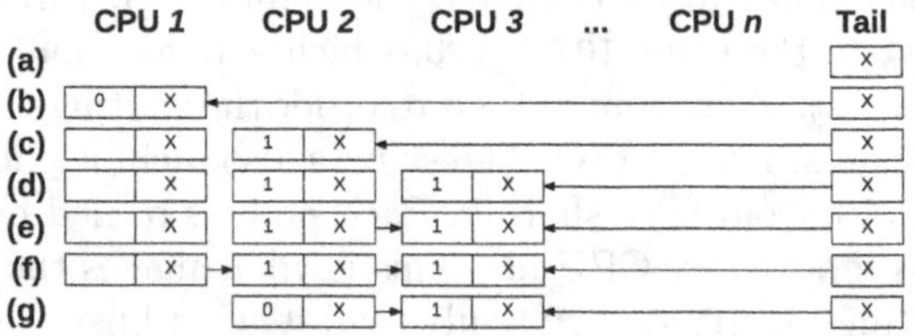

Fig. 2. A possible execution sequence for an MCS Lock.

Figure 2 illustrates a possible sequence of states taken by the algorithm. At the beginning (a), the lock is free, and CPU 1 can take it in a single atomic FAS operation (b). Since CPU 1 did not have to wait for the lock, it does not need to update its *next*-pointer. After that, CPUs 2 and 3 each try to take the lock ((c) and (d)). The last value will be updated correctly thanks to the property of the atomic expression. However, there can be some delay in-between a CPU updating the *tail* pointer, and adjusting the *next*-pointer of the previous node in the queue; as this example illustrates, that means although there are three nodes which logically makes up the queue of waiting CPUs, any subset of the next-pointers may be unset. At (e), although CPU 1 wants to release the lock, the CAS call will return false (because tail is 3, not 1). In this case, CPU 1 has to wait in a busy-loop until CPU 2 has set its *next*-pointer (f). After that, the CPU 1 can set the busy flag to FREE for the next node in the queue, CPU 2's node, which releases the lock (g).

Because the algorithm is fair, it satisfies a *liveness* property: "Suppose all clients of the lock are well-behaved, i.e. whenever they acquire a lock they release it again after some finite time, and suppose the scheduling of operations from different CPUs is fair. Then whenever mcs_acquire or mcs_release are called they will succeed within some finite time." A big part of our formal development is devoted to stating and proving this.

3 Abstraction Layers

The most distinctive thing about CertiKOS-style verification is the notion of *abstraction layers* [7]. Of course, any large-scale programming or verification project uses layers of abstraction, but typically these are merely an informal organization that the programmer has in mind when writing the program. In CertiKOS, we formalize layers as objects defined in Coq, these layers are treated as first-class objects, and we use the framework to vertically compose them. We split the MCS Lock verification into five layers, each building on the interface exposed by the layer below.

Our notion of a "layer interface" is a particular style of state machine where the transitions correspond to function calls, while a "layer" in our development is a proof of refinement between interfaces. More formally, an *abstraction layer* is a tuple (L_1, M, L_2), together with a refinement proof showing that the code M, when run on top of a system specified by the interface L_1, faithfully implements the interface L_2. Then another layer (L_2, M', L_3) can run on top of the first one. Functions in M' can call functions in M, but we only need to look at the specification L_2 to prove them correct.

The code M is a set of functions written in C or assembly, and the entire stack of layers can be compiled to executable code using a modified version of CompCert called CompCertX [7]. It is also possible to have a layer with no code at all. Such a "pure refinement" layer represents a proof that the interfaces L_1 and L_2 are equivalent. The last two layers in our development are pure refinements.

Each layer interface L is a pair $L = (A, P)$, where A is Coq data type (usually a record type) which we call the *abstract state type*, and P is a set of named *primitive specifications* which describe the behavior of C/assembly functions. Each primitive specification $\sigma \in P$ is written as a Coq function of type $\sigma : (val^* \times mem \times A) \to \mathsf{option}\ (val \times mem \times A)$. The types val and mem are borrowed from CompCert's operational semantics for C; val and val^* are the type of C values and lists of values (for the function return value and arguments), and mem is the type of C memory states.

The idea is that a pair $(m, d) : mem \times A$ represents the state of the computer. A typical refinement proof for a layer $((A_1, P_1), M, (A_2, P_2))$ will give a relation R saying that the fields in A_2 represent certain objects stored in memory. Then the high-level specifications in P_2 can refer to the abstract value d when specifications in P_1 had to talk about the memory state m. In particular, in Sect. 4.1 we will define a layer which proves a relation between the array LK (see Fig. 1) and an abstract state. The specifications in all layers about it never need to mention memory again, so they avoid all the side conditions to do with C memory accesses.

3.1 Events, Logs, and Concurrent Contexts

In order to handle concurrent programs, the verification framework imposes some structure on the specifications [9]. Each record type A must include at least a *log of events* (written l) and a *concurrent context* (written ε, further explained in Sect. 4.2). For almost all of the MCS Lock development, these are the only two fields that matter. Instead of representing the state of shared memory by an arbitrary type A, it will be represented using the log.

```
1  Inductive TicketOracleEvent :=
2    // Events for MCS-lock primitives
3    | SWAP_TAIL (bound: nat) (IS_CPU_NUM: bool) | CAS_TAIL (success : bool)
4    | GET_NEXT | SET_NEXT (old_tail: Z) | GET_BUSY (busy : bool) | SET_BUSY
5    // Events for the high-level queue-lock
6    | WAIT_LOCK (n: nat) | REL_LOCK.
7
8  Inductive SharedMemEvent := ...
```

Fig. 3. Event set for MCS Lock

An *event* is any action which has observable consequences for other CPUs. Each specification must define events for all the points in the program where it reads or writes to shared memory (but not for accesses to thread-local memory). The *log* is a list of events, representing all actions that have happened in the computer since it began running. Actions from different CPUs are interleaved in the list. When we write a specification we can chose the set of events, as long as it is fine-grained enough to capture all scheduling interleavings that may happen. Figure 3 shows the event definition used to model lock acquire and release. They correspond to the part of the MCS lock source code in Fig. 1 acquiring/releasing the lock after we show starvation freedom.

Because all CPUs see a single linear log, this model assumes that the machine is sequentially consistent. Even with this assumption, verifying the MCS algorithm is not easy (the other proofs we are aware of assume sequential consistency too), so we leave weak memory models to future work.

The first six events correspond to places where the C code reads or writes to memory, e.g. the `SWAP_TAIL bound success` event is for the operations from line 4 to 6 in Fig. 1. The events carry enough data that you can reconstruct what the state of the memory was, e.g. the second argument `IS_CPU_NUM` indicates whether the previous "last" value of MCS lock was the "`TOTAL_CPU`" value. However, there is also one non-obvious novel idea here: the first argument is the *bound number*. This plays a key role in our development. Every client that invokes `mcs_acquire` has to promise a bound for the critical section. This number does not influence the compiled code in any way, but the *specification* says that it is invalid to hold the critical section for longer than that. For a thread waiting for a lock, its wait time can be estimated based on other threads' bound number. For the lock holder, it has to guarantee to exit the critical section within its own bound. Thus, by locally showing that each thread follows this protocol, we can derive the liveness property for the whole system. (To be precise, the bound number is a limit on the number of events that can get appended to the log, see the counter `c1` in Sect. 4.4. Every CPU adds at least one event every time it "does something", e.g. each loop iteration in `mcs_release` appends a GET_NEXT event, so as we will see in Sect. 4.5 this suffices to give a bound of the number of loop iterations in the lock acquire function. In the following we often speak of "number of operations", which does not mean single CPU instructions, but instead the operations represented by particular events.)

Those six events are used to show the functional correctness of an MCS Lock. However, for clients that use the MCS Lock to build shared objects they expose too much implementation details. In Sect. 4.5 we will prove linearizability and starvation freedom, to replace them with just two events, `WAIT_LOCK` and `REL_LOCK`.

In addition to the above eight events, which are generated by the lock acquire and release functions, the clients of the lock will also generate events while they are in the critical section. Mutex locks in CertiKOS are used to protect blocks of shared memory, so we call the events generated by the client code **shared memory events**. The final specification we prove will entail that a shared memory event from CPU i can only happen in the interval between a lock acquire event for i and a lock release event for i, which is how we express the mutual exclusion property.

4   Verification—Layer by Layer

We build five layers, starting from a base layer which represents the machine model that our compiled code will run on.[1] Figure 4 shows the overall structure of our development. For simplicity the figure only includes lock primitives, and not primitives passed through from below. The arrows show dependencies between adjacent layers, for example the definition of `wait_lock` in `MMCSLockOp` uses three primitives (`mcs_swap_tail`, `mcs_set_next`, and `mcs_get_busy`) from the `MMCSLockAbsIntro` layer.

---

[1] See the long version of this paper [15] for some additional details in this section.

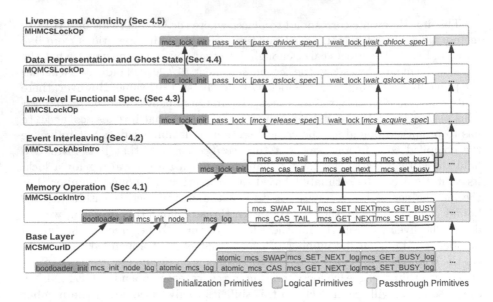

Fig. 4. MCS Lock layers

The layers `MCSMCurID` through `MMCSLockAbsIntro` introduces getter and set-ter functions for accessing memory (Sects. 4.1 and 4.2). These layers also contain logical primitives which record events to the log; we are in effect manually imple-menting a model of concurrent execution by extending a sequential operational semantics for C.

The layer `MMCSLockOp` contains the C code from Fig. 1. This layer proves low-level functional correctness, i.e. it reasons about the C code and abstracts away details about memory accesses, integer overflows, etc., to expose an equivalent specification written as a Coq function (Sect. 4.3).

The two top layers, `MQCSLockOp` and `MHMCSLockOp`, do not introduce any new primitives. They simplify the specifications of the release- and acquire lock func-tions (`pass_lock` and `wait_lock`), i.e. each layer ascribes a different specification (with a different log replay function and a set of events) to the same C function. Those specification names are notated inside the square bracket in Fig. 4.

The layer `MQMCSLockOp` adds ghost state, keeping track of a queue of waiting CPUs (Sect. 4.4). This queue is key to the liveness proof but is not explicitly represented in the C implementation. The top layer `MHMCSLockOp` proves starva-tion freedom and liveness (Sect. 4.5). This lets us ascribe atomic specifications where taking or releasing a lock generates just a single event to the log.

4.1 Memory Operations Layers

Although we glossed over this in Fig. 1, our actual C implementations of `msc_acquire` and `msc_release` do not access memory directly. Instead, they call a collection of helper functions with names like mcs_set_next. The lowest two layers in our proofs are devoted to implementing these helper functions.

We first describe the first and the lowest tuple in our proofs in Fig. 4, (MCSMCurID, M, MMCSLockIntro). All primitives defined in MCSMCurID are part of the trusted computing base, and correspond to empty functions in our compiled code. Eight of the primitives in MCSMCurID are closely related to the MCS Lock verification:

{atomic_mcs_log, atomic_mcs_SWAP, atomic_mcs_CAS, mcs_init_node_log,
mcs_GET_NEXT_log, mcs_SET_NEXT_log, mcs_GET_BUSY_log, mcs_SET_BUSY_log}

Two primitives, atomic_mcs_SWAP and atomic_mcs_CAS are for the two atomic instructions *fetch-and-store* and *compare-and-swap*, and will be further discussed below. The other six are used to update the log. As we noted in Sect. 3.1, the log is part of the abstract state. Ordinary assembly instructions only modify physical memory, not abstract state, so in order for programs to be able to append events to the log we include these six primitives in MCSMCurID. For example, the specification of mcs_SET_NEXT_log will update the log by adding one (SET_NEXT,prev_id) event. In the compiled code, these primitives appear as empty functions that do nothing, they are only used to modify the logical state.

The code M in the layer contains the functions which actually modifies the memory in the way the event announces. Each function in M calls the corresponding primitive from MCSMCurID inside the function to add the event to the log. For example, mcs_SET_NEXT, one function in M, writes to next and also calls the empty function mcs_SET_NEXT_log:

```
1 void mcs_SET_NEXT(uint lk_id, uint cpuid, uint pv_id) {
2    mcs_SET_NEXT_log(lk_id, cpuid, pv_id);
3    (LK[lk_id].ndpool[pv_id]).next = cpuid; }
```

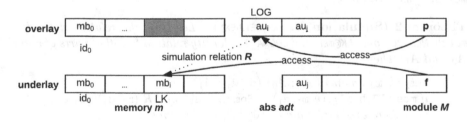

Fig. 5. The structure of the memory operations layer

The interface MMCSLockIntro contains the high level specification for each function defined in M. The high level specifications work on the log instead of the exact memory slot LK. Therefore, after proving the *refinement* between the memory (LK in Fig. 5) and the abstract state (*log* in Fig. 5), we only need to care about the abstract state.

For the refinement proof, we need two more ingredients. The first one is a *log replay function*. A log is merely a list of events, but what specifications need to know is what the state of the system will look like after those events have executed, and a replay function computes that. Different layers may define different replay functions in order to interpret the same log in a way that suits their proofs. In MMCSLockIntro, we define CalMCSLock with the type "MultiLog -> option MCSLock", where the definition of MCSLock is "MCSLOCK (tail: Z) (lock_array: ZMap.t (bool * Z))". The return type of this log replay function closely corresponds to C data structures, which makes it easy to prove the refinement. (ZMap is a finite map from Z to bool*Z.) The second ingredient is a relation R which shows the relationship between the concrete memory in underlay MCSMCurID and the abstract state in overlay MMCSLockIntro. As a part of R, we define match_MCSLOCK as follows:

Definition 1 (match_MCSLOCK). *Suppose that 'loc' is among the proper field accessors for the MCS Lock (i.e. 'last', 'ndpool[i].next', or 'ndpool[i].busy' when '$0 \leq i <$ TOTAL_CPU'). And, assuming that l is a shared log. Then define*

$$match\_MCSLOCK \ (l\text{: } Log) \ (b\text{: } block) \ loc$$
iff $(\exists \ val, \ Mem.load \ Mint32 \ m \ b \ loc = Some(val) \ \wedge \ Mem.valid\_access \ m \ b \ loc$
$\wedge \ (CalMCSLock(l) = Some(mcsval) \ \text{-> } loc_a@mcsval = val))$

when '$loc_a@mcsval$' represents the corresponding value to the 'loc_a' in the 'mcsval' and 'loc_a' corresponds to the value of 'loc'.

Intuitively, the definition says that the value that CalMCSLock calculates from the log always corresponds to the value in the memory with the same identifiers. The memory access functions Mem.load and Mem.valid_access are from CompCert's operational semantics for C. Using the definition, we prove one theorem for each primitive, which shows that the memory refines the shared log. E.g., for mcs_SET_NEXT we prove:

Theorem 2 (Simulation for mcs_SET_NEXT). *Let R be the relation defined as* match_MCSLOCK *over* LK@mem *and* LOG@A_1, *identity relation for other parts of mem, A_0 and A_1. Then*

$\forall (m_1 \ m_1' \ m_0 : mem) \ (d_0 \ : A_0) \ (d_1 \ d_1' : A_1),$
if $mcs\_SET\_NEXT_{L_1}(v, m_1, d_1) = Some(m_1', d_1') \ and \ R \ (m_1, d_1) \ (m_0, d_0),$
then there exists $(m_0' : mem) \ (d_0' : A_0), \ such \ that$
$mcs\_SET\_NEXT_{L_0}(v, m_0, d_0) = Some(m_0', d_0') \ and \ R \ (m_1', d_1') \ (m_0', d_0').$

One interesting variation is the semantics for fetch-and-store and compare-and-swap. These instructions are not formalized in the x86 assembly semantics we use, so we cannot prove that replay function is correctly defined. Instead we modify the last ("pretty-printing") phase of the compiler so that these primitive calls map to assembly instructions, and one has to trust that they match the specification.

4.2 Event Interleaving Layer

After abstracting memory accesses into the operation on the log, we then need to model possible interleaving among multiple CPUs. In our approach, this is done through a new layer which adds *context queries*.

The concurrent context ε (sometimes called the "oracle") is a function of the CPU-id and the log which has the type ε : Z -> list event -> list event. It is one component of the abstract state, and it represents *all the other CPUs*, from the perspective of code running on the current CPU. Any time a program does an operation which reads or writes shared memory, it should first query ε by giving it the current log. The oracle will reply with a list of events that other CPUs have generated since then, and we update the log by appending those new events to it.

Primitive specifications are provided read-only access to a context ε by the verification framework, and the framework also guarantees that two properties are true of ε: (1) the returned partial log from the oracle query does not contain any events generated by the given CPU-id; and (2) if we query the oracle with the well-formed shared log, the updated log after the oracle query will be well-formed.

Similar to Sect. 4.1, we provide primitives in L_0 which query ε and extend the log. Then in this second layer, we can model abstract operations with interleaving. For example, mcs_SET_NEXT can be re-written as

```
1  void mcs_set_next(uint lk_id, uint cpuid, uint pv_id){
2      mcs_log(lk_id, cpuid);
3      mcs_SET_NEXT(lk_id, cpuid, pv_id); }
```

by using the logical primitive which corresponds to the oracle query (The function mcs_log refines the semantics of atomic_mcs_log in the lowest layer by the match_MCSLOCK relation). To model the interleaving, all the setter and getter functions defined in Sect. 4.1 should be combined with the oracle query.

Trust in the Machine Model. Some of the design decisions in the memory access layers have to be trusted, so the division between machine model and implementation is unfortunately slightly blurred. Ideally, we would have a generic machine model as proposed by Gu et al. [8], where memory is partitioned into thread-local memories (no events), lock-protected memory (accesses generate PUSH/PULL events), and atomic memory (each access generates one READ/ WRITE/SWAP/etc. event). However, our starting point is the CompCert x86 semantics, which was designed for single-threaded programs, and does not come with a log, so we add a log and memory access primitives ourselves. But because the spinlock module is the only code in the OS that uses atomic memory, we do not add a generic operation called read_word etc. Instead we take a short-cut and specify the particular 6 memory accesses that the lock code uses: mcs_get_next5 etc. For these procedures to correctly express the intended semantics, there are two trusted parts we must take care to get right. First, each access to non-thread-local memory must generate an event, so we must not forget the call to mcs_SET_NEXT_log. Second, to account for interleavings between CPUs (and not accidentally assume that consecutive operations execute atomically) we must not forget the call to mcs_log after each access.

4.3   Low-Level Functional Specification

Using the primitives that we have defined in lower layers, we prove the correctness of lock acquire, mcs_acquire, and release, mcs_release. The target code in this layer is identical to the code in Fig. 1 except two aspects. First, we replaced all operations on memory with the getters and setters described in Sect. 4.2. Second, mcs_acquire has one more argument, which is the bound number for the client code of the lock.

Since the functions defined in Sect. 4.2 already abstract interleaving of multiple CPUs, the proofs in this layers work just like sequential code verification. We find out the machine state after the function call by applying the C operational semantics to our function implementation, and check that it is equal to the desired state defined in our specification.

However, writing the specifications for these functions is slightly subtle, because they contain while-loops without any obviously decreasing numbers. Since our specifications are Coq functions we need to model this by structural recursion, in some way that later will let us show the loop is terminating. So to define the semantics of mcs_wait_lock, we define an auxiliary function CalMCS_AcqWait which describes the behavior of the first n iterations of the loop: each iteration queries the environment context ε, replays the log to see if busy is now false, and appends a GET_BUSY event. If we do not succeed within n iterations the function is undefined (Coq None). Then, in the part of the specification for the acquire lock function (CalMCS_AcqWait) where we need to talk about the while loop, we say that it loops for some "sufficiently large" number of iterations CalWaitLockTime tq.

```
1      ...   match CalMCS_AcqWait (CalWaitLockTime tq) ...  with
2            | Some ... => Some ....
3            | _ => None
4          end ...
```

The function CalWaitLockTime computes a suitable number of loop iterations based on tq, the time-bounds which each of the queuing CPUs promised to respect. We will show how it is defined in Sect. 4.5. However, in *this part* of the proof, the definition doesn't matter. Computations where n reaches 0 are considered crashing, and our ultimate theorem is about safe programs, so when proving that the C code matches the specification we only need to consider cases when CalMCS_AcqWait returned (Some l). It is easy to show in a downward simulation that the C loop can match any such finite run, since the C loop can run any number of times.

4.4   Data Representation and Ghost State

From here on, we never have to think about C programs again. All the subsequent reasoning is done on Coq functions manipulating ordinary Coq data types, such as lists, finite maps, and unbounded integers. Verifying functional programs written in Coq's Gallina is exactly the situation Coq was designed to deal with. However, the data computed by the replay function in the previous layer still corresponds exactly to the array-of-structs that represents the state of the lock in memory. In particular, the intuitive reason that the algorithm is fair is that each CPU has to wait in a queue, but this conceptual queue is not identical with the linked-list in memory, because the next-pointers may not be set.

In order to keep the data-representation and liveness concerns separate, we introduce an intermediate layer, which keeps the same sequence of operations and same log of events, but manipulates an *abstracted data representation*. We provide a different replay function with the type QS_CalLock: Multi_Log -> option (nat * nat * head_status * list Z * ZSet.t * list nat). The tuple returned by this replay function provides the information we need to prove liveness. The meaning of a tuple (c1, c2, b, q, slow, t) is as follows: c1 and c2 are upper bounds on how many more operations the CPU which currently holds the lock will generate as part of the critical section and of releasing the lock, respectively. They are purely logical ghost state but can be deduced from the complete history of events in the system. b is either LHOLD or LFREE, the lock status of the head of the queue. q is the list of the CPUs currently waiting for the lock, and t is the list of bound numbers that corresponds to each element in q. slow is a finite set which represents the subset of CPUs in q that have not yet executed their *set next* operation. Our liveness proof is based on the fact that each CPU only needs to wait for CPUs that are ahead of it in q.

Invariant. The replay function plays two different roles. When it returns Some v, for some tuple v, it describes what the current state of the system is, which lets us write the specifications for the primitives. At the same time, the cases where the function is defined to return None are also important, because this can be read as a description of events that are *not* possible. For example, from inspecting the program, we know that each CPU will create exactly one SET_NEXT event before it starts generating GET_BUSY events, and this fact will be needed when doing the proofs in the later layers (Sect. 4.5). By taking advantage of the side conditions in the replay function, we can express all the invariants about the log in a single statement, "the replay function is defined":

$$\exists\ \text{c1 c2 b q s t. QS\_CalLock(l) = Some(c1, c2, b, q, s, t)}$$

To show that the ghost layer refines the previous layer, we show a one-step forward-downward refinement: if the method from the higher layer returns, then method in the lower layer returns a related value. For this particular layer the log doesn't change, so the relation in the refinement is just equality, and the programmer just has to show that the lower-level methods are at least as defined and that they return equal results for equal arguments.

4.5   Liveness and Atomicity

The specification in the previous section is still too low-level and complex to be usable by client code in the rest of the system. First, the specification of the mcs_acquire and mcs_release primitives contain loops, with complicated bounds on the number of iterations, which clients certainly will not want to reason directly about. More importantly, since the specifications generate multiple events, clients would have to show all interleavings generate equivalent results.

To solve this we propose a basic design pattern: build a new layer with *atomic specifications*, i.e. each primitive is specified to generate a single event. For an atomic layer there is a therefore a one-to-one mapping between events and primitives, and the global log can be seen as a record of which primitives were invoked in which order. Thus, the refinement proof which ascribes an atomic specification proves once and for all that overlapping and interleaved primitive invocations give correct results. In this layer, the specifications only use three kinds of events: taking the lock (WAIT_LOCK n), releasing it (PASS_LOCK), and modifications of the shared memory that the lock protects (TSHARED _).

Figure 6 shows the final specification for the wait primitive. We show this one in full detail, with no elisions, because this is the interface that clients use. First, the specification for the lock acquire function itself (mcs_wait_hlock_spec) takes the function arguments bound, index, ofs, and maps an abstract state (RData) to another. When writing this specification we chose to use two components in the abstract state, the log (multi_log) and also a field (lock) which records for each numbered lock if it is free (LockFalse) or owned by a CPU (LockOwn). The lock field is not very important, because the same information can also be computed from the log, but exposing it directly to clients is sometimes more convenient.

The specification returns None in some cases, and it is the responsibility of the client to ensure that does not happen. So clients must ensure that: the CPU is in kernel/host mode (for the memory accesses to work); the index/offset (used to compute the lock id) are in range; the CPU did not already hold the lock (LockFalse); and the log is well-formed (H_CalLock l' is defined, which will always be the case if H_CalLock l is defined). When all these preconditions are satisfied, the specification queries the context once, and appends a single new WAIT_LOCK event to the log. Figure 6 also shows the replay function H_CalLock. It has a much simpler type than QS_CalLock in the previous layer, because we have abstracted the internal state of the lock to just whether it is free (LEMPTY), held (LHOLD), and if taken, the CPU id (Some i) of the holder of the lock. Unlike the three bound numbers in the previous layer, here we omit the numbers for the internal lock operations and only keep the bound self_c for the number of events generated during the critical section. Again, it's the client's responsibility to avoid the cases when H_CalLock returns None. In particular, it is only allowed to release the lock or to generate memory events if it already holds the lock (zeq i i0), and each memory event decrements the counter, which must not reach zero. The client calling wait_lock specifies the initial value n of the counter, promising to take at most n actions within the critical section.

In the rest of the section, we show how to prove that the function does in fact satisfy this high-level atomic specification. Unlike the previous layers we considered, in this case the log in the upper layer differs from the one in the lower layer. For example, when a CPU takes the lock, the log in the upper layer

```
1  Fixpoint H_CalLock (l: MultiLog) : option (nat * head_status * option Z) :=
2    match l with
3      | nil => Some (0, LEMPTY, None)
4      | (TEVENT i e) :: l' =>
5        match H_CalLock l' with
6          | Some (S self_c', LHOLD, Some i0) =>
7            match zeq i i0, e with
8              | left _, TTICKET REL_LOCK => Some (0, LEMPTY, None)
9              | left _, TSHARED _ => Some (self_c', LHOLD, Some i0)
10             | _, _ => None end
11         | Some (_, LEMPTY, None) =>
12           match e with
13             | TTICKET (WAIT_LOCK n) => Some (n, LHOLD, Some i)
14             | _ => None end
15         | _ => None end end.
```

```
1  Definition mcs_wait_hlock_spec (bound index ofs :Z) (adt: RData) : option RData :=
2    let cpu := CPU_ID adt in
3    match (ikern adt, ihost adt, index2Z index ofs) with
4    | (true, true, Some abid) =>
5      match ZMap.get abid (multi_log adt), ZMap.get abid (lock adt) with
6      | MultiDef l, LockFalse =>
7        let to := ZMap.get abid (multi_oracle adt) in
8        let l1 := (to cpu l) ++ l in
9        let l' := (TEVENT cpu (TTICKET (WAIT_LOCK (Z.to_nat bound)))) :: l1 in
10       match H_CalLock l' with
11       | Some _ =>
12         Some adt {multi_log: ZMap.set abid (MultiDef l') (multi_log adt)}
13                  {lock: ZMap.set abid LockOwn (lock adt)}
14       | _ => None end
15     | _, _ => None end
16   | _ => None end.
```

Fig. 6. The final, atomic, specification of the aquire lock function.

just has the one atomic event (WAIT_LOCK n), while the log in the underlay has a flurry of activity (swap the tail pointer, set the next-pointer, repeatedly query the busy-flag). Because the log represents shared data, we can not use any arbitrary refinement relation R for it. Eventually the framework needs to combine the local per-CPU simulations to show that there exists a consistent global log for the entire system [9], so we need to know that all the CPUs produced equal logs. Our solution is to require the simulation relation R to be a function f. In other words, when proving the simulation, we find a function f for the logs, such that $f(l_{\text{MQMCSLockOp}}) = l_{\text{MHMCSLockOp}}$.

As for the MCS Lock, we define a function relate_mcs_log from the implementation log to the atomic log. Figure 7 shows by example what it does. It keeps the shared memory events as they are, discards the events that are generated while a CPU wait for the lock, and maps just the event that finally takes or releases the lock into WAIT_LOCK and REL_LCOK.

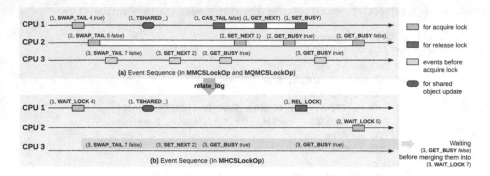

Fig. 7. Log sequence and Log refinement example

We then prove a one-step refinement theorem from the atomic specification to the implementation, in other words, that if a call to the atomic primitive returns a value, then a call to its implementation also returns with a related log:

Theorem 3 (MCS Wait Lock Exist). *Suppose* $d_{MHMCSLockOp}$ *and* $d_{MQMCSLockOp}$ *satisfy the layer invariants and are related by* relate_mcs_log$(d_{MQMCSLockOp}) = d_{MHMCSLockOp}$. *If* wait_hlock_spec$(d_{MHMCSLockOp}) =$ Some$(d'_{MHMCSLockOp})$, *then there exists some* $d'_{MQMCSLockOp}$ *which is* wait_qslock_spec$(d_{MQMCSLockOp}) = d'_{MQMCSLockOp}$ *and is related with* $d'_{MHMCSLockOp}$ *by* relate_mcs_log$(d'_{MQMCSLockOp}) = d'_{MHMCSLockOp}$.

The proof requires a *fairness assumption*. A CPU cannot take the lock until the previous CPU releases it, and the previous CPU cannot release it if it never gets to run. Specifically, we assume there exists some constant F (for "fairness") such that no CPU that enters the queue has to wait for more than F events until it runs again. The way we phrase this in Coq is quite similar to how the bound numbers c1 and c2 are handled: we define a separate replay function CalBound$_i(l)$ which "counts down" to the next time that CPU i must be scheduled, and add a hypothesis that the count never reaches zero.

We then define a natural-number valued termination measure $M_i($c1,c2, $h,q,s,l)$ This is a bound on how many events the CPU i will have to wait for in a state represented by the log l, and where QS_CalLock(l) = Some(c1,c2,h,q++i::q$_0$,s,t+n::t$_0$). Note that we partition the waiting queue into two parts q and i::q$_0$, where q represents the waiting CPUs that were ahead of i in the queue. The function M has two cases that depend on the head status.

$$M_i(\text{c1,c2,LEMPTY,q,s,l}) = \text{CalBound}_{hd(q)}(l) + (K_1(\Sigma t) + |q\cup s|) \times K_2$$
$$M_i(\text{c1,c2,LHOLD,q,s,l}) = \text{CalBound}_{hd(q)}(l) + \text{BoundValAux} \times K_2$$
$$\text{where BoundValAux} = (\text{c1+c2}+(\Sigma(\text{tl}(t)) \times K_1 + |\text{tl}(q)\cup s|)$$

In short, if the lock is not taken, the bound M is the sum of the maximum time until the first thread in the queue gets scheduled again ($\text{CalBound}_{hd(q)}(l)$), plus a constant times the sum of the number of operations to be done by the CPUs ahead of i in the queue (Σt) and the number of CPUs ahead of i which has yet to execute SET_NEXT operation ($|q \cup s|$). If the lock is currently held, then c1 + c2 is a bound of the number of operations it will do. The definition of M is justified by the following two lemmas. First, we prove that M decreases if CPU i is waiting and some other CPU j executes an event e_j.

Lemma 4 (Decreasing measure for other CPUs). *Assuming that* $QS\_CalLock(l) = Some(c1,c2,h,q_1{+}{+}i{::}q_2,s,t_1{+}{+}c{::}t_2)$, *where* $|q_1| = |t_1|$ *as well as* $QS\_CalLock(e_j{::}l) = Some(c1',c2',h',q',s',t')$ *for some* $j \neq i$ *and* $CalBound(e_j{::}l) > 0$. *Then we can split* $q' = q_1'{+}{+}i{::}q_2'$, *and* $M_i(c1',c2',h',q_1',s',t_1',e_j{::}l) < M_i(c1,c2,h,q_1,s,t_1,l)$.

The second lemma ensures that the waiting loop will eventually terminate (The preconditions that i is somewhere in the waiting queue, and that it has already left the set s, correspond the set-up which wait_lock does before it starts looping).

Lemma 5 (Loop termination). *Let's assume that* $QS\_CalLock(l) = Some(c1,c2,h,q_1{+}{+}i{::}q_2,s,t_1{+}{+}c{::}t_2)$, *where* $|q_1| = |t_1|, with\, i \notin q_1\, and\, i \notin s$. *If* $k > M_i(c1,c2,h,q_1,s,t_1)$, *then there exists* l' *such that* $CalWaitGet(k,i,l) = Some(l')$.

Now, to prove that the loop in mcs_acquire specification is defined, we just have to pick the function CalWaitLockTime so that CalWaitLockTime(t) is greater than M at that point. The rest of the simulation proof for Theorem 3 is straightforward. Except the waiting loop, other operations in the wait lock function are deterministic and finite.

4.6   From Downwards- to Upwards-Simulation

When moving from sequential to concurrent programs we must re-visit some fundamental facts about refinement proofs. Ultimately, the correctness theorem we want to prove is "all behaviors of the machine satisfy the specification". If we model the machine and the specification as two transition systems M and S, then this corresponds to *upwards simulation*: if $S \sim M$ and $M \Longrightarrow^* M'$, then $\exists S'.S' \sim M'$ and $S \Longrightarrow^* S'$, and if M is stuck then S is stuck also. But directly proving an upwards simulation is difficult. You are given a long sequence of low-level steps, and have to somehow reconstruct the high-level steps and high-level ghost state corresponding to it. One of the insights that made the CompCert project possible [18] is that as long as M is deterministic and S is not stuck, it suffices to prove a *downward simulation*: if $S \sim M$ and $S \Longrightarrow S'$, then $\exists M'.S' \sim M'$ and $M \Longrightarrow^* M'$. (The assumption that S is not stuck is standard, it corresponds to only proving refinement for "safe" clients regarding to the specifications.)

Unfortunately, concurrent programs are *not* deterministic: we want to prove that every interleaving of operations from different CPUs in the low-level machine results in correct behavior. So if we had directly modeled the implementation as a nondeterministic transition system, then we would have to work directly with upwards simulations, which would be intractable when reasoning about the low-level details of C programs.

In our approach, all the nondeterminism is isolated to the concurrent context ε. Any possible interleaving of the threads can be modelled by initializing the abstract state with a particular ε_L, and the execution proceeds deterministically from there. Therefore we can still use the Compcert/CertiKOS method of first proving a downward simulation and then concluding the existence of a upward simulation as a corollary.

5   Evaluation

Clients. The verified MCS lock code is used by multiple clients in the CertiKOS system. To be practical the design should require as little extra work as possible compared to verifying non-concurrent programs, both to better match the programmer's mental model, and to allow code-reuse from the earlier, single-processor version of CertiKOS.

```
1 uint palloc (uint cid){
2   ...
3   acquire_lock_AT();
4   ...
5   release_lock_AT();
6   return palloc free index; }
```

```
1 Inductive SharedMemEvent :=
2 | OMEME (l: list Integers.Byte.int)
3 | OATE (a: ATable)
4 | OPALLOCE (b: Z)
5 ...
```

Fig. 8. palloc Example

For this reason, we don't want our machine model to generate an event for every single memory access to shared memory. Instead we use what we call a *push/pull memory model* [8,9]. A CPU that wants to access shared memory first generates a "pull" event, which declares that that CPU now owns a particular block of memory. After it is done it generates a "push" event, which publishes the CPU's local view of memory to the rest of the system. In this way, individual memory reads and writes are treated by the same standard operational semantics as in sequential programs, but the state of the shared memory can still be replayed from the log. The push/pull operations are logical (generate no machine code) but because the replay function is undefined if two different CPUs try to pull at the same time, they force the programmer to prove that programs are well-synchronized and race-free. Like we did for atomic memory operations, we extend the machine model at the lowest layer by adding logical primitives, e.g. release_shared which takes a memory block identifier as an argument and adds a OMEME (l:list Integers.Byte.int) event to the log, where the byte list is a copy of the contents of the shared memory block when the primitive was called.

When we use `acquire/release_shared` we need a lock to make sure that only one CPU pulls, so we begin by defining combined functions `acquire_lock` which takes the lock (with a bound of 10) and then pulls, and `release_lock` which pushes and then releases the lock. The specification is similar to `pass_hlock_spec`, except it appends *two* events.

Similar to Sect. 4.5, logs for different layers can use different types of pull/push events. Figure 8(right) shows the events for the `palloc` function (which uses a lock to protect the page allocation table). The lowest layer in the palloc-verification adds `OMEME` events, while higher layers instead add (`OATE (a: ATable)`) events, where the relation between logs uses the same relation as between raw memory and abstract `ATable` data. Therefore, we write wrapper functions `acquire/release_lock_AT_spec`, where the implementation just calls `acquire/release_lock` with the particular memory block that contains the allocation table, but the specification adds an `OATE` event.

```
1 Definition release_lock_AT_spec adt := ...
2   let l' := TEVENT cpu (TTICKET REL_LOCK)::TEVENT cpu (TSHARED(OATE(AT adt)))::l
3   in match H_CalLock l' with Some _ => Some (adt { ... l' ...}) | None => None ...
1 Function palloc'_spec (n: Z) (adt: RData): option (RData * Z) :=
2   match acquire_lock_AT_spec adt with
3     | Some adt1 => match palloc_aux_spec n adt1 with
4         | Some (adt2, i) =>
5             match release_lock_AT_spec adt2 with
6               | Some adt3 => Some (adt3, i)
7               | _ => None end
8         | _ => None end
9     | _ => None end.
```

Fig. 9. Specification for `palloc`

We can then ascribe a low-level functional specification `palloc'_spec` to the `palloc` function. As shown in Fig. 9, this is decomposed into three parts, the acquire/release lock, and the specification for the critical section. The critical section spec is exactly the same in a sequential program: it does not modify the log, but instead only affects the `AT` field in the abstract data.

Then in a final, pure refinement step, we ascribe a high-level atomic specification `lpalloc_spec` to the `palloc` function. In this layer we no longer have any lock-related events at all, a call to `palloc` appends a single `OPALLOCE` event to the log. This is when we see the proof obligations related to liveness of the locks. Specifically, in order to prove the downwards refinement, we need to show that the call to `palloc'_spec` doesn't return `None`, so we need to show that `H_CalLock l'` is defined, so in particular the bound counter must not hit zero. By expanding out the definitions, we see that `palloc'_spec` takes a log l to `REL_LOCK :: (OATE (AT adt)) :: (TSHARED OPULL) :: (WAIT_LOCK 10) :: l`. The initial bound is 10, and there are two shared memory events, so the count never goes lower than 8. If a function modified more than one memory block there would be additional push- and pull-events, which could be handled by a larger initial bound.

Like all kernel-mode primitives in CertiKOS, the `palloc` function is total: if its preconditions are satisfied it always returns. So when verifying it, we show that all loops inside the critical section terminate. Through the machinery of bound numbers, this guarantee is propagated to the while-loops inside the lock implementation: because all functions terminate, they can know that other CPUs will make progress and add more events to the log, and because of the bound number, they cannot add push/pull events forever. On the other hand, the framework completely abstract away how long time (in microseconds) elapses between any two events in the log.

Code Reuse. The same `acquire/release_lock` specifications can be used for all clients of the lock. The only proofs that need to be done for a given client is the refinement into abstracted primitives like `release_lock_AT_spec` (easy if we already have a sequential proof for the critical section), and the refinement proof for the atomic primitive like `lpalloc_spec` (which is very short). We never need to duplicate the thousands of lines of proof related to the lock algorithm itself.

Using More than One Lock. The layers approach is particularly nice when verifying code that uses more than one lock. To avoid deadlock, all functions must acquire the locks in the same order, and to prove the correctness the ordering must be included in the program invariant. We *could* do such a verification in a single layer, by having a single log with different events for the two locks, with the replay function being undefined if the events are out of order. But the layers approach provides a better way. Once we have ascribed an atomic specification to `palloc`, as above, all higher layers can use it freely without even knowing that the `palloc` implementation involves a lock. For example, some function in a higher layer could acquire a lock, allocate a page, and release the lock; in such an example the order of the layers provides an order on the locks implicitly.

Proof Effort. Among all the proofs, the most challenging are the starvation freedom theorems like Theorem 3, and the functional correctness proofs for `mcs_acquire` and `mcs_release` in Sect. 4.3. The total lines of code for starvation freedom is 2.5k lines, 0.6k lines for specifications, and 1.9k lines for proofs. This is because of the subtlety of those proofs. The starvation freedom theorems require many lemmas to express properties about the algorithm state in terms of replaying the log. E.g., if $QS\_CalLock(l) = Some(c1, c2, b, q, s, t)$ and $q = nil$, then $s = \emptyset$ and $t = nil$. This fact looks trivial in a pen-and-paper proof, but requires multiple lines in the mechanized proof. The total lines of codes for the low-level functional correctness of `mcs_acquire` and `mcs_release` are $3.2\,K$ lines, 0.7k lines for specifications, and 2.5k lines for proofs. It is much bigger than other code correctness proofs for while-loops in CertiKOS, because these loops do not have any explicit decreasing value. While our proofs are completely manual, the layer-based structure should be equally helpful when using proof automation to handle individual lemmas.

As can be seen from these line counts, proofs about concurrent programs have a huge ratio of lines of proof to lines of C code. If we tried to directly verify shared objects that use locks to perform more complex operations, like thread scheduling and inter-process communication, a monolithic proof would become much bigger than the current one, and would be quite unmanageable. The modular lock specification is essential here.

6   Related Work and Conclusions

Verified System Software. CertiKOS is an end-to-end verified concurrent system showing that its assembly code indeed "implements" (contextually simulates) the high-level specification. Other verified systems [10,16,27], are single-threaded, or use a per-core big kernel lock. The Verisoft team used VCC [2] to verify spinlocks in a hypervisor by directly postulating a Hoare logic rather than building on top of an operational semantics for C, and only proved properties about the low-level primitives rather than the full functionality of the hypervisor. By contrast, CertiKOS deals with the problem of formulating a specification in a way that can be used as one layer inside a large stack of proofs. As for CertiKOS itself, while we discussed the "local" verification of a single module, other papers explain how to relate the log and context to a more realistic nondeterministic machine model [8], how to "concurrently link" the per-CPU proofs into a proof about the full system [9], and how this extends to multiple threads per CPU [9].

Fine-Grained Concurrency. The MCS algorithm uses low-level operations like CAS instead of locks. There is much research about how to reason about such programs, more than we have space to discuss here. One key choice is how much to prove. At least all operations should be linearizable [13] (a safety property). Some authors have considered mechanized verification of linearizability (e.g. [4,6]), but on abstract transition system models, not directly on executable code. The original definition of linearizability instrumented programs to record a global history of method-invocation and method-return events. However, that's not a convenient theorem statement when verifying client code. Our formulation is closer to Derrick et al. [4], who prove a simulation to a history of single atomic actions modifying abstract state. Going beyond safety, one also wants to prove a progress property such as wait-freedom [11] or (in our case) starvation-freedom [12].

Liang et al. [20] showed that the linearizability and progress properties [12] for concurrent objects is exactly equivalent to various termination-sensitive versions of the contextual simulation property. Most modern separation-style concurrent logics [5,14,23–26] do not prove the same strong termination-sensitive contextual simulation properties as our work does, so it is unclear how they can be used to prove both the linearizability and starvation-freedom properties of our MCS Lock module. Total-TaDA [24] can be used to prove the total correctness of concurrent programs but it has not been mechanized in any proof assistant and there is no formal proof that its notion of liveness is precisely equivalent to Helihy's notion of linearizability and progress properties for concurrent objects [12]. FCSL [25] attempts to build proofs of concurrent programs in a "layered" way, but it does not address the liveness properties. Many of these program logics [14,26], however, support higher-order functions which our work does not address.

Other Work on the MCS Algorithm. We are aware of two other efforts to apply formal verification methods to the MCS algorithm. Ogata and Futatsugi developed a mechanized proof using the UNITY program logic. [22] They work with an abstract transition system, not executable code. Like us, their correctness proof works by refinement (between a fine-grained and a more atomic spec) but they directly prove backward simulation.

The other MCS Lock verification we know of is by Liang and Feng [19], who define a program logic LiLi to prove liveness and linearizability properties and verify the MCS algorithm as one of their examples. The LiLi proofs are done on paper, so they can omit many "obvious" steps, and they work with a simple while-loop language instead of C. Many of the concepts in our proof are also recognizable in theirs. In their invariant and precondition they use specificational variables ta and tb (like $\mathtt{la}$ in Sect. 4.3), tl and S (like q and s in Sect. 4.4), and their termination measure $f(\mathfrak{G})$ includes the length of tl and the size of S (like M in Sect. 4.5). On the other hand, the fairness constant makes no appearance in $f(\mathfrak{G})$, because fairness assumptions are implicit in their inference rules.

A big difference between our work and LiLi is our emphasis on modularity. Between every two lines of code of a program in LiLi, you need to prove all the different invariants, down to low-level data representation in memory. In our development, these concerns are in different modules which can be completed by different programmers. Similarly, we aim to produce a stand-alone specification of the lock operations. In the LiLi example, the program being verified is an entire "increment" operation, which takes a lock, increments a variable and releases the lock. The pre/post-conditions of the code in the critical section includes the low-level implementation invariants of the lock, and the fact the lock will eventually be released is proved for the "increment" operation as a whole. Our locks are specified using *bound* numbers, so they can be used by many different methods.

Apart from modularity, one can see a more philosophical difference between the CertiKOS approach and program logics such as LiLi. Liang and Feng are constructing a program logic which is tailor-made precisely to reason about liveness properties under fair scheduling. To get a complete mechanized proof for a program in that setting would require mechanizing not only the proof of the program itself, but also the soundness proof for the logic, which is a big undertaking. Other parts of the program will favor other kinds of reasoning, for example many researchers have studied program logics with inference rules for reasoning about code *using* locks. One of the achievements of the CertiKOS style of specification is its flexibility, because the same model—a transition system with data abstraction and a log of events—works throughout the OS kernel. When we encountered a feature that required thinking about liveness and fairness, we were able to do that reasoning without changing the underlying logical framework.

Conclusion and Future Work. Using the "layers" framework by Gu et al. [7] made our MCS lock proofs modular and reusable. It also lets us verify the code from end to end and extract certified executable code. Those proofs are also combined with client code using MCS Locks, which shows they can be used in a large scale system verification without increasing the complexity dramatically. In the future, we are planning to devise generic methods for building oracles, log replay functions, liveness proofs, and so on. We intend to generalize the machine model to handle weak memory models instead of assuming sequential consistency. And we also plan to apply this approach to other concurrent algorithms.

Acknowledgments. We would like to thank our anonymous referees for helpful feedbacks that improved this paper significantly. This research is based on work supported in part by NSF grants 1521523 and 1319671 and DARPA grants FA8750-12-2-0293, FA8750-16-2-0274, and FA8750-15-C-0082. The U.S. Government is authorized to reproduce and distribute reprints for Governmental purposes notwithstanding any copyright notation thereon. The views and conclusions contained herein are those of the authors and should not be interpreted as necessarily representing the official policies or endorsements, either expressed or implied, of DARPA or the U.S. Government.

References

1. Boyd-wickizer, S., Kaashoek, M.F., Morris, R., Zeldovich, N.: Non-scalable locks are dangerous. In: Proceedings of the Ottawa Linux Symposium (OLS 2012) (2012)
2. Cohen, E., Dahlweid, M., Hillebrand, M., Leinenbach, D., Moskal, M., Santen, T., Schulte, W., Tobies, S.: VCC: a practical system for verifying concurrent C. In: Berghofer, S., Nipkow, T., Urban, C., Wenzel, M. (eds.) TPHOLs 2009. LNCS, vol. 5674, pp. 23–42. Springer, Heidelberg (2009). https://doi.org/10.1007/978-3-642-03359-9_2
3. Corbet, J.: Ticket spinlocks, February 2008. https://lwn.net/Articles/267968/
4. Derrick, J., Schellhorn, G., Wehrheim, H.: Mechanically verified proof obligations for linearizability. ACM Trans. Program. Lang. Syst. **33**(1), 1–43 (2011)
5. Dinsdale-Young, T., Dodds, M., Gardner, P., Parkinson, M.J., Vafeiadis, V.: Concurrent abstract predicates. In: D'Hondt, T. (ed.) ECOOP 2010. LNCS, vol. 6183, pp. 504–528. Springer, Heidelberg (2010). https://doi.org/10.1007/978-3-642-14107-2_24
6. Doherty, S., Groves, L., Luchangco, V., Moir, M.: Formal verification of a practical lock-free queue algorithm. In: de Frutos-Escrig, D., Núñez, M. (eds.) FORTE 2004. LNCS, vol. 3235, pp. 97–114. Springer, Heidelberg (2004). https://doi.org/10.1007/978-3-540-30232-2_7
7. Gu, R., Koenig, J., Ramananandro, T., Shao, Z., Wu, X., Weng, S.-C., Zhang, H., Guo, Y.: Deep specifications and certified abstraction layers. In: Proceedings of the 42nd ACM Symposium on Principles of Programming Languages, pp. 595–608 (2015)
8. Gu, R., Shao, Z., Chen, H., Wu, X., Kim, J., Sjoberg, V., Costanzo, D.: Certikos: an extensible architecture for building certified concurrent OS kernels. In: 12th USENIX Symposium on Operating Systems Design and Implementation (OSDI 2016). USENIX Association (2016)

9. Gu, R., Shao, Z., Wu, X., Kim, J., Koenig, J., Ramananandro, T., Sjoberg, V., Chen, H., Costanzo, D.: Language and compiler support for building certified concurrent abstraction layers. Technical report YALEU/DCS/TR-1530, Department of Computer Science, Yale University, New Haven, CT, October 2016
10. Hawblitzel, C., Howell, J., Lorch, J.R., Narayan, A., Parno, B., Zhang, D., Zill, B.: Ironclad apps: end-to-end security via automated full-system verification. In: Proceedings of the 11th USENIX Conference on Operating Systems Design and Implementation, (OSDI 2014) USENIX Association (2014)
11. Herlihy, M.: Wait-free synchronization. ACM Trans. Program. Lang. Syst. **13**(1), 124–149 (1991)
12. Herlihy, M., Shavit, N.: The Art of Multiprocessor Programming. Morgan Kaufmann, Burlington (2008)
13. Herlihy, M.P., Wing, J.M.: Linearizability: a correctness condition for concurrent objects. ACM Trans. Program. Lang. Syst. **12**(3), 463–492 (1990)
14. Jung, R., Swasey, D., Sieczkowski, F., Svendsen, K., Turon, A., Birkedal, L., Dreyer, D.: Iris: monoids and invariants as an orthogonal basis for concurrent reasoning. In: Proceedings 42nd ACM Symposium on Principles of Programming Languages, pp. 637–650 (2015)
15. Kim, J., Sjöberg, V., Gu, R., Shao, Z.: Safety and liveness of MCS lock–layer by layer (long version). Technical report YALEU/DCS/TR-1535, Department of Computer Science, Yale University, New Haven, CT, September 2017
16. Klein, G., Elphinstone, K., Heiser, G., Andronick, J., Cock, D., Derrin, P., Elkaduwe, D., Engelhardt, K., Kolanski, R., Norrish, M., et al.: seL4: formal verification of an OS kernel. In: SOSP 2009: the 22nd ACM SIGOPS Symposium on Operating Systems Principles, pp. 207–220 (2009)
17. Leroy, X.: Formal verification of a realistic compiler. Commun. ACM **52**(7), 107–115 (2009)
18. Leroy, X.: A formally verified compiler back-end. J. Autom. Reason. **43**(4), 363–446 (2009)
19. Liang, H., Feng, X.: A program logic for concurrent objects under fair scheduling. In: Proceedings of the 43rd Annual ACM SIGPLAN-SIGACT Symposium on Principles of Programming Languages, POPL 2016, pp. 385–399. ACM, New York (2016)
20. Liang, H., Hoffmann, J., Feng, X., Shao, Z.: Characterizing progress properties of concurrent objects via contextual refinements. In: D'Argenio, P.R., Melgratti, H. (eds.) CONCUR 2013. LNCS, vol. 8052, pp. 227–241. Springer, Heidelberg (2013). https://doi.org/10.1007/978-3-642-40184-8_17
21. Mellor-Crummey, J.M., Scott, M.L.: Algorithms for scalable synchronization on shared-memory multiprocessors. ACM Trans. Comput. Syst. **9**(1), 21–65 (1991)
22. Ogata, K., Futatsugi, K.: Formal verification of the MCS list-based queuing lock. In: Thiagarajan, P.S., Yap, R. (eds.) ASIAN 1999. LNCS, vol. 1742, pp. 281–293. Springer, Heidelberg (1999). https://doi.org/10.1007/3-540-46674-6_24
23. da Rocha Pinto, P., Dinsdale-Young, T., Gardner, P.: TaDA: a logic for time and data abstraction. In: Jones, R. (ed.) ECOOP 2014. LNCS, vol. 8586, pp. 207–231. Springer, Heidelberg (2014). https://doi.org/10.1007/978-3-662-44202-9_9
24. da Rocha Pinto, P., Dinsdale-Young, T., Gardner, P., Sutherland, J.: Modular termination verification for non-blocking concurrency. In: Thiemann, P. (ed.) ESOP 2016. LNCS, vol. 9632, pp. 176–201. Springer, Heidelberg (2016). https://doi.org/10.1007/978-3-662-49498-1_8
25. Sergey, I., Nanevski, A., Banerjee, A.: Mechanized verification of fine-grained concurrent programs. In: PLDI 2015, pp. 77–87 (2015)

26. Turon, A., Thamsborg, J., Ahmed, A., Birkedal, L., Dreyer, D.: Logical relations for fine-grained concurrency. In: POPL, pp. 343–356 (2013)
27. Yang , J., Hawblitzel, C.: Safe to the last instruction: automated verification of a type-safe operating system. In: Proceedings of the 2010 ACM Conference on Programming Language Design and Implementation, pp. 99–110 (2010)

Domain-Specific Languages

Palgol: A High-Level DSL for Vertex-Centric Graph Processing with Remote Data Access

Yongzhe Zhang[1,2]($\boxtimes$), Hsiang-Shang Ko[2], and Zhenjiang Hu[1,2]

[1] Department of Informatics, SOKENDAI, Shonan Village, Hayama,
Kanagawa 240-0193, Japan
[2] National Institute of Informatics, 2-1-2 Hitotsubashi, Chiyoda-ku,
Tokyo 101-8430, Japan
{zyz915,hsiang-shang,hu}@nii.ac.jp

Abstract. Pregel is a popular distributed computing model for dealing with large-scale graphs. However, it can be tricky to implement graph algorithms correctly and efficiently in Pregel's vertex-centric model, especially when the algorithm has multiple computation stages, complicated data dependencies, or even communication over dynamic internal data structures. Some domain-specific languages (DSLs) have been proposed to provide more intuitive ways to implement graph algorithms, but due to the lack of support for *remote access* — reading or writing attributes of other vertices through references — they cannot handle the above mentioned dynamic communication, causing a class of Pregel algorithms with fast convergence impossible to implement.

To address this problem, we design and implement Palgol, a more declarative and powerful DSL which supports remote access. In particular, programmers can use a more declarative syntax called *chain access* to naturally specify dynamic communication as if directly reading data on arbitrary remote vertices. By analyzing the logic patterns of chain access, we provide a novel algorithm for compiling Palgol programs to efficient Pregel code. We demonstrate the power of Palgol by using it to implement several practical Pregel algorithms, and the evaluation result shows that the efficiency of Palgol is comparable with that of hand-written code.

1 Introduction

The rapid increase of graph data calls for efficient analysis on massive graphs. Google's Pregel [9] is one of the most popular frameworks for processing large-scale graphs. It is based on the bulk-synchronous parallel (BSP) model [14], and adopts the *vertex-centric* computing paradigm to achieve high parallelism and scalability. Following the BSP model, a Pregel computation is split into *supersteps* mediated by *message passing*. Within each superstep, all the vertices execute the same user-defined function *compute()* in parallel, where each vertex can read the messages sent to it in the previous superstep, modify its own state, and send messages to other vertices. Global barrier synchronization happens at the end of each superstep, delivering messages to their designated receivers

© Springer International Publishing AG 2017
B.-Y.E. Chang (Ed.): APLAS 2017, LNCS 10695, pp. 301–320, 2017.
https://doi.org/10.1007/978-3-319-71237-6_15

before the next superstep. Despite its simplicity, Pregel has demonstrated its usefulness in implementing many interesting graph algorithms [9,10,12,15,17].

Despite the power of Pregel, it is a big challenge to implement a graph algorithm correctly and efficiently in it [17], especially when the algorithm consists of multiple stages and complicated data dependencies. For such algorithms, programmers need to write an exceedingly complicated *compute()* function as the loop body, which encodes all the stages of the algorithm. Message passing makes the code even harder to maintain, because one has to trace where the messages are from and what information they carry in each superstep. Some attempts have been made to ease Pregel programming by proposing domain-specific languages (DSLs), such as Green-Marl [7] and Fregel [2]. These DSLs allow programmers to write a program in a compositional way to avoid writing a complicated loop body, and provide neighboring data access to avoid explicit message passing. Furthermore, programs written in these DSLs can be automatically translated to Pregel by fusing the components in the programs into a single loop, and mapping neighboring data access into message passing. However, for efficient implementation, the existing DSLs impose a severe restriction on data access — each vertex can only access data on their neighboring vertices. In other words, they do not support general *remote data access* — reading or writing attributes of other vertices through references.

Remote data access is, however, important for describing a class of Pregel algorithms that aim to accelerate information propagation (which is a crucial issue in handling graphs with large diameters [17]) by maintaining a dynamic internal structure for communication. For instance, a parallel pointer jumping algorithm maintains a tree (or list) structure in a distributed manner by letting each vertex store a reference to its current parent (or predecessor), and during the computation, every vertex constantly exchanges data with the current parent (or predecessor) and modifies the reference to reach the root vertex (or the head of the list). Such computational patterns can be found in algorithms like the Shiloach-Vishkin connected component algorithm [17] (see Sect. 2.3 for more details), the list ranking algorithm (see Sect. 2.4) and Chung and Condon's minimum spanning forest (MSF) algorithm [1]. However, these computational patterns cannot be implemented with only neighboring access, and therefore cannot be expressed in any of the existing high-level DSLs.

It is, in fact, hard to equip DSLs with efficient remote reading. First, when translated into Pregel's message passing model, remote reads require multiple rounds of communication to exchange information between the reading vertex and the remote vertex, and it is not obvious how the communication cost can be minimized. Second, remote reads would introduce more involved data dependencies, making it difficult to fuse program components into a single loop. Things become more complicated when there is *chain access*, where a remote vertex is reached by following a series of references. Furthermore, it is even harder to equip DSLs with remote writes in addition to remote reads. For example, Green-Marl detects read/write conflicts, which complicate its programming model; Fregel has a simpler functional model, which, however, cannot support remote writing without major extension. A more careful design is required to make remote reads and writes efficient and friendly to programmers.

In this paper, we propose a more powerful DSL called Palgol[1] that supports remote data access. In more detail:

- We propose a new high-level model for vertex-centric computation, where the concept of *algorithmic supersteps* is introduced as the basic computation unit for constructing vertex-centric computation in such a way that remote reads and writes are ordered in a safe way.
- Based on the new model, we design and implement Palgol, a more declarative and powerful DSL, which supports both remote reads and writes, and allows programmers to use a more declarative syntax called *chain access* to directly read data on remote vertices. For efficient compilation from Palgol to Pregel, we develop a logic system to compile chain access to efficient message passing where the number of supersteps is reduced whenever possible.
- We demonstrate the power of Palgol by working on a set of representative examples, including the Shiloach-Vishkin connected component algorithm and the list ranking algorithm, which use communication over dynamic data structures to achieve fast convergence.
- The result of our evaluation is encouraging. The efficiency of Palgol is comparable with hand-written code for many representative graph algorithms on practical big graphs, where execution time varies from a 2.53% speedup to a 6.42% slowdown in ordinary cases, while the worst case is less than a 30% slowdown.

The rest of the paper is organized as follows. Section 2 introduces algorithmic supersteps and the essential parts of Palgol, Sect. 3 presents the compiling algorithm, and Sect. 4 presents evaluation results. Related work is discussed in Sect. 5, and Sect. 6 concludes this paper with some outlook.

2   The Palgol Language

This section first introduces a high-level vertex-centric programming model (Sect. 2.1), in which an algorithm is decomposed into atomic vertex-centric computations and high-level combinators, and a vertex can access the entire graph through the references it stores locally. Next we define the Palgol language based on this model, and explain its syntax and semantics (Sect. 2.2). Finally we use two representative examples — the Shiloach-Vishkin connected component algorithm (Sect. 2.3) and the list ranking algorithm (Sect. 2.4) — to demonstrate how Palgol can concisely describe vertex-centric algorithms with dynamic internal structures using remote access.

---

[1] Palgol stands for **P**regel **algo**rithmic language. The system with all implementation code and test examples is available at https://bitbucket.org/zyz915/palgol.

2.1 The High-Level Model

The high-level model we propose uses remote reads and writes instead of message passing to allow programmers to describe vertex-centric computation more intuitively. Moreover, the model remains close to the Pregel computation model, in particular keeping the vertex-centric paradigm and barrier synchronization, making it possible to automatically derive a valid and efficient Pregel implementation from an algorithm description in this model, and in particular arrange remote reads and writes without data conflicts.

In our high-level model, the computation is constructed from some basic components which we call *algorithmic supersteps*. An algorithmic superstep is a piece of vertex-centric computation which takes a graph containing a set of vertices with local states as input, and outputs the same set of vertices with new states. Using algorithmic supersteps as basic building blocks, two high-level operations *sequence* and *iteration* can be used to glue them together to describe more complex vertex-centric algorithms that are iterative and/or consist of multiple computation stages: the *sequence* operation concatenates two algorithmic supersteps by taking the result of the first step as the input of the second one, and the *iteration* operation repeats a piece of vertex-centric computation until some termination condition is satisfied.

The distinguishing feature of algorithmic supersteps is remote access. Within each algorithmic superstep (illustrated in Fig. 1), all vertices compute in parallel, performing the same computation specified by programmers. A vertex can read the fields of any vertex in the input graph; it can also write to arbitrary vertices to modify their fields, but the writes are performed on a separate graph rather than the input graph (so there are no read-write conflicts). We further distinguish *local writes* and *remote writes* in our model: local writes can only modify the current vertex's state, and are first performed on an intermediate graph (which is initially a copy of the input graph); next, remote writes are propagated to the destination vertices to further modify their intermediate states. Here, a remote write consists of a remote field, a value and an "accumulative" assignment (like += and |=), and that field of the destination vertex is modified by executing the assignment with the value on its right-hand side. We choose to support only accumulative assignments so that the order of performing remote writes does not matter.

More precisely, an algorithmic superstep is divided into two phases:

- a *local computation* (LC) phase, in which a copy of the input graph is created as the intermediate graph, and then each vertex can read the state of any vertex in the input graph, perform local computation, and modify its own state in the intermediate graph, and
- a *remote updating* (RU) phase, in which each vertex can modify the states of any vertices in the intermediate graph by sending remote writes. After all remote writes are processed, the intermediate graph is returned as the output graph.

Among these two phases, the RU phase is optional, in which case the intermediate graph produced by the LC phase is used directly as the final result.

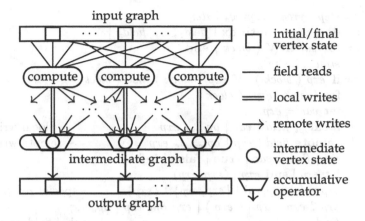

input graph

initial/final
vertex state

field reads

local writes

remote writes

intermediate graph

intermediate
vertex state

output graph

accumulative
operator

Fig. 1. In an algorithmic superstep, every vertex performs local computation (including field reads and local writes) and remote updating in order.

2.2   An Overview of Palgol

Next we present Palgol, whose design follows the high-level model we introduced above. Figure 2 shows the essential part of Palgol's syntax. As described by the syntactic category *step*, an algorithmic superstep in Palgol is a code block enclosed by "**for** *var* **in V**" and "**end**", where *var* is a variable name that can be used in the code block for referring to the current vertex (and **V** stands for the set of vertices of the input graph). Such steps can then be composed (by sequencing) or iterated until a termination condition is met (by enclosing them in "**do**" and "**until** ..."). Palgol supports several kinds of termination condition, but in this paper we focus on only one kind of termination condition called *fixed point*, since it is extensively used in many algorithms. The semantics of fixed-point iteration is iteratively running the program enclosed by **do** and **until**, until the specified fields stabilize.

Corresponding to an algorithmic superstep's remote access capabilities, in Palgol we can read a field of an arbitrary vertex using a global field access expression of the form *field* [*exp*], where *field* is a user-specified field name and *exp* should evaluate to a vertex id. Such expression can be updated by local or remote assignments, where an assignment to a remote vertex should always be accumulative and prefixed with the keyword **remote**. One more thing about remote assignments is that they take effect only in the RU phase (after the LC phase), regardless of where they occur in the program.

There are some predefined fields that have special meaning in our language. **Nbr** is the edge list in undirected graphs, and **In** and **Out** respectively store incoming and outgoing edges for directed graphs. Essentially, these are normal fields of a predefined type for representing edges, and most importantly, the compiler assumes a form of symmetry on these fields (namely that every edge is stored consistently on both of its end vertices), and uses the symmetry to produce more efficient code.

$$prog ::= step \mid prog_1 \ldots prog_n \mid iter$$
$$iter ::= \textbf{do} \langle prog \rangle \textbf{ until fix } [\ field_1, \ldots, field_n\ ]$$
$$step ::= \textbf{for } var \textbf{ in V } \langle block \rangle \textbf{ end}$$
$$block ::= stmt_1 \ldots stmt_n$$
$$stmt ::= \textbf{if } exp \langle block \rangle \mid \textbf{if } exp \langle block \rangle \textbf{ else } \langle block \rangle$$
$$\mid \quad \textbf{for } (var \leftarrow exp) \langle block \rangle$$
$$\mid \quad \textbf{let } var = exp$$
$$\mid \quad \textbf{local}_{opt}\ field\ [\ var\ ]\ op_{local}\ exp \qquad\qquad \text{– local write}$$
$$\mid \quad \textbf{remote } field\ [\ exp\ ]\ op_{remote}\ exp \qquad\quad \text{– remote write}$$
$$exp ::= int \mid float \mid var \mid \textbf{true} \mid \textbf{false} \mid \textbf{inf}$$
$$\mid \quad \textbf{fst } exp \mid \textbf{snd } exp \mid (exp, exp)$$
$$\mid \quad exp.\textbf{ref} \mid exp.\textbf{val} \mid \{exp, exp\} \mid \{exp\} \qquad \text{– specialized pair}$$
$$\mid \quad exp\ ?\ exp : exp \mid (\ exp\ ) \mid exp\ op_b\ exp \mid op_u\ exp$$
$$\mid \quad field\ [\ exp\ ] \qquad\qquad\qquad\qquad\qquad \text{– global field access}$$
$$\mid \quad func_{opt}\ [\ exp \mid var \leftarrow exp, exp_1, \ldots, exp_n\ ]$$
$$func ::= \textbf{maximum} \mid \textbf{minimum} \mid \textbf{sum} \mid \ldots$$

Fig. 2. Essential part of Palgol's syntax. Palgol is indentation-based, and two special tokens '$\langle$' and '$\rangle$' are introduced to delimit indented blocks.

The rest of the syntax for Palgol steps is similar to an ordinary programming language. Particularly, we introduce a specialized pair type (expressions in the form of $\{exp, exp\}$) for representing a reference with its corresponding value (e.g., an edge in a graph), and use **.ref** and **.val** respectively to access the reference and the value respectively, to make the code easy to read. Some functional programming constructs are also used here, like let-binding and list comprehension. There is also a foreign function interface that allows programmers to invoke functions written in a general-purpose language, but we omit the detail from the paper.

2.3   The Shiloach-Vishkin Connected Component Algorithm

Here is our first representative Palgol example: the *Shiloach-Vishkin (S-V) connected component algorithm* [17], which can be expressed as the Palgol program in Fig. 3. A traditional HashMin connected component algorithm [17] based on neighborhood communication takes time proportional to the input graph's diameter, which can be large in real-world graphs. In contrast, the S-V algorithm can calculate the connected components of an undirected graph in a logarithmic number of supersteps; to achieve this fast convergence, the capability of accessing data on non-neighboring vertices is essential.

In the S-V algorithm, the connectivity information is maintained using the classic disjoint set data structure [4]. Specifically, the data structure is a forest, and vertices in the same tree are regarded as belonging to the same connected component. Each vertex maintains a parent pointer that either points to some other vertex in the same connected component, or points to itself, in which

```
1  for u in V
2    D[u] := u
3  end
4  do
5    for u in V
6      if (D[D[u]] == D[u])
7        let t = minimum [ D[e.ref] | e <- Nbr[u] ]
8        if (t < D[u])
9          remote D[D[u]] <?= t
10     else
11         D[u] := D[D[u]]
12   end
13 until fix[D]
```

Fig. 3. The S-V algorithm in Palgol

case the vertex is the root of a tree. We henceforth use $D[u]$ to represent this pointer for each vertex u. The S-V algorithm is an iterative algorithm that begins with a forest of n root nodes, and in each step it tries to discover edges connecting different trees and merge the trees together. In a vertex-centric way, every vertex u performs one of the following operations depending on whether its parent $D[u]$ is a root vertex:

- **tree merging:** if $D[u]$ is a root vertex, then u chooses one of its neighbors' current parent (to which we give a name t), and makes $D[u]$ point to t if $t < D[u]$ (to guarantee the correctness of the algorithm). When having multiple choices in choosing the neighbors' parent p, or when different vertices try to modify the same parent vertex's pointer, the algorithm always uses the "minimum" as the tiebreaker for fast convergence.
- **pointer jumping:** if $D[u]$ is not a root vertex, then u modifies its own pointer to its current "grandfather" ($D[u]$'s current pointer). This operation reduces u's distance to the root vertex, and will eventually make u a direct child of the root vertex so that it can perform the above tree merging operation.

The algorithm terminates when all vertices' pointers do not change after an iteration, in which case all vertices point to some root vertex and no more tree merging can be performed. Readers interested in the correctness of this algorithm are referred to the original paper [17] for more details.

The implementation of this algorithm is complicated, which contains roughly 120 lines of code[2] for the *compute()* function alone. Even for detecting whether the parent vertex $D[u]$ is a root vertex for each vertex u, it has to be translated into three supersteps containing a query-reply conversation between each vertex and its parent. In contrast, the Palgol program in Fig. 3 can describe this algorithm concisely in 13 lines, due to the declarative remote access syntax. This piece of code contains two steps, where the first one (lines 1–3) performs simple

---

[2] http://www.cse.cuhk.edu.hk/pregelplus/code/apps/basic/svplus.zip.

initialization, and the other (lines 5–12) is inside an iteration as the main computation. We also use the field D to store the pointer to the parent vertex. Let us focus on line 6, which checks whether u's parent is a root. Here we simply check $D[D[u]] == D[u]$, i.e., whether the pointer of the parent vertex $D[D[u]]$ is equal to the parent's id $D[u]$. This expression is completely declarative, in the sense that we only specify what data is needed and what computation we want to perform, instead of explicitly implementing the message passing scheme.

The rest of the algorithm can be straightforwardly associated with the Palgol program. If u's parent is a root, we generate a list containing all neighboring vertices' parent id ($D[e.\mathbf{ref}]$), and then bind the minimum one to the variable t (line 7). Now t is either **inf** if the neighbor list is empty or a vertex id; in both cases we can use it to update the parent's pointer (lines 8–9) via a remote assignment. One important thing is that the parent vertex ($D[u]$) may receive many remote writes from its children, where only one of the children providing the minimum t can successfully perform the updating. Here, the statement a <?= b is an accumulative assignment, whose meaning is the same as a := min(a, b). Finally, for the **else** branch, we (locally) assign u's grandparent's id to u's D field.

2.4 The List Ranking Algorithm

Another example is the *list ranking* algorithm, which also needs communication over a dynamic structure during computation. Consider a linked list L with n elements, where each element u stores a value $val(u)$ and a link to its predecessor $pred(u)$. At the head of L is a virtual element v such that $pred(v) = v$ and $val(v) = 0$. For each element u in L, define $sum(u)$ to be the sum of the values of all the elements from u to the head (following the predecessor links). The list ranking problem is to compute $sum(u)$ for each element u. If $val(u) = 1$ for every vertex u in L, then $sum(u)$ is simply the rank of u in the list. List ranking can be solved using a typical pointer-jumping algorithm in parallel computing with a strong performance guarantee. Yan et al. [17] demonstrated how to compute the pre-ordering numbers for all vertices in a tree in $O(\log n)$ supersteps using this algorithm, as an internal step to compute bi-connected components (BCC).[3]

We give the Palgol implementation of list ranking in Fig. 4 (which is a 10-line program, whereas the Pregel implementation[4] contains around 60 lines of code). $Sum[u]$ is initially set to $Val[u]$ for every u at line 2; inside the fixed-point iteration (lines 5–9), every u moves $Pred[u]$ toward the head of the list and updates $Sum[u]$ to maintain the invariant that $Sum[u]$ stores the sum of a sublist from itself to the successor of $Pred[u]$. Line 6 checks whether u points to the virtual head of the list, which is achieved by checking $Pred[Pred[u]] == Pred[u]$, i.e., whether the current predecessor $Pred[u]$ points to itself. If the current predecessor is not the head, we add the sum of the sublist maintained in $Pred[u]$ to the

---

[3] BCC is a complicated algorithm, whose efficient implementation requires constructing an intermediate graph, which is currently beyond Palgol's capabilities. Palgol is powerful enough to express the rest of the algorithm, however.

[4] http://www.cse.cuhk.edu.hk/pregelplus/code/apps/basic/bcc.zip.

```
 1  for u in V
 2     Sum[u] := Val[u]
 3  end
 4  do
 5     for u in V
 6         if (Pred[Pred[u]] != Pred[u])
 7             Sum[u] += Sum[Pred[u]]
 8             Pred[u] := Pred[Pred[u]]
 9         end
10  until fix[Pred]
```

Fig. 4. The list ranking program

current vertex u, by reading $Pred[u]$'s Sum and $Pred$ fields and modifying u's own fields accordingly. Note that since all the reads are performed on a snapshot of the input graph and the assignments are performed on an intermediate graph, there is no need to worry about data dependencies.

3 Compiling Palgol to Pregel

In this section, we present the compiling algorithm to transform Palgol to Pregel. The task overall is complicated and highly technical, but the most challenging problem is how to translate chain access (like $D[D[u]]$) into Pregel's message passing model. We describe the compilation of chain access in Sect. 3.1, and then the compilation of a Palgol step in Sect. 3.2, and finally how to combine Palgol steps using sequence and iteration in Sect. 3.3.

3.1 Compiling Remote Reads

Our compiler currently recognizes two forms of remote reads. The first form is *chain access* expressions like $D[D[u]]$. The second form is *neighborhood access* where a vertex may use chain access to acquire data from *all* its neighbors, and this can be described using the list comprehension (e.g., line 7 in Fig. 3) or for-loop syntax in Palgol. The combination of these two remote read patterns is already sufficient to express quite a wide range of practical Pregel algorithms. Here we only present the compilation of chain access, which is novel, while the compilation of neighborhood access is similar to what has been done in Fregel.

Definition and Challenge of Compiling: A chain access is a consecutive field access expression starting from the current vertex. As an example, supposing that the current vertex is u, and D is a field for storing a vertex id, then $D[D[u]]$ is a chain access expression, and so is $D[D[D[D[u]]]]$ (which we abbreviate to $D^4[u]$ in the rest of this section). Generally speaking, there is no limitation on the depth of a chain access or the number of fields involved in the chain access.

As a simple example of the compilation, to evaluate $D[D[u]]$ on every vertex u, a straightforward scheme is a request-reply conversation which takes two rounds of communication: in the first superstep, every vertex u sends a request to (the vertex whose id is) $D[u]$ and the request message should contain u's own id; then in the second superstep, those vertices receiving the requests should extract the sender's ids from the messages, and reply its D field to them.

When the depth of such chain access increases, it is no longer trivial to find an efficient scheme, where efficiency is measured in terms of the number of supersteps taken. For example, to evaluate $D^4[u]$ on every vertex u, a simple query-reply method takes six rounds of communication by evaluating $D^2[u]$, $D^3[u]$ and $D^4[u]$ in turn, each taking two rounds, but the evaluation can actually be done in only three rounds with our compilation algorithm, which is not based on request-reply conversations.

Logic System for Compiling Chain Access: The key insight leading to our compilation algorithm is that we should consider not only the expression to evaluate but also the vertex on which the expression is evaluated. To use a slightly more formal notation (inspired by Halpern and Moses [5]), we write $\forall u. \mathrm{K}_{v(u)} e(u)$, where $v(u)$ and $e(u)$ are chain access expressions starting from u, to describe the state where every vertex $v(u)$ "knows" the value of the expression $e(u)$; then the goal of the evaluation of $D^4[u]$ can be described as $\forall u. \mathrm{K}_u D^4[u]$. Having introduced the notation, the problem can now be treated from a logical perspective, where we aim to search for a derivation of a target proposition from a few axioms.

There are three axioms in our logic system:

1. $\forall u. \mathrm{K}_u u$
2. $\forall u. \mathrm{K}_u D[u]$
3. $(\forall u. \mathrm{K}_{w(u)} e(u)) \wedge (\forall u. \mathrm{K}_{w(u)} v(u)) \implies \forall u. \mathrm{K}_{v(u)} e(u)$

The first axiom says that every vertex knows its own id, and the second axiom says every vertex can directly access its local field D. The third axiom encodes message passing: if we want every vertex $v(u)$ to know the value of the expression $e(u)$, then it suffices to find an intermediate vertex $w(u)$ which knows both the value of $e(u)$ and the id of $v(u)$, and thus can send the value to $v(u)$. As an example, Fig. 5 shows the solution generated by our algorithm to solve $\forall u. \mathrm{K}_u D^4[u]$, where each line is an instance of the message passing axiom.

Figure 6 is a direct interpretation of the implications in Fig. 5. To reach $\forall u. \mathrm{K}_u D^4[u]$, only three rounds of communication are needed. Each solid arrow represents an invocation of the message passing axiom in Fig. 5, and the dashed arrows represent two logical inferences, one from $\forall u. \mathrm{K}_u D[u]$ to $\forall u. \mathrm{K}_{D[u]} D^2[u]$ and the other from $\forall u. \mathrm{K}_u D^2[u]$ to $\forall u. \mathrm{K}_{D^2[u]} D^4[u]$.

The derivation of $\forall u. \mathrm{K}_u D^4[u]$ is not unique, and there are derivations that correspond to inefficient solutions — for example, there is also a derivation for the six-round solution based on request-reply conversations. However, when searching for derivations, our algorithm will minimize the number of rounds of communication, as explained below.

$$(\forall u.\,\mathrm{K}_u \quad u \quad) \wedge (\forall u.\,\mathrm{K}_u \quad D[u]\ ) \implies \forall u.\,\mathrm{K}_{D[u]} \quad u$$

$$(\forall u.\,\mathrm{K}_{D[u]} \quad u \quad) \wedge (\forall u.\,\mathrm{K}_{D[u]} \quad D^2[u]) \implies \forall u.\,\mathrm{K}_{D^2[u]}\, u$$

$$(\forall u.\,\mathrm{K}_{D[u]} \quad D^2[u]) \wedge (\forall u.\,\mathrm{K}_{D[u]} \quad u \quad) \implies \forall u.\,\mathrm{K}_u \quad\quad D^2[u]$$

$$(\forall u.\,\mathrm{K}_{D^2[u]} \, D^4[u]) \wedge (\forall u.\,\mathrm{K}_{D^2[u]}\, u \quad) \implies \forall u.\,\mathrm{K}_u \quad\quad D^4[u]$$

Fig. 5. A derivation of $\forall u.\,\mathrm{K}_u\, D^4[u]$

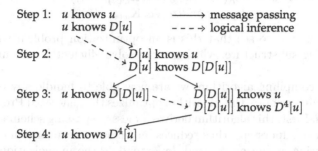

Fig. 6. Interpretation of the derivation of $\forall u.\,\mathrm{K}_u\, D^4[u]$

The Compiling Algorithm: Initially, the algorithm sets as its target a proposition $\forall u.\,\mathrm{K}_{v(u)}\, e(u)$, for which a derivation is to be found. The key problem here is to choose a proper $w(u)$ so that, by applying the message passing axiom backwards, we can get two potentially simpler new target propositions $\forall u.\,\mathrm{K}_{w(u)}\, e(u)$ and $\forall u.\,\mathrm{K}_{w(u)}\, v(u)$ and solve them respectively. The range of such choices is in general unbounded, but our algorithm considers only those simpler than $v(u)$ or $e(u)$. More formally, we say that a is a *subpattern* of b, written $a \preceq b$, exactly when b is a chain access starting from a. For example, u and $D[u]$ are subpatterns of $D[D[u]]$, while they are all subpatterns of $D^3[u]$. The range of intermediate vertices we consider is then $\mathrm{Sub}(e(u), v(u))$, where Sub is defined by

$$\mathrm{Sub}(a,b) = \{\, c \mid c \preceq a \text{ or } c \prec b \,\}$$

We can further simplify the new target propositions with the following function before solving them:

$$generalize(\forall u.\,\mathrm{K}_{a(u)}\, b(u)) = \begin{cases} \forall u.\,\mathrm{K}_u\, (b(u)/a(u)) & \text{if } a(u) \preceq b(u) \\ \forall u.\,\mathrm{K}_{a(u)}\, b(u) & \text{otherwise} \end{cases}$$

where $b(u)/a(u)$ denotes the result of replacing the innermost $a(u)$ in $b(u)$ with u. (For example, $A[B[C[u]]]/C[u] = A[B[u]]$.) This is justified because the original proposition can be instantiated from the new proposition. (For example, $\forall u.\,\mathrm{K}_{C[u]}\, A[B[C[u]]]$ can be instantiated from $\forall u.\,\mathrm{K}_u\, A[B[u]]$.)

It is now possible to find an optimal solution with respect to the following inductively defined function *step*, which calculates the number of rounds of communication for a proposition:

$$step(\forall u.\, \mathrm{K}_u\, u) \quad\;\; = 0$$
$$step(\forall u.\, \mathrm{K}_u\, D[u]) \;\;\; = 0$$
$$step(\forall u.\, \mathrm{K}_{v(u)}\, e(u)) = 1 + \min_{w(u)\in \mathrm{Sub}(e(u),v(u))} \max(x,y)$$
$$\text{where } x = step(generalize(\forall u.\, \mathrm{K}_{w(u)}\, e(u)))$$
$$y = step(generalize(\forall u.\, \mathrm{K}_{w(u)}\, v(u)))$$

It is straightforward to see that this is an optimization problem with optimal and overlapping substructure, which we can solve efficiently with memoization techniques.

With this compiling algorithm, we are now able to handle any chain access expressions. Furthermore, this algorithm optimizes the generated Pregel program in two aspects. First, this algorithm derives a message passing scheme with a minimum number of supersteps, thus reduces unnecessary cost for launching Pregel supersteps during execution. Second, by extending the memoization technique, we can ensure that a chain access expression will be evaluated exactly once even if it appears multiple times in a Palgol step, avoiding redundant message passing for the same value.

3.2 Compiling Palgol Steps

Having introduced the compiling algorithm for remote data reads in Palgol, here we give a general picture of the compilation for a single Palgol step, as shown in Fig. 7. The computational content of every Palgol step is compiled into a *main superstep*. Depending on whether there are remote reads and writes, there may be a number of *remote reading supersteps* before the main superstep, and a *remote updating superstep* after the main superstep.

We will use the main computation step of the S-V program (lines 5–12 in Fig. 3) as an illustrative example for explaining the compilation algorithm, which consists of the following four steps:

1. We first handle neighborhood access, which requires a sending superstep that provides all the remote data for the loops from the neighbors' perspective. This sending superstep is inserted as a remote reading superstep immediately before the main superstep.
2. We analyze the chain access expressions appearing in the Palgol step with the algorithm in Sect. 3.1, and corresponding remote reading supersteps are inserted in the front. (For the S-V algorithm, the only interesting chain access expression is $D[D[u]]$, which induces two remote reading supersteps realizing a request-reply conversation.)
3. Having handled all remote reads, the main superstep receives all the values needed and proceeds with the local computation. Since the local computational content of a Palgol step is similar to an ordinary programming language, the transformation is straightforward.

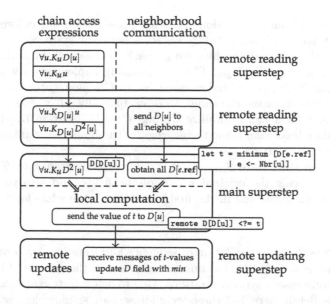

Fig. 7. Compiling a Palgol step to Pregel supersteps.

4. What remain to be handled are the remote assignments, which require sending the updating values as messages to the target vertices in the main superstep. Then an additional remote updating superstep is added after the main superstep; this additional superstep reads these messages and updates each field using the corresponding remote updating operator.

3.3 Compiling Sequences and Iterations

Finally, we look at the compilation of sequence and iteration, which assemble Palgol steps into larger programs. A Pregel program generated from Palgol code is essentially a *state transition machine* (STM) combined with computation code for each state. Every Palgol step is translated into a "linear" STM consisting of a chain of states corresponding to the supersteps like those shown in Fig. 7, and the compilation of a Palgol program starts from turning the atomic Palgol steps into linear STMs, and implements the sequence and iteration semantics to construct more complex STMs.

Compilation of sequence: To compile the sequence, we first compile the two component programs into STMs, then a composite STM is constructed by simply adding a state transition from the end state of the first STM to the start state of the second STM.

Compilation of iteration: We first compile the loop body into an STM, which starts from some state S_{start} and ends in a state S_{end}, then we extend this STM to implement the fixed-point semantics. Here we describe a generalized approach which generates a new STM starting from state $S_{start'}$ and ending in state $S_{end'}$:

314 Y. Zhang et al.

1. First, a check of the termination condition takes place right before the state S_{start}: if it holds, we immediately enters a new exit state $S_{exit'}$; otherwise we execute the body, after which we go back to the check by adding a state transition from S_{end} to S_{start}. This step actually implements a while loop.
2. The termination check is implemented by an OR aggregator to make sure that every vertex makes the same decision: basically, all vertices determine whether their local fields stabilize during a single iteration by storing the original values beforehand, and the aggregator combines the results and makes it available to all vertices.
3. We add a new start state $S_{start'}$ and make it directly transit to S_{start}. This state is for storing the original values of the fields, and also to make the termination check succeed in the first run, turning the while loop into a do-until loop.

Optimizations: In the compilation of sequence and iteration, two optimization techniques are used to reduce the number of states in the generated STMs and can remove unnecessary synchronizations. Due to space restrictions, we will not present all the details here, but these techniques share similar ideas with Green-Marl's "state merging" and "intra-loop state merging" optimizations [7]:

- *state merging*: whenever it is safe to do so, the Green-Marl compiler merges two consecutive states of vertex computation into one. In the compilation of sequence in Palgol, we can always safely merge the end state of the first STM and the start state of the second STM, resulting in a reduction of one state in the composite STM.
- *intra-loop state merging*: this optimization merges the first and last vertex-parallel states inside Green-Marl's loops. In Palgol, we can also discover such chance when iterating a linear STM inside a fixed-point iteration.

4 Experiments

In this section, we evaluate the overall performance of Palgol and the state-merging optimisations introduced in the previous section. We compile Palgol code to Pregel+[5], which is an open-source implementation of Pregel written in C++.[6] We have implemented the following six graph algorithms on Pregel+'s basic mode, which are:

- PageRank [9]
- Single-Source Shortest Path (SSSP) [9]
- Strongly Connected Components (SCC) [17]

---

[5] http://www.cse.cuhk.edu.hk/pregelplus.
[6] Palgol does not target a specific Pregel-like system. Instead, by properly implementing different backends of the compiler, Palgol can be transformed into any Pregel-like system, as long as the system supports the basic Pregel interfaces including message passing between arbitrary pairs of vertices and aggregators.

- Shiloach-Vishkin Connected Component Algorithm (S-V) [17]
- List Ranking Algorithm (LR) [17]
- Minimum Spanning Forest (MSF) [1]

Among these algorithms, SCC, S-V, LR and MSF are non-trivial ones which contain multiple computing stages. Their Pregel+ implementations are included in our repository for interested readers.

4.1 Performance Evaluation

In our performance evaluation, we use three real-world graph datasets (Facebook[7], Wikipedia[8], USA[9]) and one synthetic graph, and some detailed information is listed in Table 1. The experiment is conducted on an Amazon EC2 cluster with 16 nodes (whose instance type is m4.large), each containing 2 vCPUs and 8G memory. Each algorithm is run on the type of input graphs to which it is applicable (PageRank on directed graphs, for example) with 4 configurations, where the number of nodes changes from 4 to 16. We measure the execution time for each experiment, and all the results are averaged over three repeated experiments. The runtime results of our experiments are summarized in Table 2.

Remarkably, for most of these algorithms (PageRank, SCC, S-V and MSF), we observed highly close execution time on the compiler-generated programs and the manually implemented programs, with the performance of the Palgol programs varying between a 2.53% speedup to a 6.42% slowdown.

For SSSP, we observed a slowdown up to 29.55%. The main reason is that the human-written code utilizes Pregel's *vote_to_halt()* API to deactivate converged vertices during computation; this accelerates the execution since the Pregel system skips invoking the *compute()* function for those inactive vertices, while in Palgol, we check the states of the vertices to decide whether to perform computation. Similarly, we observed a 24% slowdown for LR, since the human-written code deactivates all vertices after each superstep, and it turns out to work correctly. While voting to halt may look important to efficiency, we would argue against supporting voting to halt as is, since it makes programs impossible to compose: in general, an algorithm may contain multiple computation stages, and

Table 1. Datasets for performance evaluation

Dataset	Type	$|V|$	$|E|$	Description
Wikipedia	Directed	18,268,992	172,183,984	The hyperlink network of Wikipedia
Facebook	Undirected	59,216,214	185,044,032	A friendship network of the Facebook
USA	Weighted	23,947,347	58,333,344	The USA road network
Random	Chain	10,000,000	10,000,000	A chain with randomly generated values

---

[7] https://archive.is/o/cdGrj/konect.uni-koblenz.de/networks/facebook-sg.
[8] http://konect.uni-koblenz.de/networks/dbpedia-link.
[9] http://www.dis.uniroma1.it/challenge9/download.shtml.

Table 2. Comparison of execution time between Palgol and Pregel+ implementation

Dataset	Algorithm	4 nodes		8 nodes		12 nodes		16 nodes		Comparison
		Pregel+	Palgol	Pregel+	Palgol	Pregel+	Palgol	Pregel+	Palgol	
Wikipedia	SSSP	8.33	10.80	4.47	5.61	3.18	3.83	2.41	2.85	18.06% – 29.55%
	PageRank	153.40	152.36	83.94	82.58	61.82	61.24	48.36	47.66	−1.62% – 2.26%
	SCC	177.51	178.87	85.87	86.52	61.75	61.89	46.64	46.33	−0.66% – 0.77%
Facebook	S-V	143.09	142.16	87.98	86.22	67.62	65.90	58.29	57.49	−2.53% – −0.65%
Random	LR	56.18	64.69	29.58	33.17	19.76	23.48	14.64	18.16	12.14% – 24.00%
USA	MSF	78.80	82.57	43.21	45.98	29.47	31.07	22.84	24.29	4.79% – 6.42%

Table 3. Comparison of the compiler-generated programs before/after optimization

Dataset	Algorithm	Number of supersteps			Execution time		
		Before	After	Comparison	Before	After	Comparison
Wikipedia	SSSP	147	50	−65.99%	5.36	2.85	−46.83%
	PageRank	93	32	−65.59%	45.57	47.66	4.58%
	SCC	3819	1278	−66.54%	106.03	46.33	−56.30%
Facebook	S-V	31	23	−25.81%	52.37	57.49	9.78%
Random	LR	77	52	−32.47%	17.54	18.16	3.51%
USA	MSF	318	192	−39.62%	26.67	24.29	−8.95%

we need to control when to end a stage and enter the next; voting to halt, however, does not help with such stage transition, since it is designed to deactivate
all vertices and end the whole computation right away.

4.2   Effectiveness of Optimization

In this subsection, we evaluate the effectiveness of the "state merging" optimization mentioned in Sect. 3.3, by generating both the optimized and unoptimized
versions of the code and executing them in the same configurations. We use all
the six graph applications in the previous experiment, and fix the number of
nodes to 16. The experiment results are shown in Table 3.

The numbers of supersteps in execution are significantly reduced, and this is
due to the fact that the main iterations in these graph algorithms are properly
optimized. For applications containing only a simple iteration like PageRank
and SSSP, we reduce nearly 2/3 supersteps in execution, which is achieved by
optimizing the three supersteps inside the iteration body into a single one. Similarly, for SCC, S-V and LR, the improvement is around 2/3, 1/4 and 1/3 due
to the reduction of one or two superstep in the main iteration(s). The MSF is a

slightly complicated algorithm containing multiple stages, and we get an overall reduction of nearly 40% supersteps in execution.

While this optimization reduces the number of supersteps, and thus the number of global synchronizations, it does not necessarily reduce the overall execution time since it incurs a small overhead for every loop. The optimization produces a tighter loop body by unconditionally sending at the end of each iteration the necessary messages for the next iteration; as a result, when exiting the loop, some redundant messages are emitted (although the correctness of the generated code is ensured). This optimization is effective when the cost of sending these redundant messages is cheaper than that of the eliminated global synchronizations. In our experiments, SSSP and SCC become twice as fast after optimization since they are not computationally intensive, and therefore the number of global synchronizations plays a more dominant role in execution time; this is not the case for the other algorithms though.

5   Related Work

Google's Pregel [9] proposed the vertex-centric computing paradigm, which allows programmers to think naturally like a vertex when designing distributed graph algorithms. Some graph-centric (or block-centric) systems like Giraph+ [13] and Blogel [16] extends Pregel's vertex-centric approach by making the partitioning mechanism open to programmers, but it is still unclear how to optimize general vertex-centric algorithms (especially those complicated ones containing non-trivial communication patterns) using such extension.

Domain-Specific Languages (DSLs) are a well-known mechanism for describing solutions in specialized domains. To ease Pregel programming, many DSLs have been proposed, such as Palovca [8], s6raph [11], Fregel [2] and Green-Marl [7]. We briefly introduce each of them below.

Palovca [8] exposes the Pregel APIs in Haskell using a monad, and a vertex-centric program is written in a low-level way like in typical Pregel systems. Since this language is still low-level, programmers are faced with the same challenges in Pregel programming, mainly having to tackle all low-level details.

At the other extreme, the s6raph system [11] is a special graph processing framework with a functional interface, which models a particular type of graph algorithms containing a single iterative computation (such as PageRank and Shortest Path) by six programmer-specified functions. However, many practical Pregel algorithms are far more complicated.

A more comparable and (in fact) closely related piece of work is Fregel [2], which is a functional DSL for declarative programming on big graphs. In Fregel, a vertex-centric computation is represented by a pure step function that takes a graph as input and produces a new vertex state; such functions can then be composed using a set of predefined higher-order functions to implement a complete graph algorithm. Palgol borrows this idea in the language design by letting programmers write atomic vertex-centric computations called Palgol steps, and put them together using two combinators, namely sequence and iteration. Compared with Fregel, the main strength of Palgol is in its remote access capabilities:

- a Palgol step consists of local computation and remote updating phases, whereas a Fregel step function can be thought of as only describing local computation, lacking the ability to modify other vertices' states;
- even when considering local computation only, Palgol has highly declarative *field access expressions* to express remote reading of arbitrary vertices, whereas Fregel allows only neighboring access.

These two features are however essential for implementing the examples in Sect. 2, especially the S-V algorithm. Moreover, when implementing the same graph algorithm, the execution time of Fregel is around an order of magnitude slower than human written code; Palgol shows that Fregels combinator-based design can in fact achieve efficiency comparable to hand-written code.

Another comparable DSL is Green-Marl [6], which lets programmers describe graph algorithms in a higher-level imperative language. This language is initially proposed for graph processing on the shared-memory model, and a "Pregel-canonical" subset of its programs can be compiled to Pregel. Since it does not have a Pregel-specific language design, programmers may easily get compilation errors if they are not familiar with the implementation of the compiler. In contrast, Palgol (and Fregel) programs are by construction vertex-centric and distinguish the current and previous states for the vertices, and thus have a closer correspondence with the Pregel model. For remote reads, Green-Marl only supports neighboring access, so it suffers the same problem as Fregel where programmers cannot fetch data from an arbitrary vertex. While it supports graph traversal skeletons like BFS and DFS, these traversals can be encoded as neighborhood access with modest effort, so it actually has the same expressiveness as Fregel in terms of remote reading. Green-Marl supports remote writing, but according to our experience, it is quite restricted, and at least cannot be used inside a loop iterating over a neighbor list, and thus is less expressive than Palgol.

6   Concluding Remarks

This paper has introduced Palgol, a high-level domain-specific language for Pregel systems with flexible remote data access, which makes it possible for programmers to express Pregel algorithms that communicate over dynamic internal data structures. We have demonstrated the power of Palgol's remote access by giving two representative examples, the S-V algorithm and the list ranking algorithm, and presented the key algorithm for compiling remote access. Moreover, we have shown that Fregels more structured approach to vertex-centric computing can achieve high efficiency — the experiment results show that graph algorithms written in Palgol can be compiled to efficient Pregel programs comparable to human written ones.

We expect Palgol's remote access capabilities to help with developing more sophisticated vertex-centric algorithms where each vertex decides its action by looking at not only its immediate neighborhood but also an extended and dynamic neighborhood. The S-V and list ranking algorithms are just a start — for a differently flavored example, graph pattern matching [3] might be greatly simplified when the pattern has a constant size and can be translated declaratively as a remote access expression deciding whether a vertex and some other "nearby" vertices exhibit the pattern.

Algorithm design and language design are interdependent, with algorithmic ideas prompting more language features and higher-level languages making it easier to formulate and reason about more sophisticated algorithms. We believe that Palgol is a much-needed advance in language design that can bring vertex-centric algorithm design forward.

Acknowledgements. We thank Dr. Kento Emoto for his advice in the design of Palgol, Mr. Smith Dhumbumroong for his help in setting up the experiments, and the reviewers for their insightful comments to improve this paper. This work was supported by JSPS KAKENHI Grant Numbers 26280020 and 17H06099.

References

1. Chung, S., Condon, A.: Parallel implementation of Borůvka's minimum spanning tree algorithm. In: IPPS, pp. 302–308. IEEE (1996)
2. Emoto, K., Matsuzaki, K., Morihata, A., Hu, Z.: Think like a vertex, behave like a function! A functional DSL for vertex-centric big graph processing. In: ICFP, pp. 200–213. ACM (2016)
3. Fard, A., Nisar, M.U., Ramaswamy, L., Miller, J.A., Saltz, M.: A distributed vertex-centric approach for pattern matching in massive graphs. In: BigData, pp. 403–411. IEEE (2013)
4. Gabow, H.N., Tarjan, R.E.: A linear-time algorithm for a special case of disjoint set union. J. Comput. System Sci. **30**(2), 209–221 (1985)
5. Halpern, J.Y., Moses, Y.: Knowledge and common knowledge in a distributed environment. J. ACM **37**(3), 549–587 (1990)
6. Hong, S., Chafi, H., Sedlar, E., Olukotun, K.: Green-Marl: a DSL for easy and efficient graph analysis. In: ASPLOS, pp. 349–362. ACM (2012)
7. Hong, S., Salihoglu, S., Widom, J., Olukotun, K.: Simplifying scalable graph processing with a domain-specific language. In: CGO, p. 208. ACM (2014)
8. Lesniak, M.: Palovca: describing and executing graph algorithms in Haskell. In: Russo, C., Zhou, N.-F. (eds.) PADL 2012. LNCS, vol. 7149, pp. 153–167. Springer, Heidelberg (2012). https://doi.org/10.1007/978-3-642-27694-1_12
9. Malewicz, G., Austern, M.H., Bik, A.J., Dehnert, J.C., Horn, I., Leiser, N., Czajkowski, G.: Pregel: a system for large-scale graph processing. In: SIGMOD, pp. 135–146. ACM (2010)
10. Quick, L., Wilkinson, P., Hardcastle, D.: Using Pregel-like large scale graph processing frameworks for social network analysis. In: ASONAM, pp. 457–463. IEEE (2012)
11. Ruiz, O.C., Matsuzaki, K., Sato, S.: s6raph: vertex-centric graph processing framework with functional interface. In: FHPC, pp. 58–64. ACM (2016)
12. Salihoglu, S., Widom, J.: Optimizing graph algorithms on Pregel-like systems. PVLDB **7**(7), 577–588 (2014)

13. Tian, Y., Balmin, A., Corsten, S.A., Tatikonda, S., McPherson, J.: From think like a vertex to think like a graph. PVLDB **7**(3), 193–204 (2013)
14. Valiant, L.G.: A bridging model for parallel computation. Commun. ACM **33**(8), 103–111 (1990)
15. Xie, M., Yang, Q., Zhai, J., Wang, Q.: A vertex centric parallel algorithm for linear temporal logic model checking in Pregel. J. Parallel Distrib. Com. **74**(11), 3161–3174 (2014)
16. Yan, D., Cheng, J., Lu, Y., Ng, W.: Blogel: a block-centric framework for distributed computation on real-world graphs. PVLDB **7**(14), 1981–1992 (2014)
17. Yan, D., Cheng, J., Xing, K., Lu, Y., Ng, W., Bu, Y.: Pregel algorithms for graph connectivity problems with performance guarantees. PVLDB **7**(14), 1821–1832 (2014)

Efficient Functional Reactive Programming
Through Incremental Behaviors

Bob Reynders[✉] and Dominique Devriese

imec - DistriNet, KU Leuven, Leuven, Belgium
{bob.reynders,dominique.devriese}@cs.kuleuven.be

Abstract. Many types of software are inherently event-driven ranging from web applications to embedded devices and traditionally, such applications are implemented using imperative callbacks. An alternative approach to writing such programs is functional reactive programming (FRP). FRP offers abstractions to make event-driven programming convenient, safe and composable, but they come at a price. FRP behaviors cannot efficiently deal with larger, incrementally constructed values such as a collection of messages or a list of connected devices. Since these situations occur naturally, it hinders the use of FRP. We report on a new FRP primitive: 'incremental behavior'. We show that the semantics fit within existing FRP semantics and that their API can be used as a foundation for more ad-hoc solutions, such as incremental collections and discrete behaviors. Finally, we present benchmarks that demonstrate the advantages of incremental behaviors in terms of reduced computation time and bandwidth.

1 Introduction

Event-driven applications are common in several domains. Traditionally, such applications are implemented using imperative callbacks. An alternative approach to writing such programs is functional reactive programming (FRP). It offers abstractions to make event-driven programming convenient, safe and composable. It has been successfully applied to both GUI programming [5], embedded devices [23], etc.

FRP semantics define two primitives: events (a stream of values at discrete times) and behaviors (time-varying values). Let us introduce these with a small example, an FRP equivalent for the common case of using event handlers to increase a mutable sum:

```
val ints: Event[Int]    = ...                        //   3, 5, 2, ...
val sum: Behavior[Int] = ints.fold†(0) { (x, y) ⇒ x + y } // 0, 3, 8, 10, ...
```

We assume the existence of `ints`, an event that contains integers. We use the `fold` † method on events to build up state.[1] It takes an initial value (0) and an

---

[1] `fold` † is marked with † for clarity since a variant named `fold` is introduced in Sect. 2.

© Springer International Publishing AG 2017
B.-Y.E. Chang (Ed.): APLAS 2017, LNCS 10695, pp. 321–338, 2017.
https://doi.org/10.1007/978-3-319-71237-6_16

accumulation function (`(x, y) => x + y`) as arguments and builds a behavior. The event's values are accumulated starting with the initial value.

An FRP application is constructed by composing *behaviors* and *events* with a set of FRP operations. It typically defines a main behavior to describe the entire application, for example `Behavior[UI]` as the main value for a GUI application.

While FRP is nice in theory, there are shortcomings that crop up when you use it in practice. This paper focuses on one of those issues.

Computational Overhead. A practical problem with FRP is that behaviors containing large incrementally constructed values often behave suboptimally, for example a chat view:

```
val msgs: Event[Message] = ...
val chat: Behavior[List[Message]] = msgs.fold†(List.empty[Message]) { (lst, m) ⇒ m :: lst }
val chatView: Behavior[List[String]] = chat.map(_.map(_.pretty))
```

From an event stream of messages (`msgs`) we accumulate the state of the program (`chat`). All the messages are concatenated into a list behavior. A view of the state is generated through `map` by pretty printing all elements.

The problem here is that FRP only keeps track of the complete values within behaviors. It does not keep track of *how* it changes. In the example above, this means that a change to `chat` (through `msgs`) is propagated to `chatView` as 'there is a new list'. The entire list in the view is then re-mapped every time a new message is added. This makes the occurrence of a new message take $\mathcal{O}(n)$ processing time instead of a possible $\mathcal{O}(1)$.

This is especially problematic since maintaining large collections in behaviors is common in lots of FRP applications: chat applications have a list of messages, social networks have news feeds, sensor networks have lists of nodes, etc. In practice this means that FRP programmers work around the problem by using events to model concepts that would fit a behavior better, such as representing the chat view not as a behavior, but as an event of added strings.

Bandwidth Overhead. Computational complexity is not the only area in which standard behaviors do not perform optimally. Bandwidth intensive operations such as saving a behavior's history to disk (for logging or debugging purposes) or sending its data across the network, are directly impacted by knowing *how* behaviors change. The multi-tier FRP-based language as proposed in [19] is a typical example where bandwidth matters. To demonstrate this problem in our chat example, we extend it to continuously broadcast to clients:

```
def broadcastToClients(b: Behavior[List[String]]) = ...
broadcastToClients(chatView)
```

In this case, there is no way to efficiently implement `broadcastToClients` since behaviors cannot express *when* or *how* values update. Its only options are to poll for changes followed by either recomputing and transmitting the differences, or by sending the entire new list. In practice this often means that functions similar to `broadcastToClients` are modeled with less appropriate abstractions such as events:

```
def broadcastToClients(init: List[String], changes: Event[List[String]])
```

In addition to reducing computational and bandwidth overhead there are other reasons to express *how* behaviors change. For example, in an FRP Html library the interface may be modeled as a `Behavior[Element]`. Compared to completely rewriting the DOM, it would be much more efficient to apply only the changes of such a behavior.

1.1 Contributions

To summarize, we make the following contributions:

- We define incremental behaviors and their API and show how they fit within existing FRP semantics.
- We show how our approach is more general than previous work such as incremental collections [14,17] and discrete behaviors [3,15,20] by implementing them into our framework. Additionally, we show how a joint API between discrete and incremental behaviors based on manually computing differences can form a middle ground between them.
- We present an implementation of incremental behaviors and incremental collections as a Scala library. We demonstrate the advantages of incremental behaviors through a performance analysis of our implementation. In the analysis we compare incremental behavior's computational and bandwidth overhead with their non-incremental counterpart.

We start by introducing FRP and incremental behaviors in Sect. 2, and we show how incremental collections and discrete behaviors can be implemented on top of their API in Sect. 3. In Sect. 4, we evaluate their performance. Section 5 discusses incremental behaviors with respect to higher-order FRP semantics. We highlight related work in Sect. 6 and conclude with future work in Sect. 7.

In addition to our own implementation, we also found an independent implementation of similar ideas in the grapefruit-frp Haskell library [12] (their incremental signals seem similar to our incremental behaviors). This implementation has not been presented in the literature and lacks some of the features described here, but we consider it as additional evidence of the value of incremental behaviors.

2 Incremental Behaviors

We present incremental behaviors, an additional primitive for functional reactive programming (FRP). All code examples use our working proof-of-concept Scala implementation and we encourage the reader to play around with it.[2] As a

---

[2] https://github.com/Tzbob/hokko.

small Scala introduction, in this paper it is sufficient to think of a `trait` as a Java-like interface, `object Foo` as a collection of static methods for `Foo` and the `case class A(x: Int)` as a data type with field `x`. Case classes can get constructed (like regular classes) through either `new A(0)` or just `A(0)`.

2.1 Functional Reactive Programming: Event and Behavior

We begin with a summary of FRP and its semantics. We focus on first-order FRP semantics that are very similar to the ones defined in [3,11]. For readers interested in higher-order FRP semantics we refer to Sect. 5. Let us go over the two main FRP primitives, event and behavior:

Events are sets of discrete values:

$$[\![Event_\tau]\!] = \{e \in \mathcal{P}(Time \times [\![\tau]\!]) \mid \forall (t, v), (t', v') \in e.\, t = t' \Rightarrow v = v'\}$$

In the denotational semantics above $[\![\alpha]\!]$ is the 'denotation' or *meaning* of α, $\{e \in \mathcal{P}(\alpha) \mid P\}$ is the set of elements e from the powerset of α for which P holds. Events are sets of $(Time, [\![\tau]\!])$ tuples that do not contain values with duplicate *Time* components.

Typical examples of these discrete values are mouse clicks or button presses. There are three core operations: `map`, `filter` and `merge` as shown in Fig. 1. We do not discuss `map` or `filter` since they behave just like their well-known collection counterparts. `merge` takes two events and returns an event that fires whenever one of the original events fire. When both fire at the same time, the given function combines both values into a single new one.

Behaviors can be thought of as values that can vary continuously over time. Semantically, behaviors of type τ are regular functions from *Time* to τ:

$$[\![Behavior_\tau]\!] = \{b \in Time \to [\![\tau]\!]\}$$

An example of a behavior is the cursor's position. A mouse is always somewhere but its position may change continuously as you move your hand. The two core operations on behaviors are: `map2` and `constant` as shown in Fig. 1. `constant` creates a behavior that never changes its value. `map2` has the ability to combine two behaviors with a function. Other convenience functions such as `map` can be defined in terms of `constant` and `map2`.

Behaviors ⇔ Events. Converting from events to behaviors and vice versa is done through two other operations: `Event.fold` [3] and `Behavior.snapshot`, also shown in Fig. 1. Folding an event is similar to folding a list, a starting value and an accumulation function is given to compute a new value whenever

---

[3] Note that to have a definable semantics for *fold* an extra restriction on events (which we omitted for brevity) is required. The occurrences in an event must be 'uniform discrete', that is, the amount of events before any time t must be finite.

```
trait Event[A] {
  def map[B](f: A ⇒ B): Event[B]
  def filter(p: A ⇒ Boolean): Event[A]
  def merge(e: Event[A])(f: (A, A) ⇒ A): Event[A]
  def fold†[B](init: B)(accum: (B, A) ⇒ B): Behavior[B]
}

trait Behavior[A] {
  def map2[B, C](b: Behavior[B])(f: (A, B) ⇒ C): Behavior[C]
  def map[B](f: A ⇒ B): Behavior[B]
  def snapshot[B, C](e: Event[B])(f: (A, B) ⇒ C): Event[C]
}
object Behavior { def constant[A]: Behavior[A] }
```

Fig. 1. Event & Behavior API

a new element arises. Its result is a behavior representing the accumulation. Snapshotting a behavior with an event inspects the value of a behavior at the rate of that event. The behavior is sampled for every change in the event by applying a combination function to the event value and the behavior's value at the time.

The FRP semantics that we just showed make a couple of design decisions that can differ from others: it is first-order instead of higher-order (see Sect. 5), it allows only one event value at a time and behaviors are defined in continuous time opposed to discrete time (see discrete behaviors in Sect. 3.2).

2.2 Motivating Example: Todo List

An example FRP program using our Scala library is shown in Fig. 2. We implement a simple todo list. We leave out most of the code and focus only on the bits that are important to this paper. The user's intent to submit his message is modeled by the `submissionE` event. The state of the todo application itself is created by accumulating all the submissions into a list behavior (`todoListB`).

We create `todoListView`, a string representation of all the entries in the list by first turning the list of entries into a pretty printed list of strings (`_.map(_.pretty)`) and then concatenating all elements with `.mkString`.

Without going into details of its implementation, we assume the `replicate` function that takes a behavior and replicates it to a different application, such as in client/server applications.

This example demonstrates the computation and bandwidth issues for large values that we discussed before. Each new submission accumulates into the application's state (`todoListB`), and the mapping to `todoListView` always recomputes the entire pretty printed string since `todoListB` does not contain information about *how* it changes. Furthermore, the `replicate` function is impossible to implement efficiently since the newly created `todoListView` behavior does not contain information about *how* it changes either. `persist` has to detect changes and either recompute the differences between two behavior values, or send the entire behavior's state.

```
case class Entry(title: String, content: String) { val pretty = s"$title\n$content" }

val submissionE: Event[Entry] = ...

val todoListB: Behavior[List[Message]] =
  submissionE.fold†(List.empty) { (lst, msg) ⇒ msg :: lst }
val todoListView: Behavior[String] = todoListB.map(_.map(_.pretty).mkString)

def replicate(b: Behavior[String]) = ...
replicate(todoListView)
```

Fig. 2. FRP todo list example

Depending on the amount of submissions, both problems can impact the user experience. A programmer has to either accept an underperforming application or remodel his code with less appropriate abstractions such as events as a workaround.

2.3 Incremental Behaviors

The purpose of our new FRP primitive, incremental behaviors, is to capture *when* behaviors change and *how* they change. Semantically we interpret them as a triple of an event (e), an initial value (v_0) and an accumulation function (f):

$$[\![IBehavior_{\tau,\delta}]\!] = \{(e, v_0, f) \in [\![Event_\delta]\!] \times [\![\tau]\!] \times ([\![\tau]\!] \times [\![\delta]\!] \rightarrow [\![\tau]\!])\}$$

An incremental behavior has two type parameters, τ denotes the behavior's value while δ is the type of its increments. The event component in the semantics refers to the increment responsible for the change in a behavior's value. The type signature of the fold † operation on events in Fig. 1 is the motivation behind the semantics. From now on we replace fold † (which creates **Behavior**s) with fold to create incremental behaviors:

```
trait Event {
  ...
  def fold[B](init: B)(accum: (B, A) ⇒ B): IBehavior[B]
}
```

Generally, an incremental behavior is a behavior that has been, or could have been, defined using fold. In other words, it can be seen as a reified fold. To work with incremental behaviors we provide the following functions: constant, incMap, incMap2, snapshot and toBehavior, shown below:

```
trait OneOrBoth[+A, +B]

case class Left[A](l: A) extends OneOrBoth[A, Nothing]
case class Right[B](r: B) extends OneOrBoth[Nothing, B]
case class Both[A, B](l: A, r: B) extends OneOrBoth[A, B]

object IBehavior {
  def constant[A, DA](init: A): IBehavior[A, DA]
}
trait IBehavior[A, DA] {
  def deltas: Event[DA]
  def incMap[B, DB](valueFun: A ⇒ B)(deltaFun: (A, DA) ⇒ DB)
                   (accumulator: (B, DB) ⇒ B): IBehavior[B, DB]
```

```
def incMap2[B, DB, C, DC](b: IBehavior[B, DB])(valueFun: (A, B) ⇒ C)
                         (deltaFun: (A, B, OneOrBoth[DA, DB]) ⇒ Option[DC])
                         (accumulator: (C, DC) ⇒ C): IBehavior[C, DC]
   def snapshot[B, C](ev: Event[B])(f: (A, B) ⇒ C): Event[C]
   def toBehavior: Behavior[A]
}
```

constant and snapshot work exactly as they do on regular behaviors by creating constants and allowing behaviors to be sampled at the rate of events. The chosen semantics for incremental behaviors make their semantic implementation trivial, but the complexity of folding events is moved to toBehavior.

It executes the fold and turns an incremental behavior into a continuous one ($Time \rightarrow \tau$):

$$toBehavior : IBehavior_{\tau,\delta} \rightarrow Behavior_\tau$$

$$[\![toBehavior]\!](\ (e, v_0, f)\ ) = \lambda t.\, f(f(...(f(v_0, d_1), ...), d_{n-1})d_n)$$

$$\textbf{if } (t_1 < ... < t_n \leq t < t_{n+1} < ...) \wedge \{(t_1, d_1), ..., (t_n, d_n), (t_{n+1}, d_{n+1})...\}\ = e$$

toBehavior defines a behavior that, upon evaluation at a time t, returns the accumulation (using f) of all event values up to time t, starting from the initial value (v_0).[4] Note that while toBehavior is an explicit method in this paper, a subclass relation between incremental behaviors and behaviors is completely reasonable.

incMap has the same purpose as a behavior's map, that is, provide a way to apply a function over the data. In the case of incremental behaviors we require three things. (1) f is the function that maps the old value of an incremental behavior to the new. (2) f_δ maps old deltas to new deltas, and (3) accumulator tells us how to put new values and new deltas back together. Note that we expect the programmer to take care of a proper relation between the old accumulator acc_{old}, f_δ, f and the new accumulator acc_{new}:

$$f(acc_{old}(\alpha, \delta_\alpha)) = acc_{new}(f(\alpha), f_\delta(\delta_\alpha)) \qquad \forall \alpha \in A.\, \forall \delta_\alpha \in DA$$

incMap2 is also more complex than a behavior's map2. But its purpose is also the same, that is, provide a way to combine two behaviors into one. Its main parameters are a second behavior and a combination function, but two additional parameters are required to produce an incremental behavior. The first, deltaFun, takes two values of the incoming behaviors as well as a value of type OneOrBoth[DA, DB]. This type contains either an increment of the first or the second behavior (of type DA resp. DB) or both. deltaFun's task is to compute an increment of type DC that represents the change (if any) that the given changes cause in the value of the resulting behavior. The final parameter accumulator tells us how to apply the new type of increments to previous values, it is the fold function for the new incremental behavior.

---

[4] This construction assumes that the event fires only a finite amount of times before any fixed time t (a property we call uniform discreteness).

Fixing Todo List. We fix the overhead issues that were present in the previous example from Fig. 2 by using incremental behaviors in Fig. 3. We omit the creation of submissionE since it is identical to the implementation in Fig. 2.

We create an incremental todo list with incremental state by using fold to create todoListIB. In this example we create an incremental version of the pretty printed todo list (todoListViewIB) by using incMap, the incremental version of map. It takes three arguments. The first defines how to create a pretty printed string from a list of entries by mapping it: _.map(_.pretty).mkString. The second defines how the deltas should change by pretty printing the old delta: _.pretty. The final argument tells us how to combine our new values with the new deltas through string concatenation: (accStr, dStr) => dStr + "n" + accStr.

The result is a version of the pretty printed todo list that is synchronized with the actual state through a time complexity of $\mathcal{O}(1)$ instead of $\mathcal{O}(n)$.[5] Similarly, replicate can now be implemented efficiently since it has access to a behavior's fine-grained change. It can directly send just a trace of its changes.

```
val todoListIB: IBehavior[List[Entry], Entry] =
    submissionE.fold(List.empty) { (list, entry) ⇒ entry :: list }
val todoListViewIB: IBehavior[String, String] =
    todoListIB.incMap { _.map(_.pretty).mkString } { _.pretty }
                       { (accStr, dStr) ⇒ dStr + "\n" + accStr }
def replicate(ib: IBehavior[String, String]) = ...
    replicate(todoListViewIB)
```

Fig. 3. FRP incremental todo list example

3   Incremental Behaviors as a Foundation

The advantages of incremental behaviors are apparent with performance improvements and the ability to model with behaviors where they are appropriate, such as using a behavior for the string representation of our todo list. However, they came at a cost, the API of incremental behaviors is more complex than their non-incremental counterparts. While the general incremental behavior API offers the most freedom, its complexity can be off-putting.

Other work on different FRP primitives such as incremental collections [14, 17] and discrete behaviors [3,15,20] provide similar benefits in certain cases while having a much simpler API. After our general proposal we now demonstrate that these other approaches can be seen as specialized versions of incremental behaviors by implementing them on top of our design.

---

[5] To keep the code concise we ignore the inefficient string operations here.

3.1   Incremental Collections

Compared to regular behaviors, it is harder to create composable incremental behaviors. Let us use `todoListIB` from Fig. 3 as an example. We create a function `toView` that takes an incremental behavior of entries and returns a view such as `todoListViewIB`:

```
def toView(ib: IBehavior[String, String]) =
  ib.incMap { _.map(_.pretty).mkString } { _.pretty }
          { (accStr, dStr) ⇒ dStr + "\n" + accStr }
val todoListIBF: IBehavior[List[Entry], Entry] =
  submissionE.fold(List.empty) { (list, e) ⇒ if (e.title.contains("FRP")) e :: list
                                  else list }
```

Using `toView` on `todoListIB` creates an incremental behavior identical to the previously defined `todoListViewIB`. We define a second version of `todoListIB` that filters out entries that do not contain FRP within their title (`todoListIBF`). Using `toView` on `todoListIBF` instead does not create a properly pretty-printed filtered to-do list version. The problem here is that, although `todoListIBF` also uses `Entry` as the type of deltas, `toView` fails to take into account the different meaning of the delta type: a delta of type `Entry` is unconditionally added to the list in `todoListIB`, but only under a certain condition in `todoListIBF`. This example illustrates a general issue with incremental behaviors: functions operating on them are now not just coupled to the representation of data but also to the representation of deltas.

However, for standard types with standard APIs (like collections), we can mitigate this problem by defining a standard type of deltas (with a standard meaning). Both [14,17] propose incremental collections in a reactive programming environment to get more efficient collection operations without adding the API complexity that incremental behaviors bring. For this section, we focus on [14]'s abstraction: an incremental sequence (`RSeq[A]`) and discuss how it can be implemented on top of incremental behaviors. From a high level you can think of it as an efficient version of `Behavior[Seq[A]]`. Its usage and API is similar to collection libraries as shown in Fig. 4.

A commonly used operation is `map`, which for reactive sequences returns a new reactive sequence. The mapped `RSeq` does not remap the entire list upon change, instead modifications to the list are processed on their own. Elements that should be inserted are mapped separately and their results are inserted directly. The same goes for deletions, which are propagated to the mapped list and directly remove an element. Other common collection operations work similarly.

```
trait RSeq[A] {
    def map[B](f: A ⇒ B): RSeq[B]
    def filter(f: A ⇒ Boolean): RSeq[A]
    def foldUndo[B](init: B)(op: (B, A) ⇒ B)(undo: (B, A) ⇒ B): Behavior[B]
    def flatMap[B](f: A ⇒ RSeq[B]): RSeq[B]
}
```

Fig. 4. Reactive sequence core API

We implement reactive sequences as a special kind of incremental behavior: `RSeq[A]` $\simeq$ `IBehavior[Vector[A], SeqDelta[A]]`. Our Scala prototype implementation of incremental behaviors also contains a collection library. It implements incremental collections by using a standard delta that models common operations such as addition or deletion. Incremental collection APIs are implemented through incremental behavior operations such as `incMap2`. It plugs into the Scala standard library and uses the appropriate collection abstractions such as traversable and sequence to provide a generic incremental API for the collection library.

In Fig. 5, we demonstrate the model of such an incremental collection. Do keep in mind that to avoid Scala-specific concepts we focus on a reactive sequence implementation for just the vector and that an implementation for generic traversables or sequences is more complex.

In short, the incremental vector that we build is a vector data structure that efficiently handles incremental changes based on incremental behaviors. As a first step we model the different types of incremental changes (`SeqDelta`s). Each increment contains a method `apply` that defines the application of the increment to a vector, for brevity we assume its implementation. The different types of increments that we support are: an insertion (`Insert`), a removal (`Remove`), an in-place update (`Update`) or a combination of other deltas (`Combined`). Insertions simply contain the element to be inserted at a specific index, removals contain the element that should be removed and updates contain an element that should replace an element on a specific index.

They correspond to the three functions that are available on the incremental vector: `updated`, `insert` and `remove` as shown in Fig. 5.

Using the model from Fig. 5, we implement a simple version of an incremental map in Fig. 6. Its created by using the incremental behavior's `incMap` function. The first argument provides a way to transform the initial vector to an initial result vector. In our case this is a simple map: `v => v.map(f)`. The second argument contains the transformation on the increments. For this we defined a helper function that applies the function f and use it accordingly: `d => mapDelta(d, f)`. The final argument defines how new deltas are applied to new values, in our case it remains the assumed `apply` method on `SeqDelta`.

For a discussion about higher order APIs on reactive sequences such as `flatMap` we refer to Sect. 5.

3.2 Discrete Behaviors

Continuous behaviors change unpredictably and continuously and their semantics are simple because their meaning are functions of time ($Time \rightarrow \tau$). But, in practice, discrete behaviors are often used [3,15,20]. The semantics provide less freedom but they express discrete changes. Essentially, they capture and expose *when* behaviors change. They are represented as an initial value and a stream of value changes:

$$[\![DBehavior_\tau]\!] = \{(e, v_0) \in [\![Event_\tau]\!] \times [\![\tau]\!]\}$$

```
type IVector[A] = IBehavior[Vector[A], SeqDelta[A]]

sealed trait SeqDelta[+A] {
  def apply(v: Vector[A]): Vector[A]
}
case class Insert[A](element: A, index: Int)            extends SeqDelta[A]
case class Remove[A](element: A)                        extends SeqDelta[A]
case class Update[A](element: A, index: Int)            extends SeqDelta[A]
case class Combined[A](d1: SeqDelta[A], d2: SeqDelta[A])  extends SeqDelta[A]

def updated[A](iv: IVector[A], updates: Event[(A, Int)]): IVector[A]
def insert[A](iv: IVector[A], insertions: Event[(A, Int)]): IVector[A]
def remove[A](iv: IVector[A], deletions: Event[Int]): IVector[A]
```

Fig. 5. Reactive sequence implementation

```
def mapDelta[A, B](d: SeqDelta[A], f: A ⇒ B): SeqDelta[B] =
  d match {
    case Insert(element, i)   ⇒ Insert(f(element), i)
    case Remove(element)      ⇒ Remove(f(element))
    case Update(element, i)   ⇒ Update(f(element), i)
    case Combined(d1, d2)     ⇒ Combined(mapDelta(d1, f), mapDelta(d2, f))
  }
def map[A, B](rseq: IVector[A])(f: A ⇒ B): IVector[B] =
  rseq.incMap(v ⇒ v.map(f))(d ⇒ mapDelta(d, f)) {
    (acc: B, delta: SeqDelta[A]) ⇒ delta.apply(acc)
  }
```

Fig. 6. Map implementation

Other than exposing the time at which they change (def changes: Event[A]), their API is identical to that of continuous behaviors.

It turns out that discrete behaviors can be implemented as a special case of incremental behaviors (DBehavior[A] ≃ IBehavior[A, A]) with a trivial implementation for the accumulator. Their simple behavior API is possible since the accumulator never changes and both types are the same, for example an implementation of map:

```
type DBehavior[A] = IBehavior[A, A]
def accumulator[A](oldV: A, newV: A) = newV
def map[A, B](b: DBehavior[A])(f: A ⇒ B): DBehavior[B] = b.incMap(f)(f)(accumulator)
```

Incremental Behaviors Through Computing Differences. There are situations where bandwidth is costly such as saving a behavior's history to disk (for logging or debugging) or sending its data across the network. When time complexity is of less concern, the API complexity of incremental methods (such as incMap2) makes them less desirable, regardless of their computational benefits.

To accommodate these scenarios we propose a way to obtain incremental behaviors through the simpler discrete behaviors:

```
trait DBehavior[A] {
  def toIBehavior[DA](diff: (A, A) ⇒ DA)(patch: (A, DA) ⇒ A): IBehavior[A, DA]
  def toIBehaviorGeneric[DA](implicit d: Delta[A, DA]): IBehavior[A, DA]
}
```

We recover increments between values by computing their differences. We require diff and patch functions to be defined with the following relation:

$patch(v_1, diff(v_2, v_1)) = v_2 \quad \forall v_1, v_2 \in A$. `diff` is used to compute differences that work as deltas and `patch` completes the incremental behavior by defining how they fold back into a value. In practice these two functions can often be derived with generic programming approaches. For example, there is a Scala library[6] which could be integrated; in this case the user would see an API like `DBehavior.toIBehaviorGeneric`. Using it is easy, for example, converting `rates`:

```
val rates: DBehavior[Set[Rate]] = ...
rates.toIBehaviorGeneric
```

4 Evaluation

Accompanying our proposed incremental behavior API is a prototype implementation of our ideas. We evaluate this prototype through some microbenchmarks to confirm our expected results. Note that neither our FRP implementation nor our incremental collection implementation were built with performance in mind and as such, overhead is not as low as it could be.[7]

Computational Performance. In Fig. 7 we demonstrate the results regarding the computational performance of incremental behaviors. This microbenchmark is similar to the todo list example of Fig. 3. We start with an initial vector of a certain amount of integers (plotted on the x-axis) and map them with a function that generates 10 random numbers. Afterwards, we update a single value in the collection and propagate the change to the mapped collection (time to update plotted on the y-axis). As a base case we use a regular push-based (discrete) behavior that contains a Scala vector from the collection library (marked `DBehavior[Vector[Int]]`). We compare the base case to three different incremental behaviors. First, a hand coded implementation using the `fold` primitive, exactly as we did in the todo list example from Fig. 3 (marked `IBehavior[Vector[Int], Int]`). Second, an implementation based on the incremental collection abstraction from Sect. 3.1 (marked `ICollection[Int, Vector[Int]]`). Finally, an implementation which starts from the base case vector and performs a naive diffing comparing all elements of the vectors in order to convert a discrete behavior into an incremental one as discussed in Sect. 3.2 (marked `DBehavior[Vector[Int]] => ICollection[Int, Vector[Int]]`).

The graphs show that, as expected, the naive approach of the regular behavior is the slowest. It remaps every element in the vector whenever a change is made since it does not propagate what changed. The hand coded example has the best performance, it is hard-coded to handle only one case, modifying the head of the collection. It maps the element in isolation and then creates a new modified

---

[6] https://github.com/stacycurl/delta.
[7] To make our benchmarks as accurate and fair as possible on the JVM, the measurements are results over multiple VM invocations, each prepared with warmup operations.

Scala vector. Similarly, the incremental collections vector also isolates changes, however it has to go through an added abstraction layer that handles other cases than just changing the head of a collection, this causes a bit of overhead. Finally, the case of recomputing the differences. Recomputing the differences trades remapping for a difference algorithm, depending on the algorithm the outcome may be worth it.

Bandwidth Overhead. In Fig. 8 we demonstrate the results of a scenario where bandwidth matters. The goal of the application is to write a trace to disk from which all versions of values can be recomputed. This mimics scenarios where bandwidth is important, such as replicating a behavior's value across the internet. Its implementation is similar to the todo list example in Fig. 3. We change one element in the collection several times and after every change we expect to be able to trace a trail of its value on disk. The most efficient implementation logs the first value in its entirety and adds differences afterwards.

We test the same four cases as the last benchmark. We can immediately see that no matter the vector's size, the incremental implementations remains constant in storage size since their differences remain identical (1 value change). Again, there is an overhead for the higher abstractions used. Extra information regarding the change to the collection is encoded by the incremental collections vector which implies a larger bandwidth footprint. The hand coded result only supports the specific case of the benchmark and logs the absolute minimum at the cost of added programmer complexity. The base case is a naive implementation that logs the entire vector every time.

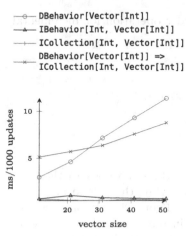

Fig. 7. Updating logged vectors

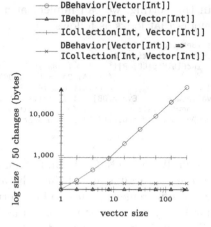

Fig. 8. Updating logged vectors

5 Discussion: Higher-Order Incremental Behaviors

In the paper we used *first-order FRP* instead of higher order FRP. Concretely, this means that we do not provide APIs that are higher-order in the sense that they work with events of events or behaviors of behaviors. A typical example is:

```
def join[A](b: Event[Event[A]]): Event[A]
```

It takes an event that fires new events and returns an event that dynamically includes other events.

Higher-order APIs is a tricky subject because the natural semantics for APIs like `join` cannot be implemented without storing or being able to recalculate all previous values of any generated behavior or event that is incorporated into the network. This implies a very high memory usage, which is known in the FRP literature as *time leaks*, see [22] for more details. Various solutions have been proposed for avoiding time leaks, often based on restricting which `Events` may fire from an argument of APIs like `join`. A particularly powerful system was presented by [13] that manages to offer very powerful higher-order FRP primitives, using temporally modal types to exclude space-time leaks and requiring explicit use of allocation tokens when retaining values accross ticks is really desired.

We do not go into more details on higher-order FRP or the ways to avoid time leaks, because we believe incremental behaviors are orthogonal to the problem. If we assume the existence of a naive higher-order `flatMap` API for standard events (as used by [7]), then we can implement a higher-order primitive for incremental behaviors. Concretely, we assume a higher-order API with the following function that lets us flatten nested events:

```
def flatMap[A, B](e: Event[A], f: A ⇒ Event[B]): Event[B]
```

In this setting, we can implement a higher-order operation for incremental behaviors that looks as follows:

```
trait IBehavior[A, DA] {
  private val initial: A
  def incFlatMap[DB, B](fa: A ⇒ IBehavior[B, DB])
                       (fb: (A, DA) ⇒ Event[DB])
                       (accumulator: (B, DB) ⇒ B): IBehavior[B, DB] = {
    val newDeltas: Event[DB] = this.deltas.flatMap(fb)
    val newInitial: B        = fa(this.initial).initial
    newDeltas.fold(newInitial)(accumulator)
  }
}
```

Similarly to `incMap`, the first argument maps the old values to the new, while the last argument redefines the accumulator. But, the second argument allows new increment events to be inserted ($DA =>$ `Event[DB]`). In other words, it enables dynamic insertion of deltas into the incremental behavior. Use of `incFlatMap` is only correct if `fa`'s behavior and `fb`'s event have the following relation: $\forall a.\, \forall da.\, fb(a, da) = fa(applyDelta(a, da)).changes$

Interestingly, this `incFlatMap` on incremental behaviors and `join` on events is all that is required to implement the missing higher order methods from reactive sequences in Sect. 3.1.

6 Related Work

We split our related work section into two categories: (1) functional reactive programming and its semantics, and (2) incremental computing, and more specifically self-adjusting computations (SAC).

Functional Reactive Programming was first introduced in FRAN [6] to write composable reactive animations. However, its proposed semantics are inherently leaky in the higher-order primitives [22, see Sect. 2]. Since then multiple revisions of the semantics were proposed [7,10,13,21,22, see among others,].

In contrast, our work focuses on extending the first-order semantics with support for explicit incremental computations. The incremental behaviors that we propose are a generalization of patterns that appear in other work like incremental lists [14,17] or discrete behaviors [3,15,20]. An implementation of incremental behaviors that is, as far as we can tell, close to the semantics proposed in this paper can be found in the grapefruit library [12], but its semantics are not written down in documentation or an accompanying paper.

Incremental Computation is a way of implementing programs that do not redo entire calculations after a change in input. We divide this work based on how much manual work a programmer has to do.

Some approaches based on memoization [18] and self-adjusting computations (SAC) [1] minimize manual interference by using dependency graphs and propagation algorithms to efficiently react to input changes. In practice, this has several similarities with FRP, which is also frequently implemented by propagating changes through dependency graphs. However, their focus and granularity differ. SAC focuses on efficiently reacting to small changes in input while FRP focuses on providing simple denotational semantics for event-driven programs. Our FRP work with incremental behaviors is a middle ground which allows programmers to manually express a finer granularity compared to traditional FRP. It allows incremental computations that use the FRP implementation's propagation and dependency tracking to be defined by the user. [4] describes a different approach to automated incremental computations. They define ILC, a static and extendable program-to-program transformation that lifts incremental computations on first-order programs to incremental computations on higher-order programs.

A different approach to automated solutions are frameworks that help programmers with writing incremental computations. Instead of trying to automate the encoding of incremental algorithms it aims to make such computations easier to write such as the reactive sequences [14]. We discuss two other examples in detail:

i3QL [16] proposes relational algebra as a suitable API for incremental computing. i3QL operators are a high-level abstraction for incremental computing implemented on top of a low-level Observable-like change-propagation framework that supports events for adding, removing and updating values. Incremental behaviors are an addition to traditional FRP to further capture when and how values change, it's more akin to the lower-level implementation of i3QL's propagation framework (which supports 'when' and 'how' natively). It would be very interesting to see to which extent incremental behaviors and FRP can be used to implement i3QL's relational algebra operators.

[8] describes a general framework in which incremental changes and their propagation are made to compose through typeclasses. They define a type class for changes:

```
class Change a where
  type Value p :: *
  ($$) :: p -> Value p -> Value p
```

A change of some type has a value to which it can be applied using the `$$` function. Incremental operations can be defined as transformation from one type to another. A transformation in its simplest form is a pair of two functions:

```
data Trans p q = Trans (Value p -> Value q) (p -> q)
```

The similarity between these transformations and our `incMap` on behaviors is interesting. `incMap` takes three functions as arguments, one turns a state `A` into another, a change `DA` into another and finally a function that defines how the new change and the new state can be combined. This corresponds exactly to the `Trans` and `Change` functionality. `Trans` defines how to convert both values and changes from one type to another while `Change` makes sure that there is a way to apply changes to a value.

Note that they propose several more complicated versions of `Trans`, e.g.:

```
data Trans p q = forall s. Trans (Value p -> (Value q, s)) (p -> s -> (q, s))
data Trans p q = Trans (forall s. Value p -> ST s (Value q, p -> ST s q))
```

The first provides access to a local pure state. Something that can be emulated with `incMap`. The second version provides *safe* access to local mutable state, something for which we do not have an alternative. Given the similarites between the two approaches a logical step for future work seems to incorporate the typeclass-based framework for incremental computing into the incremental behavior API which could give us alternative definitions such as:

```
trait ITBehavior[A: Change] {
  def incMap[B: Change](trans: Trans[A, B]): ITBehavior[B]
}
```

As a final note, Several SAC papers [2,9] refer to FRP and point out opportunities to combine the two, for example, [2] says "Although FRP research remained largely orthogonal to incremental computation, it may benefit from incremental computation, because computations performed at consecutive time steps can be similar.". Incremental behaviors may be a stepping stone towards a better integration of incremental computations in FRP.

7 Conclusion and Future Work

Functional Reactive Programming in theory is nice and simple, but in practice there are some shortcomings that prevent general use. This paper tackles one such problem, the ability to efficiently deal with large incrementally constructed values.

We presented incremental behaviors, a new FRP primitive that can express *how* and *when* values change. We show that it can be used as a foundation for other abstractions and demonstrate that its benefits are noticeable by executing a performance analysis and comparing it to traditional FRP.

As future work, applying ideas from self-adjusting computations to further automate the writing of incremental programs sounds promising. An automatic and efficient replacement to our `diff` function which converts discrete to incremental behaviors efficiently would be the ideal case.

Acknowledgments. Bob Reynders holds an SB fellowship of the Research Foundation - Flanders (FWO). Dominique Devriese holds a postdoctoral fellowship of the Research Foundation - Flanders (FWO).

References

1. Acar, U.A., Blelloch, G.E., Harper, R.: Adaptive functional programming. TOPLAS **28**(6), 990–1034 (2006)
2. Acar, U.A., Blume, M., Donham, J.: A consistent semantics of self-adjusting computation. J. Funct. Program. **23**(03), 249–292 (2013)
3. Blackheath, S.: Denotational semantics for Sodium (2015). http://blog.reactiveprogramming.org/?p=236
4. Cai, Y., Giarrusso, P.G., Rendel, T., Ostermann, K.: A theory of changes for higher-order languages: incrementalizing λ-calculi by static differentiation. In: PLDI, vol. 49, pp. 145–155. ACM (2014)
5. Czaplicki, E., Chong, S.: Asynchronous functional reactive programming for GUIs. In: PLDI, pp. 411–422. ACM (2013)
6. Elliott, C., Hudak, P.: Functional reactive animation. In: ICFP, pp. 263–273. ACM (1997)
7. Elliott, C.M.: Push-pull functional reactive programming. In: Haskell, pp. 25–36. ACM (2009)
8. Firsov, D., Jeltsch, W.: Purely functional incremental computing. In: Castor, F., Liu, Y.D. (eds.) SBLP 2016. LNCS, vol. 9889, pp. 62–77. Springer, Cham (2016). https://doi.org/10.1007/978-3-319-45279-1_5
9. Hammer, M.A., Dunfield, J., Headley, K., Labich, N., Foster, J.S., Hicks, M., Van Horn, D.: Incremental computation with names. In: OOPSLA, vol. 50, pp. 748–766. ACM (2015)
10. Jeltsch, W.: Signals, Not Generators!. Trends Funct. Program. **10**, 145–160 (2009)
11. Jeltsch, W.: Strongly typed and efficient functional reactive programming. Ph.D. thesis, Universitätsbibliothek (2011)
12. Jeltsch, W.: Grapefruit-frp: functional reactive programming core (2012). https://hackage.haskell.org/package/grapefruit-frp
13. Krishnaswami, N.R.: Higher-order functional reactive programming without space-time leaks. In: ICFP, vol. 48, pp. 221–232. ACM (2013)
14. Maier, I., Odersky, M.: Higher-order reactive programming with incremental lists. In: Castagna, G. (ed.) ECOOP 2013. LNCS, vol. 7920, pp. 707–731. Springer, Heidelberg (2013). https://doi.org/10.1007/978-3-642-39038-8_29

15. Maier, I., Rompf, T., Odersky, M.: Deprecating the observer pattern. Technical report (2010)
16. Mitschke, R., Erdweg, S., Köhler, M., Mezini, M., Salvaneschi, G.: i3ql: language-integrated live data views. In: Proceedings of the 2014 ACM International Conference on Object Oriented Programming Systems Languages & Applications, pp. 417–432. ACM (2014)
17. Prokopec, A., Haller, P., Odersky, M.: Containers and aggregates, mutators and isolates for reactive programming. In: SCALA, pp. 51–61. ACM (2014)
18. Pugh, W., Teitelbaum, T.: Incremental computation via function caching. In: POPL, pp. 315–328. ACM (1989)
19. Reynders, B., Devriese, D., Piessens, F.: Multi-tier functional reactive programming for the web. In: Onward!, pp. 55–68. ACM (2014)
20. Salvaneschi, G., Hintz, G., Mezini, M.: REScala: Bridging between object-oriented and functional style in reactive applications. In: Modularity, pp. 25–36. ACM (2014)
21. van der Ploeg, A.: Monadic functional reactive programming. In: Haskell, vol. 48(12), pp. 117–128 (2014)
22. van der Ploeg, A., Claessen, K.: Practical principled FRP: forget the past, change the future, FRPNow! In: ICFP, pp. 302–314. ACM (2015)
23. Wan, Z., Taha, W., Hudak, P.: Real-time FRP. In: ICFP, pp. 146–156. ACM (2001)

Implementing Algebraic Effects in C
"Monads for Free in C"

Daan Leijen[✉]

Microsoft Research, Redmond, USA
daan@microsoft.com

Abstract. We describe an implementation of algebraic effects and handlers as a library in standard and portable C99, where effect operations
can be used just like regular C functions. We use a formal operational
semantics to guide the C implementation at every step where an evaluation context corresponds directly to a particular C execution context.
Finally we show a novel extension to the semantics for optimized tail
resumptions and prove it sound. This gives two orders of magnitude
improvement to the performance of tail resumptive operations (up to
about 150 million operations per second on a Core i7@2.6GHz).

1 Introduction

Algebraic effects [34] and handlers [35,36] come from category theory as a way
to reason about effects. Effects come with a set of operations as their interface,
and handlers to give semantics to the operations. Any free monad [2,17,38] can
be expressed using algebraic effect handlers: the operations describe an algebra
that gives rise to a free monad, whereas the handler is the *fold* over that algebra
giving its semantics.

This makes algebraic effects highly expressive and practical, and they can
describe many control flow constructs that are usually built into a language
or compiler. Examples include, exception handling, iterators, backtracking, and
async/await style asynchronous programming. Once you have algebraic effects,
all of these abstractions can be implemented *as a library* by the user. In this
article, we describe a practical implementation of algebraic effects and handlers
as a library itself in C. In particular,

- We describe a full implementation of algebraic effects and handlers in standard and portable C99. Using effect operations is just like calling regular
  C functions. Stacks are always restored at the same location and regular C
  semantics are preserved.
- Even though the semantics of algebraic effects are simple, the implementation in C is not straightforward. We use a formal operational semantics to
  guide the C implementation at every step. In particular, we use context based
  semantics where a formal context corresponds directly to a particular C execution context.

© Springer International Publishing AG 2017
B.-Y.E. Chang (Ed.): APLAS 2017, LNCS 10695, pp. 339–363, 2017.
https://doi.org/10.1007/978-3-319-71237-6_17

– We show a novel extension to the formal semantics to describe optimized tail resumptions and prove that the extension is sound. This gives two orders of magnitude improvement to the performance of tail resumptive operations (up to about 150 million operations per second on a Core i7).

At this point using effects in C is nice, but defining handlers is still a bit cumbersome. Its interface could probably be improved by providing a C++ wrapper. For now, we mainly see the library as a target for library writers or compilers. For example, the P language [11] is a language for describing verifiable asynchronous state machines, and used for example to implement and verify the core of the USB device driver stack that ships with Microsoft Windows 8. Compiling to C involves a complex CPS-style transformation [19,26] to enable async/await style programming [5] with a `receive` statement - using the effects library this transformation is no longer necessary and we can generate straightforward C code instead. Similarly, we are integrating this library with `libuv` [29] (the asynchronous C library underlying Node [41]) enabling programming with `libuv` directly from C or C++ using async/await style abstractions [13,28].

The library is publicly available as `libhandler` under an open-source license [25]. For simplicity the description in this paper leaves out many details and error handling etc. but otherwise follows the real implementation closely. We refer the reader to the extended technical report [27] for further details and integration with C++.

2 Overview

We necessarily give a short overview here of using algebraic effects in C. For how this can look if a language natively supports effects, we refer to reader to other work [3,18,26,28,30]. Even though the theory of algebraic effects describes them in terms of monads, we use a more operational view in this article that is just as valid - and view effects as *resumable exceptions*. Therefore we start by describing how to implement regular exceptions using effect handlers.

2.1 Exceptions

Implementing exceptions as an algebraic effect is straightforward. First we declare a new effect `exn` with a single operation `raise` that takes a `const char*` argument:

```
DEFINE_EFFECT1(exn, raise)
DEFINE_VOIDOP1(exn, raise, string)
```

Later we will show exactly what these macros expand to. For now, it is enough to know that the second line defines a new operation `exn_raise` that we can call as any other C function, for example:

```
int divexn( int x, int y ) {
  return (y!=0 ? x / y : exn_raise("divide by zero")); }
```

Since using an effect operation is just like calling a regular C function, this makes the library easy to use from a user perspective.

Defining *handlers* is a bit more involved. Here is a possible handler function for our **raise** operation:

```
value handle_exn_raise(resume* r, value local, value arg) {
  printf("exception raised: %s\n", string_value(arg));
  return value_null; }
```

The value type is used here to simulate parametric polymorphism in C and is typedef'd to a long long, together with some suitable conversion macros; in the example we use string_value to cast the value back to the const char* argument that was passed to exn_raise.

Using the new operation handler is done using the handle library function. It is a bit cumbersome as we need to set up a handler definition (handlerdef) that contains a table of all operation handlers:

```
const operation _exn_ops[] = {
  { OP_NORESUME, OPTAG(exn,raise), &handle_exn_raise } };
const handlerdef _exn_def  = { EFFECT(exn), NULL, NULL, NULL, _exn_ops };

value my_exn_handle(value(*action)(value), value arg) {
  return handle(&_exn_def, value_null, action, arg); }
```

Using the handler, we can run the full example as:

```
value divide_by(value x) {
  return value_long(divexn(42,long_value(x)));
}
int main() {
  my_exn_handle( divide_by, value_long(0));
  return 0; }
```

When running this program, we'll see:

```
exception raised: divide by zero
```

A handler definition has as its last field a list of operations, defined as:

```
typedef struct _operation {
  const opkind  opkind;
  const optag   optag;
  value         (*opfun)(resume* r, value local, value arg);
} operation;
```

The operation tag optag uniquely identifies the operation, while the opkind describes the kind of operation handler:

```
typedef enum _opkind {
  OP_NULL,
  OP_NORESUME,  // never resumes
  OP_TAIL,      // only uses 'resume' in tail-call position
  OP_SCOPED,    // only uses 'resume' inside the handler
  OP_GENERAL    // 'resume' is a first-class value
} opkind;
```

These operation kinds are used for optimization and restrict what an operation handler can do. In this case we used `OP_NORESUME` to signify that our operation handler never resumes. We'll see examples of the other kinds in the following sections.

The `DEFINE_EFFECT` macro defines a new effect. For our example, it expands into something like:

```
const char*  effect_exn[3]    = {"exn","exn_raise",NULL};
const optag  optag_exn_raise = { effect_exn, 1 };
```

An effect can now be uniquely identified by the address of the `effect_exn` array, and `EFFECT(exn)` expands simply into `effect_exn`. Similarly, `OPTAG(exn,raise)` expands into `optag_exn_raise`. Finally, the `DEFINE_VOIDOP1` definition in our example expands into a small wrapper around the library `yield` function:

```
void exn_raise( const char* s ) {
  yield( optag_exn_raise, value_string(s) ); }
```

which "yields" to the innermost handler for `exn_raise`.

2.2   Ambient State

As we saw in the exception example, the handler for the `raise` operation took a `resume*` argument. This can be used to *resume* an operation at the point where it was issued. This is where the true power of algebraic effects come from (and why we can view them as resumable exceptions). As another example, we are going to implement *ambient state* [28].

```
DEFINE_EFFECT(state,put,get)
DEFINE_OP0(state,get,int)
DEFINE_VOIDOP1(state,put,int)
```

This defines a new effect `state` with the operations `void state_put(int)` and `int state_get()`. We can use them as any other C function:

```
void loop() {
  int i;
  while((i = state_get()) > 0) {
```

```
    printf("state: %i\n", i);
    state_put(i-1);
} }
```

We call this *ambient state* since it is dynamically bound to the innermost
state handler - instead of being global or local state. This captures many common patterns in practice. For example, when writing a web server, the "current"
request object needs to be passed around manually to each function in general;
with algebraic effects you can just create a `request` effect that gives access to
the current request without having to pass it explicitly to every function. The
handler for `state` uses the `local` argument to store the current state:

```
value handle_state_get( resume* r, value local, value arg ) {
  return tail_resume(r,local,local); }
value handle_state_put( resume* r, value local, value arg ) {
  return tail_resume(r,arg,value_null); }
```

The `tail_resume` (or `resume`) library function resumes an operation at its
yield point. It takes three arguments: the resumption object `r`, the new value of
the local handler state `local`, and the return value for the `yield` operation. Here
the `handle_state_get` handler simply returns the current local state, whereas
`handle_state_put` returns a null value but resumes with its local state set to
`arg`. The `tail_resume` operation can only be used in a tail-call position and
only with `OP_TAIL` operations, but it is much more efficient than using a general
`resume` function (as shown in Sect. 5).

2.3   Backtracking

> You can enter a room once, yet leave it twice.
> — Peter Landin [22, 23]

In the previous examples we looked at an abstractions that never resume (e.g.
exceptions), and an abstractions that resumes once (e.g. state). Such abstractions
are common in most programming languages. Less common are abstractions that
can resume more than once. Examples of this behavior can usually only be found
in languages like Lisp and Scheme, that implement some variant of `callcc` [40].
A nice example to illustrate multiple resumptions is the ambiguity effect:

```
DEFINE_EFFECT1(amb,flip)
DEFINE_BOOLOP0(amb,flip,bool)
```

which defines one operation `bool amb_flip()` that returns a boolean. We can
use it as:

```
bool xor() {
  bool p = amb_flip();
  bool q = amb_flip();
  return ((p || q) && !(p && q)); }
```

One possible handler just returns a random boolean on every flip:

```
value random_amb_flip( resume* r, value local, value arg ) {
  return tail_resume(r, local, value_bool( rand()%2 )); }
```

but a more interesting handler resumes *twice*: once with a `true` result, and once with `false`. That way we can return a list of all results from the handler:

```
value all_amb_flip( resume* r, value local, value arg ) {
  value xs = resume(r,local, value_bool(true));
  value ys = resume(r,local, value_bool(false)); // resume again at 'r'!
  return list_append(xs,ys); }
```

Note that the results of the `resume` operations are lists themselves since a resumption runs itself under the handler. When we run the `xor` function under the `all_amb` handler, we get back a list of all possible results of running `xor`, printed as:

```
[false,true,true,false]
```

In general, resuming more than once is a dangerous thing to do in C. When using mutable state or external resources, most C code assumes it runs at most once, for example closing file handles or releasing memory when exiting a lexical scope. Resuming again from inside such scope would give invalid results.

Nevertheless, you can make this work safely if you for example manage state using effect handlers themselves which take care of releasing resources correctly. Multiple resumptions are also needed for implementing async/await interleaving where the resumptions are safe by construction.

2.4 Asynchronous Programming

Recent work shows how to build `async/await` abstractions on top of algebraic effects [13,28]. We are using a similar approach to implement a nice interface to programming `libuv` directly in C. This is still work in progress [25] and we only sketch here the basic approach to show how algebraic effects can enable this. We define an asynchronous effect as:

```
DEFINE_EFFECT1(async,await)
int  await( uv_req_t* req );
void async_callback(uv_req_t* req);
```

The handler for `async` only needs to implement `await`. This operation receives an asynchronous `libuv` request object `uv_req_t` where it only stores its resumption in the request custom `data` field. However, it does not resume itself! Instead it returns directly to the outer `libuv` event loop which invokes the registered callbacks when an asynchronous operation completes.

```
value handle_async_await( resume* r, value local, value arg ) {
  uv_req_t* req = (uv_req_t*)ptr_value(arg);
  req->data = r;
  return value_null; }
```

We ensure that the asynchronous `libuv` functions all use the same `async_callback` function as their callback. This in turn calls the actual resumption that was stored in the `data` field by `await`:

```
void async_callback( uv_req_t* req ) {
  resume* r = (resume*)req->data;
  resume(r, req->result); }
```

In other words, instead of explicit callbacks with the current state encoded in the `data` field, the current execution context is fully captured by the first-class resumption provided by our library. We can now write small wrappers around the `libuv` asynchronous API to use the new `await` operation, for example, here is the wrapper for an asynchronous file stat:

```
int async_stat( const char* path, uv_stat_t* stat ) {
  uv_fs_t* req = (uv_fs_t*)malloc(sizeof(uv_fs_t));
  uv_stat(uv_default_loop(), req, path, async_callback);  // register
  int err = await((uv_req_t*)req);                        // and await
  *stat = req->statbuf;
  uv_fs_req_cleanup(req);
  free(req);
  return content; }
```

The asynchronous functions can be called just like regular functions:

```
uv_stat_t stat;
int err = async_stat("foo.txt", &stat);  // asynchronous!
printf("Last access time: %li\n", (err < 0 ? 0 : stat.st_atim.tv_sec));
```

This makes it much more pleasant to use `libuv` directly in C.

3   Operational Semantics

An attractive feature of algebraic effects and handlers is that they have a simple operational semantics that is well-understood. To guide our implementation in C we define a tiny core calculus for algebraic effects and handlers that is well-suited to reason about the operational behavior.

Figure 1 shows the syntax of our core calculus, λ_{eff}. This is equivalent to the definition given by Leijen [26]. It consists of basic lambda calculus extended with handler definitions h and operations op. The calculus can also be typed using regular static typing rules [18,26,37]. However, we can still give a dynamic *untyped* operational semantics: this is important in practice as it allows an implementation algebraic effects without needing explicit types at runtime.

$$
\begin{array}{llll}
\text{Expressions} & e & ::= & e(e) & \text{application} \\
& & | & \text{val } x = e;\ e & \text{binding} \\
& & | & \text{handle}_h(e) & \text{handler} \\
& & | & v & \text{value} \\
\text{Values} & v & ::= & x \mid c \mid op \mid \lambda x.\ e \\
\text{Clauses} & h & ::= & \text{return } x \to e \\
& & | & op(x) \to e;\ h & op \notin h
\end{array}
$$

Fig. 1. Syntax of expressions in λ_{eff}

Evaluation contexts:

$$
\begin{aligned}
\mathsf{E} &::= [] \mid \mathsf{E}(e) \mid v(\mathsf{E}) \mid op(\mathsf{E}) \mid \text{val } x = \mathsf{E};\ e \mid \text{handle}_h(\mathsf{E}) \\
\mathsf{X}_{op} &::= [] \mid \mathsf{X}_{op}(e) \mid v(\mathsf{X}_{op}) \mid \text{val } x = \mathsf{X}_{op};\ e \\
& \quad\ \mid \text{handle}_h(\mathsf{X}_{op}) \qquad\qquad\qquad\qquad \text{if } op \notin h
\end{aligned}
$$

Reduction rules:

$$
\begin{array}{llll}
(\delta) & c(v) & \longrightarrow & \delta(c,v) \quad \text{if } \delta(c,v) \text{ is defined} \\
(\beta) & (\lambda x.\ e)(v) & \longrightarrow & e[x \mapsto v] \\
(let) & \text{val } x = v;\ e & \longrightarrow & e[x \mapsto v]
\end{array}
$$

$$
\begin{array}{lll}
(return) & \text{handle}_h(v) & \longrightarrow & e[x \mapsto v] \\
& & \text{with} \\
& & (\text{return } x \to e) \in h
\end{array}
$$

$$
\begin{array}{lll}
(handle) & \text{handle}_h(\mathsf{X}_{op}[op(v)]) \longrightarrow e[x \mapsto v,\ resume \mapsto \lambda y.\ \text{handle}_h(\mathsf{X}_{op}[y])] \\
& \qquad \text{with} \\
& \qquad (op(x) \to e) \in h
\end{array}
$$

Fig. 2. Reduction rules and evaluation contexts

Figure 2 defines the semantics of λ_{eff} in just five evaluation rules. It has been shown that well-typed programs cannot go 'wrong' under these semantics [26]. We use two evaluation contexts: the E context is the usual one for a call-by-value lambda calculus. The X_{op} context is used for handlers and evaluates down through any handlers that do *not* handle the operation op. This is used to express concisely that the 'innermost handler' handles particular operations.

The E context concisely captures the entire evaluation context, and is used to define the evaluation function over the basic reduction rules: $\mathsf{E}[e] \longmapsto \mathsf{E}[e']$ iff $e \longrightarrow e'$. The first three reduction rules, (δ), (β), and (let) are the standard rules of call-by-value evaluation. The final two rules evaluate handlers. Rule $(return)$ applies the return clause of a handler when the argument is fully evaluated.

The next rule, $(handle)$, shows that algebraic effect handlers are closely related to delimited continuations as the evaluation rules captures a delimited 'stack' $\mathsf{X}_{op}[op(v)]$ under the handler h. Using a X_{op} context ensures by construction that only the innermost handler containing a clause for op, can handle the operation $op(v)$. Evaluation continues with the expression ϵ but besides binding the parameter x to v, also the *resume* variable is bound to the continuation: $\lambda y.\,\mathsf{handle}_h(\mathsf{X}_{op}[y])$. Applying *resume* results in continuing evaluation at X_{op} with the supplied argument as the result. Moreover, the continued evaluation occurs again under the handler h.

3.1 Dot Notation

The C implementation closely follows the formal semantics. We will see that we can consider the contexts as the current evaluation context in C, i.e. the call stack and instruction pointer. To make this more explicit, we use dot notation to express the notion of a context as call stack more clearly. We write $\cdot$ as a right-associative operator where $e\cdot e' \equiv e(e')$ and $\mathsf{E}\cdot e \equiv \mathsf{E}[e]$. Using this notation, we can for example write the (*handle*) rule as:

$$\mathsf{handle}_h\cdot \mathsf{X}_{op}\cdot op(v) \longrightarrow e[x \mapsto v,\ resume \mapsto \lambda y.\,\mathsf{handle}_h\cdot \mathsf{X}_{op}\cdot y]$$

where $(op(x) \to e) \in h$. This more clearly shows that we evaluate $op(v)$ under a current "call stack" $\mathsf{handle}_h\cdot \mathsf{X}_{op}$ (where h is the innermost handler for op as induced by the grammar of X_{op}).

4   Implementing Effect Handlers in C

The main contribution of this paper is showing how we can go from the operational semantics on an idealized lambda-calculus to an implementation as a C library. All the regular evaluation rules like application and let-bindings are already part of the C language. Of course, there are no first-class lambda expressions so we must make do with top-level functions only. So, our main challenge is to implement the (*handle*) rule:

$$\mathsf{handle}_h\cdot \mathsf{X}_{op}\cdot op(v) \longrightarrow e[x \mapsto v,\ resume \mapsto \lambda y.\,\mathsf{handle}_h\cdot \mathsf{X}_{op}\cdot y]$$

where $(op(x) \to e) \in h$. For this rule, we can view "$\mathsf{handle}_h\,.\,\mathsf{X}_{op}$" as our current execution context, i.e. as a *stack* and instruction pointer. In C, the execution context is represented by the current call stack and the current register context, including the instruction pointer. That means:

1. When we enter a handler, push a handle_h frame on the stack.
2. When we encounter an operation $op(v)$, walk down the call stack "$\mathsf{E}\cdot \mathsf{handle}_h\cdot \mathsf{X}_{op}$" until we find a handler for our operation.
3. Capture the current execution context "$\mathsf{handle}_h\cdot \mathsf{X}_{op}$" (call stack and registers) into a **resume** structure.
4. Jump to the handler h (restoring its execution context), and pass it the operation op, the argument v, and the captured resumption.

In the rest of this article, we assume that a stack always grows up with any parent frames "below" the child frames. In practice though, most platforms have downward growing stacks and the library adapts dynamically to that.

4.1 Entering a Handler

When we enter a handler, we need to push a handler frame on the stack. Effect handler frames are defined as:

```
typedef struct _handler {
  jmp_buf           entry;        // used to jump back to a handler
  const handlerdef* hdef;         // operation definitions
  volatile value    arg;          // the operation argument is passed here
  const operation*  arg_op;       // the yielded operation is passed here
  resume*           arg_resume;   // the resumption function
  void*             stackbase;    // stack frame address of the handler function
} handler;
```

Each handler needs to keep track of its `stackbase` - when an operation captures its resumption, it only needs to save the stack up to its handler's `stackbase`. The `handle` function starts by recording the `stackbase`:

```
value handle( const handlerdef* hdef,
              value (*action)(value), value arg ) {
  void* base = NULL;
  return handle_upto( hdef, &base, action, arg ); }
```

The stack base is found by taking the address of the local variable `base` itself; this is a good conservative estimate of an address just below the frame of the handler. We mark `handle_upto` as `noinline` to ensure it gets its own stack frame just above `base`:

```
noinline value handle_upto( hdef, base, action, arg ) {
  handler* h = hstack_push();
  h->hdef = hdef;
  h->stackbase = base;
  value res;
  if (setjmp(h->entry) == 0) {
    // (H1): we recorded our register context
    ...
  }
  else {
    // (H2): we long jumped here from an operation
    ...
  }
  // (H3): returning from the handler
  return res; }
```

This function pushes first a fresh `handler` on a *shadow* handler stack. In principle, we could have used the C stack to "push" our handlers simply by declaring it as a local variable. However, as we will see later, it is more convenient to maintain a separate shadow stack of handlers which is simply a thread-local array of handlers. Next the handler uses `setjmp` to save its execution context in `h->entry`. This is used later by an operation to `longjmp` back to the handler. On its invocation, `setjmp` returns always 0 and the **(H1)** block is executed next. When it is long jumped to, the **(H2)** block will execute.

For our purposes, we need a standard C compliant `setjmp`/`longjmp` implementation; namely one that just saves all the necessary registers and flags in `setjmp`, and restores them all again in `longjmp`. Since that includes the stack pointer and instruction pointer, `longjmp` will effectively "jump" back to where `setjmp` was called with the registers restored. Unfortunately, we sometimes need to resort to our own assembly implementations on some platforms. For example, the Microsoft Visual C++ compiler (`msvc`) will unwind the stack on a `longjmp` to invoke destructors and finalizers for C++ code [33]. On other platforms, not always all register context is saved correctly for floating point registers. We have seen this in library code for the ARM Cortex-M for example. Fortunately, a compliant implementation of these routines is straightforward as they just move registers to and from the `entry` block. See [27] for an example of the assembly code for `setjmp` on 32-bit x86.

4.1.1 Handling Return

The **(H1)** block in `handle_upto` is executed when `setjmp` finished saving the register context. It starts by calling the `action` with its argument:

```
if (setjmp(h->entry) == 0) {
  // (H1): we recorded our register context
  res = action(arg);
  hstack_pop();            // pop our handler
  res = hdef->retfun(res); } // invoke the return handler
```

If the action returns normally, we are in the (*return*) rule:

$$\text{handle}_h \cdot v \longrightarrow e[x \mapsto v] \quad \text{with } (\text{return} \to e) \in h$$

We have a handler `h` on the handler stack, and the result value v in `res`. To proceed, we call the return handler function `retfun` (i.e. e) with the argument `res` (i.e. $x \mapsto v$) - but only after popping the handle_h frame.

4.1.2 Handling an Operation

The **(H2)** block of `handle_upto` executes when an operation long jumps back to our handler `entry`:

```
else {
    // we long jumped here from an operation
    value    arg = h->arg;              // load our parameters
    const operation* op = h->arg_op;
    resume* resume = h->arg_resume;
    hstack_pop();                        // pop our handler
    res = op->opfun(resume,arg); }  // and call the operation
```

This is one part of the (*handle*) rule:

$$\mathsf{handle}_h \cdot \mathsf{X}_{op} \cdot op(v) \quad \longrightarrow \quad e[x \mapsto v, \; resume \mapsto \lambda y. \, \mathsf{handle}_h \cdot \mathsf{X}_{op} \cdot y]$$

where $(op(x) \to e) \in h$. At this point, the yielding operation just jumped back and the X_{op} part of the stack has been "popped" by the long jump. Moreover, the yielding operation has already captured the resumption *resume* and stored it in the handler frame `arg_resume` field together with the argument v in `arg` (Sect. 4.2). We store them in local variables, pop the handler frame handle_h, and execute the operation handler function e, namely `op->opfun`, passing the resumption and the argument.

4.2 Yielding an Operation

Calling an operation $op(v)$ is done by a function call `yield(OPTAG( op), v)`:

```
value yield(const optag* optag, value arg) {
    const operation* op;
    handler* h = hstack_find(optag,&op);
    if (op->opkind==OP_NORESUME)  yield_to_handler(h,op,arg,NULL);
                         else  return capture_resume_yield(h,op,arg); }
```

First we call `hstack_find(optag,&op)` to find the first handler on the handler stack that can handle `optag`. It returns the a pointer to the handler frame and a pointer to the operation description in `&op`. Next we make our first optimization: if the operation handler does not need a resumption, i.e. `op->opkind==OP_NORESUME`, we can pass `NULL` for the resumption and not bother capturing the execution context. In that case we immediately call `yield_to_handler` with a `NULL` argument for the resumption. Otherwise, we capture the resumption first using `capture_resume_yield`. The `yield_to_handler` function just long jumps back to the handler:

```
noreturn void yield_to_handler( handler* h, const operation* op,
                        value oparg, resume* resume ) {
    hstack_pop_upto(h);        // pop handler frames up to 'h'
    h->arg = oparg;            // pass the arguments in then handler fields
    h->arg_op = op;  h->arg_resume = resume;
    longjmp(h->entry,1); }  // and jump back down! (to (H2))
```

4.2.1   Capturing a Resumption

At this point we have a working implementation of effect handlers without
resume. The real power comes from having first-class resumptions where the
(*handle*) rule captures the resumption:

$$resume \mapsto \lambda y.\ \mathsf{handle}_h \cdot \mathsf{X}_{op} \cdot y$$

This means we need to capture the current execution context, "$\mathsf{handle}_h \cdot Xop$",
so we can later resume in the context with a result y. The execution context in
C would be the stack up to the handler together with the registers. This is done
by `capture_resume_yield`:

```
value capture_resume_yield(handler* h, const operation* op, oparg ) {
  resume* r = (resume*)malloc(sizeof(resume));
  r->refcount = 1;   r->arg = lh_value_null;
  // set a jump point for resuming
  if (setjmp(r->entry) == 0) {
    // (Y1) we recorded the register context in 'r->entry'
    void* top = get_stack_top();
    capture_cstack(&r->cstack, h->stackbase, top);
    capture_hstack(&r->hstack, h);
    yield_to_handler(h, op, oparg, r); } // back to (H2)
  else {
    // (Y2) we are resumed (and long jumped here from (R1))
    value res = r->arg;
    resume_release(r);
    return res;
  } }
```

A resumption structure is allocated first; it is defined as:

```
typedef struct _resume {
  ptrdiff_t refcount; // resumptions are heap allocated
  jmp_buf   entry;    // jump point where the resume was captured
  cstack    cstack;   // captured call stack
  hstack    hstack;   // captured handler stack
  value     arg;      // the argument to 'resume' is passed through 'arg'.
} resume;
```

Once allocated, we initialize its reference count to 1 and record the current
register context in its `entry`. We then proceed to the (`Y1`) block to capture the
current call stack and handler stack.

Capturing the handler stack is easy and `capture_hstack(&r->hstack,h)`
just copies all handlers up to and including h into r's `hstack` field (allocating
as necessary). Capturing the C call stack is a bit more subtle. To determine the
current top of the stack, we cannot use our earlier trick of just taking the address
of a local variable, for example as:

```
void* top = (void*)&top;
```

since that may underestimate the actual stack used: the compiler may have put some temporaries above the `top` variable, and ABI's like the System V amd64 include a *red zone* which is a part of the stack above the stack pointer where the compiler can freely spill registers [32, Sect. 3.2.2]. Instead, we call a child function that captures its stack top instead as a guaranteed conservative estimate:

```
noinline void* get_stack_top() {
  void* top = (void*)&top;
  return top; }
```

The above code is often found as a way to get the stack top address but it is wrong in general; an optimizing compiler may detect that the address of a local is returned which is undefined behavior in C. This allows it to return any value! In particular, both `clang` and `gcc` always return 0 with optimizations enabled. The trick is to use a separate identity function to pass back the local stack address:

```
noinline void* stack_addr( void* p ) {
  return p;
}
noinline void* get_stack_top() {
  void* top = NULL;
  return stack_addr(&top);
}
```

This code works as expected on current compilers even with aggressive optimizations enabled.

The piece of stack that needs to be captured is exactly between the lower estimate of the handler `stackbase` up to the upper estimate of our stack `top`. The `capture_cstack(&r->cstack,h->stackbase,top)` allocates a `cstack` and `memcpy`'s into that from the C stack. At this point the resumption structure is fully initialized and captures the delimited execution context. We can now use the previous `yield_to_handler` to jump back to the handler with the operation, its argument, and a first-class `resume` structure.

4.3 Resuming

Now that we can capture a resumption, we can define how to resume one. In our operational semantics, a resumption is just a lambda expression:

$$resume \mapsto \lambda y.\, \mathsf{handle}_h \cdot \mathsf{X}_{op} \cdot y$$

and resuming is just application, $\mathsf{E} \cdot resume(v) \longrightarrow \mathsf{E} \cdot \mathsf{handle}_h \cdot \mathsf{X}_{op} \cdot v$. For the C implementation, this means pushing the captured stack onto the main stacks and passing the argument v in the `arg` field of the resumption. Unfortunately, we

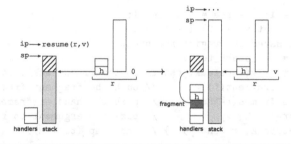

Fig. 3. Resuming a resumption r that captured the stack up to a handler h. The captured stack will overwrite the striped part of the existing stack, which is saved by a fragment handler. The argument v is passed in the **arg** field of the resumption r.

cannot just push our captured stack on the regular call stack. In C, often local variables *on the stack* are passed by reference to child functions. For example,

```
char buf[N];  snprintf(buf,N,"address of buf: %p", buf);
```

Suppose inside **snprintf** we call an operation that captures the stack. If we resume and restore the stack at a different starting location, then all those stack relative addresses are wrong! In the example, **buf** is now at a different location in the stack, but the address passed to **snprintf** is still the same.

Therefore, we must *always restore a stack at the exact same location,* and we need to do extra work in the C implementation to maintain proper stacks. In particular, when jumping back to an operation (H2), the operation may call the resumption. At that point, restoring the original captured stack will need to overwrite part of the current stack of the operation handler!

4.3.1 Fragments

This is situation is shown in Fig. 3. It shows a resumption r that captured the stack up to a handler h. The arrow from h points to the **stackbase** which is below the current stack pointer. Upon restoring the saved stack in r, the striped part of the stack is overwritten. This means:

1. We first save that part of the stack in a `fragment` which saves the register context and part of a C stack.
2. We push a special `fragment` handler frame on the handler stack just below the newly restored handler h. When h returns, we can now restore the original part of the call stack from the `fragment`.

The implementation of resuming becomes:

```
value resume(resume* r, value arg) {
  fragment* f = (fragment*)malloc(sizeof(fragment));
```

```
f->refcount = 1;   f->res = value_null;
if (setjmp(f->entry) == 0) {
  // (R1) we saved our register context
  void* top = get_stack_top();
  capture_cstack(&f->cstack, cstack_bottom(&r->cstack), top);
  hstack_push_fragment(f);        // push the fragment frame
  hstack_push_frames(r->hstack);  // push the handler frames
  r->arg = arg;                   // pass the argument to resume
  jumpto(r->cstack, r->entry); }  // and jump (to (Y2))
else {
  // (R2) we jumped back to our fragment from (H3).
  value res = f->res; // save the resume result to a local
  hstack_pop(hs);     // pop our fragment frame
  return res;         // and return the resume result
} }
```

The `capture_cstack` saves the part of the current stack that can be overwritten into our fragment. Note that this may capture an "empty" stack if the stack happens to be below the part that is restored. This only happens with resumptions though that escape the scope of an operation handler (i.e. *non-scoped* resumptions). The `jumpto` function restores an execution context by restoring a C stack and register context. We discuss the implementation in the next section.

First, we need to supplement the handler function `handle_upto` to take `fragment` handler frames into account. In particular, every handler checks whether it has a fragment frame below it: if so, it was part of a resumption and we need to restore the original part of the call stack saved in the fragment. We add the following code to (H3):

```
noinline value handle_upto( hdef, base, action, arg ) {
  ...
  // (H3): returning from the handler
  fragment* f = hstack_try_pop_fragment();
  if (f != NULL) {
    f->res = res;                  // pass the result
    jumpto(f->cstack,f->entry); // and restore the fragment (to (R2))
  }
  return res; }
```

Here we use the same `jumpto` function to restore the execution context. Unwinding through fragments also needs to be done with care to restore the stack correctly; See [27] for further details.

4.3.2   Jumpto: Restoring an Execution Context

The `jumpto` function takes a C stack and register context and restores the C stack at the original location and long jumps. We cannot implement this directly though as:

```
noreturn void jumpto( cstack* c, jmp_buf* entry ) {
  // wrong!
  memcpy(c->base,c->frames,c->size);  // restore the stack
  longjmp(*entry,1); }                // restore the registers
```

In particular, the memcpy may well overwrite the current stack frame of jumpto, including the entry variable! Moreover, some platforms use a longjmp implementation that aborts if we try to jump up the stack [15].

The trick is to do jumpto in two parts: first we reserve in jumpto enough stack space to contain the stack we are going to restore and a bit more. Then we call a helper function _jumpto to actually restore the context. This function is now guaranteed to have a proper stack frame that will not be overwritten:

```
noreturn noinline
void _jumpto( byte* space, cstack* c, jmp_buf* entry ) {
  space[0] = 0;                       // make sure is live
  memcpy(c->base,c->frames,c->size);  // restore the stack
  longjmp(*entry,1);                  // restore the registers
}
noreturn void jumpto(cstack* cstack, jmp_buf* entry ) {
  void*     top   = get_stack_top();
  ptrdiff_t extra = top - cstack_top(cstack);
  extra += 128;             // safety margin
  byte* space = alloca(extra);  // reserve enough stack space
  _jumpto(space,cstack,entry); }
```

As before, for clarity we left out error checking and assume the stack grows up and extra is always positive. By using alloca we reserve enough stack space to restore the cstack safely. We pass the space parameter and write to it to prevent optimizing compilers to optimize it away as an unused variable.

4.4 Performance

To measure the performance of operations in isolation, we use a simple loop that calls a work function. The native C version is:

```
int counter_native(int i) {
  int sum = 0;  while (i > 0) { sum += work(i); i-; }
  return sum; }
```

The effectful version mirrors this but uses a *state* effect to implement the counter, performing two effect operations per loop iteration:

```
int counter() {
  int i; int sum = 0;
  while ((i = state_get()) > 0) {
    sum += work(i);
    state_put(i - 1);  }
  return sum; }
```

Compiler	Native (s)	Effects (s)	Slowdown	Operation Cost	Ops/s
msvc 2015 /02	0.00057	0.1852	326×	162 · sqrt	$1.158 \cdot 10^6$
clang 3.8.0 -03	0.00056	0.1565	279×	139 · sqrt	$1.402 \cdot 10^6$
gcc 5.4.0 -03	0.00056	0.1883	336×	167 · sqrt	$1.193 \cdot 10^6$

Fig. 4. Performance using full resumptions. All measurements are on a 2016 Surface Book with an Intel Core i7-6600U at 2.6 GHz with 8GB ram (LPDDR3-1866) using 64-bit Windows 10 & Ubuntu 16.04. The benchmark ran for 100000 iterations. The *Native* version is a plain C loop, while the *Effect* version uses effect handlers to implement state. *Operation cost* is the approximate cost of an effect operation relative to a double precision *sqrt* instruction. *Ops/s* are effect operations per second performed without doing any work.

The `work` function is there to measure the relative performance; the native C loop is almost "free" on a modern processors as it does almost nothing with a loop variable in a register. The work function performs a square root operation:

```
noinline int work(int i) {  return (int)(sqrt((double)i)); }
```

This gives us a baseline to compare how expensive effect operations are compared to the cost of a square root instruction. Figure 4 shows the results of running 100,000 iteration on a 64-bit platform. The effectful version is around 300× times slower, and we can execute about 1.3 million of effect operations per second.

The reason for the somewhat slow execution is that we capture many resumptions and fragments, moving a lot of memory and putting pressure on the allocator. There are various ways to optimize this. First of all, we almost never need a *first-class* resumption that can escape the scope of the operation. For example, if we use a `OP_NORESUME` operation that never resumes, we need to capture no state and the operation can be as cheap as a `longjmp`.

Another really important optimization opportunity is *tail resumptions*: these are resumes in a tail-call position in the operation handler. In the benchmark, each `resume` remembers its continuation in a fragment so it can return execution there - just to return directly without doing any more work! This leads to an ever growing handler stack with fragment frames on it. It turns out that in practice, almost *all* operation implementations use `resume` in a tail-call position. And fortunately, we can optimize this case nicely giving orders of magnitude improvement.

5   Optimized Tail Resumptions

In this section we expand on the earlier observation that tail resumptions can be implemented more efficiently. We consider in particular a operation handler of the form $(op(x) \rightarrow resume(e)) \in h$ where $resume \notin \mathsf{fv}(e)$. In that case:

$\mathsf{handle}_h \cdot \mathsf{X}_{op} \cdot op(v) \longrightarrow$
$resume(e)[x \mapsto v, \ resume \mapsto \lambda y. \ \mathsf{handle}_h \cdot \mathsf{X}_{op} \cdot y]$
$\quad \longrightarrow \{ \ resume \notin e \ \}$
$(\lambda y. \ \mathsf{handle}_h \cdot \mathsf{X}_{op} \cdot y)(e[x \mapsto v])$
$\quad \longrightarrow^* \{ \ e[x \mapsto v] \longrightarrow^* v' \ \}$
$(\lambda y. \ \mathsf{handle}_h \cdot \mathsf{X}_{op} \cdot y)(v') \longrightarrow$
$\mathsf{handle}_h \cdot \mathsf{X}_{op} \cdot v'$

Since we end up with the same stack, $\mathsf{handle}_h \cdot \mathsf{X}_{op}$, we do not need to capture and restore the context $\mathsf{handle}_{op} \cdot \mathsf{X}_{op}$ at all but can directly evaluate the operation expression e as if it was a regular function call! However, if we leave the stack in place, we need to take special precautions to ensure that any operations yielded in the evaluation of $e[x \mapsto v]$ are not handled by any handler in $\mathsf{handle}_h \cdot \mathsf{X}_{op}$.

5.1 A Tail Optimized Semantics

In order to evaluate such tail resumptive expressions under the stack $\mathsf{handle}_{op} \cdot \mathsf{X}_{op}$, but prevent yielded operations from being handled by handlers in that stack, we introduce a new *yield* frame $\mathsf{yield}_{op}(e)$. Intuitively, a piece of stack of the from $\mathsf{handle}_{op} \cdot \mathsf{X}_{op} \cdot \mathsf{yield}_{op}$ can be ignored - the yield_{op} specifies that any handlers up to h (where $op \in h$) should be skipped when looking for an operation handler.

This is made formal in Fig. 5. We have a new evaluation context F that evaluates under the new yield expression, and we define a new handler context Y_{op} that is like X_{op} but now also skips over parts of the handler stack that are skipped by yield frames, i.e. it finds the innermost handler that is not skipped.

The reduction rules in Fig. 5 use a new reduction arrow $\overset{-}{\longrightarrow}$ to signify that this reduction can contain yield_{op} frames. The first five rules are equivalent to the usual rules except that the the (*handle*) rule uses the Y_{op} context now instead of X_{op} to correctly select the innermost handler for op skipping any handlers that are part of a $\mathsf{handle}_h \cdot \mathsf{Y}_{op} \cdot \mathsf{yield}_{op}$ (with $op \in h$) sequence.

The essence of our optimization is in the (*thandle*) rule which applies when the *resume* operation is only used in the tail-position. In this case we can (1) keep the stack *as is*, just pushing a yield_{op} frame, and (2) we can skip capturing a resumption and binding *resume* since $resume \notin \mathsf{fv}(e)$. The "unbound" tail *resume* is now handled explicitly in the (*tail*) rule: it can just pop the yield_{op} frame and continue evaluation under the original stack.

5.1.1 Soundness
We would like to preserve the original semantics with our new optimized rules: if we reduce using our new $\overset{-}{\longrightarrow}$ reduction, we should get the same result if we reduce using the original reduction rule $\longrightarrow$. To state this formally, we define a

Evaluation contexts:

$$\mathsf{F} \quad ::= \quad [] \mid \mathsf{F}(e) \mid v(\mathsf{F}) \mid op(\mathsf{F}) \mid \mathsf{val}\, x = \mathsf{F};\ e \mid \mathsf{handle}_h(\mathsf{F}) \mid \mathsf{yield}_{op}(\mathsf{F})$$

$$\mathsf{Y}_{op} \quad ::= \quad [] \mid \mathsf{Y}_{op}(e) \mid v(\mathsf{Y}_{op}) \mid op(\mathsf{Y}_{op}) \mid \mathsf{val}\, x = \mathsf{Y}_{op};\ e$$
$$\mid \quad \mathsf{handle}_h(\mathsf{Y}_{op}) \qquad\qquad\qquad\qquad \text{if } op \notin h$$
$$\mid \quad \mathsf{handle}_h(\mathsf{Y}_{op'}[\mathsf{yield}_{op'}(\mathsf{Y}_{op})]) \qquad\qquad \text{if } op' \in h$$

New Reduction rules:

$$(\textit{handle}) \quad \mathsf{handle}_h \cdot \mathsf{Y}_{op} \cdot op(v) \ \overset{\cdot}{\longrightarrow}\ e[x \mapsto v,\ \textit{resume} \mapsto \lambda y.\, \mathsf{handle}_h \cdot \mathsf{Y}_{op} \cdot y]$$
$$\text{with} \quad (op(x) \to e) \in h$$

$$(\textit{thandle}) \quad \mathsf{handle}_h \cdot \mathsf{Y}_{op} \cdot op(v) \ \overset{\cdot}{\longrightarrow}\ \mathsf{handle}_h \cdot \mathsf{Y}_{op} \cdot \mathsf{yield}_{op} \cdot \textit{resume}(e)[x \mapsto v]$$
$$\text{with} \quad (op(x) \to \textit{resume}(e)) \in h$$
$$\textit{resume} \notin \mathsf{fv}(e)$$

$$(\textit{tail}) \quad \mathsf{handle}_h \cdot \mathsf{Y}_{op} \cdot \mathsf{yield}_{op} \cdot \textit{resume}(v) \ \overset{\cdot}{\longrightarrow}\ \mathsf{handle}_h \cdot \mathsf{Y}_{op} \cdot v \quad \text{with } (op \in h)$$

Fig. 5. Optimized reduction rules with yield frames. Rules (δ), (β), (let), and $(return)$ are the same as in Fig. 2.

ignore function on expression, $\overline{e}$, and contexts $\overline{\mathsf{F}}$ and $\overline{\mathsf{Y}}$. This function removes any $\mathsf{handle}_h \cdot \mathsf{Y}_{op} \cdot \mathsf{yield}_{op}$ sub expressions where $op \in h$, effectively turning any of our extended expressions into an original one, and taking F to E, and Y_{op} to X_{op}. Using this function, we can define soundness as:

Theorem 1 *(Soundness).* If $\mathsf{F} \cdot e \overset{\cdot}{\longrightarrow} \mathsf{F} \cdot e'$ then $\overline{\mathsf{F}} \cdot \overline{e} \longrightarrow \overline{\mathsf{F}} \cdot \overline{e'}$.

The proof is given in [27].

5.2 Implementing Tail Optimized Operations

Implementing tail resumptions only needds a modification to yielding operations:

```
value yield(const optag* optag, value arg) {
  const operation* op;
  handler* h = hstack_find(optag,&op);
  if (op->opkind==OP_NORESUME)  yield_to_handler(h,op,arg,NULL);
  else if (op->opkind==OP_TAIL) {
    hstack_push_yield(h);               // push a yield frame
    value res = op->opfun(NULL,op,arg); // call operation directly
    hstack_pop_yield();                 // pop the yield again
    return res;
  }
  else return capture_resume_yield(h,op,arg); }
```

Compiler	Native (s)	Effects (s)	Slowdown	Operation Cost	Ops/s
msvc 2015 /O2	0.059	0.197	3.3×	1.15 · sqrt	$134 \cdot 10^6$
clang 3.8.0 -O3	0.059	0.153	2.6×	0.79 · sqrt	$150 \cdot 10^6$
gcc 5.4.0 -O3	0.059	0.167	2.8×	0.90 · sqrt	$141 \cdot 10^6$

Fig. 6. Performance using tail optimized resumptions. Same benchmark as in Fig. 4 but with 1010^6 iterations.

We simply add a new operation kind OP_TAIL that signifies that the operation is a tail resumption, i.e. the operation promises to end in a tail call to tail_resume. We then push a yield frame, and directly call the operation. It will return with the final result (as a tail_resume) and we can pop the yield frame and continue. We completely avoid capturing the stack and allocating memory. The tail_resume is now just an identity function:

```
value tail_resume(const resume* r, value arg) { return arg; }
```

In the real implementation, we do more error checking and also allow OP_TAIL operations to not resume at all (and behave like and OP_NORESUME). We also need to adjust the hstack_find and hstack_pop_uptofunctions to skip over handlers as designated by the yield frames.

5.3 Performance, Again

With our new optimized implementation of tail-call resumptions, let's repeat our earlier *counter* benchmark of Sect. 4.4. Figure 6 shows the new results where we see three orders of magnitude improvements and we can perform up to 150 million (!) tail resuming operations per second with the clang compiler. That is quite good as that is only about 18 cycles on our processor running at 2.6GHz.

6   What Doesn't Work?

Libraries for co-routines and threading in C are notorious for breaking common C idioms. We believe that the structured and scoped form of algebraic effects prevents many potential issues. Nevertheless, with stacks being copied, we make certain assumptions about the runtime:

- We assume that the C stack is contiguous and does not move. This is the case for all major platforms. For platforms that support "linked" stacks, we could even optimize our library more since we can then capture a piece of stack by reference instead of copying! The "not moving" assumption though means we cannot resume a resumption on another thread than where it was captured. Otherwise any C idioms work as expected and arguments can be passed by stack reference. Except.

- When calling `yield` and `(tail_)resume`, we cannot pass parameters by stack reference but must allocate them in the heap instead. We feel this is a reasonable restriction since it only applies to new code specifically written with algebraic effects. When running in debug mode the library checks for this.
- For resumes in the scope of a handler, we always restore the stack and fragments at the exact same location as the handler stack base. This way the stack is always valid and can be unwound by other tools like debuggers. This is not always the case for a first-class resumption that escapes the handler scope - in that case a resumption stack may restore into an arbitrary C stack, and the new C stack is (temporarily) only valid above the resume base. We have not seen any problems with this though in practice with either `gdb` or Microsoft's debugger and profiler. Of course, in practice almost all effects use either tail resumptions or resumptions that stay in the scope of the handler. The one exception is the `async` effect but that in that case we still happen to resume at the right spot since we always resume from the same event loop.

7   Related Work

This is the first library to implement algebraic effects and handlers for the C language, but many similar techniques have been used to implement co-routines [21, Sect. 1.4.2] and cooperative threading [1,4,6,7,12]. In particular, stack copying/switching, and judicious use of `longjmp` and `setjmp` [15]. Many of these libraries have various drawbacks though and restrict various C idioms. For example, most co-routines libraries require a fixed C stack [9,10,16,24,39], move stack locations on resumptions [31], or restrict to one-shot continuations [8].

We believe that is mostly a reflection that general co-routines and first-class continuations (`call/cc`) are *too* general - the simple typing and added structure of algebraic effects make them more safe by construction. As Andrej Bauer, co-creator of the Eff [3] language puts it: *effects+handlers* are to *delimited continuations* as what *while* is to *goto* [20].

Recently, there are various implementations of algebraic effects, either embedded in Haskell [20,42], or built into a language, like Eff [3], Links [18], Frank [30], and Koka [26]. Most closely related to this article is Multi-core OCaml [13,14] which implements algebraic effects natively in the OCaml runtime system. To prevent copying the stack, it uses multiple stacks in combination with explicit copying when resuming more than once.

Multi-core OCaml supports *default* handlers [13]: these are handlers defined at the outermost level that have an implicit `resume` over their result. These are very efficient and implemented just as a function call. Indeed, these are a special case of the tail-resumptive optimization shown in Sect. 5.1: the implicit `resume` guarantees that the resumption is in a tail-call position, while the outermost level ensures that the handler stack is always empty and thus does not need a $yield_{op}$ frame specifically but can use a simple flag to prevent handling of other operations.

8 Conclusion

We described a library that provides powerful new control abstractions in C. For the near future we plan in integrate this into a compiler backend for the P language [11], and to create a nice wrapper for `libuv`. As part of the P language backend, we are also working on a C++ interface to our library which requires special care to run destructors correctly (see [27] for details).

References

1. Abadi, M., Plotkin, G.: A model of cooperative threads. Log. Methods Comput. Sci. **6**(4:2), 1–39 (2010). https://doi.org/10.2168/LMCS-6(4:2)2010
2. Awodey, S.: Category Theory. Oxford Logic Guides, vol. 46. Oxford University Press, Oxford (2006)
3. Bauer, A., Pretnar, M.: Programming with algebraic effects and handlers. J. Log. Algebr. Methods Program. **84**(1), 108–123 (2015). https://doi.org/10.1016/j.jlamp.2014.02.001
4. Berry, D., Milner, R., Turner, D.N.: A semantics for ML concurrency primitives. In: Proceedings of the 19th ACM SIGPLAN-SIGACT Symposium on Principles of Programming Languages, POPL 1992, pp. 119–129, Albuquerque, New Mexico, USA (1992). https://doi.org/10.1145/143165.143191
5. Bierman, G., Russo, C., Mainland, G., Meijer, E., Torgersen, M.: Pause 'n' Play: formalizing asynchronous C$^\sharp$. In: Noble, J. (ed.) ECOOP 2012. LNCS, vol. 7313, pp. 233–257. Springer, Heidelberg (2012). https://doi.org/10.1007/978-3-642-31057-7_12
6. Boudol, G.: Fair cooperative multithreading. In: Caires, L., Vasconcelos, V.T. (eds.) CONCUR 2007. LNCS, vol. 4703, pp. 272–286. Springer, Heidelberg (2007). https://doi.org/10.1007/978-3-540-74407-8_19
7. Boussinot, F.: FairThreads: mixing cooperative and preemptive threads in C. Concur. Comput. Pract. Exp. **18**(5), 445–469 (2006). https://doi.org/10.1002/cpe.v18:5
8. Bruggeman, C., Waddell, O., Dybvig, R.K.: Representing control in the presence of one-shot continuations. In: Proceedings of the ACM SIGPLAN 1996 Conference on Programming Language Design and Implementation, PLDI 1996, pp. 99–107, Philadelphia, Pennsylvania, USA (1996). https://doi.org/10.1145/231379.231395
9. Buhr, P.A., Stroobosscher, R.A.: The uSystem: providing light-weight concurrency on shared-memory multiprocessor computers running UNIX. Softw. Pract. Exp. **20**(9), 929–963 (1990)
10. Cox, R.: Libtask (2005). https://swtch.com/libtask
11. Desai, A., Gupta, V., Jackson, E., Qadeer, S., Rajamani, S., Zufferey, D.: P: safe asynchronous event-driven programming. In: Proceedings of the 34th ACM SIG-PLAN Conference on Programming Language Design and Implementation, PLDI 2013, pp. 321–332, Seattle, Washington, USA (2013). https://doi.org/10.1145/2491956.2462184
12. Dijkstra, E.W.: Cooperating sequential processes. In: Hansen, P.B. (ed.) The Origin of Concurrent Programming, pp. 65–138. Springer, New York (2002)
13. Dolan, S., Eliopoulos, S., Hillerström, D., Madhavapeddy, A., Sivaramakrishnan, K.C., White, L.: Concurrent system programming with effect handlers. In: Proceedings of the Symposium on Trends in Functional Programming, TFP 2017, May 2017

14. Dolan, S., White, L., Sivaramakrishnan, K.C., Yallop, J., Madhavapeddy, A.: Effective concurrency through algebraic effects. In: OCaml Workshop, September 2015
15. Engelschall, R.S.: Portable multithreading: the signal stack trick for user-space thread creation. In: Proceedings of the Annual Conference on USENIX Annual Technical Conference, ATEC 2000, pp. 20–31, San Diego, California (2000)
16. Finch, T.: Coroutines in Less than 20 Lines of Standard C. http://fanf.livejournal.com/105413.html. Blog post
17. Forster, Y., Kammar, O., Lindley, S., Pretnar, M.: On the expressive power of user-defined effects: effect handlers, monadic reflection, delimited control. In: Proceedings of the 22nd ACM SIGPLAN International Conference on Functional Programming, ICFP 2017 (2017). arXiv:1610.09161
18. Hillerström, D., Lindley, S.: Liberating effects with rows and handlers. In: Proceedings of the 1st International Workshop on Type-Driven Development, TyDe 2016, Nara, Japan, pp. 15–27 (2016). https://doi.org/10.1145/2976022.2976033
19. Hillerström, D., Lindley, S., Atkey, R., Sivaramakrishnan, K.C.: Continuation passing style for effect handlers. In: 2nd International Conference on Formal Structures for Computation and Deduction, FSCD 2017, vol. 84 (2017). https://doi.org/10.4230/LIPIcs.FSCD.2017.18
20. Kammar, O., Lindley, S., Oury, N.: Handlers in action. In: Proceedings of the 18th ACM SIGPLAN International Conference on Functional Programming, ICFP 2013, pp. 145–158. ACM, New York (2013). https://doi.org/10.1145/2500365.2500590
21. Knuth, D.: The Art of Computer Programming, vol. 1. Addison-Wesley, Redwood City (1997)
22. Landin, P.J.: A Generalization of Jumps and Labels. UNIVAC systems programming research (1965)
23. Landin, P.J.: A generalization of jumps and labels. High. Order Symb. Comp. **11**(2), 125–143 (1998). https://doi.org/10.1023/A:1010068630801
24. Lehmann, M.: Libcoro (2006). http://software.schmorp.de/pkg/libcoro.html
25. Leijen, D.: Libhandler (2017). https://github.com/koka-lang/libhandler
26. Leijen, D.: Type directed compilation of row-typed algebraic effects. In: Proceedings of the 44th ACM SIGPLAN Symposium on Principles of Programming Languages (POPL 2017), Paris, France, pp. 486–499, January 2017. https://doi.org/10.1145/3009837.3009872
27. Leijen, D.: Implementing Algebraic Effects in C. MSR-TR-2017-23. Microsoft Research technical report, June 2017
28. Leijen, D.: Structured asynchrony using algebraic effects. In: Proceedings of the 2nd ACM SIGPLAN Workshop on Type-Driven Development, TyDe 2017, Oxford, UK, September 2017. https://doi.org/10.1145/3122975.3122977
29. Libuv. https://github.com/libuv/libuv
30. Lindley, S., McBride, C., McLaughlin, C.: Do Be Do Be Do. In: Proceedings of the 44th ACM SIGPLAN Symposium on Principles of Programming Languages (POPL 2017), Paris, France, pp. 500–514, January 2017. https://doi.org/10.1145/3009837.3009897
31. Magi, S.: Libconcurrency (2008). https://code.google.com/archive/p/libconcurrency
32. Matz, M., Hubička, J., Jaeger, A., Mitchell, M.: System V application binary interface: AMD64 architecture processor supplement, April 2017. http://chamilo2.grenet.fr/inp/courses/ENSIMAG3MM1LDB/document/doc_abi_ia64.pdf
33. MSDN. Using Setjmp and Longjmp (2017). https://docs.microsoft.com/en-us/cpp/cpp/using-setjmp-longjmp

34. Plotkin, G.D., Power, J.: Algebraic operations and generic effects. Appl. Categ. Struct. **11**(1), 69–94 (2003). https://doi.org/10.1023/A:1023064908962
35. Plotkin, G., Pretnar, M.: Handlers of algebraic effects. In: Castagna, G. (ed.) ESOP 2009. LNCS, vol. 5502, pp. 80–94. Springer, Heidelberg (2009). https://doi.org/10.1007/978-3-642-00590-9_7
36. Plotkin, G.D., Pretnar, M.: Handling algebraic effects. Log. Methods Comput. Sci. **9**(4) (2013). https://doi.org/10.2168/LMCS-9(4:23)2013
37. Pretnar, M.: Inferring algebraic effects. Log. Methods Comput. Sci. 10(3) (2014). https://doi.org/10.2168/LMCS-10(3:21)2014
38. Swierstra, W.: Data types à la carte. J. Funct. Program. **18**(4), 423–436 (2008). https://doi.org/10.1017/S0956796808006758
39. Tatham, S.: Coroutines in C (2000). https://www.chiark.greenend.org.uk/sgtatham/coroutines.html
40. Thielecke, H.: Using a continuation twice and its implications for the expressive power of Call/CC. High. Order Symb. Comput. **12**(1), 47–73 (1999). https://doi.org/10.1023/A:1010068800499
41. Tilkov, S., Vinoski, S.: NodeJS: using javascript to build high-performance network programs. IEEE Internet Comput. **14**, 80–83 (2010)
42. Wu, N., Schrijvers, T., Hinze, R.: Effect handlers in scope. In: Proceedings of the 2014 ACM SIGPLAN Symposium on Haskell, Haskell 2014, Göthenburg, Sweden, pp. 1–12 (2014). https://doi.org/10.1145/2633357.2633358

Sound and Efficient Language-Integrated Query
Maintaining the ORDER

Oleg Kiselyov[(⊠)] and Tatsuya Katsushima

Tohoku University, Sendai, Japan
oleg@okmij.org

Abstract. As SQL moved from the English-like language for ad hoc queries by business users to its present status as the universal relational database access, the lack of abstractions and compositionality in the original design is felt more and more acute. Recently added subqueries and common table expressions compensate, albeit generally inefficiently. The inadequacies of SQL motivated language-integrated query systems such as (T-)LINQ, which offer an applicative, programming-like query language compiled to efficient SQL.

However, the seemingly straightforward ranking operations ORDER BY and LIMIT are not supported efficiently, consistently or at all in subqueries. The SQL standard defines their behavior only when applied to the whole query. Language-integrated query systems do not support them either: naively extending ranking to subexpressions breaks the distributivity laws of UNION ALL underlying optimizations and compilation.

We present the first compositional semantics of ORDER BY and LIMIT, which reproduces in the limit the standard-prescribed SQL behavior but also applies to arbitrarily composed query expressions and preserves the distributivity laws. We introduce the relational calculus SQUR that includes ordering and subranging and whose normal forms correspond to efficient, portable, subquery-free SQL. Treating these operations as effects, we describe a type-and-effect system for SQUR and prove its soundness. Our denotational semantics leads to the provably correctness-preserving normalization-by-evaluation. An implementation of SQUR thus becomes a sound and efficient language-integrated query system maintaining the ORDER.

1 Introduction

Language-integrated query is "smooth integration" of database queries with a conventional programming language [1,4]. Not only do we access (generally external) relational data as if they were local arrays of records. Not only do we type-check queries as ordinary programs. Mainly, we use the abstraction facilities of the programming language – functions, modules, classes, etc. – to parameterize queries, reuse old queries as parts of new ones, and compile query libraries. Reflecting operations on database relations in the type system is the old problem with good solutions [3]. Query reuse and composition, detailed below, is more difficult: as we are about to see, the seemingly straightforward operation to sort

© Springer International Publishing AG 2017
B.-Y.E. Chang (Ed.): APLAS 2017, LNCS 10695, pp. 364–383, 2017.
https://doi.org/10.1007/978-3-319-71237-6_18

the query results – patterned after ORDER BY of SQL – wreaks havoc with the existing approaches to query composition. It hence acts quite like a side effect. Seemingly simple, the more one (or stackoverflow users) thinks about it, the more problematic edge cases come to light. A formal treatment is called for, which we develop in this paper in terms of a denotational approach.

1.1 Query Composition

Since query composition is the central, and subtle problem, we introduce it in more detail. The query language of this section is SQL, although the rest of the paper uses the calculus SQUR that is more regular and suited for formal analysis. However, an implementation of SQUR still eventually produces SQL, the *lingua franca* of relational databases. Therefore, understanding the SQL behavior is crucial. Besides, SQL compositions here and their problems in Sect. 1.2 occur in the wild, as seen, e.g., on `stackoverflow` and in training literature.

Consider a sample database table **employee** that lists, among others, employee names, their departments and the hourly wage. The following query then

QE $\stackrel{def}{=}$ SELECT E.* FROM employee **as** E WHERE E.wage > 20

reports employees paid at twice the minimum wage. One may also think of the query as building a filtered table: a subset of well-paid employees. As typical, the department in the **employee** table is mentioned by its **deptID** and so not informative for people outside the company. Suppose there is a table **department** with the descriptive name for each department, along with other data. A more presentable **employee** report is then obtained by the so-called join query, which all relational database systems are meant to run well:

QD $\stackrel{def}{=}$ SELECT E.*, D.name FROM employee **as** E, department **as** D
         WHERE E.deptID $=$ D.deptID

Queries QE and QD are useful on their own; one may imagine them stored in a library. It is also useful to combine them, so to report well-paid employees with descriptive department names. We would like to reuse the queries without changing them except for substituting table names.

There have been three approaches to query composition, shown in the order of increasing performance[1].

temporary table One may store the results of QE in a (temporary) table subemp and then perform QD in which **employee** is replaced with the filtered subemp. The latter table can be 'virtual': a (non-materialized) view or a so-called common table expression shown below:

   with subemp $\{QE\}$ $QD[employee := subemp]$

---

[1] To obtain an informative report one may, in principle, run QE first and for each resulting record, query **department** for the descriptive department name. Such 'composition' essentially executes as many department queries as there are well-paid employees and leads to the 'query avalanche' well explained in [4]. In this paper we consider only those compositions that result in a single query.

where QE and QD above are meant to be replaced with the respective SQL statements; [*old* := *new*] stands for substitution. No full subemp is created; instead, QE runs incrementally.

subquery Another way to compose QE and QD is to consider the query QE as a table on its own and substitute it for the original employee table in QD:

$QD[employee := QE]$

Thus QE will run as a subquery of QD^2. Subqueries have generally better performance: the optimizer may rewrite a subquery into a simple join (like the one shown below), which can then be further optimized. The rewriting is by no means guaranteed[3].

rewriting into flat SQL After composing QE and QD as above, rather than sending the result to the ('black-box') database engine we re-write it ourselves into a subquery-free (i.e., 'flat') SQL using equational laws:

```
SELECT E.*, D.name FROM employee as E, department as D
     WHERE E.deptID = D.deptID AND E.wage > 20
```

This is the most performant approach, and in fact recommended in vendor and training literature. The database user is supposed to do the rewriting. Language-integrated query, as an intermediary between the programmers and SQL, aims to isolate them from the vagaries of SQL – in particular, to perform such re-writing automatically. We demonstrate it in Sect. 2.

1.2   Ordering

Ordering of the query results at first glance appears straightforward: for example, the following modification to QE

QEO $\overset{def}{=}$ SELECT E.* FROM employee as E WHERE E.wage > 20 ORDER BY E.wage

lists employees in the increasing order of their wages. As for instance, the Oracle documentation puts it, "Use the ORDER BY clause to order rows returned by the [SELECT] statement. Without an ORDER BY clause, no guarantee exists that the same query executed more than once will retrieve rows in the same order."[4] It takes time for the second part of the quote to sink in, however. We shall see the examples momentarily.

This seemingly simple ORDER BY feature wrecks all three approaches to compositionality described above. Consider the temporary table approach, with the ordered QEO in place of QE: **with** subemp$\{QEO\}$ $QD[employee := subemp]$. To order the filtered employee table, it first has to be fully constructed, and then sorted (at least that is what PostgreSQL does). Therefore, QEO cannot run

---

[2] Such subqueries in the FROM SQL clause are sometimes called 'derived tables' or 'inlined views'.

[3] For example, MySQL 5.7 never re-writes and hence optimizes subqueries in the FROM clause: http://dev.mysql.com/doc/refman/5.7/en/subquery-restrictions.html.

[4] https://docs.oracle.com/cd/B28359_01/server.111/b28286/statements_10002.htm#sthref6708.

incrementally; it requires space for the filtered data and sorting. Unfortunately, this expense is all for naught: the rows of the entire composed query are still reported in unpredictable order. Recall, unless ORDER BY is attached to the whole query (QD is our example), nothing certain can be said about the order of its results. Expensive useless operations are not the feature one wishes for in a practical system.

If we substitute QEO for employee as a (derived) table in QD, we end up with a subquery containing ORDER BY. According to the Microsoft SQL server documentation, "The ORDER BY clause is not valid in views, inline functions, derived tables, and subqueries, unless either the TOP or OFFSET and FETCH clauses are also specified. When ORDER BY is used in these objects, the clause is used only to determine the rows returned by the TOP clause or OFFSET and FETCH clauses. The ORDER BY clause does not guarantee ordered results when these constructs are queried, unless ORDER BY is also specified in the query itself."[5] Thus composing of ORDER BY queries is not just about poor performance. It could be no performance at all: dynamic error when trying to run the composed query.

Attempting to rewrite the ordered subquery into flat SQL is just as problematic: Re-writing relies on equational laws [6], many of which are no longer valid in the presence of ordering naively extended to subqueries. As an example, consider one of the equational laws (called ForUnionAll1 in [6,13]), applied when a subquery is a UNION ALL of two smaller queries Q1 and Q2:

```
SELECT * FROM (Q1 UNION ALL Q2) WHERE exp ≡
   (SELECT * FROM Q1 WHERE exp) UNION ALL (SELECT * FROM Q2 WHERE exp)
```

For the ordered query, the analogous distributivity no longer holds:

```
SELECT * FROM (Q1 UNION ALL Q2) WHERE exp ORDER BY eo ≢
(SELECT * FROM Q1 WHERE exp ORDER BY eo) UNION ALL
   (SELECT * FROM Q2 WHERE exp ORDER BY eo)
```

Indeed, the left-hand-side query gives the results in a definite order whereas the right-hand-side does not. (With subranging, LIMIT...OFFSET, the failure of distributivity is even more evident.) Incidentally, in our semantics of ordering and subranging, distributivity does hold: see Sect. 4.

Composing queries with ORDER BY is not contrived: 'real-life' database programmers regularly do that and are regularly confused by the inconsistent, puzzling, vendor- and version–specific responses of database engines, as amply documented in stackoverflow and other fora. For example,

"Query with ORDER BY in a FROM subquery produces unordered result. Is this a bug? Below is an example of this:

```
SELECT field1, field2
   FROM ( SELECT field1, field2 FROM table₁ ORDER BY field2 alias
```

returns a result set that is not necessarily ordered by field2."[6]

---

[5] https://msdn.microsoft.com/en-us/library/ms188385.aspx.

[6] https://mariadb.com/kb/en/mariadb/why-is-order-by-in-a-from-subquery-ignored/.

"I am using an application (MapServer) that wraps SQL statements, so that the ORDER BY statement is in the inner query. E.g.

SELECT * FROM (SELECT ID, GEOM, Name FROM t ORDER BY Name) as tbl

The application has many different database drivers. I mainly use the MS SQL Server driver, and SQL Server 2008. This throws an error if an ORDER BY is found in a subquery."[7]

One may find many more such discussions[8] by googling "ORDER BY derived table". The semantics presented in the paper not only answers these questions but also shows how to transform the problematic queries into portable SQL.

1.3 Contributions

If we are to talk to a relational database and obtain sorted results, we have to send the SQL code with ORDER BY attached where the SQL standard expects to see it, to the whole SELECT statement. If we are to freely compose and reuse the already built queries, we quickly end up with ORDER BY appearing in subexpressions, often where the SQL standard does not expect to see it. It is not clear what such composed queries actually mean, let alone how to transform them to the ones that can be *portably* executed on various database systems. (Many systems, e.g., PostgreSQL, Oracle, DB2, and MySQL support nested ORDER BY, but *each* differently.) In short, the problem is that neither the SQL standard, nor its realizations, nor the existing language-integrated query systems supporting ordering give a compositional semantics to ORDER BY.

We present the first compositional treatment of ORDER BY and the related LIMIT... OFFSET – and its application for optimizing composed queries to yield efficient and *portable* SQL. Specifically,

- We present a new language-integrated query calculus SQUR[9] with the denotational, and hence, compositional semantics. The semantics is strikingly, ridiculously simple, requiring *no* domain calculus, no complete partial orders, no lifted types. As the price for simplicity, bare SQUR, like the old SQL, lacks abstractions and is cumbersome to use. Unlike SQL, however, SQUR is composable and hence easily embeddable into a rich metalanguage, which provides modules, combinators, and other syntax sugar. To demonstrate[10], we have embedded SQUR into OCaml (see below).

---

[7] http://dba.stackexchange.com/questions/82930/database-implementations-of-order-by-in-a-subquery.

[8] http://stackoverflow.com/questions/18031421/the-order-by-clause-is-invalid-in-views-inline-functions-derived-tables-subqu, https://www.sqlservercentral.com/Forums/Topic1079476-391-1.aspx.

[9] The name, just like QueΛ of [13], is a pun for old-timers.

[10] A simpler example of embedding a bare, first-order calculus into a rich, functional (meta)language is described in http://okmij.org/ftp/tagless-final/nondet-effect.html.

- Using the non-standard domain of partially-known values we design a normalization-by-evaluation algorithm, which normalizes a SQUR query into the form easily convertible to the *portable* flat SQL. We hence re-implement QUEΛ [13] and reproduce its (and T-LINQ [4]) results. The earlier research relied on the (syntactic) normalization-by-rewriting and hence had to contend with confluence and termination. Our, semantic, normalization is deterministic by construction and is easily shown total;
- We extend the core SQUR with ordering and subranging, maintaining the denotational, compositional treatment and the normalization-by-evaluation. Our semantics of ranking coincides with the SQL semantics when applied to the whole query. Our semantics preserves the distributivity laws of UNION ALL whereas the naively understood ordering and subranging do not.
- We treat ordering and subranging as effects, and design the corresponding type-and-effect system. The types tell when subqueries can be eliminated and when they have to be turned into virtual tables (common-table expressions).

The calculus has been implemented by embedding into OCaml in the tagless-final style, resulting in a sound and efficient language-integrated–query system. The implementation is available at http://okmij.org/ftp/meta-programming/Sqr/ but is not described here for the lack of space.

The structure of the paper is as follows. The next section introduces the core SQUR: first, by examples and then formally. We give the denotational semantics, the type system, and the semantic proof of the type soundness. Section 3 describes the normalization-by-evaluation for the core calculus, and the generation of flat SQL. Section 4 adds sorting and the limiting of the query output. We then review the related work and conclude.

2   Core SQUR

This section presents the core calculus, to be extended with ranking in Sect. 4.

Before the formal presentation (formal definition in Sect. 2.1, type system Sect. 2.2, denotational semantics Sect. 2.3), we introduce SQUR informally, on examples from Sect. 1.1. The query QE that listed high-paid employees looks in SQUR as follows:

```
defn Q_e:
  for (e ← table employee) where e.wage>20 yield e
```

The first line is not part of SQUR (hence the different font): it is mere a presentation tool to attach the name to a query for easy reference. One may think that SQUR is to be subjected to a C-like preprocessor (although we certainly have in mind something more refined: see the accompanying code). The query QD attaching meaningful department names to employees is

```
defn Q_d emp:
  for (e ← emp) for (d ← table department)
  where e.deptID = d.deptID yield <name=e.name, dep=d.name, wage=e.wage>
```

This definition is parameterized by the source of the employee records.

For the presentable report of high-paid employees we compose the two queries, simply as $Q_d\ Q_e$. After desugaring/preprocessing (i.e., inlining the definitions and substituting the parameters) we obtain

```
for (e ← for(e ← table employee) where e.wage>20 yield e)
for (d ← table department)
  where e.deptID = d.deptID yield <name=e.name, dep=d.name, wage=e.wage>
```

which can be interpreted as SQL with the nested SELECTs (derived tables), as described in Sect. 1.1. The paper [13] has explained in detail why subqueries are suboptimal. Normalizing that query gives

```
for (e ← table employee)
for (d ← table department)
  where e.deptID = d.deptID && e.wage>20
  yield <name=e.name, dep=d.name, wage=e.wage>
```

which corresponds to the simple and efficient flat query at the end of Sect. 1.1. Section 3 explains the normalization, and Sect. 3.2 SQL generation, in detail. But first we have to formally introduce SQUR.

2.1   SQUR, Formally

The basic SQUR is formally defined in Fig. 1. It is reminiscent of nested relational calculus [14]. One of the most glaring, although essentially minor differences, is the absence of lambda-abstractions and applications. SQUR hence is not (an extension of) lambda-calculus. Database systems generally do not support first-class functions in queries; hence the lack of lambda-abstractions in SQUR is not an expressiveness limitation in that respect. Furthermore, SQUR is designed for language-*integrated* queries: it is intended to be 'preprocessed', that is, embedded into a host language, and hence to take advantage of the host language's abstraction mechanisms such as first-class functions, modules, etc.

We use x,y for variables, c for integer, boolean, etc. and table constants, n and m for numeric literals, l for record labels. The sequence of items $e_1, ..., e_n$ is abbreviated as e,.... For clarity, Fig. 1 defines only one basic operation: addition. Others are analogous and are silently added when needed. Types of SQUR are base types b, record types $<l_1:b,...>$ where $l_1, ..., l_n$ are field labels, and bag types t bag where t is a base or a record type. Bag types can be annotated with the set of effects ϵ; if empty, it is frequently elided. Effects come into play only in Sect. 4; for now we can assume them empty and ignore.

Besides constants, variable references and primitive operations, the language supports record construction $<l_1=e_1,l_2=e_2,...>$ and record field l_i projection $e.l_i$, bag comprehensions **for**$(x\leftarrow e_1)$ e_2, and the bag concatenation $e_1 \uplus e_2$ patterned after SQL's UNION ALL. The body of **for** extends as far to the right as possible (similarly for **where** and **yield**). Intuitively, **where** e_1e_2 evaluates to the empty bag if e_1 is false; **yield** e produces the singleton bag with the result of e. The language has table constants representing database tables (plus the special constant bag_empty) with their own type t tbl. The expression table e turns a table into a bag; the need to distinguish table constants comes during normalization and SQL conversion. Since the language has no first-class functions, we assume from the outset that all variable names (appearing in comprehensions) are unique.

Variables	x,y,z...
Constants	c (integers, booleans, tables, etc.)
Numeric Literals	n, m
Record Labels	l
Effect Annotations	ϵ
Base Types	b ::= int | bool | string
Flat Types	t ::= b | <l:b,...>
Types	s ::= t | t bag^ϵ | t tbl
Type Environment	Γ ::= x:t, y:t tbl, ...

Expressions e ::= c \| x \| e + e \| <l=e,...> \| e.l \| for(x←e) e \| e ⊎ e
  \| **where** e e \| **yield** e \| table e

Fig. 1. Syntax of core SQUR

2.2 Type System

The type system is presented in Fig. 2. The (Const) rule shows the typing of a single base-type constant **true** and the single table constant employee. Other constants are analogous. The type environment Γ contains only the bindings with flat types and table types (we see the latter bindings only in Sect. 4). As one may expect from the typing of empty containers in general, bag_empty can bear any element type and any effect annotation. From now on, we only deal with well-typed SQUR terms.

$$\frac{}{\Gamma \vdash \textbf{true}: bool}\ Const \qquad \frac{}{\Gamma \vdash employee: <name:string,\ deptID:int,\ wage:int> tbl}\ Const$$

$$\frac{}{\Gamma \vdash bag\_empty: t\ bag^\epsilon}\ Empty \qquad \frac{x:t \in \Gamma}{\Gamma \vdash x:\ t}\ Var \qquad \frac{\Gamma \vdash e_1: int \quad \Gamma \vdash e_2: int}{\Gamma \vdash e_1 + e_2:\ int}\ Op$$

$$\frac{\Gamma \vdash e:\ t\ tbl}{\Gamma \vdash table\ e\ :\ t\ bag^\phi}\ Table \qquad \frac{\Gamma \vdash e:\ b\ ...}{\Gamma \vdash <l=e,...>:\ <l:b,...>}\ Rec \qquad \frac{\Gamma \vdash e:\ <l:b,...>}{\Gamma \vdash e.l_i:\ b_i}\ Proj$$

$$\frac{\Gamma \vdash e_1:\ t\ bag^\epsilon \quad \Gamma \vdash e_2:\ t\ bag^\epsilon}{\Gamma \vdash e_1\ \uplus\ e_2:\ t\ bag^\epsilon}\ UnionAll \qquad \frac{\Gamma \vdash e:t}{\Gamma \vdash \textbf{yield}\ e:\ t\ bag^\phi}\ Yield$$

$$\frac{\Gamma \vdash e_1:\ bool \quad \Gamma \vdash e_2:\ t\ bag^\epsilon}{\Gamma \vdash \textbf{where}\ e_1\ e_2:\ t\ bag^\epsilon}\ Where \qquad \frac{\Gamma \vdash e_1:\ t_1\ bag^\phi \quad \Gamma,x:t_1 \vdash e_2:\ t_2\ bag^\epsilon}{\Gamma \vdash \textbf{for}(x \leftarrow e_1)\ e_2:\ t_2\ bag^\epsilon}\ For$$

Fig. 2. Type system

The next section presents the (denotational) dynamic semantics and proves the type system sound.

2.3   Denotational Semantics

The denotational semantics of SQUR is set-theoretic and Church-style (that is, only typed expressions are given meaning). Figure 3 presents semantic domains and defines $T[s]$ that maps SQUR's type s to a semantic domain, which is an ordinary set. If A_1 and A_2 are sets, we write $l_1 : A_1 \times l_2 : A_2$ for a labeled product: the set of pairs $<l_1{:}a_1,l_2{:}a_2>$, $a_1 \in A_1, a_2 \in A_2$. The components of the pair are identified by their labels l_i rather than their position. If p is such a labeled pair, we write $p.l_i$ to access the l_i-th component, and $p \times l_3 : a_3$ to extend the pair with a new component. We write $\{\{a, ...\}\}$ for a multiset with elements a_i, and $\{\{A\}\}$ for the set of multisets whose elements come from the set A.

$$
\begin{array}{lll}
T[\text{int}] & = \mathbb{N} & \text{set of integers} \\
T[\text{bool}] & = \{T, F\} & \text{booleans} \\
T[\text{string}] & = \mathbb{S} & \text{set of strings} \\
T[<l_1{:}b_1,\dots,l_n{:}b_n>] & = l_1{:}T[b_1] \times \cdots \times l_n{:}T[b_n] & \text{labeled product} \\
T[\text{t tbl}] & = \{\{T[t]\}\} & \text{set of multisets of elements of type } T[t] \\
T[\text{t bag}] & = \{\{T[t]\}\} & \text{set of multisets of elements of type } T[t] \\
T[x_1{:}t_1,\dots,x_n{:}t_n] & = x_1{:}T[t_1] \times \cdots \times x_n{:}T[t_n] & \text{interpretation of the environment}
\end{array}
$$

Fig. 3. Semantic domains and the interpretation of types

The semantic function $\mathcal{E}\Gamma \vdash e : s]\rho_\Gamma$ in Fig. 4 maps a type judgment and the environment to an element of $T[s]$. Here ρ_Γ is an element of the labeled product $T[\Gamma]$. We added the if-then-else conditional to our mathematical notation for writing denotations, overload $\cup$ to mean the set or multiset union, and write $\{\{... \mid \ x{\leftarrow}A\}\}$ for a multiset comprehension.

It is clear from Fig. 4 that $\mathcal{E}[-]\rho$ is the total map. Hence

Theorem 1 (Type Soundness). *For any* $\rho_\Gamma \in T[\Gamma]$, $\mathcal{E}\Gamma \vdash e : s]\rho_\Gamma \in T[s]$.

$$
\begin{aligned}
&\mathcal{E}[\Gamma \vdash c{:}\ s]\ \rho && \in\ T[s] \\
&\mathcal{E}[\Gamma \vdash \text{bag\_empty}{:}\ t\ \text{bag}]\ \rho && =\ \{\{\}\} \\
&\mathcal{E}[\Gamma \vdash x{:}\ t]\ \rho && =\ \rho.x \\
&\mathcal{E}[\Gamma \vdash e_1 + e_2{:}\ \text{int}]\ \rho && =\ \mathcal{E}[\Gamma \vdash e_1{:}\ \text{int}]\rho + \mathcal{E}[\Gamma \vdash e_2{:}\ \text{int}]\rho \\
&\mathcal{E}[\Gamma \vdash <l{=}e,\dots>{:}\ <l{:}b,\dots>]\ \rho && =\ <l{:}\mathcal{E}[\Gamma \vdash e{:}b]\rho,\dots> \\
&\mathcal{E}[\Gamma \vdash e.l_i{:}\ b_i]\ \rho && =\ (\mathcal{E}[\Gamma \vdash e{:}\ <l{:}b,\dots>]\rho).l_i \\
&\mathcal{E}[\Gamma \vdash e_1 \uplus e_2{:}\ t\ \text{bag}]\ \rho && =\ \mathcal{E}[\Gamma \vdash e_1{:}\ t\ \text{bag}]\rho \cup \mathcal{E}[\Gamma \vdash e_2{:}\ t\ \text{bag}]\rho \\
&\mathcal{E}[\Gamma \vdash \textbf{yield}\ e{:}\ t\ \text{bag}]\ \rho && =\ \{\{\ \mathcal{E}[\Gamma \vdash e{:}\ t]\rho\ \}\} \\
&\mathcal{E}[\Gamma \vdash \textbf{where}\ e_1\ e{:}\ t\ \text{bag}]\ \rho && =\ \textbf{if}\ \mathcal{E}[\Gamma \vdash e_1{:}\ \text{bool}]\rho\ \textbf{then}\ \mathcal{E}[\Gamma \vdash e{:}\ t\ \text{bag}]\rho\ \textbf{else}\ \{\{\}\} \\
&\mathcal{E}[\Gamma \vdash \text{table}\ e{:}\ t\ \text{bag}]\ \rho && =\ \mathcal{E}[\Gamma \vdash e{:}\ t\ \text{tbl}]\rho \\
&\mathcal{E}[\Gamma \vdash \textbf{for}(x{\leftarrow}e_1)\ e{:}\ t\ \text{bag}]\ \rho && =\ \bigcup\{\{\ \mathcal{E}[\Gamma,x{:}t_1 \vdash e{:}\ t\ \text{bag}]\ (\rho \times x : x')\ \mid \\
& && \qquad\qquad x'{\leftarrow}\mathcal{E}[\Gamma \vdash e_1{:}\ t_1\ \text{bag}]\rho\ \}\}
\end{aligned}
$$

Fig. 4. Denotational semantics of Core SQUR

The semantics of $e_1 \uplus e_2$ clearly shows that the UNION ALL operation is associative and commutative. Moreover, the following distributive laws hold (which is easy to verify by applying the semantic function to both sides of the equations). These laws, among others, underlie the normalization-by-rewriting of [4,6].

Theorem 2 (Distributive Equational Laws of UNION ALL).

$$
\begin{aligned}
\mathsf{for}\,(x \leftarrow e_1 \uplus e_2)\, e &\equiv (\mathsf{for}\,(x{\leftarrow}e_1)\, e) \;\uplus\; (\mathsf{for}\,(x{\leftarrow}e_2)\, e) \\
\mathsf{for}\,(x \leftarrow e)\, e_1 \uplus e_2 &\equiv (\mathsf{for}\,(x{\leftarrow}e)\, e_1) \;\uplus\; (\mathsf{for}\,(x{\leftarrow}e)\, e_2) \\
\mathsf{where}\; e\; e_1 \uplus e_2 &\equiv (\mathsf{where}\; e\; e_1) \;\uplus\; (\mathsf{where}\; e\; e_2)
\end{aligned}
$$

3   Normalization-by-Evaluation

The just described denotational semantics may be regarded as an interpreter of SQUR queries over an in-memory database of lists of records. Our motivation however is to run SQUR over external relational databases. Therefore, this section interprets SQUR expressions as SQL statements – i.e., gives a different semantics to SQUR, over the domain of SQL queries.

The problem is not trivial: as we saw in Sect. 2 earlier and see again later, only a subset of SQUR expressions can be easily translated to 'flat' SQL queries. A solution suggested in Cooper [6] is to re-write, if possible, the expressions outside the easily-translatable subset into that good subset. For the simple language corresponding to our Core SQUR, Cooper (later followed by [4]) introduced a set of rewriting rules, proved they are type- and semantic- preserving, confluent and terminating, and the resulting normal forms are easily-translatable to SQL. No such rules are known for the language extended with ordering, grouping, etc.

We take an approach radically different from [6] and its followers: semantic, rather than syntactic. We *start* with the 'normal form' for SQUR expressions, specifically designed to be easily convertible to SQL. We then show how to compute that normal form, through deterministic evaluation. The totality of evaluation proves that all SQUR expressions are translatable to SQL. The denotational approach makes it rather easy to show the type and semantics preservation of this normalization by evaluation.

We define the normalization-by-evaluation as giving another, non-standard interpretation of SQUR, into different semantic domains. This section defines new semantic functions $\mathcal{T}^n[-]$ and $\mathcal{E}^n[-]$, clause by clause. The environments and variables are handled as before:

$$
\begin{aligned}
\mathcal{T}^n[x_1{:}t_1,\dots,x_n{:}t_n] &= x_1{:}\mathcal{T}^n[t_1] \times \cdots \times x_n{:}\mathcal{T}^n[t_n] \\
\mathcal{E}^n[\Gamma \vdash x{:}\, t]\, \rho &= \rho.x
\end{aligned}
$$

The new semantic domains will include, in one form or another, sets of all SQUR terms of type s, which we denote as $\mathbb{E}_s$. The terms are generally open, so, strictly speaking we have to index $\mathbb{E}$ not only by the type but also by the corresponding typing environment. To keep the notation readable (and writable), however, we make the typing environment implicit. For base types (we only show int), the new domain is the disjoint union (sum) of $T[\mathsf{b}]$ and $\mathbb{E}_\mathsf{b}$. To simplify the notation, we explicitly write only the inr tag of the sum, and elide inl. We also show the relevant clauses of a new semantic function, $\mathcal{I}[-]\colon T^n[\mathsf{s}] \to \mathbb{E}_\mathsf{s}$, called *reification*. It is in some sense (made precise later) an 'inverse' of evaluation, producing the SQUR expression with the given (non-standard) meaning.

$$
\begin{aligned}
T^n[\mathsf{int}] &= \mathbb{N} \oplus \mathbb{E}_{\mathsf{int}} \\
\mathcal{E}^n[\Gamma \vdash \mathsf{0}\colon \mathsf{int}]\,\rho &= 0 \quad \text{(other integer constants are similar)} \\
\mathcal{E}^n[\Gamma \vdash \mathsf{e_1 + e_2}\colon \mathsf{int}]\,\rho &= add\ (\mathcal{E}^n[\Gamma \vdash \mathsf{e_1}\colon \mathsf{int}]\,\rho)\ (\mathcal{E}^n[\Gamma \vdash \mathsf{e_2}\colon \mathsf{int}]\,\rho) \text{ where} \\
\quad add\ 0\ \mathrm{x} &= \mathrm{x} \\
\quad add\ \mathrm{x}\ 0 &= \mathrm{x} \\
\quad add\ n\ m &= n + m \quad n, m \in \mathbb{N} \\
\quad add\ \mathrm{x}\ \mathrm{y} &= inr\ (\mathcal{I}[\mathsf{x}] + \mathcal{I}[\mathsf{y}]) \\
\mathcal{I}[0] &= 0 \\
\mathcal{I}[inr\ \mathsf{e}] &= \mathsf{e}
\end{aligned}
$$

The standard and non-standard semantics thus differ in assigning meaning to open expressions: the former interprets, say, x+1 to mean a $\mathbb{N} \to \mathbb{N}$ function (viz., the increment). On the other hand, the non-standard semantics interprets the same expression as itself (plus the implicit typing environment associating x with int). The non-standard domain is hence the domain of partially-known values, familiar from partial evaluation, also known as a glued domain [7].

The interpretation of record types is similar:

$$
\begin{aligned}
T^n[<\mathsf{l}{:}\mathsf{b},\ldots>] &= \mathsf{l}{:}T^n[\mathsf{b}] \times \cdots \oplus \mathbb{E} \\
\mathcal{E}^n[\Gamma \vdash <\mathsf{l}{=}\mathsf{e},\ldots>\colon <\mathsf{l}{:}\mathsf{b},\ldots>]\,\rho &= <\mathsf{l}{:}\mathcal{E}^n[\Gamma \vdash \mathsf{e}{:}\mathsf{b}]\rho,\ldots> \\
\mathcal{E}^n[\Gamma \vdash \mathsf{e}.\mathsf{l}_i\colon \mathsf{b}_i]\,\rho &= prj_{l}\ (\mathcal{E}^n[\Gamma \vdash \mathsf{e}\colon <\mathsf{l}{:}\mathsf{b},\ldots>]\rho) \text{ where} \\
\quad prj_{l}\ <\mathsf{l}{:}x,\ldots> &= x \\
\quad prj_{l}\ (inr\ \mathsf{e}) &= inr\ \mathsf{e}.\mathsf{l} \\
\mathcal{I}[<\mathsf{l}{:}x,\ldots>] &= <\mathsf{l}{:}\mathcal{I}[x],\ldots> \\
\mathcal{I}[inr\ \mathsf{e}] &= \mathsf{e}
\end{aligned}
$$

The non-standard semantic domain for bag types is quite more complex. Formally, the meaning of a t bag expression is a multiset whose elements (to be called primitive comprehensions) are triples (ts, y, w) where w is the non-standard boolean representing the guard of the comprehension; y is the meaning of the (generic) comprehension element and ts is the set of pairs (x,m) where m is a table constant of type t' tbl for some t' and x: t' is a fresh variable. We will use a special notation for such triple: $\mathbf{fors(x{\leftarrow}m\ldots)}\ \mathbf{whr}\ w\ \mathbf{yld}\ y$, which should remind one of SQUR's repeated comprehension expressions (with $n \geq 0$)

for $(\mathsf{x_1} \leftarrow$ table $\mathsf{m_1})\ \ldots$ for$(\mathsf{x_n} \leftarrow$ table $\mathsf{m_n})$ **where** w **yield** y

We write $\mathbb{M}$ for the set of table constants. The reification clause should explain the intent behind our representation of bags. As we shall see later, the representation is also good for converting to SQL.

$$\mathcal{T}^n[\text{t bag}] \qquad\qquad = \{\{\text{ fors}(\text{x}\leftarrow\mathbb{M}\ldots)\text{ whr }\mathcal{T}^n[\text{bool}]\text{ yld }\mathcal{T}^n[\text{t}]\ \}\}$$

$$\mathcal{E}^n[\Gamma \vdash \text{bag\_empty: t bag}]\ \rho\ = \{\{\}\}$$

$$\mathcal{E}^n[\Gamma \vdash \text{e}_1 \uplus \text{e}_2\text{: t bag}]\ \rho\ = \mathcal{E}^n[\Gamma \vdash \text{e}_1\text{: t bag}]\rho \cup \mathcal{E}^n[\Gamma \vdash \text{e}_2\text{: t bag}]\rho$$

$$\mathcal{E}^n[\Gamma \vdash \textbf{yield}\ \text{e: t bag}]\ \rho\ = \{\{\text{ fors ()}\text{ whr }T\text{ yld }\mathcal{E}[\Gamma \vdash \text{e: t}]\rho\ \}\}$$

$$\mathcal{E}^n[\Gamma \vdash \textbf{table}\ \text{m: t bag}]\ \rho\ = \{\{\text{ fors (u}\leftarrow\text{m)}\text{ whr }T\text{ yld u}\ \}\}\text{ and u is fresh}$$

$$\mathcal{E}^n[\Gamma \vdash \textbf{where}\ \text{e}_1\ \text{e: t bag}]\ \rho\ = where'\ (\mathcal{E}^n[\Gamma \vdash \text{e}_1\text{: bool}]\rho)\ (\mathcal{E}^n[\Gamma \vdash \text{e: t bag}]\rho)\text{ where}$$

$$\qquad where'\ T\ xs \qquad\qquad = xs$$

$$\qquad where'\ F\ xs \qquad\qquad = \{\{\}\}$$

$$\qquad where'\ t\ xs \qquad\qquad = \{\{\text{ fors (x}\leftarrow\text{m}\ldots)\text{ whr }w \wedge t\text{ yld }y$$
$$\qquad\qquad\qquad\qquad\qquad\qquad\quad |\ \text{ fors (x}\leftarrow\text{m}\ldots)\text{ whr }w\text{ yld }y \leftarrow xs\}\}$$

$$\mathcal{E}^n[\Gamma \vdash \textbf{for}(\text{x}\leftarrow\text{e}_1)\ \text{e: t bag}]\ \rho\ =$$
$$\qquad \{\{\text{ fors (x'}\leftarrow\text{m'},\ldots\text{x''}\leftarrow\text{m''},\ldots)\text{ whr }w' \wedge w''\text{ yld }y''\ |$$
$$\qquad\qquad \text{fors (x'}\leftarrow\text{m'}\ldots)\text{ whr }w'\text{ yld }y' \leftarrow \mathcal{E}^n[\Gamma \vdash \text{e}_1\text{: t}_1\text{ bag}]\rho,$$
$$\qquad\qquad \text{fors (x''}\leftarrow\text{m''}\ldots)\text{ whr }w''\text{ yld }y'' \leftarrow \mathcal{E}^n[\Gamma,\text{x:t}_1 \vdash \text{e: t bag}](\rho\times\text{x:}y')\ \}\}$$

$$\mathcal{I}[\{\{\}\}] \qquad\qquad\qquad = \text{bag\_empty}$$

$$\mathcal{I}[xs] \qquad\qquad\qquad\ = \uplus \{\{\ \textbf{for}(\text{x}\leftarrow\textbf{table}\ \text{m})\ldots\ \textbf{where}\ \mathcal{I}[w]\ \textbf{yield}\ \mathcal{I}[y]\ |$$
$$\qquad\qquad\qquad\qquad\qquad \text{fors(x}\leftarrow\text{m}\ldots)\text{ whr }w\text{ yld }y \leftarrow xs\}\}$$
$$\qquad\qquad\qquad\qquad (\text{the } \textbf{where} \text{ clause is omitted if } w \text{ is } T)$$

A primitive table and **yield** are straightforward to interpret as primitive comprehensions. The operation $\uplus$, like in the standard semantics, joins the multisets. The **where** operation pushes its boolean guard down to the whr w of a primitive comprehension. The **for** operation is interpreted as a nested comprehension. The SQUR implementation realizes the non-standard evaluation $\mathcal{E}^n[-]$ as another tagless-final interpreter of SQUR's expressions.

3.1 Formal Properties of NBE

The mere inspection of $\mathcal{E}^n[-]$ shows it to be total and hence well-defined, giving another denotational semantics of SQUR. Recall, $\mathcal{I}[-]: \mathcal{T}^n[\text{s}] \rightarrow \mathbb{E}_{\text{s}}$ takes the non-standard interpretation of a SQUR expression ('semantics') and picks an expression ('syntax') with that meaning. Such an operation is typically called 'reify'; see the tutorial [7] for more discussion. Clearly, $\mathcal{I}[-]$ picks an expression of the same type as the original one. We have been implicit about the environments however. The following proposition, which follows from a more careful analysis of $\mathcal{E}^n[-]$ and $\mathcal{I}[-]$, recovers the environments.

Proposition 1 (Type Preservation). *For all* $\Gamma \vdash \text{e : s}$ *and* $\rho \in \mathcal{T}^n[\Gamma]$*, it holds* $\Gamma' \vdash \mathcal{I}[\mathcal{E}^n[\text{e}]\rho]$*, where* Γ' *lists the variables in the domain of* ρ *and their types.*

As an example, consider

x:<l_1:int,l_2:int,l_3:int>, y:int ⊢ x.l_1 + x.l_2 + x.l_3 + y:int

Interpreting it in the environment ρ =< x :< l_1 : $inr\, u_1, l_2$: $inr\, u_2 + 2, l_3 = 3$>, y : 4 > and reifying gives u_1 : int, u_2 : int ⊢ $u_1 + (u_2 + 2) + 7$: int.

Theorem 3 (Soundness of NBE). *For all* SQUR *expressions* $\Gamma \vdash$ e : s, *and environments* ρ *and* ρ' *of appropriate types,* $\mathcal{E}[\mathcal{I}[\mathcal{E}^n[e]\rho]]\rho'$ *is equal to* $\mathcal{E}[e](\mathcal{E}[\mathcal{I}[\rho]]\rho')$.

The non-standard interpretation is thus consistent with the standard denotational semantics in Sect. 2.3. For closed e the theorem states that $\mathcal{I}[\mathcal{E}^n[e]<>]$ is equal (i.e., has the equal denotation) to e. Hence $\mathcal{I}[-]$ is the left inverse of $\mathcal{E}^n[-]$. The proof is straightforward and is outlined in the Appendix.

3.2   Normal Forms and SQL Generation

Definition 1 (Normal form). *We call* $\mathcal{I}[\mathcal{E}^n[e]<>]$ *the normal form* $\mathcal{N}[e]$ *of a closed term* e

Proposition 2 (Correctness of normal form). *If* e *is a closed term of the type* s, *then: (a)* $\mathcal{N}[e]$ *exists; (b)* ⊢ $\mathcal{N}[e]$: s; *(c)* $\mathcal{N}[\mathcal{N}[e]] = \mathcal{N}[e]$; *(d)* $\mathcal{E}[e] = \mathcal{E}[\mathcal{N}[e]]$.

That is, the normalization is total, type-preserving, idempotent, and meaning preserving. The totality comes from the fact that $\mathcal{E}^n[-]$ and $\mathcal{I}[-]$ are total; (b) is Proposition 1; (d) is a corollary of Theorem 3, and (c) is easy to verify by inspection of $\mathcal{E}^n[-]$. The fact that $\mathcal{N}[$table m$]$ is **for**(x←table m) **yield** x tells that our normal forms are eta-long.

We can now complete our program of interpreting every well-typed SQUR expression of a bag type as a SQL query. First we apply the normalization-by-evaluation to obtain the normal form $\mathcal{N}[e]$, which is designed to be easily mapped to a flat SQL query. Actually, it is simpler use the result of $\mathcal{E}^n[e]$ directly. Recall, if e is a closed expression of a bag type, $\mathcal{E}^n[e]<>$ is a multiset of primitive comprehensions {{ fors (x←m...) whr w yld y }} where m are table constants. A primitive comprehension is straightforward to convert to a SELECT statement: the table constants m, ... become the FROM list of the SELECT statement, w becomes the WHERE condition and y becomes the SELECT list. If the multiset of primitive comprehensions has more than one element, the resulting SELECTs are UNION ALL-ed together.

The approach presented so far handles the same language-integrated query language as QueΛ and T-LINQ [4], eventually producing the same SQL code as in those two previous approaches (SQUR in Fig. 1 does not include EXIST queries, but our implementation of SQUR does).

An example is given in Sect. 2, when describing the SQL code eventually obtained for the composition of the sample queries, Q_e and Q_d.

4   Ordering

SQL has operations to sort the results of a query or extract a particular range of rows, as discussed in Sect. 1.2. The query in the right-hand column is the example from Sect. 1.2, sorting the filtered list of employees.

defn Q_{eo}:
  for(e ← table employee) where e.wage>20
    ordering_wage e.wage yield e
	SELECT E.∗ FROM employee as E
	WHERE E.wage > 20
	ORDER BY E.wage

whereas the following one returns only the first three rows of the sorted table starting from the second one.

defn Q_{el}:
  for(e ← table employee) where e.wage>20
    limit (3,1) ordering_wage e.wage yield e
	SELECT E.∗ FROM employee as E
	WHERE E.wage > 20
	ORDER BY E.wage
	LIMIT 3 OFFSET 1

To write these queries in SQUR we add the operations ordering and limit, as illustrated in the left-hand column of the tables. Formally the operations are defined as (Fig. 5).

Ordering Effects o:[olabel,. . .], l:(n,m)
Ordering Labels owage,. . .
Expressions   e +:= ordering_wage e_1 e | limit (n,m) e | let table x = e in e

Fig. 5. Syntax of ordering and ranging operations

We assume a countable supply of ordering operations ordering_l, each with its own effect label ol; we show only one such operation ordering_wage and its effect label owage; the others are analogous. An implementation of SQUR is presumed to be able to declare ordering operations and the corresponding labels (e.g., using generative modules). Following the earlier conventions, expressions e in ordering_l e_1e and limit(n,m) e continue as far right as possible, saving us parentheses. The ordering is ascending; this is not a limitation since the key is an arbitrary integer expression, which can always be adjusted for the desired ordering. The directive limit (n,m) e extracts n elements starting from m from the sequence obtained by sorting the *final* bag result; the type system ensures the presence of ordering defining the sorting keys. We also added let table, the let-expression specialized for bags, to be used shortly.

In SQL, ORDER BY and LIMIT...OFFSET are to be applied at the end, to the results of the query – at the top-level, so to speak. When reusing previously written queries as part of new ones, the originally 'top-level' forms quickly become buried in subexpressions. Here is an example of a query composition, reusing Q_{eo}:

defn Q_{eo2}:
  for (e ← Q_{eo}) for (d ← table department)
  where e.deptID = d.deptID ordering_dept d.deptID
  yield <name=e.name, dep=d.name, wage=e.wage>

(assume Q_{eo} in the above expression is substituted with the corresponding query). Naively doing such composition in SQL results in

```
SELECT E.name, D.name, E.wage FROM (SELECT E.* FROM employee as E WHERE
      E.wage > 20 ORDER BY E.wage) AS E, department as D
WHERE E.deptID = D.deptID ORDER BY D.deptID
```

with ORDER BY in a subquery – which is either slow and wasteful, or even not allowed at all, as we saw in Sect. 1.2.

To allow compositionality we do not impose syntactic restrictions on ordering and limit: they may in principle appear anywhere within a query. We do however wish to preserve the intent of SQL of treating these operations as directives, to be applied to the end-result of a query. Thus, ordering and limiting are *effects*. Even if ordering and limit may be buried and duplicated, they have an effect, which is noticed, accumulated, and applied to the query results. In the type system the effects appear as the annotation on the bag type, as shown in the extended type system in Fig. 6. We have refined the (For) rule, whose justification will become clear from the dynamic semantics explained below. The ordering effect annotation o : [label,...] is parameterized by the list of ordering labels. The limit annotation l:(n,m) is indexed by the subranging parameters. They are statically known integers and do not require dependent types. They can be simply realized using OCaml modules.

$$\frac{\Gamma \vdash e_1: \text{int} \qquad \Gamma \vdash e: t\ \text{bag}\hat{\ }\epsilon \qquad \epsilon \subseteq \{o:[lb,\dots]\}}{\Gamma \vdash \textbf{ordering\_wage}\ e_1\ e\ :\ t\ \text{bag}\hat{\ }\{o:[owage,lb,\dots]\}}\ \text{Ordering}$$

$$\frac{\Gamma \vdash e: t\ \text{bag}\hat{\ }\epsilon \qquad \epsilon = \{o:[lb,\dots]\}}{\Gamma \vdash \textbf{limit}\ (n,m)\ e\ :\ t\ \text{bag}\hat{\ }(\epsilon \cup \{l:(n,m)\})}\ \text{Limit}$$

$$\frac{\Gamma \vdash e_1: t_1\ \text{bag}\hat{\ }\epsilon_1 \qquad \epsilon_1 \subseteq \{o:[lb,\dots]\} \qquad \Gamma,x:t_1 \vdash e_2: t_2\ \text{bag}\hat{\ }\epsilon}{\Gamma \vdash \textbf{for}(x\leftarrow e_1)\ e_2: t_2\ \text{bag}\hat{\ }\epsilon}\ \text{For}$$

$$\frac{\vdash e_1: t_1\ \text{bag}\hat{\ }\epsilon_1 \qquad \Gamma,y:t_1\ \text{tbl} \vdash e_2: t_2\ \text{bag}\hat{\ }\epsilon}{\Gamma \vdash \textbf{let}\ \text{table}\ y=e_1\ \textbf{in}\ e_2: t_2\ \text{bag}\hat{\ }\epsilon}\ \text{Let}$$

Fig. 6. Type system with ordering operations

The type system reflects several arbitrary choices, as we explain later. For example, in the (Ordering) rule, **ordering_wage** e_1 e adds the corresponding ordering label owage before other ordering effect labels associated with e. As extensively discussed back in Sect. 1.2, ORDER BY in subexpressions, unless accompanied by LIMIT, makes no sense and we (along with several real database systems) ignore it, which is reflected in the denotational semantics below.

The extended normalization-by-evaluation normalizes Q_{eo2} into

```
defn Qⁿₑₒ₂:
  for (e ← table employee)
  for (d ← table department)
  where e.deptID = d.deptID && e.wage>20
  ordering_dept d.deptID
  yield <name=e.name, dep=d.name, wage=e.wage>
```

```
SELECT E.name, D.name, E.wage
FROM employee as E, department as D
WHERE E.deptID = D.deptID AND
    E.wage > 20
ORDER BY D.deptID
```

eliminating the nested ORDER BY (as well as the subquery). The result is easily convertible to flat SQL, shown on the right.

If we attempt to write Q_{eo2} with the subranged Q_{el} in place of Q_{eo}, it will not type check: whereas Q_{eo} has the effect annotation $\{o : [owage]\}$, Q_{el} has $\{l : (3, 1), o : [owage]\}$. The (For) typing rule for $\textbf{for}(x \leftarrow e_1)\ e_2$ does not permit the subranging $l:(n,m)$ effect annotation on e_1. That is, ordering with the limit cannot be eliminated from a subquery, resulting in the performance hit. One has to use let-table, to make the performance implications explicit:

```
defn Qₑₒₗ₂:
  let table t = Qₑₗ in
  for (e ← table t) for (d ← table department)
  where e.deptID = d.deptID ordering_dept d.deptID
  yield <name=e.name, dep=d.name, wage=e.wage>
```

which translates to SQL with common table expressions

```
WITH t8 AS (SELECT E.* FROM employee as E
            WHERE E.wage > 20 ORDER BY E.wage LIMIT 3 OFFSET 1)
SELECT t9.name, t7.name, t9.wage FROM department AS t7, t8 AS t9
WHERE t9.deptID = t7.deptID ORDER BY t7.deptID
```

The denotational semantics of SQUR extended with ordering and subranging is subtle. It is rather surprising how little has changed: only the interpretation of **for** is updated, and only slightly (Fig. 7).

As before, an expression of the $\texttt{t bag}^{\wedge}\epsilon$ type is interpreted as a multiset, whose elements are (typically records) $T[t]$. If the effect annotation ϵ includes ordering $o : [label,...]$, we add to $T[t]$ a new field o, a tuple of sorting keys (which SQUR takes, without loss of generality, to be integers). If the $l:(n,m)$ annotation is also present, we add yet another field, l, with the pair of integers n and m. The type system ensures that the field has the same value across all elements of a multiset (and so it could be factored out, as our OCaml implementation actually does). The interpretation of **for** is changed to ignore the extra fields in the comprehended multiset (the l field should be absent to start with, according to the type system). The type system ensures that in $e_1 \uplus e_2$, both expressions have the same effect annotations: the same subranging and the same sorting keys. Therefore, taking, as before, the multiset union of $\mathcal{E}[e_1]\rho$ and $\mathcal{E}[e_2]\rho$ is meaningful. It is easy to verify that type soundness (Theorem 1) is preserved.

We now have to distinguish the denotation of an expression from the denotation of the whole program. The latter is computed by the semantic function $\mathcal{M}[-]$ that maps a closed term of a bag type to a *sequence* of elements. For an expression e without the ordering annotation, $\mathcal{M}[-]$ converts the multiset $\mathcal{E}[e]<>$ to a sequence of some non-deterministic order. If the ordering annotation is present, however, $\mathcal{M}[-]$ uses the o:keys field to sort the elements (removing

$\mathcal{T}[\text{t bag}^\wedge\phi]$ $= \{\{\ \mathcal{T}[\text{t}]\ \}\}$

$\mathcal{T}[\text{t bag}^\wedge\{\text{o:[lb,}\ldots]\}]$ $= \{\{\ \mathcal{T}[\text{t}] \times \text{o:}(\mathbb{N} \times \ldots)\ \}\}$

$\mathcal{T}[\text{t bag}^\wedge\{\text{o:[lb,}\ldots],\text{l:(n,m)}\}]$ $= \{\{\ \mathcal{T}[\text{t}] \times \text{o:}(\mathbb{N} \times \ldots) \times \text{l:}(\mathbb{N} \times \mathbb{N})\ \}\}$

$\mathcal{E}[\Gamma \vdash \textbf{for}(\text{x}{\leftarrow}e_1)\ e\text{: t bag}^\wedge\epsilon]\ \rho$ $=$
$\quad \bigcup\{\{\ \mathcal{E}[\Gamma,\text{x:}t_1 \vdash e\text{: t bag}^\wedge\epsilon]\ (\rho \times x : x')\ |\ x' \times \text{o:}\_ {\leftarrow} \mathcal{E}[\Gamma \vdash e_1\text{: }t_1\text{ bag}^\wedge\epsilon']\rho\ \}\}$

$\mathcal{E}[\Gamma \vdash \textbf{ordering\_lb}\ e_1\ e\text{: t bag}^\wedge\{\text{o:[lb]}\}]\ \rho$ $=$
$\quad \{\{\ x \times \text{o:}[\mathcal{E}[e_1]\rho]\ |\ x \leftarrow \mathcal{E}[\Gamma \vdash e\text{: t bag}^\wedge\phi]\rho\ \}\}$

$\mathcal{E}[\Gamma \vdash \textbf{ordering\_lb}\ e_1\ e\text{: t bag}^\wedge\epsilon]\ \rho$ $=$
$\quad \{\{\ x \times \text{o:}[\mathcal{E}[e_1]\rho,\text{lb'},\ldots]\ |\ x \times \text{o:[lb'},\ldots] \leftarrow \mathcal{E}[\Gamma \vdash e\text{: t bag}^\wedge\epsilon_1]\rho\ \}\}$
$\quad$ where $\epsilon_1{=}\{\text{o:[lb'},\ldots]\}$ and $\epsilon{=}\{\text{o:[lb,lb'},\ldots]\}$

$\mathcal{E}[\Gamma \vdash \textbf{limit}\ (\text{n,m})\ e\text{: t bag}^\wedge\{\epsilon \cup \text{l:(n,m)}\}]\ \rho =$
$\quad \{\{\ x \times \text{l:(n,m)}\ |\ x \leftarrow \mathcal{E}[\Gamma \vdash e\text{: t bag}^\wedge\epsilon]\rho\ \}\}$

$\mathcal{E}[\Gamma \vdash \textbf{let}\ \text{table y}{=}e_1\ \textbf{in}\ e\text{: t bag}^\wedge\epsilon]\ \rho$ $=$
$\quad \mathcal{E}[\Gamma,\text{y:}t_1\ \text{tbl} \vdash e\text{: t bag}^\wedge\epsilon]\ (\rho \times \text{y:}\mathcal{M}[\vdash e_1\text{: }t_1\ \text{bag}^\wedge\epsilon_1])$

$\mathcal{M}[\vdash e\text{: t bag}^\wedge\phi]$ $= \mathcal{E}[\vdash e\text{: t bag}^\wedge\phi]{<>}$

$\mathcal{M}[\vdash e\text{: t bag}^\wedge\epsilon]$ $=$
$\quad subrange\ (\text{n,m}) \circ sort\ \text{keys}\ \{\{\ x\ |\ x \times \text{o:keys} \times \text{l:(n,m)} \leftarrow \mathcal{E}[\vdash e\text{: t bag}^\wedge\epsilon]{<>}\ \}\}$
$\quad$ (no subranging if the l annotation is absent)

Fig. 7. Denotational semantics of SQUR with ordering and limit

the field from the result). If the l:(n,m) annotation is also present, the (n,m) subsequence is extracted afterwards. $\mathcal{M}[-]$ hence corresponds to the semantics of ordering and subranging defined in SQL: sorting and limiting are applied at the end of query processing.

Since UNION ALL has the same denotation as in Core SQUR, it is still commutative and associative, and the distributivity laws (Theorem 2) still hold:

Theorem 4 (Distributive Equational Laws of UNION ALL).

$\begin{array}{lll}
\textbf{for}\,(x \leftarrow e_1 \uplus e_2)\ e & \equiv\ (\textbf{for}\,(x{\leftarrow}e_1)\ e) & \uplus\ (\textbf{for}\,(x{\leftarrow}e_2)\ e) \\
\textbf{for}\,(x \leftarrow e)\ e_1 \uplus e_2 & \equiv\ (\textbf{for}\,(x{\leftarrow}e)\ e_1) & \uplus\ (\textbf{for}\,(x{\leftarrow}e)\ e_2) \\
\textbf{where}\ e\ e_1 \uplus e_2 & \equiv\ (\textbf{where}\ e\ e_1) & \uplus\ (\textbf{where}\ e\ e_2) \\
\textbf{ordering_}lb\ e\ (e_1 \uplus e_2) & \equiv\ (\textbf{ordering_}lb\ e\ e_1) & \uplus\ (\textbf{ordering_}lb\ e\ e_2) \\
\textbf{limit}\ (n,m)\ (e_1 \uplus e_2) & \equiv\ (\textbf{limit}\ (n,m)\ e_1) & \uplus\ (\textbf{limit}\ (n,m)\ e_2)
\end{array}$

That is quite unexpected, if one were to take ordering and limit naively, as sorting and subranging of their argument expressions. One surely would not think of UNION ALL to be distributive, let alone symmetric. The distributivity across ordering and limit is particularly outrageous. It is worth stressing again that ordering and limit are directives. The expression ordering $e_1 e$ does *not* immediately sort the bag e; neither does **limit** $(1,0)$ e mean taking the first element of the bag e (which is meaningless since bags, as multisets, have no definite order).

In defining the semantics of ordering and limit, we had to resolve a number of essentially arbitrary choices:

- in a nested ordering e_1 ordering e_2 e, should e_1 be the major sort key, or e_2? We chose e_1.
- in a nested subranging **limit** (n_1, m_1) **limit** (n_2, m_2) e, should the outer limit take effect over the inner, or the inner overriding outer, or somehow be combined? Or the nesting of limit should be outlawed by the time system? We chose the latter. Multiple limits are still possible; on has to explicitly use **let** table to force subranging and other effects of an intermediary expression.
- should ordering e_1 **limit** (n,m) e be allowed (without the explicit **let** table)? We chose against it, since e_1 as the major sort key affects the subranging.

One may argue for different choices: after all, SQL gives no guidance since the standard only talks about ORDER BY when attached to the top-most SELECT. The choices are up to us to make. However we – or the reader – choose, our denotational framework trivially accommodates any choice.

The presented denotational semantics can then be generalized to the normalization-by-evaluation semantics, similar to the approach illustrated in Sect. 3. The only significant change is to add to the triple **fors** $(x \leftarrow m \ldots)$ **whr** w **yld** y two extra fields, for the ordering keys and subranging, depending on the effect annotations. For the lack of space, we refer to the SQUR implementation for details.

The non-standard interpretation can again be converted to SQL. The example SQL code at the beginning of this section was the output of such conversion.

5   Related Work

Language-integrated query as a research area was established with the nested relational calculus (NRC) in [2,14]. Specifically, integration of relational algebra into a typed functional language was pioneered in [3]. Although some versions of NRC [10, Corollary 3.3] can express ordering (called 'rank assignment' in that paper), it is what Sect. 4 has called the 'naive' ordering, whose serious drawbacks have been explained in Sect. 1.2.

Our approach may superficially be seen as an extension of a long line of work starting from Cooper [6] and Microsoft LINQ, and continuing through T-LINQ [4,13]. None of them considered ordering and subranging. Our use of effects is notably different from Cooper's and our integration with the host language is less tight and more stylized. Compared to T-LINQ, SQUR has no quotation. As we have already emphasized, SQUR has no functions and is not an extension of lambda-calculus. Although SQUR is superficially similar to QUEΛ of Suzuki et al., it has no first-class functions, its dynamic semantics is given denotationally rather than operationally, the soundness of its type system is proven semantically rather than syntactically. Finally, SQUR relies on the normalization-by-evaluation (NBE) rather than on repeated, and hopefully convergent, re-writing.

The language-integrated query systems SML# [12] and Haskell's Opaleye [8] and HRR [9] also deal with ordering. They do not present relational data as local arrays to iterate over. They have rather complicated type system. The published materials describe no compositional semantics. Mainly, these systems consider no query normalization and optimizations, relying on subqueries to achieve compositionality – hence exhibit the problems described in Sect. 1.2 and may generate broken queries.

We owe a great debt to Dybjer and Filinski's tutorial on normalization-by-evaluation [7]. The many similarities in our NBE approaches are not accidental. One notable difference is our use of the tagless-final approach, which let us index semantic domains by the object types without resorting to dependent types. Therefore, all our interpreters are patently total and hence easier to see correct. Also, we do not define any reduction-based semantics or the corresponding reduction equational theory.

Normalization in embedded languages is thoroughly discussed by Najd et al. in [11]. However, they consider quite a more complicated problem of so-called quoted DSLs, where quoted expressions may contain higher-order constructs such as function applications. The latter are to be eliminated in the course of normalization, and the subformula property sees to it. The normalization procedure of their QDSL operates on 'syntax', a representation of a QDSL expression. We, on the other hand, deal with 'semantics', with a representation of the meaning of a SQUR expression. Since our SQUR does not have functions, there are no β-redices or other higher-order constructs to eliminate.

6   Conclusions

We have presented the new, denotational approach to language-integrated query based on the calculus SQUR. We support query composition and reuse, and still are able to generate efficient flat SQL for interaction with external databases. The key feature is the normalization-by-evaluation (NBE), facilitated by the denotational semantics, which converts a query to the normal form from which flat SQL can be easily generated. Unlike the previous syntactic, rewriting-rule–based approaches, NBE is deterministic and can easily be proven total. Notably, it can be extended to support such SQL features as ordering and subranging of the eventual query results. The denotational approach goes hand-in-hand with the embedding SQUR in the tagless-final style.

In the future work we extend the approach to GROUP BY and aggregation. It is also interesting to further explicate the equational laws induced by the semantics of ordering, grouping and subranging, with [5] for inspiration.

Acknowledgments. We thank anonymous reviewers for many very helpful comments and suggestions. This work was partially supported by JSPS KAKENHI Grant Number 17K00091.

References

1. Atkinson, M.P., Buneman, O.P.: Types and persistence in database programming languages. ACM Comput. Surv. **19**(2), 105–170 (1987)
2. Buneman, P., Naqvi, S., Tannen, V., Wong, L.: Principles of programming with complex objects and collection types. Theor. Comput. Sci. **149**(1), 3–48 (1995)
3. Buneman, P., Ohori, A.: Polymorphism and type inference in database programming. ACM Trans. Database Syst. **21**(1), 30–76 (1996)
4. Cheney, J., Lindley, S., Wadler, P.: A practical theory of language-integrated query. In: ICFP 2013, pp. 403–416. ACM, New York (2013)
5. Chu, S., Weitz, K., Cheung, A., Suciu, D.: HoTTSQL: proving query rewrites with univalent SQL semantics. CoRR abs/1607.04822 (2016). http://arxiv.org/abs/1607.04822
6. Cooper, E.: The script-writer's dream: how to write great SQL in your own language, and be sure it will succeed. In: Gardner, P., Geerts, F. (eds.) DBPL 2009. LNCS, vol. 5708, pp. 36–51. Springer, Heidelberg (2009). https://doi.org/10.1007/978-3-642-03793-1_3
7. Dybjer, P., Filinski, A.: Normalization and partial evaluation. In: Barthe, G., Dybjer, P., Pinto, L., Saraiva, J. (eds.) Applied Semantics. LNCS, vol. 2395, pp. 137–192. Springer, Heidelberg (2002). https://doi.org/10.1007/3-540-45699-6_4
8. Ellis, T.: Opaleye. https://github.com/tomjaguarpaw/haskell-opaleye. Accessed Dec 2014
9. Hibino, K., Murayama, S., Yasutake, S., Kuroda, S., Yamamoto, K.: Haskell relational record. http://khibino.github.io/haskell-relational-record/. Accessed May 2017
10. Libkin, L., Wong, L.: Conservativity of nested relational calculi with internal generic functions. Inf. Process. Lett. **49**(6), 273–280 (1994)
11. Najd, S., Lindley, S., Svenningsson, J., Wadler, P.: Everything old is new again: quoted domain-specific languages. In: PEPM, pp. 25–36. ACM (2016)
12. Ohori, A., Ueno, K.: Making Standard ML a practical database programming language. In: ICFP 2011, pp. 307–319. ACM, New York (2011)
13. Suzuki, K., Kiselyov, O., Kameyama, Y.: Finally, safely-extensible and efficient language-integrated query. In: Proceedings of the PEPM, pp. 37–48. ACM (2016)
14. Breazu-Tannen, V., Buneman, P., Wong, L.: Naturally embedded query languages. In: Biskup, J., Hull, R. (eds.) ICDT 1992. LNCS, vol. 646, pp. 140–154. Springer, Heidelberg (1992). https://doi.org/10.1007/3-540-56039-4_38

Semantics

A Computational Interpretation of Context-Free Expressions

Martin Sulzmann[1]([✉]) and Peter Thiemann[2]

[1] Faculty of Computer Science and Business Information Systems,
Karlsruhe University of Applied Sciences,
Moltkestrasse 30, 76133 Karlsruhe, Germany
martin.sulzmann@hs-karlsruhe.de
[2] Faculty of Engineering, University of Freiburg,
Georges-Köhler-Allee 079, 79110 Freiburg, Germany
thiemann@acm.org

Abstract. We phrase parsing with context-free expressions as a type
inhabitation problem where values are parse trees and types are context-
free expressions. We first show how containment among context-free
and regular expressions can be reduced to a reachability problem by
using a canonical representation of states. The proofs-as-programs principle yields a computational interpretation of the reachability problem
in terms of a coercion that transforms the parse tree for a context-free
expression into a parse tree for a regular expression. It also yields a partial coercion from regular parse trees to context-free ones. The partial
coercion from the trivial language of all words to a context-free expression corresponds to a predictive parser for the expression.

1 Introduction

In the context of regular expressions, there have been a number of works which
give a *computational* interpretation of regular expressions. For example, Frisch
and Cardelli [4] show how to phrase the regular expression parsing problem as a
type inhabitation problem. Parsing usually means that for an input string that
matches a regular expression we obtain a parse tree which gives a precise explanation which parts of the regular expression have been matched. By interpreting
parse trees as values and regular expressions as types, parsing can be rephrased
as type inhabitation as shown by Frisch and Cardelli. Henglein and Nielsen [6]
as well Lu and Sulzmann [8,12], formulate containment of regular expressions
as a type conversion problem. From a containment proof, they derive a transformation (a type coercion) from parse trees of one regular expression into parse
trees of the other regular expression.

This paper extends these ideas to the setting of context-free expressions.
Context-free expressions extend regular expressions with a least fixed point operator, so they are effectively equivalent to context-free grammars. An essential new
idea is to phrase the containment problem among context-free expressions and

© Springer International Publishing AG 2017
B.-Y.E. Chang (Ed.): APLAS 2017, LNCS 10695, pp. 387–405, 2017.
https://doi.org/10.1007/978-3-319-71237-6_19

regular expressions as a reachability problem [11], where states are represented
by regular expressions and reachable states are Brzozowski-style derivatives [3].
By characterizing the reachability problem in terms of a natural-deduction style
proof system, we can apply the proofs-are-programs principle to extract the coercions that implement the desired transformation between parse trees.

In summary, our contributions are:

- an interpretation of context-free expressions as types which are inhabited by
  valid parse trees (Sect. 3);
- a reduction of containment among context-free expressions and regular
  expressions to a reachability problem (Sect. 4);
- a formal derivation of coercions between context-free and regular parse trees
  extracted from a natural-deduction style proof of context-free reachability
  (Sect. 5).

The online version of this paper contains an appendix with proofs and further
details.[1]

2   Preliminaries

This section introduces some basic notations, recalls definitions like the languages of regular and context-free expressions, and restates some known results
for Brzozowski style derivatives.

Let Σ be a finite set of symbols with x, y, and z ranging over Σ. We write
Σ^* for the set of finite words over Σ, ε for the empty word, and $v \cdot w$ for the
concatenation of words v and w. A language is a subset of Σ^*.

Definition 1 (Regular Expressions). *The set RE of regular expressions is
defined inductively by*

$$r, s ::= \phi \mid \varepsilon \mid x \in \Sigma \mid (r + s) \mid (r \cdot s) \mid (r^*)$$

We omit parentheses by assuming that * binds tighter than · and · binds tighter
than +.

Definition 2 (Regular Languages). *The meaning function L maps a regular
expression to a language. It is defined inductively as follows:*

$$L(\phi) = \{\}. \ L(\varepsilon) = \{\varepsilon\}. \ L(x) = \{x\}. \ L(r+s) = L(r) \cup L(s). \ L(r \cdot s) = \{v \cdot w \mid v \in L(r) \wedge w \in L(s)\}. \ L(r^*) = \{w_1 \cdot \ldots \cdot w_n \mid n \geq 0 \wedge \forall i \in \{1, \ldots, n\}. \ w_i \in L(r)\}.$$

We say that regular expressions r and s are equivalent, $r \equiv s$, if $L(r) = L(s)$.

Definition 3 (Nullability). *A regular expression r is nullable if $\varepsilon \in L(r)$.*

The *derivative* of a regular expression r with respect to some symbol x, written
$d_x(r)$, is a regular expression for the left quotient of $L(r)$ with respect to x. That
is, $L(d_x(r)) = \{w \in \Sigma^* \mid x \cdot w \in L(r)\}$. A derivative $d_x(r)$ can be computed by
recursion over the structure of the regular expression r.

---

[1] https://arxiv.org/abs/1708.07366.

Definition 4 (Brzozowski Derivatives [3])

$$d_x(\phi) = \phi \qquad\qquad\qquad d_x(\varepsilon) = \phi$$

$$d_x(y) = \begin{cases} \varepsilon \;\; if\; x = y \\ \phi \;\; otherwise \end{cases} \qquad\qquad d_x(r + s) = d_x(r) + d_x(s)$$

$$d_x(r \cdot s) = \begin{cases} d_x(r) \cdot s \qquad\qquad if\; \varepsilon \notin \mathrm{L}(r) \\ d_x(r) \cdot s + d_x(s) \;\; otherwise \end{cases} d_x(r^*) = d_x(r) \cdot r^*$$

Example 1. The derivative of $(x+y)^*$ with respect to symbol x is $(\varepsilon+\phi) \cdot (x+y)^*$. The calculation steps are as follows:

$$d_x((x+y)^*) = d_x(x+y) \cdot (x+y)^* = (d_x(x) + d_x(y)) \cdot (x+y)^* = (\varepsilon + \phi) \cdot (x+y)^*$$

Theorem 1 (Expansion [3]). *Every regular expression r can be represented as the sum of its derivatives with respect to all symbols. If $\Sigma = \{x_1, \ldots, x_n\}$, then*

$$r \equiv x_1 \cdot d_{x_1}(r) + \ldots + x_n \cdot d_{x_n}(r)(+\varepsilon \;\; if\; r \;\; nullable).$$

Definition 5 (Descendants and Similarity). *A descendant of r is either r itself or the derivative of a descendant. We say r and s are similar, written $r \sim s$, if one can be transformed into the other by finitely many applications of the rewrite rules (Idempotency) $r + r \sim r$, (Commutativity) $r + s \sim s + r$, (Associativity) $r + (s + t) \sim (r + s) + t$, (Elim1) $\varepsilon \cdot r \sim r$, (Elim2) $\phi \cdot r \sim \phi$, (Elim3) $\phi + r \sim r$, and (Elim4) $r + \phi \sim r$.*

Lemma 1. *Similarity is an equivalence relation that respects regular expression equivalence: $r \sim s$ implies $r \equiv s$.*

Theorem 2 (Finiteness [3]). *The elements of the set of descendants of a regular expression belong to finitely many similarity equivalence classes.*

Similarity rules (Idempotency), (Commutativity), and (Associativity) suffice to achieve finiteness. Elimination rules are added to obtain a compact *canonical representative* for an equivalence class of similar regular expressions. The canonical form is obtained by systematic application of the similarity rules in Definition 5. We enforce right-associativity of concatenated expressions, sort alternative expressions according to their size and their first symbol, and concatenations lexicographically, assuming an arbitrary total order on Σ. We further remove duplicates and apply elimination rules exhaustively (the details are standard [5]).

Definition 6 (Canonical Representatives). *For a regular expression r, we write $cnf(r)$ to denote the canonical representative among all expressions similar to r. We write $D(r)$ for the set of canonical representatives of the finitely many dissimilar descendants of r.*

Example 2. If we assume $x < t$, then $cnf((\varepsilon + \phi) \cdot (x + y)^*) = (x + y)^*$.

Context-free expressions [13] extend regular expressions with a least fixed point operator μ. Our definition elides the Kleene star operator because it can be defined with the fixed point operator: $e^* = \mu\alpha.e \cdot \alpha + \varepsilon$.

Definition 7 (Context-Free Expressions). *Let A be a denumerable set of placeholders disjoint from Σ. The set CFE of context-free expressions is defined inductively by*

$$e, f ::= \phi \mid \varepsilon \mid x \in \Sigma \mid \alpha \in A \mid e + f \mid e \cdot f \mid \mu\alpha.e$$

We only consider closed context-free expressions where (A) all placeholders are bound by some enclosing μ-operator and (B) the placeholder introduced by a μ-operator is distinct from all enclosing μ-bindings. Requirement (A) guarantees that reduction of a context-free expression does not get stuck whereas requirement (B) avoids name clashes when manipulating a context-free expression.

While Winter et al. [13] define the semantics of a context-free expression by coalgebraic means, we define its meaning with a reduction semantics.

Definition 8 (Big-Step Semantics). *The reduction relation $\Rightarrow \subseteq CFE \times \Sigma^*$ is defined inductively by the following inference rules.*

$$\frac{}{\varepsilon \Rightarrow \varepsilon} \quad \frac{}{x \Rightarrow x} \quad \frac{e \Rightarrow w}{e + f \Rightarrow w} \quad \frac{f \Rightarrow w}{e + f \Rightarrow w} \quad \frac{e \Rightarrow v \quad f \Rightarrow w}{e \cdot f \Rightarrow v \cdot w} \quad \frac{[\alpha \mapsto \mu\alpha.e](e) \Rightarrow w}{\mu\alpha.e \Rightarrow w}$$

In the last rule, we write $[\alpha \mapsto \mu\alpha.e](e)$ to denote the expression obtained by replacing all occurrences of placeholder α in e by $\mu\alpha.e$. If $\mu\alpha.e$ is closed, then requirement (B) ensures that there is no inadvertent capture of placeholders.

We further define $L(e) = \{w \in \Sigma^* \mid e \Rightarrow w\}$.

As an immediate consequence of the last rule, we see that unfolding does not affect the language.

Lemma 2. $L(\mu\alpha.e) = L([\alpha \mapsto \mu\alpha.e](e))$.

Definition 9 (Containment). *Let e be a context-free expression or regular expression and let r be a regular expression. We define $e \leq r$ iff $L(e) \subseteq L(r)$.*

We express partial functions as total functions composed with lifting as follows. Let A and B be sets. The set *Maybe B* consists of elements which are either *Nothing* or of the form *Just b*, for $b \in B$. Thus a total function f' of type $A \to Maybe\ B$ corresponds uniquely to a partial function f from A to B: for $a \in A$, if $f(a)$ is not defined, then $f'(a) = Nothing$; if $f(a) = b$ is defined, then $f'(a) = Just\ b$; and vice versa.

3   Parsing as Type Inhabitation

Parsing for regular expressions has been phrased as a type inhabitation problem [4]. We follow suit and generalize this approach to parsing for context-free expressions. For our purposes, parse trees are generated by the following grammar.

Definition 10 (Parse Trees for context-free expressions)

$$p, q :: = \text{EPS} \mid \text{SYM } x \mid \text{INL } p \mid \text{INR}q \mid \text{SEQ } p \; q \mid \text{FOLD } p$$

Like a derivation tree for a context-free grammar, a parse tree is a structured representation of the derivation of a word from some context-free expression. The actual word can be obtained by flattening the parse tree.

Definition 11 (Flattening)

$$flatten(\text{EPS}) = \varepsilon \qquad\qquad flatten(\text{SYM } x) = x$$

$$flatten(\text{INL } p) = flatten(p) \qquad\qquad flatten(\text{INR } q) = flatten(q)$$

$$flatten(\text{SEQ } p \; q) = flatten(p) \cdot flatten(q) \qquad flatten(\text{FOLD } p) = flatten(p)$$

Compared to derivation trees whose signatures depend on the underlying grammar, parse trees are generic, but their validity depends on the particular context-free expression. The connection between parse trees and context-free expressions is made via the following typing relation where we interpret context-free expressions as types and parse trees as values.

Definition 12 (Valid Parse Trees, $\vdash p : e$)

$$\vdash \text{EPS} : \varepsilon \qquad\qquad \vdash \text{SYM } x : x \qquad\qquad \frac{\vdash p : e \quad \vdash q : f}{\vdash \text{SEQ } p \; q : e \cdot f}$$

$$\frac{\vdash p : e}{\vdash \text{INL } p : e + f} \qquad \frac{\vdash p : f}{\vdash \text{INR } p : e + f} \qquad \frac{\vdash p : [\alpha \mapsto \mu\alpha.e](e)}{\vdash \text{FOLD } p : \mu\alpha.e}$$

We consider ε as a singleton type with value EPS as its only inhabitant. The concatenation operator $\cdot$ effectively corresponds to a pair where pair values are formed via the binary constructor SEQ. We treat $+$ as a disjoint sum with the respective injection constructors INL and INR. Recursive μ-expressions represent iso-recursive types with FOLD denoting the isomorphism between the unrolling of a recursive type and the recursive type itself.

The following results establish that parse trees obtained via the typing relation can be related to words derivable in the language of context-free expression and vice versa.

Lemma 3. *Let e be a context-free expression and w be a word. If $e \Rightarrow w$, then there exists a parse tree p such that $\vdash p : e$ where $flatten(p) = w$.*

Lemma 4. *Let e be a context-free expression and p a parse tree. If $\vdash p : e$, then $e \Rightarrow flatten(p)$.*

Example 3. Let $p = \text{FOLD } (\text{INL } (\text{SEQ } (\text{SYM } x) \; (\text{SEQ } (\text{INR EPS}) \; (\text{SYM } x))))$ be a parse tree and consider the expression $e = \mu\alpha.x \cdot \alpha + \varepsilon$. We find that $\vdash p : e$ and $flatten(p) = x \cdot x$.

Instead of tackling the parsing problem, we solve the more general problem of coercing parse trees of context-free expressions into parse trees of regular expressions and vice versa.

4   Containment via Reachability

In this section, we consider the problem of determining containment $(e \leq r)$? between a context-free language represented by some expression e and a regular language represented by regular expression r. This problem is decidable. The standard algorithm constructs a context-free grammar for the intersection $L(e) \cap \overline{L(r)}$ and tests it for emptiness.

We proceed differently to obtain some computational content from the proof of containment. We first rephrase the containment problem "$(e \leq r)$?" as a reachability problem. In Sect. 5, we extract computational content by deriving suitable coercions as mappings between the respective parse trees of e and r.

There are coercions in both directions, which correspond to embedding-projection pairs:

1. a total coercion from $L(e)$ to $L(r)$ as a mapping of type $e \to r$ and
2. a partial coercion from $L(r)$ to $L(e)$ as a mapping of type $r \to Maybe\ e$,

The partial coercion under 4 can be considered as a parser specialized to words from $L(r)$. Thus, the partial coercion from $\Sigma^* \to Maybe\ e$ is a general parser for $L(e)$.

We say that a regular expression r' is reachable from $e \in CFE$ and r if there is some word $w \in L(e)$ such that $L(r') = w/L(r) = \{v \in \Sigma^* \mid w \cdot v \in L(r)\}$. To obtain a finite representation, we define reachability in terms of canonical representatives of derivatives.

Definition 13 (Reachability). *Let e be a context-free expression and r a regular expression. We define the set of reachable expressions as $reach(e, r) = \{cnf(d_w(r)) \mid w \in \Sigma^*, e \Rightarrow w\}$.*

Theorem 3. *Let e be a context-free expression and r be a regular expression. Then $e \leq r$ iff each expression in $reach(e, r)$ is nullable.*

By finiteness of dissimilar descendants the set $reach(e, r)$ is finite and can be computed effectively via a least fixed point construction. Thus, we obtain a new algorithm for containment by reduction to decidable reachability and nullability.

Instead of showing the least fixed point construction, we give a characterization of the set of reachable expressions in terms of a natural-deduction style proof system. The least fixed point construction follows from the proof rules.

The system in Fig. 1 defines the judgment $r \overset{e}{\rightsquigarrow} S$ where $e \in CFE$, r a regular expression, and S is a set of regular expressions in canonical form. It makes use of a set Γ of hypothetical proof judgments of the same form. The meaning of a judgment is that S (over)approximates $reach(e, r)$ (see upcoming Lemmas 5 and 6).

$$\boxed{\Gamma \vdash r \overset{e}{\leadsto} S}$$

(Eps) $\Gamma \vdash r \overset{\varepsilon}{\leadsto} \{cnf(r)\}$ (Phi) $\Gamma \vdash r \overset{\phi}{\leadsto} \{\}$ (Sym) $\Gamma \vdash r \overset{x}{\leadsto} \{cnf(d_x(r))\}$

$$\text{(Alt)} \quad \frac{\Gamma \vdash r \overset{e}{\leadsto} S_1 \quad \Gamma \vdash r \overset{f}{\leadsto} S_2}{\Gamma \vdash r \overset{e+f}{\leadsto} S_1 \cup S_2}$$

$$\text{(Seq)} \quad \frac{\Gamma \vdash r \overset{e}{\leadsto} \{r_1, \ldots, r_n\} \quad \Gamma \vdash r_i \overset{f}{\leadsto} S_i \text{ for } i = 1, \ldots, n}{\Gamma \vdash r \overset{e \cdot f}{\leadsto} S_1 \cup \ldots \cup S_n}$$

$$\text{(Rec)} \quad \frac{\Gamma \cup \{r \overset{\mu\alpha.f}{\leadsto} S\} \vdash r \overset{[\alpha \mapsto \mu\alpha.f](f)}{\leadsto} S}{\Gamma \vdash r \overset{\mu\alpha.f}{\leadsto} S} \qquad \text{(Hyp)} \quad \frac{r \overset{\mu\alpha.f}{\leadsto} S \in \Gamma}{\Gamma \vdash r \overset{\mu\alpha.f}{\leadsto} S}$$

Fig. 1. Reachability proof system

The interesting rules are (Rec) and (Hyp). In rule (Hyp), we look up a proof judgment for a context-free expression with topmost operator μ from the assumption set Γ. Such proof judgments are added to Γ in rule (Rec). Hence, we can make use of to be verified proof judgments in subsequent proof steps. Hence, the above proof system is defined coinductively. Soundness of the proof system is guaranteed by the fact that we unfold the fixpoint operator μ in rule (Rec). We can indeed show soundness and completeness: the set $reach(e, r)$ is derivable and any derivable set S is a superset of $reach(e, r)$.

Lemma 5. *Let e be a context-free expression and r be a regular expression. Then, $\vdash r \overset{e}{\leadsto} reach(e, r)$ is derivable.*

Lemma 6. *Let e be a context-free expression, r be a regular expression and S be a set of expressions such that $\vdash r \overset{e}{\leadsto} S$. Then, we find that $S \supseteq reach(e, r)$.*

Example 4. Consider $e = \mu\alpha.x \cdot (\alpha \cdot y) + \varepsilon$ and $r = x^* \cdot y^*$. It is easy to see that $reach(e, r) = \{r, y^*\}$. Indeed, we can verify that $\{\} \vdash r \overset{e}{\leadsto} \{r, y^*\}$ is derivable.

$$\text{(Rec)} \cfrac{\text{(Alt)} \cfrac{\text{(Seq)} \cfrac{\text{(Seq)} \cfrac{\begin{array}{l}\text{(Hyp)} \; \{r \overset{e}{\leadsto} \{r, y^*\}\} \vdash r \overset{e}{\leadsto} \{r, y^*\} \checkmark \\ \text{(Sym)} \; \{r \overset{e}{\leadsto} \{r, y^*\}\} \vdash r \overset{y}{\leadsto} \{y^*\} \checkmark \\ \text{(Sym)} \; \{r \overset{e}{\leadsto} \{r, y^*\}\} \vdash y \overset{y}{\leadsto} \{y^*\} \checkmark\end{array}}{\{r \overset{e}{\leadsto} \{r, y^*\}\} \vdash r \overset{e \cdot y}{\leadsto} \{y^*\}} \quad \text{(Sym)} \; \{r \overset{e}{\leadsto} \{r, y^*\}\} \vdash r \overset{x}{\leadsto} \{r\} \checkmark}{\{r \overset{e}{\leadsto} \{r, y^*\}\} \vdash r \overset{x \cdot (e \cdot y)}{\leadsto} \{y^*\}} \quad \text{(Eps)} \; \{r \overset{e}{\leadsto} \{r, y^*\}\} \vdash r \overset{\varepsilon}{\leadsto} \{r\} \checkmark}{\{r \overset{e}{\leadsto} \{r, y^*\}\} \vdash r \overset{x \cdot (e \cdot y) + \varepsilon}{\leadsto} \{r, y^*\}}}{\{\} \vdash r \overset{e}{\leadsto} \{r, y^*\}}$$

We first apply rule (Rec) followed by (Alt). One of the premises of (Alt) can be verified immediately via (Eps) as indicated by $\checkmark$. For space reasons, we write premises on top of each other. Next, we apply (Seq) where one of the premises can be verified immediately again. Finally, we find another application of (Seq). $\{r \overset{e}{\rightsquigarrow} \{r, y^*\}\} \vdash r \overset{e}{\rightsquigarrow} \{r, y^*\}$ holds due to (Hyp). Because the reachable set contains two elements, r and y^*, we find two applications of (Sym) and we are done.

Example 5. As a special case, consider $e = \mu\alpha.\alpha$ where $reach(e, r) = \{\}$ for any regular expression r. The reachability proof system over-approximates and indeed we find that $\vdash r \overset{\mu\alpha.\alpha}{\rightsquigarrow} S$ for any S as shown by the following derivation

$$(\text{Rec}) \frac{(\text{Hyp})\ \{r \overset{\mu\alpha.\alpha}{\rightsquigarrow} S\} \vdash r \overset{\mu\alpha.\alpha}{\rightsquigarrow} S}{\vdash r \overset{\mu\alpha.\alpha}{\rightsquigarrow} S}$$

5   Coercions

Our proof system for the reachability judgment $r \overset{e}{\rightsquigarrow} S$ in Fig. 1 provides a coinductive characterization of the set of reachable expressions. Now we apply the proofs-are-programs principle to derive coercions from derivation trees for reachability. As the proof system is coinductive, we obtain recursive coercions from applications of the rules (Rec) and (Hyp).

Our first step is to define a term language for coercions, which are functions on parse trees. This language turns out to be a lambda calculus (lambda abstraction, function application, variables) with recursion and pattern matching on parse trees.

Definition 14 (Coercion Terms). *Coercion terms c and patterns pat are inductively defined by*

$$c \ ::= v \mid k \mid \lambda v.c \mid c\ c \mid \text{rec } x.c \mid \text{case } c \text{ of } [pat_1 \Rightarrow c_1, \ldots, pat_n \Rightarrow c_n]$$
$$pat ::= v \mid k\ pat_1 \ldots pat_{arity(k)}$$

where v range overs a denumerable set of variables disjoint from Σ and constructors k are taken from the set $\mathcal{K} = \{\text{Eps}, \text{Seq}, \text{Inl}, \text{Inr}, \text{Fold}, Just, Nothing, (\_,\_)\}$. Constructors $\text{Eps}, \ldots, \text{Fold}$ are used in the formation of parse trees. Constructors Just and Nothing belong to the Maybe type that arises in the construction of partial coercions. The binary constructor $(\_,\_)$ builds a pair. The function $arity(k)$ defines the arity of constructor k. Patterns are linear (i.e., all pattern variables are distinct) and we write $\lambda pat.c$ as a shorthand for $\lambda v.\text{case } v \text{ of } [pat \Rightarrow c]$.

We give meaning to coercions in terms of a standard denotational semantics where values are elements of a complete partial order formed over the set of parse trees and function space. We write η to denote the mapping from variables to values and $[\![c]\!]\eta$ to denote the meaning of coercions where η defines the meaning of free variables in c. In case c is closed, we simply write $[\![c]\!]$.

Earlier work shows how to construct coercions that demonstrate containment among regular expressions [8,12]. These works use a specialized representation for Kleene star which would require to extend Definitions 10 and 12. We avoid any special treatment of the Kleene star by considering r^* an abbreviation for $\mu\alpha.r \cdot \alpha + \varepsilon$. The representations suggested here is isomorphic to the one used in previous work [8,12]. We summarize their main results. We adopt the convention that t refers to parse trees of regular expressions, b refers to coercions manipulating regular parse trees. We write $b : r \to s$ to denote a coercion of type $r \to s$, and we use $\vdash_r t : r$ for the regular typing judgment.

Definition 15 (Parse Trees for Regular Expressions)

$$t ::= \text{Eps} \mid \text{Sym } x \mid \text{Inl } t \mid \text{Inr } t \mid \text{Seq } t\, t \mid \text{Fold } t$$

Definition 16 (Valid Regular Parse Trees, $\vdash_r t : r$)

$$\vdash_r \text{Eps} : \varepsilon \qquad \vdash_r \text{Sym } x : x \qquad \frac{\vdash_r t_1 : r \quad \vdash_r t_2 : s}{\vdash_r \text{Seq } t_1\, t_2 : r \cdot s} \qquad \frac{\vdash_r t : r}{\vdash_r \text{Inl } t : r + s}$$

$$\frac{\vdash_r t : s}{\vdash_r \text{Inr } t : r + s} \qquad \vdash_r \text{Fold } (\text{Inr Eps}) : r^*$$

$$\frac{\vdash_r t_1 : r \quad \vdash_r t_2 : r^*}{\vdash_r \text{Fold } (\text{Inl } (\text{Seq } t_1\, t_2)) : r^*}$$

Lemma 7 (Regular Coercions [8,12]). *Let r and s be regular expressions such that $r \le s$. There is an algorithm to obtain coercions $b_1 : r \to s$ and $b_2 : s \to$ Maybe r such that (1) for any $\vdash_r t : r$ we have that $\vdash_r b_1 (t) : s$, $\llbracket b_1 (t) \rrbracket = t'$ for some t' and flatten(t) = flatten(t'), and (2) for any $\vdash_r t : s$ where flatten(t) $\in L(r)$ we have that $\llbracket b_2 (t) \rrbracket =$ Just t' for some t' where $\vdash_r t' : r$ and flatten(t) = flatten(t'), and (3) for any $\vdash_r t : s$ where flatten(t) $\notin L(r)$, $b_2 (t) =$ Nothing.*

We refer to b_1 as the *upcast* coercion and to b_2 as the *downcast* coercion, indicated by $r \le^{b_1} s$ and $r \le_{b_2} s$, respectively. Upcasting means that any parse tree for the smaller language can be coerced into a parse tree for the larger language. On the other hand, a parse tree can only be downcast if the underlying word belongs to the smaller language.

We wish to extend these results to the containment $e \le r$ where e is a context-free expression and r is a regular expression. In the first step, we build a (reachability upcast) coercion c which takes as inputs a parse tree of e and a proof that e is contained in r. The latter comes in the form of the reachability set $reach(e, r)$, which we canonicalize to $+reach(e, r)$ as follows: For a set $R = \{r_1, \ldots, r_n\}$ of canonical regular expressions, we define $+R = cnf(r_1 + \ldots + r_n)$ where we set $+\{\} = \phi$.

$$\boxed{\Delta \vdash^{\Uparrow} c : \mathtt{U}(e,r)}$$

$$(\text{Eps})_u \ \frac{cnf(r) \leq^b r \qquad c = \lambda(\text{Eps},t).b\ (t)}{\Delta \vdash^{\Uparrow} c : \mathtt{U}(\varepsilon,r)}$$

$$(\text{Sym})_u \ \frac{x \cdot cnf(d_x(r)) \leq^b r \qquad c = \lambda(v,t).b\ (\text{Seq}\ v\ t)}{\Delta \vdash^{\Uparrow} c : \mathtt{U}(x,r)}$$

$$(\text{Alt})_u \ \frac{\begin{array}{cc} \Delta \vdash^{\Uparrow} c_1 : \mathtt{U}(e,r) & \Delta \vdash^{\Uparrow} c_2 : \mathtt{U}(f,r) \\ +reach(e,r) \leq_{b_1} +reach(e+f,r) & + reach(f,r) \leq_{b_2} +reach(e+f,r) \end{array} \\ \begin{array}{l} c = \lambda(p,t).\,\mathsf{case}\ p\ \mathsf{of}\ [\\ \qquad \text{INL}\ p_1 \Rightarrow \mathsf{case}\ (b_1\ (t))\ \mathsf{of}\ [Just\ t_1 \Rightarrow c_1\ (p_1,t_1)], \\ \qquad \text{INR}\ p_2 \Rightarrow \mathsf{case}\ (b_2\ (t))\ \mathsf{of}\ [Just\ t_2 \Rightarrow c_2\ (p_2,t_2)]] \end{array}}{\Delta \vdash^{\Uparrow} c : \mathtt{U}(e+f,r)}$$

$$(\text{Seq})_u \ \frac{\Delta \vdash^{\Uparrow} c_1 : \mathtt{U}(e,r) \qquad \Delta \vdash^{\Uparrow} c_2 : \mathtt{U}(f,+reach(e,r)) \\ c = \lambda(\text{Seq}\ p_1\ p_2,t).c_1\ (p_1,c_2\ (p_2,t))}{\Delta \vdash^{\Uparrow} c : \mathtt{U}(e \cdot f,r)}$$

$$(\text{Rec})_u \ \frac{v_{\alpha.e,r} \notin \Delta \qquad \Delta \cup \{v_{\alpha.e,r} : \mathtt{U}(\mu\alpha.e,r)\} \vdash^{\Uparrow} c' : \mathtt{U}([\alpha \mapsto \mu\alpha.e](e),r) \\ c = \mathsf{rec}\ v_{\alpha.e,r}.\lambda(\text{Fold}\ p,t).c'\ (p,t)}{\Delta \vdash^{\Uparrow} c : \mathtt{U}(\mu\alpha.e,r)}$$

$$(\text{Hyp})_u \ \frac{(v_{\alpha.e,r} : \mathtt{U}(\mu\alpha.e,r)) \in \Delta}{\Delta \vdash^{\Uparrow} v_{\alpha.e,r} : \mathtt{U}(\mu\alpha.e,r)}$$

Fig. 2. Reachability upcast coercions

Reachability coercions are derived via the judgment $\Delta \vdash^{\Uparrow} c : \mathtt{U}(e,r)$, which states that under environment Δ an upcast coercion c of type $\mathtt{U}(e,r)$ can be constructed. Environments Δ are defined by $\Delta ::= \{\} \mid \{v : \mathtt{U}(e,r)\} \mid \Delta \cup \Delta$ and record coercion assumptions, which are needed to construct recursive coercions. We interpret $\mathtt{U}(e,r)$ as the type $(e \times +reach(e,r)) \to r$. Figure 2 contains the proof rules which are derived from Fig. 1 by decorating each rule with an appropriate coercion term. If Δ is empty, we write $\vdash^{\Uparrow} c : \mathtt{U}(e,r)$ for short.

The proof rules in Fig. 2 are decidable in the sense that it is decidable if $\Delta \vdash^{\Uparrow} c : \mathtt{U}(e,r)$ can be derived. This property holds because proof rules are syntax-directed and $reach(e,r)$ is decidable. We can also attempt to infer c where we either fail or succeed in a finite number of derivation steps.

Lemma 8 (Upcast Soundness). *Let e be a context-free expression and r be a regular expression such that $\vdash^{\Uparrow} c : U(e, r)$ for some coercion c. Let p and t be parse trees such that $\vdash p : e$ and $\vdash_r t : {+}reach(e, r)$ where $flatten(t) \in L(d_{flatten(p)}(r))$. Then, we find that $[\![c\,((p, t))]\!] = t'$ for some t' where $\vdash t' : r$ and $flatten(p) = flatten(t')$.*

The assumption $flatten(t) \in L(d_{flatten(p)}(r))$ guarantees that e's parse tree p in combination with ${+}reach(e, r)$'s parse tree t allows us to build a parse tree for r.

For example, consider rule $(Alt)_u$. Suppose $e + f$ parses some input word w because e parses the word w. That is, w's parse tree has the form $p = \text{INL } p_1$. As we have proofs that $e \le r$ and $f \le r$, the downcast $b_1 \, (t)$ cannot fail and yields $Just\ t_1$. Formally, we have $\vdash p_1 : e$ and conclude that $flatten(p) = flatten(p_1) \in L(e)$. By Lemma 4, $e \Rightarrow flatten(p_1)$ and therefore we find that $d_{flatten(p_1)}(r)$ is similar to an element of $reach(e, r)$. Because $flatten(t) \in L(d_{flatten(p)}(r))$ we conclude that $flatten(t) \in L({+}reach(e, r))$. By Lemma 7, it must be that $b_1\,(t) = Just\ t_1$ for some t_1 where $\vdash t_1 : {+}reach(e, r)$. By induction the result holds for c_1 and hence we can establish the result for c.

In rule $(Seq)_u$, we exploit the fact that ${+}reach(e \cdot f, r) = {+}reach(f, {+}reach(e, r))$. So, we use coercion c_2 to build a parse tree of ${+}reach(e, r)$ given parse trees of f and ${+}reach(e \cdot f, r)$. Then, we build a parse tree of r by applying c_1 to parse trees of e and ${+}reach(e, r)$.

Due to the coinductive nature of the coercion proof system, coercion terms may be recursive as evidenced by rule $(Rec)_u$. Soundness is guaranteed by the assumption that the set of reachable states is non-empty. As we find a parse tree of that type, progress is made when building the coercion for the unfolded μ-expression. Unfolding must terminate because there are only finitely many combinations of unfolded subterms of the form $\mu\alpha.e$ and regular expressions r. The latter are drawn from the finitely many dissimilar descendant of some r. Hence, resulting coercions must be well-defined as stated in the above result.

Example 6. We show how to derive $\vdash^{\Uparrow} c_0 : U(e, r)$ where $e = \mu\alpha.x \cdot (\alpha \cdot y) + \varepsilon$, $r = x^* \cdot y^*$ and $reach(e, r) = \{r, y^*\}$. The shape of the derivation tree corresponds to the derivation we have seen in Example 4.

$$
(\text{REC})_u \dfrac{ (\text{ALT})_u \dfrac{ (\text{SEQ})_u \dfrac{ (\text{SEQ})_u \dfrac{ \begin{array}{c} (\text{Hyp})_u\ \ \Delta \vdash^{\Uparrow} c_7 : U(e, r)\checkmark \\ (\text{Sym})_u\ \ \Delta \vdash^{\Uparrow} c_6 : U(y, r + y^*)\checkmark \end{array} }{ \Delta \vdash^{\Uparrow} c_5 : U(e \cdot y, r) } \quad (\text{Sym})_u\ \ \Delta \vdash^{\Uparrow} c_4 : U(x, r)\checkmark }{ \Delta \vdash^{\Uparrow} c_3 : U(x \cdot (e \cdot y), r) } \qquad (\text{Eps})_u\ \ \mathfrak{C}_2 }{ \Delta \vdash^{\Uparrow} c_1 : U(x \cdot (e \cdot y) + \varepsilon, r) } }{ \vdash^{\Uparrow} c_0 : U(e, r) }
$$

For space reasons, we use $\mathfrak{C}_2$ for $\Delta \vdash^{\Uparrow} c_2 : U(\varepsilon, r)\checkmark$. We fill in the details by following the derivation tree from bottom to top. We set $\Delta = \{v_{\alpha.e,r} : U(e, r)\}$.

From the first $(Rec)_u$ step we conclude $c_0 = \mathsf{rec}\ v_{\alpha.e,r}.\lambda(\mathrm{FOLD}\ p,t).c_1\ (p,t)$. Next, we find $(Alt)_u$ which yields

$$c_1 = \lambda(p,t).\mathsf{case}\ p\ \mathsf{of}\ [$$
$$\mathrm{INL}\ p_1 \Rightarrow \mathsf{case}\ (b_1\ (t))\ \mathsf{of}\ [Just\ t_1 \Rightarrow c_3\ (p_1,t_1)],$$
$$\mathrm{INR}\ p_2 \Rightarrow \mathsf{case}\ (b_2\ (t))\ \mathsf{of}\ [Just\ t_2 \Rightarrow c_2\ (p_2,t_2)]]$$

We consider the definition of the auxiliary regular (downcast) coercions b_1 and b_2. We have that $+reach(x \cdot (e \cdot y) + \varepsilon, r) = r + y^*$, $+reach(\varepsilon, r) = r$ and $+reach(x \cdot (e \cdot y), r) = y^*$. Hence, we need to derive $y^* \leq_{b_1} r + y^*$ and $r \leq_{b_2} r + y^*$.

Recall the requirement (2) for downcast coercions. See Lemma 7. We first consider $y^* \leq_{b_1} r + y^*$. The right component of the sum can be straightforwardly coerced into a parse tree of y^*. For the left component we need to check that the leading part is effectively empty. Recall that Kleene star is represented in terms of μ-expressions. Following Definition 16, an empty parse tree for Kleene star equals $\mathrm{FOLD}\ (\mathrm{INR}\ \mathrm{EPS})$. Thus, we arrive at the following definition for b_1.

$$b_1 = \lambda t.\mathsf{case}\ t\ \mathsf{of}\ [$$
$$\mathrm{INL}\ (\mathrm{SEQ}\ (\mathrm{FOLD}\ \mathrm{INR}\ \mathrm{EPS})\ v) \Rightarrow Just\ v,$$
$$\mathrm{INL}\ v \Rightarrow Nothing,$$
$$\mathrm{INR}\ v \Rightarrow Just\ v]$$

$$\overline{\qquad\qquad y^* \leq_{b_1} r + y^* \qquad\qquad}$$

The derivation of $r \leq_{b_2} r + y^*$ follows a similar pattern. As both expressions r and $r + y^*$ are equal, the downcast never fails here.

$$b_2 = \lambda t.\mathsf{case}\ t\ \mathsf{of}\ [$$
$$\mathrm{INL}\ v \Rightarrow Just\ v,$$
$$\mathrm{INR}\ v \Rightarrow Just\ (\mathrm{SEQ}\ (\mathrm{FOLD}\ \mathrm{INR}\ \mathrm{EPS})\ v)]$$

$$\overline{\qquad\qquad r \leq_{b_2} r + y^* \qquad\qquad}$$

Next, consider the premises of the $(Alt)_u$ rule. For $\Delta \vdash^{\Uparrow} c_2 : U(\varepsilon, r)$ by definition $c_2 = \lambda(\mathrm{EPS},t).b_3\ (t)$ where $r \leq^{b_3} r$ which can be satisfied by $b_3 = \lambda v.v$. For $\Delta \vdash^{\Uparrow} c_3 : U(x \cdot (e \cdot y), r)$ we find by definition $c_3 = \lambda(\mathrm{SEQ}\ p_1\ p_2,t).c_4\ (p_1, c_5\ (p_2,t))$.

It follows some $(Seq)_u$ step where we first consider $\Delta \vdash^{\Uparrow} c_4 : U(x, r)$. By definition of $(Sym)_u$ and $cnf(d_r(x)) = r$ we have that $c_4 = \lambda(v,t).b_4\ (\mathrm{SEQ}\ v\ t)$ where $x \cdot r \leq^{b_4} r$. Recall $r = x^* \cdot y^*$. So, upcast b_4 injects x into x^*'s parse tree. Recall the representation of parse trees for Kleene star in Definition 16.

$$b_4 = \lambda(\mathrm{SEQ}\ v\ (\mathrm{SEQ}\ t_1\ t_2)).\mathrm{SEQ}\ (\mathrm{FOLD}\ (\mathrm{INL}\ (\mathrm{SEQ}\ v\ t_1)))\ t_2$$

Next, we consider $\Delta \vdash^{\Uparrow} c_5 : \mathtt{U}(e \cdot y, r)$ where we find another $(Seq)_u$ step. Hence, $c_5 = \lambda(\mathrm{SEQ}\ p_1\ p_2, t).c_7\ (p_1, c_6\ (p_2, t))$. By $(Hyp)_u$, we have that $c_7 = v_{\alpha.e,r}$. To obtain $\Delta \vdash^{\Uparrow} c_6 : \mathtt{U}(y, r + y^*)$ we apply another $(Sym)_u$ step and therefore $c_6 = \lambda(v, t).b_5\ (\mathrm{SEQ}\ v\ t)$. The regular (upcast) coercion b_5 is derived from $y \cdot y^* \leq^{b_5} r + y^*$ because $cnf(d_y(r + y^*)) = y^*$. Its definition is as follows.

$$b_5 = \lambda(\mathrm{SEQ}\ v\ t).\mathrm{INR}\ (\mathrm{FOLD}\ (\mathrm{INL}\ (\mathrm{SEQ}\ v\ t)))$$

This step completes the example.

Remark 1 (Ambiguities). Example 6 shows that coercions may be ambiguous in the sense that there are several choices for the resulting parse trees. For example, in the construction of the regular (upcast) coercion $y \cdot y^* \leq^{b_5} x^* \cdot y^* + y^*$ we choose to inject y into the right component of the sum. The alternative is to inject y into the left component by making the x^* part empty.

$$b_5' = \lambda(\mathrm{SEQ}\ v\ t).\mathrm{INL}\ (\mathrm{SEQ}\ (\mathrm{FOLD}\ (\mathrm{INR}\ \mathrm{EPS}))\ (\mathrm{FOLD}\ (\mathrm{INL}\ (\mathrm{SEQ}\ v\ t))))$$

Both choices are valid. To obtain deterministic behavior of coercions we can apply a disambiguation strategy (e.g., favoring left-most alternatives). A detailed investigation of this topic is beyond the scope of the present work.

Based on Lemma 8 we easily obtain an upcast coercion to transform e's parse tree into a parse tree of r. As $e \leq r$ if all elements in $reach(e, r)$ are nullable, we simply need to provide an empty parse tree for $+reach(e, r)$. The upcoming definition of $mkE()$ supplies such parse trees. It requires to check for nullability of context-free expression. This check is decidable as shown by the following definition.

Definition 17 (CFE Nullability)

$$\begin{aligned}
\mathcal{N}(\phi) = \mathcal{N}(x) &= False & \mathcal{N}(e + f) &= \mathcal{N}(e) \vee \mathcal{N}(f) \\
\mathcal{N}(\varepsilon) &= True & \mathcal{N}(e \cdot f) &= \mathcal{N}(e) \wedge \mathcal{N}(f) \\
\mathcal{N}(\alpha) &= False & \mathcal{N}(\mu\alpha.e) &= \mathcal{N}(e)
\end{aligned}$$

Lemma 9. *Let e be a context-free expression. Then, $\mathcal{N}(e)$ holds iff $\varepsilon \in L(e)$.*

Based on the nullability check, we can derive empty parse trees (if they exist).

Definition 18 (Empty Parse Tree)

$$mkE(\varepsilon) \quad = \mathrm{EPS} \qquad mkE(e + f) = \begin{cases} \mathrm{INL}\ mkE(e) & \text{if } \mathcal{N}(e) \\ \mathrm{INR}\ mkE(f) & \text{otherwise} \end{cases}$$

$$mkE(\mu\alpha.e) = \mathrm{FOLD}\ mkE(e) \quad mkE(e \cdot f) \quad = \mathrm{SEQ}\ mkE(e)\ mkE(f)$$

Lemma 10. *Let e be a context-free expression such that $\mathcal{N}(e)$. Then, we find that $\vdash mkE(e) : e$ and $flatten(mkE(e)) = \varepsilon$.*

We summarize the construction of upcast coercions for context-free and regular expressions in containment relation.

Theorem 4 (Upcast Coercions). *Let e be a context-free expression and r be a regular expression such that $e \leq r$ and $\vdash^{\Uparrow} c' : \mathtt{U}(e, r)$ for some coercion c'. Let $c = \lambda x.c'\ (x, mkE(+reach(e, r)))$. Then, we find that c is well-typed with type $e \to r$ where for any $\vdash p : e$ we have that $[\![c\ (p)]\!] = t'$ for some t' where and $\vdash t' : r$ and $flatten(p) = flatten(t')$.*

In analogy to the construction of upcast coercions, we can build a proof system for the construction of downcast coercions. Each such downcast coercion c has type $\mathtt{D}(e, r)$ where $\mathtt{D}(e, r)$ corresponds to $r \to Maybe\ (e \times +reach(e, r))$. That is, a parse tree of r can possibly be coerced into a parse tree of e and some residue which is a parse tree of $+reach(e, r)$. See Fig. 3.

Rule $(\mathrm{Eps})_d$ performs a change in representation. The downcast will always succeed. Rule $(\mathrm{Sym})_d$ applies the regular downcast b to split r's parse tree into x and the parse tree of the (canonical) derivative. The resulting downcast will not succeed if there is no leading x.

In case of a sum, rule $(\mathrm{Alt})_d$ first tests if we can downcast r's parse tree into a parse tree of the left component e and $+reach(e, r)$. If yes, we upcast $+reach(e, r)$'s parse tree into a parse tree of $+reach(e + f, r)$. Otherwise, we check if a downcast into f and $+reach(f, r)$ is possible.

In rule $(\mathrm{Seq})_d$, we first check if we can obtain parse trees for e and residue $+reach(e, r)$. Otherwise, we immediately reach failure. From $+reach(e, r)$'s parse tree we then attempt to extract f's parse tree and residue $+reach(f, +reach(e, r))$ which we know is equivalent to $+reach(e \cdot f, r)$. Hence, we combine the parse trees of e and f via SEQ and only need to pass through the residue.

As in case of upcast coercions, downcast coercions may be recursive. See rules $(\mathrm{Rec})_d$ and $(\mathrm{Hyp})_d$. In case the downcast yields the parse tree p' of the unfolding, we apply FOLD. The residue t' can be passed through as we find that $+reach(\mu\alpha.e, r) = +reach([\alpha \mapsto \mu\alpha.e](e), r)$.

Lemma 11 (Downcast Soundness). *Let e be a context-free expression and r be a regular expression such that $\Delta \vdash_{\Downarrow} c : \mathtt{D}(e, r)$ for some coercion c. Let t be such that $\vdash t : r$ and $[\![c\ (t)]\!] = Just\ (p, t')$ for some p and t'. Then, we have that $\vdash p : e$, $\vdash t' : +reach(e, r)$ and $flatten(t) = flatten(p)$.*

$$\boxed{\Delta \vdash_{\Downarrow} c : \mathtt{D}(e,r)}$$

$$(\text{Eps})_d \; \frac{r \leq^b cnf(r) \qquad c = \lambda t.Just\ (\text{Eps}, b\ (t))}{\Delta \vdash_{\Downarrow} c : \mathtt{D}(\varepsilon, r)}$$

$$(\text{Sym})_d \; \frac{x \cdot cnf(d_x(r)) \leq_b r}{c = \lambda t.\mathsf{case}\ (b\ (t))\ \mathsf{of}\ [Nothing \Rightarrow Nothing,\ Just\ (\text{Seq}\ x'\ t') \Rightarrow Just\ (x', t')]}{\Delta \vdash_{\Downarrow} c : \mathtt{D}(x, r)}$$

$$(\text{Alt})_d \; \frac{\begin{array}{c} \Delta \vdash_{\Downarrow} c_1 : \mathtt{D}(e, r) \qquad \Delta \vdash_{\Downarrow} c_2 : \mathtt{D}(f, r) \\ +reach(e, r) \leq^{b_1} +reach(e+f, r) \qquad +reach(f, r) \leq^{b_2} +reach(e+f, r) \\ c = \lambda t.\,\mathsf{case}\ (c_1\ (t))\ \mathsf{of} \\ [Nothing \Rightarrow \mathsf{case}\ (c_2\ (t))\ \mathsf{of} \\ [Nothing \Rightarrow Nothing, \\ Just\ (p_2, t_2) \Rightarrow Just\ (\text{Inr}\ p_2, b_2\ (t_2))], \\ Just\ (p_1, t_1) \Rightarrow Just\ (\text{Inl}\ p_1, b_1\ (t_1))] \end{array}}{\Delta \vdash_{\Downarrow} c : \mathtt{D}(e+f, r)}$$

$$(\text{Seq})_d \; \frac{\begin{array}{c} \Delta \vdash_{\Downarrow} c_1 : \mathtt{D}(e, r) \qquad \Delta \vdash_{\Downarrow} c_2 : \mathtt{D}(f, +reach(e, r)) \\ c = \lambda t.\,\mathsf{case}\ (c_1\ (t))\ \mathsf{of} \\ [Nothing \Rightarrow Nothing, \\ Just\ (p_1, t_1) \Rightarrow \mathsf{case}\ (c_2\ (t_1))\ \mathsf{of} \\ [Nothing \Rightarrow Nothing, \\ Just\ (p_2, t_2) \Rightarrow Just\ (\text{Seq}\ p_1\ p_2, t_2)]] \end{array}}{\Delta \vdash_{\Downarrow} c : \mathtt{D}(e \cdot f, r)}$$

$$(\text{Rec})_d \; \frac{\begin{array}{c} v_{\alpha.e,r} \notin \Delta \quad \Delta \cup \{(v_{\alpha.e,r} : \mathtt{D}(\mu\alpha.e, r))\} \vdash_{\Downarrow} c' : \mathtt{D}([\alpha \mapsto \mu\alpha.e](e), r) \\ c = \mathsf{rec}\ v_{\alpha.e,r}.\lambda t.\ \mathsf{case}\ (c'\ (t))\ \mathsf{of} \\ [Nothing \Rightarrow Nothing, \\ Just\ (p', t') \Rightarrow Just\ (\text{Fold}\ p', t')] \end{array}}{\Delta \vdash_{\Downarrow} c : \mathtt{D}(\mu\alpha.e, r)}$$

$$(\text{Hyp})_d \; \frac{(v_{\alpha.e,r} : \mathtt{D}(\mu\alpha.e, r)) \in \Delta}{\Delta \vdash_{\Downarrow} v_{\alpha.e,r} : \mathtt{D}(\mu\alpha.e, r)}$$

Fig. 3. Reachability downcast coercions

Example 7. We consider the derivation of $\vdash_{\Downarrow} c_0 : \mathtt{D}(e, r)$ where $e = \mu\alpha.x \cdot (\alpha \cdot y) + \varepsilon$, $r = x^* \cdot y^*$ and $reach(e, r) = \{r, y^*\}$. The downcast coercion attempts to turn a parse of r into a parse tree of e and some residual parse tree of $+reach(e, r)$.

The construction is similar to Example 6. We consider the downcast coercions resulting from $(\text{Rec})_d$ and $(\text{Alt})_d$.

$$c_0 : D(e, r) \;=\; \text{rec } v_{\alpha.e,r}.\lambda t.\text{case } (c_1 \ (t)) \text{ of}$$
$$[Nothing \Rightarrow Nothing,$$
$$Just \ (p', t') \Rightarrow Just \ (\text{FOLD } p', t')]$$

$$c_1 : D(x \cdot (e \cdot y) + \varepsilon, r) \;=\; \lambda t.\text{case } (c_2 \ (t)) \text{ of}$$
$$[Nothing \Rightarrow \text{case } (c_3 \ (t)) \text{ of}$$
$$[Nothing \Rightarrow Nothing,$$
$$Just \ (p_2, t_2) \Rightarrow Just \ (\text{INR} p_2, b_2 \ (t_2))],$$
$$Just \ (p_1, t_1) \Rightarrow Just \ (\text{INL } p_1, b_1 \ (t_1))]$$

where $r \leq^{b_1} r + y^*$ $r \leq^{b_2} r + y^*$ $b_1 = \text{INR}$ $b_2 = \text{INL}$

The auxiliary coercion c_2 greedily checks for a leading symbol x. Otherwise, we pick the base case $(\text{Eps})_d$ where the entire input becomes the residue. This is dealt with by coercion c_3.

$$c_3 : D(\varepsilon, r) \;=\; \lambda t.Just \ (\text{EPS}, b_3 \ (t))$$
$$\text{where } cnf(r) = r \quad b_3 = \lambda x.x \quad r \leq^{b_3} cnf(r))$$

Coercion c_2 first checks for x, then recursively calls (in essence) c_0, followed by a check for y. Here are the details.

$$c_2 : D(x \cdot (e \cdot y), r) \;=\; \lambda t.\text{case } (c_4 \ (t)) \text{ of}$$
$$[Nothing \Rightarrow Nothing,$$
$$Just \ (p_1, t_1) \Rightarrow \text{case } (c_5 \ (t_1)) \text{ of}$$
$$[Nothing \Rightarrow Nothing,$$
$$Just \ (p_2, t_2) \Rightarrow Just \ (\text{SEQ } p_1 \ p_2, t_2)]]$$

Auxiliary coercion c_4 checks for x and any residue is passed on to coercion c_5.

$$c_4 : D(x, r) \;=\; \lambda t.\text{case } (b_4 \ (t)) \text{ of } [Nothing \Rightarrow Nothing, \ Just \ (\text{SEQ } x' \ t') \Rightarrow Just \ (x', t')]$$
$$\text{where } cnf(d_x(r)) = r \quad x \cdot r \leq_{b_4} r$$

$$b_4 = \lambda \text{SEQ } t_1 \ t_2.\text{case } t_1 \text{ of } [$$
$$\text{FOLD INR EPS} \Rightarrow Nothing,$$
$$\text{FOLD INL } (\text{SEQ } t_3 \ t_4) \Rightarrow Just \ (\text{SEQ } t_3 \ (\text{SEQ } t_4 \ t_3))]$$

In coercion c_5, we check for e which then leads to the recursive call.

$$c_5 : D(e \cdot y, r) \;=\; \lambda t.\text{case } (c_7 \ (t)) \text{ of}$$
$$[Nothing \Rightarrow Nothing,$$
$$Just \ (p_1, t_1) \Rightarrow \text{case } (c_6 \ (t_1)) \text{ of}$$
$$[Nothing \Rightarrow Nothing,$$
$$Just \ (p_2, t_2) \Rightarrow Just \ (\text{SEQ } p_1 \ p_2, t_2)]]$$
$$c_7 : D(e, r) \;=\; v_{\alpha.e,r}$$

Finally, coercion c_6 checks for y

$$c_6 : D(y, r + y^*) \;=\; \lambda t.\,\mathsf{case}\ (b_6\ (t))\ \mathsf{of}\ [$$
$$Nothing \Rightarrow Nothing,$$
$$Just\ (\mathrm{SEQ}\ x'\ t') \Rightarrow Just\ (x', t')]$$
$$\text{where } cnf(d_y(r + y^*)) = y^*\ y \cdot y^* \leq_{b_6} r + y^*$$
$$b_6 = \lambda t.\,\mathsf{case}\ t\ \mathsf{of}\ [$$
$$\mathrm{INL}\ \mathrm{SEQ}\ t_1\ t_2 \Rightarrow b_6'\ (t_2),$$
$$\mathrm{INR}\ t \Rightarrow b_6'\ (t)]$$
$$y \cdot y^* \leq_{b_6'} y^*$$
$$b_6' = \lambda t.\,\mathsf{case}\ t\ \mathsf{of}\ [$$
$$\mathrm{FOLD}\ \mathrm{INR}\ \mathrm{EPS} \Rightarrow Nothing,$$
$$\mathrm{FOLD}\ \mathrm{INL}\ (\mathrm{SEQ}\ t_1\ t_2) \Rightarrow Just\ (\mathrm{SEQ}\ t_1\ t_2)]$$

Consider input $t = \mathrm{SEQ}\ t_1\ t_2$ where $t_1 = \mathrm{FOLD}\ (\mathrm{INL}\ \mathrm{SEQ}\ x\ (\mathrm{FOLD}\ (\mathrm{INR}\ \mathrm{EPS})))$, $t_2 = \mathrm{FOLD}\ (\mathrm{INL}\ \mathrm{SEQ}\ y\ (\mathrm{FOLD}\ (\mathrm{INR}\ \mathrm{EPS})))$, $\vdash t : r$ and $flatten(t) = x \cdot y$. Then $[\![c_0\ (t)]\!] = Just\ (p, t')$ where $p = \mathrm{FOLD}\ (\mathrm{INL}\ \mathrm{SEQ}\ x\ (\mathrm{SEQ}\ (\mathrm{FOLD}\ (\mathrm{INR}\ \mathrm{EPS}))\ y))$ and $\vdash p : e$ and $flatten(p) = x \cdot y$. For residue t' we find $flatten(t') = \varepsilon$. This completes the example.

Any context-free expression e is contained in the regular language Σ^*. We wish to derive a downcast coercion for this containment which effectively represents a parser for $L(e)$. That is, the parser maps a parse tree for $w \in \Sigma^*$ (which is isomorphic to w) to a parse tree $\vdash p : e$ with $w = flatten(p)$ if $w \in L(e)$. However, our parser, like any predictive parser, is sensitive to the shape of context-free expressions. So, we need to syntactically restrict the class of context-free expressions on which our parser can be applied.

Definition 19 (Guarded Context-Free Expressions).   *A context-free expression is* guarded *if the expression is of the following shape:*

$$e, f ::= \phi \mid \varepsilon \mid x \in \Sigma \mid \alpha \in A \mid e + f \mid e \cdot f \mid \mu\alpha.g$$
$$g \quad ::= x \cdot e \mid \varepsilon \mid x \cdot e + g$$

where for each symbol x there exists at most one guard $x \cdot e$ in g.

For any context-free expression we find an equivalent guarded variant. This follows from the fact that guarded expressions effectively correspond to context-free grammars in Greibach Normal Form. We additionally impose the conditions that guards x are unique and ε appears last. This ensures that the parser leaves no residue behind.

Theorem 5 (Predictive Guarded Parser). *Let e be a guarded context-free expression and r be a regular expression such that $e \leq r$ and $\Delta \vdash_{\Downarrow} c' : D(e, r)$ for some coercion c'. Let $c = \lambda x.\mathsf{case}\ (c'\ (x))\ \mathsf{of}\ [Nothing \Rightarrow Nothing, Just\ (p, t') \Rightarrow Just\ p]$ Then, we find that c is well-typed with type $r \to Maybe\ e$ and terminates for any input $t \vdash t : r$ If $[\![c\ (t)]\!] = Just\ p$ for some p, then we have that $\vdash p : e$ and $flatten(t) = flatten(p)$.*

Guardedness is essential as shown by the following examples. Consider $e' = \mu\alpha.\varepsilon + x \cdot (\alpha \cdot y)$, $r = x^* \cdot y^*$. The difference to e from Example 7 is that subexpression ε appears in leading position. Hence, the guardedness condition is violated. The downcast coercion for this example (after some simplifications) has the form $c_0 = \lambda t.(\text{FOLD }(\text{INL EPS}), t)$. As we can see no input is consumed at all. We return the trivial parse term and the residue t contains the unconsumed input. As an example for a non-terminating parser consider $e' = \mu\alpha.\alpha \cdot x + \varepsilon$ and $r = (x+y)^*$. Again the guardedness condition is violated because subexpression α is not guarded. The coercion resulting from $\vdash_{\Downarrow} c'_0 : \text{D}(e', r)$ has (after some simplifications) the following form $c'_0 = \text{rec } v.\lambda t.\text{case } v \ (t) \text{ of } \ldots$. Clearly, this parser is non-terminating which is no surprise as the context-free expression is left-recursive.

6   Related Work and Conclusion

Our work builds upon prior work in the setting of regular expressions by Frisch and Cardelli [4], Henglein and Nielsen [6] and Lu and Sulzmann [8,12], as well as Brandt and Henglein's coinductive characterization of recursive type equality and subtyping [2]. We extend these ideas to the case of context-free expressions and their parse trees.

Standard methods for constructing predictive parsers (e.g., recursive descent) are presented in any textbook on compiler construction [1]. But the standard methods are tied to parse from a single regular input language, Σ^*, whereas our approach provides specialized parsers from an arbitrary regular language. These parsers will generally be more deterministic, fail earlier, etc. because they are exploiting knowledge about the input.

Based on our results we obtain a predictive parser for guarded context-free expressions. Earlier work in this area extends Brzozowski-style derivatives [3] to the context-free setting while we use plain regular expression derivatives in combination with reachability. Examples may be found in the work by Krishnaswami [7], Might, Darais and Spiewak [10], and Winter, Bonsangue, and Rutten [13]. Krishnaswami [7] shows how to elaborate general context-free expressions into some equivalent guarded form and how to transform guarded parse trees into their original representation. We could integrate this elaboration/transformation step into our approach to obtain a geneneral, predictive parser for context-free expressions.

Marriott, Stuckey, and Sulzmann [9] show how containment among context-free languages and regular languages can be reduced to a reachability problem [11]. While they represent languages as context-free grammars and deterministic finite automata, we rely on context-free expressions, regular expressions, and specify reachable states in terms of Brzozowski-style derivatives [3]. This step is essential to obtain a characterization of the reachability problem in terms of a natural-deduction style proof system. By applying the proofs-are-programs principle we derive upcast and downcast coercions to transform parse trees of context-free and regular expressions. These connections are not explored in any prior work.

Acknowledgments. We thank the APLAS'17 reviewers for their constructive feedback.

References

1. Aho, A.V., Sethi, R., Ullman, J.D.: Compilers: Principles, Techniques, and Tools. Addison-Wesley Longman Publishing Co. Inc., Boston (1986)
2. Brandt, M., Henglein, F.: Coinductive axiomatization of recursive type equality and subtyping. Fundam. Inf. **33**(4), 309–338 (1998)
3. Brzozowski, J.A.: Derivatives of regular expressions. J. ACM **11**(4), 481–494 (1964)
4. Frisch, A., Cardelli, L.: Greedy regular expression matching. In: Díaz, J., Karhumäki, J., Lepistö, A., Sannella, D. (eds.) ICALP 2004. LNCS, vol. 3142, pp. 618–629. Springer, Heidelberg (2004). https://doi.org/10.1007/978-3-540-27836-8_53
5. Grabmayer, C.: Using proofs by coinduction to find "Traditional" proofs. In: Fiadeiro, J.L., Harman, N., Roggenbach, M., Rutten, J. (eds.) CALCO 2005. LNCS, vol. 3629, pp. 175–193. Springer, Heidelberg (2005). https://doi.org/10.1007/11548133_12
6. Henglein, F., Nielsen, L.: Regular expression containment: coinductive axiomatization and computational interpretation. In: Proceedings of POPL 2011, pp. 385–398. ACM (2011)
7. Krishnaswami, N.R.: A typed, algebraic approach to parsing (2017). https://www.cl.cam.ac.uk/nk480/parsing.pdf
8. Lu, K.Z.M., Sulzmann, M.: An implementation of subtyping among regular expression types. In: Chin, W.-N. (ed.) APLAS 2004. LNCS, vol. 3302, pp. 57–73. Springer, Heidelberg (2004). https://doi.org/10.1007/978-3-540-30477-7_5
9. Marriott, K., Stuckey, P.J., Sulzmann, M.: Resource usage verification. In: Ohori, A. (ed.) APLAS 2003. LNCS, vol. 2895, pp. 212–229. Springer, Heidelberg (2003). https://doi.org/10.1007/978-3-540-40018-9_15
10. Might, M., Darais, D., Spiewak, D.: Parsing with derivatives: a functional pearl. In: Proceedings of ICFP 2011, pp. 189–195. ACM (2011)
11. Reps, T.: Program analysis via graph reachability. In: Proceedings of ILPS 1997, pp. 5–19. MIT Press, Cambridge, MA, USA (1997)
12. Sulzmann, M., Lu, K.Z.M.: A type-safe embedding of XDuce into ML. Electron. Notes Theor. Comput. Sci. **148**(2), 239–264 (2006)
13. Winter, J., Bonsangue, M.M., Rutten, J.J.M.M.: Coalgebraic characterizations of context-free languages. Log. Methods Comput. Sci. **9**(3), 1–39 (2013)

Partiality and Container Monads

Tarmo Uustalu[1] and Niccolò Veltri[1,2(✉)]

[1] Department of Software Science, Tallinn University of Technology,
Akadeemia tee 21B, 12618 Tallinn, Estonia
{tarmo,niccolo}@cs.ioc.ee
[2] IT University of Copenhagen,
Rued Langgaards Vej 7, 2300 Copenhagen S, Denmark

Abstract. We investigate monads of partiality in Martin-Löf type theory, following Moggi's general monad-based method for modelling effectful computations. These monads are often called lifting monads and appear in category theory with different but related definitions. In this paper, we unveil the relationship between containers and lifting monads. We show that the lifting monads usually employed in type theory can be specified in terms of containers. Moreover, we give a precise characterization of containers whose interpretations carry a lifting monad structure. We show that these conditions are tightly connected with Rosolini's notion of dominance. We provide several examples, putting particular emphasis on Capretta's delay monad and its quotiented variant, the non-termination monad.

1 Introduction

Martin-Löf type theory is a total language, meaning that every definable function is necessarily total. This is a fundamental requirement guaranteeing the consistency of the type system. Therefore the implementation of partial functions in type theory requires the employment of ad-hoc techniques. A comprehensive overview of such techniques has been recently given by Bove et al. [5].

In this work, we investigate monads of partiality, following Moggi's general monad-based method for modelling effectful computations [16]. The study of monads of partiality in type theory, in particular aimed at the representation of possibly non-terminating computations (non-termination from iteration), has been an active area of research in recent years [3,7,8,14].

Monads of partiality have also been intensively studied in category theory. These monads are often called *lifting monads* and appear in the literature with different but related definitions. The oldest one, originated in the area of topos theory, is the notion of partial map classifier [15]. A monad T on a category $\mathbb{C}$ is a partial map classifier if every partial map $f : X \rightharpoonup Y$ in $\mathbb{C}$, to be thought of as a total map from a certain subset of X into Y, is in one-to-one correspondence with a map $\hat{f} : X \rightarrow TY$. Another notion of lifting monad is given by Cockett and Lack's classifying monads [10]. They can be thought of as abstract partial map classifiers, in the sense that their Kleisli category is an abstract category

© Springer International Publishing AG 2017
B.-Y.E. Chang (Ed.): APLAS 2017, LNCS 10695, pp. 406–425, 2017.
https://doi.org/10.1007/978-3-319-71237-6_20

of partial maps, viz., a restriction category [9]. For a base category with finite products, Bucalo et al. [6] have given another notion of lifting monad, that they call equational lifting monads. These monads enjoy a more concise algebraic characterization than classifying monads. Moreover, equational lifting monads are a subclass of classifying monads.

In this paper, we investigate the connection between lifting monads and containers [1] in type theory. We noticed that the monads of partiality most commonly employed in type theory can be specified by containers:

- The maybe monad can be defined as $\mathsf{Maybe}\, X =_{\mathrm{df}} \Sigma s : \mathsf{Bool}. ((s = \mathsf{ok}) \to X)$ where $\mathsf{Bool} = \{\mathsf{ok}, \mathsf{err}\}$.
- The different definitions of the monad for non-termination [3,8] are isomorphic to $X_\perp =_{\mathrm{df}} \Sigma s : \mathsf{S}. ((s = \top) \to X)$ where S is a type called the Sierpinski set [13] or Rosolini's dominance [19].
- The full partial map classifier, classifying all partial maps, can be defined as $\mathsf{PMC}\, X =_{\mathrm{df}} \Sigma s : \Omega. ((s = 1) \to X)$ where Ω is the type of all propositions. In the type theory that we consider, $(s = 1) = s$.

The types Bool, S and Ω have to be thought as types of truth values classifying decidable, semidecidable and all subobjects respectively. The specific elements $\mathsf{ok} : \mathsf{Bool}$, $\top : \mathsf{S}$ and $1 : \Omega$ are the truth values corresponding to truth.

Ahman et al. [2,21] have given an algebraic characterization of containers whose interpretations carry a monad structure. We build on their work and give an algebraic characterization of containers whose interpretations carry a lifting monad structure. We show that different notions of lifting monad give rise to different characterizations. In particular, we give a new algebraic description of dominances, a notion first introduced by Rosolini for the specification of partial map classifiers in topos theory [19].

Our motivation for studying the relationship between containers and lifting monad comes from the fact that different notions of lifting monad are difficult to get an intuition for and compare in the abstract. Containers are a more concrete setting where the fine differences between them become easier to see and appreciate. For partiality specifically, containers provide a separation between reasoning about the partiality effect of a computation (which is all about shapes) and its functional content (which is about assignments of values to positions).

There is also some simplification to the metatheory of non-termination. The container approach allowed Chapman et al. [8] to define the non-termination monad in homotopy type theory avoiding the axiom of countable choice by using standard higher inductive types. This was an improvement over Altenkirch et al.'s [3] earlier solution that required higher inductive-inductive types.

The paper is organized as follows. In Sect. 2, we give an overview of some notion of lifting monads that appear in category theory. In Sect. 3, we revise containers and mnd-containers (containers interpreting into monads). In Sect. 4, we derive algebraic conditions on containers that makes their interpretations carry a lifting monad structure. Moreover, we give a new algebraic description of dominances. In Sect. 5, we give several examples, with special emphasis on the non-termination monad, used to classify partial maps with semidecidable domain of definedness in type theory. Finally, in Sect. 6, we draw some conclusions and we discuss future work.

We have fully formalized the development of the paper in the dependently typed programming language Agda [17]. The code is available at http://cs.ioc. ee/~niccolo/partialcont/; it uses Agda version 2.5.2 and Agda Standard Library version 0.13.

The Type-Theoretical Framework. We work in Martin-Löf type theory extended with the following extensional concepts: function extensionality (pointwise equal functions are equal) and proposition extensionality (logically equivalent propositions are equal). Equivalently, we could work in homotopy type theory, where function and proposition extensionality are consequences of the univalence axiom.

We assume uniqueness of identity proofs, which corresponds to working with 0-truncated types in homotopy type theory.

We revise a couple of basic definitions. A type X is a *proposition*, if any two of its inhabitants are equal: $\mathsf{isProp}\, X =_{\mathrm{df}} \Pi x_1\, x_2 : X.\, x_1 = x_2$. A type X is called *contractible*, if there exists $x : X$ such that every other element of X is equal to x: $\mathsf{isContr}\, X =_{\mathrm{df}} \Sigma x : X.\, \Pi x' : X.\, x = x'$.

2   Lifting Monads

In this section, we revise the different definitions of lifting monads appearing in category theory and how these notions relate to each other.

A few words on notation. Given a monad (T, η, μ), we write $f^* : T X \to T Y$ for the Kleisli extension of the map $f : X \to T Y$. Moreover, we write $g \diamond f$ for the composition of $f : X \to T Y$ and $g : Y \to T Z$ in the Kleisli category of T.

We start with Cockett and Lack's classifying monads [10].

Definition 1. An *almost-classifying monad* on a category $\mathbb{C}$ is a monad (T, η, μ) with an operation $\overline{(-)}$, called *restriction*, sending any map $f : X \to T Y$ into a map $\overline{f} : X \to T X$ subject to the following conditions:

> **CM1** $f \diamond \overline{f} = f$,
> **CM2** $\overline{g} \diamond \overline{f} = \overline{f} \diamond \overline{g}$,
> **CM3** $\overline{g} \diamond \overline{f} = \overline{g \diamond \overline{f}}$,
> **CM4** $\overline{g} \diamond f = f \diamond \overline{g \diamond f}$,
> **CM5** $\overline{\eta_Y \circ h} = \eta_X$, for $h : X \to Y$.

We call it a *classifying monad*, if it also satisfies

> **CM6** $\overline{\mathsf{id}_{TX}} = T\eta_X$.

The restriction of a map $f : X \to T Y$ should be thought of as a "partial identity function" on X, a kind of a specification, in the form of a map, of the "domain of definedness" of f (which need not be present in the category as an object).

Conditions CM1-4 stipulate that the Kleisli category of T is a restriction category. Condition CM5 states that pure maps, i.e., maps in the base category $\mathbb{C}$, are total. The additional condition CM6 of a classifying monad is more technical. It was postulated by Cockett and Lack in order to connect classifying monads and partial map classifiers, or more generally, classified restriction categories and classified $\mathcal{M}$-categories (Theorem 3.6 of [10]), $\mathcal{M}$-categories being Robinson and Rosolini's [18] framework for partiality.

Together with CM5, the condition CM4 implies CM1:

$$f \diamond \overline{f} = f \diamond \overline{\eta_Y \diamond f} \overset{\text{CM4}}{=} \overline{\eta_Y} \diamond f \overset{\text{CM5}}{=} \eta_Y \diamond f = f$$

A more specific notion of lifting monads is given by effective classifying monads [10]. Recall that a natural transformation is called Cartesian, if all of its naturality squares are pullbacks. A monad (T, η, μ) is said to be Cartesian, if η and μ are Cartesian.

Definition 2. A classifying monad $(T, \eta, \mu, \overline{(-)})$ is called *effective*, if η is Cartesian, pullbacks along η_X exist and are preserved by T.

An effective classifying monad is always Cartesian. Effective classifying monads are the same thing as *partial map classifiers* (Theorem 5.8 of [10]). This means that, given an effective classifying monad $(T, \eta, \mu, \overline{(-)})$, there exists an isomorphism $\mathbb{C}(X, TY) \cong \mathsf{Par}_\mathcal{M}(\mathbb{C})(X, Y)$, where the category $\mathsf{Par}_\mathcal{M}(\mathbb{C})$ has the same objects of $\mathbb{C}$ and it has spans

$$
\begin{array}{ccc}
 & X' & \\
{}^{m}\swarrow & & \searrow^{f} \\
X & & Y
\end{array}
$$

as morphisms between X and Y, where the left leg m is a monic map belonging to the collection $\mathcal{M}$. Intuitively, an element of $\mathsf{Par}_\mathcal{M}(\mathbb{C})(X, Y)$ is a partial map from X to Y. The left leg of the span specifies its domain of definedness.

Bucalo et al. [6] introduced the notion of equational lifting monad. Recall that a monad (T, η, μ) on a category $\mathbb{C}$ with finite products, equipped with a left strength $\psi_{X,Y} : X \times TY \to T(X \times Y)$, is called *commutative*, if the following diagram commutes:

$$
\begin{array}{ccc}
TX \times TY & \xrightarrow{\psi_{TX,Y}} & T(TX \times Y) \qquad \textbf{(CommM)} \\
{}^{\phi_{X,TY}}\downarrow & & \downarrow^{\phi^*_{X,Y}} \\
T(X \times TY) & \xrightarrow{\psi^*_{X,Y}} & T(X \times Y)
\end{array}
$$

where the right strength $\phi_{X,Y} : TX \times Y \to T(X \times Y)$ is defined as $\phi_{X,Y} =_{\text{df}} T\,\mathsf{swap} \circ \psi_{X,Y} \circ \mathsf{swap}$.

Definition 3. A commutative monad (T, η, μ, ψ) is called an *equational lifting monad*, if the following diagram commutes:

$$
\begin{array}{ccc}
TX & \xrightarrow{\;\;\Delta\;\;} & TX \times TX \\
{\scriptstyle T\Delta}\downarrow & & \downarrow{\scriptstyle \psi_{TX,X}} \\
T(X \times X) & \xrightarrow[T(\eta_X \times \mathrm{id}_X)]{} & T(TX \times X)
\end{array}
\qquad (\textbf{EqLM})
$$

Every equational lifting monad is canonically a classifying monad. Its restriction operation is defined with the aid of the strength:

$$
\bar{f} =_{\mathrm{df}} X \xrightarrow{\langle \mathrm{id}_X, f \rangle} X \times TY \xrightarrow{\psi_{X,Y}} T(X \times Y) \xrightarrow{T\pi_0} TX \qquad (\star)
$$

Cockett and Lack showed that there exist classifying monads on categories with finite products which are not equational lifting monads [10].

Notice that, in order to construct an almost-classifying monad, we can relax condition EqLM above and consider Cockett and Lack's copy monads [11].

Definition 4. A *copy monad* is a commutative monad (T, η, μ, ψ) for which the following diagram commutes:

$$
\begin{array}{ccc}
TX & \xrightarrow{\;\;\Delta\;\;} & TX \times TX \\
{\scriptstyle T\Delta}\downarrow & & \downarrow{\scriptstyle \psi_{TX,X}} \\
T(X \times X) & \xleftarrow[\phi^*_{X,X}]{} & T(TX \times X)
\end{array}
\qquad (\textbf{CopyM})
$$

Every equational lifting monad is a copy monad:

$$
\phi^* \circ \psi \circ \Delta = \phi^* \circ T\langle \eta, \mathrm{id} \rangle = (\phi \circ (\eta \times \mathrm{id}) \circ \Delta)^* = (\eta \circ \Delta)^* = T\Delta
$$

Every copy monad is canonically an almost-classifying monad. Its restriction operation is defined as the one of equational lifting monads $(\star)$.

3   Container Monads

Containers [1] serve as a "syntax" of a wide class of set functors; we call these set functors *container functors*. Many constructions on set functors can be carried out on the level of containers. Their concreteness makes containers a useful tool for enumerative combinatorics of container functors with special structure or properties.

In this paper, we are specifically interested in container functors with a monad structure. These were characterized by Ahman et al. [2,21].

A *container* is given by a set S (of shapes) and an S-indexed family P of sets (of positions in each shape).

A container determines a set functor $[\![S, P]\!]^c =_{df} T$ where $T X =_{df} \Sigma s : S.$ $P s \to X$ and $T f =_{df} \lambda(s, v). (s, f \circ v)$.

We will not discuss container morphisms and their interpretation here. But containers form a category **Cont** and interpretation $[\![-]\!]^c$ makes a fully-faithful functor between **Cont** and $[\mathbf{Set}, \mathbf{Set}]$.

There is an identity container defined by $\mathsf{Id}^c =_{df} (1, \lambda * . 1)$. Containers can be composed, composition is defined by $(S, P) \cdot^c (S', P') =_{df} (\Sigma s : S.$ $P s \to S', \lambda(s, v). \Sigma p : P s. P' (v p))$.

Identity and composition of containers provide a monoidal category structure on **Cont**. Interpretation $[\![-]\!]^c$ is a monoidal functor between $(\mathbf{Cont}, \mathsf{Id}^c, \cdot^c)$ and $([\mathbf{Set}, \mathbf{Set}], \mathsf{Id}, \cdot)$.

We call a *mnd-container* a container (S, P) with operations

- $\mathsf{e} : S$,
- $\bullet : \varPi s : S. (P s \to S) \to S$,
- $q_0 : \varPi s : S. \varPi v : P s \to S. P (s \bullet v) \to P s$,
- $q_1 : \varPi s : S. \varPi v : P s \to S. \varPi p : P (s \bullet v). P (v (v \diagdown_s p))$

(where we write $q_0 \, s \, v \, p$ as $v \diagdown_s p$ and $q_1 \, s \, v \, p$ as $p \diagup_v s$) satisfying

- $s \bullet (\lambda\_. \mathsf{e}) = s$,
- $\mathsf{e} \bullet (\lambda\_. s) = s$,
- $(s \bullet v) \bullet (\lambda p''. w (v \diagdown_s p'') (p'' \diagup_v s)) = s \bullet (\lambda p'. v p' \bullet w p')$,
- $(\lambda\_. \mathsf{e}) \diagdown_s p = p$,
- $p \diagup_{\lambda\_. s} \mathsf{e} = p$,
- $v \diagdown_s ((\lambda p''. w (v \diagdown_s p'') (p'' \diagup_v s)) \diagdown_{s \bullet v} p) = (\lambda p'. v p' \bullet w p') \diagdown_s p$,
- $((\lambda p''. w (v \diagdown_s p'') (p'' \diagup_v s)) \diagdown_{s \bullet v} p) \diagup_v s =$
  $$\text{let } u \leftarrow \lambda p'. v p' \bullet w p' \text{ in } w (u \diagdown_s p) \diagdown_{v (u \diagdown_s p)} (p \diagup_u s),$$
- $p \diagup_{\lambda p''. w (v \diagdown_s p'') (p'' \diagup_v s)} (s \bullet v) =$
  $$\text{let } u \leftarrow \lambda p'. v p' \bullet w p' \text{ in } (p \diagup_u s) \diagup_{w (u \diagdown_s p)} v (u \diagdown_s p).$$

The data $(\mathsf{e}, \bullet)$ are like a monoid structure on S modulo the 2nd argument of the multiplication being not an element of S, but a function from $P s$ to S where s is the 1st argument. Similarly, introducing the visual $\diagdown, \diagup$ notation for the data q_0, q_1 helps us see that they are reminiscent of a biaction (a pair of agreeing right and left actions) of this monoid-like structure on P. But here a further difference is also that P is not a set, but a S-indexed family of sets.

An mnd-container $(S, P, \mathsf{e}, \bullet, \diagdown, \diagup)$ interprets into a monad $[\![S, P, \mathsf{e}, \bullet, \diagdown, \diagup]\!]^{mc} =_{df} (T, \eta, \mu)$ where

- $T =_{df} [\![S, P]\!]^c$
- $\eta \, x =_{df} (\mathsf{e}, \lambda p. x)$
- $\mu (s, v) =_{df} \text{let } (v_0 \, p, v_1 \, p) \leftarrow v p \text{ in } (s \bullet v_0, \lambda p. v_1 (v_0 \diagdown_s p) (p \diagup_{v_0} s))$

We omit the definition of mnd-container morphisms and their interpretation. We note that mnd-containers form a category **MCont** whose identity and composition are inherited from **Cont**. Interpretation $[\![-]\!]^{mc}$ is a fully-faithful functor between **MCont** and **Monad**(**Set**).

Mnd-containers are in a bijection with containers whose interpretation carries a monad structure. The reason is, we could say, that they are in a bijection with monoid objects in the monoidal category $(\mathbf{Cont}, \mathsf{Id}^c, \cdot^c)$.

Moving from sets of objects to categories, one can observe that the functor $[\![-]\!]^{mc} : \mathbf{MCont} \to \mathbf{Monad}(\mathbf{Set})$ is the pullback of the fully-faithful functor $[\![-]\!]^c : \mathbf{Cont} \to [\mathbf{Set}, \mathbf{Set}]$ along $U : \mathbf{Monad}(\mathbf{Set}) \to [\mathbf{Set}, \mathbf{Set}]$ and the category $\mathbf{MCont}$ is isomorphic to the category of monoids in $(\mathbf{Cont}, \mathsf{Id}^c, \cdot^c)$.

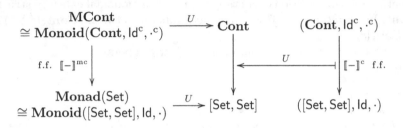

As an example, we look at the container syntax for the list functor and the standard monad structure on it.

The relevant container is (S, P) where $S =_{\mathrm{df}} \mathbb{N}$, $P\, s =_{\mathrm{df}} [0..s]$. The corresponding functor is T where $T\, X =_{\mathrm{df}} \Sigma s : \mathbb{N}.\ [0..s] \to X \cong \mathsf{List}\, X$.

This container extends to an mnd-container by

- $\mathsf{e} =_{\mathrm{df}} 1$,
- $s \bullet v =_{\mathrm{df}} \sum_{p:[0..s)} v\, p$,
- $v \searrow_s p =_{\mathrm{df}}$ greatest $p_0 : [0..s)$ such that $\sum_{p':[0..p_0)} v\, p' \leq p$,
- $p \nearrow_v s =_{\mathrm{df}} p - \sum_{p':[0..v \searrow_s p)} v\, p'$

The corresponding monad structure on T is the standard list monad with $\eta\, x =_{\mathrm{df}} [x]$, $\mu\, xss =_{\mathrm{df}} \mathsf{concat}\, xss$.

The list mnd-container example can be generalized in the following way. Let $(O, \#, \mathsf{id}, \circ)$ be some non-symmetric operad, i.e., let O be a set of operations, $\# : O \to \mathbb{N}$ a function fixing the arity of each operation and $\mathsf{id} : O$ and $\circ : \Pi o : O.\,(\#o \to O) \to O$ an identity operation and a parallel composition operator, with $\#\,\mathsf{id} = 1$ and $\#\,(o \circ v) = \sum_{i:[0..\#\,o)} \#\,(v\,i)$, satisfying the equations of a non-symmetric operad. We can take $S =_{\mathrm{df}} O$, $P\, o =_{\mathrm{df}} [0..\#\,o)$, $\mathsf{e} =_{\mathrm{df}} \mathsf{id}$, $\bullet =_{\mathrm{df}} \circ$ and $\searrow, \nearrow$ analogously to the definition of the (standard) list mnd-container. This choice of $(S, P, \mathsf{e}, \bullet, \searrow, \nearrow)$ gives a mnd-container. The list mnd-container corresponds to a special case where there is exactly one operation for every arity, in which situation we can w.l.o.g. take $O = \mathbb{N}$, $\#\,o = o$. Keeping this generalization of the list monad example in mind, we can think of mnd-containers as a generalization of non-symmetric operads where the argument places of an operation are identified nominally rather than positionally, operations may also have infinite arities, and, importantly, arguments may be discarded and duplicated in composition.

Altenkirch and Pinyo [4] have proposed to think of an mnd-container $(S, P, \mathsf{e}, \bullet, \searrow, \nearrow)$ as a "lax" $(1, \Sigma)$ type universe à la Tarski, namely, to view S as a universe of types ("codes for types"), P as an assignment of a set to each type, e as a type 1, • as a Σ-type former, $\diagdown$ and $\diagup$ as first and second projections from the denotation of a Σ-type. The laxity here is that we have functions $\lambda_-.* : P\,\mathsf{e} \to 1$ and $\lambda p.\,(v \diagdown_s p, p \diagup_v s) : P\,(s \bullet v) \to \Sigma p : P\,s.\,P\,(v\,p)$, but they are not isomorphisms.

The interpretation of an mnd-container $(S, P, \mathsf{e}, \bullet, \diagdown, \diagup)$ is a Cartesian monad if and only if the functions $\lambda_-.* : P\,\mathsf{e} \to 1$ and $\lambda p.\,(v \diagdown_s p, p \diagup_v s) : P\,(s \bullet v) \to \Sigma p : P\,s.\,P\,(v\,p)$ are isomorphisms. (We will prove the condition for Cartesianness of η in Lemma 11).

The list mnd-container satisfies these conditions and the list monad is Cartesian.

Cartesian mnd-containers can be thought of as (proper) operads with possibly infinitary operations and as (proper) $(1, \Sigma)$ type universes.

4   Containers of Partiality

Let $(S, P, \mathsf{e}, \bullet, \diagdown, \diagup)$ be an mnd-container and let (T, η, μ) be its interpretation into a monad. We now derive conditions on the mnd-container under which the monad is a lifting monad (in some sense or other).

4.1   Classifying Monads

We start with classifying monads. We restrict our attention to classifying monads whose restriction operation is defined as in $(\star)$.

We have that $\overline{f}\,x = (s, \lambda_-.\,x)$, if $f\,x = (s, h)$. If additionally $g\,x = (s', h')$, then $g^*\,(\overline{f}\,x) = (s \bullet (\lambda_-.\,s'), \lambda_-.\,h'(p \diagup_{\lambda_-.\,s'} s))$.

We already know that CM1 is derivable from CM4 and CM5.

Lemma 1. *CM2 holds if and only if the following condition holds:*

A2 $s \bullet (\lambda_-.\,s') = s' \bullet (\lambda_-.\,s)$

Proof. Given $f : X \to T\,Y, g : X \to T\,Z, x : X$, let $(s, h) = f\,x$ and $(s', h') = g\,x$. We have:

$$\overline{g}^*\,(\overline{f}\,x) = \overline{g}^*\,(s, \lambda_-.\,x) = (s \bullet (\lambda_-.\,s'), \lambda_-.\,x)$$

$$\overline{f}^*\,(\overline{g}\,x) = \overline{f}^*\,(s', \lambda_-.\,x) = (s' \bullet (\lambda_-.\,s), \lambda_-.\,x)$$

It is easy to see that A2 implies CM2. Vice versa, CM2 implies A2 by choosing $f, g : 1 \to T\,1, f * =_{\mathrm{df}}(s, \lambda_-.\,*)$ and $g * =_{\mathrm{df}}(s', \lambda_-.\,*)$.   □

Lemma 2. *CM3 holds always.*

Proof. Given $f : X \to T\,Y, g : X \to T\,Z, x : X$, let $(s, h) = f\,x$ and $(s', h') = g\,x$. We have $\overline{g}^*\,(\overline{f}\,x) = (s \bullet (\lambda_-.\,s'), \lambda_-.\,x)$ and $\overline{g^* \circ \overline{f}}\,x = (s \bullet (\lambda_-.\,s', \lambda_-.\,x))$.   □

Lemma 3. *CM4 holds if and only if the following two conditions hold:*

- **A4** $(s \bullet v) \bullet (\lambda_-.\, s) = s \bullet v$
- **A4'** $p \nearrow_{\lambda_-.\, s} (s \bullet v) = v \searrow_s p$

Proof. Given $f : X \to TY, g : Y \to TZ, x : X$, let $(s, h) = f\, x$ and $v = \pi_0 \circ g \circ h : P\, s \to S$. We have:

$$\overline{g}^* (f\, x) = \overline{g}^* (s, h) = (s \bullet v, \lambda p.\, h\, (v \searrow_s p))$$

$$f^* (\overline{g^* \circ f}\, x) = f^* (s \bullet v, \lambda_-.x) = ((s \bullet v) \bullet (\lambda_-.\, s), \lambda p.\, h\, (p \nearrow_{\lambda_-.\, s} (s \bullet v)))$$

It is easy to see that A4 and A4' imply CM4. Vice versa, CM4 implies A4 and A4' by choosing $f : 1 \to T\, (P\, s), f\, *=_{\mathrm{df}}(s, \mathsf{id})$ and $g : P\, s \to T\, 1, g\, p=_{\mathrm{df}}(v\, p, \lambda_-.\, *)$. $\qquad\square$

Lemma 4. *CM5 holds always.*

Proof. Immediate. $\qquad\qquad\qquad\qquad\qquad\qquad\qquad\qquad\qquad\qquad\qquad\qquad\square$

It is worth noting that the condition A2 is similar to commutativity and condition A4 to left regularity of a binary operation.

In summary, we obtain the following characterization of containers whose interpretation carry an almost-classifying monad structure.

Theorem 1. *The interpretation of an mnd-container $(S, P, \mathsf{e}, \bullet, \searrow, \nearrow)$ is an almost-classifying monad with restriction operation defined as in $(\star)$ if and only if it satisfies A2, A4 and A4'.*

We proceed to classifying monads and analyze condition CM6.

Lemma 5. *CM6 holds if and only if the following two conditions hold:*

B $P\, s \to s = \mathsf{e}$
C $\mathsf{isProp}\,(P\, s)$

Proof. ($\Rightarrow$) Assume CM6. Let $s : S$, we define $t : T\, (P\, s), t =_{\mathrm{df}} (s, \mathsf{id}_{P\, s})$. We have:

$$\overline{\mathsf{id}_{T\,(P\, s)}}\, t = (s, \lambda_-.\, (s, \mathsf{id}_{P\, s}))$$

$$T\, \eta_{P\, s}\, t = (s, (\lambda q.\, (\mathsf{e}, (\lambda_-.\, q))))$$

CM6 implies, in particular, that the functions $g =_{\mathrm{df}} \lambda_-.\, (s, \mathsf{id}_{P\, s})$ and $h =_{\mathrm{df}} \lambda q.\, (\mathsf{e}, \lambda_-.\, q)$ of type $P\, s \to T\, (P\, s)$ are equal.
In order to conclude B, let $p : P\, s$. Applying both functions g and h to p, we obtain $(s, \mathsf{id}_{P\, s}) = (\mathsf{e}, \lambda_-.\, p)$, and in particular $s = \mathsf{e}$.

In order to conclude C, let $p, q : P\, s$. Applying both functions g and h to p, we obtain $(s, \mathsf{id}_{P\, s}) = (\mathsf{e}, \lambda_-.\, p)$. Applying both functions g and h to q, we obtain $(s, \mathsf{id}_{P\, s}) = (\mathsf{e}, \lambda_-.\, q)$. In particular, we have $(\mathsf{e}, \lambda_-.\, p) = (\mathsf{e}, \lambda_-.\, q)$ and therefore $p = q$.

($\Leftarrow$) Assume B and C. Let $(s,g) : TX$. We have $\overline{\mathsf{id}_{TX}}\,(s,g) = (s, \lambda_{-}.\,(s,g))$ and $T\,\eta_X\,(s,g) = (s, \lambda p.\,(\mathsf{e}, \lambda_{-}.\,g\,p))$. B and C imply that these two terms are equal. $\square$

For container monads, we have that CM6 implies CM4.

Lemma 6. *B implies A4; C implies A4'.*

Proof. Assume B. Let $s : S$, $v : Ps \to S$.

$$(s \bullet v) \bullet (\lambda_{-}.\,s) \overset{\mathrm{B}}{=} (s \bullet v) \bullet (\lambda_{-}.\,\mathsf{e}) = s \bullet v$$

Assuming also C, we derive immediately A4', since the latter is an equation between positions. $\square$

In summary, we obtain the following characterization of containers whose interpretations carry a classifying monad structure.

Theorem 2. *The interpretation of an mnd-container $(S, P, \mathsf{e}, \bullet, \diagdown, \diagup)$ is a classifying monad with restriction operation defined as in ($\star$) if and only if it satisfies A2, B and C.*

As we have shown in the Lemma 6, condition C implies the position equation A4'. Analogously, condition C trivializes all position equations from the definition of mnd-container.

4.2   Copy Monads and Equational Lifting Monads

We now move to the characterization of containers whose interpretations carry a copy monad structure or an equational lifting monad structure.

The left strength ψ, when applied to a term $(s,h) : TX$, returns $\psi\,(x,(s,h)) = (s, \lambda p.\,(x, h\,p))$, while the right strength ϕ symmetrically returns $\phi\,((s,h),y) = (s, \lambda p.\,(h\,p, y))$.

Lemma 7. *CommM holds if and only if both A2 and the following condition hold:*

A2' $(\lambda_{-}.\,s')\diagdown_s p = p\diagup_{\lambda_{-}.\,s} s'$

Proof. Given $(s,h) : TX$ and $(s',h') : TY$, we have:

$$\psi^*\,(\phi\,((s,h),(s',h'))) = \psi^*\,(s, \lambda p.\,(h\,p, (s',h')))$$
$$= (s \bullet (\lambda_{-}.\,s'), \lambda p.\,(h\,(\lambda_{-}.s' \diagdown_s p), h'\,(p\diagup_{\lambda_{-}.s'} s)))$$

$$\phi^*\,(\psi\,((s,h),(s',h'))) = \phi^*\,(s', \lambda p.\,((s,h), h'\,p))$$
$$= (s' \bullet (\lambda_{-}.\,s), \lambda p.\,(h\,(p\diagup_{\lambda_{-}.s} s'), h'\,(\lambda_{-}.s \diagdown_{s'} p)))$$

It is easy to see that A2 and A2' imply CommM. Vice versa, CommM implies both A2 and A2' by choosing $h =_{\mathrm{df}} \mathsf{id}_{P\,s}$ and $h' =_{\mathrm{df}} \mathsf{id}_{P\,s'}$. $\square$

Lemma 8. *CopyM holds if and only if the following conditions hold:*

A1 $s \bullet (\lambda_-. s) = s$
A1' $p \uparrow_{\lambda_-s} s = p$
A1'' $(\lambda_-. s) \nwarrow_s p = p$

Proof. Given $(s, h) : T X$, we have:

$$\phi^* \left(\psi \left((s, h), (s, h) \right) \right) = \left(s \bullet (\lambda_-. s), \lambda p. \left(h \left(p \uparrow_{\lambda_-s} s \right), h \left(\lambda_-.s \nwarrow_s p \right) \right) \right)$$

$$T \Delta (s, h) = (s, \lambda p. (h\, p, h\, p))$$

It is easy to check that A1, A1' and A1'' imply CopyM. Vice versa, CopyM implies A1, A1' and A1'' by choosing $h =_{\mathrm{df}} \mathsf{id}_{P\,s}$. □

Condition A1 is a version of idempotence of a binary operation.

In summary, we obtain the following characterization of containers whose interpretations carry a copy monad structure.

Theorem 3. *The interpretation of an mnd-container $(S, P, \mathsf{e}, \bullet, \nwarrow, \uparrow)$ is a copy monad if and only if it satisfies A1, A1', A1'', A2 and A2'.*

The following lemma shows that the set of conditions characterizing almost-classifying monads in Theorem 1 implies the set of conditions characterizing copy monads in Theorem 3.

Lemma 9. *A4 implies A1. A4 and A4' imply A1' and A1''. Moreover, conditions A2, A4 and A4' imply A2'.*

Proof. Assume A4. Given $s : S$, we have:

$$s \bullet (\lambda_-. s) = (s \bullet (\lambda_-. \mathsf{e})) \bullet (\lambda_-. s) \stackrel{\mathrm{A4}}{=} s \bullet (\lambda_-. \mathsf{e}) = s$$

Assume also A4'. Given $s : S$ and $p : P(s \bullet (\lambda_-. s))$, we have:

$$p \uparrow_{\lambda_-s} s = p \uparrow_{\lambda_-s} (s \bullet (\lambda_-. \mathsf{e})) \stackrel{\mathrm{A4'}}{=} (\lambda_-. \mathsf{e}) \nwarrow_s p = p$$

$$(\lambda_-. s) \nwarrow_s p \stackrel{\mathrm{A4'}}{=} p \uparrow_{\lambda_-s} (s \bullet (\lambda_-. s)) \stackrel{\mathrm{A1}}{=} p \uparrow_{\lambda_-s} s = p$$

Now assume also A2. Given $s, s' : S$ and $p : P(s \bullet (\lambda_-. s'))$, we have:

$$p \uparrow_{\lambda_-s} s' \stackrel{\mathrm{A1'}}{=} (p \uparrow_{\lambda_-s' \bullet (\lambda_-.s)} (s' \bullet (\lambda_-. s))) \uparrow_{\lambda_-s} s'$$
$$= p \uparrow_{\lambda_-s} ((s' \bullet (\lambda_-. s)) \bullet (\lambda_-. s'))$$
$$\stackrel{\mathrm{A4}}{=} p \uparrow_{\lambda_-s} (s' \bullet (\lambda_-. s)) \stackrel{\mathrm{A2}}{=} p \uparrow_{\lambda_-s} (s \bullet (\lambda_-. s'))$$
$$\stackrel{\mathrm{A4'}}{=} (\lambda_-. s') \nwarrow_s p$$

□

Remember that every copy monad is canonically an almost-classifying monad. Theorems 1 and 3 together with Lemma 9 tell us that the converse holds, if the underlying functor of the monad is specified by a container and if restriction is given as in (⋆).

Corollary 1. *The interpretation of an mnd-container is a copy monad if and only if it is an almost-classifying monad with restriction operation defined as in (⋆).*

We now move on to equational lifting monads.

Lemma 10. *EqLM holds if and only if B and C hold.*

Proof. Given $(s, h) : T X$, we have:

$$\psi\left(\Delta\left(s, h\right)\right) = \left(s, \lambda p.\left(\left(s, h\right), h\, p\right)\right)$$

$$T\left(\eta \times \mathrm{id}\right)\left(T\, \Delta\left(s, h\right)\right) = \left(s, \left(\eta \times \mathrm{id}\right) \circ \Delta \circ h\right) = \left(s, \lambda p.\left(\left(\mathsf{e}, \lambda\_.\, h\, p\right), h\, p\right)\right)$$

It is easy to check that B and C imply EqLM. Vice versa, EqLM implies both B and C by choosing $h =_{\mathrm{df}} \mathrm{id}_{P\,s}$. □

Analogously to Lemma 6, it is easy to see C implies A1', A1'', A2', as these are all position equations.

In summary, we obtain the following characterization of containers whose interpretations carry an equational lifting monad structure.

Theorem 4. *The interpretation of an mnd-container $(S, P, \mathsf{e}, \bullet, \backslash, \mathord{\nearrow})$ is an equational lifting monad if and only if it satisfies A2, B and C.*

Remember that every equational lifting monad is canonically a classifying monad. Theorems 2 and 4 tell us that the converse holds, if the monad is specified by a container and if restriction is given as in (⋆).

Corollary 2. *The interpretation of an mnd-container is an equational lifting monad if and only if it is a classifying monad with restriction operation defined as in (⋆).*

4.3   Effective Classifying Monads

We move to effective classifying monads. As usual, we restrict our attention to classifying monads whose restriction operation is defined as in (⋆).

In **Set**, all pullbacks exist and any container functor preserves all of them. This means that in the category of sets and functions, an effective classifying monad is a classifying monad with Cartesian η.

Lemma 11. *The unit η is Cartesian if and only if the following condition holds:*

D isContr $(P\,\mathsf{e})$

Proof. ($\Leftarrow$) Assume D. We are given the following data:

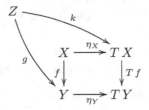

We have to construct a unique map $u : Z \to X$ such that $f \circ u = g$ and $\eta_X \circ u = k$. Given $z : Z$, if $k\,z = (s, h)$, then the commutativity of the outermost square gives us $s = $ e and $f\,(h\,p) = g\,z$ for all $p : P$e, since we have:

$$\eta_Y\,(g\,z) = (\mathsf{e}, \lambda\_.\,g\,z)$$
$$T\,f\,(k\,z) = (s, f \circ h)$$

By D, we are given an element $p : P$e, so we define $u\,z =_{\mathrm{df}} h\,p$. We immediately have $f\,(u\,z) = g\,z$. Moreover, $\eta_X\,(u\,z) = (\mathsf{e}, \lambda\_.\,h\,p)$ which is equal to $k\,z$ since $h\,p = h\,q$ for all $q : P$e by D.

Let $u' : Z \to X$ be another mediating map. In particular, we have $\eta_X\,(u'\,z) = k\,z$, which implies $u'\,z = h\,p = u\,z$.

($\Rightarrow$) Assume that η is Cartesian. We consider the following diagram:

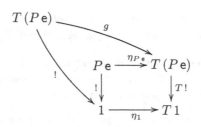

where $g\,(s, h) =_{\mathrm{df}} (\mathsf{e}, \mathrm{id}_{P\,\mathsf{e}})$. Since the outermost diagram commutes, there exists a unique mediating map $u : T\,(P\,\mathsf{e}) \to P\,\mathsf{e}$. In particular, $P\,\mathsf{e}$ is inhabited by $u\,(\mathsf{e}, \mathrm{id}_{P\,\mathsf{e}})$. It remains to show that $P\,\mathsf{e}$ is a proposition. Let $(s, h) : T\,(P\,\mathsf{e})$. We know that $\eta_{P\,\mathsf{e}}\,(u\,(s, h)) = g\,(s, h)$, i.e., $(\mathsf{e}, \lambda\_.\,u\,(s, h)) = (\mathsf{e}, \mathrm{id}_{P\,\mathsf{e}})$. Then for all $p : P\,\mathsf{e}$, we have $p = u\,(s, h)$. So in particular $p = u\,(\mathsf{e}, \mathrm{id}_{P\,\mathsf{e}})$. Therefore $P\,\mathsf{e}$ is contractible. $\quad\square$

Theorem 2 and Lemma 11 tell us that the interpretation of an mnd-container $(S, P, \mathsf{e}, \bullet, \nwarrow, \nearrow)$ is an effective classifying monad with restriction operation defined as in ($\star$) if and only if satisfies A2, B, C and D.

Conditions B, C and D, when considered together, are very powerful. Assuming conditions B and D, we obtain that $P\,s$ is logically equivalent to $s = \mathsf{e}$. The left-to-right direction is given by B. Vice versa, if $s = \mathsf{e}$, then $P\,s = P\,\mathsf{e}$ and therefore $P\,s$ holds by D. Assuming also C (and remembering that we are assuming proposition extensionality), we obtain $P\,s = (s = \mathsf{e})$. Therefore, for containers whose interpretation extends to an effective classifying monad, P cannot be chosen, it is uniquely determined.

Mnd-containers whose interpretation carry an effective classifying monad structure can be given a more concise characterization.

Definition 5. An *effective classifier* is a set S equipped with operations

- $e : S$
- $\bullet : \Pi s : S. ((s = e) \to S) \to S$
- $q_0 : \Pi s : S. \Pi v : (s = e) \to S. s \bullet v = e \to s = e$
- $q_1 : \Pi s : S. \Pi v : (s = e) \to S. \Pi p : s \bullet v = e \to v (q_0 \, s \, v \, p) = e$

satisfying $s \bullet (\lambda_-. e) = s$ (i.e., the first shape equation of an mnd-container, henceforth denoted **RU**) and A2.

Theorem 5. *The interpretation of an mnd-container $(S, P, e, \bullet, \diagdown, \diagup)$ is an effective classifying monad with restriction operation defined as in $(\star)$ (so that, in particular, $P s = (s = e)$) if and only if $(S, e, \bullet \diagdown, \diagup)$ is an effective classifier.*

Proof. We only need to show the right-to-left direction. In particular, we only need to check that, using RU and A2, it is possible to derive all the equations of mnd-containers. We know that the position equations hold since $s = e$ is a proposition for all $s : S$.

The first shape equation is RU, so we only need to derive the other two. Notice that RU and A2 imply that the type family $\lambda s. (s = e)$ is injective, i.e., if $s = e \leftrightarrow s' = e$ then $s = s'$. In fact, from $s = e \to s' = e$ and $s' = e \to s = e$, we obtain two proofs, $r_1 : s \bullet (\lambda_-. e) = s \bullet (\lambda_-. s')$ and $r_2 : s' \bullet (\lambda_-. e) = s' \bullet (\lambda_-. s)$. Therefore we have:

$$s \overset{\text{RU}}{=} s \bullet (\lambda_-. e) \overset{r_1}{=} s \bullet (\lambda_-. s') \overset{\text{A2}}{=} s' \bullet (\lambda_-. s) \overset{r_2}{=} s' \bullet (\lambda_-. e) \overset{\text{RU}}{=} s' \qquad (1)$$

Then, in order to prove $e \bullet (\lambda_-. s) = s$, it is sufficient to construct the two implications $s = e \to e \bullet (\lambda_-. s) = e$ and $e \bullet (\lambda_-. s) = e \to s = e$. The first implication follows from RU, the second from the type of q_0.

The third shape equation is similarly derived employing the injectivity of $\lambda s. (s = e)$. $\qquad \square$

4.4 Dominances

Traditionally, in topos theory partial map classifiers are specified by dominances, introduced by Rosolini in his PhD thesis [19]. Dominances are used to characterize the domain of definedness of partial maps, generalizing the notion of subobject classifier. In type theory, the notion of dominance was reformulated by Escardó and Knapp [14]. Here we give a definition which is equivalent to theirs.

Definition 6. A *dominance* is a set with operations

- $[\![-]\!] : D \to \Omega$,
- $1_D : D$,
- $\Sigma_D : \Pi X : D.\,([\![X]\!] \to D) \to D$

satisfying

- isInj $[\![-]\!]$,
- $[\![1_D]\!] = 1$,
- $[\![\Sigma_D\,X\,Y]\!] = \Sigma x : [\![X]\!].\,[\![Y\,x]\!]$.

The predicate isInj states the injectivity of a function. The type Ω is the type of all propositions, $\Omega =_{\mathrm{df}} \Sigma X : \mathcal{U}.\,\mathsf{isProp}\,X$.

In other words, a dominance is a set of (unique codes of) propositions closed under 1 and Σ. Interestingly, the notion of dominance is equivalent to the one of effective classifier.

Theorem 6. *A set carries a dominance structure if and only it carries an effective classifier structure.*

Proof. Let D be a set with a dominance structure.

First notice that, by the injectivity of $[\![-]\!]$ and the fact that $[\![1_D]\!] = 1$, we have $[\![X]\!] = (X = 1_D)$. Indeed, by injectivity of $[\![-]\!]$, we have $([\![X]\!] = [\![1_D]\!]) \leftrightarrow (X = 1_D)$. By proposition extensionality therefore $([\![X]\!] = [\![1_D]\!]) = (X = 1_D)$. Because $[\![1_D]\!] = 1$, we have $([\![X]\!] = [\![1_D]\!]) = ([\![X]\!] = 1)$. If $[\![X]\!]$, then $[\![X]\!] \leftrightarrow 1$, so by propositional extensionality also $[\![X]\!] = 1$. Conversely, if $[\![X]\!] = 1$, then trivially $[\![X]\!] \leftrightarrow 1$ and further $[\![X]\!]$. So $[\![X]\!] \leftrightarrow ([\![X]\!] = 1)$. Hence by propositional extensionality one last time, $[\![X]\!] = ([\![X]\!] = 1)$. In summary, $[\![X]\!] = ([\![X]\!] = 1) = ([\![X]\!] = [\![1_D]\!]) = (X = 1_D)$.

The type D is equipped with the following effective classifier structure:

- $\mathsf{e} =_{\mathrm{df}} 1_D$,
- $X \bullet Y =_{\mathrm{df}} \Sigma_D\,X\,Y$,
- q_0 and q_1 are definable, since we have $[\![\Sigma_D\,X\,Y]\!] = \Sigma x : [\![X]\!].\,[\![Y\,x]\!]$, which is equivalent to $(\Sigma_D\,X\,Y = 1_D) \leftrightarrow \Sigma p : (X = 1_D).\,(Y\,p = 1_D)$. Using the latter logical equivalence, it is easy to prove both RU and A2.

Vice versa, let S be a set with an effective classifier structure. Then it is equipped with the following dominance structure:

- $[\![s]\!] =_{\mathrm{df}} (s = \mathsf{e})$,
- $1_D =_{\mathrm{df}} \mathsf{e}$,
- $\Sigma_D\,s\,v =_{\mathrm{df}} s \bullet v$,
- $[\![-]\!]$ is injective. The proof of this fact corresponds to Eq. (1) in the proof of Theorem 5,
- $[\![1_D]\!] = 1$ is trivially true,

– $[\![\Sigma_D \, s \, v]\!] = \Sigma p : [\![s]\!] . [\![v \, p]\!]$ holds. Indeed, using proposition extensionality, we only have to show that the two propositions are logically equivalent. Unfolding the definitions, we have that the left-to-right implication $s \bullet v = \mathsf{e} \rightarrow \Sigma p : s = \mathsf{e}. v \, p = \mathsf{e}$ corresponds precisely to the conjunction of q_0 and q_1. For the right-to-left implication, if $p : s = \mathsf{e}$ and $v \, p = \mathsf{e}$, then we have:

$$s \bullet v \overset{p,q}{=} \mathsf{e} \bullet (\lambda_-. \mathsf{e}) \overset{\mathsf{RU}}{=} \mathsf{e}$$

$\square$

Theorem 6 shows that effective classifiers are the same as dominances. But the definition of effective classifier is more concise and easier to work with.

5 Examples

Imposed simultaneously, the characterizing conditions of effective classifying monads, i.e., conditions A2, B, C and D, are very strong and constrain the monad very much. But when some of them are dropped, more examples arise. In this section, we give examples of lifting monads specified by containers.

Maybe Monad, Exception Monad. The maybe monad $T \, X =_{\mathrm{df}} X + 1$, or the exception monad with one exception, can be alternatively defined as the interpretation of the container $S =_{\mathrm{df}} \{\mathsf{ok}, \mathsf{err}\}$, $P \, \mathsf{ok} =_{\mathrm{df}} 1$, $P \, \mathsf{err} =_{\mathrm{df}} 0$. The mnd-container data are given by $\mathsf{e} =_{\mathrm{df}} \mathsf{ok}$, $\mathsf{ok} \bullet v =_{\mathrm{df}} v *$, $\mathsf{err} \bullet \_ =_{\mathrm{df}} \mathsf{err}$. These data satisfy all of A2, B, C and D. In fact, the maybe monad is the partial map classifier classifying partial maps with decidable domain of definedness.

One could ask if the exception monad with more than one exception carries the structure of a lifting monad. The answer is no. The exception monad with two exceptions, i.e., $T \, X =_{\mathrm{df}} X + 2$, can be alternatively defined as the interpretation of the container $S =_{\mathrm{df}} \{\mathsf{ok}, \mathsf{err}_0, \mathsf{err}_1\}$, $P \, \mathsf{ok} =_{\mathrm{df}} 1$, $P \, \mathsf{err}_i =_{\mathrm{df}} 0$. The mnd-container data are given by $\mathsf{e} =_{\mathrm{df}} \mathsf{ok}$, $\mathsf{ok} \bullet v =_{\mathrm{df}} v *$, $\mathsf{err}_i \bullet \_ =_{\mathrm{df}} \mathsf{err}_i$. These data satisfy B, C and D, but falsify A2, since $\mathsf{err}_0 \bullet (\lambda_-. \mathsf{err}_1) \neq \mathsf{err}_1 \bullet (\lambda_-. \mathsf{err}_0)$.

Delay Monad. The underlying functor of Capretta's delay monad [7] is defined as the following coinductive type:

$$\frac{x : X}{\mathsf{now}\, x : \mathsf{D}\, X} \qquad \frac{c : \mathsf{D}\, X}{\mathsf{later}\, c : \mathsf{D}\, X}$$

It can be alternatively defined as the interpretation of the container $S =_{\mathrm{df}} \mathsf{coN}$, $P \, n =_{\mathrm{df}} n {\downarrow}$ where $\mathsf{coN} =_{\mathrm{df}} \mathsf{D}\, 1$ is the set of conatural numbers and $\downarrow$ is the convergence predicate defined inductively by the rules

$$\frac{}{0^{\downarrow} : 0{\downarrow}} \qquad \frac{n{\downarrow}}{\mathsf{suc}^{\downarrow} : (\mathsf{suc}\, n){\downarrow}}$$

We can define $\mathsf{e} =_{\mathrm{df}} 0$, $0 \bullet v =_{\mathrm{df}} v \, 0^{\downarrow}$, $\mathsf{suc}\, n \bullet v =_{\mathrm{df}} \mathsf{suc}\, (n \bullet v \circ \mathsf{suc}^{\downarrow})$. These data specify the monad structure introduced by Capretta [7], which validate A2, C and

D, but neither A4 nor B. A4 fails since $n \bullet (\lambda\_. m) = n + m$, and therefore generally $(n \bullet v) \bullet (\lambda\_. n) \neq n \bullet v$. B fails since $n\downarrow$ does not generally imply $n = 0$.

If we instead define $\mathsf{suc}\, n \bullet v =_{\mathrm{df}} \mathsf{suc}\, (n \bullet \mathsf{pred} \circ v \circ \mathsf{suc}^\downarrow)$, we also validate A4. In fact, now we have $n \bullet (\lambda\_. m) = \max(n, m)$. Therefore $(n \bullet v) \bullet (\lambda\_. n) = n \bullet v$. With this alternative definition of the operation $\bullet$, the delay datatype carries an almost-classifying monad structure.

Non-termination Monad. To modify the delay monad example to validate B too, we can quotient coN by weak bisimilarity $\approx$ defined by $n \approx m =_{\mathrm{df}} n\downarrow \leftrightarrow m\downarrow$, i.e., $S =_{\mathrm{df}} \mathsf{coN}/\approx$. The new set S is typically called the *Sierpinski set* [13] or *Rosolini's dominance* [19]. The definitions of P and e are easily adjusted to this change: $P\, n =_{\mathrm{df}} n = [0]$, where $[m]$ indicate the equivalence class of m wrt. the equivalence relation $\approx$, and $\mathsf{e} =_{\mathrm{df}} [0]$. In order to lift the operation $\bullet$ to the quotient, it is necessary to invoke a choice principle. Chapman et al. [8] solve this issue assuming the axiom of countable choice, a semi-classical principle recently proved to be non-derivable in type theory [12]. A different solution is given by Escardó and Knapp [14] assuming the axiom of propositional choice from Rosolini propositions, i.e., propositions X for which the type $\|\Sigma n : \mathsf{coN}.\,(n\downarrow \leftrightarrow X)\|$ is inhabited, where $\|A\|$ is the propositional truncation of the type A [20, Chap. 6.9]. It does not matter which version of $\bullet$ we lift to the quotient, addition or maximum, the resulting monad structure on the quotient is the same.

We call the interpretation of this mnd-container the *non-termination monad*.[1] It is the partial map classifier classifying partial maps with semidecidable domain of definedness.

The Sierpinski set can also be defined from scratch in homotopy type theory as a higher inductive type without recourse to the choice principle.

A first construction like this was given by Altenkirch et al. [3] using higher inductive-inductive types. They defined a datatype $X_\perp$ as the free ω-complete pointed partial order on a type X. The join constructor $\bigcup$ has to take as input increasing streams of elements in $X_\perp$ (arbitrary streams do not have joins). Since this constructor has to take an increasingness proof as an argument, they had to use higher inductive-inductive types. They showed that the type $X_\perp$ is isomorphic to $\mathsf{D}\, X/\approx$ under the assumption of countable choice. The Sierpinski set arises as $1_\perp$.

An alternative construction of the Sierpinski set was given by Chapman et al. [8] using standard higher inductive types. They defined the Sierpinski set S as the free countably-complete join semilattice on the unit type 1. This is to say that S is the countable powerset of 1. They noticed that the Sierpinski set can be specified using a join constructor $\bigvee$ that takes as input arbitrary streams of elements of $1_\perp$, not only the increasing ones. They showed that the types S and $1_\perp$ are isomorphic, which in turns also shows that S is isomorphic to $\mathsf{coN}/\approx$ under the assumption of countable choice.

---

[1] It is also called the partiality monad, but we want to use a more specific term here.

Full Partial Map Classifier. The *full partial map classifier*, i.e., the partial map classifier classifying all partial maps, can be defined as the interpretation of the container $S =_{\text{df}} \Omega$, $P\,X =_{\text{df}} X$ where Ω is the type of all propositions introduced in Sect. 4.4.[2] The mnd-container data is given by $e =_{\text{df}} 1$, $X \bullet Y =_{\text{df}} \Sigma x : X.\,Y\,x$. Notice that the latter type is a proposition, when X is a proposition and $Y\,x$ is a proposition for all $x : X$. These data satisfy all of A2, B, C and D.

Terminal Monad. The terminal monad $T\,X =_{\text{df}} 1$ can be alternatively defined as the interpretation of the container $S =_{\text{df}} 1$, $P\,* =_{\text{df}} 0$. The mnd-container data are trivial. These data satisfy A2, B and C, but falsify D, since $P\,*$ does not hold. The terminal monad is an example of a classifying monad that is not effective.

6   Conclusions

In this paper, we continued the study of monads of partiality in Martin-Löf type theory. In particular, we studied the connection between such monads and containers. Building on work by Ahman et al. [2,21] on container comonads and container monads, we gave an algebraic characterization of containers whose interpretation carries a lifting monad structure.

We considered several notion of lifting monad from category theory: classifying monads [10], equational lifting monads [6], copy monads [11] and effective classifying monads [10], corresponding to partial map classifiers [15]. A byproduct of our investigation is the result that, for container monads, equational lifting monads are the same as classifying monads with restriction operation defined as in ($\star$). Similarly, copy monads are the same as almost-classifying monads with restriction operation defined as in ($\star$). Moreover, we discovered a new concise alternative definition of dominance [19] in type theory.

Recently, Uustalu and Veltri [22] introduced ω-complete pointed classifying monads, which are those classifying monads whose Kleisli category is ω**CPPO**-enriched wrt. the "less defined than" order on homsets induced by the restriction operation. These monads are used for modelling potential non-termination. Examples include the non-termination monad of Sect. 5, which is the initial ω-complete pointed classifying monad, and the full partial map classifier of Sect. 5. In future work, we plan to extend the characterization developed in this paper to containers whose interpretation carries a ω-complete pointed classifying monad structure. When considering the effective case, those containers should correspond to dominances closed under countable joins.

Acknowledgements. We are thankful to Thorsten Altenkirch and Martín Escardó for discussions and valuable hints.

This research was supported by the ERDF funded Estonian national CoE project EXCITE and the Estonian Ministry of Education and Research institutional research grant IUT33-13.

---

[2] Notice that, if $X : \mathcal{U}$, then $[\![S, P]\!]^c\,X : \mathcal{U}_1$, i.e., $[\![S, P]\!]^c$ would not be an endofunctor. But if $X : \mathcal{U}_1$, then also $[\![S, P]\!]^c\,X : \mathcal{U}_1$. Therefore we think of $[\![S, P]\!]^c$ as a monad on $\mathcal{U}_1$.

References

1. Abbott, M., Altenkirch, T., Ghani, N.: Containers: constructing strictly positive types. Theor. Comput. Sci. **342**(1), 3–27 (2005)
2. Ahman, D., Chapman, J., Uustalu, T.: When is a container a comonad? Log. Methods Comput. Sci. **10**(3), article 14 (2014)
3. Altenkirch, T., Danielsson, N.A., Kraus, N.: Partiality, revisited. The partiality monad as a quotient inductive-inductive type. In: Esparza, J., Murawski, A.S. (eds.) FoSSaCS 2017. LNCS, vol. 10203, pp. 534–549. Springer, Heidelberg (2017). https://doi.org/10.1007/978-3-662-54458-7_31
4. Altenkirch, T., Pinyo, G.: Monadic containers and universes (abstract). In: Kaposi, A. (ed.) Abstracts of 23rd International Conference on Types for Proofs and Programs, TYPES 2017, pp. 20–21. Eötvös Lórand University, Budapest (2017)
5. Bove, A., Krauss, A., Sozeau, M.: Partiality and recursion in interactive theorem provers–an overview. Math. Struct. Comput. Sci. **26**(1), 38–88 (2016)
6. Bucalo, A., Führmann, C., Simpson, A.: An equational notion of lifting monad. Theor. Comput. Sci. **294**(1–2), 31–60 (2003)
7. Capretta, V.: General recursion via coinductive types. Log. Methods Comput. Sci. **1**(2), Article 1 (2005)
8. Chapman, J., Uustalu, T., Veltri, N.: Quotienting the delay monad by weak bisimilarity. Math. Struct. Comput. Sci. (to appear)
9. Cockett, J.R.B., Lack, S.: Restriction categories I: categories of partial maps. Theor. Comput. Sci. **270**(1–2), 223–259 (2002)
10. Cockett, J.R.B., Lack, S.: Restriction categories II: partial map classification. Theor. Comput. Sci **294**(1–2), 61–102 (2003)
11. Cockett, J.R.B., Lack, S.: Restriction categories III: colimits, partial limits, and extensivity. Math. Struct. Comput. Sci. **17**(4), 775–817 (2007)
12. Coquand, T., Mannaa, B., Ruch, F.: Stack semantics of type theory. In: Proceedings of 32th Annual ACM/IEEE Symposium on Logic in Computer Science, LICS 2017 (2017)
13. Escardó, M.H.: Synthetic topology of data types and classical spaces. Electron. Notes Theor. Comput. Sci. **87**, 21–156 (2004)
14. Escardó, M.H., Knapp, C.M.: Partial elements and recursion via dominances in univalent type theory. In: Goranko, V., Dam, M. (eds.) Proceedings of 26th EACSL Annual Conference on Computer Science Logic, CSL 2017, Leibniz International Proceedings in Informatics, vol. 82, article 21. Dagstuhl Publishing, Saarbrücken/Wadern (2017)
15. Johnstone, P.T.: Topos Theory. London Mathematical Society Monographs, vol. 10. Cambridge University Press, Cambridge (1977)
16. Moggi, E.: Notions of computation and monads. Inf. Comput. **93**(1), 55–92 (1991)
17. Norell, U.: Dependently typed programming in Agda. In: Koopman, P., Plasmeijer, R., Swierstra, D. (eds.) AFP 2008. LNCS, vol. 5832, pp. 230–266. Springer, Heidelberg (2009). https://doi.org/10.1007/978-3-642-04652-0_5
18. Robinson, E., Rosolini, G.: Categories of partial maps. Inf. Comput. **79**(2), 95–130 (1988)
19. Rosolini, G.: Continuity and Effectiveness in Topoi. DPhil thesis, University of Oxford (1986)
20. Univalent Foundations Program, The: Homotopy Type theory: Univalent Foundations of Mathematics. Institute for Advanced Study, Princeton, NJ (2013). http://homotopytypetheory.org/book

21. Uustalu, T.: Container combinatorics: monads and lax monoidal functors. In: Mousavi, M.R., Sgall, J. (eds.) TTCS 2017. LNCS, vol. 10608, pp. 91–105. Springer, Heidelberg (2017). https://doi.org/10.1007/978-3-319-68953-1_8
22. Uustalu, T., Veltri, N.: The delay monad and restriction categories. In: Hung, D.V., Kapur, D. (eds.) ICTAC 2017. LNCS, vol. 10580, pp. 32–50. Springer, Heidelberg (2017). https://doi.org/10.1007/978-3-319-67729-3_3

The Negligible and Yet Subtle Cost of Pattern Matching

Beniamino Accattoli$^{(\boxtimes)}$ and Bruno Barras

INRIA, UMR 7161, LIX, École Polytechnique, Palaiseau, France
{beniamino.accattoli,bruno.barras}@inria.fr

Abstract. The model behind functional programming languages is the *closed* λ-*calculus*, that is, the fragment of the λ-calculus where evaluation is weak (*i.e.* out of abstractions) and terms are closed. It is well-known that the number of β (*i.e.* evaluation) steps is a reasonable cost model in this setting, for all natural evaluation strategies (call-by-name/value/need). In this paper we try to close the gap between the closed λ-calculus and actual languages, by considering an extension of the λ-calculus with pattern matching. It is straightforward to prove that β plus matching steps provide a reasonable cost model. What we do then is finer: we show that β steps only, without matching steps, provide a reasonable cost model also in this extended setting—morally, pattern matching comes for free, complexity-wise. The result is proven for all evaluation strategies (name/value/need), and, while the proof itself is simple, the problem is shown to be subtle. In particular we show that qualitatively equivalent definitions of call-by-need may behave very differently.

1 Introduction

Functional programming languages are modeled on the λ-calculus. More precisely, on the dialect in which evaluation is *weak*, that is, it does not enter function bodies, and terms are closed—we refer to this setting as to the *closed* λ-*calculus*. In contrast to other models such as Turing machines, in the λ-calculus it is far from evident that the number of evaluation steps is a reasonable cost model for time. Its evaluation rule, β-reduction, is in fact a complex, non-atomic operation, for which there exist *size exploding families*, *i.e.* families of programs whose code grows at an exponential rate with respect to the number of β-reductions.

The time cost models of the closed λ-*calculus.* Since the work of Blelloch and Greiner [17], it is known that the number of β-steps in the call-by-value closed λ-calculus can indeed be considered as a reasonable cost model. Roughly, one can consider β as an (almost) atomic operation, counting 1 (actually a cost bound by the size of the initial term) for each step. The key point is that β can be *simulated* efficiently, using simple forms of shared evaluation such as environment-based

---

This work is part of a wider research effort, the COCA HOLA project [3].

© Springer International Publishing AG 2017
B.-Y.E. Chang (Ed.): APLAS 2017, LNCS 10695, pp. 426–447, 2017.
https://doi.org/10.1007/978-3-319-71237-6_21

abstract machines, circumventing size explosion. Sands, Gustavsson, and Moran have then showed that ordinary abstract machines for call-by-name and call-by-need closed λ-calculi are also reasonable [34]. Similar results have also been obtained by Martini and Dal Lago (by combining the results in [21,22]), and then the whole question has been finely decomposed and studied by Accattoli, Barenbaum, Mazza, and Sacerdoti Coen [6,14]. It is thus fair to say that the number of β-steps is *the* time cost model of the closed λ-calculus.

Functional programming languages and the negligible cost hypothesis. There is a gap between the closed λ-calculus and an actual functional language, that usually has various constructs and evaluation rules in addition to β-reduction. From the cited results it would easily follow that the number of β-steps plus the steps for the additional constructs is a reasonable cost model. In practice, however, a more parsimonious cost model is used: for functional programs the number of function calls (aka β-reductions) is usually considered as (an upper bound on) its time complexity—this is done for instance by Charguéraud and Pottier in [18]. The implicit hypothesis is that the cost of β-reduction dominates the cost of all these additional rules, so that it is fair to ignore them, complexity-wise—that is, they can be considered to have zero cost. To the best of our knowledge, however, such a *negligible cost hypothesis* has never been proved.

The cost of pattern matching. This paper is a first step towards proving the negligible cost hypothesis. Here, we extend the study of cost models to the closed λ-calculus with constructors and pattern matching. It turns out that the problem is subtler than what folklore suggests: evaluation steps related to pattern matching can easily be exponential in the number of β-steps—*i.e.* they are far from being dominated by β. We show, however, that evaluation can be *simulated* so that matching steps are tamed. The cost of pattern matching is proved to be indeed negligible: matching steps can be assigned zero cost, as they are linear in the number of β-steps and the size of the initial term, the two key parameters in the study of cost models. Therefore, our results provide formal arguments supporting common practice, despite the apparently bad behavior of pattern matching.

In contrast to the ordinary closed λ-calculus, where call-by-name/value/need strategies can be treated with the same techniques, for pattern matching these evaluation strategies behave less uniformly. Namely:

- *Call-by-name (CbN) explodes*: we show that in CbN there are *matching exploding families*, that is, families $\{t_n\}_{n\in\mathbb{N}}$ of terms where t_n evaluates in n β-steps and 2^n matching steps, suggesting that the cost of pattern matching is far from being negligible.
- *Call-by-value (CbV) is reasonable*: the explosion of matching steps in CbN is connected to the re-evaluation of function arguments, it is then natural to look at the CbV case, where arguments are evaluated once and for all. It turns out that in CbV matchings are negligible, namely they are *bilinear*, that is, linear in the number of β-steps and the size of the initial term, and that such a bound is tight.

- *Call-by-need (CbNeed) is sometimes reasonable*: CbNeed is halfway CbN and CbV, as it is operationally equivalent to CbN but it avoids the re-evaluation of arguments as in CbV—in particular CbNeed rests on *values*. The problem here is subtle, and amounts to how values are defined. If constructors are always considered as values, independently of the shape of their arguments, then there are matching exploding families similar—but trickier—to those affecting CbN. If constructors are considered as values only when they are applied to variables, then one can adapt the proof used for CbV, and show that matchings are negligible.
- *Call-by-name (CbN) is reasonable, actually*: being operationally equivalent to CbN, CbNeed can be seen as an efficient simulation of CbN, proving that the matching exploding families of CbN are a circumventable problem, similarly to the size exploding families for β-reduction.

The context of the paper. The problem of the cost of pattern matching arises as an intermediate steps in a more ambitious research program, going beyond the negligible cost hypothesis. Our real goal in fact is the complexity analysis of the abstract machine at work in the kernel of Coq[1] [20]. Such a machine has been designed and partially studied by Barras in his PhD thesis [16], and provides a lightweight approach compared to the compilation scheme by Grégoire and Leroy described in [25]. It is used to decide convertibility of terms, which is the bottleneck of the type-checking (and thus proof-checking) algorithm. It is at the same time one of the most sophisticated and one of the most used abstract machines for the λ-calculus. The goal is to prove it *reasonable*, that is, to show that the overhead of the machine is polynomial in the number of β-steps and in the size of the initial term, and eventually design a new machine along the way, if the existing one turns out to be unreasonable.

Barras' machine executes a language that is richer than λ-calculus. In particular, it includes constructors and pattern matching, to which the paper is devoted—this justifies the choice of the particular presentation of pattern matching that we adopt, rather than other formalisms such as Cirstea and Kirchner's *rewriting calculus* [19], Klop, van Oostrom, and de Vrijer's λ-*calculus with patterns* [29], or Jay and Kesner's *pure pattern calculus* [26]. The machine actually implements call-by-need strong (*i.e.* under abstraction) evaluation, while here we only deal with the closed case. This is done for the sake of simplicity, because the subtleties concerning pattern matching are already visible at the closed level, but also because the closed case is of wider interest, being the one modeling functional programming languages.

The value of the paper. To our knowledge, our work is the first study of the asymptotic cost of pattern matching in a functional setting. As we explained, this paper provides an example of the subtleties hidden in passing from the

---

[1] The kernel of Coq is the subset of the codebase which ensures that only valid proofs are accepted. Hence the use of an abstract machine, which has a better ratio efficiency/complexity than the use of a compiler or a naive interpreter.

ideal, abstract setting of the closed λ-calculus to an actual, concrete functional language—and the case we study here is still quite abstract—motivating further complexity analyses of programming features beyond the core of the λ-calculus. Another interesting point is the fact that the study of cost models is used to discriminate between different presentations of CbNeed that would otherwise seem equivalent. Said differently, complexity and cost models are used here as language design principles.

The style of the paper. We adopt a lightweight, minimal style, focusing on communicating ideas rather than providing a comprehensive treatment of the calculi under study. The style is akin to that of a *functional pearl*—the reasoning is in fact simple, not far from a pearl. A more thorough study is left to an eventual longer version of this work. In particular, our results are proved using simple calculi with explicit substitutions (ES) inspired by the *linear substitution calculus*—a variation over a λ-calculus with ES by Robin Milner [32] developed by Accattoli and Kesner [2,8]—in which both the search of the redex and α-renaming are left to the meta-level. To be formal, we should make both tasks explicit in the form of an abstract machine. The work of Accattoli and coauthors [4,6,9] has however repeatedly showed that these tasks require an overhead linear in the number of β-steps and the size of the initial term, and in some cases even logarithmic in the size of the initial term (see the companion paper [7])—in the terminology of this paper, the costs of *search* and α-*renaming* are negligible.

At the technical level, for the study of cost models we mostly adopt the techniques and the terminology (linear substitution calculus, subterm invariant, harmony, etc.) developed by Accattoli and his coauthors (Dal Lago, Barenbaum, Mazza, Sacerdoti Coen, Guerrieri) in [4,6,9–11].

2   Call-by-Name and Matching Explosion

Here we consider the case of the CbN closed λ-calculus extended with constructors and pattern matching. Since the aim is to show a degeneracy, we proceed quickly (omitting the error handling, for instance), delaying a more formal treatment to the next section on CbV, where we show a positive result.

Constructors and pattern matching. The language is the ordinary λ-calculus extended with a fixed finite set of constructors $c_1, \ldots c_k$—therefore, k is a constant parameter of the language. Each constructor c_i takes a fixed number k_{c_i} (≥ 0) of arguments, *e.g.* $c_i(t_1, \ldots, t_{k_{c_i}})$. Constructors are supposed to be fully applied from the beginning, and the application of constructors to their arguments is *not* the application of the λ-calculus—that is, we write $c_i(t_1, \ldots, t_{k_{c_i}})$ and not $c_i t_1, \ldots, t_{k_{c_i}}$, thus ruling out partial applications such as *e.g.* $c_i t_1$ (assuming that $k_{c_i} > 1$). There also is a pattern matching operator $\mathsf{case}\, t\, \{b\}$, where b is a set of branches—since k is fixed, for the sake of simplicity we assume that every $\mathsf{case}\, t\, \{b\}$ has a branch for every constructor. Namely:

$$
\begin{aligned}
\text{TERMS} \quad & t, u ::= x \mid \lambda x.t \mid t\, u \mid c_i(t) \mid \mathsf{case}\, t\, \{b\} \\
\text{BRANCHES} \quad & b ::= c_i(\boldsymbol{x}) \Rightarrow \boldsymbol{u_i}
\end{aligned}
$$

where the bold font denotes vectors according to the following conventions:

- t is the notation for a vector of terms $t_1, \ldots, t_n$, whose length is left implicit as much as possible;
- $c_i(t)$ and $c_i(x)$ assume that t and x have the right arity k_{c_i}, and
- $c_i(x) \Rightarrow u_i$ is a compact notation for $c_1(x) \Rightarrow u_1, \ldots, c_k(x) \Rightarrow u_k$.

Moreover, $c_i(x_1, \ldots, x_{k_{c_i}}) \Rightarrow u_i$ binds the variables $x_1, \ldots, x_{k_{c_i}}$ in u_i. Finally, the size of a term is the number of its term constructors (that is, the number of productions used to derive it using the grammar for terms), and it is noted $|t|$.

Evaluation. The small-steps operational semantics is the usual one for CbN, extended with an evaluation context and a rewriting rule for pattern matching.

CBN EVALUATION CONTEXTS $C ::= \langle \cdot \rangle \mid Ct \mid \text{case } C\{b\}$

RULE AT TOP LEVEL	CONTEXTUAL CLOSURE	
$(\lambda x.t)u \mapsto_\beta t\{x \leftarrow u\}$	$C\langle t \rangle \to_\beta C\langle u \rangle$	if $t \mapsto_\beta u$
$\text{case } c_i(t)\{c_i(x) \Rightarrow u_i\} \mapsto_{\text{case}} u_i\{x \leftarrow t\}$	$C\langle t \rangle \to_{\text{case}} C\langle u \rangle$	if $t \mapsto_{\text{case}} u$

To help the reader getting used to our notations, let us unfold the $\mapsto_{\text{case}}$ rule:

$$\text{case } c_i(t_1, \ldots, t_{k_{c_i}})\{c_1(x) \Rightarrow u_1, \ldots, c_k(x) \Rightarrow u_k\} \mapsto_{\text{case}}$$
$$u_i\{x_1 \leftarrow t_1\} \ldots \{x_{k_{c_i}} \leftarrow t_{k_{c_i}}\}$$

The union of $\to_\beta$ and $\to_{\text{case}}$ is noted $\to_{\text{CbN}}$. A derivation $d : t \to^* u$ is a potentially empty sequence of evaluation $\to_\beta$ and $\to_{\text{case}}$ steps, whose length/number of β steps/number of $\to_{\text{case}}$ steps is denoted by $|d|/|d|_\beta/|d|_{\text{case}}$. As it is standard, we silently work modulo α-equivalence.

The matching exploding family. We already have enough ingredients to build a matching exploding family. Consider a zeroary constructor 0. Now, define the following family of closed terms:

$$t_1 := \lambda x.\text{case } x \{0 \Rightarrow \text{case } x \{0 \Rightarrow 0\}\}$$
$$t_{n+1} := \lambda x.(t_n(\text{case } x \{0 \Rightarrow \text{case } x \{0 \Rightarrow 0\}\}))$$

Our exploding family is actually given by $\{t_n 0\}_{n \in \mathbb{N}}$, for which we want to prove that $t_n 0 \to_\beta^n \to_{\text{case}}^{2^n} 0$. To this aim, we need the following auxiliary family:

$$u_0 := 0 \qquad u_{n+1} := \text{case } u_n \{0 \Rightarrow \text{case } u_n \{0 \Rightarrow 0\}\})$$

Now, in two steps, we prove a slightly more general statement, namely $t_n u_k \to_\beta^n$ $u_{n+k} \to_{\text{case}}^{2^{n+k}} 0$.

Proposition 1

1. Linear β prefix: *there exists a derivation* $d_n : t_n u_k \to_\beta^n u_{n+k}$ *for* $n \geq 1$ *and* $k \geq 0$;
2. Exponential pattern matching suffix: *there exists a derivation* $e_n : u_n \to_{\mathsf{case}}^* 0$ *with* $|e_n| = \Omega(2^n)$ *for* $n \geq 1$.
3. Matching exploding family: *there exists a derivation* $f_n : t_n 0 \to^* 0$ *with* $|t_n 0| = O(n)$, $|f_n|_\beta = n$, *and* $|f_n| = \Omega(2^n)$.

Proof. Point 3 is obtained by concatenating Point 1 and Point 2.
Point 1 and Point 2 are by induction on n. Cases:

– *Base case, i.e.* $n = 1$.
    1. *Linear β prefix*: the derivation d_1 is given by

$$
\begin{aligned}
t_1 u_k &= (\lambda x.\mathsf{case}\, x\, \{0 \Rightarrow \mathsf{case}\, x\, \{0 \Rightarrow 0\}\}) u_k \\
&\to_\beta \mathsf{case}\, u_k\, \{0 \Rightarrow \mathsf{case}\, u_k\, \{0 \Rightarrow 0\}\}) \quad = u_{k+1}
\end{aligned}
$$

   2. *Exponential pattern matching suffix*: the derivation e_1 given by the following sequence has indeed $2^1 = 2$ steps, as required:

$$
\begin{aligned}
u_1 &= \mathsf{case}\, 0\, \{0 \Rightarrow \mathsf{case}\, 0\, \{0 \Rightarrow 0\}\}) \\
&\to_{\mathsf{case}} \mathsf{case}\, 0\, \{0 \Rightarrow 0\} \qquad\qquad \to_{\mathsf{case}} 0
\end{aligned}
$$

– *Inductive case*
   1. *Linear β prefix*: the derivation d_{n+1} is given by

$$
\begin{aligned}
t_{n+1} u_k &= (\lambda x.(t_n \mathsf{case}\, x\, \{0 \Rightarrow \mathsf{case}\, x\, \{0 \Rightarrow 0\}\})) u_k \\
&\to_\beta t_n \mathsf{case}\, u_k\, \{0 \Rightarrow \mathsf{case}\, u_k\, \{0 \Rightarrow 0\}\})) \\
&= t_n u_{k+1} \\
(\text{by i.h.}) &\xrightarrow{d_n}_\beta^n u_{n+k+1}
\end{aligned}
$$

   2. *Exponential pattern matching suffix*: the derivation e_{n+1} is given by:

$$
\begin{aligned}
u_{n+1} &= \mathsf{case}\, u_n\, \{0 \Rightarrow \mathsf{case}\, u_n\, \{0 \Rightarrow 0\}\}) \\
(\text{by i.h.}) &\xrightarrow{e_n}^* \mathsf{case}\, 0\, \{0 \Rightarrow \mathsf{case}\, u_n\, \{0 \Rightarrow 0\}\}) \\
&\to_{\mathsf{case}} \mathsf{case}\, u_n\, \{0 \Rightarrow 0\} \\
(\text{by i.h.}) &\xrightarrow{e_n}^* \mathsf{case}\, 0\, \{0 \Rightarrow 0\} \qquad\qquad \to_{\mathsf{case}} 0
\end{aligned}
$$

Now, $|e_{n+1}| = 2 + 2 \cdot |e_n| =_{i.h.} 2 + 2 \cdot \Omega(2^n) = \Omega(2^{n+1})$. $\qquad\square$

3 Call-by-Value, LIME, and the Bilinear Bound

It is easy to see that the matching exploding family of the previous section does not explode if evaluated according to the CbV strategy. Said differently, the problem seems to be about the re-evaluation of arguments.

We prove here that for the CbV closed λ-calculus extended with constructors and pattern matching the number of β-steps (alone, *i.e.* without matching steps) is a reasonable cost model. Despite the absence of matching explosion, to reach our goal we have to address the underlying size explosion problem that affects every λ-calculus with a small-step operational semantics, and so we have to adopt sharing and an abstract machine-like formalism. In the terminology of the introduction, we have to define a framework *simulating* the small-step calculus, in order to tame size explosion.

Therefore, we switch from a small-step operational semantics to a *micro*-step one, that is, we replace β-reduction $\rightarrow_\beta$ and meta-level substitution $t\{x\leftarrow u\}$ with a *multiplicative* rule $\rightarrow_m$, turning a β-redex $(\lambda x.t)u$ into an explicit, delayed substitution $t[x\leftarrow u]$, and an *exponential* rule $\rightarrow_e$, replacing one variable occurrence at the time, when it ends up in evaluation position. The terminology *multiplicative/exponential* comes from the connection with linear logic, that is however kept hidden here—see [6] for more details—just bear in mind that the exponential rule does not have an exponential cost, the name is due to other reasons.

For the sake of simplicity, we define the micro-step calculus but not the small-step one, and thus we also omit the study of the correspondence between the two. It would be obtained by simply unfolding the explicit substitutions (ES), and it is standard—see [4] for a detailed similar study in CbN. The only point that is important is that in such a correspondence there is a bijection between the evaluation steps at the two levels, except for the exponential steps, that vanish, because ES are unfolded by the correspondence. In particular, the number of multiplicative and β-steps coincide, and they can thus be identified for our complexity analyses.

Introducing LIME. Our proof uses a new simple formalism, the *LInear Matching calculus by valuE* (shortened *LIME*), that is a variation over other formalisms studied by Accattoli and coauthors (the *value substitution calculus* [13], the *GLAM abstract machine* [9], and the *micro-substituting abstract machine* [4]).

Let us explain how to classify LIME in the zoo of decompositions of the λ-calculus. There are three tasks that in the λ-calculus are left implicit or at the meta-level and that are addressed by finer frameworks such as abstract machines or calculi with ES:

1. *Substitution*: delaying and decomposing the substitution process;
2. *Search*: searching for the next redex to reduce;
3. *Names*: handling/avoiding α-renaming.

The original approach to calculi with ES [1] addressed all these tasks. With time, it was realized that the handling of names could be safely left implicit, see Kesner's [28] for a survey. More recently, also the search of the redex has been factored out, bringing it back to the implicit level, making ES act at a distance, without percolating through the term. The paradigmatic framework of this simpler, *at a distance* approach is the *linear substitution calculus* (LSC), a variation over a λ-calculus with ES by Robin Milner [32] developed by Accattoli and Kesner [2,8]—a LSC-like calculus is used in forthcoming Sect. 4. LIME, as the

LSC, addresses only the substitution task, letting the other two implicit. Here, however, we add a further simplification: it groups all ES in a global environment, in a way inspired by abstract machines and at work also in Accattoli's [4]. The literature of course contains also other formalisms employing a global environment or factoring out the search of the redex, at least [23,24,27,34–36,38], but usually developed focusing on other points.

The only data structure in LIME is the global environment E for delayed substitutions. With respect to abstract machines, the idea is that the transitions for the search of the redex are omitted (together with the related data structures, such as stacks and dumps), because the transitions corresponding to β, matching, and substitution transitions are expressed via evaluation contexts. For what concerns α-renaming, we follow the same approach used in the mainstream approach to the λ-calculus, leaving it at the meta-level and applying it on-the-fly. Our choice is justified by the fact that, as already pointed out in the introduction, previous work has repeatedly showed that the costs of handling *search* and *names* explicitly are negligible, when one is interested is showing that the overhead is not exponential.

Our result is that the number of steps of LIME is bilinear, that is, linear in the number of β-steps and the size of the initial term, that are the two fundamental parameters in the study of cost models. Additionally, we show that our bound is tight. Making search and names explicit usually has only an additional bilinear cost, that would not change the asymptotic behavior. The choice of omitting them, then, is particularly reasonable.

Defining LIME. The idea is that a term t is paired with an environment E, to form a program p. There is a special program err, denoting that an error occurred, that can happen in two cases: because of a pattern matching on an abstraction, or the application of a constructor to a further argument—the two cases are spelled out by the forthcoming rewriting rules. Evaluation is right-to-left, and values include abstractions, error, and constructors applied recursively to values. In particular, variables are excluded from values as it is standard in the literature on abstract machines, see [14]. The language is thus defined by:

$$
\begin{array}{rl}
\text{TERMS} & t,u ::= x \mid \lambda x.t \mid t\,u \mid \mathsf{c}(t) \mid \mathsf{case}\,t\,\{b\} \mid \mathsf{err} \\
\text{BRANCHES} & b ::= \mathsf{c}_i(\boldsymbol{x}) \Rightarrow \boldsymbol{u}_i \\
\text{VALUES} & v,w ::= \lambda x.t \mid \mathsf{c}(v) \mid \mathsf{err} \\
\text{ENVIRONMENTS} & E ::= \epsilon \mid [x\!\leftarrow\!v]::E \\
\text{PROGRAMS} & p ::= (t,E)
\end{array}
$$

$$
\text{EVAL. CONTEXTS} \quad C ::= \langle \cdot \rangle \mid tC \mid Cv \mid \mathsf{c}(t,\dots,C,\dots,v) \mid \mathsf{case}\,C\,\{b\}
$$

Note that the definition of evaluation contexts forces the evaluation of constructor arguments, from right to left. Most of the time we write programs (t,E) without the parentheses, *i.e.* simply as $t\,E$. Evaluation $\to_{\mathsf{cbv}}$ is the relation obtained as the union of the following rewriting rules (m for *multiplicative* and e for *exponential*). They are not defined at top level and then closed by evaluation context but are defined directly at the global level (by means of evaluation contexts, of course):

$$
\begin{aligned}
C\langle(\lambda x.t)\ v\rangle\ E &\to_{\mathtt{m}} & C\langle t\rangle\ [x{\leftarrow}v]{::}E \\
C\langle x\rangle\ E{::}[x{\leftarrow}v]{::}E' &\to_{\mathtt{e}} & C\langle v\rangle\ E{::}[x{\leftarrow}v]{::}E' \\
C\langle\mathsf{case}\ \mathsf{c}_i(v)\,\{\mathsf{c}_j(x)\Rightarrow u_j\}\rangle\ E &\to_{\mathtt{case}} & C\langle u_i\rangle\ [x{\leftarrow}v]{::}E \\
C\langle\mathsf{case}\ \lambda x.t\,\{b\}\rangle\ E &\to_{\mathtt{err_1}} & \mathsf{err}\ \epsilon \\
C\langle\mathsf{c}_i(v)\ t\rangle\ E &\to_{\mathtt{err_2}} & \mathsf{err}\ \epsilon
\end{aligned}
$$

where rule $\to_{\mathtt{case}}$ has been written compactly. Its explicit form is

$$
\begin{aligned}
C\langle\mathsf{case}\ \mathsf{c}_i(v_1,\ldots,v_{k_{c_i}})\,\{\mathsf{c}_j(x)\Rightarrow u_j\}\rangle\ E \\
\to_{\mathtt{case}} C\langle u_i\rangle\ [x_1{\leftarrow}v_1]\ldots[x_{k_{c_i}}{\leftarrow}v_{k_{c_i}}]{::}E
\end{aligned}
$$

As before, a derivation $d : t \to^*_{\mathsf{CbV}} u$ is a potentially empty sequence of evaluation steps, whose length/number of $\to_a$ steps is denoted by $|d|/|d|_a$ for $a \in \{\mathtt{m}, \mathtt{e}, \mathtt{case}, \mathtt{err_1}, \mathtt{err_2}\}$.

The free and bound variables of a term are defined as expected—**err** has no free variables. The free variables of a program are defined by looking at environments from the end, as follows:

$$
\mathtt{fv}(t,\epsilon) := \mathtt{fv}(t) \qquad \mathtt{fv}(t,E{::}[x{\leftarrow}v]) := (\mathtt{fv}(t,E)\setminus\{x\})\cup\mathtt{fv}(v)
$$

As expected, a program is *closed* if its set of free variables is empty. As it is standard, we silently work modulo α-equivalence.

Progress and harmony. The choice of LIME for our study is justified by the similarity with the formalisms used in the studies on functional cost models [4,6,9,11] and with the one used in the Coq abstract machine designed by Barras [16]. A further justification is the fact that it is conservative with respect to CbV closed λ-calculus in a sense that we are now going to explain.

A fundamental property of the CbV closed λ-calculus is that terms either evaluate to a value or they diverge. This property has been highlighted and called *progress* by Wright and Felleisen [39] and later extensively used by Pierce [33], among others. In these studies, however, the property is studied in relationship to a typing system, as a tool to prove its soundness (*typed programs cannot go wrong*). Accattoli and Guerrieri in [11] focus on it in an *untyped* setting and call it *harmony* because it expresses a form of internal completeness, in two ways. First, it shows that in the closed λ-calculus CbV can be seen as a notion of *call-by-normal-form*. Note the subtlety: one cannot define call-by-normal-form evaluation directly, because one needs evaluation to define normal forms—a call-by-normal-form calculus thus requires a certain harmony in its definition. Second, the property shows that the restriction to CbV β-reduction has an impact on the order in which redexes are evaluated, but evaluation never gets stuck, as every β-redex will eventually become a CbV β-redex and be fired, unless evaluation diverges (and with no need of types). In [11], harmony is showed to hold for the *fireball calculus*, an extension of the CbV closed λ-calculus with open terms. LIME rests on closed terms but adds constructors and pattern matching, and so its harmony does not follow from the one of the closed λ-calculus.

Now, we show that LIME is harmonious—types have no role here, so we prefer to refer to *harmony* rather than to *progress*. Let us stress however that harmony has no role in the complexity analysis, it is presented here only to show that LIME is not ad-hoc.

Harmony is generally showed for single steps, showing that a term either reduces or it is a value.

Proposition 2 (Progress/harmony for LIME). *Let (t, E) be a closed program. Then either $(t, E) \to_{\mathsf{Cbv}} (u, E')$ or t is a value.*

Proof. By induction on t. Cases:

- *Value, i.e. $t = v$.* Then no rules apply;
- *Variable, i.e. $t = x$.* Note that E contains a substitution $[x \leftarrow v]$ because the program is closed, and so $\to_{\mathsf{e}}$ applies.
- *Application, i.e. $t = u\ s$.* The *i.h.* on (s, E) gives
  - s reduces. Then so does (t, E);
  - s is a value. The *i.h.* on (u, E) gives
    - u reduces. Then so does (t, E);
    - u is a value. Then either $\to_{\mathsf{m}}$ (if u is an abstraction) or $\to_{\mathsf{err}_2}$ (if u is a constructor) applies.
- *Constructor that is not a value, i.e. $t = \mathsf{c}(\boldsymbol{u})$.* Then there is a rightmost argument s in $\boldsymbol{u}$ that is not a value. By *i.h.*, (s, E) reduces, and so does $(\mathsf{c}(\boldsymbol{u}), E)$.
- *Match, i.e. $t = \mathsf{case}\ u\ \{b\}$.* The *i.h.* on (u, E) gives:
  - u reduces. Then so does (t, E);
  - u is a constructor. Then $\to_{\mathsf{case}}$ applies;
  - u is an abstraction. Then $\to_{\mathsf{err}_1}$ applies.   □

Complexity analysis. For complexity analyses, one usually assumes that the initial program p comes with an empty environment, that is, $p = (t_0, \epsilon)$. The two fundamental parameters for analyses of a derivation $d : (t_0, \epsilon) \to^*_{\mathsf{Cbv}} q$ are

1. *Length of its small-step evaluation*: the number $|d|_{\mathsf{m}}$ of m-steps in the derivation d, that morally is the number of β-steps at the omitted small-step level.
2. *Input*: the size $|t_0|$ of the initial term t_0;

Our aim is to show that the length $|d|$ of a d is bilinear, that is, linear in $|d|_{\mathsf{m}}$ and $|t_0|$. Since error-handling rules can only appear once, and only at the end of a derivation, they do not really play a role. Therefore, the goal is to prove that the number of exponential $\to_{\mathsf{e}}$ and matching $\to_{\mathsf{case}}$ steps is bilinear. To prove it, we need the following measure $|\cdot|_{\mathsf{v}}$ of terms and programs (where k is the number of constructors in the language and k_{c_i} is the arity of the i-th constructor), that simply counts the number of free variable occurrences and of case constructs out of abstractions, *i.e.* of the locations where $\to_{\mathsf{e}}$ and $\to_{\mathsf{case}}$ steps can act:

$$|x|_{\mathsf{v}} := 1 \qquad\qquad |\lambda x.t|_{\mathsf{v}} := 0 \qquad\qquad |\mathsf{err}|_{\mathsf{v}} := 0$$

$$|t\ u|_{\mathsf{v}} := |t|_{\mathsf{v}} + |u|_{\mathsf{v}} \quad |\mathsf{c}_i(t)|_{\mathsf{v}} := \Sigma_{j=1}^{k_{\mathsf{c}_i}} |t_j|_{\mathsf{v}} \quad |(t, E)|_{\mathsf{v}} := |t|_{\mathsf{v}}$$

$$|\mathsf{case}\, t\, \{\mathsf{c}_i(\boldsymbol{x}) \Rightarrow \boldsymbol{u_i}\}|_{\mathsf{v}} := 1 + |t|_{\mathsf{v}} + max\{|u_i|_{\mathsf{v}} \mid i = 1, \ldots, k\}$$

Note that for the branches of a case construct we use the *max*, because only one of them is selected by $\to_{\mathsf{case}}$ while the others are discarded. The measure is extended to evaluation contexts by setting $|\langle\cdot\rangle|_{\mathsf{v}} := 0$ and defining it on the other cases as for terms. The following properties of the measure follow immediately from the definition:

Lemma 3 (Basic properties of the measure)

1. Values: $|v|_{\mathsf{v}} = 0$ for every value v.
2. Size Upper Bound: $|t|_{\mathsf{v}} \le |t|$ for every term t.
3. Context Factorization: $|C\langle t\rangle|_{\mathsf{v}} = |C|_{\mathsf{v}} + |t|_{\mathsf{v}}$.

From these properties a straightforward inspection of the rules shows, as expected, that

Lemma 4 (Exponential and matching rules decrease the measure). *If* $(t, E) \to_a (u, E')$ *then* $|(t, E)|_{\mathsf{v}} > |(u, E')|_{\mathsf{v}}$ *for* $a \in \{\mathsf{e}, \mathsf{case}\}$.

Lemma 4 implies that the length of a sequence of exponential and matching steps is bounded by the measure of the code at the beginning of the sequence, that by Lemma 3.2 is bounded by the size of that code. To conclude, we have to establish the connection between multiplicative steps and code sizes. It turns out that $\to_{\mathsf{m}}$ can increase the measure only by an amount bounded by the size of the initial term. This property follows by an invariant known as *the subterm property*, that relates the size of terms along the derivation with the size of the initial one. It is the key property for complexity analyses, playing a role akin to that of the cut-elimination theorem for sequent calculi, or of the subformula property for proof search. It does not hold in the ordinary λ-calculus, because it requires meta-level substitution to be decomposed in micro-steps. It can instead be found in many abstract machines and other setting decomposing β-reduction.

The subterm property can be formulated in various ways. Sometimes it states that the size of duplicated subterms is bounded by the size of the initial term. In LIME, it takes a different form. The multiplicative rule $\to_{\mathsf{m}}$ can increase the measure because it opens an abstraction, that being a value has measure 0, and potentially exposes new free variable occurrences and case constructs. Therefore, the important point is to bound the size of abstraction bodies, which is why the property takes the following form.

Lemma 5 (LIME subterm property). *Let* $d : (t_0, \epsilon) \to^*_{\mathsf{CbV}} (u, E)$ *be a LIME derivation. Then the size of every abstraction in* u *and* E *is bounded by the size* $|t_0|$ *of the initial term.*

Proof. By induction on the length of the derivation d. The base case $|d| = 0$ is immediate. For a non-empty derivation consider the last step $(s, E') \to_{\mathsf{CbV}} (u, E)$.

By *i.h.*, the statement holds for (s, E'). The rules may move abstractions from s to E' or vice-versa, but they never substitute inside abstractions (evaluation contexts are weak, *i.e.* they do not go under abstraction) nor create them out of the blue. ☐

Let us stress why the property requires meta-level substitution to be decomposed: it is only because LIME never replaces variable occurrences under abstraction that the size of abstractions does not grow.

We can then conclude with the bound on the length of derivations.

Theorem 6 (LIME bilinear bound). *Let* $d : (t_0, \epsilon) \to^*_{\mathsf{CbV}} (u, E)$ *be a LIME derivation. Then* $|d| = O(|t_0| \cdot (|d|_\mathsf{m} + 1))$.

Proof. First of all, note that a error-handling rules can appear only at the end of the evaluation process, and they end it. So, we omit them, and consider them included in the *big O* notation, in the additive constant.

The measure is non-negative, and at the beginning is bound by the size $|t_0|$ of the initial term, by the size upper bound (Lemma 3.2). Rules $\to_\mathsf{e}$ and $\to_\mathsf{case}$ decrease the size, that is increased only by the multiplicative rule $\to_\mathsf{m}$ that opens an abstraction (whose content was ignored by the measure before) but the increment given by the body of the abstraction is bound by the size of the initial term by the subterm property (plus the size upper bound and the context factorization of the measure). Thus the number of $\to_\mathsf{e}$ and $\to_\mathsf{case}$ steps is bound by $|t_0| \cdot (|d|_\mathsf{m} + 1)$. Finally, one has to add the multiplicative steps themselves, and the eventual final error step—therefore, $|d| = O(|t_0| \cdot (|d|_\mathsf{m} + 1))$. ☐

Tightness of the bilinear bound, and the increased number of exponentials. We finish this study by showing that this bound is asymptotically optimal, that is, by showing a family of derivations reaching the bilinear bound. Our family is a diverging one, obtained by a simple hack of the famous diverging term $\delta\delta$. Of course, the example can be made terminating at the cost of some additional technicalities, we use a diverging family only for the sake of simplicity.

Before giving the example, let us point out a subtlety. Theorem 6 states in particular that the number of exponential steps is bilinear. Accattoli and Sacerdoti Coen have shown that in the CbV (and CbNeed) closed λ-calculus (that is, without pattern matching) a stronger bound holds: exponentials do not depend on the size of the initial term, and are linear only in the number of β-steps. It is natural to wonder whether in LIME the bilinearity involves only matching steps, and so exponentials are actually linear, or if instead both matching and exponential steps are bilinear. The example shows that both are bilinear.

For the example, we consider a unary constructor c and a zeroary constructor 0, but for the sake of conciseness the matching constructs in the family will specify only one branch. Define:

$$C_0 := (y\ y)\ \langle\cdot\rangle \qquad\qquad \delta_n := \lambda y.\lambda x_n.C_n\langle x_n\rangle$$
$$C_{n+1} := \mathsf{case\ c}(\langle\cdot\rangle)\ \{\mathsf{c}(x_n) \Rightarrow C_n\langle x_n\rangle\} \qquad t_n := (\delta_n\ \delta_n)\ 0$$

Note that

$$
\begin{aligned}
(C_n\langle 0\rangle, E) \;=\;\; & (\mathsf{case}\, \mathsf{c}(0)\,\{\mathsf{c}(x_{n-1}) \Rightarrow C_{n-1}\langle x_{n-1}\rangle\}, E) \\
\to_{\mathsf{case}}\; & (C_n\langle x_{n-1}\rangle, [x_{n-1}{\leftarrow}0]{::}E) \\
\to_{\mathsf{e}}\; & (C_{n-1}\langle 0\rangle, [x_{n-1}{\leftarrow}0]{::}E)
\end{aligned}
$$

And so we can iterate, obtaining the derivation:

$$
\begin{aligned}
(C_n\langle 0\rangle, E)\;\;\;=\;\;\; & (\mathsf{case}\, \mathsf{c}(0)\,\{\mathsf{c}(x_{n-1}) \Rightarrow C_{n-1}\langle x_{n-1}\rangle\}, E) \\
(\to_{\mathsf{case}}\to_{\mathsf{e}})^n\;\; & (C_0\langle 0\rangle, [x_0{\leftarrow}0]{::}\ldots{::}[x_{n-1}{\leftarrow}0]{::}E)
\end{aligned}
$$

Defining $E_0 := [x_0{\leftarrow}0]{::}\ldots{::}[x_{n-1}{\leftarrow}0]$ we then have $(C_n\langle 0\rangle, E)\;(\to_{\mathsf{case}}\to_{\mathsf{e}})^n\;(C_0\langle 0\rangle, E_0{::}E)$. Starting from t_n and a generic environment E, we obtain the following derivation d (that does not in fact depend on E):

$$
\begin{aligned}
(t_n, E)\;\;\;\;\;=\;\;\; & (((\lambda y.\lambda x_n.C_n\langle x_n\rangle)\,\delta_n)\,0, E) \\
\to_{\mathtt{m}}\; & ((\lambda x_n.C_n\langle x_n\rangle)0, [y{\leftarrow}\delta_n]{::}E) \\
\to_{\mathtt{m}}\; & (C_n\langle x_n\rangle, [x_n{\leftarrow}0]{::}[y{\leftarrow}\delta_n]{::}E) \\
\to_{\mathsf{e}}\; & (C_n\langle 0\rangle, [x_n{\leftarrow}0]{::}[y{\leftarrow}\delta_n]{::}E) \\
(\to_{\mathsf{case}}\to_{\mathsf{e}})^n\; & (C_0\langle 0\rangle, E_0{::}[x_n{\leftarrow}0]{::}[y{\leftarrow}\delta_n]{::}E) \\
=\; & ((y\,y)0, E_0{::}[x_n{\leftarrow}0]{::}[y{\leftarrow}\delta_n]{::}E) \\
\to_{\mathsf{e}}\; & ((y\,\delta_n)0, E_0{::}[x_n{\leftarrow}0]{::}[y{\leftarrow}\delta_n]{::}E) \\
\to_{\mathsf{e}}\; & ((\delta_n\,\delta_n)0, E_0{::}[x_n{\leftarrow}0]{::}[y{\leftarrow}\delta_n]{::}E) \\
=\; & (t_n, E_0{::}[x_n{\leftarrow}0]{::}[y{\leftarrow}\delta_n]{::}E)
\end{aligned}
$$

More compactly, $(t_n, E) \to^*_{\mathsf{CbV}} (t_n, E')$ with $O(1)$ (namely 2) $\to_{\mathtt{m}}$ steps and $\Omega(n)$ $\to_{\mathsf{case}}$ and $\Omega(n)$ $\to_{\mathsf{e}}$ steps. Now, consider the m-th iteration d^m of d starting from (t_n, ϵ). Since the size of the initial term is proportional to n (*i.e.* $|t_n| = \Theta(n)$), the number of steps in d^m is linear in the size of the initial term t_n, and each iteration is enabled by a $\beta/\mathtt{m}$ step, so it is also linear in the number of β-steps. That is, we obtained that both $|d^m|_{\mathsf{e}}$ and $|d^m|_{\mathsf{case}}$ have lower bound $\Omega(|t_n|\cdot |d^m|_{\mathtt{m}})$, reaching the bilinear upper bound for both kinds of step.

4   Call-by-Need, LINED, and the Bilinear Bound

CbNeed evaluation is the variation over CbV where arguments that are not needed are not evaluated, so that the cases in which CbV diverges but CbN terminates are avoided, marrying the efficiency of CbV with the better behavior with respect to termination of CbN—classic references on CbNeed are [15, 30, 31, 36, 37].

Being based on CbV, CbNeed rests on values, and for our study the key point turns out to be the definition of values in the case of constructors. In this section constructors are values only when their arguments are variables. Under this hypothesis, we can smoothly adapt the proof of the previous section, and show that pattern matching is negligible. In the next section we shall study the variant in which every constructor is considered as a value, independently of the shape of its arguments.

Here we adopt the presentation of CbNeed of Accattoli, Barenbaum, and Mazza [6], resting on the linear substitution calculus. With respect to LIME, the only difference is that the environment is integrated inside the term itself and the notion of program disappears—in CbNeed is not possible to disentangle the term and the environment, unless more data structures are used. Let us call this framework *LINED*, for *LInear matching calculus by NEeD*.

The grammar of LINED is:

$$
\begin{array}{rl}
\text{Terms} & t, u ::= x \mid \lambda x.t \mid t\,u \mid \mathsf{c}(t) \mid \mathsf{case}\,t\,\{b\} \mid \mathsf{err} \mid t[x\!\leftarrow\!u] \\
\text{Branches} & b ::= \mathsf{c}_i(x) \Rightarrow u_i \\
\text{Values} & v, w ::= \lambda x.t \mid \mathsf{c}(x) \mid \mathsf{err}
\end{array}
$$

$$
\begin{array}{rl}
\text{Subs. Contexts} & L ::= \langle \cdot \rangle \mid L[x\!\leftarrow\!t] \\
\text{Eval. Contexts} & N, M ::= \langle \cdot \rangle \mid N\,t \mid N[x\!\leftarrow\!u] \mid M\langle x\rangle[x\!\leftarrow\!N] \mid \mathsf{case}\,N\,\{b\} \\
\text{Answers} & a ::= L\langle v\rangle
\end{array}
$$

where $t[x\!\leftarrow\!u]$ is called an *explicit substitution* (ES) and binds x in t—it is absolutely equivalent to write let $x = u$ in t, it is just more concise. Note the category of answers, that are simply values in an environment.

The key point for CbNeed evaluation is the case $M\langle x\rangle[x\!\leftarrow\!N]$ in the definition of evaluation contexts (where we implicitly assume that M does not bind x), whose role is to move evaluation inside the ES/environment $[x\!\leftarrow\!N]$.

Rewriting rules. Now that the environment is entangled with the term, most rules have to work up to a segment of the environment, that is, a substitution context L. This is standard in the framework of the linear substitution calculus. All rules but the last one ($\to_{\mathsf{err}_3}$, that is a global rule) are defined at top level and then closed by evaluation contexts:

RULES AT TOP LEVEL (PLUS $\to_{\mathsf{err}_3}$)

$$
\begin{array}{rcll}
L\langle\lambda x.t\rangle\,u & \mapsto_{\mathsf{m}} & L\langle t[x\!\leftarrow\!u]\rangle \\
N\langle x\rangle[x\!\leftarrow\!L\langle v\rangle] & \mapsto_{\mathsf{e}} & L\langle N\langle v\rangle[x\!\leftarrow\!v]\rangle \\
\mathsf{case}\,L\langle\mathsf{c}_i(y)\rangle\,\{\mathsf{c}_i(x)\Rightarrow u_i\} & \mapsto_{\mathsf{case}} & L\langle u_i[x\!\leftarrow\!y]\rangle \\
\mathsf{c}(t) & \mapsto_{\mathsf{cstr}} & \mathsf{c}(x)[x\!\leftarrow\!t] & \text{if } t \neq y \\
\mathsf{case}\,L\langle\lambda x.t\rangle\,\{b\} & \mapsto_{\mathsf{err}_1} & \mathsf{err} \\
L\langle\mathsf{c}(x)\rangle\,t & \mapsto_{\mathsf{err}_2} & \mathsf{err} \\
N\langle\mathsf{err}\rangle & \to_{\mathsf{err}_3} & \mathsf{err}
\end{array}
$$

CONTEXTUAL CLOSURE

$$
N\langle t\rangle \to_a N\langle u\rangle \quad \text{if } t \mapsto_a u \qquad \text{for } a \in \{\mathsf{m}, \mathsf{e}, \mathsf{cstr}, \mathsf{case}, \mathsf{err}_1, \mathsf{err}_2\}
$$

We use $\to_{\mathsf{CbNeed}}$ to denote the union of all these rules. Note the side condition $t \neq y$ for $\mapsto_{\mathsf{cstr}}$: it is a compact way of saying that at least one term in t is not a variable, whose aim is to avoid silly diverging derivations. The rule can be optimized by avoiding to replace those elements in t that are already variables, but to show that the overhead is not exponential this is not needed. Note also that rule $\to_{\mathsf{case}}$ now asks the arguments of the constructor to match to be variables, because if they are not then $\to_{\mathsf{cstr}}$ applies first.

Harmony. As for LIME, harmony holds for LINED, and, as before, we show it to stress that LINED is not an ad-hoc framework. Here, however, it is formulated in a slightly different way, on open terms. The reason is that in the case of a term of the form $t[x \leftarrow u]$, the subterm t—to which we want to apply the inductive hypothesis—might be open even when the whole term is closed. Therefore harmony has now a new, third case for open terms: closed terms however cannot fall in this category, and so on them harmony takes its usual form.

Proposition 7 (Progress/harmony for LINED). *Let t be a term of LINED. Either $t \rightarrow_{\texttt{CbNeed}} u$, or t is an answer, or t is an open term of the form $N\langle x \rangle$ where N does not bind x.*

Proof. By induction on t. Cases:

- *Value, i.e. $t = v$.* Then t is an answer (and it is not of the two other forms).
- *Variable, i.e. $t = x$.* Then t is an open term.
- *Application, i.e. $t = u\,s$.* The *i.h.* on u gives
  - *u reduces or is open.* Then so does t;
  - *u is a constructor value in a substitution context.* Then $\rightarrow_{\texttt{err}_2}$ applies;
  - *u is an abstraction in a substitution context.* Then $\rightarrow_{\texttt{m}}$ applies.
  - *u is an error in a substitution context.* Then $\rightarrow_{\texttt{err}_3}$ applies.
- *Substitution, i.e. $t = u[x \leftarrow s]$.* The *i.h.* on u gives
  - *u reduces or is open with head variable not x.* Then so does t;
  - *u is open with hereditary head variable x.* Then $\rightarrow_{\texttt{e}}$ applies;
  - *u is an answer.* Then so is t.
- *Constructor that is not a value, i.e. $t = \texttt{c}(\boldsymbol{u})$.* Then $\rightarrow_{\texttt{cstr}}$ applies.
- *Match, i.e. $t = \texttt{case}\,u\,\{b\}$.* The *i.h.* on u gives:
  - *u reduces or is open.* Then so does t;
  - *u is a constructor value in a substitution context.* Then $\rightarrow_{\texttt{case}}$ applies;
  - *u is an abstraction in a substitution context.* Then $\rightarrow_{\texttt{err}_1}$ applies.
  - *u is an error in a substitution context.* Then $\rightarrow_{\texttt{err}_3}$ applies.   □

Complexity analysis. The bounds for LINED are obtained following the same reasoning done for LIME, but using a slightly different measure. There are two differences. First, in LINED evaluation enters inside ES, so now the measure takes them into account. Second, in LINED the analysis has to bound also the number of $\rightarrow_{\texttt{cstr}}$ steps, not present in LIME. Accordingly, the measure now counts 1 for every constructor out of abstractions. The measure $|\cdot|_{\texttt{n}}$ for LINED is thus defined by:

$$|x|_{\texttt{n}} := 1 \qquad |v|_{\texttt{n}} := 0 \qquad |t[x \leftarrow u]|_{\texttt{n}} := |t|_{\texttt{n}} + |u|_{\texttt{n}}$$

$$|t\,u|_{\texttt{n}} := |t|_{\texttt{n}} + |u|_{\texttt{n}} \qquad |\texttt{c}_i(\boldsymbol{t})|_{\texttt{n}} := 1 + \Sigma_{j=1}^{k_{\texttt{c}_i}}|t_j|_{\texttt{n}}$$

$$|\texttt{case}\,t\,\{\texttt{c}_i(\boldsymbol{x}) \Rightarrow \boldsymbol{u_i}\}|_{\texttt{n}} := 1 + |t|_{\texttt{n}} + max\{k_{\texttt{c}_i} + |u_i|_{\texttt{n}} \mid i = 1, \dots, k\}$$

Note that also the definition on case constructs is different with respect to the measure for LIME, as it now adds k_{c_i}. The reason: $\rightarrow_{\mathsf{case}}$ creates k_{c_i} ES that in LINED contribute to the measure, while in LIME they do not.

As before, the measure is extended to evaluation contexts by setting $|\langle\cdot\rangle|_v := 0$ and defining it on the other cases as for terms. The following properties of the measure follow immediately from the definition:

Lemma 8 (Basic properties of the measure)

1. Size Upper Bound: $|t|_n \leq |t|$ for every term t.
2. Context Factorization: $|N\langle t\rangle|_n = |N|_n + |t|_n$ and in particular $|L\langle t\rangle|_n = |L|_n + |t|_n$.

Next, we show that the measure decreases with the rules other than the multiplicative one, standing for β, and the error handling rules (that are trivial).

Lemma 9 (Exponential, matching and constructor rules decrease the measure). If $t \rightarrow_a u$ then $|t|_n > |u|_n$ for $a \in \{\mathsf{e}, \mathsf{case}, \mathsf{cstr}\}$.

Proof

– *Exponential:* $t = N\langle x\rangle[x{\leftarrow}L\langle v\rangle] \rightarrow_{\mathsf{e}} L\langle N\langle v\rangle[x{\leftarrow}v]\rangle = u$. Then:

$$|N\langle x\rangle[x{\leftarrow}L\langle v\rangle]|_n = 1 + |N|_n + 0 + |L|_n >$$
$$0 + |N|_n + 0 + |L|_n = |L\langle N\langle v\rangle[x{\leftarrow}v]\rangle|_n$$

– *Matching:* $t = \mathsf{case}\, L\langle c_i(y)\rangle\, \{c_i(x) \Rightarrow u_i\} \rightarrow_{\mathsf{case}} L\langle u_i[x{\leftarrow}y]\rangle = u$. Then:

$$|t|_n = 1 + 0 + |L|_n + max\{k_{c_j} + |u_j|_n \mid j = 1,\dots,k\}$$
$$> |L|_n + k_{c_i} + |u_i|_n \qquad\qquad = |L\langle u_i[x{\leftarrow}y]\rangle|_n$$

– *Constructor:* $t = c(t) \rightarrow_{\mathsf{cstr}} c(x)[x{\leftarrow}t] = u$. We have:

$$|c(t)|_n = 1 + \Sigma|t|_n > 0 + \Sigma|t|_n = |c(x)[x{\leftarrow}t]|_n$$

□

As for LIME, the bilinear bound rests on a subterm property. Both the property and the bound are proved exactly as in the CbV case. Moreover, the example showing that the bound for LIME is tight applies also to LINED.

Lemma 10 (LINED subterm property). Let $d : t_0 \rightarrow^*_{\mathsf{CbNeed}} u$ be a LINED derivation. Then the size of every abstraction in u and is bounded by the size $|t_0|$ of the initial term.

Theorem 11 (LINED bilinear bound). Let $d : t_0 \rightarrow^*_{\mathsf{CbNeed}} u$ be a LINED derivation. Then $|d| = O(|t_0| \cdot (|d|_m + 1))$.

5   Call-by-Need, ExpLINED, and Matching Explosion

Here we consider ExpLINED, a variant of LINED where constructors are always considered as values, not only when they are applied to variables. The effect of this change is dramatic: it re-introduces matching explosions, even if arguments are still evaluated once and for all, because constructors then can be exploited to block the evaluation of subterms. This case study is used to stress two facts: first, the no negligible cost hypothesis for pattern matching is less obvious than it seems, and second, the study of cost models can be used as a language design principle, to discriminate between different and yet equivalent operational semantics[2].

ExpLINED. For the sake of conciseness and readability, ExpLINED is defined by pointing out the differences with respect to LINED, rather than repeating all the definitions. The grammar of values of ExpLINED is:

$$v :: = \lambda x.t \mid \mathtt{err} \mid \mathtt{c}(t)$$

Dynamically, rule $\to_{\mathtt{cstr}}$ is removed while $\to_{\mathtt{case}}$ is slightly modified, to fire with every constructor, independently of the shape of its arguments:

$$\mathtt{case}\, L\langle \mathtt{c}_i(t)\rangle\, \{\mathtt{c}_i(x) \Rightarrow u_i\} \to_{\mathtt{case}} L\langle u_i[x{\leftarrow}t]\rangle$$

Matching exploding family. We are now going to define a matching exploding family. The idea is similar to that of the family for CbN, that is, to repeatedly trigger the evaluation of arguments—in CbN we used arguments of β-redexes, now we exploit constructor arguments. The family is trickier to define and analyze. In fact, the definition of the family requires a delicate decomposition via contexts, and the calculations are more involved. Moreover, it took us a lot more time to find it. The trick, however, is essentially the same used for CbN.

As before, we use two constructors $\mathtt{c}$, that is unary, and 0, that is zeroary. We introduce various notions of contexts, and the exploding family is given by $D_n\langle t_n\rangle$, but we decompose the analysis in two steps.

Terms and contexts are then defined by:

$$E_n := \mathtt{case}\, x_n\, \{\mathtt{c}(y) \Rightarrow \mathtt{case}\, y\, \{0 \Rightarrow \langle\cdot\rangle\}\}$$
$$t_n := E_n\langle E_n\langle 0\rangle\rangle$$

$$\begin{array}{ll} C_1 := \langle\cdot\rangle[x_1{\leftarrow}\mathtt{c}(0)] & D_1 := (\lambda x_1.\langle\cdot\rangle)\mathtt{c}(0) \\ C_{n+1} := C_n\langle\langle\cdot\rangle[x_{n+1}{\leftarrow}\mathtt{c}(t_n)]\rangle & D_{n+1} := D_n\langle(\lambda x_{n+1}.\langle\cdot\rangle)\mathtt{c}(t_n)\rangle \end{array}$$

---

[2] We do not prove the equivalence between the two formulations of CbNeed studied in the paper, but the difference is essentially that in one case $\mathtt{c}(t)$ is reduced to $\mathtt{c}(x)[x{\leftarrow}t]$ (via $\to_{\mathtt{cstr}}$) while in the other case it is left unchanged—the two calculi compute the same result, up to substitutions, just with very different complexities.

Proposition 12

1. Linear multiplicative prefix: *for any term u there exists a derivation d_n :* $D_n\langle u\rangle \to_{\mathtt{m}}^n C_n\langle u\rangle$;
2. Exponential pattern matching suffix: *if N does not capture x_n then there exists a context L and a derivation $e_n : C_n\langle N\langle t_n\rangle\rangle \to^* C_n\langle N\langle L\langle 0\rangle\rangle\rangle$ with $|e_n|_{\mathtt{case}} = \Omega(2^{n+1})$ and $|e_n|_{\mathtt{e}} = \Omega(2^{n+1})$.*
3. Matching exploding family: *there exists a context L and a derivation $f_n : D_n\langle t_n\rangle \to^* C_n\langle L\langle 0\rangle\rangle$ with $|D_n\langle t_n\rangle| = O(n)$, $|f_n|_{\mathtt{m}} = n$, $|f_n|_{\mathtt{case}} = \Omega(2^{n+1})$, and $|f_n|_{\mathtt{e}} = \Omega(2^{n+1})$.*

Proof Point 3 is obtained by concatenating Point 1 and Point 2 (taking the empty evaluation context $N = \langle\cdot\rangle$).

Point 1 and Point 2 are by induction on n. Cases:

- *Base case, i.e. $n = 1$.*
  1. *Linear multiplicative prefix*: the derivation d_1 is given by

  $$D_1\langle u\rangle = (\lambda x_1.u)\mathtt{c}(0)$$
  $$\to_{\mathtt{m}} u[x_1\leftarrow\mathtt{c}(0)] = C_1\langle u\rangle$$

  2. *Exponential pattern matching suffix*: the first part of the evaluation e_1 of the statement is given by

  $$
  \begin{aligned}
  C_1\langle N\langle t_1\rangle\rangle &= N\langle t_1\rangle[x_1\leftarrow\mathtt{c}(0)]\\
  &= N\langle\mathtt{case}\,x_1\,\{\mathtt{c}(y) \Rightarrow \mathtt{case}\,y\,\{0 \Rightarrow E_n\langle 0\rangle\}\}\rangle[x_1\leftarrow\mathtt{c}(0)]\\
  &\to_{\mathtt{e}} N\langle\mathtt{case}\,\mathtt{c}(0)\,\{\mathtt{c}(y) \Rightarrow \mathtt{case}\,y\,\{0 \Rightarrow E_n\langle 0\rangle\}\}\rangle[x_1\leftarrow\mathtt{c}(0)]\\
  &\to_{\mathtt{case}} N\langle\mathtt{case}\,y\,\{0 \Rightarrow E_n\langle 0\rangle\}[y\leftarrow 0]\rangle[x_1\leftarrow\mathtt{c}(0)]\\
  &\to_{\mathtt{e}} N\langle\mathtt{case}\,0\,\{0 \Rightarrow E_n\langle 0\rangle\}[y\leftarrow 0]\rangle[x_1\leftarrow\mathtt{c}(0)]\\
  &\to_{\mathtt{case}} N\langle E_n\langle 0\rangle[y\leftarrow 0]\rangle[x_1\leftarrow\mathtt{c}(0)]
  \end{aligned}
  $$

  Let us now expand E_n and continue with the second part of e_1:

  $$
  \begin{aligned}
  &N\langle E_n\langle 0\rangle[y\leftarrow 0]\rangle[x_1\leftarrow\mathtt{c}(0)]\\
  ={}& N\langle\mathtt{case}\,x_1\,\{\mathtt{c}(z) \Rightarrow \mathtt{case}\,z\,\{0 \Rightarrow 0\}\}[y\leftarrow 0]\rangle[x_1\leftarrow\mathtt{c}(0)]\\
  \to_{\mathtt{e}}{}& N\langle\mathtt{case}\,\mathtt{c}(0)\,\{\mathtt{c}(z) \Rightarrow \mathtt{case}\,z\,\{0 \Rightarrow 0\}\}[y\leftarrow 0]\rangle[x_1\leftarrow\mathtt{c}(0)]\\
  \to_{\mathtt{case}}{}& N\langle\mathtt{case}\,z\,\{0 \Rightarrow 0\}[z\leftarrow 0][y\leftarrow 0]\rangle[x_1\leftarrow\mathtt{c}(0)]\\
  \to_{\mathtt{e}}{}& N\langle\mathtt{case}\,0\,\{0 \Rightarrow 0\}[z\leftarrow 0][y\leftarrow 0]\rangle[x_1\leftarrow\mathtt{c}(0)]\\
  \to_{\mathtt{case}}{}& N\langle 0[z\leftarrow 0][y\leftarrow 0]\rangle[x_1\leftarrow\mathtt{c}(0)]\\
  ={}& N\langle L\langle 0\rangle\rangle[x_1\leftarrow\mathtt{c}(0)]\\
  ={}& C_1\langle N\langle L\langle 0\rangle\rangle\rangle
  \end{aligned}
  $$

  where $|e_1|_{\mathtt{case}} = 4 = \Omega(2^{1+1})$ and $|e_1|_{\mathtt{e}} = 4 = \Omega(2^{1+1})$.
- *Inductive case.*
  1. *Linear multiplicative prefix*: note that C_n is an evaluation context for every n. Then d_{n+1} is given by

  $$
  \begin{aligned}
  D_{n+1}\langle u\rangle ={}& D_n\langle(\lambda x_{n+1}.u)\mathtt{c}(t_n)\rangle\\
  \text{(by i.h.)} \overset{d_n}{\to_{\mathtt{m}}^n}{}& C_n\langle(\lambda x_{n+1}.u)\mathtt{c}(t_n)\rangle\\
  \to_{\mathtt{m}}{}& C_n\langle u[x_{n+1}\leftarrow\mathtt{c}(t_n)]\rangle = C_{n+1}\langle u\rangle
  \end{aligned}
  $$

2. *Exponential pattern matching suffix*: note that $E_n\langle u\rangle$ has the form $N_u\langle x_n\rangle$ with $N_u = \mathsf{case}\,\langle\cdot\rangle\,\{\mathsf{c}(y) \Rightarrow \mathsf{case}\,y\,\{0 \Rightarrow u\}\}$, and so $t_n = E_n\langle E_n\langle 0\rangle\rangle = N_{E_n\langle 0\rangle}\langle x_n\rangle$ and $E_n\langle 0\rangle = N_0\langle x_n\rangle$. The derivation e_{n+1} is constructed as follows. It starts with

$$
\begin{aligned}
&\quad C_{n+1}\langle N\langle t_{n+1}\rangle\rangle \\
=\;& C_n\langle N\langle t_{n+1}\rangle[x_{n+1}\leftarrow\mathsf{c}(t_n)]\rangle \\
=\;& C_n\langle N\langle N_{E_{n+1}\langle 0\rangle}\langle x_{n+1}\rangle\rangle[x_{n+1}\leftarrow\mathsf{c}(t_n)]\rangle \\
\rightarrow_{\mathsf{e}}\;& C_n\langle N\langle N_{E_{n+1}\langle 0\rangle}\langle\mathsf{c}(t_n)\rangle\rangle[x_{n+1}\leftarrow\mathsf{c}(t_n)]\rangle \\
\rightarrow_{\mathsf{case}}\;& C_n\langle N\langle\mathsf{case}\,y\,\{0 \Rightarrow E_{n+1}\langle 0\rangle\}[y\leftarrow t_n]\rangle[x_{n+1}\leftarrow\mathsf{c}(t_n)]\rangle
\end{aligned}
$$

Now, let us set $N' := N\langle\mathsf{case}\,y\,\{0 \Rightarrow E_{n+1}\langle 0\rangle\}[y\leftarrow\langle\cdot\rangle]\rangle[x_{n+1}\leftarrow\mathsf{c}(t_n)]$. Then, e_{n+1} continues as follows

$$
\begin{aligned}
&\quad C_n\langle N\langle\mathsf{case}\,y\,\{0 \Rightarrow E_{n+1}\langle 0\rangle\}[y\leftarrow t_n]\rangle[x_{n+1}\leftarrow\mathsf{c}(t_n)]\rangle \\
=\;& C_n\langle N'\langle t_n\rangle\rangle \\
(\text{by } i.h.)\quad \overset{e_n}{\rightarrow^*}\;& C_n\langle N'\langle L\langle 0\rangle\rangle\rangle \\
=\;& C_n\langle N\langle\mathsf{case}\,y\,\{0 \Rightarrow E_{n+1}\langle 0\rangle\}[y\leftarrow L\langle 0\rangle]\rangle[x_{n+1}\leftarrow\mathsf{c}(t_n)]\rangle \\
\rightarrow_{\mathsf{e}}\;& C_n\langle N\langle L\langle\mathsf{case}\,0\,\{0 \Rightarrow E_{n+1}\langle 0\rangle\}[y\leftarrow 0]\rangle\rangle[x_{n+1}\leftarrow\mathsf{c}(t_n)]\rangle \\
\rightarrow_{\mathsf{case}}\;& C_n\langle N\langle L\langle E_{n+1}\langle 0\rangle[y\leftarrow 0]\rangle\rangle[x_{n+1}\leftarrow\mathsf{c}(t_n)]\rangle
\end{aligned}
$$

Using the equality $E_{n+1}\langle 0\rangle = N_0\langle x_{n+1}\rangle$, we continue with

$$
\begin{aligned}
&\quad C_n\langle N\langle L\langle E_{n+1}\langle 0\rangle[y\leftarrow 0]\rangle\rangle[x_{n+1}\leftarrow\mathsf{c}(t_n)]\rangle \\
=\;& C_n\langle N\langle L\langle N_0\langle x_{n+1}\rangle[y\leftarrow 0]\rangle\rangle[x_{n+1}\leftarrow\mathsf{c}(t_n)]\rangle \\
\rightarrow_{\mathsf{e}}\;& C_n\langle N\langle L\langle N_0\langle\mathsf{c}(t_n)\rangle[y\leftarrow 0]\rangle\rangle[x_{n+1}\leftarrow\mathsf{c}(t_n)]\rangle \\
=\;& C_n\langle N\langle L\langle\mathsf{case}\,\mathsf{c}(t_n)\,\{\mathsf{c}(z) \Rightarrow \mathsf{case}\,z\,\{0 \Rightarrow 0\}\}[y\leftarrow 0]\rangle\rangle[x_{n+1}\leftarrow\mathsf{c}(t_n)]\rangle \\
\rightarrow_{\mathsf{case}}\;& C_n\langle N\langle L\langle\mathsf{case}\,z\,\{0 \Rightarrow 0\}[z\leftarrow t_n][y\leftarrow 0]\rangle\rangle[x_{n+1}\leftarrow\mathsf{c}(t_n)]\rangle
\end{aligned}
$$

Now, let us set $N'' := N\langle L\langle\mathsf{case}\,z\,\{0 \Rightarrow 0\}[z\leftarrow\langle\cdot\rangle][y\leftarrow 0]\rangle\rangle[x_{n+1}\leftarrow\mathsf{c}(t_n)]$. Then, e_{n+1} continues and ends as follows

$$
\begin{aligned}
&\quad C_n\langle N\langle L\langle\mathsf{case}\,z\,\{0 \Rightarrow 0\}[z\leftarrow t_n][y\leftarrow 0]\rangle\rangle[x_{n+1}\leftarrow\mathsf{c}(t_n)]\rangle \\
=\;& C_n\langle N''\langle t_n\rangle\rangle \\
(\text{by } i.h.)\quad \overset{e_n}{\rightarrow^*}\;& C_n\langle N''\langle L'\langle 0\rangle\rangle\rangle \\
=\;& C_n\langle N\langle L\langle\mathsf{case}\,z\,\{0 \Rightarrow 0\}[z\leftarrow L'\langle 0\rangle][y\leftarrow 0]\rangle\rangle[x_{n+1}\leftarrow\mathsf{c}(t_n)]\rangle \\
\rightarrow_{\mathsf{e}}\;& C_n\langle N\langle L\langle L'\langle\mathsf{case}\,0\,\{0 \Rightarrow 0\}[z\leftarrow 0]\rangle[y\leftarrow 0]\rangle\rangle[x_{n+1}\leftarrow\mathsf{c}(t_n)]\rangle \\
\rightarrow_{\mathsf{case}}\;& C_n\langle N\langle L\langle L'\langle 0[z\leftarrow 0]\rangle[y\leftarrow 0]\rangle\rangle[x_{n+1}\leftarrow\mathsf{c}(t_n)]\rangle \\
=\;& C_n\langle N\langle L\langle L''\langle 0\rangle\rangle[x_{n+1}\leftarrow\mathsf{c}(t_n)]\rangle \\
=\;& C_{n+1}\langle N\langle L''\langle 0\rangle\rangle\rangle
\end{aligned}
$$

Now, $|e_{n+1}|_{\mathsf{case}} = 4 + 2\cdot|e_n|_{\mathsf{case}} =_{i.h.} 4 + 2\cdot\Omega(2^{n+1}) = \Omega(2^{(n+1)+1})$ and $|e_{n+1}|_{\mathsf{e}} = 4 + 2\cdot|e_n|_{\mathsf{e}} =_{i.h.} 4 + 2\cdot\Omega(2^{n+1}) = \Omega(2^{(n+1)+1})$. $\qquad\square$

6   Conclusions

Contributions. For functional programming languages, it is generally assumed that the number of function calls, aka β-steps, is a reasonable cost model, since all other operations are dominated by the cost of β-steps. This paper shows that such a *negligible cost hypothesis* is less obvious than it seems at first sight, by considering constructors and pattern matching and showing that in CbN the number of pattern matching steps can be exponential in the number of β-steps. Furthermore, it shows that matching explosions are possible also in CbNeed, if evaluation is defined naively.

On the positive side, we showed that in CbV, and for a less naive formulation of CbNeed, the cost of pattern matching is indeed negligible: the number of matching steps is bilinear, that is, linear in the number of β-steps and in the size of the initial term. Summing up, we confirmed the negligible cost hypothesis for pattern matching, pointing out at the same time its subtleties. A novelty, is the use of cost models as a language design principle, to discriminate—in this paper—between otherwise equivalent formulations of CbNeed.

Coq and further extensions. The main motivation behind our work is the development of the analysis of the Coq abstract machine, that executes a language richer than the λ-calculus, including in particular pattern matching. To that aim, our CbNeed formalism, LINED, has to be further extended with fixpoints, and evaluation has to be generalized as to handle open terms and go under abstraction. Here we omitted the study of fixpoints because they behave like β-redexes, being function calls, and their cost is not negligible, *i.e.* they have to be counted for complexity analyses. Moreover, all our results smoothly scale up to languages with fixpoints, without surprises. We plan to include them in a longer, journal version of this work. Open terms and evaluation under abstraction instead require more sophisticated machineries [5,9–12], whose adaptation to CbNeed and pattern matching is under development.

It would also be interesting to study other features of programming languages, such as first-class (delimited) continuations or other forms of effects, even if they are not part of the language executed by the Coq abstract machine.

Acknowledgements. This work has been partially funded by the ANR JCJC grant COCA HOLA (ANR-16-CE40-004-01).

References

1. Abadi, M., Cardelli, L., Curien, P.L., Lévy, J.J.: Explicit substitutions. J. Funct. Program. **1**(4), 375–416 (1991)
2. Accattoli, B.: An abstract factorization theorem for explicit substitutions. In: RTA, pp. 6–21 (2012)
3. Accattoli, B.: COCA HOLA (2016). https://sites.google.com/site/beniaminoaccattoli/coca-hola

4. Accattoli, B.: The complexity of abstract machines. In: WPTE@FSCD 2016, pp. 1–15 (2016)
5. Accattoli, B.: The useful MAM, a reasonable implementation of the strong λ-calculus. In: Väänänen, J., Hirvonen, Å., de Queiroz, R. (eds.) WoLLIC 2016. LNCS, vol. 9803, pp. 1–21. Springer, Heidelberg (2016). https://doi.org/10.1007/978-3-662-52921-8_1
6. Accattoli, B., Barenbaum, P., Mazza, D.: Distilling abstract machines. In: ICFP 2014, pp. 363–376. ACM (2014)
7. Accattoli, B., Barras, B.: Environments and the complexity of abstract machines (2017). Accepted to PPDP 2017
8. Accattoli, B., Bonelli, E., Kesner, D., Lombardi, C.: A nonstandard standardization theorem. In: POPL, pp. 659–670 (2014)
9. Accattoli, B., Coen, C.S.: On the relative usefulness of fireballs. In: LICS 2015, pp. 141–155. IEEE Computer Society (2015)
10. Accattoli, B., Dal Lago, U.: (Leftmost-outermost) beta reduction is invariant, indeed. Logical Methods Comput. Sci. **12**(1), 1–46 (2016)
11. Accattoli, B., Guerrieri, G.: Open call-by-value. In: Igarashi, A. (ed.) APLAS 2016. LNCS, vol. 10017, pp. 206–226. Springer, Cham (2016). https://doi.org/10.1007/978-3-319-47958-3_12
12. Accattoli, B., Guerrieri, G.: Implementing open call-by-value. In: Dastani, M., Sirjani, M. (eds.) FSEN 2017. LNCS, vol. 10522, pp. 1–19. Springer, Cham (2017). https://doi.org/10.1007/978-3-319-68972-2_1
13. Accattoli, B., Paolini, L.: Call-by-value solvability, revisited. In: Schrijvers, T., Thiemann, P. (eds.) FLOPS 2012. LNCS, vol. 7294, pp. 4–16. Springer, Heidelberg (2012). https://doi.org/10.1007/978-3-642-29822-6_4
14. Accattoli, B., Sacerdoti Coen, C.: On the value of variables. In: Kohlenbach, U., Barceló, P., de Queiroz, R. (eds.) WoLLIC 2014. LNCS, vol. 8652, pp. 36–50. Springer, Heidelberg (2014). https://doi.org/10.1007/978-3-662-44145-9_3
15. Ariola, Z.M., Felleisen, M.: The call-by-need lambda calculus. J. Funct. Program. **7**(3), 265–301 (1997)
16. Barras, B.: Auto-validation d'un système de preuves avec familles inductives. Ph.D. thesis, Université Paris 7 (1999)
17. Blelloch, G.E., Greiner, J.: Parallelism in sequential functional languages. In: FPCA 1995, pp. 226–237. ACM (1995)
18. Charguéraud, A., Pottier, F.: Machine-checked verification of the correctness and amortized complexity of an efficient union-find implementation. In: Urban, C., Zhang, X. (eds.) ITP 2015. LNCS, vol. 9236, pp. 137–153. Springer, Cham (2015). https://doi.org/10.1007/978-3-319-22102-1_9
19. Cirstea, H., Kirchner, C.: The rewriting calculus - part I. Logic J. IGPL **9**(3), 339–375 (2001)
20. Coq Development Team: The coq proof-assistant reference manual, version 8.6 (2016). http://coq.inria.fr
21. Dal Lago, U., Martini, S.: Derivational complexity is an invariant cost model. In: van Eekelen, M., Shkaravska, O. (eds.) FOPARA 2009. LNCS, vol. 6324, pp. 100–113. Springer, Heidelberg (2010). https://doi.org/10.1007/978-3-642-15331-0_7
22. Dal Lago, U., Martini, S.: On constructor rewrite systems and the lambda-calculus. In: Albers, S., Marchetti-Spaccamela, A., Matias, Y., Nikoletseas, S., Thomas, W. (eds.) ICALP 2009. LNCS, vol. 5556, pp. 163–174. Springer, Heidelberg (2009). https://doi.org/10.1007/978-3-642-02930-1_14
23. Danvy, O., Zerny, I.: A synthetic operational account of call-by-need evaluation. In: PPDP 2013, pp. 97–108. ACM (2013)

24. Fernández, M., Siafakas, N.: New developments in environment machines. Electr. Notes Theor. Comput. Sci. **237**, 57–73 (2009)
25. Grégoire, B., Leroy, X.: A compiled implementation of strong reduction. In: ICFP 2002, pp. 235–246. ACM (2002)
26. Jay, C.B., Kesner, D.: First-class patterns. J. Funct. Program. **19**(2), 191–225 (2009)
27. Jeannin, J., Kozen, D.: Computing with capsules. J. Automata Lang. Comb. **17**(2–4), 185–204 (2012)
28. Kesner, D.: The theory of calculi with explicit substitutions revisited. In: Duparc, J., Henzinger, T.A. (eds.) CSL 2007. LNCS, vol. 4646, pp. 238–252. Springer, Heidelberg (2007). https://doi.org/10.1007/978-3-540-74915-8_20
29. Klop, J.W., van Oostrom, V., de Vrijer, R.C.: Lambda calculus with patterns. Theor. Comput. Sci. **398**(1–3), 16–31 (2008)
30. Launchbury, J.: A natural semantics for lazy evaluation. In: POPL 1993, pp. 144–154. ACM Press (1993)
31. Maraist, J., Odersky, M., Wadler, P.: The call-by-need lambda calculus. J. Funct. Program. **8**(3), 275–317 (1998)
32. Milner, R.: Local bigraphs and confluence: two conjectures. Electr. Notes Theor. Comput. Sci. **175**(3), 65–73 (2007)
33. Pierce, B.C.: Types and Programming Languages. MIT Press, Cambridge (2002)
34. Sands, D., Gustavsson, J., Moran, A.: Lambda calculi and linear speedups. In: Mogensen, T.Æ., Schmidt, D.A., Sudborough, I.H. (eds.) The Essence of Computation. LNCS, vol. 2566, pp. 60–82. Springer, Heidelberg (2002). https://doi.org/10.1007/3-540-36377-7_4
35. Sergey, I., Vytiniotis, D., Peyton Jones, S.L.: Modular, higher-order cardinality analysis in theory and practice. In: POPL 2014, pp. 335–348 (2014)
36. Sestoft, P.: Deriving a lazy abstract machine. J. Funct. Program. **7**(3), 231–264 (1997)
37. Wadsworth, C.P.: Semantics and pragmatics of the lambda-calculus. Ph.D. thesis, Oxford (1971). Chapter 4
38. Walker, D.: Substructural type systems. In: Pierce, B.C. (ed.) Advanced Topics in Types and Programming Languages, pp. 3–43. The MIT Press (2004)
39. Wright, A.K., Felleisen, M.: A syntactic approach to type soundness. Inf. Comput. **115**(1), 38–94 (1994)

A Lambda Calculus for Density Matrices with Classical and Probabilistic Controls

Alejandro Díaz-Caro$^{(\boxtimes)}$

Universidad Nacional de Quilmes & CONICET,
Roque Sáenz Peña 352, B1876BXD Bernal, Buenos Aires, Argentina
alejandro.diaz-caro@unq.edu.ar

Abstract. In this paper we present two flavors of a quantum extension to the lambda calculus. The first one, λ_ρ, follows the approach of classical control/quantum data, where the quantum data is represented by density matrices. We provide an interpretation for programs as density matrices and functions upon them. The second one, λ_ρ°, takes advantage of the density matrices presentation in order to follow the mixed trace of programs in a kind of generalised density matrix. Such a control can be seen as a weaker form of the quantum control and data approach.

Keywords: Lambda calculus · Quantum computing · Density matrices · Classical control

1 Introduction

In the last decade several quantum extensions to lambda calculus have been investigated,e.g. [5,6,11,19,22,23,31]. In all of those approaches, the language chosen to represent the quantum state are vectors in a Hilbert space. However, an alternative formulation of quantum mechanics can be made using density matrices. Density matrices provide a way to describe a quantum system in which the state is not fully known. More precisely, density matrices describe quantum systems in a mixed state, that is, a statistical set of several quantum states. All the postulates of quantum mechanics can be described in such a formalism, and hence, also quantum computing can be done using density matrices.

The first postulate states that a quantum system can be fully described by a density matrix ρ, which is a positive operator with trace (tr) one. If a system is in state ρ_i with probability p_i, then the density matrix of the system is $\sum_i p_i \rho_i$. The second postulate states that the evolution of a quantum system ρ is described with a unitary operator U by $U\rho U^\dagger$, where $U^\dagger$ is the adjoint operator of U. The third postulate states that the measurement is described by a set of measurement operators $\{\pi_i\}_i$ with $\sum_i \pi_i^\dagger \pi_i = \mathsf{I}$, so that the output of the measurement is i, with probability $\mathsf{tr}(\pi_i^\dagger \pi_i \rho)$, leaving the sate of the system

---

A. Díaz-Caro—Supported by projects STIC-AmSud 16STIC05 FoQCoSS, PICT 2015-1208 and the Laboratoire International Associé "INFINIS".

B.-Y.E. Chang (Ed.): APLAS 2017, LNCS 10695, pp. 448–467, 2017.
https://doi.org/10.1007/978-3-319-71237-6_22

as $\frac{\pi_i \rho \pi_i^\dagger}{\text{tr}(\pi_i^\dagger \pi_i \rho)}$. The fourth postulate states that from two systems ρ and ρ', the composed one can be described by the tensor product of those $\rho \otimes \rho'$.

Naturally, if we want to use the output of a measurement as a condition in the classical control, we need to know that output. However, density matrices can still be used as a way to compare processes before running them. For example the process of tossing a coin, and according to its result, applying Z or not to a balanced superposition, and the process of tossing a coin and not looking at its result, may look quite different in most quantum programming languages. Yet both processes output the same density matrix, and so they are indistinguishable.

In [20], Selinger introduced a language of quantum flow charts, and an interpretation of his language into a CPO of density matrices. After this paper, the language of density matrices has been widely used in quantum programming, e.g. [9,14,15,25,28]. Indeed, the book "Foundations of Quantum Programming" [27] is entirely written in the language of density matrices. Yet, as far as we know, no lambda calculus for density matrix have been proposed.

Apart from the distinction of languages by how they treat the quantum states (vectors in a Hilbert space or density matrices), we also can distinguish the languages on how the control is considered: either quantumly or classically. The idea of quantum data/classical control stated by Selinger in [20] induced a quantum lambda calculus in this paradigm [22]. Later, this calculus was the base to construct the programming language Quipper [16], an embedded, scalable, functional programming language for quantum computing. The concept of quantum data/classical control declares that quantum computers will run in a specialized device attached to a classical computer, and it is the classical computer which will instruct the quantum computer what operations to perform over which qubits, and then read the classical result after a measurement. It is a direct consequence from the observation that quantum circuits are classical (i.e. one cannot superpose circuits or measure them). Several studies have been done under this paradigm, e.g. [2,16,19,22,31].

Dually to the quantum data/classical control paradigm, there is what we can call the quantum data and control paradigm. The idea is to provide a computational definition of the notions of vector space and bilinear functions. In the realm of quantum walks, quantum control is not uncommon (e.g. [1,3]). Also, several high-level languages on quantum control have been proposed in the past (e.g. [2,8,29,30]), however, up to now, no complete lambda-calculus with quantum control have been proposed. We benefit, though, from the long line of works in this direction [4–7,13].

In this paper, we propose a quantum extension to the lambda calculus, λ_ρ, in the quantum data/classical control paradigm, where the quantum data is given by density matrices, as first suggested by Selinger's interpretation of quantum flow charts [20]. Then, we propose a modification of such a calculus, called λ_ρ°, in which we generalise the density matrices to the classical control: That is, after a measurement, we take all the possible outcomes in a kind of generalised density matrix of arbitrary terms. The control does not become quantum, since it is not possible to superpose programs in the quantum sense. However, we consider the density matrix of the mixed state of programs arising from a measurement. Therefore, this can be considered as a kind of probabilistic control, or even another way, perhaps weaker, of quantum control.

Outline of the Paper. In Sect. 2 we introduce the typed calculus λ_ρ, which manipulates density matrices, and we give two interpretations of the calculus. One where the terms are interpreted into a generalisation of mixed states, and another where the terms are interpreted into density matrices. Then we prove some properties of those interpretations. In Sect. 3 we introduce a modification of λ_ρ, called λ_ρ°, where the output of a measurement produce a sum with all the possible outputs. We then extend the interpretation of λ_ρ to accommodate λ_ρ°, and prove its basic properties. In Sect. 4 we prove the Subject Reduction (Theorem 4.4) and Progress (Theorem 4.7) properties for both calculi. In Sect. 5 we give two interesting examples, in both calculi. Finally, in Sect. 6, we conclude and discuss some future work. A long version of this paper, with detailed proofs in a 10-pages appendix, has been submitted to the arXiv [10].

2   Classical-Control Calculus with Probabilistic Rewriting

2.1   Definitions

The grammar of terms, given in Table 1, have been divided in three categories.

1. Standard lambda calculus terms: Variables from a set Vars, abstractions and applications.
2. The four postulates of quantum mechanics, with the measurement postulate restricted to measurements in the computational basis[1]: ρ^n to represent the density matrix of a quantum system. $U^n t$ to describe its evolution. $\pi^n t$ to measure it. $t \otimes t$ to describe the density matrix of a composite system (that is, a non entangled system composed of two subsystems).
3. Two constructions for the classical control: a pair (b^m, ρ^n), where b^m is the output of a measurement in the computational basis and ρ^n is the resulting density matrix, and the conditional letcase construction reading the output of the measurement.

The rewrite system, given in Table 2, is described by the relation $\longrightarrow_p$, which is a probabilistic relation where p is the probability of occurrence. If U^m is applied to ρ^n, with $m \leq n$, we write $\overline{U^m}$ for $U^m \otimes I^{n-m}$. Similarly, we write $\overline{\pi^m}$ when we apply this measurement operator to ρ^n for $\{\pi_0 \otimes I^{n-m}, \ldots, \pi_{2^m-1} \otimes I^{n-m}\}$. If the unitary U^m needs to be applied, for example, to the last m qubits of ρ^n instead of the first m, we will need to use the unitary transformation $I^{n-m} \otimes U^m$ instead. And if it is applied to the qubits k to $k+m$, then, we can use $\overline{I^{k-1} \otimes U^m}$.

---

[1] A generalisation to any arbitrary measurement can be considered in a future, however, for the sake of simplicity in the classical control, we consider only measurements in the computational basis, which is a common practice in quantum lambda calculi [11,17,19,21,22,31].

Table 1. Grammar of terms of λ_ρ.

$$
\begin{aligned}
t &:= x \mid \lambda x.t \mid tt & \text{(Standard lambda calculus)}\\
&\mid \rho^n \mid U^n t \mid \pi^n t \mid t \otimes t & \text{(Quantum postulates)}\\
&\mid (b^m, \rho^n) \mid \mathsf{letcase}\ x = r\ \text{in}\ \{t, \ldots, t\} & \text{(Classical control)}
\end{aligned}
$$

where:

- $n, m \in \mathbb{N}$, $m \le n$.
- ρ^n is a density matrix of n-qubits, that is, a positive $2^n \times 2^n$-matrix with trace 1.
- $b^m \in \mathbb{N}$, $0 \le b^m < 2^m$.
- $\{t, \ldots, t\}$ contains 2^m terms.
- U^n is a unitary operator of dimension $2^n \times 2^n$, that is, a $2^n \times 2^n$-matrix such that $(U^n)^\dagger = (U^n)^{-1}$.
- $\pi^n = \{\pi_0, \ldots, \pi_{2^n - 1}\}$, describes a quantum measurement in the computational basis, where each π_i is a projector operator of dimension 2^n projecting to one vector of the canonical base.

This rewrite system assumes that after a measurement, the result is known. However, since we are working with density matrices we could also provide an alternative rewrite system where after a measurement, the system turns into a mixed state. We left this possibility for Sect. 3.

The type system, including the grammar of types and the derivation rules, is given in Table 3. The type system is affine, so variables can be used at most once, forbidding from cloning a density matrix.

Example 2.1. The teleportation algorithm, while it is better described by pure states, can be expressed in the following way:

Let $\beta_{00} = \frac{1}{2}(|00\rangle\langle 00| + |00\rangle\langle 11| + |11\rangle\langle 00| + |11\rangle\langle 11|)$. Then, the following term expresses the teleportation algorithm.

$$\lambda x.\mathsf{letcase}\ y = \pi^2(\mathsf{H}^1(\mathsf{Cnot}^2(x \otimes \beta_{00})))\ \text{in}\ \{y, \mathsf{Z}_3 y, \mathsf{X}_3 y, \mathsf{Z}_3 \mathsf{X}_3 y\}$$

where $\mathsf{Z}_3 = I \otimes I \otimes \mathsf{Z}^1$ and $\mathsf{X}_3 = I \otimes I \otimes \mathsf{X}^1$.

The type derivation is as follows.

$$
\cfrac{
  \cfrac{
    \cfrac{
      y:3 \vdash y:3
    }{}\,\text{ax}
    \quad
    \cfrac{
      \cfrac{y:3 \vdash y:3}{y:3 \vdash \mathsf{Z}_3 y:3}\text{ax}
      \;
      \cfrac{y:3 \vdash y:3}{y:3 \vdash \mathsf{X}_3 y:3}\text{ax,u}
      \;
      \cfrac{\cfrac{y:3 \vdash y:3}{y:3 \vdash \mathsf{X}_3 y:3}\text{ax}}{y:3 \vdash \mathsf{Z}_3 \mathsf{X}_3 y:3}\text{u}
    }{}
    \quad
    \cfrac{
      \cfrac{
        \cfrac{x:1 \vdash x:1 \;\text{ax} \quad \vdash \beta_{00}:2\;\text{ax}_\rho}{x:1 \vdash x \otimes \beta_{00}:3}\otimes
      }{x:1 \vdash \mathsf{Cnot}^2(x \otimes \beta_{00}):3}\,\text{u}
    }{
      \cfrac{x:1 \vdash \mathsf{H}^1(\mathsf{Cnot}^2(x \otimes \beta_{00})):3}{x:1 \vdash \pi^2(\mathsf{H}^1(\mathsf{Cnot}^2(x \otimes \beta_{00}))):(2,3)}\text{u}
    }
  }{
    x:1 \vdash \mathsf{letcase}\ y = \pi^2(\mathsf{H}^1(\mathsf{Cnot}^2(x \otimes \beta_{00})))\ \text{in}\ \{y, \mathsf{Z}_3 y, \mathsf{X} y, \mathsf{Z}_3 \mathsf{X}_3 y\}:3
  }\,\text{lc}
}{
  \vdash \lambda x.\mathsf{letcase}\ y = \pi^2(\mathsf{H}^1(\mathsf{Cnot}^2(x \otimes \beta_{00})))\ \text{in}\ \{y, \mathsf{Z}_3 y, \mathsf{X}_3 y, \mathsf{Z}_3 \mathsf{X}_3 y\}:1 \multimap 3
}\,\multimap_i
$$

Table 2. Rewrite system for λ_ρ.

$$(\lambda x.t)r \longrightarrow_1 t[r/x]$$

$$U^m \rho^n \longrightarrow_1 \rho'^n \qquad \text{with } \rho'^n = \overline{U^m}\rho^n\overline{U^m}^\dagger$$

$$\pi^m \rho^n \longrightarrow_{p_i} (i, \rho_i^n) \qquad \text{with } \begin{cases} p_i = \mathsf{tr}(\overline{\pi_i}^\dagger \overline{\pi_i} \rho^n) \\ \rho_i^n = \frac{\overline{\pi_i}\rho^n\overline{\pi_i}^\dagger}{p_i} \end{cases}$$

$$\rho \otimes \rho' \longrightarrow_1 \rho'' \qquad \text{with } \rho'' = \rho \otimes \rho'$$

$$\mathsf{letcase}\ x = (b^m, \rho^n)\ \mathsf{in}\ \{t_0, \ldots, t_{2^m-1}\} \longrightarrow_1 t_{b^m}[\rho^n/x]$$

$$\frac{t \longrightarrow_p r}{\lambda x.t \longrightarrow_p \lambda x.r} \qquad \frac{t \longrightarrow_p r}{ts \longrightarrow_p rs} \qquad \frac{t \longrightarrow_p r}{st \longrightarrow_p sr} \qquad \frac{t \longrightarrow_p r}{U^n t \longrightarrow_p U^n r}$$

$$\frac{t \longrightarrow_p r}{\pi^n t \longrightarrow_p \pi^n r} \qquad \frac{t \longrightarrow_p r}{t \otimes s \longrightarrow_p r \otimes s} \qquad \frac{t \longrightarrow_p r}{s \otimes t \longrightarrow_p s \otimes r}$$

$$\frac{t \longrightarrow_p r}{\mathsf{letcase}\ x = t\ \mathsf{in}\ \{s_0, \ldots, s_n\} \longrightarrow_p \mathsf{letcase}\ x = r\ \mathsf{in}\ \{s_0, \ldots, s_n\}}$$

Table 3. Type system for λ_ρ.

$$A := n \mid (m,n) \mid A \multimap A$$

where $m \leq n \in \mathbb{N}$.

$$\frac{}{\Gamma, x : A \vdash x : A}\ \mathsf{ax} \qquad \frac{\Gamma, x : A \vdash t : B}{\Gamma \vdash \lambda x.t : A \multimap B}\ \multimap_i \qquad \frac{\Gamma \vdash t : A \multimap B \quad \Delta \vdash r : A}{\Gamma, \Delta \vdash tr : B}\ \multimap_e$$

$$\frac{}{\Gamma \vdash \rho^n : n}\ \mathsf{ax}_\rho \qquad \frac{\Gamma \vdash t : n}{\Gamma \vdash U^m t : n}\ \mathsf{u} \qquad \frac{\Gamma \vdash t : n}{\Gamma \vdash \pi^m t : (m,n)}\ \mathsf{m} \qquad \frac{\Gamma \vdash t : n \quad \Delta \vdash r : m}{\Gamma, \Delta \vdash t \otimes r : n+m}\ \otimes$$

$$\frac{}{\Gamma \vdash (b^m, \rho^n) : (m,n)}\ \mathsf{ax_{am}} \qquad \frac{x : n \vdash t_0 : A \quad \ldots \quad x : n \vdash t_{2^m-1} : A \quad \Gamma \vdash r : (m,n)}{\Gamma \vdash \mathsf{letcase}\ x = r\ \mathsf{in}\ \{t_0, \ldots, t_{2^m-1}\} : A}\ \mathsf{lc}$$

2.2 Interpretation

We give two interpretations for terms. One, noted by $(\!|\cdot|\!)$, is the interpretation of terms into density matrices and functions upon them, and the other, noted by $[\![\cdot]\!]$, is a more fine-grained interpretation, interpreting terms into a generalisation of mixed states. In particular, we want $[\![\pi^n\rho^n]\!] = \{(\mathsf{tr}(\pi_i^\dagger \pi_i \rho^n), \frac{\pi_i \rho^n \pi_i^\dagger}{\mathsf{tr}(\pi_i^\dagger \pi_i \rho^n)})\}_i$, while $(\!|\pi^n\rho|\!) = \sum_i \pi_i \rho^n \pi_i^\dagger$. However, since the letcase construction needs also to distinguish each possible result of a measurement, we will carry those results in the interpretation $[\![\cdot]\!]$, making it a set of triplets instead of a set of tuples.

Let $\mathbb{N}^\varepsilon = \mathbb{N}_0 \cup \{\varepsilon\}$, so terms are interpreted into sets of triplets (p, b, e) with $p \in \mathbb{R}_+^{\leq 1}$, representing the probability, $b \in \mathbb{N}^\varepsilon$, representing the output of a measurement if it occurred, and $e \in [\![A]\!]$ for some type A and an interpretation $[\![\cdot]\!]$ on types yet to define. In addition, we consider that the sets $\{\dots, (p, b, e), (q, b, e), \dots\}$ and $\{\dots, (p+q, b, e), \dots\}$ are equal. Finally, we define the weight function as $\mathsf{w}(\{(p_i, b_i, e_i)\}_i) = \sum_i p_i$. We are interested in sets S such that $\mathsf{w}(S) = 1$.

The interpretation of types is given in Table 4. $\mathcal{D}_n$ is the set of density matrices of n-qubits, that is $\mathcal{D}_n = \{\rho \mid \rho \in \mathcal{M}_{2^n \times 2^n}^+ \text{ such that } \mathsf{tr}(\rho) = 1\}$, where $\mathcal{M}_{2^n \times 2^n}^+$ is the set of positive matrices of size $2^n \times 2^n$. $P(b, A)$ is the following property: $[A = \vec{B} \multimap (m, n) \implies b \neq \varepsilon]$, where $\vec{A} \multimap B$ is any of B, $A \multimap B$, $A_1 \multimap A_2 \multimap B, \dots, A_1 \multimap \cdots \multimap A_n \multimap B$. We also establish the convention that $P(\{(p_i, b_i, e_i)\}_i, A) = \bigwedge_i P(b_i, A)$. Finally, we write $\mathsf{trd}(S) = \{e \mid (p, b, e) \in S\}$.

Table 4. Interpretation of types

$$[\![n]\!] = \mathcal{D}_n$$
$$[\![(m, n)]\!] = \mathcal{D}_n$$
$$[\![A \multimap B]\!] = \{f \mid \forall e \in [\![A]\!], \forall b \in \mathbb{N}^\varepsilon \text{ s.t. } P(b, A),$$
$$\mathsf{trd}(f(b, e)) \subseteq [\![B]\!], \mathsf{w}(f(b, e)) = 1 \text{ and } P(f(b, e), B)\}$$

Let $E = \bigcup_{A \in \mathsf{Types}} [\![A]\!]$. We denote by θ to a valuation $\mathsf{Vars} \to \mathbb{N}^\varepsilon \times E$. Then, we define the interpretation of terms with respect to a given valuation θ in Table 5.

Definition 2.2. $\theta \vDash \Gamma$ *if and only if, for all* $x : A \in \Gamma$, $\theta(x) = (b, e)$ *with* $e \in [\![A]\!]$, *and* $P(b, A)$.

Lemma 2.3 states that a term with type (m, n) (or an arrow type ending in (m, n)), will be the result of a measurement, and hence, its interpretation will carry the results $b_i \neq \varepsilon$.

Lemma 2.3. *Let* $\Gamma \vdash t : \vec{A} \multimap (m, n)$, $\theta \vDash \Gamma$, *and* $[\![t]\!]_\theta$ *be well-defined. Then,* $[\![t]\!]_\theta = \{(p_i, b_i, e_i)\}_i$ *with* $b_i \neq \varepsilon$ *and* $e_i \in [\![\vec{A} \multimap (m, n)]\!]_\theta$.

Proof. By induction on the type derivation. □

Lemma 2.4 states that the interpretation of a typed term is well-defined.

Lemma 2.4. *If* $\Gamma \vdash t : A$ *and* $\theta \vDash \Gamma$, *then* $\mathsf{w}([\![t]\!]_\theta) = 1$, *and* $\mathsf{trd}([\![t]\!]_\theta) \subseteq [\![A]\!]$.

Proof. By induction on t. □

Table 5. Interpretation of terms

$$[\![x]\!]_\theta = \{(1, b, e)\} \text{ where } \theta(x) = (b, e)$$

$$[\![\lambda x.t]\!]_\theta = \{(1, \varepsilon, (b, e) \mapsto [\![t]\!]_{\theta, x=(b,e)})\}$$

$$[\![tr]\!]_\theta = \{(p_i q_j h_{ijk}, b''_{ijk}, g_{ijk}) \,|\, [\![r]\!]_\theta = \{(p_i, b_i, e_i)\}_i,$$
$$[\![t]\!]_\theta = \{(q_j, b'_j, f_j)\}_j \text{ and}$$
$$f_j(b_i, e_i) = \{(h_{ijk}, b''_{ijk}, g_{ijk})\}_k\}$$

$$[\![\rho^n]\!]_\theta = \{(1, \varepsilon, \rho^n)\}$$

$$[\![U^n t]\!]_\theta = \{(p_i, \varepsilon, \overline{U^n}\rho_i\overline{U^n}^\dagger) \,|\, [\![t]\!]_\theta = \{(p_i, b_i, \rho_i)\}_i\}$$

$$[\![\pi^m t]\!]_\theta = \left\{\left(p_j \mathsf{tr}(\overline{\pi_i}^\dagger \overline{\pi_i}\rho_j), i, \frac{\overline{\pi_i}\rho_j\overline{\pi_i}^\dagger}{\mathsf{tr}(\overline{\pi_i}^\dagger\overline{\pi_i}\rho_j)}\right) \,\Big|\, [\![t]\!]_\theta = \{(p_j, b_j, \rho_j)\}_j\right\}$$

$$[\![t \otimes r]\!]_\theta = \{(p_i q_j, \varepsilon, \rho_i \otimes \rho'_j) \,|\, [\![t]\!]_\theta = \{(p_i, b_i, \rho_i)\}_i \text{ and}$$
$$[\![r]\!]_\theta = \{(q_j, b'_j, \rho'_j)\}_j\}$$

$$[\![(b^m, \rho^n)]\!]_\theta = \{(1, b^m, \rho^n)\}$$

$$[\![\text{letcase } x = r \text{ in } \{t_0, \ldots, t_{2^m-1}\}]\!]_\theta = \{(p_i q_{ij}, b'_{ij}, e_{ij}) \,|$$
$$[\![r]\!]_\theta = \{(p_i, b_i, \rho_i)\}_i \text{ and}$$
$$[\![t_{b_i}]\!]_{\theta, x=(\varepsilon, \rho_i)} = \{(q_{ij}, b'_{ij}, e_{ij})\}_j\}$$

Since the interpretation $[\![\cdot]\!]$ of a term is morally a mixed state, the interpretation $(\!|\cdot|\!)$, which should be the density matrix of such a state, is naturally defined using the interpretation $[\![\cdot]\!]$.

Definition 2.5. *Let* $e \in [\![A]\!]$ *for some* A, θ *a valuation, and* t *be a term such that* $[\![t]\!]_\theta = \{(p_i, b_i, e_i)\}_i$. *We state the convention that* $(b, e) \mapsto \sum_i p_i e_i = \sum_i p_i((b, e) \mapsto e_i)$. *We define* $[e]$ *and* $(\!|t|\!)_\theta$ *by mutual recursion as follows:*

$$[\rho] = \rho$$

$$[(b, e) \mapsto [\![t]\!]_{\theta, x=(b,e)}] = (b, e) \mapsto (\!|t|\!)_{\theta, x=(b,e)}$$

$$(\!|t|\!)_\theta = \sum_i p_i [e_i]$$

Lemma 2.6. (Substitution). *Let* $[\![r]\!]_\theta = \{(p_i, b_i, e_i)\}_i$, *then*

$$(\!|t[r/x]|\!)_\theta = \sum_i p_i (\!|t|\!)_{\theta, x=(b_i, e_i)}$$

Proof. By induction on t. However, we enforce the hypothesis by also showing that if $[\![t]\!]_{\theta, x=(b_i, e_i)} = \{(q_{ij}, b'_{ij}, \rho_{ij})\}_j$, then $[\![t[r/x]]\!]_\theta = \{(p_i q_{ij}, b'_{ij}, \rho_{ij})\}_{ij}$. We use five auxiliary results (cf. appendix in [10] for more details). □

Theorem 2.7 shows how the interpretation $(\!|\cdot|\!)$ of a term relates to all its reducts.

Theorem 2.7. *If* $\Gamma \vdash t : A$, $\theta \vDash \Gamma$ *and* $t \longrightarrow_{p_i} r_i$, *with* $\sum_i p_i = 1$, *then* $(\!| t |\!)_\theta = \sum_i p_i (\!| r_i |\!)_\theta$.

Proof. By induction on the relation $\longrightarrow_p$.   □

3 Probabilistic-Control Calculus with No-Probabilistic Rewriting

3.1 Definitions

In the previous sections we have presented an extension to lambda calculus to handle density matrices. The calculus could have been done using just vectors, because the output of a measurement is not given by the density matrix of the produced mixed state, instead each possible output is given with its probability. In this section, we give an alternative presentation, named λ_ρ°, where we can make the most of the density matrices setting.

In Table 6 we give a modified grammar of terms for λ_ρ° in order to allow for linear combination of terms. We follow the grammar of the algebraic lambda-calculi [6,7,24].

Table 6. Grammar of terms of λ_ρ°.

$t := x \mid \lambda x.t \mid tt$	(Standard lambda calculus)
$\mid \rho^n \mid U^n t \mid \pi^n t \mid t \otimes t$	(Quantum postulates)
$\mid \sum_{i=1}^{n} p_i t_i \mid \mathsf{letcase}^\circ \; x = r \; \text{in} \; \{t, \ldots, t\}$	(Probabilistic control)

where $p_i \in (0,1]$, $\sum_{i=1}^{n} p_i = 1$, and $\sum$ is considered modulo associativity and commutativity (cf. for example [6]).

The new rewrite system is given by the non-probabilistic relation $\rightsquigarrow$, described in Table 7. The measurement does not reduce, unless it is the parameter of a $\mathsf{letcase}^\circ$. Therefore, if only a measurement is needed, we can encode it as:
$$\mathsf{letcase}^\circ \; x = \pi^m \rho^n \; \text{in} \; \{x, \ldots, x\} \rightsquigarrow \sum_i p_i \rho_i^n \rightsquigarrow \rho'$$

where $\rho' = \sum_i \overline{\pi}_i \rho^n \overline{\pi}_i^\dagger$. The rationale is that in this version of the calculus, we can never look at the result of a measurement. It will always produce the density matrix of a mixed-state. As a consequence, the $\mathsf{letcase}^\circ$ constructor rewrites to a sum of terms.

The type system for λ_ρ°, including the grammar of types and the derivation rules, is given in Table 8. The only difference with the type system of λ_ρ

Table 7. Rewrite system of λ_ρ°.

$$(\lambda x.t)r \rightsquigarrow t[r/x]$$

$$\mathsf{letcase}^\circ \; x = \pi^m \rho^n \text{ in } \{t_0, \ldots, t_{2^m} - 1\} \rightsquigarrow \sum_i p_i t_i[\rho_i^n/x] \quad \text{with } \begin{cases} \rho_i^n = \dfrac{\pi_i \rho^n \pi_i^\dagger}{p_i} \\ p_i = \mathrm{tr}(\pi_i^\dagger \pi_i \rho^n) \end{cases}$$

$$U^m \rho^n \rightsquigarrow \rho'^n \qquad\qquad \text{with } \overline{U^m} \rho^n \overline{U^m}^\dagger = \rho'^n$$

$$\rho \otimes \rho' \rightsquigarrow \rho'' \qquad\qquad\quad \text{with } \rho'' = \rho \otimes \rho'$$

$$\sum_i p_i \rho_i \rightsquigarrow \rho' \qquad\qquad\quad \text{with } \rho' = \sum_i p_i \rho_i$$

$$\sum_i p_i t \rightsquigarrow t$$

$$\left(\sum_i p_i t_i\right)r \rightsquigarrow \sum_i p_i(t_i r)$$

$$\frac{t \rightsquigarrow r}{\lambda x.t \rightsquigarrow \lambda x.r} \qquad \frac{t \rightsquigarrow r}{ts \rightsquigarrow rs} \qquad \frac{t \rightsquigarrow r}{st \rightsquigarrow sr} \qquad \frac{t \rightsquigarrow r}{U^n t \rightsquigarrow U^n r}$$

$$\frac{t \rightsquigarrow r}{\pi^n t \rightsquigarrow \pi^n r} \qquad \frac{t \rightsquigarrow r}{t \otimes s \rightsquigarrow r \otimes s} \qquad \frac{t \rightsquigarrow r}{s \otimes t \rightsquigarrow s \otimes r}$$

$$\frac{t_j \rightsquigarrow r_j}{\sum_{i=1}^n p_i t_i \rightsquigarrow \sum_{i=1}^n p_i r_i} \;\; (\forall i \neq j, t_i = r_j)$$

$$\frac{t \rightsquigarrow r}{\mathsf{letcase}^\circ \; x = t \text{ in } \{s_0, \ldots, s_{2^m-1}\} \rightsquigarrow \mathsf{letcase}^\circ \; x = r \text{ in } \{s_0, \ldots, s_{2^m-1}\}}$$

(cf. Table 3), is that rule $\mathsf{ax}_{\mathsf{am}}$ is no longer needed, since (b^m, ρ^n) is not in the grammar of λ_ρ°, and there is a new rule $(+)$ typing the generalised mixed states. We use the symbol $\Vdash$ for λ_ρ° to distinguish it from $\vdash$ used in λ_ρ.

Example 3.1. The teleportation algorithm expressed in λ_ρ in Example 2.1, is analogous for λ_ρ°, only changing the term $\mathsf{letcase}$ by $\mathsf{letcase}^\circ$. Also, the type derivation is analogous. The difference is in the reduction. Let ρ be the density matrix of a given quantum state (mixed or pure). Let

$$\rho_0^3 = \rho \otimes \beta_{00}, \qquad \rho_1^3 = (\mathsf{Cnot} \otimes I)\rho_0^3, \qquad \text{and} \qquad \rho_2^3 = (\mathsf{H} \otimes I \otimes I)\rho_1^3.$$

The trace of the teleportation of ρ in λ_ρ is the following:

$$(\lambda x.\mathsf{letcase} \; y = \pi^2(\mathsf{H}^1(\mathsf{Cnot}^2(x \otimes \beta_{00}))) \text{ in } \{y, \mathsf{Z}_3 y, \mathsf{X}_3 y, \mathsf{Z}_3 \mathsf{X}_3 y\})\rho$$
$$\longrightarrow_1 \mathsf{letcase} \; y = \pi^2(\mathsf{H}^1(\mathsf{Cnot}^2(\rho \otimes \beta_{00}))) \text{ in } \{y, \mathsf{Z}_3 y, \mathsf{X}_3 y, \mathsf{Z}_3 \mathsf{X}_3 y\}$$
$$\longrightarrow_1 \mathsf{letcase} \; y = \pi^2(\mathsf{H}^1(\mathsf{Cnot}^2 \rho_0^3)) \text{ in } \{y, \mathsf{Z}_3 y, \mathsf{X}_3 y, \mathsf{Z}_3 \mathsf{X}_3 y\}$$
$$\longrightarrow_1 \mathsf{letcase} \; y = \pi^2(\mathsf{H}^1 \rho_1^3) \text{ in } \{y, \mathsf{Z}_3 y, \mathsf{X}_3 y, \mathsf{Z}_3 \mathsf{X}_3 y\}$$
$$\longrightarrow_1 \mathsf{letcase} \; y = \pi^2 \rho_2^3 \text{ in } \{y, \mathsf{Z}_3 y, \mathsf{X}_3 y, \mathsf{Z}_3 \mathsf{X}_3 y\} \tag{1}$$

Table 8. Type system for λ_ρ°.

$$A := n \mid (m, n) \mid A \multimap A$$

where $m \le n \in \mathbb{N}$.

$$\frac{}{\Gamma, x : A \Vdash x : A} \text{ ax} \qquad \frac{\Gamma, x : A \Vdash t : B}{\Gamma \Vdash \lambda x.t : A \multimap B} \multimap_i \qquad \frac{\Gamma \Vdash t : A \multimap B \quad \Delta \Vdash r : A}{\Gamma, \Delta \Vdash tr : B} \multimap_e$$

$$\frac{}{\Gamma \Vdash \rho^n : n} \text{ ax}_\rho \qquad \frac{\Gamma \Vdash t : n}{\Gamma \Vdash U^m t : n} \text{ u} \qquad \frac{\Gamma \Vdash t : n}{\Gamma \Vdash \pi^m t : (m, n)} \text{ m} \qquad \frac{\Gamma \Vdash t : n \quad \Delta \Vdash r : m}{\Gamma, \Delta \Vdash t \otimes r : n + m} \otimes$$

$$\frac{x : n \Vdash t_0 : A \quad \ldots \quad x : n \Vdash t_{2^m - 1} : A \quad \Gamma \Vdash r : (m, n)}{\Gamma \Vdash \mathsf{letcase}^\circ \ x = r \text{ in } \{t_0, \ldots, t_{2^m - 1}\} : A} \text{ lc}$$

$$\frac{\Gamma \Vdash t_1 : A \quad \ldots \quad \Gamma \Vdash t_n : A \quad \sum_{i=1}^n p_i = 1}{\Gamma \Vdash \sum_{i=1}^n p_i t_i : A} +$$

From (1), there are four possible reductions. For $i = 0, 1, 2, 3$, let $p_i = \mathrm{tr}(\pi_i^\dagger \pi_i \rho_2^3)$ and $\rho_{3i}^3 = \frac{\pi_i \rho_2^3 \pi_i^\dagger}{p_i}$. Then,

- $(1) \longrightarrow_{p_0}$ letcase $y = (0, \rho_{30}^3)$ in $\{y, Z_3 y, X_3 y, Z_3 X_3 y\} \longrightarrow_1 \rho_{30}^3 = \rho.$
- $(1) \longrightarrow_{p_1}$ letcase $y = (1, \rho_{31}^3)$ in $\{y, Z_3 y, X_3 y, Z_3 X_3 y\} \longrightarrow_1 Z_3 \rho_{31}^3 \longrightarrow_1 \rho.$
- $(1) \longrightarrow_{p_2}$ letcase $y = (2, \rho_{32}^3)$ in $\{y, Z_3 y, X_3 y, Z_3 X_3 y\} \longrightarrow_1 X_3 \rho_{32}^3 \longrightarrow_1 \rho.$
- $(1) \longrightarrow_{p_3}$ letcase $y = (3, \rho_{33}^3)$ in $\{y, Z_3 y, X_3 y, Z_3 X_3 y\} \longrightarrow_1 Z_3 X_3 \rho_{33}^3 \longrightarrow_1 \rho.$

On the other hand, the trace of the same term, in λ_ρ°, would be analogous until (1), just using $\rightsquigarrow$ instead of $\longrightarrow_1$. Then:

$$(1) \rightsquigarrow p_0 \rho + p_1 Z_3 \rho_{31}^3 + p_2 X_3 \rho_{32}^3 + p_3 Z_3 X_3 \rho_{33}^3 \rightsquigarrow^* \sum_{i=0}^3 p_i \rho_{30}^3 \rightsquigarrow \left(\sum_{i=0}^3 p_i\right) \rho \rightsquigarrow \rho$$

3.2 Interpretation

The interpretation of λ_ρ given in Sect. 2.2 considers already all the traces. Hence, the interpretation of λ_ρ° can be obtained from a small modification of it. We only need to drop the interpretation of the term that no longer exists, (b^m, ρ^n), and add an interpretation for the new term $\sum_i p_i t_i$ as follows:

$$\left[\!\left[\sum_i p_i t_i\right]\!\right]_\theta = \{(p_i q_{ij}, b_{ij}, e_{ij}) \mid [\![t_i]\!]_\theta = \{(q_{ij}, b_{ij}, e_{ij})\}_j\}$$

The interpretation of $\mathsf{letcase}^\circ$ is the same as the interpretation of letcase.

Then, we can prove a theorem (Theorem 3.4) for λ_ρ° analogous to Theorem 2.7.

We need the following auxiliary Lemmas.

Lemma 3.2. *If $\Gamma \Vdash t : A$ and $\theta \vDash \Gamma$, then $(\!|\sum_i p_i t_i|\!)_\theta = \sum_i p_i (\!|t_i|\!)_\theta$*

Proof. Let $[\![t_i]\!]_\theta = \{(q_{ij}, b_{ij}, e_{ij})\}_j$. Then, we have $(\!|\sum_i p_i t_i|\!)_\theta = \sum_{ij} p_i q_{ij} e_{ij} = \sum_i p_i \sum_j q_{ij} e_{ij} = \sum_i p_i (\!|t_i|\!)_\theta$. $\qquad\square$

Lemma 3.3. *Let $[\![r]\!]_\theta = \{(p_i, b_i, e_i)\}_i$, then $(\!|t[r/x]|\!)_\theta = \sum_i p_i (\!|t|\!)_{\theta, x=(b_i, e_i)}$.*

Proof. The proof of the analogous Lemma 2.6 in λ_ρ follows by induction on t. Since the definition of $[\![\cdot]\!]$ is the same for λ_ρ than for λ_ρ°, we only need to check the only term of λ_ρ° which is not a term of λ_ρ: $\sum_j q_j t_j$. Using Lemma 3.2, and the induction hypothesis, we have $(\!|(\sum_j q_j t_j)[r/x]|\!)_\theta = (\!|(\sum_j q_j (t_j[r/x]))|\!)_\theta = \sum_j q_j (\!|t_j[r/x]|\!)_\theta = \sum_j q_j \sum_i p_i (\!|t_j|\!)_{\theta, x=(b_i, e_i)} = \sum_i p_i (\!|\sum_j q_j t_j|\!)_{\theta, x=(b_i, e_i)}$. $\qquad\square$

Theorem 3.4. *If $\Gamma \Vdash t : A$, $\theta \vDash \Gamma$ and $t \rightsquigarrow r$, then $(\!|t|\!)_\theta = (\!|r|\!)_\theta$.*

Proof. By induction on the relation $\rightsquigarrow$. Rules $(\lambda x.t)r \rightsquigarrow t[r/x]$, $U^m \rho^n \rightsquigarrow \rho'$ and $\rho \otimes \rho' \rightsquigarrow \rho''$ are also valid rules for relation $\longrightarrow_1$, and hence the proof of these cases are the same than in Theorem 2.7. $\qquad\square$

4   Subject Reduction and Progress

In this section we state and prove the subject reduction and progress properties on both, λ_ρ and λ_ρ° (Theorems 4.4 and 4.7 respectively).

Lemma 4.1 (Weakening)

- *If $\Gamma \vdash t : A$ and $x \notin FV(t)$, then $\Gamma, x : B \vdash t : A$.*
- *If $\Gamma \Vdash t : A$ and $x \notin FV(t)$, then $\Gamma, x : B \Vdash t : A$.*

Proof. By a straightforward induction on the derivation of $\Gamma \vdash t : A$ and on $\Gamma \Vdash t : A$. $\qquad\square$

Lemma 4.2 (Strengthening)

- *If $\Gamma, x : A \vdash t : B$ and $x \notin FV(t)$, then $\Gamma \vdash t : B$.*
- *If $\Gamma, x : A \Vdash t : B$ and $x \notin FV(t)$, then $\Gamma \Vdash t : B$.*

Proof. By a straightforward induction on the derivation of $\Gamma, x : A \vdash t : B$ and $\Gamma, x : A \Vdash t : B$. $\qquad\square$

Lemma 4.3 (Substitution)

- *If $\Gamma, x : A \vdash t : B$ and $\Delta \vdash r : A$ then $\Gamma, \Delta \vdash t[r/x] : B$.*
- *If $\Gamma, x : A \Vdash t : B$ and $\Delta \Vdash r : A$ then $\Gamma, \Delta \Vdash t[r/x] : B$.*

Proof. By induction on t. $\qquad\square$

Theorem 4.4 (Subject reduction)

- *If $\Gamma \vdash t : A$, and $t \longrightarrow_p r$, then $\Gamma \vdash r : A$.*
- *If $\Gamma \Vdash t : A$, and $t \rightsquigarrow r$, then $\Gamma \Vdash r : A$.*

Proof. By induction on the relations $\longrightarrow_p$ and $\rightsquigarrow$. □

Definition 4.5 (Values)

- *A value in λ_ρ is a term v defined by the following grammar:*

$$w := x \mid \lambda x.v \mid w \otimes w$$
$$v := w \mid \rho^n \mid (b^m, \rho^n).$$

- *A value in λ_ρ° (or value°) is a term v defined by the following grammar:*

$$w := x \mid \lambda x.v \mid w \otimes w \mid \sum_i p_i w_i \text{ with } w_i \neq w_j \text{ if } i \neq j$$

$$v := w \mid \rho^n$$

Lemma 4.6

1. *If v is a value, then there is no t such that $v \longrightarrow_p t$ for any p.*
2. *If v is a value°, then there is no t such that $v \rightsquigarrow t$.*

Proof. By induction on v in both cases. □

Theorem 4.7 (Progress)

1. *If $\vdash t : A$, then either t is a value or there exist n, $p_1, \ldots, p_n$, and $r_1, \ldots, r_n$ such that $t \longrightarrow_{p_i} r_i$.*
2. *If $\Vdash t : A$ and $A \neq (m, n)$, then either t is a value° or there exists r such that $t \rightsquigarrow r$.*

Proof. We relax the hypotheses and prove the theorem for open terms as well. That is:

1. If $\Gamma \vdash t : A$, then either t is a value, there exist n, $p_1, \ldots, p_n$, and $r_1, \ldots, r_n$ such that $t \longrightarrow_{p_i} r_i$, or t contains a free variable, and t does not rewrite.
2. If $\Gamma \Vdash t : A$, then either t is a value°, there exists r such that $t \rightsquigarrow r$, or t contains a free variable, and t does not rewrite.

In both cases, we proceed by induction on the type derivation. □

5   Examples

Example 5.1. Consider the following experiment: Measure some ρ and then toss a coin to decide whether to return the result of the measurement, or to give the result of tossing a new coin.

The experiment in λ_ρ. This experiment can be implemented in λ_ρ as follows:

$$(\text{letcase } y = \pi^1|+\rangle\langle+| \text{ in } \{\lambda x.x, \lambda x.\text{letcase } w = \pi^1|+\rangle\langle+| \text{ in } \{w, w\}\})$$

$$(\text{letcase } z = \pi^1\rho \text{ in } \{z, z\})$$

Trace: We give one possible probabilistic trace. Notice that, by using different strategies, we would get different derivation trees. We will not prove confluence in this setting (cf. [12] for a full discussion on the notion of confluence of probabilistic rewrite systems), but we conjecture that such a property is meet.

We use the following notations:

$$s = \pi^1|+\rangle\langle+|$$
$$t_0 = \lambda x.x$$
$$t_1 = \lambda x.\text{letcase } w = s \text{ in } \{w, w\}$$
$$\rho = \frac{3}{4}|0\rangle\langle0| + \frac{\sqrt{3}}{4}|0\rangle\langle1| + \frac{\sqrt{3}}{4}|1\rangle\langle0| + \frac{1}{4}|1\rangle\langle1|$$
$$r_1 = \text{letcase } y = s \text{ in } \{t_0, t_1\}$$
$$r_2 = \text{letcase } z = \pi^1\rho \text{ in } \{z, z\}$$
$$l_x = \text{letcase } y = (x, |x\rangle\langle x|) \text{ in } \{y, y\} \text{ with } x = 0, 1$$
$$r_1^x = \text{letcase } y = (x, |x\rangle\langle x|) \text{ in } \{t_0, t_1\} \text{ with } x = 0, 1$$

Using this notation, the probabilistic trace is given by the tree in Table 9. Therefore, with probability $\frac{5}{8}$ we get $|0\rangle\langle0|$, and with probability $\frac{3}{8}$ we get $|1\rangle\langle1|$. Thus, the density matrix of this mixed state is $\frac{5}{8}|0\rangle\langle0| + \frac{3}{8}|1\rangle\langle1|$.

Typing:

$$\cfrac{\cfrac{\dfrac{}{y:1, x:1, w:1 \vdash w:1} \text{ ax} \quad \dfrac{}{y:1, x:1, w:1 \vdash w:1} \text{ ax}}{\cfrac{y:1, x:1 \vdash \text{letcase } w = \pi^1|+\rangle\langle+| \text{ in } \{w, w\}:1}{y:1 \vdash \lambda x.\text{letcase } w = \pi^1|+\rangle\langle+| \text{ in } \{w, w\}:1 \multimap 1} \multimap_i}}{\quad} \qquad \cfrac{\dfrac{\vdash |+\rangle\langle+|:1}{\vdash \pi^1|+\rangle\langle+|:(1,1)} \text{ ax}_\rho}{} \text{ m} \atop \text{lc}$$

$$\text{(2)}$$

$$\cfrac{\dfrac{\dfrac{}{y:1, x:1 \vdash x:1} \text{ ax}}{y:1 \vdash \lambda x.x:1 \multimap 1} \multimap_i \qquad \dfrac{\vdots}{y:1 \vdash t_1:1 \multimap 1} \text{(2)} \qquad \dfrac{\dfrac{\vdash |+\rangle\langle+|:1}{\vdash \pi^1|+\rangle\langle+|:(1,1)} \text{ ax}_\rho}{} \text{ m}}{\vdash \text{letcase } y = \pi^1|+\rangle\langle+| \text{ in } \{t_0, t_1\}:1 \multimap 1} \text{ lc}$$

$$\text{(3)}$$

Table 9. Trace of the λ_ρ term implementing the experiment of Example 5.1.

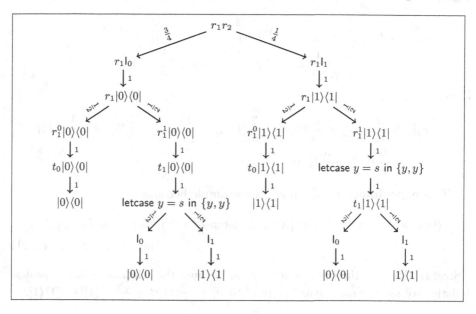

$$\frac{\vdots}{\vdash \text{letcase } y = \pi^1|+\rangle\langle+| \text{ in } \{t_0, t_1\} : 1 \multimap 1} \text{ (3)} \quad \frac{z : 1 \vdash z : 1 \text{ ax} \quad \dfrac{\dfrac{\vdash \rho : 1}{\vdash \pi^1\rho : (1,1)} \text{ ax}_\rho}{\vdash \text{letcase } z = \pi^1\rho \text{ in } \{z, z\} : 1} \text{ m}}{\vdash (\text{letcase } y = \pi^1|+\rangle\langle+| \text{ in } \{t_0, t_1\})(\text{letcase } z = \pi^1\rho \text{ in } \{z, z\}) : 1} \multimap_e$$

Interpretation:

$$[\![s]\!]_\emptyset = \{(\tfrac{1}{2}, 0, |0\rangle\langle0|), (\tfrac{1}{2}, 1, |1\rangle\langle1|)\}$$

$$[\![t_0]\!]_{y=(\varepsilon,|0\rangle\langle0|)} = \{(1, \varepsilon, (\mathsf{b}, \mathsf{e}) \mapsto \{(1, \mathsf{b}, \mathsf{e})\})\}$$

$$[\![t_1]\!]_{y=(\varepsilon,|1\rangle\langle1|)} = \{(1, \varepsilon, (\mathsf{b}, \mathsf{e}) \mapsto \{(\tfrac{1}{2}, \varepsilon, |0\rangle\langle0|), (\tfrac{1}{2}, \varepsilon, |1\rangle\langle1|)\})\}$$

$$[\![r_1]\!]_\emptyset = \{(\tfrac{1}{2}, \varepsilon, (\mathsf{b}, \mathsf{e}) \mapsto \{(\tfrac{1}{2}, \varepsilon, |0\rangle\langle0|), (\tfrac{1}{2}, \varepsilon, |1\rangle\langle1|)\}), (\tfrac{1}{2}, \varepsilon, (\mathsf{b}, \mathsf{e}) \mapsto \{(1, \mathsf{b}, \mathsf{e})\})\}$$

$$[\![\pi^1\rho]\!]_\emptyset = \{(\tfrac{3}{4}, 0, |0\rangle\langle0|), (\tfrac{1}{4}, 1, |1\rangle\langle1|)\}$$

$$[\![r_2]\!]_\emptyset = \{(\tfrac{3}{4}, \varepsilon, |0\rangle\langle0|), (\tfrac{1}{4}, \varepsilon, |1\rangle\langle1|)\}$$

Then,

$$[\![r_1 r_2]\!]_\emptyset = \{(\frac{3}{16}, \varepsilon, |0\rangle\langle 0|), (\frac{1}{16}, \varepsilon, |0\rangle\langle 0|), (\frac{3}{16}, \varepsilon, |1\rangle\langle 1|),$$
$$(\frac{1}{16}, \varepsilon, |1\rangle\langle 1|), (\frac{3}{8}, \varepsilon, |0\rangle\langle 0|), (\frac{1}{8}, \varepsilon, |1\rangle\langle 1|)\}$$

Hence,

$$(\![r_1 r_2]\!)_\emptyset = \frac{3}{16}|0\rangle\langle 0| + \frac{1}{16}|0\rangle\langle 0| + \frac{3}{16}|1\rangle\langle 1| + \frac{1}{16}|1\rangle\langle 1| + \frac{3}{8}|0\rangle\langle 0| + \frac{1}{8}|1\rangle\langle 1|$$
$$= \frac{5}{8}|0\rangle\langle 0| + \frac{3}{8}|1\rangle\langle 1|$$

The experiment in λ_ρ°. In λ_ρ°, the example becomes:

$$t := (\text{letcase}^\circ \; y = \pi^1|+\rangle\langle+| \text{ in } \{\lambda x.x, \lambda x.\text{letcase}^\circ \; w =\pi^1|+\rangle\langle+| \text{ in } \{w, w\}\})$$
$$(\text{letcase}^\circ \; z = \pi^1\rho \text{ in } \{z, z\})$$

Trace: In this case the trace is not a tree, because the relation $\leadsto$ is not probabilistic. We use the same ρ as before: $\frac{3}{4}|0\rangle\langle 0| + \frac{\sqrt{3}}{4}|1\rangle\langle 0| + \frac{\sqrt{3}}{4}|0\rangle\langle 1| + \frac{1}{4}|1\rangle\langle 1|$.

$$t \leadsto (\text{letcase}^\circ \; y = \pi^1|+\rangle\langle+| \text{ in } \{\lambda x.x, \lambda x.\text{letcase}^\circ \; w = \pi^1|+\rangle\langle+| \text{ in } \{w, w\}\})$$
$$(\frac{3}{4}|0\rangle\langle 0| + \frac{1}{4}|1\rangle\langle 1|)$$
$$\leadsto (\frac{1}{2}\lambda x.x + \frac{1}{2}\lambda x.\text{letcase}^\circ \; w = \pi^1|+\rangle\langle+| \text{ in } \{w, w\})(\frac{3}{4}|0\rangle\langle 0| + \frac{1}{4}|1\rangle\langle 1|)$$
$$\leadsto (\frac{1}{2}\lambda x.x + \frac{1}{2}(\lambda x.\frac{1}{2}|0\rangle\langle 0| + \frac{1}{2}|1\rangle\langle 1|))(\frac{3}{4}|0\rangle\langle 0| + \frac{1}{4}|1\rangle\langle 1|)$$
$$\leadsto \frac{1}{2}((\lambda x.x)(\frac{3}{4}|0\rangle\langle 0| + \frac{1}{4}|1\rangle\langle 1|))$$
$$+ \frac{1}{2}((\lambda x.\frac{1}{2}|0\rangle\langle 0| + \frac{1}{2}|1\rangle\langle 1|)(\frac{3}{4}|0\rangle\langle 0| + \frac{1}{4}|1\rangle\langle 1|))$$
$$\leadsto \frac{1}{2}((\lambda x.x)(\frac{3}{4}|0\rangle\langle 0| + \frac{1}{4}|1\rangle\langle 1|)) + \frac{1}{2}(\frac{1}{2}|0\rangle\langle 0| + \frac{1}{2}|1\rangle\langle 1|)$$
$$\leadsto \frac{1}{2}(\frac{3}{4}|0\rangle\langle 0| + \frac{1}{4}|1\rangle\langle 1|) + \frac{1}{2}(\frac{1}{2}|0\rangle\langle 0| + \frac{1}{2}|1\rangle\langle 1|)$$
$$\leadsto \frac{5}{8}|0\rangle\langle 0| + \frac{3}{8}|1\rangle\langle 1|$$

Typing and Interpretation: Since t does not contain sums, its typing is analogous to the term in λ_ρ, as well as the interpretation.

Example 5.2. In [18, p. 371] there is an example of the freedom in the operator-sum representation by showing two quantum operators, which are actually the same. One is the process of tossing a coin and, according to its results, applying I or Z to a given qubit The second is the process performing a projective measurement with unknown outcome to the same qubit. These operations can be encoded in λ_ρ by:

$$O_1 = \lambda y.\text{letcase } x = \pi^1|+\rangle\langle+| \text{ in } \{y, Zy\}$$
$$O_2 = \lambda y.\text{letcase } x = \pi^1 y \text{ in } \{x, x\}$$

with $\pi^1 = \{|0\rangle\langle0|, |1\rangle\langle1|\}$.

Let us apply those operators to the qubit $\rho = \frac{3}{4}|0\rangle\langle0| + \frac{\sqrt{3}}{4}|0\rangle\langle1| + \frac{\sqrt{3}}{4}|1\rangle\langle0| + \frac{1}{4}|1\rangle\langle1|$. We can check that the terms $O_1\rho$ and $O_2\rho$ have different interpretations $\llbracket \cdot \rrbracket$. Let $\rho^- = Z\rho Z^\dagger$, then

$$\llbracket(\lambda y.\text{letcase } x = \pi^1|+\rangle\langle+| \text{ in } \{y, Zy\})\rho\rrbracket_\emptyset = \{(\frac{1}{2}, \varepsilon, \rho), (\frac{1}{2}, \varepsilon, \rho^-)\}$$

$$\llbracket(\lambda y.\text{letcase } x = \pi^1 y \text{ in } \{x, x\})\rho\rrbracket_\emptyset = \{(\frac{3}{4}, \varepsilon, |0\rangle\langle0|), (\frac{1}{4}, \varepsilon, |1\rangle\langle1|)\}$$

However, they have the same interpretation $\llparenthesis \cdot \rrparenthesis$.

$$\llparenthesis(\lambda y.\text{letcase } x = \pi^1|+\rangle\langle+| \text{ in } \{y, Zy\})\rho\rrparenthesis_\emptyset$$
$$= \frac{1}{2}\rho + \frac{1}{2}\rho^-$$
$$= \frac{3}{4}|0\rangle\langle0| + \frac{1}{4}|1\rangle\langle1|$$
$$= \llparenthesis(\lambda y.\text{letcase } x = \pi^1 y \text{ in } \{x, x\})\rho\rrparenthesis_\emptyset$$

Table 10. Trace of the terms $O_1\rho$ from Example 5.2 in λ_ρ.

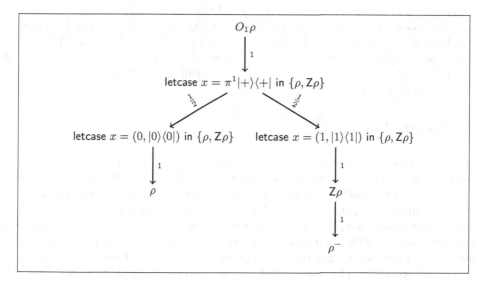

Table 11. Trace of the term $O_2\rho$ from Example 5.2 in λ_ρ.

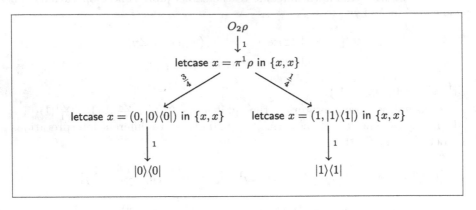

The trace of $O_1\rho$ is given in Table 10, and the trace of $O_2\rho$ in Table 11. The first term produces ρ, with probability $\frac{1}{2}$, and ρ^-, with probability $\frac{1}{2}$, while the second term produces either $|0\rangle\langle 0|$ with probability $\frac{3}{4}$ or $|1\rangle\langle 1|$, with probability $\frac{1}{4}$.

However, if we encode the same terms in λ_ρ°, we can get both programs to produce the same density matrix:

$$O_1^\circ = \lambda y.\text{letcase}^\circ\ x = \pi^1|+\rangle\langle +| \text{ in } \{y, Zy\}$$
$$O_2^\circ = \lambda y.\text{letcase}^\circ\ x = \pi^1 y \text{ in } \{x, x\}$$

The traces of $O_1^\circ\rho$ and $O_2^\circ\rho$ are as follow:

$O_1^\circ\rho$
$= (\lambda y.\text{letcase}^\circ\ x = \pi^1|+\rangle\langle +| \text{ in } \{y, Zy\})\rho$
$\rightsquigarrow \text{letcase}^\circ\ x = \pi^1|+\rangle\langle +| \text{ in } \{\rho, Z\rho\}$
$\rightsquigarrow (\frac{1}{2}\rho) + (\frac{1}{2}Z\rho)$
$\rightsquigarrow (\frac{1}{2}\rho) + (\frac{1}{2}\rho^-)$
$\rightsquigarrow \frac{3}{4}|0\rangle\langle 0| + \frac{1}{4}|1\rangle\langle 1|$

$O_2^\circ\rho$
$= (\lambda y.\text{letcase}^\circ\ x = \pi^1 y \text{ in } \{x, x\})\rho$
$\rightsquigarrow \text{letcase}^\circ\ x = \pi^1\rho \text{ in } \{x, x\})$
$\rightsquigarrow (\frac{3}{4}|0\rangle\langle 0|) + (\frac{1}{4}|1\rangle\langle 1|)$
$\rightsquigarrow \frac{3}{4}|0\rangle\langle 0| + \frac{1}{4}|1\rangle\langle 1|$

6   Conclusions

In this paper we have presented the calculus λ_ρ, which is a quantum data/classical control extension to the lambda calculus where the data is manipulated by density matrices. The main importance of this calculus is its interpretation into density matrices, which can equate programs producing the same density matrices. Then, we have given a second calculus, λ_ρ°, where the density matrices are generalised to accommodate arbitrary terms, and so, programs producing the same density matrices, rewrite to such a matrix, thus, coming closer to its interpretation. The control of λ_ρ° is not classical nor quantum, however it can be seen as a weaker version of the quantum control approach. It is indeed not classical control because a generalised density matrix of terms is allowed ($\sum_i p_i t_i$). It is not quantum control because superposition of programs are not allowed (indeed, the previous sum is not a quantum superposition since all the p_i are positive and so no interference can occur). However, it is quantum in the sense that programs in a kind of generalised mixed-states are considered. We preferred to call it *probabilistic control.*

As depicted in Example 5.2, the calculus λ_ρ° allows to represent the same operator in different ways. Understanding when two operators are equivalent is important from a physical point of view: it gives insights on when two different physical processes produce the same dynamics. To the best of our knowledge, it is the first lambda calculus for density matrices.

Future work and open questions. As pointed out by Bădescu and Panangaden [8], one of the biggest issues with quantum control is that it does not accommodate well with traditional features from functional programming languages like recursion. Ying [26] went around this problem by introducing a recursion based on second quantisation. Density matrices are DCPOs with respect to the Löwner order. Is the form of weakened quantum control suggested in this paper monotone? Can it be extended with recursion? Could this lead to a concrete quantum programming language, like Quipper [16]?

All these open questions are promising new lines of research that we are willing to follow. In particular, we have four ongoing works trying to answer some of these questions:

- The most well studied quantum lambda calculus is, without doubt, Selinger-Valiron's λ_q [22]. Hence, we are working on the mutual simulations between λ_ρ and λ_q, and between λ_ρ° and a generalisation of λ_q into mixed states.
- We are also working on a first prototype of an implementation of λ_ρ°.
- We are studying extensions to both λ_ρ and λ_ρ° with recursion and with polymorphism.
- Finally, we are studying a more sophisticated denotational semantics for both calculi than the one given in this paper. We hope such a semantics to be adequate and fully abstract.

Acknowledgements. We want to thank the anonymous reviewer for some important references and suggestions on future lines of work.

References

1. Aharonov, D., Ambainis, A., Kempe, J., Vazirani, U.: Quantum walks on graphs. In: Proceedings of the Thirty-Third Annual ACM Symposium on Theory of Computing, STOC 2001, pp. 50–59. ACM (2001)
2. Altenkirch, T., Grattage, J.J.: A functional quantum programming language. In: Proceedings of LICS-2005, pp. 249–258. IEEE Computer Society (2005)
3. Ambainis, A., Bach, E., Nayak, A., Vishwanath, A., Watrous, J.: One-dimensional quantum walks. In: Proceedings of the Thirty-Third Annual ACM Symposium on Theory of Computing, STOC 2001, pp. 37–49. ACM (2001)

4. Arrighi, P., Díaz-Caro, A.: A System F accounting for scalars. Logical Methods Comput. Sci. **8**(1:11) (2012)
5. Arrighi, P., Díaz-Caro, A., Valiron, B.: The vectorial λ-calculus. Inf. Comput. **254**(1), 105–139 (2017)
6. Arrighi, P., Dowek, G.: Lineal: A linear-algebraic lambda-calculus. Logical Methods Comput. Sci. **13**(1:8) (2017)
7. Assaf, A., Díaz-Caro, A., Perdrix, S., Tasson, C., Valiron, B.: Call-by-value, call-by-name and the vectorial behaviour of the algebraic λ-calculus. Logical Methods Comput. Sci. **10**(4:8) (2014)
8. Bădescu, C., Panangaden, P.: Quantum alternation: prospects and problems. In: Heunen, C., Selinger, P., Vicary, J. (eds.) Proceedings of QPL-2015. Electronic Proceedings in Theoretical Computer Science, vol. 195, pp. 33–42 (2015)
9. D'Hondt, E., Panangaden, P.: Quantum weakest preconditions. Mathe. Struct. Comput. Sci. **16**, 429–451 (2006)
10. Díaz-Caro, A.: A lambda calculus for density matrices with classical and probabilistic controls. arXiv:1705.00097 (extended version with a 10-pages appendix with proofs) (2017)
11. Díaz-Caro, A., Dowek, G.: Typing quantum superpositions and measurements. To appear in LNCS 10687 (TPNC 2017)
12. Díaz-Caro, A., Martínez, G.: Confluence in probabilistic rewriting. LSFA, to appear in ENTCS (2017)
13. Díaz-Caro, A., Petit, B.: Linearity in the non-deterministic call-by-value setting. In: Ong, L., de Queiroz, R. (eds.) WoLLIC 2012. LNCS, vol. 7456, pp. 216–231. Springer, Heidelberg (2012). https://doi.org/10.1007/978-3-642-32621-9_16
14. Feng, Y., Duan, R., Ying, M.: Bisimulation for quantum processes. ACM SIGPLAN Notices (POPL 2011) **46**(1), 523–534 (2011)
15. Feng, Y., Yu, N., Ying, M.: Model checking quantum markov chains. J. Comput. Syst. Sci. **79**(7), 1181–1198 (2013)
16. Green, A.S., Lumsdaine, P.L., Ross, N.J., Selinger, P., Valiron, B.: Quipper: a scalable quantum programming language. ACM SIGPLAN Notices (PLDI 2013) **48**(6), 333–342 (2013)
17. Dal Lago, U., Masini, A., Zorzi, M.: Confluence results for a quantum lambda calculus with measurements. Electron. Notes Theor. Comput. Sci. **270**(2), 251–261 (2011)
18. Nielsen, M., Chuang, I.: Quantum Computation and Quantum Information. Cambridge University Press, Cambridge (2000)
19. Pagani, M., Selinger, P., Valiron, B.: Applying quantitative semantics to higher-order quantum computing. ACM SIGPLAN Notices (POPL 2014) **49**(1), 647–658 (2014)
20. Selinger, P.: Towards a quantum programming language. Mathe. Struct. Comput. Sci. **14**(4), 527–586 (2004)
21. Selinger, P., Valiron, B.: Quantum lambda calculus. In: Gay, S., Mackie, I. (eds.) Semantic Techniques in Quantum Computation, Chap. 9, pp. 135–172. Cambridge University Press (2009)
22. Selinger, P., Valiron, B.: A lambda calculus for quantum computation with classical control. Mathe. Struct. Comput. Sci. **16**(3), 527–552 (2006)
23. van Tonder, A.: A lambda calculus for quantum computation. SIAM J. Comput. **33**, 1109–1135 (2004)
24. Vaux, L.: The algebraic lambda calculus. Mathe. Struct. Comput. Sci. **19**, 1029–1059 (2009)

25. Ying, M.: Floyd-hoare logic for quantum programs. ACM Trans. Program. Lang. Syst. **33**(6), 19:1–19:49 (2011)
26. Ying, M.: Quantum recursion and second quantisation. arXiv:1405.4443 (2014)
27. Ying, M.: Foundations of Quantum Programming. Elsevier (2016)
28. Ying, M., Ying, S., Wu, X.: Invariants of quantum programs: characterisations and generation. ACM SIGPLAN Notices (POPL 2017) **52**(1), 818–832 (2017)
29. Ying, M., Yu, N., Feng, Y.: Defining quantum control flow. arXiv:1209.4379 (2012)
30. Ying, M., Yu, N., Feng, Y.: Alternation in quantum programming: from superposition of data to superposition of programs. arXiv:1402.5172 (2014)
31. Zorzi, M.: On quantum lambda calculi: a foundational perspective. Mathe. Struct. Comput. Sci. **26**(7), 1107–1195 (2016)

Numerical Reasoning

Compact Difference Bound Matrices

Aziem Chawdhary$^{(\boxtimes)}$ and Andy King

University of Kent, Canterbury CT2 7NF, UK
aziem@chawdhary.co.uk

Abstract. The Octagon domain, which tracks a restricted class of two-variable inequalities, is the abstract domain of choice for many applications because its domain operations are either quadratic or cubic in the number of program variables. Octagon constraints are classically represented using a Difference Bound Matrix (DBM), where the entries in the DBM store bounds c for inequalities of the form $x_i - x_j \leqslant c$, $x_i + x_j \leqslant c$ or $-x_i - x_j \leqslant c$. The size of such a DBM is quadratic in the number of variables, giving a representation which can be excessively large for number systems such as rationals. This paper proposes a compact representation for DBMs, in which repeated numbers are factored out of the DBM. The paper explains how the entries of a DBM are distributed, and how this distribution can be exploited to save space and significantly speed-up long-running analyses. Moreover, unlike sparse representations, the domain operations retain their conceptually simplicity and ease of implementation whilst reducing memory usage.

1 Introduction

The Octagon domain [18] is a widely deployed [6] abstract domain, whose popularity stems from the polynomial complexity of its domain operations [2,9,18] and ease of implementation [13]. Systems of octagon constraints are conventionally represented [18] using difference bound matrices (DBMs). DBMs were originally devised for modelling (time) [10,16] differences where each difference constraint $x_i - x_j \leqslant c$ bounds a difference $x_i - x_j$ with a constant c. For a set of program variables $\{x_0, \ldots, x_{n-1}\}$, an inequality $x_i - x_j \leqslant c$ can be represented by storing c at the i, j entry of an $n \times n$ matrix, which is the DBM. The absence of an upper bound on $x_i - x_j$ is indicated by an entry of ∞. A DBM thus gives a natural representation for a system of n^2 difference constraints. Moreover, a Floyd-Warshall style, $O(n^3)$, all-pairs shortest path algorithm can be applied to check satisfiability and derive a canonical representation.

By working over an augmented set of variables $\{x'_0, \ldots, x'_{2n-1}\}$ and defining $x'_{2i} = x_i$ and $x'_{2i+1} = -x_i$, algorithms for manipulating difference constraints can be lifted to octagonal constraints [18]. Moreover, because of redundancy induced by the encoding, it is not necessary to deploy a DBM of dimension $2n \times 2n$, but instead the DBM can be packed into an array of size $2n(n+1)$. Nevertheless, space consumption is a problem for large n.

© Springer International Publishing AG 2017
B.-Y.E. Chang (Ed.): APLAS 2017, LNCS 10695, pp. 471–490, 2017.
https://doi.org/10.1007/978-3-319-71237-6_23

Space consumption is not just a space problem: memory needs to be allocated, initialised and managed, all of which take time. Running Callgrind [25] on an off-the-shelf abstract interpreter (EVA [8]), equipped with the de-facto implementation of Octagons (Apron [13]) on AES-128 code (taes of Table 1) revealed that 36% of all the function calls emanated from qmpq_init which merely allocates memory and initialises the state of a rational number. When working over rationals, these indirect costs dampen or mask algorithmic improvements obtained by refactoring [2] and reformulating [9] domain operations.

One solution is to abandon rationals for floats [14,23], which is less than satisfactory for the purposes of verification. Another recent trend is adopt a sparse representation [11,14], sacrificing the simplicity and regularity of DBMs which, among other things, makes DBMs amenable to parallelisation [3]. Instead, this paper proposes compact DBMs (CoDBMs) which exploit a previously overlooked property: the number of different DBM entries is typically small. This allows common matrix entries to be shared and reused across all CoDBMs, reducing memory pressure and factoring out repeated initialisation. To summarise, this paper makes the following contribution to the representation of DBMs and octagonal analysis in particular:

- It reports the relative frequency of read and write to DBMs, as well the total number of distinct numbers that arise during the lifetime of octagonal analyses using DBMs. These statistics justify the CoDBM construction.
- It proposes CoDBMs for improving the memory consumption of DBMs, which does not compromise the conceptual simplicity of DBMs or their regular structure, important to algorithmic efficiency.
- It provides experimental evidence which shows that the extra overheads induced by reading and writing to a CoDBM are repaid, often significantly, by the savings in memory allocation and initialisation.
- It analyses the performance gains in terms of the number of memory references and percentage of cache misses, explaining why the auxiliary data-structure used for reading a CoDBM has good locality of reference.

2   The Octagon Domain and Its Representation

An octagonal constraint [2,17,18] is a two variable inequality of the syntactic form $x_i - x_j \leqslant c$, $x_i + x_j \leqslant c$ or $-x_i - x_j \leqslant c$ where c is a constant, and x_i and x_j are drawn from a finite set of program variables $\{x_0, \ldots, x_{n-1}\}$. This class includes unary inequalities $x_i + x_i \leqslant c$ and $-x_i - x_i \leqslant c$ which express interval constraints. An octagon is a set of points satisfying a system of octagonal constraints. The octagon domain over $\{x_0, \ldots, x_{n-1}\}$ is the set of all octagons defined over $\{x_0, \ldots, x_{n-1}\}$.

Implementations of the octagon domain reuse machinery developed for solving difference constraints of the form $x_i - x_j \leqslant c$. An octagonal constraint over $\{x_0, \ldots, x_{n-1}\}$ can be translated [18] to a pair of difference constraints over an augmented set of variables $\{x'_0, \ldots, x'_{2n-1}\}$, which are interpreted by $x'_{2i} = x_i$ and $x'_{2i+1} = -x_i$. The translation proceeds as follows:

$$
\begin{aligned}
x_i - x_j \leqslant c &\rightsquigarrow \quad x'_{2i} - x'_{2j} \leqslant c \ \wedge x'_{2j+1} - x'_{2i+1} \leqslant c \\
x_i + x_j \leqslant c &\rightsquigarrow x'_{2i} - x'_{2j+1} \leqslant c \ \wedge \quad x'_{2j} - x'_{2i+1} \leqslant c \\
-x_i - x_j \leqslant c &\rightsquigarrow x'_{2i+1} - x'_{2j} \leqslant c \ \wedge \quad x'_{2j+1} - x'_{2i} \leqslant c \\
x_i \leqslant c &\rightsquigarrow x'_{2i} - x'_{2i+1} \leqslant 2c \\
-x_i \leqslant c &\rightsquigarrow x'_{2i+1} - x'_{2i} \leqslant 2c
\end{aligned}
$$

A difference bound matrix (DBM) [10,16], which is a square matrix of dimension $n \times n$, is commonly used to represent a systems of n^2 (syntactically irredundant [15]) difference constraints over n variables. The entry $\mathbf{m}_{i,j}$ that represents the constant c of the inequality $x_i - x_j \leqslant c$ where $i, j \in \{0, \ldots, n-1\}$. Since an octagonal constraint system over n variables translates to a difference constraint system over $2n$ variables, a DBM representing an octagon has dimension $2n \times 2n$.

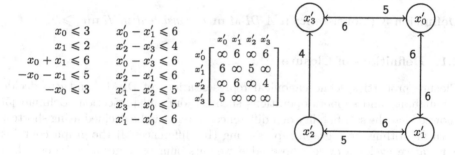

$$
\begin{aligned}
x_0 &\leqslant 3 \\
x_1 &\leqslant 2 \\
x_0 + x_1 &\leqslant 6 \\
-x_0 - x_1 &\leqslant 5 \\
-x_0 &\leqslant 3
\end{aligned}
\qquad
\begin{aligned}
x'_0 - x'_1 &\leqslant 6 \\
x'_2 - x'_3 &\leqslant 4 \\
x'_0 - x'_3 &\leqslant 6 \\
x'_2 - x'_1 &\leqslant 6 \\
x'_1 - x'_2 &\leqslant 5 \\
x'_3 - x'_0 &\leqslant 5 \\
x'_1 - x'_0 &\leqslant 6
\end{aligned}
\qquad
\begin{array}{c}
\quad x'_0 \ x'_1 \ x'_2 \ x'_3 \\
\begin{array}{c}
x'_0 \\ x'_1 \\ x'_2 \\ x'_3
\end{array}
\left[
\begin{array}{cccc}
\infty & 6 & \infty & 6 \\
6 & \infty & 5 & \infty \\
\infty & 6 & \infty & 4 \\
5 & \infty & \infty & \infty
\end{array}
\right]
\end{array}
$$

Fig. 1. Example of an octagonal system and its DBM representation

Example 1. Figure 1 serves as an example of how an octagon translates to a system of differences. The entries of the DBM correspond to the constants in the difference constraints. Note how differences which are (syntactically) absent from the system lead to entries which take a symbolic value of ∞. Observe too how that DBM defines an adjacency matrix for the illustrated graph where the weight of a directed edge abuts its arrow.

The interpretation of a DBM representing an octagon is different to a DBM representing difference constraints. Consequently there are two concretisations for DBMs: one for interpreting differences and another for interpreting octagons, although the latter is defined in terms of the former.

Definition 1. *Concretisation for rational ($\mathbb{Q}^n$) solutions:*

$$
\begin{aligned}
\gamma_{diff}(\mathbf{m}) &= \{\langle v_0, \ldots, v_{n-1}\rangle \in \mathbb{Q}^n \mid \forall i, j . v_i - v_j \leqslant \mathbf{m}_{i,j}\} \\
\gamma_{oct}(\mathbf{m}) &= \{\langle v_0, \ldots, v_{n-1}\rangle \in \mathbb{Q}^n \mid \langle v_0, -v_0, \ldots, v_{n-1}, -v_{n-1}\rangle \in \gamma_{diff}(\mathbf{m})\}
\end{aligned}
$$

where the concretisation for integer ($\mathbb{Z}^n$) solutions can be defined analogously.

Example 2. Since octagonal inequalities are modelled as two related differences, the DBM of Fig. 1 contains duplicated entries, for instance, $\mathbf{m}_{1,2} = \mathbf{m}_{3,0}$.

Operations on a DBM representing an octagon must maintain equality between the two entries that share the same constant of an octagonal inequality. This requirement leads to the notion of coherence:

Definition 2 (Coherence). *A DBM* $\mathbf{m}$ *is coherent iff* $\forall i.j.\mathbf{m}_{i,j} = \mathbf{m}_{\bar{\jmath},\bar{\imath}}$ *where* $\bar{\imath} = i + 1$ *if* i *is even and* $i - 1$ *otherwise.*

Example 3. Observe from Fig. 1 that $\mathbf{m}_{0,3} = 6 = \mathbf{m}_{2,1} = \mathbf{m}_{\bar{3},\bar{0}}$. Coherence holds in a degenerate way for unary inequalities, note $\mathbf{m}_{2,3} = 4 = \mathbf{m}_{2,3} = \mathbf{m}_{\bar{3},\bar{2}}$.

Care should be taken to preserve coherence when manipulating DBMs, either by carefully designing algorithms or by using a data structure that enforces coherence [17, Sect. 4.5], as realised in the Apron library [13]. Finally to check if a DBM represents a satisfiable octagonal system, we have the following notion:

Definition 3 (Consistency). *A DBM* $\mathbf{m}$ *is consistent iff* $\forall i.\mathbf{m}_{i,i} \geqslant 0$.

2.1 Definitions of Closure

Closure properties define canonical representations of DBMs, and can decide satisfiability and support operations such as join and projection. Bellman [5] showed that the satisfiability of a difference system can be decided using shortest path algorithms on a graph representing the differences. If the graph contains a negative cycle (a cycle whose edge weights sum to a negative value) then the difference system is unsatisfiable. The same applies for DBMs representing octagons. Closure propagates all the implicit (entailed) constraints in a system, leaving each entry in the DBM with the sharpest possible constraint entailed between the variables. Closure is formally defined below:

$$
\begin{array}{c}
\begin{array}{cccc} x'_0 & x'_1 & x'_2 & x'_3 \end{array} \\
\begin{array}{c} x'_0 \\ x'_1 \\ x'_2 \\ x'_3 \end{array}
\left[\begin{array}{cccc}
11 & 6 & 11 & 6 \\
6 & 11 & 5 & 9 \\
9 & 6 & 11 & 4 \\
5 & 11 & 16 & 11
\end{array}\right]
\qquad
\begin{array}{c}
\begin{array}{cccc} x'_0 & x'_1 & x'_2 & x'_3 \end{array} \\
\begin{array}{c} x'_0 \\ x'_1 \\ x'_2 \\ x'_3 \end{array}
\left[\begin{array}{cccc}
0 & 6 & 11 & 6 \\
6 & 0 & 5 & 9 \\
9 & 6 & 0 & 4 \\
5 & 11 & 16 & 0
\end{array}\right]
\qquad
\begin{array}{c}
\begin{array}{cccc} x'_0 & x'_1 & x'_2 & x'_3 \end{array} \\
\begin{array}{c} x'_0 \\ x'_1 \\ x'_2 \\ x'_3 \end{array}
\left[\begin{array}{cccc}
0 & 6 & 11 & 5 \\
6 & 0 & 5 & 5 \\
5 & 5 & 0 & 4 \\
5 & 11 & 16 & 0
\end{array}\right]
\end{array}
$$

Fig. 2. DBM after shortest path, closed DBM and strongly closed DBM

Definition 4 (Closure). *A DBM* $\mathbf{m}$ *is closed iff*

- $\forall i.\mathbf{m}_{i,i} = 0$
- $\forall i, j, k.\mathbf{m}_{i,j} \leqslant \mathbf{m}_{i,k} + \mathbf{m}_{k,j}$

Example 4. The DBM of Fig. 1 is not closed. By running an all-pairs shortest path algorithm the left DBM of Fig. 2 is obtained. Shortest path algorithms derive all constraints implied by the original system. Notice the diagonal has non-negative elements implying that the constraint system is satisfiable. Once satisfiability has been established, the diagonal values are set to zero to satisfy the requirements of closure, giving the middle (closed) DBM.

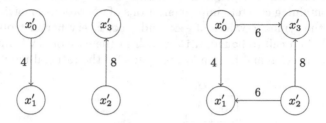

Fig. 3. Two representations of the same octagon constraints $x_0 \leqslant 2$, $x_1 \leqslant 4$

Closure by itself is not enough to provide a canonical form for DBMs representing octagons. A stronger notion is required called strong closure [17,18]:

Definition 5 (Strong closure). *A DBM* **m** *is strongly closed iff*

– **m** *is closed*
– $\forall i, j . \mathbf{m}_{i,j} \leqslant \mathbf{m}_{i,\bar{\imath}}/2 + \mathbf{m}_{\bar{\jmath},j}/2$

The strong closure of DBM m can be computed by propagating the following the property: if $x'_j - x'_{\bar{\jmath}} \leqslant c_1$ and $x'_{\bar{\imath}} - x'_i \leqslant c_2$ both hold then $x'_j - x'_i \leqslant (c_1 + c_2)/2$ also holds. This sharpens the bound on the difference $x'_j - x'_i$ using the two unary constraints encoded by $x'_j - x'_{\bar{\jmath}} \leqslant c_1$ and $x'_{\bar{\imath}} - x'_i \leqslant c_1$, namely, $2x'_j \leqslant c_1$ and $-2x'_i \leqslant c_2$. Note that this constraint propagation is not guaranteed to occur with a shortest path algorithm since there is not necessarily a path from a $\mathbf{m}_{i,\bar{\imath}}$ and $\mathbf{m}_{\bar{\jmath},j}$. An example in Fig. 3 illustrates such a situation: the two graphs represent the same octagon, but a shortest path algorithm will not propagate constraints on the left graph; hence strengthening is needed to bring the two graphs to the same normal form. Strong closure yields a canonical representation: there is a unique strongly closed DBM for any (non-empty) octagon [18]. Thus any semantically equivalent octagonal constraint systems are represented by the same strongly closed DBM. Strengthening is the act of computing strong closure.

Example 5. The right DBM of Fig. 2 gives the strong closure of the middle DBM of the same figure.

Thus the overall algorithm for computing the strong closure of an octagonal DBM is to first run a closure algorithm, check for consistency by searching for a negative entry in the diagonal, and then apply strengthening [9,18]. These closure algorithms are not detailed for reasons of brevity; they are a (long) study in their own right [2,9,18], and the CoDBM representation, and its relationship to a DBM, can be followed without detailed understanding of these algorithms.

2.2 Apron Library

The Apron library is the most widely used Octagon domain implementation [13].
The Apron library is implemented in C, with bindings for C++, Java and OCaml.
The library implements the box, polyhedra and octagon abstract domains. Various number systems are supported by the Apron library, such as single-precision
floats and GNU multiple-precision (GMP) rationals. Numbers are represented
by a type bound_t, which depending on compile time options will select a specific
header file containing concrete implementations of operations involving numbers
extended to the symbolic values of $-\infty$ and $+\infty$. Every bound_t object has to
be initialised via a call to bound_init, which in the case of GMP rationals will
call a malloc function and heap allocate space for the rational number.

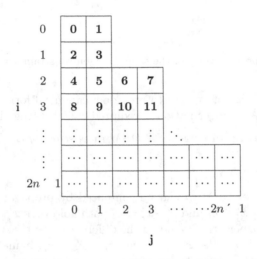

Fig. 4. Half-matrix representation of a DBM

DBMs are stored in memory by taking advantage of the half-matrix nature
of octagonal DBMs which follows by coherence. A (linear) array of bound_t
objects is then used to represent the half-matrix, as shown in Fig. 4. If $i \geqslant j$ or
$i = \bar{j}$ then the entry at (i, j) in the DBM is stored at index $j + \lfloor i^2/2 \rfloor$ in the
array. Otherwise (i, j) is stored at the index location reserved for entry $(\bar{j}, \bar{i})$. A
DBM of size n requires an array of size $2n(n + 1)$ which gives a significant space
reduction.

However, DBMs are still not compact: if a rational occurs repeatedly in a
DBM then each occurrence of that number is heap allocated separately.

3 Compact DBMs

The rationale for compact DBMs (CoDBMs) is to redistribute the cost of memory allocation and initialisation, and do so in a way that is sensitive to the

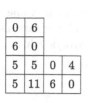
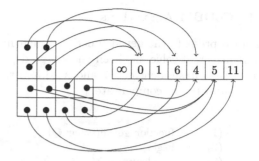

Fig. 5. Example illustrating the difference between DBMs and CoDBMs

relative frequency of DBM reads to DBM writes, whilst improving locality of reference.

CoDBMs are difference bound matrices where the entries are identifiers, rather than numeric values, and the identifiers are interpreted and maintained with the aid of two arrays, namely values and sorted. Conceptually, CoDBMs differ from DBMs by storing numbers in a common shared array, and elements in the DBM refer to these rather than storing the numeric bound itself, as shown in Fig. 5.

The array values has size elements and has elements of type $\mathbb{Q} \cup \{\infty\}$. The values array is used to map an identifier, which is an integer, to its value. It is used when reading an entry in a CoDBM. Dually, the array sorted is used when writing an entry to a CoDBM. This array is indexed from 0, contains size records, where each record has value and id fields of type $\mathbb{Q} \cup \{\infty\}$ and $\mathbb{N}$ respectively. This array records all CoDBM entry values which have been seen thus far, including ∞, with their identifiers. The records are arranged in strictly ascending order, using the value field as the key. The ordering provides an efficient way of searching to determine whether a value has been encountered previously. If found, the id field gives the corresponding identifier.

An identifier of 0 is preassigned for the symbolic value ∞. This is achieved by initialising the values and sorted arrays so that $\text{values}[0] = \infty$, $\text{sorted}[0].\text{value} = \infty$ and $\text{sorted}[0].\text{id} = 0$. Finally, identifiers are allocated in increasing order, and next is used to record the next available unused identifier; it is initialised to 1, since 0 is used to identify ∞.

3.1   CoDBM Data-Structure Invariants

The next, size and values and sorted arrays are maintained to satisfy the following invariants:

- $\text{values}[0] = \infty$
- $1 \leqslant \text{next} \leqslant \text{size}$
- $\forall 0 < i < \text{next}.(\text{sorted}[i-1].\text{value} < \text{sorted}[i].\text{value})$
- $\forall 0 \leqslant i < \text{next}.\exists 0 \leqslant j < \text{next}.(\text{sorted}[j].\text{value} = \text{values}[i] \wedge \text{sorted}[j].\text{id} = i)$

3.2 CoDBM Algorithms

Figure 6 presents the get_id function which maps its single argument, value, to an identifier. If value has been encountered previously, its identifier is returned, otherwise a fresh identified is allocated and returned, and the arrays values and sorted adjusted to compensate.

```
(1)      function get_id(value: ℚ)
(2)      begin
(3)          lower ← 0;
(4)          upper ← next - 1;
(5)
(6)          while (lower ≤ upper)
(7)          begin
(8)              mid ←(lower + upper) div 2;
(9)              if (value < sorted[mid].value) upper ← mid - 1;
(10)             else if (value > sorted[mid].value) lower ← mid + 1;
(11)             else return sorted[mid].id;
(12)         end
(13)
(14)         if (next ≥ size)
(15)             return lower;
(16)         else
(17)         begin
(18)             for (i = next; i > lower; i ← i - 1)
(19)             begin
(20)                 sorted[i].value ← sorted[i - 1].value;
(21)                 sorted[i].id ← sorted[i - 1].id;
(22)             end
(23)
(24)             sorted[lower].value ← value;
(25)             sorted[lower].id ← next;
(26)             values[next] ← value;
(27)
(28)             next ← next + 1
(29)             return sorted[lower].id;
(30)         end
```

Fig. 6. Searching and extending the sorted and values arrays (with idealised arithmetic)

The get_id function applies binary (or half-interval) search [26] on lines 3–12. Line 8 assigns mid to the semi-sum of lower and upper using integer division, which rounds towards 0. The while loop will terminate within $\lceil \log_2(\text{size}) \rceil + 1$ iterations, either returning the identifier of value, or exiting at line 14 with lower = upper + 1. To see this, let lower$'$ and upper$'$ denote the values of these variables on loop exit, and their unprimed counterparts denote their values at the start of the last iteration. Hence lower $\leq$ upper and lower$'$ > upper$'$.

If upper$'$ = mid $-$ 1 then mid $-$ 1 = upper$'$ $<$ lower$'$ = lower $\leqslant$ mid hence lower = mid whence upper$'$ = mid $-$ 1 = lower $-$ 1 = lower$'$ $-$ 1. Conversely if lower$'$ = mid $+$ 1 it likewise follows that lower$'$ = upper$'$ $+$ 1.

The exit condition lower = upper $+$ 1 indicates where to insert a new record for value in sorted. Observe that if $0 \leqslant i <$ lower then sorted$[i]$.value $<$ value and conversely if upper $< i <$ next then sorted$[i]$.value $>$ value. In particular sorted[upper].value $<$ value $<$ sorted[lower].value indicating that the value record needs to be inserted at position lower of sorted, once the record at this position and the higher positions are all shuffled along. The for loop commencing at line 18 enacts the shuffle and lines 24 and 25 adjust the record at position lower record value and its identifier next. Line 26 updates values to map the identifier next to value. The next counter is updated at line 18 and the identifier for value returned at line 29.

The check at line 14 detects whether the capacity of the arrays values and sorted are exceeded. Suppose this line is reached. Because values and sorted are initialised to store the value ∞ (coupled with the 0 identifier) it follows value $\neq \infty$ hence value $\in \mathbb{Q}$. Thus there exists a recorded value (even if it is ∞) which is strictly larger than value and indeed value $<$ sorted[lower].value. Moreover sorted[lower $-$ 1].value = sorted[upper].value $<$ value hence lower is the identifier for the smallest value strictly larger than value. This provides a way to update a CoDBM entry with a relaxed value when one does not want to resize the arrays. This, in effect, widening the CoDBM in a way that is sensitive to space capacity. For completeness, Fig. 7 shows how the entries of a CoDBM are read and written, where for a CoDBM of dimension n, i is an index into the linear array of identifiers, hence $0 \leqslant i < 2n(n+1)$.

Finally to remark on complexity, the set_ddbm_entry function resides in $O(n)$, where n is the size of the value and sorted arrays, because of the potential for copying in the get_id function. The get_ddbm_entry function is in $O(1)$.

```
(1)  procedure set_ddbm_entry(ddbm: N*, i: N, value: Q)
(2)  begin
(3)      ddbm[i] ← get_id(value);
(4)  end
(5)
(6)  function get_ddbm_entry(ddbm: N*, i: N)
(7)  begin
(8)   return values[ddbm[i]];
(9)  end
```

Fig. 7. Reading (getting) and writing (setting) an entry of a CoDBM

3.3 Binary Search with Machine Arithmetic

By way of a postscript, Fig. 8 gives a revised version of get_id which is sensitive to the limitations of machine arithmetic. Since natural numbers are used for identifiers it is natural to employ unsigned integers. However, if lower = upper = 0 then mid = 0 hence mid − 1 will underflow at line 9. The listing in Fig. 8 avoids this adding a positive offset of 1 to lower and upper to give lower' and upper' which is duly compensated for at line 13. Overflow will not occur on mid' + 1 at line 10, however, if size, hence next, is strictly smaller than the largest representable number. Another subtlety is that the semi-sum (lower + upper) div 2 on line 8 of Fig. 6 can overflow [22]. Hence the alternative formulation of lower' + ((upper' − lower') div 2) in Fig. 8.

```
(1)      function get_id(value: ℚ)
(2)      begin
(3)          lower' ← 1;
(4)          upper' ← next;
(5)
(6)          while (lower' ≤ upper')
(7)          begin
(8)              mid' ← lower' + ((upper' - lower') div 2);
(9)              if (value < sorted[mid' - 1].value) upper' ← mid' - 1;
(10)             else if (value > sorted[mid' - 1].value) lower' ← mid' + 1;
(11)             else return sorted[mid' - 1].id;
(12)         end
(13)         lower ← lower' - 1
...          ...
(31)     end
```

Fig. 8. Searching and extending the sorted and values arrays (with machine arithmetic)

4   Experiments

The abstract interpretation plugin for Frama-C, EVA [8], was used for gathering salient statistics on octagons, and then comparing CoDBMs against DBMs. The statistics were gathered on a Linux box equipped with 128 GB of RAM and dual 2.0 GHz Intel Xeon E5-2650 processors. EVA has options to use the Apron library [13], a widely-used numerical domain library, with implementations of polyhedra, boxes (intervals) and octagons. EVA is a prototype analyser for C99, and as such does not provide state-of-the-art optimisations such as automatic variable clustering [12] or access-based localisation [4]; which precludes the analysis of very large programs. Therefore, Table 1 lists modestly sized programs drawn from the Frama-C open source case studies repository (github.com/Frama-C/open-source-case-studies), which were used for benchmarking. The case studies repository was designed to test the default value analysis plugin of Frama-C, and not the EVA plugin, and in fact some of the case studies did not terminate using the EVA plugin with the octagon domain.

Table 1. Benchmarks

Abbrv	Benchmark	LOC	Description
lev	levenstein	187	Levenstein string distance library
sol	solitaire	334	card cipher
2048	2048	435	2048 game
kh	khash	652	hash code from klib C library
taes	Tiny-AES	813	portable AES-128 implementation
qlz	qlz	1168	fast compression library
mod	libmodbus	7685	library to interact with Modbus protocol
mgmp	mini-gmp	11787	subset of GMP library
unq	unqlite	64795	embedded NoSQL DB
bzip	bzip-single-file	74017	bzip single file for static analysis benchmarking

4.1 Execution Time

Table 2 reports the headline results, giving both the key statistics, and timing information. The #Ids and #Entries columns give, respectively, the total number of identifiers allocated using CoDBMs, and the exact number of matrix entries required across all DBMs. The former details how many rationals need be stored for CoDBMs; the latter for DBMs. The upper graph of Fig. 9 illustrates these numbers, showing that the reduction in memory allocation and initialisation is typically by three orders of magnitude. The #Reads and #Writes columns report the total number of reads and writes to the difference matrices (which is the same for both DBMs and CoDBMs). The lower graph of Fig. 9 illustrates these as proportions, showing that there are typically 2 and 3 times as many reads

Table 2. Experimental statistics (tabulated)

Abbrv	#Ids	#Entries	#Reads	#Writes	DBM time	CoDBM time	Speedup
lev	900	795345356	221230162	76969699	14.18	10.59	25%
sol	2161	3044202788	565119059	258963325	45.44	33.70	25%
2048	358	1919995058	445261291	144479736	24.44	16.53	32%
kh	196	30165440	8465749	3640830	1.37	1.32	3%
taes	140	106396722938	–	–	803.30	505.90	37%
qlz	10	69126	17216	13742	1.32	1.41	−7%
mod	3627	45157313792	1921289169	661225970	336.22	214.10	36%
mgmp	126	101752918	22603122	8805323	2.01	1.56	22%
unq	–	–	–	–	1.50	1.56	−4%
bzip	262	373715276692	–	–	591.85	196.69	66%
total					1821.63	983.36	46%

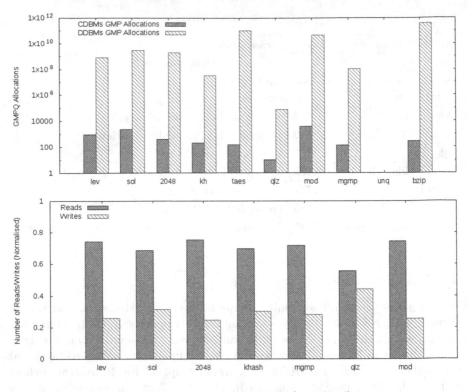

Fig. 9. Experimental statistics (visualised)

as writes to the difference matrices entries over the lifetime of an analysis. The exception is unq. (Statistics are omitted for runs with excessively long traces.)

The table also reports the total execution time, in seconds, for the DBM and CoDBM analyses to parse their input, reach the fixpoint, and then output their results (which were identical). The last row totals the execution times over all benchmarks. CoDBMs are faster than DBMs on the longer-running analyses. The unq benchmark is a surprising corner case which does not produce any two variable constraints, and thus does not create any difference matrices. This gives an inexplicable slowdown, possibly due to an increase in code size. CoDBMs give a modest slowdown for qlz, presumably because of the higher proportion of writes to reads; elsewhere CoDBMs give a significant speedup.

4.2   Memory Consumption

Table 3 shows end-to-end memory consumption statistics of each Frama-C benchmark. Memory consumption was measured using the GNU time utility which returns the maximum resident set size of the process during its lifetime. The results show that memory consumption is reduced in all but one of the benchmarks. Memory consumption is most notably reduced for the longer running benchmarks, with bzip showing the greatest reduction. Overall, the results show that the CoDBM representation has a positive effect in reducing the memory usage of the Apron library.

Table 3. Memory usage statistics (in Kb)

Benchmark	DBM	CoDBM	Reduction (%)
lev	3317872	2531096	23.71
sol	11694896	7538160	35.54
2048	6389484	3584856	43.89
kh	284776	198656	30.24
taes	35453276	32361744	8.72
qlz	332252	331788	0.14
mod	51832508	31831468	38.59
mgmp	443932	236236	46.79
unq	207332	208560	−0.59
bzip	11047816	5781492	47.67
Total	121335932	84604056	30.27

4.3   Cache Behaviour

Modern processors have become reliant on caching as the speed of the core has steadily outstripped the clock frequency of the memory bus and the performance of RAM. For example, the 2.0 GHz Xeon (Sandy Bridge) E5-2650 has a separate level 1 instruction cache and level 1 data cache, and unified caches at level 2 and 3. The latency of the level 3 cache is 28 cycles, whereas the latency of RAM is 28 cycles plus 49 ns [21], which equates to $28 + (49 \times 10^{-9}) \times (2 \times 10^9) = 218$ cycles. This underscores the importance of reducing cache misses, even by small percentages, and the role of temporal and spatial locality to the performance of DBMs and CoDBMs. Reading an element from a CoDBM incurs an extra layer of indirection compared to a DBM and writing to a CoDBM can incur multiple memory references, so one might expect these additional memory references to put pressure on the cache and worsen memory performance. This section thus investigates the memory behaviour of CoDBMs.

Table 4 summarises memory and cache statistics for CoDBMs and DBMs gathered with Cachegrind [19]. Cachegrind simulates a theoretical architecture with a first-level data (D1) cache, first-level instruction (I1) cache and a last-level (LL) unified data and instruction cache. LL hints at the way Cachegrind abstracts a three cache architecture: it auto-detects the cache configuration (cache size, associativity and line size) and sets LL to model the L3 rather than the L2 cache. This is because missing L3 has more effect on runtime than

Table 4. Cachegrind statistics: DBMs upper-half; CoDBMs lower-half

Activity		lev	sol	2048	kh	teas	qlz	mod	mgmp	unq	bzip
D refs	r	22b	14b	63b	825m	696b	358m	379b	3b	5b	1125b
	w	17b	11b	48b	559m	511b	207m	285b	2b	3b	918b
	t	**39b**	**25b**	**111b**	**1,384m**	**1,207b**	**566m**	**665b**	**6b**	**8b**	**2044b**
D1 misses	r	1.8%	2.1%	2.0%	2.0%	2.0%	1.9%	1.9%	1.9%	1.4%	2.5%
	w	1.6%	1.9%	1.6%	2.0%	1.6%	2.5%	1.6%	2.0%	2.9%	1.8%
	t	**1.7%**	**2.0%**	**1.8%**	**2.0%**	**1.8%**	**2.1%**	**1.8%**	**2.0%**	**2.0%**	**2.2%**
LL misses	r	0.1%	0.1%	0.1%	0.0%	0.5%	0.0%	0.1%	0.0%	0.1%	0.2%
	w	0.5%	0.7%	0.5%	0.3%	0.6%	0.3%	0.8%	0.3%	0.1%	1.1%
	t	**0.1%**	**0.1%**	**0.1%**	**0.1%**	**0.5%**	**0.1%**	**0.2%**	**0.1%**	**0.1%**	**0.3%**
D refs	r	16b	8b	35b	681m	512b	205m	200b	2.5b	5b	234b
	w	9b	5b	20b	407m	258b	104m	106b	1.4b	3b	92b
	t	**25b**	**13b**	**55b**	**1,088m**	**771b**	**310m**	**306b**	**4b**	**8b**	**326b**
D1 misses	r	0.7%	1.2%	0.7%	1.6%	0.3%	2.4%	0.4%	1.2%	1.4%	0.4%
	w	0.9%	1.4%	1.1%	1.9%	0.5%	2.3%	0.8%	1.9%	2.9%	0.6%
	t	**0.8%**	**1.3%**	**0.9%**	**1.7%**	**0.4%**	**2.4%**	**0.5%**	**1.4%**	**2.0%**	**0.4%**
LL misses	r	0.0%	0.0%	0.0%	0.0%	0.0%	0.0%	0.0%	0.0%	0.1%	0.0%
	w	0.0%	0.7%	0.5%	0.3%	0.2%	0.5%	0.5%	0.2%	0.1%	0.0%
	t	**0.0%**	**0.1%**	**0.0%**	**0.0%**	**0.0%**	**0.1%**	**0.0%**	**0.0%**	**0.1%**	**0.0%**

missing L2. Although Cachegrind abstracts the cache structure of a Xeon, it nevertheless reports accurate counts for the total number of memory references.

While data handling is determined by the programmer in the design of the data-structures, the compiler itself will generate the low-level instructions, and normally do so in way that aids spacial and temporal locality. Indeed the I1 statistics for the DBM and CoDBM code are almost identical, and therefore not discussed further.

Number of Memory References. Table 4 focuses on D1 and LL misses, and the number of memory references (D refs). The table presents the total number of D refs (t), as well as the number of reads (r) and writes (w), where k, m and b respectively denote the multipliers 10^3, 10^6 and 10^9. The table also details the number of cache misses for D1 and LL, expressed as a percentage of the total number of memory references. These statistics are augmented with percentages for the number of misses on read and write. The upper portion of the table presents the statistics for DBMs; the lower for CoDBMs.

The main result is that, with the exception of unq, the number of reads and writes to memory are both reduced with CoDBMs. For 2048, mod and bzip in particular, the difference to the number of writes is considerable and reflects the CoDBM design which factors out shared sub-structure in the difference matrix. Specifically, each distinct number is allocated and initialised exactly once over the lifetime of the whole analysis. Thus, when a fresh CoDBM is created, in contrast with a DBM, it is not necessary to allocate fresh memory for each rational stored in the CoDBM: only those few, if any, which have not been encountered previously. In fact, the most common use-case for CoDBM creation involves merely allocating the matrix of identifiers and then setting each cell of the matrix to the identifier for ∞. This initialises the matrix to represent a system of vacuous difference constraints. CoDBM creation thus saves many memory references, particularly writes, relative to DBMs. Copying a CoDBM likewise avoids multiple memory allocations and initialisations, since only the matrix of identifiers need be created and then copied over one-by-one, again saving many memory references, mainly writes, relative to the equivalent operation on a DBM.

Furthermore, although reading an entry of a CoDBM requires one extra memory reference per read, for an incremental closure algorithm [9], the total number of reads is actually is only linear in the size of the matrix which, in turn, is quadratic in the number of program variables. Moreover, incremental closure is the most frequently applied domain operation, after the creation and copying a difference matrix. In fact, with code hoisting, the inner loop of incremental closure (which dominates the overall cost) requires just one read operation per iteration [9]. Hence the increase in memory references though the reads of incremental closure is more than compensated by the reduction obtained by factoring out matrix sub-structure, and the subsequent reduction in memory allocation and initialisation.

As a final check, taes was again instrumented with Callgrind, which revealed that the number of calls to gmpq_init drops from 36% of the total using DBMs to 12% using CoDBMs. This is not reduced to zero because of the need to store intermediate rational numbers in various domain operations.

Locality of the Memory References. The D1 and LL misses reported in Table 4 act as a proxy for temporal and spatial locality and suggest that, despite the extra reference incurred on each read, there is an overall, sometimes dramatic, improvement to locality. The significant result here is that in the majority of cases the number of LL misses reduce to 0%. We suspect that locality is improved, in part, because a CoDBM is denser than the equivalent DBM so that a single cache line stores more CoDBM entries than DBM entries. Moreover, the values and sorted arrays are often much smaller than a moderately sized CoDBM, which is itself much smaller than the corresponding DBM. This again is good for locality. The table also explains the slowdown on qlz: although the number of memory references almost halve, the number of D1 misses increase, which illustrates the importance of locality.

But Fig. 10 reveals a more subtle explanation for locality. Figure 10 gives distributions of the identifiers which arise on CoDBM reads during the analysis of taes, lev and sol. For a given prefix of the values array, each distribution gives the total number of times the array prefix is used to map an identifier to a value. The distributions are normalised. It is interesting to see that accesses cluster at the bottom end of values, implying that there is both temporal and

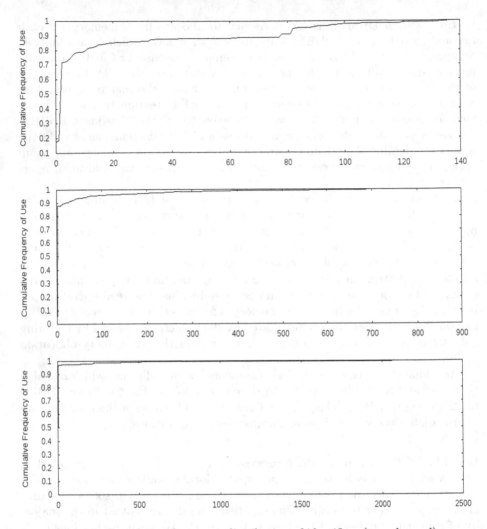

Fig. 10. Cumulative frequency distribution of identifiers (taes, lev, sol)

spacial locality to the way the array is accessed. In fact, for taes, the first 7 elements of values attract over 75% of the reads, and for both lev and sol the first 3 elements are responsible for over 75% of the reads. This bias is not unique to taes, lev and sol; it is a general pattern.

This pattern of access suggests that the portion of values needed for a read is likely to reside in a cache line. This stems from the way identifiers are created on demand when a matrix is updated with a previously unseen number. Numbers which arise with highest frequency tend to be encountered earlier in the lifetime of an analysis hence are inclined to be assigned smaller identifiers, giving the biased frequency distributions of Fig. 10. Moreover, the preallocated value ∞, needed for space widening, is also accessed with high frequency.

The first few iterations of the while loop at line 6 of Fig. 6 are not likely to be conducive to locality, which suggests that a high proportion of writes to reads is likely to degrade locality, which squares with unq.

5   Related Work

A DBM can track any octagonal constraint between any pair of two variables, whether that constraint is needed or not. In response, variable clustering has been proposed [6,17,24] for grouping variables into sets which scope the relationships which are tracked. However, deciding variable groupings is an art, although there has been recent progress made in its automation [12].

Other remedies for the size of DBMs include sparse analyses [20] and access-based localisation techniques [4]. Access-based localisation uses scoping heuristics to adjust the size of the DBM to those variables that can actually be updated [4]. Sparse analyses generalise access-based localisation techniques, using data dependencies to adjust the size of abstract states propagated to method calls: [20] defines a generic technique to apply sparse techniques to abstract interpretation and combines this with variable packing to scale an octagon based abstract interpreter for C programs. Variable clustering, access-based localisation and sparse frameworks are orthogonal to our work, and can take advantage of the CoDBMs introduced in this paper.

Sparse matrix representations have been proposed for Octagons [14] and Differences [11] as an alternative to DBMs, but these representations sit at odds with the simplicity of the original domains algorithms. The desirable property of strong closure [18] (the normal form for Octagons) does not hold for a sparse representation, motivating the need to rework the domain operations in order to retain precision [14]. The CoDBM representation proposed in this paper is reminiscent of a sparse set representation [7], which likewise uses two arrays. The key difference is that sparse sets use their two arrays to reference one another to speed up set operations. They are also limited to a fixed size universe. CoDBMs, on the other hand, uses a single lookup table to store all rational numbers occurring in all the difference matrices and moreover the elements of the difference matrices are not prescribed upfront.

There is a trend towards using doubles instead of rationals so as to take advantage of modern instruction sets [23]. In contrast, we aim to retain the precision of rationals and not sacrifice performance for soundness. The memory footprint of a DBM directly relates to the underlying arithmetic: a double requires 8 bytes in the IEEE 754-1983 standard and a rational number at least 12 bytes using the GNU multiple precision library applied in Apron [13]. But if space is the primary concern, then a CoDBM over rationals will be smaller than its corresponding DBM over doubles.

6   Discussion

CoDBMs are designed to change the economy of difference matrices: the overheads of memory management in DBMs are exchanged in CoDBMs for the costs of reading the matrix through an indirection and writing to the matrix through search. Callgrind instrumentation shows that one hot spot occurs at lines 9 and 10 of the get_id function, in comparing rational numbers. If the writes to the matrix have temporal locality, then a splay trees [1] could improve search by ensuring that recently accessed rationals will require fewer comparisons to be found again. Alternatively hashing could reduce the number of comparisons, while matching the conceptual simplicity of Octagons.

We suspect that CoDBMs will confer further advantages for parallelisation where multiple processes increase the size of the working set, and exert additional pressure on the caches. It is worth noting that CoDBMs were designed to counter the size of DBMs, but actually are faster too. As qlz illustrates, the key difference is not the number of memory references, but locality. Moreover, as CPUs continue to out pace memory, locality will only become a more important issue in the implementation and realisation of abstract domains.

Finally, it is important to emphasise that CoDBMs are not a substitute for variable clustering and access-based localisation: these are orthogonal techniques that can benefit from CoDBMs.

7   Conclusions

This paper proposes CoDBMs as a compact, new representation for difference bound matrices (DBMs) in which each distinct rational number in the DBM is assigned a unique (small) identifier. The identifier is then stored as an entry in the matrix as a substitute for the number it represents. The matrix is used in tandem with two arrays. The first array, used for reading the matrix, maps the identifier to its number. The second array is ordered, used for writing to the matrix, maps a number to its identifier (to provide a partial inverse). CoDBMs retain the regular structure of DBMs, hence the simple, attractive loop structures of their domain operations, but also reduce space consumption while improving cache behaviour, and speeding up long-running analyses.

Acknowledgements. We thank Colin King at Canonical Limited for his tireless patience and help with the performance analysis which underpinned this work.

References

1. Allen, B., Munro, I.: Self-organizing binary search trees. J. ACM **25**(4), 526–535 (1978)
2. Bagnara, R., Hill, P.M., Zaffanella, E.: Weakly-relational shapes for numeric abstractions: improved algorithms and proofs of correctness. Form. Methods Syst. Des. **35**(3), 279–323 (2009)
3. Banterle, F., Giacobazzi, R.: A fast implementation of the octagon abstract domain on graphics hardware. In: Nielson, H.R., Filé, G. (eds.) SAS 2007. LNCS, vol. 4634, pp. 315–332. Springer, Heidelberg (2007). https://doi.org/10.1007/978-3-540-74061-2_20

4. Beckschulze, E., Kowalewski, S., Brauer, J.: Access-based localization for octagons. Electron. Notes Theor. Comput. Sci. **287**, 29–40 (2012)
5. Bellman, R.: On a routing problem. Q. Appl. Math. **16**, 87–90 (1958)
6. Blanchet, B., Cousot, P., Cousot, R., Feret, J., Mauborgne, L., Miné, A., Monniaux, D., Rival, X.: A static analyzer for large safety-critical software. In: PLDI, pp. 196–207 (2003)
7. Briggs, P., Torczon, L.: An efficient representation for sparse sets. ACM Lett. Program. Lang. Syst. **2**(1–4), 59–69 (1993)
8. Bühler, D., Cuoq, P., Yakobowski, B., Lemerre, M., Maroneze, A., Perrelle, V., Prevosto, V.: The EVA Plug-in. CEA LIST, Software Reliability Laboratory, Saclay, France, F-91191 (2017). https://frama-c.com/download/frama-c-value-analysis.pdf
9. Chawdhary, A., Robbins, E., King, A.: Simple and efficient algorithms for octagons. In: Garrigue, J. (ed.) APLAS 2014. LNCS, vol. 8858, pp. 296–313. Springer, Cham (2014). https://doi.org/10.1007/978-3-319-12736-1_16
10. Dill, D.L.: Timing assumptions and verification of finite-state concurrent systems. In: Sifakis, J. (ed.) CAV 1989. LNCS, vol. 407, pp. 197–212. Springer, Heidelberg (1990). https://doi.org/10.1007/3-540-52148-8_17
11. Gange, G., Navas, J.A., Schachte, P., Søndergaard, H., Stuckey, P.J.: Exploiting sparsity in difference-bound matrices. In: Rival, X. (ed.) SAS 2016. LNCS, vol. 9837, pp. 189–211. Springer, Heidelberg (2016). https://doi.org/10.1007/978-3-662-53413-7_10
12. Heo, K., Oh, H., Yang, H.: Learning a variable-clustering strategy for octagon from labeled data generated by a static analysis. In: Rival, X. (ed.) SAS 2016. LNCS, vol. 9837, pp. 237–256. Springer, Heidelberg (2016). https://doi.org/10.1007/978-3-662-53413-7_12
13. Jeannet, B., Miné, A.: Apron: a library of numerical abstract domains for static analysis. In: Bouajjani, A., Maler, O. (eds.) CAV 2009. LNCS, vol. 5643, pp. 661–667. Springer, Heidelberg (2009). https://doi.org/10.1007/978-3-642-02658-4_52
14. Jourdan, J.-H.: Verasco: a formally verified C static analyzer. Ph.D. thesis, Université Paris Diderot (Paris 7) Sorbonne Paris Cité, May 2016
15. Lassez, J.-L., Huynh, T., McAloon, K.: Simplication and elimination of redundant linear arithmetic constraints. In: Constraint Logic Programming, pp. 73–87. MIT Press (1993)
16. Measche, M., Berthomieu, B.: Time Petri-nets for analyzing and verifying time dependent communication protocols. In: Rudin, H., West, C. (eds.) Protocol Specification, Testing and Verification III, pp. 161–172. North-Holland (1983)
17. Miné, A.: Weakly relational numerical abstract domains. Ph.D. thesis, École Polytechnique En Informatique (2004)
18. Miné, A.: The octagon abstract domain. HOSC **19**(1), 31–100 (2006)
19. Nethercote, N.: Dynamic binary analysis and instrumentation. Ph.D. thesis, Trinity College, University of Cambridge (2004)
20. Oh, H., Heo, K., Lee, W., Lee, W., Park, D., Kang, J., Yi, K.: Global sparse analysis framework. ACM TOPLAS **36**(3), 8:1–8:44 (2014)
21. Pavlov, I.: Lempel-Ziv-Markov chain algorithm CPU benchmarking (2017). http://www.7-cpu.com/
22. Ruggieri, S.: On computing the semi-sum of two integers. Inf. Process. Lett. **87**(2), 67–71 (2003)
23. Singh, G., Püschel, M., Vechev, M.: Making numerical program analysis fast. In: PLDI, pp. 303–313. ACM Press (2015)

24. Venet, A., Brat, G. Precise and efficient static array bound checking for large embedded C programs. In: PLDI, pp. 31–242 (004)
25. Weidendorfer, J., Kowarschik, M., Trinitis, C.: A tool suite for simulation based analysis of memory access behavior. In: Bubak, M., van Albada, G.D., Sloot, P.M.A., Dongarra, J. (eds.) ICCS 2004. LNCS, vol. 3038, pp. 440–447. Springer, Heidelberg (2004). https://doi.org/10.1007/978-3-540-24688-6_58
26. Williams Jr., L.F.: A modification to the half-interval search (binary search) method. In: Proceedings of the 14th ACM Southeast Conference, pp. 95–101 (1976)

Sharper and Simpler Nonlinear Interpolants for Program Verification

Takamasa Okudono[1]([✉]), Yuki Nishida[2], Kensuke Kojima[2], Kohei Suenaga[2,3],
Kengo Kido[1,4], and Ichiro Hasuo[5]

[1] University of Tokyo, Tokyo, Japan
tokudono@is.s.u-tokyo.ac.jp
[2] Kyoto University, Kyoto, Japan
[3] JST PRESTO, Kyoto, Japan
[4] JSPS Research Fellow, Tokyo, Japan
[5] National Institute of Informatics, Tokyo, Japan

Abstract. *Interpolation* of jointly infeasible predicates plays important roles in various program verification techniques such as invariant synthesis and CEGAR. Intrigued by the recent result by Dai et al. that combines real algebraic geometry and SDP optimization in synthesis of polynomial interpolants, the current paper contributes its enhancement that yields *sharper* and *simpler* interpolants. The enhancement is made possible by: theoretical observations in real algebraic geometry; and our continued fraction-based algorithm that rounds off (potentially erroneous) numerical solutions of SDP solvers. Experiment results support our tool's effectiandveness; we also demonstrate the benefit of sharp and simple interpolants in program verification examples.

Keywords: Program verification · Interpolation · Nonlinear interpolant · Polynomial · Real algebraic geometry · SDP optimization · Numerical optimization

1 Introduction

Interpolation for Program Verification. *Interpolation* in logic is a classic problem. Given formulas φ and ψ that are jointly unsatisfiable (meaning $\models \varphi \wedge \psi \Rightarrow \bot$), one asks for a "simple" formula ξ such that $\models \varphi \Rightarrow \xi$ and $\models \xi \wedge \psi \Rightarrow \bot$. The simplicity requirement on ξ can be a formal one (like the *common variable condition*, see Definition 2.6) but it can also be informal, like "ξ is desirably much simpler than φ and ψ (that are gigantic)." Anyway the intention is that ξ should be a simple witness for the joint unsatisfiability of φ and ψ, that is, an "essential reason" why φ and ψ cannot coexist.

This classic problem of interpolation has found various applications in static analysis and program verification [11,13,15,21–23]. This is particularly the case with techniques based on automated reasoning, where one relies on symbolic *predicate abstraction* in order to deal with infinite-state systems like (behaviors of) programs. It is crucial for the success of such techniques that we discover "good"

© Springer International Publishing AG 2017
B.-Y.E. Chang (Ed.): APLAS 2017, LNCS 10695, pp. 491–513, 2017.
https://doi.org/10.1007/978-3-319-71237-6_24

predicates that capture the essence of the systems' properties. Interpolants—as simple witnesses of incompatibility—have proved to be potent candidates for these "good" predicates.

Interpolation via Optimization and Real Algebraic Geometry. A lot of research efforts have been made towards efficient interpolation algorithms. One of the earliest is [5]: it relies on *Farkas' lemma* for synthesizing linear interpolants (i.e. interpolants expressed by linear inequalities). This work and subsequent ones have signified the roles of *optimization* problems and their algorithms in efficient synthesis of interpolants.

In this line of research we find the recent contribution by Dai et al. [8] remarkable, from both theoretical and implementation viewpoints. Towards synthesis of *nonlinear* interpolants (that are expressed by polynomial inequalities), their framework in [8] works as follows.

– On the theory side it relies on *Stengle's Positivstellensatz*—a fundamental result in *real algebraic geometry* [3,34]—and relaxes the interpolation problem to the problem of finding a suitable "disjointness certificate." The latter consists of a few polynomials subject to certain conditions.
– On the implementation side it relies on state-of-the-art *SDP solvers* to efficiently solve the SDP problem that results from the above relaxation.

In [8] it is reported that the above framework successfully synthesizes nontrivial nonlinear interpolants, where some examples are taken from program verification scenarios.

Contribution. The current work contributes an enhancement of the framework from [8]. Our specific concerns are in *sharpness* and *simplicity* of interpolants.

Example 1.1 (sharp interpolant). Let $\mathcal{T} := (y > x \land x > -y)$ and $\mathcal{T}' := (y \leq -x^2)$. These designate the blue and red areas in the figure, respectively. We would like an interpolant $\mathcal{S}$ so that $\mathcal{T}$ implies $\mathcal{S}$ and $\mathcal{S}$ is disjoint from $\mathcal{T}'$. Note however that such an interpolant $\mathcal{S}$ must be "sharp." The areas of $\mathcal{T}$ and $\mathcal{T}'$ almost intersect with each other at $(x, y) = (0, 0)$. That is, the conditions $\mathcal{T}$ and $\mathcal{T}'$ are barely disjoint in the sense that, once we replace $>$ with $\geq$ in $\mathcal{T}$, they are no longer disjoint. (See Definition 3.1 for formal definitions.)

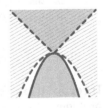

The original framework in [8] fails to synthesize such "sharp" interpolants; and this failure is theoretically guaranteed (see Sect. 3.1). In contrast our modification of the framework succeeds: it yields an interpolant $8y + 4x^2 > 0$ (the green hatched area).

Example 1.2 (simple interpolant). Let $\mathcal{T} := (y \geq x^2 + 1)$ and $\mathcal{T}' := (y \leq -x^2 - 1)$ The implementation aiSat [6] of the workflow in [8] succeeds and synthesizes an interpolant $284.3340y + 0.0012x^2y > 0$. In contrast our tool synthesizes $5y + 2 > 0$ that is much simpler.

The last two examples demonstrate two issues that we found in the original framework in [8]. Our enhanced framework shall address these issues of sharpness and simplicity, employing the following two main technical pieces.

The first piece is *sharpened Positivstellensatz-inspired relaxation* (Sect. 3). We start with the relaxation in [8] that reduces interpolation to finding polynomial certificates. We devise its "sharp" variant that features: use of *strict inequalities* $>$ (instead of *disequalities* $\neq$); and a corresponding adaptation of Positivstellensatz that uses a notion we call *strict cone*. Our sharpened relaxation allows encoding to SDP problems, much like in [8].

The second technical piece that we rely on is our continued fraction-based *rounding algorithm*. We employ the algorithm in what we call the *rounding-validation loop* (see Sect. 4), a workflow from [12] that addresses the challenge of *numerical errors*.

Numerical relaxation of problems in automated reasoning—such as the SDP relaxation in [8] and in the current work—is nowadays common, because of potential performance improvement brought by numerical solvers. However a numerical solution is subject to numerical errors, and due to those errors, the solution may not satisfy the original constraint. This challenge is identified by many authors [2,12,17,27,28,30].

Moreover, even if a numerical solution satisfies the original constraint, the solution often involves floating-point numbers and thus is not simple. See Example 1.2, where one may wonder if the coefficient 0.0012 should be simply 0. Such complication is a disadvantage in applications in program verification, where we use interpolants as candidates for "useful" predicates. These predicates should grasp essence and reflect insights of programmers; it is our hypothesis that such predicates should be simple. Similar arguments have been made in previous works such as [16,35].

To cope with the last challenges of potential unsoundness and lack of simplicity, we employ a workflow that we call the *rounding-validation loop*. The workflow has been used e.g. in [12]; see Fig. 1 (p. 14) for a schematic overview. In the "rounding" phase we apply our continued fraction-based rounding algorithm to a candidate obtained as a numerical solution of an SDP solver. In the "validation" phase the rounded candidate is fed back to the original constraints and their satisfaction is checked by purely symbolic means. If validation fails, we increment the *depth* of rounding—so that the candidate becomes less simple but closer to the original candidate—and we run the loop again.

Example 1.3 (invalid interpolant candicate). Let $\mathcal{T} =$ $(y \leq -1), \mathcal{T}' = (x^2 + y^2 < 1)$, as shown in the figure. These are barely disjoint and hence the algorithm in [8] does not apply to it. In our workflow, the first interpolant candidate that an SDP solver yields is $f(x,y) \geq 0$, where

$$f(x,y) = \begin{pmatrix} -3.370437975 + 8.1145 \times 10^{-14}x - 2.2469y + 1.1235y^2 - 2.2607 \times 10^{-10}y^3 + \\ 9.5379 \times 10^{-11}x^2 - 2.2607 \times 10^{-10}x^2y - 4.8497 \times 10^{-11}x^2y^2 - 1.1519 \times \\ 10^{-14}x^3 + 4.8935 \times 10^{-11}x^4 - 9.7433 \times 10^{-11}y^4 \end{pmatrix}.$$

Being the output of a numerical solver the coefficients are far from simple integers. Here coefficients in very different scales coexist—for example one may wonder if the coefficient 8.1145×10^{-14} for x could just have been 0. Worse, the above candidate is in fact not an interpolant: $x = 0, y = -1$ is in the region of $\mathcal{T}$ but we have $f(0, -1) < 0$.

By subsequently applying our rounding-validation loop, we eventually obtain a candidate $34y^2 - 68y - 102 \geq 0$, and its validity is guaranteed by our tool.

This workflow of the rounding-validation loop is adopted from [12]. Our technical contribution lies in the rounding algorithm that we use therein. It can be seen an extension of the well-known rounding procedure by *continued fraction expansion*. The original procedure, employed e.g. in [27], rounds a real number into a rational number (i.e. a ratio $k_1 : k_2$ between two integers). In contrast, our current extension rounds a ratio $r_1 : \cdots : r_n$ between n real numbers into a simpler ratio $k_1 : \cdots : k_n$.

We have implemented our enhancement of [8]; we call our tool SSINT (*Sharp and Simple Interpolants*). Our experiment results support its effectiveness: the tool succeeds in synthesizing sharp interpolants (while the workflow in [8] is guaranteed to fail); and our program verification examples demonstrate the benefit of sharp and simple interpolants (synthesized by our tool) in verification. The latter benefit is demonstrated by the following example; the example is discussed in further detail later in Sect. 5.

Example 1.4 (program verification). Consider the imperative program in Listing 1.1 (p. 17). Let us verify its assertion (the last line) by *counterexample-guided abstraction refinement (CEGAR)* [4], in which we try to synthesize suitable predicates that separate the reachable region (that is under-approximated by finitely many samples of execution traces) and the unsafe region $((xa) + 2(ya) < 0)$. The use of interpolants as candidates for such separating predicates has been advocated by many authors, including [13].

Let us say that the first execution trace we sampled is the one in which the while loop is not executed at all ($1 \to 2 \to 3 \to 4 \to 16$ in line numbers). Following the workflow of CEGAR by interpolation, we are now required to compute an interpolant of $\mathcal{T} := (xa = 0 \wedge ya = 0)$ and $\mathcal{T}' := ((xa) + 2(ya) < 0)$. Because $\mathcal{T}$ and $\mathcal{T}'$ are "barely disjoint" (in the sense of Example 1.1, that is, the closures of $\mathcal{T}$ and $\mathcal{T}'$ are no longer disjoint), the procedure in [8] cannot generate any interpolant. In contrast, our implementation—based on our refined use of Stengle's positivstellensatz, see Sect. 3—successfully discovers an interpolant $(xa) + 2(ya) \geq 0$. This interpolant happens to be an invariant of the program and proves the safety of the program.

Later in Sect. 5 we explain this example in further detail.

Related Work. Aside from the work by Dai et al. [8] on which we are based, there are several approaches to polynomial interpolation in the literature. Gan et al. [9] consider interpolation for polynomial inequalities that involve uninterpreted functions, with the restriction that the degree of polynomials is quadratic. An earlier work with a similar aim is [18] by Kupferschmid et al. Gao and

Zufferey [10] study nonlinear interpolant synthesis over real numbers. Their method can handle transcendental functions as well as polynomials. Interpolants are generated from refutation, and represented as union of rectangular regions. Because of this representation, although their method enjoys δ-completeness (a notion of approximate completeness), it cannot synthesize sharp interpolants like Example 1.1. Their interpolants tend to be fairly complicated formulas, too, and therefore would not necessarily be suitable for applications like program verification (where we seek simple predicates; see Sect. 5).

Putinar's positivstellensatz [29] is a well-known variation of Stengle's positivstellensatz; it is known to allow simpler SDP relaxation than Stengle's. However it does not suit the purpose of the current paper because: (1) it does not allow mixture of strict and non-strict inequalities; and (2) it requires a compactness condition. There is a common trick to force strict inequalities in a framework that only allows non-strict inequalities, namely to add a small perturbation. We find that this trick does not work in our program verification examples; see Sect. 5.

The problem with numerical errors in SDP solving has been discussed in the literature. Harrison [12] is one of the first to tackle the problem: the work introduces the workflow of the rounding-validation loop; the rounding algorithm used there increments a denominator at each step and thus is simpler than our continued fraction-based one. The same rounding algorithm is used in [2], as we observe in the code. Peyrl and Parrilo [27], towards the goal of sum-of-square decomposition in rational coefficients, employs a rounding algorithm by continued fractions. The difference from our current algorithm is that they apply continued fraction expansion to each of the coefficients, while our generalized algorithm simplifies the ratio between the coefficients altogether. The main technical novelty of [27] lies in identification of a condition for validity of a rounded candidate. This framework is further extended in Kaltofen et al. [17] for a different optimization problem, combined with the Gauss–Newton iteration.

More recently, an approach using a simultaneous Diophantine approximation algorithm—that computes the best approximation within a given bound of denominator—is considered by Lin et al. [20]. They focus on finding a rational fine approximation to the output of SDP solvers, and do not aim at simpler certificates. Roux et al. [30] proposes methods that guarantee existence of a solution relying on numerical solutions of SDP solvers. They mainly focus on strictly feasible problems, and therefore some of our examples in Sect. 5 are out of their scope. Dai et al. [7] address the same problem of numerical errors in the context of barrier-certificate synthesis. They use *quantifier elimination* (QE) for validation, while our validation method relies on a well-known characterization of positive semidefiniteness (whose check is less expensive than QE; see Sect. 4.2).

Future Work. The workflow of the rounding-validation loop [12] is simple but potentially effective: in combination with our rounding algorithm based on continued fractions, we speculate that the workflow can offer a general methodology for coping with numerical errors in verification and in symbolic reasoning. Certainly our current implementation is not the best of the workflow: for example, the validation phase of Sect. 4 could be further improved by techniques from interval arithmetic, e.g. from [31].

Collaboration between numerical and symbolic computation in general (like in [1]) interests us, too. For example in our workflow (Fig. 1, p. 14) there is a disconnection between the SDP phase and later: passing additional information (such as gradients) from the SDP phase can make the rounding-validation loop more effective.

Our current examples are rather simple and small. While they serve as a feasibility study of the proposed interpolation method, practical applicability of the method in the context of program verification is yet to be confirmed. We plan to conduct more extensive case studies, using common program verification benchmarks such as in [33], making comparison with other methods, and further refining our method in its course.

Organization of the Paper. In Sect. 2 we review the framework in [8]. Its lack of sharpness is established in Sect. 3.1; this motivates our sharpened Positivstellensatz-inspired relaxation of interpolation in Sect. 3.2. In Sect. 4 we describe our whole workflow and its implementation, describing the rounding-validation loop and the continued fraction-based algorithm used therein. In Sect. 5 we present experimental results and discuss the benefits in program verification. Some proofs and details are deferred to appendices in [24].

2   Preliminaries

Here we review the previous interpolation algorithm by Dai et al. [8]. It is preceded by its mathematical bedrock, namely Stengle's Positivstellensatz [34].

2.1   Real Algebraic Geometry and Stengle's Positivstellensatz

We write X for a sequence $X_1, X_2, \ldots, X_k$ of variables, and $\mathbb{R}[X]$ for the set of polynomials in $X_1, \ldots, X_k$ over $\mathbb{R}$. We sometimes write $f(X)$ for a polynomial $f \in \mathbb{R}[X]$ in order to signify that the variables in f are restricted to those in X.

Definition 2.1 (SAS$\neq$). A *semialgebraic system with disequalities* (SAS$_{\neq}$) T, in variables $X_1, X_2, \ldots, X_k$, is a sequence

$$T = \begin{pmatrix} f_1(X) \geq 0, \ \ldots, \ f_s(X) \geq 0, & g_1(X) \neq 0, \ \ldots, \ g_t(X) \neq 0, \\ h_1(X) = 0, \ \ldots, \ h_u(X) = 0 \end{pmatrix} \quad (1)$$

of *inequalities* $f_i(X) \geq 0$, *disequalities* $g_j(X) \neq 0$ and *equalities* $h_k(X) = 0$. Here $f_i, g_j, h_k \in \mathbb{R}[X]$ are polynomials, for $i \in [1, s], j \in [1, t]$ and $k \in [1, u]$.

For the SAS$_{\neq}$ T in (1) in k variables, we say $x \in \mathbb{R}^k$ *satisfies* T if $f_i(x) \geq 0$, $g_j(x) \neq 0$ and $h_k(x) = 0$ hold for all i, j, k. We let $[\![T]\!] \subseteq \mathbb{R}^k$ denote the set of all such x, that is, $[\![T]\!] := \{x \in \mathbb{R}^k \mid x \text{ satisfies } T\}$.

Definition 2.2 (cone, multiplicative monoid, ideal). A set $C \subseteq \mathbb{R}[X]$ is a *cone* if it satisfies the following closure properties: (1) $f, g \in C$ implies $f + g \in C$; (2) $f, g \in C$ implies $fg \in C$; and (3) $f^2 \in C$ for any $f \in \mathbb{R}[X]$.

A set $M \subseteq \mathbb{R}[X]$ is a *multiplicative monoid* if it satisfies the following: (1) $1 \in M$; and (2) $f, g \in M$ implies $fg \in M$.

A set $I \subseteq \mathbb{R}[X]$ is an *ideal* if it satisfies: (1) $0 \in I$; (2) $f, g \in I$ implies $f + g \in I$; and (3) $fg \in I$ for any $f \in \mathbb{R}[X]$ and $g \in I$.

For a subset A of $\mathbb{R}[X]$, we write: $\mathcal{C}(A)$, $\mathcal{M}(A)$, and $\mathcal{I}(A)$ for the smallest cone, multiplicative monoid, and ideal, respectively, that includes A.

The last notions encapsulate closure properties of inequality/disequality/equality predicates, respectively, in the following sense. The definition of $[\![T]\!] \subseteq \mathbb{R}^k$ is in Definition 2.1.

Lemma 2.3. *Let $x \in \mathbb{R}^k$ and $f_i, g_j, h_k \in \mathbb{R}[X]$.*

1. *If $x \in [\![f_1 \geq 0, \ldots, f_s \geq 0]\!]$, then $f(x) \geq 0$ for all $f \in \mathcal{C}(f_1, \ldots, f_s)$.*
2. *If $x \in [\![g_1 \neq 0, \ldots, g_t \neq 0]\!]$, then $g(x) \neq 0$ for all $g \in \mathcal{M}(g_1, \ldots, g_t)$.*
3. *If $x \in [\![h_1 = 0, \ldots, h_u = 0]\!]$, then $h(x) = 0$ for all $h \in \mathcal{I}(h_1, \ldots, h_u)$.*

□

The following theorem is commonly attributed to [34]. See also [3].

Theorem 2.4 (Stengle's Positivstellensatz). *Let T be the $SAS_{\neq}$ in (1) (Definition 2.1). It is infeasible (meaning $[\![T]\!] = \emptyset$) if and only if there exist $f \in \mathcal{C}(f_1, \ldots, f_s)$, $g \in \mathcal{M}(g_1, \ldots, g_t)$ and $h \in \mathcal{I}(h_1, \ldots, h_u)$ such that $f + g^2 + h = 0$.*

□

The polynomials f, g, h can be seen as an *infeasible certificate* of the $SAS_{\neq}$ T. The "if" direction is shown easily: if $x \in [\![T]\!]$ then we have $f(x) \geq 0$, $g(x)^2 > 0$ and $h(x) = 0$ (by Lemma 2.3), leading to a contradiction. The "only if" direction is nontrivial and remarkable; it is however not used in the algorithm of [8] nor in this paper.

SOS polynomials play important roles, both theoretically and in implementation.

Definition 2.5 (sum of squares (SOS)). A polynomial is called a *sum of squares (SOS)* if it can be written in the form $p_1^2 + \cdots + p_N^2$ (for some polynomials $p_1, \ldots, p_N$). Note that $\mathcal{C}(\emptyset)$ is exactly the set of sums of squares (Definition 2.2).

2.2 The Interpolation Algorithm by Dai et al.

Definition 2.6 (interpolant). Let T and T' be $SAS_{\neq}$'s, in variables X, Y and in X, Z, respectively, given in the following form. Here we assume that each variable in X occurs both in T and T', and that $Y \cap Z = \emptyset$.

$$T = \begin{pmatrix} f_1(X, Y) \geq 0, & \ldots, & f_s(X, Y) \geq 0, & g_1(X, Y) \neq 0, & \ldots, & g_t(X, Y) \neq 0, \\ h_1(X, Y) = 0, & \ldots, & h_u(X, Y) = 0 \end{pmatrix}$$

$$T' = \begin{pmatrix} f'_1(X, Z) \geq 0, & \ldots, & f'_{s'}(X, Z) \geq 0, & g'_1(X, Z) \neq 0, & \ldots, & g'_{t'}(X, Z) \neq 0, \\ h'_1(X, Z) = 0, & \ldots, & h'_{u'}(X, Z) = 0 \end{pmatrix}$$

$$(2)$$

Assume further that T and T' are *disjoint*, that is, $[\![T]\!] \cap [\![T']\!] = \emptyset$.
An SAS$_\neq$ S is an *interpolant* of T and T' if it satisfies the following:

1. $[\![T]\!] \subseteq [\![S]\!]$;
2. $[\![S]\!] \cap [\![T']\!] = \emptyset$; and
3. (the *common variable condition*) the SAS$_\neq$ S is in the variables $\boldsymbol{X}$, that is, S contains only those variables which occur both in T and T'.

Towards efficient synthesis of nonlinear interpolants Dai et al. [8] introduced a workflow that hinges on the following variation of Positivstellensatz.

Theorem 2.7 (disjointness certificate in [8, Sect. 4]). *Let T, T' be the SAS$_\neq$'s in (2). Assume there exist*

$$
\begin{array}{ll}
\tilde{f} \in \mathcal{C}(f_1, \ldots, f_s, f'_1, \ldots, f'_{s'}), & g \in \mathcal{M}(g_1, \ldots, g_t, g'_1, \ldots, g'_{t'}) \quad and \\
\tilde{h} \in \mathcal{I}(h_1, \ldots, h_u, h'_1, \ldots, h'_{u'}), & such\ that\ \ 1 + \tilde{f} + g^2 + \tilde{h} = 0.
\end{array}
\tag{3}
$$

Assume further that $\tilde{f}$ allows a decomposition $\tilde{f} = f + f'$, with some $f \in \mathcal{C}(f_1, \ldots, f_s)$ and $f' \in \mathcal{C}(f'_1, \ldots, f'_{s'})$. (An element $\tilde{h}$ in the ideal always allows a decomposition $\tilde{h} = h + h'$ such that $h \in \mathcal{I}(h_1, \ldots, h_u)$ and $h' \in \mathcal{I}(h'_1, \ldots, h'_{u'})$.)

Under the assumptions T and T' are disjoint. Moreover the SAS$_\neq$

$$
S := \left(1/2 + f + g^2 + h > 0 \right)
\tag{4}
$$

satisfies the conditions of an interpolant of T and T' (Definition 2.6), except for Condition 3. (the common variable condition).

Proof. The proof is much like the "if" part of Theorem 2.4. It suffices to show that S is an interpolant; then the disjointness of T and T' follows.

To see $[\![T]\!] \subseteq [\![S]\!]$, assume $\boldsymbol{x} \in [\![T]\!]$. Then we have $f(\boldsymbol{x}) \geq 0$ and $h(\boldsymbol{x}) = 0$ by Lemma 2.3; additionally $\left(g(\boldsymbol{x}) \right)^2 \geq 0$ holds too. Thus $1/2 + f(\boldsymbol{x}) + \left(g(\boldsymbol{x}) \right)^2 + h(\boldsymbol{x}) \geq 1/2 > 0$ and we have $\boldsymbol{x} \in [\![S]\!]$.

To see $[\![S]\!] \cap [\![T']\!] = \emptyset$, we firstly observe that the following holds for any $\boldsymbol{x}$.

$$
\begin{aligned}
0 &= 1 + f(\boldsymbol{x}) + f'(\boldsymbol{x}) + \left(g(\boldsymbol{x}) \right)^2 + h(\boldsymbol{x}) + h'(\boldsymbol{x}) \quad \text{by (3)} \\
&= \left(1/2 + f(\boldsymbol{x}) + (g(\boldsymbol{x}))^2 + h(\boldsymbol{x}) \right) + \left(1/2 + f'(\boldsymbol{x}) + h'(\boldsymbol{x}) \right).
\end{aligned}
\tag{5}
$$

Assume $\boldsymbol{x} \in [\![S]\!] \cap [\![T']\!]$. By $\boldsymbol{x} \in [\![S]\!]$ we have $1/2 + f(\boldsymbol{x}) + (g(\boldsymbol{x}))^2 + h(\boldsymbol{x}) > 0$; and by $\boldsymbol{x} \in [\![T']\!]$ we have $f'(\boldsymbol{x}) \geq 0$ and $h'(\boldsymbol{x}) = 0$ (Lemma 2.3), hence $1/2 + f'(\boldsymbol{x}) + h'(\boldsymbol{x}) \geq 1/2 > 0$. Thus the right-hand side of (5) is strictly positive, a contradiction. $\qquad\square$

Note that we no longer have completeness: existence of an interpolant like (4) is not guaranteed. Nevertheless Theorem 2.7 offers a sound method to construct an interpolant, namely by finding a suitable disjointness certificate f, f', g, h, h'.

The interpolation algorithm in [8] is shown in Algorithm 1, where search for a disjointness certificate f, f', g, h, h' is relaxed to the following problem.

Algorithm 1. The interpolation algorithm by Dai et al. [8]. Here $\mathbf{2} = \{0,1\}$

1: **input**: SAS$_{\neq}$'s $\mathcal{T}, \mathcal{T}'$ in (2), and $b \in \mathbb{N}$ (the maximum degree)
2: **output**: either an interpolant $\mathcal{S}$ of $\mathcal{T}$ and $\mathcal{T}'$, or FAIL
3: $h := (\prod_{i=1}^{t} g_i)(\prod_{i'=1}^{t'} g_{i'}')$; $g := h^{\lfloor b/2 \deg(h) \rfloor}$ {g is roughly of degree $b/2$}
4: Solve PDioph^{SOS} to find $(\overrightarrow{\alpha}, \overrightarrow{\alpha'}, \overrightarrow{\beta}, \overrightarrow{\beta'})$. Here:

 - $\alpha_i \in \mathcal{C}(\emptyset)_{\leq b}$ (for $i \in \mathbf{2}^s$) and $\alpha_{i'}' \in \mathcal{C}(\emptyset)_{\leq b}$ (for $i' \in \mathbf{2}^{s'}$) are SOSs,
 - $\beta_j \in \mathbb{R}[\boldsymbol{X}]_{\leq b}$ (for $j \in [1, u]$) and $\beta_{j'}' \in \mathbb{R}[\boldsymbol{X}]_{\leq b}$ (for $j' \in [1, u']$) are polynomials,
 - and they are subject to the constraint

$$1 + \sum_{i \in \mathbf{2}^s} \alpha_i f_1^{i_1} \cdots f_s^{i_s} + \sum_{i' \in \mathbf{2}^{s'}} \alpha_{i'}' f_1'^{i_1'} \cdots f_{s'}'^{i_{s'}'} + g^2 + \sum_{j=1}^{u} \beta_j h_j + \sum_{j'=1}^{u'} \beta_{j'}' h_{j'}' = 0. \quad (6)$$

(Such $(\overrightarrow{\alpha}, \overrightarrow{\alpha'}, \overrightarrow{\beta}, \overrightarrow{\beta'})$ may not be found, in which case return FAIL)
5: $f := \sum_{i \in \mathbf{2}^s} \alpha_i f_1^{i_1} \cdots f_s^{i_s}$; $h := \sum_{j=1}^{u} \beta_j h_j$
6: **return** $\mathcal{S} := (1/2 + f + g^2 + h > 0)$

Definition 2.8 (PDioph^{SOS}). Let PDioph^{SOS} stand for the following problem.

Input: polynomials $\varphi_1, \ldots, \varphi_n, \psi_1, \ldots, \psi_m, \xi \in \mathbb{R}[\boldsymbol{X}]$, and
             maximum degrees $d_1, \ldots, d_n, e_1, \ldots, e_m \in \mathbb{N}$
Output: SOSs $s_1 \in \mathcal{C}(\emptyset)_{\leq d_1}, \ldots, s_n \in \mathcal{C}(\emptyset)_{\leq d_n}$ and
             polynomials $t_1 \in \mathbb{R}[\boldsymbol{X}]_{\leq e_1}, \ldots, t_m \in \mathbb{R}[\boldsymbol{X}]_{\leq e_m}$
             such that $s_1 \varphi_1 + \cdots + s_n \varphi_n + t_1 \psi_1 + \cdots + t_m \psi_m + \xi = 0$

Here $\mathbb{R}[\boldsymbol{X}]_{\leq e}$ denotes the set of polynomials in $\boldsymbol{X}$ whose degree is no bigger than e. Similarly $\mathcal{C}(\emptyset)_{\leq d}$ is the set of SOSs with degree $\leq d$.

The problem PDioph^{SOS} is principally about finding polynomials s_i, t_j subject to $\sum_i s_i \varphi_i + \sum_j t_j \psi_j + \xi = 0$; this problem is known as *polynomial Diophantine equations*. In PDioph^{SOS} SOS requirements are additionally imposed on part of a solution (namely s_i); degrees are bounded, too, for algorithmic purposes.

In Algorithm 1 we rely on Theorem 2.7 to generate an interpolant: roughly speaking, one looks for a disjointness certificate f, f', g, h, h' within a predetermined maximum degree b. This search is relaxed to an instance of PDioph^{SOS} (Definition 2.8), with $n = 2^s + 2^{s'}$, $m = u + u'$, and $\xi = 1 + g^2$, as in Line 4. The last relaxation, introduced in [8], is derived from the following representation of elements of the cone $\mathcal{C}(\overrightarrow{f}, \overrightarrow{f'})$, the multiplicative monoid $\mathcal{M}(\overrightarrow{g}, \overrightarrow{g'})$ and the ideal $\mathcal{I}(\overrightarrow{h}, \overrightarrow{h'})$, respectively.

 - Each element h of $\mathcal{I}(\overrightarrow{h}, \overrightarrow{h'})$ is of the form $h = \sum_{j=1}^{u} \beta_j h_j + \sum_{j'=1}^{u'} \beta_{j'}' h_{j'}'$, where $\beta_j, \beta_{j'} \in \mathbb{R}[\boldsymbol{X}]$. This is a standard fact in ring theory.
 - Each element of $\mathcal{M}(\overrightarrow{g}, \overrightarrow{g'})$ is given by the product of finitely many elements from $\overrightarrow{g}, \overrightarrow{g'}$ (here multiplicity matters). In Algorithm 1 a polynomial g is

fixed to a "big" one. This is justified as follows: in case the constraint (6) is satisfiable using a smaller polynomial g' instead of g, by multiplying the whole equality (6) by $1 + (g/g')^2$ we see that (6) is satisfiable using g, too.

– For the cone $\mathcal{C}(\overrightarrow{f}, \overrightarrow{f'})$ we use the following fact (here $\mathbf{2} = \{0,1\}$). The lemma seems to be widely known but we present a proof in Appendix A.1 in [24] for the record.

Lemma 2.9. *An arbitrary element f of the cone $\mathcal{C}(f_1, \dots, f_s)$ can be expressed as $f = \sum_{i \in \mathbf{2}^s} \alpha_i f_1^{i_1} \dots f_s^{i_s}$, using SOSs α_i (where $i \in \mathbf{2}^s$).*   □

The last representation justifies the definition of f and h in Algorithm 1 (Line 5). We also observe that Line 6 of Algorithm 1 corresponds to (4) of Theorem 2.7.

In implementing Algorithm 1 the following fact is crucial (see [8, Sect. 3.5] and also [25,26] for details): the problem PDioph^{SOS} (Definition 2.8) can be reduced to an SDP problem, the latter allowing an efficient solution by state-of-the-art SDP solvers. It should be noted, however, that numerical errors (inevitable in interior point methods) can pose a serious issue for our application: the constraint (6) is an equality and hence fragile.

3   Positivstellensatz and Interpolation, Revisited

3.1   Analysis of the Interpolation Algorithm by Dai et al.

Intrigued by its solid mathematical foundation in real algebraic geometry as well as its efficient implementation that exploits state-of-the-art SDP solvers, we studied the framework by Dai et al. [8] (it was sketched in Sect. 2.2). In its course we obtained the following observations that motivate our current technical contributions.

We first observed that Algorithm 1 from [8] fails to find "sharp" interpolants for "barely disjoint" predicates (see Example 1.1). This turns out to be a general phenomenon (see Proposition 3.3).

Definition 3.1 (symbolic closure). Let $\mathcal{T}$ be the SAS$_{\neq}$'s in (1). The *symbolic closure* $\mathcal{T}_{\bullet}$ of $\mathcal{T}$ is the SAS$_{\neq}$ that is obtained by dropping all the disequality constraints $g_j(\mathbf{x}) \neq 0$ in $\mathcal{T}$.

$$\mathcal{T}_{\bullet} = \big(f_1(\mathbf{X}, \mathbf{Y}) \geq 0, \ \dots, \ f_s(\mathbf{X}, \mathbf{Y}) \geq 0, \ h_1(\mathbf{X}, \mathbf{Y}) = 0, \ \dots, \ h_u(\mathbf{X}, \mathbf{Y}) = 0 \big) \tag{7}$$

The intuition of symbolic closure of $\mathcal{T}$ is to replace all strict inequalities $g'_j(\mathbf{X}, \mathbf{Y}) > 0$ in $\mathcal{T}$ with the corresponding non-strict ones $g'_j(\mathbf{X}, \mathbf{Y}) \geq 0$. Since only $\geq, \neq$ and $=$ are allowed in SAS$_{\neq}$'s, strict inequalities $g'_j(\mathbf{X}, \mathbf{Y}) > 0$ are presented in the SAS$_{\neq}$ $\mathcal{T}$ by using both $g'_j(\mathbf{X}, \mathbf{Y}) \geq 0$ and $g'_j(\mathbf{X}, \mathbf{Y}) \neq 0$. The last definition drops the latter disequality ($\neq$) requirement.

The notion of symbolic closure most of the time coincides with closure with respect to the usual Euclidean topology, but not in some singular cases. See Appendix B in [24].

Definition 3.2 (bare disjointness). Let $\mathcal{T}$ and $\mathcal{T}'$ be $\mathrm{SAS}_{\neq}$'s. $\mathcal{T}$ and $\mathcal{T}'$ are *barely disjoint* if $[\![\mathcal{T}]\!] \cap [\![\mathcal{T}']\!] = \emptyset$ and $[\![\mathcal{T}_\bullet]\!] \cap [\![\mathcal{T}'_\bullet]\!] \neq \emptyset$.

An interpolant $\mathcal{S}$ of barely disjoint $\mathrm{SAS}_{\neq}$'s $\mathcal{T}$ and $\mathcal{T}'$ shall be said to be *sharp*.

An example of barely disjoint $\mathrm{SAS}_{\neq}$'s is in Example 1.1: $(0,0) \in [\![\mathcal{T}_\bullet]\!] \cap [\![\mathcal{T}'_\bullet]\!] \neq \emptyset$.

Algorithm 1 does not work if the $\mathrm{SAS}_{\neq}$'s $\mathcal{T}$ and $\mathcal{T}'$ are only barely disjoint. In fact, such failure is theoretically guaranteed, as the following result states. Its proof (in Appendix A.2 in [24]) is much like for Theorem 2.7.

Proposition 3.3. *Let $\mathcal{T}$ and $\mathcal{T}'$ be the $\mathrm{SAS}_{\neq}$'s in (2). If $\mathcal{T}$ and $\mathcal{T}'$ are barely disjoint (in the sense of Definition 3.2), there do not exist polynomials $\tilde{f} \in \mathcal{C}(\overrightarrow{f}, \overrightarrow{f'})$, $g \in \mathcal{M}(\overrightarrow{g}, \overrightarrow{g'})$ and $\tilde{h} \in \mathcal{I}(\overrightarrow{h}, \overrightarrow{h'})$ such that $1 + \tilde{f} + g^2 + \tilde{h} = 0$.* □

The conditions in Proposition 3.3 on the polynomials $\tilde{f}, g, \tilde{h}$ are those for disjointness certificates for $\mathcal{T}$ and $\mathcal{T}'$ (Theorem 2.7). As a consequence: if $\mathcal{T}$ and $\mathcal{T}'$ are only barely disjoint, interpolation relying on Theorem 2.7—that underlies the framework in [8]—never succeeds.

3.2 Interpolation via Positivstellensatz, Sharpened

The last observation motivates our "sharper" variant of Theorem 2.7—a technical contribution that we shall present shortly in Theorem 3.8. We switch input formats by replacing disequalities $\neq$ (Definition 2.1) with $<$. This small change turns out to be useful when we formulate our main result (Theorem 3.8).

Definition 3.4 ($\mathrm{SAS}_<$). A *semialgebraic system with strict inequalities* ($\mathrm{SAS}_<$) $\mathcal{T}$, in variables $X_1, X_2, \ldots, X_k$, is a sequence

$$\mathcal{T} = \begin{pmatrix} f_1(\boldsymbol{X}) \geq 0, & \ldots, & f_s(\boldsymbol{X}) \geq 0, & g_1(\boldsymbol{X}) > 0, & \ldots, & g_t(\boldsymbol{X}) > 0, \\ h_1(\boldsymbol{X}) = 0, & \ldots, & h_u(\boldsymbol{X}) = 0 \end{pmatrix} \quad (8)$$

of inequalities $f_i(\boldsymbol{X}) \geq 0$, *strict inequalities* $g_j(\boldsymbol{X}) > 0$ and equalities $h_k(\boldsymbol{X}) = 0$. Here $f_i, g_j, h_k \in \mathbb{R}[\boldsymbol{X}]$ are polynomials; $[\![\mathcal{T}]\!] \subseteq \mathbb{R}^k$ is defined like in Definition 2.1.

$\mathrm{SAS}_<$'s have the same expressive power as $\mathrm{SAS}_{\neq}$'s, as witnessed by the following mutual translation. For the $\mathrm{SAS}_{\neq}$ $\mathcal{T}$ in (1), the $\mathrm{SAS}_<$ $\tilde{\mathcal{T}} := \left(f_i(\boldsymbol{X}) \geq 0, g_j^2(\boldsymbol{X}) > 0, h_k(\boldsymbol{X}) = 0 \right)_{i,j,k}$ satisfies $[\![\mathcal{T}]\!] = [\![\tilde{\mathcal{T}}]\!]$. Conversely, for the $\mathrm{SAS}_<$ $\mathcal{T}$ in (8), the $\mathrm{SAS}_{\neq}$ $\widehat{\mathcal{T}} := \left(f_i(\boldsymbol{X}) \geq 0, g_j^2(\boldsymbol{X}) \geq 0, g_j^2(\boldsymbol{X}) \neq 0, h_k(\boldsymbol{X}) = 0 \right)_{i,j,k}$ satisfies $[\![\mathcal{T}]\!] = [\![\widehat{\mathcal{T}}]\!]$.

One crucial piece for Positivstellensatz was the closure properties of inequalities/disequalities/equalities encapsulated in the notions of cone/multiplicative monoid/ideal (Lemma 2.3). We devise a counterpart for strict inequalities.

Definition 3.5 (strict cone). A set $S \subseteq \mathbb{R}[\boldsymbol{X}]$ is a *strict cone* if it satisfies the following closure properties: (1) $f, g \in S$ implies $f + g \in S$; (2) $f, g \in S$ implies $fg \in S$; and (3) $r \in S$ for any positive real $r \in \mathbb{R}_{>0}$. For a subset A of $\mathbb{R}[\boldsymbol{X}]$, we write $\mathcal{SC}(A)$ for the smallest strict cone that includes A.

Lemma 3.6. *Let* $\boldsymbol{x} \in \mathbb{R}^k$ *and* $g_j \in \mathbb{R}[\boldsymbol{X}]$. *If* $\boldsymbol{x} \in [\![g_1 > 0, \ldots, g_t > 0]\!]$, *then* $g(\boldsymbol{x}) > 0$ *for all* $g \in \mathcal{SC}(g_1, \ldots, g_t)$. $\qquad\square$

We can now formulate adaptation of Positivstellensatz. Its proof is in Appendix A.3 in [24].

Theorem 3.7 (Positivstellensatz for SAS$_<$). *Let* T *be the SAS$_<$ in (8). It is infeasible (i.e.* $[\![T]\!] = \emptyset$) *if and only if there exist* $f \in \mathcal{C}(f_1, \ldots, f_s, g_1, \ldots, g_t)$, $g \in \mathcal{SC}(g_1, \ldots, g_t)$ *and* $h \in \mathcal{I}(h_1, \ldots, h_u)$ *such that* $f + g + h = 0$. $\qquad\square$

From this we derive the following adaptation of Theorem 2.7 that allows to synthesize sharp interpolants. The idea is as follows. In Theorem 2.7, the constants 1 (in (3)) and 1/2 (in (4)) are there to enforce strict positivity. This is a useful trick but sometimes too "dull": one can get rid of these constants and still make the proof of Theorem 2.7 work, for example when $g(\boldsymbol{x})$ happens to belong to $\mathcal{M}(g_1, \ldots, g_t)$ instead of $\mathcal{M}(g_1, \ldots, g_t, g_1', \ldots, g_{t'}')$.

Theorem 3.8 (disjointness certificate from strict cones). *Let* T *and* T' *be the following SAS$_<$'s, where* $\boldsymbol{X}$ *denotes the variables that occur in both of* T, T'.

$$T = \begin{pmatrix} f_1(\boldsymbol{X}, \boldsymbol{Y}) \geq 0, \;\ldots, \; f_s(\boldsymbol{X}, \boldsymbol{Y}) \geq 0, & g_1(\boldsymbol{X}, \boldsymbol{Y}) > 0, \;\ldots, \; g_t(\boldsymbol{X}, \boldsymbol{Y}) > 0, \\ h_1(\boldsymbol{X}, \boldsymbol{Y}) = 0, \;\ldots, \; h_u(\boldsymbol{X}, \boldsymbol{Y}) = 0 \end{pmatrix},$$

$$T' = \begin{pmatrix} f_1'(\boldsymbol{X}, \boldsymbol{Z}) \geq 0, \;\ldots, \; f_{s'}'(\boldsymbol{X}, \boldsymbol{Z}) \geq 0, & g_1'(\boldsymbol{X}, \boldsymbol{Z}) > 0, \;\ldots, \; g_{t'}'(\boldsymbol{X}, \boldsymbol{Z}) > 0, \\ h_1'(\boldsymbol{X}, \boldsymbol{Z}) = 0, \;\ldots, \; h_{u'}'(\boldsymbol{X}, \boldsymbol{Z}) = 0 \end{pmatrix}.$$

$$(9)$$

Assume there exist

$$f \in \mathcal{C}(f_1, \ldots, f_s, g_1, \ldots, g_t), \quad f' \in \mathcal{C}(f_1', \ldots, f_{s'}', g_1', \ldots, g_{t'}'),$$
$$g \in \mathcal{SC}(g_1, \ldots, g_t), \quad h \in \mathcal{I}(h_1, \ldots, h_u), \quad \text{and} \quad h' \in \mathcal{I}(h_1', \ldots, h_{u'}')$$
$$\text{such that} \quad f + f' + g + h + h' = 0. \qquad (10)$$

Then the SAS$_<$'s T *and* T' *are disjoint. Moreover the SAS$_<$*

$$S := (f + g + h > 0) \qquad (11)$$

satisfies the conditions of an interpolant of T *and* T' *(Definition 2.6), except for Condition 3. (the common variable condition).* $\qquad\square$

The proof is like for Theorem 2.7. We also have the following symmetric variant.

Algorithm 2. Our interpolation algorithm based on Theorem 3.8. Here $\mathbf{2} = \{0, 1\}$ and $\sigma(b) = \{(k_1, \ldots, k_t) \in \mathbb{N}^t \mid k_1 + \cdots + k_t \leq b + 1\}$

1: **input:** SAS$_<$'s $\mathcal{T}, \mathcal{T}'$ in (9), and $b \in \mathbb{N}$ (the maximum degree)
2: **output:** either an interpolant $\mathcal{S}$ of $\mathcal{T}$ and $\mathcal{T}'$, or FAIL
3: Solve (an extension of) PDioph^{SOS} to find $(\overrightarrow{\alpha}, \overrightarrow{\alpha'}, \overrightarrow{\beta}, \overrightarrow{\beta'}, \overrightarrow{\gamma})$. Here:

- $\alpha_{ij} \in \mathcal{C}(\emptyset)_{\leq b}$ (for $i \in \mathbf{2}^s$, $j \in \mathbf{2}^t$) and $\alpha'_{i',j'} \in \mathcal{C}(\emptyset)_{\leq b}$ (for $i' \in \mathbf{2}^{s'}$, $j' \in \mathbf{2}^{t'}$) are SOSs,
- $\beta_j \in \mathbb{R}[\boldsymbol{X}]_{\leq b}$ (for $j \in [1, u]$) and $\beta'_{j'} \in \mathbb{R}[\boldsymbol{X}]_{\leq b}$ (for $j' \in [1, u']$) are polynomials,
- and $\gamma_k \in \mathbb{R}_{\geq 0}$ (for $k \in \sigma(b)$) are nonnegative real numbers,

that are subject to the constraints

$$
\begin{aligned}
&\sum_{i \in \mathbf{2}^s, j \in \mathbf{2}^t} \alpha_{ij} f_1^{i_1} \cdots f_s^{i_s} g_1^{j_1} \cdots g_t^{j_t} \\
&+ \sum_{i' \in \mathbf{2}^{s'}, j' \in \mathbf{2}^{t'}} \alpha'_{i'j'} f_1'^{i'_1} \cdots f_{s'}'^{i'_{s'}} g_1'^{j'_1} \cdots g_{t'}'^{j'_{t'}} \\
&+ \sum_{k \in \sigma(b)} \gamma_k g_1^{k_1} \cdots g_t^{k_t} + \sum_{j=1}^{u} \beta_j h_j + \sum_{j'=1}^{u'} \beta'_{j'} h'_{j'} = 0,
\end{aligned}
\tag{12}
$$

$$
\sum_{k \in \sigma(b)} \gamma_k \geq 1, \quad \text{and}
\tag{13}
$$

some equality constraints that forces the common variable condition.   (14)

(Such $(\overrightarrow{\alpha}, \overrightarrow{\alpha'}, \overrightarrow{\beta}, \overrightarrow{\beta'}, \overrightarrow{\gamma})$ may not be found, in which case return FAIL)
4: $f := \sum_{i \in \mathbf{2}^s, j \in \mathbf{2}^t} \alpha_{ij} f_1^{i_1} \cdots f_s^{i_s} g_1^{j_1} \cdots g_t^{j_t}$; $g := \sum_{k \in \sigma(b)} \gamma_k g_1^{k_1} \cdots g_t^{k_t}$; $h := \sum_{j=1}^{u} \beta_j h_j$
5: **return** $\mathcal{S} := (f + g + h > 0)$

Theorem 3.9. *Assume the conditions of Theorem 3.8, but let us now require $g \in \mathcal{SC}(g_1', \ldots, g_{t'}')$ (instead of $g \in \mathcal{SC}(g_1, \ldots, g_t)$). Then $\mathcal{S} = (f + h \geq 0)$ is an interpolant of $\mathcal{T}$ and $\mathcal{T}'$ (except for the common variable condition).*   □

Example 3.10. Let us apply Theorem 3.8 to $\mathcal{T} = (-y > 0)$ and $\mathcal{T}' = (y - x \geq 0, y + x \geq 0)$ (these are only barely disjoint). There exists a disjointness certificate f, f', g, h, h': indeed, we can take $f = 0 \in \mathcal{C}(-y)$, $f' = 2y = (y - x) + (y + x) \in \mathcal{C}(y - x, y + x)$, $g = 2(-y) \in \mathcal{SC}(-y)$, and $h = h' = 0 \in \mathcal{I}(\emptyset)$; for these we have $f + f' + g + h + h' = 0$. This way an interpolant $\mathcal{S} = (f + g + h > 0) = (-2y > 0)$ is derived.

Remark 3.11. Our use of strict cones allows to use a polynomial g in (11). This is in contrast with g^2 in (4) and yields an interpolant of a potentially smaller degree.

We derive an interpolation algorithm from Theorem 3.8; see Algorithm 2. An algorithm based on Theorem 3.9 can be derived similarly, too.

Algorithm 2 reduces search for a disjointness certificate f, f', g, h, h' (from Theorem 3.8) to a problem similar to PDioph^{SOS} (Line 3). Unlike the original definition of PDioph^{SOS} (Definition 2.8), here we impose additional constraints (13–14) other than the equality (12) that comes from (10). It turns out that, much like PDioph^{SOS} allows relaxation to SDP problems [8,25,26], the problem in Line 3 can also be reduced to an SDP problem.

The constraint (13) is there to force $g = \sum_{k \in \mathbf{b}^t} \gamma_k g_1^{k_1} \cdots g_t^{k_t}$ (see (4)) to belong to the *strict* cone $\mathcal{SC}(g_1, \ldots, g_t)$. A natural requirement $\sum_{k \in \mathbf{b}^t} \gamma_k > 0$ for that purpose does not allow encoding to an SDP constraint so we do not use it. Our relaxation from $\sum_{k \in \mathbf{b}^t} \gamma_k > 0$ to $\sum_{k \in \mathbf{b}^t} \gamma_k \geq 1$ is inspired by [32]; it does not lead to loss of generality in our current task of finding polynomial certificates.

The constraints (14) are extracted in the following straightforward manner: we look at the coefficient of each monomial in $f + g + h$ (see Line 5); and for each monomial that involves variables other than $\mathbf{X}$ we require the coefficient to be equal to 0. The constraint is linear in the SDP variables, that we can roughly consider as the coefficients of the monomials in $\overrightarrow{\alpha}, \overrightarrow{\alpha'}, \overrightarrow{\beta}, \overrightarrow{\beta'}, \overrightarrow{\gamma}$.

Derivation of Algorithm 2 from Theorem 3.9 also relies on the following analogue of Lemma 2.9. Its proof is in Appendix A.4 in [24].

Lemma 3.12. *An arbitrary element of the strict cone $\mathcal{SC}(f_1, \ldots, f_s)$ can be expressed as $\sum_{i \in \mathbb{N}^s} \alpha_i f_1^{i_1} \cdots f_s^{i_s}$, where $\alpha_i \in \mathbb{R}_{\geq 0}$ are nonnegative reals (for $i \in \mathbb{N}^s$) such that: there exists i such that $\alpha_i > 0$; and $\alpha_i \neq 0$ for only finitely many i.* □

To summarize: our analysis of the framework of [8] has led to a new algorithm (Algorithm 2) that allows "sharp" interpolation of barely disjoint SASs. This algorithm is based on strict inequalities ($>$) instead of disequalities ($\neq$); we introduced the corresponding notion of *strict cone*. The algorithm allows solution by numeric SDP solvers. Moreover we observe that the common variable condition—that seems to be only partially addressed in [8]—allows encoding as SDP constraints.

We conclude by noting that our algorithm (Algorithm 2) generalizes Algorithm 1 from [8]. More specifically, given SAS$_{\neq}$'s $\mathcal{T}$ and $\mathcal{T}'$ that are disjoint, if Algorithm 1 finds an interpolant, then Algorithm 2 also finds an interpolant after suitable translation of $\mathcal{T}$ and $\mathcal{T}'$ to SAS$_<$'s. See Appendix C in [24].

4   Implementation: Numerical Errors and Rounding

Our implementation, that we named SSInt (*Sharp and Simple Interpolants*), is essentially Algorithm 2; in it we use an SDP solver to solve Line 3. Specifically we use the SDP solver SDPT3 [36] via YALMIP as the backend.

The biggest issue in the course of implementation is *numerical errors*—they are inevitable due to (numerical) interior point methods that underlie most state-of-the-art SDP solvers. For one thing, we often get incorrect interpolants due to numerical errors (Example 1.3). For another, in the context of program verification simpler interpolants are often more useful, reflecting simplicity of human insights (see Sect. 1). Numerical solutions, on the contrary, do not very often provide humans with clear-cut understanding.

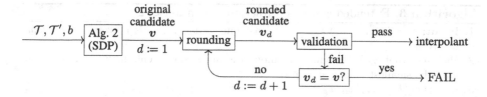

Fig. 1. The workflow of our tool SSInt

In our implementation we cope with numerical errors by *rounding* numbers. More specifically we round *ratios* $x_1 : x_2 : \cdots : x_n$ because our goal is to simplify a polynomial inequality $f + g + h > 0$ (imagine the ratio between coefficients). For this purpose we employ an extension of *continued fraction expansion*, a procedure used e.g. for the purpose of *Diophantine approximation* [19] (i.e. finding the best rational approximation k_1/k_2 of a given real r). Concretely, our extension takes a ratio $x_1 : \cdots : x_n$ of natural numbers (and a parameter d that we call *depth*), and returns a simplified ratio $y_1 : \cdots : y_n$.

Overall the workflow of our tool SSInt is as in Fig. 1.

- We first run Algorithm 2. Its output—more precisely the solution of the SDP problem in Line 3—may not yield an interpolant, due to numerical errors. The output is therefore called a *candidate* v.
- We then round the candidate v iteratively, starting with the depth $d = 1$ (the coarsest approximation that yields the simplest candidate v_1) and incrementing the depth d. The bigger the depth d is, the less simple and the closer to the original v the rounded candidate v_d becomes.
- In each iteration we check if the candidate v_d yields a valid interpolant. This *validation* phase is conducted purely symbolically, ensuring soundness of our tool.
- Our rounding algorithm eventually converges and we have $v_d = v$ for a sufficiently large d (Lemma 4.1). In case we do not succeed by then we return FAIL.

In other words, we try candidates $v_1, v_2, \ldots$, from simpler to more complex, until we obtain a symbolically certified interpolant (or fail). This is the *rounding and validation* workflow that we adopted from [12].

Our workflow involves another parameter $c \in \mathbb{N}$ that we call *precision*. It is used in an empirical implementation trick that we apply to the original candidate v: we round it off to c decimal places.

The tool SSInt is implemented in OCaml. When run with SAS$_<$'s $\mathcal{T}$, $\mathcal{T}'$ (and a parameter $b \in \mathbb{N}$ for the maximum degree, see Algorithm 2) as input, the tool generates MATLAB code that conducts the workflow in Fig. 1. The latter relies on the SDP solver SDPT3 [36] via YALMIP as the backend.

Algorithm 3. Extended continued fraction expansion CFE

1: **input:** $x = (x_1, \ldots, x_n) \in \mathbb{N}^n$ (at least one of $x_1, \ldots, x_n$ is nonzero), and *depth*
   $d \in \mathbb{N}_{>0}$
2: Pick p so that x_p is the smallest among the nonzero elements in $x_1, \ldots, x_n$
   (say the smallest among such p's)
3: $a := (\lfloor x_1/x_p \rfloor, \ldots, \lfloor x_n/x_p \rfloor)$
4: **if** $d = 1$ **then**
5:     $y := a/\gcd(a)$
6:     **return** y
7: **else**
8:     $r := (x_1 - a_1 x_p, \ldots, \overset{\overset{p-1}{\vee}}{x_{p-1} - a_{p-1}x_p}, \overset{\overset{p}{\vee}}{x_p}, \overset{\overset{p+1}{\vee}}{x_{p+1} - a_{p+1}x_p}, \ldots, x_n - a_n x_p)$
9:     $r' := \mathsf{CFE}(r, d-1)$ {a recursive call}
10:    $y := (a_1 r'_p + r'_1, \ldots, \overset{\overset{p-1}{\vee}}{a_{p-1}r'_p + r'_{p-1}}, \overset{\overset{p}{\vee}}{r'_p}, \overset{\overset{p+1}{\vee}}{a_{p+1}r'_p + r'_{p+1}}, \ldots, a_n r'_p + r'_n)$
11:    **return** $y/\gcd(y)$
12: **end if**

4.1 Rounding

Continued fraction expansion is a well-known method for rounding a real number to a rational; it is known to satisfy an optimality condition called *Diophantine approximation*. One can think of it as a procedure that simplifies ratios $x_1 : x_2$ of two numbers.

d	$\mathsf{CFE}(x,d)$
1	$(15, 1, 6)$
2	$(31, 2, 13)$
3	$(172, 11, 71)$
4	$(204, 13, 84)$
5	$(11515, 735, 4747)$
6	$(81389, 5195, 33552)$
7	$(174293, 11125, 71851)$
8	$(174293, 11125, 71851)$
x	$(871465, 55625, 359255)$

In our tool we use our extension of the procedure that simplifies ratios $x_1 : \cdots : x_n$. It is the algorithm CFE in Algorithm 3. An example is in the above table, where $x = (871465, 55625, 359255)$. One sees that the ratio gets more complicated as the depth d becomes bigger. For the depth $d = 7, 8$ the output is equivalent to the input x.

Our algorithm CFE enjoys the following pleasant properties. Their proofs are in Appendix A.5 in [24].

Lemma 4.1. *1. (Convergence) The output $\mathsf{CFE}(x, d)$ stabilizes for sufficiently large d; moreover the limit coincides with the input ratio x. That is: for each x there exists M such that $\mathsf{CFE}(x, M) = \mathsf{CFE}(x, M+1) = \cdots = x$ (as ratios).*
2. *(Well-definedness) CFE respects equivalence of ratios. That is, if $x, x' \in \mathbb{N}^n$ represent the same ratio, then $\mathsf{CFE}(x, d) = \mathsf{CFE}(x', d)$ (as ratios) for each d.* □

The algorithm CFE takes a positive ratio x as input. In the workflow in Fig. 1 CFE is applied to ratios with both positive and negative numbers; we deal with such input by first taking absolute values and later adjusting signs.

4.2 Validation

Potential unsoundness of verification methods due to numerical errors has been identified as a major challenge (see e.g. [2,12,17,27,28,30]). In our tool we enforce soundness (i.e. that the output is indeed an interpolant) by the validation phase in Fig. 1.

There the candidate v_d in question is fed back to the constraints in (the SDP problem that is solved in) Algorithm 2,[1] and we check the constraints are satisfied. The check must be symbolic. For equality constraints such symbolic check is easy. For semidefiniteness constraints, we rely on the following well-known fact: a symmetric real matrix M is positive semidefinite if and only if all the principal minors of M are nonnegative. This characterization allows us to check semidefiniteness using only addition and multiplication. We find no computation in our validation phase to be overly expensive. This is in contrast with QE-based validation methods employed e.g. in [7]: while symbolic and exact, the CAD algorithm for QE is known to be limited in scalability.

5   Experiments

We now present some experiment results. In the first part we present some simple geometric examples that call for "sharp" interpolants; in the second we discuss some program verification scenarios. These examples demonstrate our tool's capability of producing simple and sharp interpolants, together the benefits of such interpolants in program verification techniques.

The experiments were done on Apple MacBook Pro with 2.7 GHz Intel Core i5 CPU and 16 GB memory. As we described in Sect. 4, our tool SSINT consists of OCaml code that generates MATLAB code; the latter runs the workflow in Fig. 1. Running the OCaml code finishes in milliseconds; running the resulting

Table 1. Experiment results. $\mathcal{T}$ and $\mathcal{T}'$ are inputs, and $\mathcal{S}$ is our output (see Fig. 2 too). The "time" column shows the execution time (in seconds) of the generated MATLAB code, b and c show the successful choice of parameters, and d is the depth for which the workflow in Fig. 1 terminated.

	$\mathcal{T}$	$\mathcal{T}'$	$\mathcal{S}$	Time [s]	b	c	d
1	$y > x, x > -y$	$0 \geq y$	$4y > 0$	2.19	0	5	1
2	$y \leq 0$	$y > x^2$	$-2y \geq 0$	5.68	2	3	1
3	$y > x, x > -y$	$y \leq x, x \leq -y$	$4y > 0$	2.67	0	5	1
4	$y > x, x > -y$	$y \leq -x^2$	$8y + 4x^2 > 0$	5.09	2	1	1
5	$y \leq -1$	$x^2 + y^2 < 1$	$34y^2 - 68y - 102 \geq 0$	7.58	2	5	3
6	$x^2 + (y-1)^2 \leq 1$	$x^2 + (y-2)^2 > 4$	FAIL	14.0	2	5	8
7	$x^2 + (y+1)^2 \leq 1$	$x^2 + (y-1)^2 < 1$	$18x^2y - 14x^2y^2 - 144y$ $+28y^2 - 7x^4 + 18y^3 - 7y^4 \geq 0$	6.45	2	2	2
8	$x \geq z^2$	$x < -y^2$	$2x \geq 0$	7.67	2	3	1
9	$(y \geq (x-1)^2) \vee$ $(y > (x+1)^2)$	$(y < -(x-1)^2) \vee$ $(y \leq -(x+1)^2)$	$((586x + 293y + 119 > 0) \wedge (333y \geq 0)) \vee$ $((333y > 0) \wedge (374y - 748x - 117 \geq 0))$	43.7	2	3	3

---

[1]   In Algorithm 2 we introduced the constraint $\sum_{k \in \mathbf{b}^t} \gamma_k \geq 1$ in (13) as a relaxation of a natural constraint $\sum_{k \in \mathbf{b}^t} \gamma_k > 0$; see Sect. 3.2. In the validation phase of our implementation we wind back the relaxation $\sum_{k \in \mathbf{b}^t} \gamma_k \geq 1$ to the original constraint with > 0.

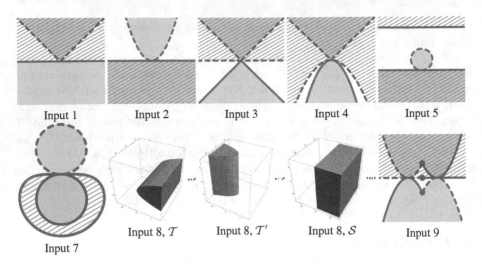

Input 1   Input 2   Input 3   Input 4   Input 5

Input 8, $\mathcal{T}$ Input 8, $\mathcal{T}'$ Input 8, $\mathcal{S}$ Input 9

Input 7

Fig. 2. Interpolants from Table 1. The blue, orange and green areas are for $\mathcal{T}$, $\mathcal{T}'$, $\mathcal{S}$, respectively. (Color figure online)

MATLAB code takes longer, typically for seconds. The execution time shown here is the average of 10 runs.

Our tool has two parameters: the maximum degree b and precision c (Sect. 4). In all our examples the common variable condition (in Definition 2.6) is successfully enforced.

Geometric Examples. Table 1 summarizes the performance of our tool on interpolation problems. For the input 6, we tried parameters $(b, c) = (1, 1), (1, 2), \ldots, (1, 5)$ and $(2, 5)$ but all failed, leading to FAIL in Fig. 1. The input 9 contains disjunction, which is not allowed in SAS$_<$'s. It is dealt with using the technique described in [8, Sect. 3.1]: an interpolant of $\mathcal{T}$ and $\mathcal{T}'$ is given by $\bigvee_i \bigwedge_j \mathcal{S}_{ij}$, where $\mathcal{S}_{ij}$ is an interpolant of each pair of disjuncts $\mathcal{T}_i$ and $\mathcal{T}'_j$ of $\mathcal{T}$ and $\mathcal{T}'$, respectively.

Listing 1.1. Code 1.3 of [8]

```
1   real x,y;
2   real xa = 0;
3   real ya = 0;
4   while(nondet()){
5     x = xa + 2*ya;
6     y = -2*xa + ya;
7     x++;
8     if(nondet()){
9       y = y + x;
10    }else{
11      y = y - x;
12    }
13    xa = x - 2*y;
14    ya = 2*x + y;
15  }
16  assert(xa + 2*ya >= 0);
```

Listing 1.2. Constant Acceleration

```
1   real x,v;
2   (x, v) = (0, 0);
3   while(nondet()){
4     (x, v) = (x+2*v, v+2);
5   }
6     assert(x >= 0);
```

$$\mathcal{T} = \begin{pmatrix} (xa) + 2(ya) \geq 0, \ x = (xa) + 2(ya), \\ y = -2(xa) + (ya), \ x_1 = x + 1, \\ y_1 = x_1 + y, \ (xa_1) = x_1 - 2y_1, \\ (ya_1) = 2x_1 + y_1 \end{pmatrix}$$

Fig. 3. The SAS for an execution of the code in Listing 1.1

Program Verification Example I: Infeasibility Checking. Consider the code in Listing 1.1; this is from [8, Sect. 7]. We shall solve Subproblem 1 in [8, Sect. 7]: if the property $(xa) + 2(ya) \geq 0$ holds at Line 5, then it holds too after the execution along $5 \rightarrow 6 \rightarrow 7 \rightarrow 8 \rightarrow 9 \rightarrow 13 \rightarrow 14$. The execution is expressed as the SAS T in Fig. 3. Then our goal is to show that the negation $T' = ((xa_1) + 2(ya_1) < 0)$ of the desired property is disjoint from T.

Our tool yields $S = (8 - 14(ya_1) - 7(xa_1) \geq 0)$ as an interpolant of these T and T' (in 14.1 s, with parameters $b = 0, c = 3$ and depth $d = 11$). The interpolant witnesses disjointness. Our interpolant is far simpler than the interpolant given in [8].[2]

Here the simplicity of our interpolant brings *robustness* as its benefit. Consider the other path $5 \rightarrow \cdots \rightarrow 8 \rightarrow 11 \rightarrow 13 \rightarrow 14$ of execution from Line 5 to 14, and let T_0 be the SAS that expresses the execution. It turns out that our interpolant S in the above is at the same time an interpolant of T_0 and T'. Thus our algorithm has managed, aiming at simpler interpolants, to automatically discover $-14(ya) - 7(xa)$ (that is, $(xa) + 2(ya)$) as a value that is significant regardless of the choice made in Line 8.

Program Verification Example II: CEGAR. This is the example we discussed in Example 1.4. Here we provide further details, aiming at readers familiar with CEGAR.

One of the most important applications of interpolation in verification is in *counterexample-guided abstraction refinement (CEGAR)* [4]. There an interpolant S is used as (a candidate for) the "essential reason" to distinguish positive examples T from negative counterexamples T'.

As an example let us verify Listing 1.1 by CEGAR. Starting from the empty set of abstraction predicates, CEGAR would find the path $p_1 := (1 \rightarrow 2 \rightarrow 3 \rightarrow 4 \rightarrow 16)$ as a counterexample.[3] This counterexample path turns out to be spurious: let $T := (xa = 0, ya = 0)$ express the path and $T' := ((xa) + 2(ya) < 0)$ express the negation of the assertion; our tool SSINT yields $189346(xa) + 378692(ya) \geq 0$ (i.e. $(xa) + 2(ya) \geq 0$) as an interpolant, proving their disjointness. For the interpolation the tool SSINT took 4.32 s; we used the parameters $b = 0$ and $c = 5$.

Consequently we add $(xa) + 2(ya) \geq 0$ as a new abstraction predicate and run the CEGAR loop again. This second run succeeds, since $(xa) + 2(ya) \geq 0$ turns out to be a suitable invariant for the loop in Line 4. We conclude safety of Listing 1.1.

We tried to do the same with the tool aiSat [6,8] instead of our SSINT. It does not succeed in interpolating $T = (xa = 0, ya = 0)$ and $T' = ((xa) + 2(ya) <$

---

[2] An interpolant $716.77 + 1326.74(ya) + 1.33(ya)^2 + 433.90(ya)^3 + 668.16(xa) - 155.86(xa)(ya) + 317.29(xa)(ya)^2 + 222.00(xa)^2 + 592.39(xa)^2(ya) + 271.11(xa)^3 > 0$ is given in [8]. We note that, to show disjointness of T and T', an interpolant of any splitting of $T \cup T'$ would suffice. It is not specified [8] which splitting they used.

[3] Here we use a *path-based* CEGAR workflow that uses an execution path as a counterexample. Since we do not have any abstraction predicates, xa and ya can be any integer; in this case the assertion in Line 16 can potentially fail.

0), since sharpness is required here (Proposition 3.3). As a workaround we tried strengthening $\mathcal{T}' = ((xa) + 2(ya) < 0)$ into $\mathcal{T}_0' = ((xa) + 2(ya) \leq -10^{-7})$; aiSat then succeeded and yielded an interpolant $\mathcal{S} = (137.3430 + 5493721088(ya) + 2746860544(xa) > 0)$. This predicate, however, cannot exclude the spurious path p_1 because $\mathcal{S}$ and the negation $(xa) + 2(ya) < 0$ of the assertion are satisfiable with $xa = 0$ and $ya = -1.25 \times 10^{-8}$.

Program Verification Example III: CEGAR. Here is another CEGAR example. Consider the code in Listing 1.2 that models movement with constant acceleration. We initially have the empty set of abstraction predicates. After the first run of the CEGAR loop we would obtain a counterexample path $p_1 := (1 \rightarrow 2 \rightarrow 3 \rightarrow 6)$; note that, since there are no predicates yet, x can be anything and thus the assertion may fail.

We let $\mathcal{T}_1 := (x = 0, v = 0)$ express the counterexample p_1 and $\mathcal{T}_1' := (x < 0)$ express the negation of the assertion. For these $\mathcal{T}_1, \mathcal{T}_1'$ our tool SSINT synthesizes $\mathcal{S}_1 := (2x \geq 0)$ as their interpolant (in 1.92 s, with $b = 0$, $c = 5$, and $d = 1$).

Thus we add $2x \geq 0$ as an abstraction predicate and run the CEGAR loop again. We would then find the path $p_2 := (1 \rightarrow 2 \rightarrow 3 \rightarrow 4 \rightarrow 5 \rightarrow 6)$ as a counterexample—note that the previous counterexample p_1 is successfully excluded by the new predicate $2x \geq 0$. Much like before, we let $\mathcal{T}_2 := (v_1 = 0)$ express an initial segment of the path p_2 and let $\mathcal{T}_2' := (x_1 = 0, v_2 = v_1 + 2, x_2 = x_1 + 2v_1, x_2 < 0)$ express the rest of the path p_2 (together with the negation of the assertion), and we shall look for their interpolant $\mathcal{S}_2$ as the witness of infeasibility of the path p_2. SSINT succeeds, yielding $\mathcal{S}_2 := (8v_1 \geq 0)$ in 2.87 s with $b = 0, c = 5, d = 1$.

In the third run of the CEGAR loop we use both $2x \geq 0$ and $8v \geq 0$ (from $\mathcal{S}_1, \mathcal{S}_2$) as abstraction predicates. The proof then succeeds and we conclude safety of Listing 1.2.

We did not succeed in doing the same with aiSat. In the first CEGAR loop an interpolant of $\mathcal{T}_1$ and $\mathcal{T}_1'$ cannot be computed because it has to be sharp. As we did in the previous example we could strengthen $\mathcal{T}_1'$ to $\mathcal{T}_1'' := (x \leq 10^{-7})$ and use an interpolant of $\mathcal{T}_1$ and $\mathcal{T}_1''$ instead for the next iteration. aiSat generated an interpolant $3790.1050 + 75802091520.0000x > 0$ of $\mathcal{T}_1$ and $\mathcal{T}_1''$; however this fails to exclude the spurious counterexample path p_1.

Overall this example demonstrates that sharpness of interpolants can be a decisive issue in their application in program verification.

Acknowledgments. Thanks are due to Eugenia Sironi, Gidon Ernst and the anonymous referees for their useful comments. T.O., K. Kido and I.H. are supported by JST ERATO HASUO Metamathematics for Systems Design Project (No. JPMJER1603), and JSPS Grants-in-Aid No. 15KT0012 & 15K11984. K. Kojima is supported by JST CREST. K.S. is supported by JST PRESTO No. JPMJPR15E5 and JSPS Grants-in-Aid No. 15KT0012. K. Kido is supported by JSPS Grant-in-Aid for JSPS Research Fellows No. 15J05580.

References

1. Anai, H., Parrilo, P.A.: Convex quantifier elimination for semidefinite programming. In: Proceedings of the International Workshop on Computer Algebra in Scientific Computing, CASC (2003)
2. Besson, F.: Fast reflexive arithmetic tactics the linear case and beyond. In: Altenkirch, T., McBride, C. (eds.) TYPES 2006. LNCS, vol. 4502, pp. 48–62. Springer, Heidelberg (2007). https://doi.org/10.1007/978-3-540-74464-1_4
3. Bochnak, J., Coste, M., Roy, M.F.: Real Algebraic Geometry. Springer, New York (1999)
4. Clarke, E.M., Grumberg, O., Jha, S., Lu, Y., Veith, H.: Counterexample-guided abstraction refinement for symbolic model checking. J. ACM **50**(5), 752–794 (2003). https://doi.org/10.1145/876638.876643
5. Colón, M., Sankaranarayanan, S., Sipma, H.: Linear invariant generation using non-linear constraint solving. In: Hunt Jr., Somenzi [14], pp. 420–432
6. Dai, L.: The tool aiSat. github.com/djuanbei/aiSat. Accessed 17 Jan 2017
7. Dai, L., Gan, T., Xia, B., Zhan, N.: Barrier certificates revisited. J. Symb. Comput. **80**, 62–86 (2017). https://doi.org/10.1016/j.jsc.2016.07.010
8. Dai, L., Xia, B., Zhan, N.: Generating non-linear interpolants by semidefinite programming. In: Sharygina, N., Veith, H. (eds.) CAV 2013. LNCS, vol. 8044, pp. 364–380. Springer, Heidelberg (2013). https://doi.org/10.1007/978-3-642-39799-8_25
9. Gan, T., Dai, L., Xia, B., Zhan, N., Kapur, D., Chen, M.: Interpolant synthesis for quadratic polynomial inequalities and combination with *EUF*. In: Olivetti, N., Tiwari, A. (eds.) IJCAR 2016. LNCS (LNAI), vol. 9706, pp. 195–212. Springer, Cham (2016). https://doi.org/10.1007/978-3-319-40229-1_14
10. Gao, S., Zufferey, D.: Interpolants in nonlinear theories over the reals. In: Chechik, M., Raskin, J.-F. (eds.) TACAS 2016. LNCS, vol. 9636, pp. 625–641. Springer, Heidelberg (2016). https://doi.org/10.1007/978-3-662-49674-9_41
11. Gurfinkel, A., Rollini, S.F., Sharygina, N.: Interpolation properties and SAT-based model checking. In: Van Hung, D., Ogawa, M. (eds.) ATVA 2013. LNCS, vol. 8172, pp. 255–271. Springer, Cham (2013). https://doi.org/10.1007/978-3-319-02444-8_19
12. Harrison, J.: Verifying nonlinear real formulas via sums of squares. In: Schneider, K., Brandt, J. (eds.) TPHOLs 2007. LNCS, vol. 4732, pp. 102–118. Springer, Heidelberg (2007). https://doi.org/10.1007/978-3-540-74591-4_9
13. Henzinger, T.A., Jhala, R., Majumdar, R., McMillan, K.L.: Abstractions from proofs. In: Jones, N.D., Leroy, X. (eds.) Proceedings of the 31st ACM SIGPLAN-SIGACT Symposium on Principles of Programming Languages, POPL 2004, Venice, Italy, January 14–16, 2004. pp. 232–244. ACM (2004). http://dl.acm.org/citation.cfm?id=964001
14. Hunt Jr., W.A., Somenzi, F. (eds.): CAV 2003. LNCS, vol. 2725. Springer, Heidelberg (2003). https://doi.org/10.1007/b11831
15. Jhala, R., McMillan, K.L.: Interpolant-based transition relation approximation. In: Etessami, K., Rajamani, S.K. (eds.) CAV 2005. LNCS, vol. 3576, pp. 39–51. Springer, Heidelberg (2005). https://doi.org/10.1007/11513988_6
16. Jhala, R., McMillan, K.L.: A practical and complete approach to predicate refinement. In: Hermanns, H., Palsberg, J. (eds.) TACAS 2006. LNCS, vol. 3920, pp. 459–473. Springer, Heidelberg (2006). https://doi.org/10.1007/11691372_33

17. Kaltofen, E., Li, B., Yang, Z., Zhi, L.: Exact certification of global optimality of approximate factorizations via rationalizing sums-of-squares with floating point scalars. In: Sendra, J.R., González-Vega, L. (eds.) Symbolic and Algebraic Computation, International Symposium, ISSAC 2008, Linz/Hagenberg, Austria, July 20–23, 2008, Proceedings, pp. 155–164. ACM (2008). http://doi.acm.org/10.1145/1390768.1390792

18. Kupferschmid, S., Becker, B.: Craig interpolation in the presence of non-linear constraints. In: Fahrenberg, U., Tripakis, S. (eds.) FORMATS 2011. LNCS, vol. 6919, pp. 240–255. Springer, Heidelberg (2011). https://doi.org/10.1007/978-3-642-24310-3_17

19. Lang, S.: Introduction to Diophantine Approximations. Springer Books on Elementary mathematics. Springer, New York (1995). https://doi.org/10.1007/978-1-4612-4220-8

20. Lin, W., Wu, M., Yang, Z., Zeng, Z.: Proving total correctness and generating preconditions for loop programs via symbolic-numeric computation methods. Front. Comput. Sci. 8(2), 192–202 (2014). https://doi.org/10.1007/s11704-014-3150-6

21. McMillan, K.L.: Interpolation and sat-based model checking. In: Hunt Jr., Somenzi [14], pp. 1–13

22. McMillan, K.L.: Applications of craig interpolants in model checking. In: Halbwachs, N., Zuck, L.D. (eds.) TACAS 2005. LNCS, vol. 3440, pp. 1–12. Springer, Heidelberg (2005). https://doi.org/10.1007/978-3-540-31980-1_1

23. McMillan, K.L.: Lazy abstraction with interpolants. In: Ball, T., Jones, R.B. (eds.) CAV 2006. LNCS, vol. 4144, pp. 123–136. Springer, Heidelberg (2006). https://doi.org/10.1007/11817963_14

24. Okudono, T., Nishida, Y., Kojima, K., Suenaga, K., Kido, K., Hasuo, I.: Sharper and simpler nonlinear interpolants for program verification. CoRR abs/1709.00314 (2017)

25. Parrilo, P.: Structured semidefinite programs and semialgebraic geometry methods in robustness and optimization. Ph.D. thesis, California Inst. of Tech. (2000)

26. Parrilo, P.A.: Semidefinite programming relaxations for semialgebraic problems. Math. Program. 96(2), 293–320 (2003). https://doi.org/10.1007/s10107-003-0387-5

27. Peyrl, H., Parrilo, P.A.: Computing sum of squares decompositions with rational coefficients. Theor. Comput. Sci. 409(2), 269–281 (2008). https://doi.org/10.1016/j.tcs.2008.09.025

28. Platzer, A., Quesel, J.-D., Rümmer, P.: Real world verification. In: Schmidt, R.A. (ed.) CADE 2009. LNCS (LNAI), vol. 5663, pp. 485–501. Springer, Heidelberg (2009). https://doi.org/10.1007/978-3-642-02959-2_35

29. Putinar, M.: Positive polynomials on compact semi-algebraic sets. Indiana Univ. Math. Journ. 42(3), 969–984 (1993)

30. Roux, P., Voronin, Y.-L., Sankaranarayanan, S.: Validating numerical semidefinite programming solvers for polynomial invariants. In: Rival, X. (ed.) SAS 2016. LNCS, vol. 9837, pp. 424–446. Springer, Heidelberg (2016). https://doi.org/10.1007/978-3-662-53413-7_21

31. Rump, S.: Verification of positive definiteness. BIT Numer. Math. 46(2), 433–452 (2006). https://doi.org/10.1007/s10543-006-0056-1

32. Rybalchenko, A., Sofronie-Stokkermans, V.: Constraint solving for interpolation. In: Cook, B., Podelski, A. (eds.) VMCAI 2007. LNCS, vol. 4349, pp. 346–362. Springer, Heidelberg (2007). https://doi.org/10.1007/978-3-540-69738-1_25

33. Sharma, R., Gupta, S., Hariharan, B., Aiken, A., Liang, P., Nori, A.V.: A data driven approach for algebraic loop invariants. In: Felleisen, M., Gardner, P. (eds.) ESOP 2013. LNCS, vol. 7792, pp. 574–592. Springer, Heidelberg (2013). https://doi.org/10.1007/978-3-642-37036-6_31

34. Stengle, G.: A Nullstellensatz and a Positivstellensatz in semialgebraic geometry. Math. Ann. **207**(2), 87–97 (1974). https://doi.org/10.1007/BF01362149

35. Terauchi, T.: Explaining the effectiveness of small refinement heuristics in program verification with CEGAR. In: Blazy, S., Jensen, T. (eds.) SAS 2015. LNCS, vol. 9291, pp. 128–144. Springer, Heidelberg (2015). https://doi.org/10.1007/978-3-662-48288-9_8

36. Toh, K.C., Todd, M., Tütüncü, R.H.: Sdpt3 - a matlab software package for semi-definite programming. Optim. Methods Softw. **11**, 545–581 (1999)

A Nonstandard Functional
Programming Language

Hirofumi Nakamura[1]([✉]), Kensuke Kojima[1,2], Kohei Suenaga[1,3],
and Atsushi Igarashi[1]

[1] Graduate School of Informatics, Kyoto University, Kyoto, Japan
hnakamura@fos.kuis.kyoto-u.ac.jp
[2] JST CREST, Tokyo, Japan
[3] JST PRESTO, Tokyo, Japan

Abstract. *Nonstandard programming languages* are the languages that
deal with *hyperreal numbers*—real numbers extended with *infinitesimal*
(i.e., smaller than any positive real) numbers—whose theory is given by
nonstandard analysis (NSA). Nonstandard imperative language **While**$^\mathbf{dt}$
and nonstandard stream-processing language **SProc**$^\mathbf{dt}$ have been proposed so far and applied to hybrid system modeling and verification. We
introduce a nonstandard *functional* language NSF. We extend a simply
typed functional language with a constant **dt** that denotes an infinitesimal number and define its denotational semantics. The major challenge
consists in giving the semantics of functions of an arbitrarily high order.
To this end, we introduce **-cpos*, a nonstandard counterpart of the standard domains.

1 Introduction

1.1 Background: Nonstandard Programming Languages

Suenaga and Hasuo proposed an imperative programming language **While**$^\mathbf{dt}$
equipped with a *positive infinitesimal* constant—a positive number that is
strictly less than any positive real number [23]. The following program describes
their language.

Example 1. The following imperative program initializes t to 0 and increments
it by **dt** until t reaches 1: $t := 0;$ **while** $(t < 1)$ $\{t := t + \mathbf{dt}\}$. The constant **dt**
denotes a positive infinitesimal value. Therefore, we would like this program to
terminate after "executing" the loop *infinitely many* (i.e. $\frac{1}{\mathbf{dt}}$) times; the value of
t at the end of the program should be infinitely close to 1.

Their motivation behind **While**$^\mathbf{dt}$ is modeling and reasoning about systems
that exhibit continuous dynamics. The following example illustrates how this is
achieved in their framework.

Example 2. The solution of an initial value problem (IVP) $\frac{dx}{dt} = v, \frac{dv}{dt} =$
$-\frac{1}{10}, x(0) = 0, v = 1$ is modeled by the following **While**$^\mathbf{dt}$ program:

$$x := 0; v := 1; \mathbf{while}\ (v > 0)\ \{(x, v) := (x + v \times \mathbf{dt}, v - \frac{1}{10} \times \mathbf{dt})\}.$$

© Springer International Publishing AG 2017
B.-Y.E. Chang (Ed.): APLAS 2017, LNCS 10695, pp. 514–533, 2017.
https://doi.org/10.1007/978-3-319-71237-6_25

In each iteration, this program updates the values of x and v to those of **dt** seconds later. We would like the result of the computation to be infinitely close to the true solution of the IVP.

They gave a formal semantics of **While**$^{\mathbf{dt}}$ and a program logic **Hoare**$^{\mathbf{dt}}$ [23]. They also implemented an automated verifier of hybrid systems based on **Hoare**$^{\mathbf{dt}}$ [9] and applied it to a model of a railway management system to show the feasibility of their idea. They also proposed a stream-processing language **SProc**$^{\mathbf{dt}}$ that is equipped with an infinitesimal constant [24].

The formal semantics of these languages is not trivial because the denotations obtained by the usual fixpoint semantics do not capture the intuition explained above. The usual fixpoint semantics, which gives the denotation as the least fixpoint of a Scott-continuous generating function, captures a *finite-step* execution of a program, whereas the denotation of the programs in Examples 1 and 2 require an *infinite-step* "execution": Finitely many iterations of the loop in Example 1 can bring the value of t only to another infinitesimal value, not a value infinitely close to 1 as we described.

They addressed this issue by using *nonstandard analysis (NSA)* [18]. NSA, proposed by Robinson [18], is a method to consistently extend the theory of reals with infinitesimal and infinite numbers. NSA constructs the set of *hyperreals* $^*\mathbb{R}$ that is an extension of the set of reals $\mathbb{R}$ with the infinitesimal and infinite numbers.

One notable property of NSA is that the extended theory satisfies *transfer principle*: The theorems that hold in the original theory are inherited to the nonstandard theory. For example, the theorem $\forall r \in \mathbb{R}. \exists s \in \mathbb{R}. r < s$, where $\mathbb{R}$ is the set of reals, holds in the theory of reals; therefore, the property $\forall r \in {}^*\mathbb{R}. \exists s \in {}^*\mathbb{R}. r < s$ holds where $^*\mathbb{R}$ is the set of hyperreals.

The semantics of **While**$^{\mathbf{dt}}$ and **SProc**$^{\mathbf{dt}}$ is obtained by applying the same construction as that of $^*\mathbb{R}$ to the denotation function of the standard counterparts of these languages. The resulting denotation handles infinitesimal values consistently. By virtue of the transfer principle, the metatheories of these languages are almost the same as their standard counterparts.

1.2   This Work: *Functional* Nonstandard Programming Language

The present paper proposes a *functional* nonstandard programming language. Our language NSF (for **N**on**S**tandard **F**unctional language) is a simply typed functional programming language equipped with an infinitesimal constant. The following example informally describes an NSF program.

Example 3. The following NSF program defines a function D:

$$\text{let } D = \lambda f.\lambda x.\frac{f\left(x + \frac{\mathbf{dt}}{2}\right) - f\left(x - \frac{\mathbf{dt}}{2}\right)}{\mathbf{dt}}.$$

It takes a function f of type $\mathcal{R} \to \mathcal{R}$, where $\mathcal{R}$ is the type of the hyperreals, and returns $\lambda x.\frac{f\left(x+\frac{\mathbf{dt}}{2}\right)-f\left(x-\frac{\mathbf{dt}}{2}\right)}{\mathbf{dt}}$. This returned function computes the value that is infinitely close to the derivative of f if f is (a good encoding of) a differentiable function (Lemma 10).

Example 4. The following NSF program defines a function S:

$$\textbf{let rec } S \; s \; t \; f = \textbf{if } t \leq s \textbf{ then } 0 \textbf{ else } (f \; t) \times \textbf{dt} + S \; s \; (t - \textbf{dt}) \; f.$$

This function takes two arguments s and t of type $\mathcal{R}$ and one argument f of type $\mathcal{R} \to \mathcal{R}$. If f is Riemann integrable, then S computes a hyperreal number that is infinitely close to $\int_s^t f(t)dt$ if $s < t$ (Lemma 11).

We give a formal semantics of NSF by using NSA. The strategy is the same as the previous nonstandard languages: introducing a nonstandard counterpart of the standard domain of Scott-style denotational semantics. One of the major challenges is accommodating first-class functions of arbitrarily high order; the previous nonstandard languages do not deal with higher-order functions. Due to this feature, we build the semantic domain called **-cpo* that includes higher-order functions.

We remark that NSF is a theoretical programming language. We do *not*, at least currently, consider the execution of an NSF program on a computer; such execution requires representing and manipulating nonzero infinitesimal values, which is seemingly not possible. This is in accord with the previous nonstandard programming languages [9,23,24]. We rather intend NSF to be used for modeling systems in which continuous dynamics is involved and, in future, manipulating and verifying the modeled systems.

Despite its theoretical nature, we believe that NSF is already interesting in various aspects. One of these aspects is in Sect. 6.2, where we present a proof of the fundamental theorem of calculus (i.e., the equation $\frac{d}{dx} \int_s^x f(t)dt = f(x)$ for a continuous $f : \mathbb{R} \to \mathbb{R}$) using a program transformation for NSF programs. Although such syntactic reasoning is a familiar method to the researchers of programming languages, as far as we know, it is not well-developed for the systems that exhibit continuous dynamics.

1.3   Structure of the Present Paper

The outline of the paper is as follows: Sect. 2 introduces the notion of ultrapower and a basic part of NSA; Sect. 3 is a primer of general NSA that we need in the present paper; Sect. 4 defines the semantic domain that is used in the semantics of NSF; Sect. 5 defines the syntax and the denotational semantics of NSF; Sect. 6 gives several examples of NSF programs; Sect. 7 discusses related work; and Sect. 8 concludes.For the proofs of the statements, readers are referred to a full version of the paper at http://www.fos.kuis.kyoto-u.ac.jp/~ksuenaga/doc/paper/aplas2017full.pdf.

Notations. We write $\mathbb{N}$ for the set of natural numbers, $\mathbb{R}$ for the set of reals, and $\mathcal{P}(X)$ for the powerset of X. For a given set S, we write $(s_i \in S)_{i \in \mathbb{N}}$ for an element of $S^{\mathbb{N}}$; we often write (s_i) omitting the part $\in S$ and the part $(-)_{i \in \mathbb{N}}$. Given an equivalence relation $R \subseteq S \times S$, an equivalence class of $s \in S$ is written $[s]_R$; we may omit the subscript R if it is clear.

2   Nonstandard Analysis on Reals

The *nonstandard analysis (NSA)* concerns constructing a *nonstandard model* of a theory $\mathcal{T}$ from its standard model; we are especially interested in the case where $\mathcal{T}$ is the theory of reals. In order to make the presentation of this construction easier to understand, this section presents the construction of the set of hyperreals. Section 3 extends this construction to accommodate other entities such as (a certain subset of) functions from hyperreals to hyperreals.

This section and Sect. 3 are intended for fixing definitions and presenting relevant results rather than the presentation of the full NSA. We refer the reader to the textbook by Goldblatt [7] and Loeb et al. [14] for the detailed exposition.

The set of hyperreals $^*\mathbb{R}$ is obtained by applying *ultrapower construction* to the set $^*\mathbb{R}$. In order to define this construction in Definition 4, we need to introduce *ultrafilter* (Definition 1) and *ultrapower* (Definition 3).

Definition 1 (Ultrafilter). *A set $\mathcal{F} \subseteq \mathcal{P}(\mathbb{N})$ is called a* proper filter *if it satisfies: (1) $\emptyset \notin \mathcal{F}$; (2) $A, B \in \mathcal{F}$ implies $A \cap B \in \mathcal{F}$; and (3) $A \in \mathcal{F}$ and $A \subseteq B$ implies $B \in \mathcal{F}$. A proper filter $\mathcal{F}$ is called an* ultrafilter *if either $A \in \mathcal{F}$ or $\mathbb{N} \setminus A \in \mathcal{F}$ holds for any $A \subseteq \mathbb{N}$.*

The set $\mathcal{F}^{co} := \{S \subseteq \mathbb{N} \mid \mathbb{N} \setminus S \text{ is a finite set}\}$ is a proper filter (called the *cofinite filter*). Using Zorn's lemma, we can show that there exists an ultrafilter containing $\mathcal{F}^{co}$; we fix one of such ultrafilters and hereafter call it $\mathcal{F}$.

Remark 1. If $\mathbb{N} \setminus S$ is a finite set, then $S \in \mathcal{F}^{co}$; therefore $S \in \mathcal{F}$. $\mathcal{F}$ also contains an element that does not belong to $\mathcal{F}^{co}$. Indeed, let S be the set of all the even numbers (i.e., $\{0, 2, 4, \ldots\}$); then $\mathbb{N} \setminus S$ is the set of all the odd numbers (i.e., $\{1, 3, 5, \ldots\}$). Although neither S nor $\mathbb{N} \setminus S$ belongs to $\mathcal{F}^{co}$, exactly one of those two sets belongs to $\mathcal{F}$ from the definition of an ultrafilter.

Our main use of the ultrafilter $\mathcal{F}$ is the following definition of *ultrapower*.

Definition 2. *Let S be a set. The relation $\sim \subseteq S^{\mathbb{N}} \times S^{\mathbb{N}}$, parameterized by a set S, is defined as follows: $(s_i)_{i \in \mathbb{N}} \sim (s'_i)_{i \in \mathbb{N}}$ if and only if $\{i \in \mathbb{N} \mid s_i = s'_i\} \in \mathcal{F}$. The relation $\sim$ is an equivalence relation; one can prove it by using the properties of a filter.*

Definition 3 (Ultrapower). *Let S be a set. The* ultrapower *of S is the quotient set $S^{\mathbb{N}}/\sim$; we write it $\prod_{\mathcal{F}} S$. By definition, an element of the ultrapower of S is of the form $[(s_i \in S)_{i \in \mathbb{N}}]_\sim$ —an equivalence class of the sequence $(s_i \in S)_{i \in \mathbb{N}}$. We often write it $[(s_i \in S)_{i \in \mathbb{N}}]_\mathcal{F}$, or simply $[s_i]_\mathcal{F}$.*

We define the set of hyperreals $^*\mathbb{R}$ as the ultrapower of $\mathbb{R}$.

Definition 4 (Ultrapower construction on $\mathbb{R}$). *The set $^*\mathbb{R} := \{[\mathbf{r}]_\mathcal{F} \mid \mathbf{r} \in \mathbb{R}^{\mathbb{N}}\}$ is called the set of* hyperreals; *notice that $^*\mathbb{R}$ is equal to $\prod_{\mathcal{F}} \mathbb{R}$. The set $\mathbb{R}$ can be embedded into $^*\mathbb{R}$ by the injection $r \in \mathbb{R} \mapsto [(r \in \mathbb{R})_{i \in \mathbb{N}}]_\mathcal{F} \in {}^*\mathbb{R}$. (Note that $[(r \in \mathbb{R})_{i \in \mathbb{N}}]_\mathcal{F}$ is the equivalence class of a constant sequence $[(r, r, \ldots)]_\mathcal{F}$.) We hereafter identify $r \in \mathbb{R}$ with $[(r \in \mathbb{R})_{i \in \mathbb{N}}]_\mathcal{F}$. We also define the set of* hypernatural numbers $^*\mathbb{N}$ *by $\{[\mathbf{n}]_\mathcal{F} \mid \mathbf{n} \in \mathbb{N}^{\mathbb{N}}\}$; embedding of $\mathbb{N}$ to $^*\mathbb{N}$ is also defined in the same way. Notice that $^*\mathbb{N} \subseteq {}^*\mathbb{R}$.*

The operations and the relations over $\mathbb{R}$ are *enlarged* to $^*\mathbb{R}$ as follows, whose well-definedness can be proved by using the properties of the ultrafilter $\mathcal{F}$ [7, Chap. 3].

Definition 5 (Enlarged function and relation). *For a function $f : \mathbb{R}^n \to \mathbb{R}$, its enlargement $^*f : (^*\mathbb{R})^n \to {}^*\mathbb{R}$ of f is defined by $^*f(\langle [r_i^1]_{\mathcal{F}}, \ldots, [r_i^n]_{\mathcal{F}} \rangle) = [f(r_i^1, \ldots, r_i^n)]_{\mathcal{F}}$. Similarly, the enlargement of an n-ary relation $S \subseteq \mathbb{R}^n$ is defined by $\{\langle [r_i^1]_{\mathcal{F}}, \ldots, [r_i^n]_{\mathcal{F}} \rangle \mid \{i \in \mathbb{N} \mid \langle r_i^1, \ldots, r_i^n \rangle \in S\} \in \mathcal{F}\}$.*

Example 5 (*$^*+$*). By definition, the enlargement of the addition $+ : \mathbb{R} \times \mathbb{R} \to \mathbb{R}$ is given by:

$$[(r_i \in \mathbb{R})_i]_{\mathcal{F}} \; {}^*+ \; [(s_i \in \mathbb{R})_i]_{\mathcal{F}} := [(r_i + s_i \in \mathbb{R})_i]_{\mathcal{F}}.$$

The operator $^*+$ is an extension of the standard $+$. Indeed, for $r, s \in \mathbb{R}$, its embedding to $^*\mathbb{R}$ is $[(r)_{i \in \mathbb{N}}]_{\mathcal{F}}$ and $[(s)_{i \in \mathbb{N}}]_{\mathcal{F}}$, respectively; therefore, $[(r)_{i \in \mathbb{N}}]_{\mathcal{F}} \; {}^*+ \; [(s)_{i \in \mathbb{N}}]_{\mathcal{F}} = [(r+s)_{i \in \mathbb{N}}]_{\mathcal{F}}$, which is the embedding of $r + s \in \mathbb{R}$ to $^*\mathbb{R}$.

Example 6 (*$^*<$*). Consider the relation $< \; \subseteq \mathbb{R} \times \mathbb{R}$. By definition, $^*< \; \subseteq {}^*\mathbb{R} \times {}^*\mathbb{R}$ is the relation such that $[(r_i)_i]_{\mathcal{F}} \; {}^*< \; [(s_i)_i]_{\mathcal{F}}$ if and only if $\{i \in \mathbb{N} \mid r_i < s_i\} \in \mathcal{F}$. We can show that $^*<$ is an extension of $<$ in the same way as Example 5.

Let $\partial := [(\frac{1}{i+1})_i]_{\mathcal{F}}$. We can show that $\partial \; {}^*< \; r$ for *any* positive $r \in \mathbb{R}$. By definition, $\partial \; {}^*< \; r$ is equivalent to $\{i \in \mathbb{N} \mid \frac{1}{i+1} < r\} \in \mathcal{F}$. Because there are only finitely many $i \in \mathbb{N}$ such that $\frac{1}{i+1} \geq r$, the set $\{i \in \mathbb{N} \mid \frac{1}{i+1} < r\}$ is cofinite, and thus belongs to $\mathcal{F}$ (recall Remark 1).

If there is no confusion, we simply write $+$ for $^*+$, $\leq$ for $^*\leq$, and similarly for other symbols (e.g., $-$, $\times$, $/$, $|-|$).

Definition 6. *Let $r \in {}^*\mathbb{R}$. We say that r is* finite *if there is $r' \in \mathbb{R}$ such that $|r| < r'$, and* infinite *otherwise; r is said to be* infinitesimal *if $|r| < r'$ for any positive $r' \in \mathbb{R}$; r is said to be* standard *if there is $r' \in \mathbb{R}$ such that $r = {}^*r'$, and* nonstandard *otherwise.*

One can prove that the element $[(\frac{1}{i+1})_i]_{\mathcal{F}}$ is a positive infinitesimal element. Similarly, we can prove that $[(i)_i]_{\mathcal{F}}$, which equals $\frac{1}{\partial} - 1$, is an *infinite* element. Notice that there are infinitely many infinitesimal and infinite elements in $^*\mathbb{R}$; for example, $\partial, 2\partial, 3\partial, \ldots$ are all infinitesimals; $\frac{1}{\partial}, \frac{1}{2\partial}, \frac{1}{3\partial}, \ldots$ are all infinite numbers.

For $r, r' \in {}^*\mathbb{R}$, we write $r \simeq r'$ if $r - r'$ is infinitesimal. We can show that, for any finite $r \in {}^*\mathbb{R}$, there uniquely exists $s \in \mathbb{R}$ such that $r \simeq s$; we call such s *standard part* of r and note as $sh(r)$.

We use the following result in Sect. 6.

Lemma 1 ([7, **Theorem 7.1.3**]). *$f : \mathbb{R} \to \mathbb{R}$ is continuous (in the sense of the standard analysis) at $c \in \mathbb{R}$ if and only if $(^*f)(x) \simeq (^*f)(c)$ for any $x \in {}^*\mathbb{R}$ such that $x \simeq c$.*

The following lemma is an easy implication of Theorem 8.1.1 in Goldblatt [7].

Lemma 2. *Suppose* $f : \mathbb{R} \to \mathbb{R}$ *is differentiable at* $r \in \mathbb{R}$ *and* $L = f'(r)$ *for some* $L \in \mathbb{R}$. *Then,* $L \simeq \frac{(^*f)(r+\frac{\theta}{2}) - (^*f)(r-\frac{\theta}{2})}{\theta}$.

The following lemma is easily obtained from Corollary 1.11.2 of Loeb et al. [14].

Lemma 3. *If* $f \in \mathbb{R} \to \mathbb{R}$ *is continuous on* $[s,t]$ *for* $s,t \in \mathbb{R}$, *then* $(^*sum)(s,t,^*f,\varepsilon) \simeq \int_s^t f(x)dx$ *for any positive infinitesimal* ε, *where* $sum(s,t,f,h) := \sum_{j=0}^{\lceil \frac{t-s}{h} \rceil - 1} f(t - jh) \times h$.

3 General NSA

Section 2 presents the construction of $^*\mathbb{R}$, presents the construction of the operators and the relations on $^*\mathbb{R}$, and shows that $^*\mathbb{R}$ contains infinitesimal and infinite elements. However, these are not enough for the denotational semantics of NSF because it contains functions of arbitrarily high orders whereas Sect. 2 mentions only first-order functions and relations on $^*\mathbb{R}$.

This section presents how NSA extends to higher-order entities such as higher-order functions. Following the traditional way of developing NSA, we define (1) the *universe* $V(\mathbb{R})$ of mathematical objects including higher-order entities from the set of base entities $\mathbb{R}$; (2) a metalanguage $\mathcal{L}$ that asserts mathematical statements on $V(\mathbb{R})$; and (3) a mapping $^*(-) : V(\mathbb{R}) \to V(^*\mathbb{R})$ that embeds every standard entity into the nonstandard universe, not only $\mathbb{R}$ and the first-order operations/relations on $\mathbb{R}$. The mapping $^*(-)$ has a useful property called *transfer principle*: A valid $\mathcal{L}$ formula Φ remains valid if we replace every $v \in V(\mathbb{R})$ that appears in Φ with $^*v \in V(^*\mathbb{R})$.

3.1 Universe

Definition 7. *Let* X *be a set of* base entities. *The* universe $V(X)$ *is defined as follows:* $V_0(X) := X$; $V_{i+1}(X) := V_i(X) \cup \mathcal{P}(V_i(X))$; *and* $V(X) := \bigcup_{i \in \mathbb{N}} V_i(X)$. *We write* V_i *for the set* $V_i(\mathbb{R})$ *and* V *for the set* $V(\mathbb{R})$. *If* $v \in V_i(\mathbb{R})$ *and* $v \notin V_{i-1}(\mathbb{R})$, *we write* **rank**$(v)$ *for* i.

Informally speaking, the universe $V(\mathbb{R})$ contains everything that we need to conduct mathematics on the real numbers.[1] We can encode common mathematical entities such as Cartesian products, relations, sequences, and functions by using elements in $V(\mathbb{R})$.

We use the following definition in Sect. 3.3:

Definition 8 (Bounded ultrapower). *The* bounded ultrapower *of* V *is the set* $\prod_{\mathcal{F}} V_0(\mathbb{R}) \cup \bigcup_{n=1}^{\infty} \prod_{\mathcal{F}} (V_n(\mathbb{R}) \setminus V_{n-1}(\mathbb{R}))$; *we write this set* $\prod_{\mathcal{F}}^0 V$.

$\prod_{\mathcal{F}}^0 V$ is the subset of the ultrapower of V where each element is constructed from sequences of elements of the same rank.

---

[1] The set $V(\mathbb{R})$ is also called the *superstructure* over $\mathbb{R}$ in the literature [7].

3.2   Language $\mathcal{L}$

Definition 9 (Language $\mathcal{L}$). *Let v be a metavariable that ranges over the set of the constant symbols for the elements of the universe $V(\mathbb{R})$; x be a metavariable that ranges over a countably infinite set of variables. The syntax of $\mathcal{L}$ is defined by the following BNF:*

$$
\begin{aligned}
\mathcal{L}\ terms &\quad t ::= v \mid x \mid \langle t_1, \ldots, t_n \rangle \mid t_1(t_2) \\
Atomic\ formulae\ \phi &::= t_1 = t_2 \mid t_1 \in t_2 \\
Formulae &\quad \Phi ::= \phi \mid \Phi_1 \wedge \Phi_2 \mid \Phi_1 \vee \Phi_2 \mid \Phi_1 \Rightarrow \Phi_2 \\
&\quad\quad\ \mid \neg\Phi \mid \forall x \in t.\Phi \mid \exists x \in t.\Phi
\end{aligned}
$$

$\mathcal{L}$ is a language of the first-order logic over the universe V. An $\mathcal{L}$ *term* is either a constant symbol v for an element in V, a variable x, a tuple of terms $\langle t_1, \ldots, t_n \rangle$, or a function application $t_1(t_2)$; by abusing the notation, we do not distinguish the constant symbol v from the element denoted by v. An atomic predicate of $\mathcal{L}$ is either the equality $t_1 = t_2$ or the membership relation $t_1 \in t_2$. An $\mathcal{L}$ formula is an ordinary first-order formula, except that a quantified variable x is bounded by a term t, the set that x ranges over. We do not present the formal semantics of the language $\mathcal{L}$ because its syntax is self-explanatory. The set of the free variables and the bound variables of a formula Φ is defined as usual. We call a closed $\mathcal{L}$ formula a *sentence*.

Example 7. The following $\mathcal{L}$ formulae $BinRel(X,r)$, $Refl(X,r)$, $Trans(X,r)$, and $AntiSym(X,r)$ assert that r is a binary relation over a set X, relation r is reflexive, relation r is transitive, and relation r is antisymmetric, respectively:

$$
\begin{aligned}
BinRel(X,r) &:= \forall x \in r.\exists y \in X.\exists z \in X.x = \langle y,z \rangle \\
Refl(X,r) &:= \forall x \in X.\langle x,x \rangle \in r \\
Trans(X,r) &:= \forall x,y,z \in X.\langle x,y \rangle \in r \wedge \langle y,z \rangle \in r \Rightarrow \langle x,z \rangle \in r \\
AntiSym(X,r) &:= \forall x,y \in X.\langle x,y \rangle \in r \wedge \langle y,x \rangle \in r \Rightarrow x = y.
\end{aligned}
$$

We write $Poset(X,r)$ for the conjunction of these four formulas. $Poset(\mathbb{R}, \leq)$, where $\leq\ \in V$ is the ordinary order on real numbers, is a valid sentence.

3.3   Ultrapower Construction

We define the map $^*(-) : V(\mathbb{R}) \to V(^*\mathbb{R})$ so that the following property holds.

Property 1 (Transfer principle). An $\mathcal{L}$ sentence Φ is valid if and only if $^*\Phi$, the formula obtained by replacing every constant v in Φ with $^*v$, is valid.

In the following, we detail the definition of the map $^*(-)$ to make the present paper self-contained; the textbook by Loeb et al. [14] has a more detailed explanation. One can safely skip this section for understanding the rest of the paper.

In the definition of $^*(-)$, we use the following binary relation over the ultrapower.

Definition 10 ($\in_\mathcal{F}$). *For* $[(a_i)_i]_\mathcal{F}$ *and* $[(b_i)_i]_\mathcal{F}$, *we write* $[(a_i)_i]_\mathcal{F} \in_\mathcal{F} [(b_i)_i]_\mathcal{F}$ *if* $\{i \in \mathbb{N} \mid a_i \in b_i\} \in \mathcal{F}$.

Definition 11 ($^*(-)$). *The map* $^*(-)$ *is a composition* $M \circ e$ *of two maps* $e : V(\mathbb{R}) \to \prod_\mathcal{F}^0 V$ *and* $M : \prod_\mathcal{F}^0 V \to V(^*\mathbb{R})$. *(See Definition 8 for the definition of* $\prod_\mathcal{F}^0 V$.*) The map* e *is defined by* $e(v) := [(v)_{i \in \mathbb{N}}]_\mathcal{F} = [(v, v, \dots)]_\mathcal{F}$. *The map* M, *called* Mostowski collapse, *is defined by induction on* n *as follows:*

$$M([(r_i \in \mathbb{R})_{i \in \mathbb{N}}]_\mathcal{F}) := [(r_i \in \mathbb{R})_{i \in \mathbb{N}}]_\mathcal{F}$$

$$M([(S_i \in (V_{n+1} \setminus V_n))_{i \in \mathbb{N}}]_\mathcal{F})$$

$$:= \left\{ M([(s_i \in (V_k \setminus V_{k-1}))_{i \in \mathbb{N}}]_\mathcal{F}) \,\middle|\, \begin{array}{l} [(s_i \in (V_k \setminus V_{k-1}))_{i \in \mathbb{N}}]_\mathcal{F} \in_\mathcal{F} \\ {[(S_i \in (V_{n+1} \setminus V_n))_{i \in \mathbb{N}}]_\mathcal{F}}, \text{ and} \\ 0 \le k \le n \end{array} \right\},$$

where V_{-1} *is defined to be* $\emptyset$.

The map M takes $[(v_i)_i]_\mathcal{F} \in \prod_\mathcal{F}^0 V$; if it consists of a sequence of elements in $V_0(\mathbb{R})$ (i.e., if the sequence consists of reals), then M returns it without change; if the argument consists of a sequence of elements in $V_{n+1}(\mathbb{R})$ (i.e., if it is an equivalence class of a sequence of some sets), then the map M gathers element s_i from each S_i so that $[s_i]_\mathcal{F} \in_\mathcal{F} [S_i]_\mathcal{F}$. This $[s_i]_\mathcal{F}$ is recursively passed to M.

We describe how this definition works by example.

Example 8. By definition, $^*r = M(e(r)) = M([(r \in \mathbb{R})_{i \in \mathbb{N}}]_\mathcal{F}) = [(r \in \mathbb{R})_{i \in \mathbb{N}}]_\mathcal{F}$ for $r \in \mathbb{R}$. This coincides with how we identify $r \in \mathbb{R}$ with $^*r \in {}^*\mathbb{R}$ (Definition 4).

Example 9. $M(e(\mathbb{R})) = M([(\mathbb{R} \in V_1(\mathbb{R}) \setminus V_0(\mathbb{R}))_{i \in \mathbb{N}}]_\mathcal{F}) = \{M([r_i]_\mathcal{F}) \mid [r_i]_\mathcal{F} \in_\mathcal{F} [\mathbb{R}]_\mathcal{F}\} = \{[r_i]_\mathcal{F} \mid [r_i]_\mathcal{F} \in_\mathcal{F} [\mathbb{R}]_\mathcal{F}\}$ by definition. This is the same as the definition of $^*\mathbb{R}$ in Definition 4; therefore we can identify $^*\mathbb{R}$ constructed previously and the image of $\mathbb{R}$ under the map $^*(-)$.

Lemma 4 ([14, **Proposition 2.5.5**]). *Let* $[a_i]_\mathcal{F}$, $[a_i^{(1)}]_\mathcal{F}, \dots, [a_i^{(n)}]_\mathcal{F}$, $[b_i]_\mathcal{F}$, $[c_i]_\mathcal{F}$, *and* $[f_i]_\mathcal{F}$ *be members of* $\prod_\mathcal{F}^0 V$. *Let* $\bowtie$ *be* $=$ *or* $\in$. *The following statements hold.*

1. $M([a_i]_\mathcal{F}) \bowtie M([c_i]_\mathcal{F})$ *if and only if* $\{i \in \mathbb{N} \mid a_i \bowtie c_i\} \in \mathcal{F}$.
2. $\{M([a_i^{(1)}]_\mathcal{F}), \dots, M([a_i^{(n)}]_\mathcal{F})\} \bowtie M([c_i]_\mathcal{F})$ *if and only if* $\{i \in \mathbb{N} \mid \{a_i^{(1)}, \dots, a_i^{(n)}\} \bowtie c_i\} \in \mathcal{F}$.
3. $\langle M[a_i^{(1)}]_\mathcal{F}), \dots, M[a_i^{(n)}]_\mathcal{F}) \rangle \bowtie M([c_i]_\mathcal{F})$ *if and only if* $\{i \in \mathbb{N} \mid \langle a_i^{(1)}, \dots, a_i^{(n)} \rangle \bowtie c_i\} \in \mathcal{F}$.
4. $(M([f_i]))(M([a_i^{(1)}]_\mathcal{F}), \dots, M([a_i^{(n)}]_\mathcal{F}))$ *is defined and equals* $M([c_i]_\mathcal{F})$ *if and only if* $\{i \in \mathbb{N} \mid f_i(a_i^{(1)}, \dots, a_i^{(n))}$ *is defined and equals* $c_i\} \in \mathcal{F}$

The following is an easy corollary of this lemma.

Corollary 1. *Let* $[a_i^{(1)}]_\mathcal{F}, \dots, [a_i^{(n)}]_\mathcal{F}$ *be elements of* $\prod_\mathcal{F}^0 V$, *and* $f \in V$. *Then, we have* $(^*f)([a_i^{(1)}]_\mathcal{F}, \dots, [a_i^{(n)}]_\mathcal{F}) = [f(a_i^{(1)}, \dots, a_i^{(n)})]_\mathcal{F}$.

Example 10. The function $+ : \mathbb{R} \times \mathbb{R} \to \mathbb{R}$ is in V. We can show that the function $^*+ = M(e(+))$ is equal to $\langle [(r_i)_{i \in \mathbb{N}}]_\mathcal{F}, [(s_i)_{i \in \mathbb{N}}]_\mathcal{F} \rangle \mapsto [(r_i + s_i)_{i \in \mathbb{N}}]_\mathcal{F}$; this coincides with Example 5.

3.4 Transfer Principle, Formally

The mapping $^*(-)$ defined in Definition 11 satisfies the transfer principle (Property 1). To state this property formally, we define $^*\Phi$ below. We introduce a language for asserting properties of elements of $^*V(\mathbb{R})$.

Definition 12 (Language $^*\mathcal{L}$). *The language $^*\mathcal{L}$ is obtained from $\mathcal{L}$ by changing the range of v to $^*V(\mathbb{R})$. The operator * that maps an $\mathcal{L}$ formula to a $^*\mathcal{L}$ formula is defined as follows:*

$$
\begin{aligned}
^*v &:= \text{the symbol for the corresponding element in } {}^*V(\mathbb{R}) \\
^*x &:= x \\
^*\langle t_1, \ldots, t_n \rangle &:= \langle {}^*t_1, \ldots, {}^*t_n \rangle \\
^*(t_1(t_2)) &:= {}^*t_1({}^*t_2) \\
^*(t_1 \diamond t_2) &:= {}^*t_1 \diamond {}^*t_2 \text{ where } \diamond \in \{=, \in\} \\
^*(\Phi_1 \bowtie \Phi_2) &:= {}^*\Phi_1 \bowtie {}^*\Phi_2 \text{ where } \bowtie \in \{\wedge, \vee, \Rightarrow\} \\
^*(\neg \Phi) &:= \neg\, {}^*\Phi \\
^*(Qx \in t.\Phi) &:= (Qx \in {}^*t.\, {}^*\Phi) \text{ where } Q \in \{\forall, \exists\}
\end{aligned}
$$

Then, Property 1 can be restated formally as follows.

Theorem 1 (Transfer principle). *An $\mathcal{L}$ sentence Φ is valid if and only if a $^*\mathcal{L}$ sentence $^*\Phi$ is valid.*

Remark 2. We note that all constant symbols of this language have the form $^*v$ for some $v \in V(\mathbb{R})$. Hence, for example, $\exists x \in {}^*\mathbb{R}.\forall y \in \mathbb{R}.x > y$ is not expressible as $^*\Phi$, since it is known that $\mathbb{R} \notin {}^*V(\mathbb{R})$. This "formula" states the existence of an infinite element, and this statement is indeed true, but this fact cannot be obtained by using the transfer principle.

3.5 Internal and External Entities

It is known that there is $v \in V({}^*\mathbb{R})$ such that $v \notin {}^*S$ for any $S \in V(\mathbb{R})$ [14]. This implies that not every set in $V({}^*\mathbb{R})$ can be obtained by enlarging a standard set. The following definition of *internality* and *externality* captures this feature of $^*(-)$.

Definition 13 (Internal and external entities). *An element $v \in V({}^*\mathbb{R})$ is called* internal *if there exists a standard set $S \in V(\mathbb{R})$ such that $v \in {}^*S$; otherwise, it is called* external.

We can reason about properties of internal entities by using Theorem 1.

Example 11. $\mathbb{R}$, $\mathbb{N}$, and $I := \{\mathbf{r} \in {}^*\mathbb{R} \mid \mathbf{r} \text{ is infinitesimal}\}$ are all external [14].

4 Transferring the Domain Theory

Denotational semantics of the standard simply typed functional languages with recursion often uses cpos as domains of the denotation (e.g., [22]). We use cpos enlarged by $^*(-)$, which we call *-cpos*, in the denotational semantics of NSF in Sect. 5.2. This section gives the definitions and the properties of these $*$-cpos.

This strategy of using enlarged cpos has been used in a nonstandard imperative language [9,10,23] and nonstandard stream-processing languages [2,24]. This section is based on the work by Kido et al. [10], in which they consider the nonstandard counterpart of standard cpos obtained by enlarging standard cpos (they call an enlarged cpo a *hyperdomain*); comparison with their work is in Sect. 7; we extend their development with various types of values including higher-order functions.

We write $Cpo(D, \sqsubseteq)$ and $Conti_{D_1, \sqsubseteq_1, D_2, \sqsubseteq_2}(f)$ for $\mathcal{L}$-formulae stating that $\langle D, \sqsubseteq \rangle$ is a cpo, and f is a Scott-continuous function from $\langle D_1, \sqsubseteq_1 \rangle$ to $\langle D_2, \sqsubseteq_2 \rangle$, respectively (their concrete definitions are found in Kido et al. [10]).

Definition 14 (*-cpo). *If $\langle D, \sqsubseteq \rangle$ is a cpo, then $\langle {}^*D, {}^*\!\sqsubseteq \rangle$ is said to be a $*$-cpo.*

The following is an immediate consequence of the transfer principle (Theorem 1).

Lemma 5. $^*(Cpo(D, \sqsubseteq))$ *is valid if $\langle D, \sqsubseteq \rangle$ is a cpo.*

Definition 15 (*-continuous function). *Let $\langle {}^*D_1, {}^*\!\sqsubseteq_1 \rangle$ and $\langle {}^*D_2, {}^*\!\sqsubseteq_2 \rangle$ be $*$-cpos. A function $f : {}^*D_1 \to {}^*D_2$ is said to be $*$-Scott-continuous or simply $*$-continuous if it satisfies $^*(Conti_{D_1, \sqsubseteq_1, D_2, \sqsubseteq_2})(f)$. We write ${}^*D_1 \to_{*\text{-}cont} {}^*D_2$ for the set of $*$-continuous functions from ${}^*D_1$ to ${}^*D_2$.*

We use the following results, which are stated in Kido et al. [10].

Lemma 6. *Let $\langle {}^*D_1, {}^*\!\sqsubseteq_1 \rangle$ and $\langle {}^*D_2, {}^*\!\sqsubseteq_2 \rangle$ be $*$-cpos. Then, $f \in {}^*D_1 \to_{*\text{-}cont} {}^*D_2$ is an internal entity.*

Lemma 7 (Fixpoint theorem). *If $\langle {}^*D, {}^*\!\sqsubseteq \rangle$ is a $*$-cpo and $f : {}^*D \to {}^*D$ is a $*$-continuous function, then f has the least fixpoint in ${}^*D$.*

Lemma 7 justifies the following definition.

Definition 16 ($*\mu$). *Let $\langle {}^*D, {}^*\!\sqsubseteq \rangle$ be a $*$-cpo and $f : {}^*D \to {}^*D$ be a $*$-continuous function. We write ${}^*\mu f$ for the least fixpoint of f; we regard ${}^*\mu$ as an operator.*

Definition 17. *We write $\mathbb{R}_\perp$ for the set $\mathbb{R} \cup \{\perp\}$ where $\perp$ is a special element that does not appear elsewhere. The order $\sqsubseteq \subseteq \mathbb{R}_\perp \times \mathbb{R}_\perp$ is defined by $x \sqsubseteq y \iff x = \perp \lor x = y$; the set $\mathbb{R}_\perp$ is a cpo with respect to this order.*

Lemma 8. *If $\langle D_1, \sqsubseteq_1 \rangle$ and $\langle D_2, \sqsubseteq_2 \rangle$ are cpos, then so are the following:*

1. $\langle D_1 \times D_2, \sqsubseteq_\times \rangle$, where $\langle d_1, d_2 \rangle \sqsubseteq_\times \langle d_1', d_2' \rangle$ if and only if $d_1 \sqsubseteq_1 d_1' \land d_2 \sqsubseteq_2 d_2'$;

2. $\langle D_1 \to_{ct} D_2, \sqsubseteq_\to \rangle$, where $D_1 \to_{ct} D_2$ is the set of Scott-continuous functions from D_1 to D_2, and $f_1 \sqsubseteq_\to f_2$ if and only if $f_1(d) \sqsubseteq_2 f_2(d)$ for all $d \in D_1$.

The category **CPO** of cpos and Scott-continuous functions between them forms a cartesian closed category (CCC) with product $\times$ and exponential $\to_{ct}$ introduced above. By using Theorem 1, we obtain a CCC structure on the category of *-cpos and *-continuous functions.

Lemma 9. *The category* ***CPO** *of* *-cpos and *-continuous functions is a CCC.*

Proof. A product of *-cpos $^*D_1$ and $^*D_2$ is given by $^*(D_1 \times D_2)$, which is equal to $^*D_1 \times \, ^*D_2$ (with projections $^*\pi_i$, where $\pi_i : D_1 \times D_2 \to D_i$ are projections in **CPO**). Their universal property is proved as follows. Because $D_1 \times D_2$ is a product in **CPO**, we have: for any cpo D and Scott-continuous functions $f : D \to D_1$ and $g : D \to D_2$, there exists unique $h : D \to D_1 \times D_2$ such that $f = \pi_1 \circ h$ and $g = \pi_2 \circ h$. This is a property expressible by an $\mathcal{L}$ formula, and therefore by transfer principle (Theorem 1), we have: for any *-cpo $^*D$ and *-continuous functions $f : {}^*D \to {}^*D_1$ and $g : {}^*D \to {}^*D_2$, there exists unique $h : {}^*D \to {}^*(D_1 \times D_2)$ such that $f = {}^*\pi_1 \circ h$ and $g = {}^*\pi_2 \circ h$. This is the universal property for a product in ***CPO**. A terminal object is given by one-element *-cpo, and an exponential is given by $^*(D_1 \to_{ct} D_2)$, which is equal to $^*D_1 \to_{*-cont} {}^*D_2$. Their universal properties are proved similarly. $\square$

We can also see that the fixed-point operator $^*\mu$ introduced in Definition 16 is a morphism in ***CPO**. Indeed, it is well-known that μ is Scott-continuous, and hence $^*\mu$ is *-continuous.

5   NSF

Having set up the domain, we define the syntax, the type system, and the denotational semantics of NSF.

5.1   Syntax and Type System

The following BNF defines the syntax of NSF.

Environment $\Gamma \; ::= \; \emptyset \mid \Gamma, x : \tau$
Type $\tau \; ::= \; \mathcal{R} \mid \tau_1 \to \tau_2$
Term $M \; ::= \; x \mid \mathbf{r} \mid \mathbf{dt} \mid M_1 \, M_2$
                $\mid \; \mathbf{rec}(f^{\tau_1}, x^{\tau_2}, M) \mid M_1 \bowtie M_2 \mid \text{if } M_1 \text{ then } M_2 \text{ else } M_3,$

where $\bowtie \; \in \; \{+, -, \times, /\}$. We use x and $\mathbf{r}$ for variables and constant symbols for real numbers, respectively. The symbol $\mathbf{dt}$ is for an infinitesimal number; the denotational semantics introduced later is parameterized over choices of the denotation of $\mathbf{dt}$. The term $\mathbf{rec}(f^{\tau_1}, x^{\tau_2}, M)$ is a recursive function, where f is the function being defined, and x is its argument. The type annotation τ_1 is that of the whole function; τ_2 is the type of the argument x. The term $M_1 \, M_2$

applies M_1 to M_2. The term $M_1 \bowtie M_2$, where $\bowtie \in \{+, -, \times, /\}$, is an arithmetic operation on hyperreals. We often write $\frac{M_1}{M_2}$ instead of M_1/M_2 for the sake of readability. In a conditional expression **if** M_1 **then** M_2 **else** M_3, M_2 is evaluated if M_1 evaluates to a nonnegative hyperreal, and otherwise M_3 is evaluated. The free and bound variables are defined as usual; we write $\mathbf{FV}(M)$ for the set of the free variables of M. We often omit type annotations in a term.

A *type* τ is either $\mathcal{R}$ for hyperreals, or $\tau_1 \to \tau_2$ for (∗-continuous) functions. A *type environment* Γ is a list $x_1 : \tau_1, \ldots, x_n : \tau_n$ of variable bindings to types. We write $\Gamma(x) = \tau$ if $x : \tau$ is the rightmost binding of x in Γ.

We write $\lambda x^\tau.M$ for $\mathbf{rec}(f^{\tau \to \tau'}, x^\tau, M)$ if f does not freely occur in M. We write **let** $x^\tau = M_1$ **in** M_2 for $(\lambda x^\tau.M_2) \, M_1$. We write **let rec** $f^{\tau_1 \to \tau_2} x^{\tau_1} = M_1$ **in** M_2 for **let** $f^{\tau_1 \to \tau_2} = \mathbf{rec}(f^{\tau_1 \to \tau_2}, x^{\tau_1}, M_1)$ **in** M_2. We often omit the "**in** M_2" part of the notations above if we present a top-level definition.

Example 12. The following function computes the factorial of x if x is a natural number: $\mathbf{rec}(fact^{\mathcal{R} \to \mathcal{R}}, x^{\mathcal{R}}, \textbf{if } x - 1 \textbf{ then } x \times fact \, (x - 1) \textbf{ else } 1)$.

In the rest of this paper, we use the following functions encoding Boolean operations and predicates over hyperreals; recall that **if** M_1 **then** M_2 **else** M_3 evaluates M_1 to a hyperreal r and then evaluates M_2 if $r \geq 0$ and M_3 if $r < 0$.

let *not* $= \lambda x.\textbf{if } x \textbf{ then } -1 \textbf{ else } 1$ **let** *and* $= \lambda x.\lambda y.\textbf{if } x \textbf{ then } y \textbf{ else } -1$
let *or* $= \lambda x.\lambda y.\textbf{if } x \textbf{ then } 1 \textbf{ else } y$ **let** *le* $= \lambda x.\lambda y.y - x$
let *eq* $= \lambda x.\lambda y.and \, (le \, x \, y) \, (le \, y \, x)$

Example 13 (Infinite sum). The following function Σ computes the value of $(f \, x) + (f(x + 1)) + \cdots + (f \, (x + \frac{1}{\mathbf{dt}}))$:

let rec $\Sigma = \lambda f.\lambda x.\textbf{if } le \, (1/\mathbf{dt}) \, x \textbf{ then } 0 \textbf{ else } (f \, x) + (\Sigma \, f \, (x + 1))$.

Here, $1/\mathbf{dt}$ denotes a positive infinite hyperreal; therefore, the function Σ computes an infinite sum if x is a finite hyperreal. For example, the value of $\Sigma \, (\lambda x.\frac{1}{x \times x}) \, 1$ is (infinitely close to) $\pi^2/6$.

The type judgment $\Gamma \vdash M : \tau$ reads "the term M has type τ under the type environment Γ," and defined by the standard rules listed in Fig. 1.

$$\frac{\Gamma(x) = \tau}{\Gamma \vdash x : \tau}(\text{T-Var}) \qquad \frac{}{\Gamma \vdash r : \mathcal{R}}(\text{T-Const}) \qquad \frac{}{\Gamma \vdash \mathbf{dt} : \mathcal{R}}(\text{T-Dt})$$

$$\frac{\Gamma, f : \tau_1 \to \tau_2, x : \tau_1 \vdash M : \tau_2}{\Gamma \vdash \mathbf{rec}(f^{\tau_1 \to \tau_2}, x^{\tau_1}, M) : \tau_1 \to \tau_2}(\text{T-Rec}) \qquad \frac{\Gamma \vdash M_1 : \tau_1 \to \tau_2 \qquad \Gamma \vdash M_2 : \tau_1}{\Gamma \vdash M_1 \, M_2 : \tau_2}(\text{T-App})$$

$$\frac{\Gamma \vdash M_1 : \mathcal{R} \qquad \Gamma \vdash M_2 : \mathcal{R}}{\Gamma \vdash M_1 \bowtie M_2 : \mathcal{R}}(\text{T-Op}) \qquad \frac{\Gamma \vdash M_1 : \mathcal{R} \qquad \Gamma \vdash M_2 : \tau \qquad \Gamma \vdash M_3 : \tau}{\Gamma \vdash \textbf{if } M_1 \textbf{ then } M_2 \textbf{ else } M_3 : \tau}(\text{T-If})$$

Fig. 1. Typing rules.

5.2   Denotational Semantics

We define the denotational semantics of NSF by using *-cpos given in the last section. In this semantic domain, by using the least fixed-point operator $^*\mu$ in Definition 16, we can give the denotation that matches with our intuition; we observe that our definition indeed works by several examples in Sect. 6.

We describe the concrete definitions in what follows. We start from the semantics of types and type environments.

Definition 18 (Denotation of types). *The denotation of type τ, written as $[\![\tau]\!]$, is inductively defined by $[\![\mathcal{R}]\!] := {}^*\mathbb{R}_\bot$ and $[\![\tau_1 \to \tau_2]\!] := [\![\tau_1]\!] \to_{*\text{-}cont} [\![\tau_2]\!]$. The denotation of type environment Γ, written as $[\![\Gamma]\!]$, is defined by $[\![\emptyset]\!] := \{\bot\}$ and $[\![\Gamma, x : \tau]\!] := [\![\Gamma]\!] \times [\![\tau]\!]$.*

The semantics of the type $\mathcal{R}$ is $^*\mathbb{R} \cup \{\bot\}$; the semantics of the function type $\tau_1 \to \tau_2$ is the set of the *-continuous functions (Definition 15) from $[\![\tau_1]\!]$ to $[\![\tau_2]\!]$.

We give the semantics of terms by induction on the derivation of type judgments $\Gamma \vdash M : \tau$.

Definition 19 (Denotation of terms). *The denotation of a well-typed term M, written as $[\![\Gamma \vdash M : \tau]\!]_\partial$ where ∂ is a (fixed) infinitesimal value, is defined as follows.*

$$[\![x_1 : \tau_1, \ldots, x_n : \tau_n \vdash x_i : \tau_i]\!]_\partial (d_1, \ldots, d_n) := d_i$$
$$[\![\Gamma \vdash \mathbf{r} : \mathcal{R}]\!]_\partial (\vec{d}) := {}^*\mathbf{r}$$
$$[\![\Gamma \vdash \mathbf{dt} : \mathcal{R}]\!]_\partial (\vec{d}) := \partial$$
$$[\![\Gamma \vdash M_1\, M_2 : \tau]\!]_\partial (\vec{d}) := [\![\Gamma \vdash M_1 : \tau' \to \tau]\!]_\partial (\vec{d}) ([\![\Gamma \vdash M_2 : \tau']\!]_\partial (\vec{d}))$$
$$[\![\Gamma \vdash \mathbf{rec}(f^{\tau_1 \to \tau_2}, x^{\tau_1}, M) : \tau_1 \to \tau_2]\!]_\partial (\vec{d})$$
$$\quad := {}^*\mu(d_f \mapsto (d_x \mapsto [\![\Gamma, f : \tau_1 \to \tau_2, x : \tau_1 \vdash M : \tau_2]\!]_\partial (\vec{d}, d_f, d_x)))$$
$$[\![\Gamma \vdash M_1 \bowtie M_2 : \mathcal{R}]\!]_\partial (\vec{d}) := [\![\bowtie]\!]([\![\Gamma \vdash M_1 : \mathcal{R}]\!]_\partial (\vec{d}), [\![\Gamma \vdash M_2 : \mathcal{R}]\!]_\partial (\vec{d}))$$
$$[\![\Gamma \vdash \mathbf{if}\ M_1\ \mathbf{then}\ M_2\ \mathbf{else}\ M_3 : \tau]\!]_\partial (\vec{d})$$
$$\quad := ({}^*ifz)([\![\Gamma \vdash M_1 : \mathcal{R}]\!]_\partial (\vec{d}), [\![\Gamma \vdash M_2 : \tau]\!]_\partial (\vec{d}), [\![\Gamma \vdash M_3 : \tau]\!]_\partial (\vec{d}))$$

where $[\![\bowtie]\!]$ is given by $^*\bowtie$, the enlargement of the standard arithmetic operation extended to $\mathbb{R}_\bot$ by $v \bowtie \bot = \bot \bowtie v = \bot$ for $v \in \mathbb{R}_\bot$; we define $v/0 = \bot$. The function ifz is defined by $ifz(\bot, x, y) := \bot$, $ifz(r, x, y) := x$ if $r \geq 0$, and $ifz(r, x, y) := y$ otherwise.

As is the standard practice in denotational semantics, the denotation $[\![x_1 : \tau_1, \ldots, x_n : \tau_n \vdash M : \tau]\!]_\partial$ of term M of type τ under type environment $x_1 : \tau_1, \ldots, x_n : \tau_n$ is defined by induction on the typing derivation (for detailed explanation, see [22]); it is a *-continuous function from $[\![x_1 : \tau_1, \ldots, x_n : \tau_n]\!]$ to $[\![\tau]\!]$ that takes a tuple of values $v_1, \ldots, v_n$ to which $x_1, \ldots, x_n$ are bound and returns the result of evaluating M. This denotation is parameterized over the denotation of $\mathbf{dt}$ (i.e., ∂).

We give brief explanations to the cases that are peculiar to NSF.

- $[\![\Gamma \vdash \mathbf{dt} : \mathcal{R}]\!]_\partial$: The denotation of $\mathbf{dt}$ is set to ∂, the parameter ∂ of the function $[\![-]\!]_\partial$.
- $[\![\Gamma \vdash \mathbf{rec}(f^{\tau_1 \to \tau_2}, x^{\tau_1}, M) : \tau_1 \to \tau_2]\!]_\partial$: By the inversion of the typing rules, the judgment $\Gamma, f : \tau_1 \to \tau_2, x : \tau_1 \vdash M : \tau_2$ holds; the denotation of $\Gamma \vdash \mathbf{rec}(f^{\tau_1 \to \tau_2}, x^{\tau_1}, M) : \tau_1 \to \tau_2$ is obtained as the least fixpoint of $[\![\Gamma, f : \tau_1 \to \tau_2, x : \tau_1 \vdash M : \tau_2]\!]_\partial$ on the argument corresponding to f by $^*\mu$ (Definition 16). The least fixpoint indeed exists because the function $(d_f \mapsto (d_x \mapsto [\![\Gamma, f : \tau_1 \to \tau_2, x : \tau_1 \vdash M : \tau_2]\!]_\partial(\overrightarrow{d}, d_f, d_x)))$ is *-continuous (Theorem 2).

In the rest of this paper, we often omit the parameter ∂ for readability if the choice of ∂ is not important or is clear from the context. Furthermore, we sometimes abbreviate $[\![\Gamma \vdash M : \tau]\!]_\partial$ to $[\![M]\!]_\partial$, if there is no confusion.

Theorem 2 (Well-definedness). *If* $\Gamma \vdash M : \tau$, *then* $[\![\Gamma \vdash M : \tau]\!]_\partial \in [\![\Gamma]\!] \to_{*\text{-}cont} [\![\tau]\!]$.

6 Examples

This section presents encoding of several operations in the mathematical analysis and shows how NSF semantics can be used to reason about the properties of this encoding. In this section, the word "continuous" is used to mean the continuity in mathematical analysis instead of the Scott-continuity.

6.1 Operations in Mathematical Analysis

Recall the following functions D and S in Examples 3 and 4:

$$\mathbf{let}\ D = \lambda f.\lambda x. \frac{f\ (x + \frac{\mathbf{dt}}{2}) - f\ (x - \frac{\mathbf{dt}}{2})}{\mathbf{dt}}$$
$$\mathbf{let\ rec}\ S\ s = \lambda t.\lambda f.\mathbf{if}\ t \leq s\ \mathbf{then}\ 0\ \mathbf{else}\ (f\ t) \times \mathbf{dt} + S\ s\ (t - \mathbf{dt})\ f.$$

Notice that these functions are higher-order functions: D has type $(\mathcal{R} \to \mathcal{R}) \to \mathcal{R} \to \mathcal{R}$; S has type $\mathcal{R} \to \mathcal{R} \to (\mathcal{R} \to \mathcal{R}) \to \mathcal{R}$.

By using the denotational semantics of NSF, we can prove that the encoding by these functions is correct.

Lemma 10. *Let* $f \in \mathbb{R} \to \mathbb{R}$ *be a differentiable function,* $f' \in \mathbb{R} \to \mathbb{R}$ *be the derivative of* f, *and* M_f *be a closed NSF term* M_f *that satisfies* $\emptyset \vdash M_f : \mathcal{R} \to \mathcal{R}$. *Suppose that* $\frac{1}{\partial}[\![\emptyset \vdash M_f : \mathcal{R} \to \mathcal{R}]\!]_\partial(r) \simeq \frac{1}{\partial}(^*f)(r)$ *for any finite* $r \in {}^*\mathbb{R}$. *Then,* $[\![\emptyset \vdash D\ M_f : \mathcal{R} \to \mathcal{R}]\!]_\partial(r) \simeq f'(r)$ *for any* $r \in \mathbb{R}$.[2]

---

[2] This lemma requires the condition $\frac{1}{\partial}[\![\emptyset \vdash M_f : \mathcal{R} \to \mathcal{R}]\!]_\partial(r) \simeq \frac{1}{\partial}(^*f)(r)$, which is stronger than $[\![\emptyset \vdash M_f : \mathcal{R} \to \mathcal{R}]\!]_\partial(r) \simeq (^*f)(r)$. This stronger condition is indeed necessary. For example, if $M_f = \mathbf{if}\ 0 \leq t\ \mathbf{then}\ \mathbf{dt}\ \mathbf{else}\ 0$ and $(^*f)(r) = 0$ for all r, then they satisfy the weaker condition, but $[\![D\ M_f]\!]_\partial(0) = 1 \neq 0 = f'(0)$.

Lemma 11. *Let* $f \in \mathbb{R} \to \mathbb{R}$ *be a Riemann-integrable function,* $s, t \in \mathbb{R}$ *such that* $s < t$, *and* M_f *be a closed NSF term such that* $\emptyset \vdash M_f : \mathcal{R} \to \mathcal{R}$. *Suppose that* $[\![\emptyset \vdash M_f : \mathcal{R} \to \mathcal{R}]\!]_\partial(r) \simeq {}^*f(r)$ *for any finite* $r \in {}^*\mathbb{R}$. *Then,* $[\![\emptyset \vdash S \ s \ t \ M_f : \mathcal{R}]\!]_\partial \simeq (\int_s^t f(x)dx)$.

Using the same strategy as that for Lemma 11, we can prove the following lemma, which intuitively means that the function S "terminates" for any f, s, and x; we will use this lemma later.

Lemma 12. $[\![f : \mathcal{R} \to \mathcal{R}, s : \mathcal{R}, x : \mathcal{R} \vdash S \ (x - \frac{dt}{2}) \ s \ f : \mathcal{R}]\!]_\partial(d_f, d_s, d_x) \neq \perp$ *for any* $d_f \in {}^*(\mathbb{R} \to \mathbb{R})$ *and* $d_s, d_x \in {}^*\mathbb{R}$.

An important consequence of Lemma 11 is that NSF can encode a solution of (a certain class of) ordinary differential equations. Consider the following initial value problem: $\frac{df}{dt} = g(t)$ and $f(x_0) = f_0$ where $g \in \mathbb{R} \to \mathbb{R}$ is Lipschitz continuous and $x_0, f_0 \in \mathbb{R}$. It is well-known that the unique solution of this initial value problem is $f(t) = f_0 + \int_{x_0}^t g(x)dx$. Therefore, by Lemma 11, the following function $\lambda t^{\mathcal{R}}.(f_0 + S \ x_0 \ t \ M_g)$ returns a value infinitely close to ${}^*f(t)$ for any $t \in {}^*\mathbb{R}$ such that $t > x_0$ if $[\![\emptyset \vdash M_g : \mathcal{R} \to \mathcal{R}]\!](r) \simeq {}^*g(r)$ for any finite $r \in {}^*\mathbb{R}$.

Lemma 13. *Let* $g \in \mathbb{R} \to \mathbb{R}$ *be Lipschitz continuous and* $x_0, f_0 \in \mathbb{R}$. *If* $[\![\emptyset \vdash M_g : \mathcal{R} \to \mathcal{R}]\!]_\partial(r) \simeq {}^*g(r)$ *for any finite* $r \in {}^*\mathbb{R}$, *then* $[\![\emptyset \vdash \lambda t^{\mathcal{R}}.(f_0 + S \ x_0 \ t \ M_g) : \mathcal{R} \to \mathcal{R}]\!]_\partial(r_t)$ *is infinitely close to the solution of the initial value problem* $\frac{df}{dt} = g(t); f(x_0) = f_0$ *if* $r_t \in {}^*\mathbb{R} > x_0$.

6.2 Fundamental Theorem of Calculus

The equation $\frac{d}{dx} \int_s^x f(t)dt = f(x)$, known as the *fundamental theorem of calculus*, is expressed by NSF as follows.

Theorem 3. *Suppose that* D *and* S *are defined as in Examples 3 and 4, respectively, and let* g *be* $[\![f : \mathcal{R} \to \mathcal{R}, s : \mathcal{R} \vdash D \ (\lambda x^{\mathcal{R}}.S \ s \ x \ f) : \mathcal{R} \to \mathcal{R}]\!]_\partial$. *Then* $g(d_f, d_s, d_x) \simeq d_f(d_x)$ *for any continuous* $d_f \in {}^*(\mathbb{R} \to \mathbb{R})$, *and* $d_s, d_x \in {}^*\mathbb{R}$ *such that* $d_x + \frac{\partial}{2} > d_s$.

Although we can prove this theorem by working on the definition of $[\![-]\!]$ directly, we use a *syntactic* inference in our proof. We use the β-equivalence, which is the least congruence closed under the rules in Fig. 2.

$$\frac{}{(\mathbf{rec}(f^{\tau_1 \to \tau_2}, x^{\tau_1}, M)) \ N \cong_\beta [\mathbf{rec}(f^{\tau_1 \to \tau_2}, x^{\tau_1}, M)/f, N/x]M} (\text{E-RecBeta})$$

$$\frac{({}^*\mathbf{r} \geq 0)}{\mathbf{if} \ \mathbf{r} \ \mathbf{then} \ M_1 \ \mathbf{else} \ M_2 \cong_\beta M_1}(\text{E-Then}) \qquad \frac{({}^*\mathbf{r} < 0)}{\mathbf{if} \ \mathbf{r} \ \mathbf{then} \ M_1 \ \mathbf{else} \ M_2 \cong_\beta M_2}(\text{E-Else})$$

Fig. 2. β-equivalence rules.

Theorem 4 (Soundness of $\cong_\beta$). *If $\Gamma \vdash M : \tau$ and $\Gamma \vdash M' : \tau$ and $M \cong_\beta M'$, then $[\![\Gamma \vdash M : \tau]\!] = [\![\Gamma \vdash M' : \tau]\!]$.*

Proof (of Theorem 3). First, notice that

$$D \; (\lambda x^{\mathcal{R}}.S \; s \; x \; f)$$
$$\cong_\beta \lambda x^{\mathcal{R}}.\frac{(\lambda x^{\mathcal{R}}.S \; s \; x \; f) \; (x + \frac{\mathbf{dt}}{2}) - (\lambda x^{\mathcal{R}}.S \; s \; x \; f)(x - \frac{\mathbf{dt}}{2})}{\mathbf{dt}}$$
$$\cong_\beta \lambda x^{\mathcal{R}}.\frac{(S \; s \; (x + \frac{\mathbf{dt}}{2}) \; f) - S \; (x - \frac{\mathbf{dt}}{2}) \; s \; f)}{\mathbf{dt}}$$
$$\cong_\beta \lambda x^{\mathcal{R}}.(\lambda y^{\mathcal{R}}.\frac{(y - S \; (x - \frac{\mathbf{dt}}{2}) \; s \; f)}{\mathbf{dt}}) \; (S \; (x + \frac{\mathbf{dt}}{2}) \; s \; f)$$
$$\cong_\beta \lambda x^{\mathcal{R}}.(\lambda y^{\mathcal{R}}.\frac{(y - (S \; (x - \frac{\mathbf{dt}}{2}) \; s \; f))}{\mathbf{dt}}) \left(\begin{array}{l} \mathbf{if} \; le \; (x + \frac{\mathbf{dt}}{2}) \; s \; \mathbf{then} \; 0 \\ \mathbf{else} \; \mathbf{dt} \times f \; (x + \frac{\mathbf{dt}}{2}) + S \; (x + \frac{\mathbf{dt}}{2} - \mathbf{dt}) \; s \; f \end{array} \right)$$

Let

$$M := \lambda y^{\mathcal{R}}.\frac{(y - (S \; (x - \frac{\mathbf{dt}}{2}) \; s \; f))}{\mathbf{dt}},$$

$$N' := \mathbf{dt} \times f \; (x + \frac{\mathbf{dt}}{2}) + S \; (x + \frac{\mathbf{dt}}{2} - \mathbf{dt}) \; s \; f,$$

$$N := \mathbf{if} \; le \; (x + \frac{\mathbf{dt}}{2}) \; s \; \mathbf{then} \; 0 \; \mathbf{else} \; N',$$

$$\Gamma := f : \mathcal{R} \to \mathcal{R}, s : \mathcal{R}, \quad \Gamma' := \Gamma, x : \mathcal{R}.$$

Then, because $d_x + \frac{\partial}{2} > d_s$,

$$[\![\Gamma' \vdash N : \mathcal{R}]\!](d_f, d_s, d_x) = [\![ifz]\!](d_s - d_x - \frac{\partial}{2}, 0, [\![N']\!](d_f, d_s, d_x)) = [\![N']\!](d_f, d_s, d_x).$$

Therefore, by using Theorem 4 and Definition 19, we have

$$[\![\Gamma \vdash D \; (\lambda x^{\mathcal{R}}.S \; s \; x \; f) : \mathcal{R} \to \mathcal{R}]\!](d_f, d_s)(d_x)$$
$$= [\![\Gamma \vdash \lambda x^{\mathcal{R}}.M \; N : \mathcal{R} \to \mathcal{R}]\!](d_f, d_s)(d_x)$$
$$= [\![\Gamma \vdash \lambda x^{\mathcal{R}}.M \; N' : \mathcal{R} \to \mathcal{R}]\!](d_f, d_s)(d_x)$$
$$= [\![\Gamma \vdash \lambda x^{\mathcal{R}}.\frac{N' - (S \; (x - \frac{\mathbf{dt}}{2}) \; s \; f)}{\mathbf{dt}} : \mathcal{R} \to \mathcal{R}]\!](d_f, d_s)(d_x).$$

The last step uses $\cong_\beta$. Then, by using the definition of $[\![-]\!]$ and Lemma 12, $(S \; (x - \frac{\mathbf{dt}}{2}) \; s \; f)$ cancels and therefore this is equal to $[\![\lambda x^{\mathcal{R}}.\frac{(\mathbf{dt} \times f \; (x + \frac{\mathbf{dt}}{2}))}{\mathbf{dt}}]\!](d_f, d_s)(d_x) = d_f(d_x + \frac{\partial}{2})$; hence, $g(d_f, d_s, d_x) = d_f(d_x + \frac{\partial}{2}) \simeq d_f(d_x)$ because d_f is continuous (Lemma 1). $\qquad\square$

6.3 Generalized European Train Control System

European Train Control System (ETCS) is an autonomous model of train control. Hasuo and Suenaga [9] encoded a simplified ETCS model with **While**$^{\mathbf{dt}}$ and verified it. This section, putting verification aside, shows how NSF models the simplified ETCS example.

Our system is described by the following state variables: z for the position of the train which runs along a one-dimensional line; v for the velocity of the train; and a for the acceleration rate of the train. These variables are called *system variables* in the following. The train first accelerates itself in acceleration rate a_0. During the acceleration, the train senses its position every ε seconds; we assume that the sensed position does not contain any noise. If the distance between the wall, located at m, and the train is less than s (i.e., if $m - z < s$), then the train sets the acceleration rate to $-b$. The initial position of the train is z_0; the initial velocity is v_0. The values a_0, ε, m, s, b, z_0, and v_0 are the parameters of the system. Hasuo and Suenaga [9] showed that their verifier could compute a precondition on the parameters so that the train does not hit the wall, that is, $z \not\geq m$.

We can model this system by the following program in NSF (extended with tuples and syntax for ML-like function definitions):

```
let rec etcs emu z v a =
    let (z', v', a') = emu z v a 0 in
    if le (m − z') s then etcs z' v' (−b) else etcs z' v' a₀

let rec emu_noslip z v a t =
    if and (le t ε) (le 0 v)
    then emu_noslip (z + v × dt) (v + a × dt) a (t + dt)
    else (z, v, a)

etcs emu_noslip z₀ v₀ a₀
```

The function *etcs* models the behavior of the train. Beside the system variables, it takes a function *emu* as an argument. The function *emu* takes the current values of the system variables and returns their new values of ε seconds later. The train chooses the acceleration rate during the next ε seconds from the new position z' of the train. The code above also shows a function *emu_noslip* that computes the values of the system variables of ε seconds later following the differential equation $\frac{dx}{dt} = v$, $\frac{dv}{dt} = a$. (The functions *and* and *le* are defined in Sect. 5.1.)

The parameterization of the function *etcs* with a higher-order function *emu* exhibits a merit of a functional nonstandard programming language. Suppose we need to model a variant of ETCS in which the rail is slippery. The only thing we need is to designate a function that computes the new values of system variable of ε seconds later:

```
let rec emu_rainy z v a t =
    if and (le t ε) (le 0 v)
    then emu_rainy (z + v × dt) (v + r × a × dt) a (t + dt)
    else (z, v, a)

etcs emu_rainy z₀ v₀ a₀
```

To model the train on slippery rail, the function *emu_rainy* discounts the acceleration rate by a constant r in computing the new value. This function is passed to the function *etcs*, which is not changed. Compare this modeling with that by Hasuo and Suenaga [9], in which they hardcoded the evolution of the train.

7 Related Work

Suenaga and Hasuo proposed an imperative nonstandard programming language **While**^{dt} [23] and a Lustre-like stream-processing nonstandard programming language **SProc**^{dt} [24]. They define the denotational semantics of these languages by transferring the semantics of their standard counterparts (a WHILE language for **While**^{dt}; a standard stream-processing language, for **SProc**^{dt}). NSF incorporates functions of arbitrarily high order whereas they do not deal with procedures [23] or deal with only first-order functions [24]. This difference is reflected in the semantic domain; we need the category ****CPO** (see Sect. 4) that constitutes a CCC structure whereas they only need simpler ones.

Combination of the nonstandard analysis and the domain theory is found in Beauxis et al. [2]. They introduced the notion of *internal domain* to give the semantics of continuous-time Kahn networks. Concretely, $\langle M([D_i]_{\mathcal{F}}), M([\preceq_i]_{\mathcal{F}}) \rangle$ is an internal domain if $\langle D_i, \preceq_i \rangle$ is a cpo for every i where $M(-)$ is the Mostowski collapse in Definition 11. A *-cpo is an internal domain but the converse is not true.[3] More precise investigation of our work (e.g., such as interpreting their work using *-cpos and our work using internal domains) is an important topic but currently left as future work.

Kido et al. [10], in their full version, provided the complete definition of the $\mathcal{L}$ formulae that specify cpos and Scott-continuous functions. They transfer these formulae to define *-cpos and *-continuous functions. Our development in Sect. 4 is based on their work. Our contribution is that we show that the category ***CPO** has the structure of CCC (Lemma 9). The structure of the *-cpos and *-continuous functions as CCC is paramount for the well-definedness of the denotational semantics (Theorem 2).

Sanders [21] applied the proof-mining method proposed by Kohlenbach [12] to the internal set theory (IST) [17], an axiomatization of the nonstandard analysis. The proof mining is a sequence of conversions to extract information related to computation. He showed that the proof-mining technique applied to IST can extract (what he calls) computational information from a theorem of NSA. Our work puts emphasis on NSF as a programming language to describe a computation that uses nonstandard entities. We, therefore, took the current programming-language-theoretic development (i.e., defining the syntax of NSF first, defining the semantics of it, and then proving metatheorems), rather than their proof-theoretic development.

Combination of NSA and the programming languages (in a broad sense) has been investigated in the context of the theory of automata [3,4,16,20], proof

---

[3] $\langle M([D_i]_{\mathcal{F}}), M([\preceq_i]_{\mathcal{F}}) \rangle$ is an internal domain but not a *-cpo if $D_i := \{0, 1, \ldots, i, \bot\}$ and $\preceq_i \subseteq D_i \times D_i$ is defined by $x \preceq_i y \iff x = \bot \vee x = y$.

assistants [5,6], process networks [2,21]. Studying the relation of NSF and these languages is an important future direction.

8 Conclusion

We defined the nonstandard functional programming language NSF. This language is an extension of a simply typed functional language with a constant **dt** that denotes an infinitesimal number. The denotational semantics of NSF, which is proved to be well-defined, is given by *-cpos obtained by enlarging standard cpos.

To exemplify the reasoning using NSF, we proved several theorems about NSF programs including one that encodes the fundamental theorem of calculus (Theorem 3). We believe that the proof of Theorem 3 is interesting in that it uses semantics-preserving successive program transformations.

As a future direction, we are interested in (semi-)automated static verification for NSF programs. In this regard, a previous nonstandard programming language **While**^{dt} is equipped with a verification framework **Hoare**^{dt} [23], which was based on Hoare logic. Based on **Hoare**^{dt}, they implemented a verifier; their implementation automatically verified the behavior of a train control system encoded as a **While**^{dt} program [9]. Kido et al. proposed an abstract interpretation framework for **While**^{dt} [10], which is used to automatically verify several hybrid systems. Automated static verification of functional programs is recently a very hot topic [1,8,11,13,15,19]. We are currently trying to apply these techniques to NSF programs.

Acknowledgments. We appreciate the anonymous reviewers for their comments. This work was supported in part by JST CREST (Kojima), JST PRESTO No. JPMJPR15E5 (Suenaga), and MEXT KAKENHI Grant Number 15H05706 (Igarashi).

References

1. Asada, K., Sato, R., Kobayashi, N.: Verifying relational properties of functional programs by first-order refinement. In: PEPM 2015, pp. 61–72 (2015)
2. Beauxis, R., Mimram, S.: A non-standard semantics for Kahn networks in continuous time. In: CSL 2011, pp. 35–50 (2011)
3. Benveniste, A., Bourke, T., Caillaud, B., Pouzet, M.: Non-standard semantics of hybrid systems modelers. J. Comput. Syst. Sci. **78**(3), 877–910 (2012)
4. Bliudze, S., Krob, D.: Modelling of complex systems: systems as dataflow machines. Fundam. Inform. **91**(2), 251–274 (2009)
5. Cowles, J.R., Gamboa, R.: Equivalence of the traditional and non-standard definitions of concepts from real analysis. In: Proceedings Twelfth International Workshop on the ACL2 Theorem Prover and its Applications, pp. 89–100 (2014)
6. Gamboa, R., Kaufmann, M.: Nonstandard analysis in ACL2. J. Autom. Reasoning **27**(4), 323–351 (2001)
7. Goldblatt, R.: Lectures on the Hyperreals: An Introduction to Nonstandard Analysis. Springer, New York (1998)

8. Hashimoto, K., Unno, H.: Refinement type inference via horn constraint optimization. In: Blazy, S., Jensen, T. (eds.) SAS 2015. LNCS, vol. 9291, pp. 199–216. Springer, Heidelberg (2015). https://doi.org/10.1007/978-3-662-48288-9_12
9. Hasuo, I., Suenaga, K.: Exercises in *Nonstandard Static Analysis* of hybrid systems. In: Madhusudan, P., Seshia, S.A. (eds.) CAV 2012. LNCS, vol. 7358, pp. 462–478. Springer, Heidelberg (2012). https://doi.org/10.1007/978-3-642-31424-7_34
10. Kido, K., Chaudhuri, S., Hasuo, I.: Abstract interpretation with infinitesimals. In: Jobstmann, B., Leino, K.R.M. (eds.) VMCAI 2016. LNCS, vol. 9583, pp. 229–249. Springer, Heidelberg (2016). https://doi.org/10.1007/978-3-662-49122-5_11
11. Kobayashi, N.: Model checking higher-order programs. J. ACM **60**(3), 20:1–20:62 (2013)
12. Kohlenbach, U.: Applied Proof Theory: Proof Interpretations and their Use in Mathematics. Springer Monographs in Mathematics. Springer, New York (2008)
13. Kuwahara, T., Sato, R., Unno, H., Kobayashi, N.: Predicate abstraction and CEGAR for disproving termination of higher-order functional programs. In: Kroening, D., Păsăreanu, C.S. (eds.) CAV 2015. LNCS, vol. 9207, pp. 287–303. Springer, Cham (2015). https://doi.org/10.1007/978-3-319-21668-3_17
14. Loeb, P.A., Wolff, M. (eds.): Nonstandard Analysis for the Working Mathematician. Mathematics and its Applications, vol. 510. Kluwer Academic Publishers, Dordrecht (2000)
15. Murase, A., Terauchi, T., Kobayashi, N., Sato, R., Unno, H.: Temporal verification of higher-order functional programs. In: Bodík, R., Majumdar, R. (eds.) POPL 2016, pp. 57–68. ACM (2016)
16. Nakamura, K., Fusaoka, A.: An analysis of the fuller phenomenon on transfinite hybrid automata. In: Majumdar, R., Tabuada, P. (eds.) HSCC 2009. LNCS, vol. 5469, pp. 450–454. Springer, Heidelberg (2009). https://doi.org/10.1007/978-3-642-00602-9_33
17. Nelson, E.: Internal set theory: a new approach to nonstandard analysis. Bull. Amer. Math. Soc. **83**(6), 1165–1198 (1977)
18. Robinson, A.: Non-standard Analysis. Princeton University Press, Princeton (1996)
19. Rondon, P.M., Kawaguchi, M., Jhala, R.: Liquid types. In: PLDI 2008, pp. 159–169 (2008)
20. Rust, H.: Operational Semantics for Timed Systems. LNCS, vol. 3456. Springer, Heidelberg (2005). https://doi.org/10.1007/978-3-540-32008-1
21. Sanders, S.: The computational content of nonstandard analysis. In: Proceedings Sixth International Workshop on Classical Logic and Computation, CL&C 2016, Porto, Portugal, 23th June 2016, pp. 24–40 (2016)
22. Streicher, T.: Domain-Theoretic Foundations of Functional Programming. World Scientific, Singapore (2007)
23. Suenaga, K., Hasuo, I.: Programming with infinitesimals: a WHILE-language for hybrid system modeling. In: Aceto, L., Henzinger, M., Sgall, J. (eds.) ICALP 2011. LNCS, vol. 6756, pp. 392–403. Springer, Heidelberg (2011). https://doi.org/10.1007/978-3-642-22012-8_31
24. Suenaga, K., Sekine, H., Hasuo, I.: Hyperstream processing systems: nonstandard modeling of continuous-time signals. In: POPL 2013, pp. 417–430 (2013)

Counterexample-Guided Bit-Precision Selection

Shaobo He[(✉)] and Zvonimir Rakamarić

School of Computing, University of Utah, Salt Lake City, UT, USA
{shaobo,zvonimir}@cs.utah.edu

Abstract. Static program verifiers based on *satisfiability modulo theories* (SMT) solvers often trade precision for scalability to be able to handle large programs. A popular trade-off is to model bitwise operations, which are expensive for SMT solving, using uninterpreted functions over integers. Such an over-approximation improves scalability, but can introduce undesirable false alarms in the presence of bitwise operations that are common in, for example, low-level systems software. In this paper, we present our approach to diagnose the spurious counterexamples caused by this trade-off, and leverage the learned information to lazily and gradually refine the precision of reasoning about bitwise operations in the whole program. Our main insight is to employ a simple and fast type analysis to transform both a counterexample and program into their more precise versions that block the diagnosed spurious counterexample. We implement our approach in the SMACK software verifier, and evaluate it on the benchmark suite from the International Competition on Software Verification (SV-COMP). The evaluation shows that we significantly reduce the number of false alarms while maintaining scalability.

1 Introduction

Advances in *satisfiability modulo theories* (SMT) solving [3] have significantly enhanced the potential of program verifiers and checkers to reason about large-scale software systems. For instance, SLAM [2] has helped developers to find important bugs in Windows device drivers. The Linux Driver Verification project [19] that uses BLAST [13] and CPAchecker [5] has reported a large number of bugs in Linux drivers. SAGE [12] has been regularly finding security-critical bugs in large Microsoft applications such as media players.

A major obstacle that still often prevents software developers from adopting program verifiers is a high rate of false alarms. A recent survey conducted inside Microsoft shows that most developers are willing to accept only up to 5% false alarm rate [7], which is much smaller than what most state-of-the-art program analyzers can achieve. There are several reasons for such low tolerance to false alarms. First, false alarms can take a long time to triage, therefore significantly impeding developers' productivity. Second, trivial false alarms compromise developers' confidence in using program verifiers. Finally, if a threshold is set for reporting alarms, true bugs can be masked in the presence of many false alarms.

This work was supported in part by NSF award CNS 1527526.

B.-Y.E. Chang (Ed.): APLAS 2017, LNCS 10695, pp. 534–553, 2017.
https://doi.org/10.1007/978-3-319-71237-6_26

In SMT-based program verifiers, false alarms usually arise from a trade-off between the efficiency of the underlying theory solvers and complete modeling of program semantics. For example, low-level programming languages such as C contain bitwise operations. While the commonly used SMT theory of integers is scalable, it cannot be used to efficiently and precisely model such program constructs. Hence, in practice, verifiers often rely on uninterpreted functions over unbounded integers to over-approximate bitwise operations. This design choice aims to improve scalability at the expense of occasionally losing precision — it does not miss bugs, but can introduce false alarms. On the other hand, it is not difficult for program verifiers to model these behaviors precisely using the theory of bit-vectors instead of integers. However, scalability suffers since the theory of bit-vectors is typically much slower. Moreover, manually deciding which theory to use reduces the usability of program verifiers since users have to determine the necessity for bit-precision, which may not be obvious even for medium-sized programs. For example, bit-field manipulations in C typically compile to bitwise operations. Users of a program verifier that operates on a compiler intermediate representation (or even binary) may not be aware of such details, and would fail to enable the theory of bit-vectors even though a verifier maybe supports it.

In this paper, we propose an automatic counterexample-guided abstraction refinement (CEGAR) [8] approach to gradually on-demand (i.e., lazily) improve bit-precision of SMT-based verifiers. Our approach is based on the observation that the precision of only a subset of bitwise operations is relevant for proving program assertions. Therefore, enabling bit-precision everywhere is an overkill that degrades scalability. We start with a program that uses uninterpreted integer functions to model bitwise operations, iteratively convert spurious bit-imprecise counterexamples to precise ones using type unification, and then propagate the learned type information to the input program until either the program verifies or a real counterexample is found. Our goal is to focus on the bitwise operations that affect the correctness of user provided assertions. Our main contribution is to employ a simple and fast type analysis to assign precise bit-vector types to imprecise uninterpreted bitwise operations and propagate the learned type information throughout the program. We implement our approach as an extension of the SMACK software verification toolchain [21,23]. We perform an empirical evaluation on benchmarks used in the International Competition on Software Verification (SV-COMP) [25], and show that it automatically removes a large proportion of false alarms while maintaining scalability.

2   Background

In this section, we describe the SMACK software verification toolchain and the simple intermediate verification language that our approach takes as input.

2.1   SMACK Software Verification Toolchain

SMACK is an SMT-based static assertion checker that targets languages compilable to the LLVM *intermediate representation* (IR) [17]. Currently, SMACK

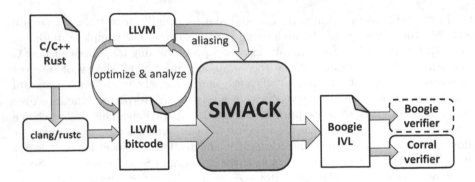

Fig. 1. SMACK software verification toolchain

mainly targets C programs, and adding support for C++ and Rust is work in progress. By default, SMACK verifies user-provided assertions up to a selected loop/recursion bound. SMACK can also automatically generate assertions to check domain-specific properties such as memory safety and signed integer overflows. Figure 1 shows the SMACK verification toolchain. We first obtain LLVM IR code (bitcode) of the input program using a specific compiler front-end (e.g., clang/clang++ for C/C++). The main SMACK module then translates LLVM IR into the Boogie *intermediate verification language* (IVL) [10,20] by encoding the semantics of LLVM IR instructions into Boogie. Finally, SMACK integrates multiple Boogie verifiers, and the generated Boogie program is verified using a chosen back-end verifier. In this work, we use Corral [16] as the Boogie verifier because it is scalable and can produce precise error traces; Corral internally invokes SMT solver Z3 [9]. Although we instantiate our approach using SMACK, Corral, and Z3, any verifier combination would suffice that operates on a statically-typed input IVL and produces precise counterexamples.

During the translation, SMACK performs analysis and optimization of the input LLVM IR program to simplify the downstream verification process. One such analysis is the data structure analysis (DSA) [18] provided by LLVM. SMACK uses it as a precise alias analysis to split the input program heap into distinct regions such that pointers referring to two regions can never alias [22]. Each region is translated into a separate memory map (i.e., array) in the Boogie program, which often greatly improves scalability since the number of updates of each individual map is reduced. In situations where the DSA-based alias analysis is imprecise, typically due to low-level pointer manipulations, smaller number of memory maps with more updates each are generated — this can lead to a significant performance penalty as we observe in our empirical evaluation.

By default, SMACK uses Boogie integer type to represent both LLVM pointer type and integer types with certain bit widths. Bitwise operations are overapproximated using uninterpreted functions and thus results of such operations are arbitrary integers. We refer to such a setup that uses the theory of integers as the integer mode of SMACK. In addition to using imprecise bitwise operations, the integer mode does not capture either the wrap-around behavior of unsigned integer overflows or casts between signed and unsigned numbers, which can result in both false alarms and missed bugs. We consider this to be an orthogonal issue that can be handled by, for example, injecting overflow checks into the program, and we only consider false alarms resulting from the over-approximation of bit-wise operations. The precision with respect to bitwise operations can be tuned up by enabling the bit-vector mode of SMACK where LLVM scalar types are translated to fixed-size bit-vector types in Boogie. However, our experience in applying SMACK on real-world programs indicates that the bit-vector mode is much less scalable than the integer mode.

2.2 Simple Intermediate Verification Language

A Boogie program generated by SMACK consists of a set of global variables, procedures, and functions. Each procedure contains a set of basic blocks, each of which consists of a series of commands. SMACK translates most LLVM IR instructions to Boogie commands that are either assignments or procedure calls. The left-hand side of such an assignment is a variable corresponding to the result of the instruction while the right-hand side is either another variable or application of a Boogie function representing the operation of the instruction. The syntax of Boogie programs generated by SMACK is shown in Fig. 2. Pointer type **ref** is a synonym of integer type $int32$ or $int64$ depending on the architecture. Integer type Γ_{int} is a synonym of the Boogie integer type **int** which is only used in the integer mode. Instead, Boogie bit-vector type Γ_{bv} only shows up in the programs generated by SMACK in the bit-vector mode.

$$
\begin{aligned}
\Gamma_{int} &::= int1 \mid int8 \mid int16 \mid int32 \mid int64 \\
\Gamma_{bv} &::= bv1 \mid bv8 \mid bv16 \mid bv32 \mid bv64 \\
\Gamma_{scalar} &::= \textbf{bool} \mid \textbf{ref} \mid \Gamma_{int} \mid \Gamma_{bv} \\
\Gamma &::= \Gamma_{scalar} \mid [\textbf{ref}]\Gamma_{scalar} \\
x &\in \textbf{Var} \\
lit &::= true \mid false \mid intlit \mid bvlit \\
pred &::= {==} \mid {!=} \\
binop_{ia} &::= \textsf{add} \mid \textsf{sub} \mid \textsf{mul} \mid \textsf{udiv} \mid \textsf{sdiv} \mid \textsf{urem} \mid \textsf{srem} \\
binop_{bw} &::= \textsf{and} \mid \textsf{or} \mid \textsf{lshr} \mid \textsf{ashr} \mid \textsf{shl} \mid \textsf{xor} \\
binop &::= binop_{ia} \mid binop_{bw} \mid compop \mid castop \\
e &::= x \mid lit \mid e_1 \; pred \; e_2 \mid uop(e) \mid binop(e_1, e_2) \mid \\
&\quad load(x, e_1) \mid store(x, e_1, e_2) \\
cmd &::= x := e \mid \textbf{assert } e \mid \textbf{assume } e \mid \textbf{call } x := p(e_i)
\end{aligned}
$$

Fig. 2. Subset of Boogie IVL that SMACK emits. We only show the syntax up to Boogie commands.

```
#include "smack.h"                  procedure main() returns(r:int32) {
#include <stdlib.h>                    var p0, p1, p5, p7: ref;
                                       var i2, i3, i6, i8, i11: int32;
typedef struct                         var i4, i9: int1;
{
  int x;                               $bb0:
} S;                                   call p0 := malloc(4);
                                       p1 := bitcast.ref.ref(p0);
int f(int* p)                          call i2 := __nondet_int();
{                                      call i3 := __nondet_int();
  return *p & 0xf;                     i4 := ne.i32(i3, 0);
}                                      goto $bb1, $bb2;

int main()                             $bb1:
{                                      assume (i4 == 1); p5 := p1;
  S* s = (S*)malloc(sizeof(S));        call i6 := f(p5); p7 := p1;
  unsigned y = __nondet_int();         M.0 := store.i32(M.0, p7, i6);
                                       i8 := i2; goto $bb3;
  if (__nondet_int()) {
    s->x = foo(&s->x);                 $bb2:
  }                                    assume !((i4 == 1));
  else {                               ...
    assume(y < 4U);                    i8 := i11; goto $bb3;
    y >>= 2U;                          ... }
  }                                  procedure f($p:ref) returns(r:int32) {
                                       var i0, i1: int32;
  if (s->x >= 16)                      i0 := load.i32(M.0, $p);
    assert(!y);                        i1 := and.i32(i0, 15);
}                                      r := i1; return; }
```

Fig. 3. C program with bitwise operations and part of its Boogie IVL translation

SMACK translation decorates each function name with types of its arguments and result. For example, function add.i32 expects the types of its operands to be *int*32 and returns an integer value of the same type. There will be an incarnation of each binary function (*binop*) for the integer mode and the bit-vector mode, respectively. Function add.bv32 is the counterpart of add.i32 in the bit-vector mode which takes two 32 bit bit-vectors as arguments and returns their sum. Functions encoding bitwise operations ($binop_{bw}$) are uninterpreted in the integer mode while implemented precisely as wrappers to Z3 built-in bit-vector functions in the bit-vector mode. Figure 3 shows a C program and a code snippet of its Boogie IVL translation.

An important feature of Corral that we leverage is that it can generate error trace programs. An error trace program produced by Corral represents an error path that starts from the program entry and ends with an assertion failure. It is a regular Boogie IVL program and follows the syntax defined in Fig. 2. The main difference from the input program is that procedure bodies in the error trace program follow a single control flow path. Hence, verifying the error trace program and its transformation only requires unrolling depth one and is generally much faster than verifying the entire program.

3   Approach

In this section, we present our counterexample-guided approach to reduce the number of false alarms due to imprecise modeling of bitwise operations. It is an iterative algorithm that keeps refining the program to verify based on the feedback provided by the already refined error trace programs.

Figure 4 presents the pseudocode of our approach. We define it as a tail-recursive function cexg which consists of the following steps. First, the Boogie verifier (function verify) is called to verify the input program P. If the program verifies or the verification is inconclusive (i.e., timeout), function cexg exits with the result returned by the verifier. If a bug is reported and the error trace program representing it is generated, then we check if the error trace program contains any uninterpreted functions corresponding to bitwise operations. If not, this counterexample is considered feasible and presented to the user. Otherwise, our approach transforms the error trace program to a more precise version with respect to bitwise operations (function transform). Then, the verifier is invoked to verify it. If the verification result is false or timeout, the error trace is feasible after the refinement or its feasibility cannot be determined given the time limit. In both cases, function cexg terminates and returns a more precise error trace or timeout status, respectively. On the other hand, when the verification succeeds, we know that the counterexample is spurious. Hence, the input program P is updated to a new program P' using function update, which removes the spurious counterexample according to the type equivalence classes EC^t learned from the error trace. Finally, function cexg recurs with P' being the input program. In

```
Function cexg(P):
    result, trace = verify(P)
    if result ∈ {true, timeout} then
        return result
    else
        if binop_bw exists and remains uninterpreted then
            trace', EC^t = transform(trace)
            result = verify(trace')
            if result ∈ {false, timeout} then
                return result, trace'
            else
                P' = update(EC^t, P)
                return cexg(P')
            end
        else
            return result, trace
        end
    end
end
```

Fig. 4. Pseudocode of our approach

the rest of this section, we describe the transformation function transform and the update function update in details.

3.1 Program Transformation

The transformation implemented by the function transform is based on a simple type analysis. The basic idea is that a new base type representing bit-vectors is created and the types of variables or expressions involved in uninterpreted bitwise operations are assigned to this type. The transformed program returned by function transform is thus more precise than the input program because any uninterpreted bitwise operations are replaced with their precise bit-vector counterparts during the transformation. To discover which types should be updated to bit-vectors, we generate type constraints in terms of equalities and the result of solving these constraints gives us an over-approximation of such types. Finally, we simply rewrite the program to install the type updates. Figure 5 demonstrates the three phases of transforming an error trace program of the program in Fig. 3 when the condition of the first if statement is true.

Generating Type Constraints. Recall that Boogie programs generated by SMACK leverage integer types of LLVM IR that specify the bit-width of each type. For the purpose of generating type constraints, two base types are introduced into our type system: integer int and bit-vector bv. The integer bit-width information contained in the original LLVM IR types is sufficient to rewrite integer subtypes to more precise corresponding bit-vector subtypes. For example, the type of the local variable i1 of procedure f in Fig. 3 is $int32$. If the type gets lifted to bv, we can easily rewrite it as $bv32$ since its original type name contains the bit-width of integers that it represents.

Figure 6 formalizes the rules used to generate type constraints. The basic idea of type constraint generation is that whenever an uninterpreted bitwise operation

$$t_{m-p5} = t_{m-p1}$$
$$t_{m-p5} = t_{f-\$p}$$
$$t_{m-i8} = t_{m-i2}$$
$$t_{f-i0} = t_{f-load.i32(M.0,\$p)}$$
$$t_{f-load.i32(M.0,\$p)} = t_{M.0-val}$$
$$t_{f-i1} = t_{f-and.i32(i0,15)}$$
$$t_{f-and.i32(i0,15)} = t_{f-i0} = BV$$

$$t_{m-p7} = t_{m-p1}$$
$$t_{m-i6} = t_{f-r}$$
$$t_{m-i6} = t_{M.0-val}$$

$$t_{m-p1}, t_{m-p5}, t_{m-p7}, t_{f-\$p}$$
$$t_{m-i8}, t_{m-i2}$$
$$t_{m-i6}, t_{f-r}, t_{M.0-val}, t_{f-i0}, t_{f-i1}$$
$$t_{f-load.i32(M.0,\$p)}, t_{f-and.i32(i0,15)}, BV$$

```
M.0 : [ref]bv8;
procedure main() returns(r:int32) {
  var $i6 : bv32;
  ...
  $bb1:
  assume (i4 == 1); p5 := p1;
  call i6 := f(p5); p7 := p1;
  M.0 := store.bytes.32(M.0, p7, i6);
  i8 := i2; goto $bb3;
  ... }
procedure f($p:ref) returns(r:bv32){
  var i0, i1: bv32;
  i0 := load.bytes.32(M.0, $p);
  i1 := and.bv32(i0, 15bv32);
  r := i1; return; }
```

Fig. 5. The left part shows the type constraints and solution for block $bb1 of procedure main and the body of procedure f. Procedure name main is abbreviated as m in the type variables. Equivalence classes are separated by dotted lines. The right part is the snippet of the transformed program according to the solution.

$$\dfrac{\Gamma \vdash binop_{bw}(e_1, e_2) : t \quad \Gamma \vdash e_1 : t_1 \quad \Gamma \vdash e_2 : t_2}{t_1 = t_2 = t = BV} \qquad \dfrac{\Gamma \vdash op(\vec{e_i}) : t \quad \Gamma \vdash e_i : t_i}{t_i = t}$$

$$\dfrac{\Gamma \vdash load(M, e) : t \quad \Gamma \vdash M : t_1 \rightarrow t_2}{t_2 = t} \qquad \dfrac{P \vdash x := e \quad \Gamma \vdash x : t_1 \quad \Gamma \vdash e : t_2}{t_1 = t_2}$$

$$\dfrac{\Gamma \vdash store(M, e_1, e_2) : t_1 \rightarrow t_2 \quad \Gamma \vdash M : t_3 \rightarrow t_4 \quad \Gamma \vdash e_2 : t_5}{t_2 = t_4 = t_5}$$

$$\dfrac{\Gamma \vdash e_1 \; pred \; e_2 : \mathbf{bool} \quad \Gamma \vdash e_1 : t_1 \quad \Gamma \vdash e_2 : t_2}{t_1 = t_2}$$

$$\dfrac{P \vdash call \; x := p(\vec{e_i}) \quad \Gamma \vdash e_i : t_{ai} \quad \Gamma \vdash x : t \quad \Gamma \vdash p : t_{pi} \rightarrow t_r}{t_{ai} = t_{pi} \quad t = t_r}$$

Fig. 6. Type rules for generating type constraints. We introduce a type variable for each expression (except literals) and a special type constant BV. Symbol $binop_{bw}$ refers to uninterpreted integer functions that over-approximate bitwise operations. Symbol op refers to the union of uop and $binop$ (excluding $binop_{bw}$) from Fig. 2.

is observed, we change the types of the operands as well as the expression into bv. On the other hand, we simply equate the types of operands and results for other operations. For the example in Fig. 3, the types of variable i0 and expression and.i32(i0, 15) in procedure f are assigned to bv since and.i32 is an uninterpreted function over integers used to model bitwise AND operation. On the other hand, the type of variable i3 is just equal to that of the inequality expression ne.i32(i3, 0) in procedure main.

The type of *load* expression or the value argument e_2 in the *store* expression is consistent with the type of the map argument M's range. The type of map domain is forced to be *int* by not generating type constraints associated with it. We place such a restriction because we observed that combining the theory of bit-vectors and theory of arrays is generally slow, especially for the case where bit-vector types are map domain types. However, we do not restrict the type of pointers to *int*. For example, the updated type of variable p7 in Fig. 3 could be bv. Therefore, an expression of type bv is cast to *int* during the rewriting stage when it is used as the pointer argument of *load* and *store* expressions. On the other hand, we do not introduce casts from *int* to bv for two reasons. First, integer to bit-vector cast is an extremely expensive operation for Z3. Second, the input integer value of such a cast must be constrained since the resulting bit-vector has only a finite set of values, thereby increasing the complexity of modeling and reasoning about the program. The cast operations *castop* in Fig. 2 include functions representing LLVM cast instructions (e.g., zext, trunc, ptrtoint). We keep the source type and the destination type as the same base type and thus equate them. The same rule also applies to the comparison operations *compop* in our language that correspond to LLVM comparison instructions.

Solving Type Constraints. Since all the type constraints generated are equivalence relations, we use a simple unification algorithm that unifies constraints and produces a number of disjoint sets that consist of type variables that are equivalent. We call these sets *equivalence classes*, and all type variables in an equivalence class have the same base type. If an equivalence class contains BV, then all the type variables in this class have type bv. On the other hand, a variable or expression keeps its original type if BV is not in the equivalence class where its type variable is.

Rewriting Programs. Once the generated type constraints are solved, we recursively rewrite the input program based on the computed solution. The declared types of variables are changed to fixed-size bit-vector types if their corresponding identifier expressions have base type bv. For map variables, only their range types can be lifted. Integer constants are simply replaced with their bit-vector counterparts if the expressions where they are used have type bv.

For function applications, recall that there is an integer version and a bit-vector version for each function in the Boogie program generated by SMACK. Therefore, we simply replace the integer version with the bit-vector version if the type is decided to be bv and recur to its arguments. Since we would like to keep the type of map domains as integer, casts from bv to int (implemented as Z3 built-in function bv2int) are added to expressions which have type bv and are used to index maps. For this reason, the pointer argument of functions *load* and *store* may be encapsulated with function bv2int.

Note that the concrete type of a *load* expression or the value argument of a *store* expression can be different from the range type of the map passed as the first argument, although their base types are the same. For example, the type of expression load.i32(M.0, $p) in Fig. 3 is $int32$ while the type of M.0 is [ref]$int8$. This often happens when the alias analysis employed by SMACK is imprecise and results in a large number of multi-type accesses to a single map. The range type of such map is $int8$, which indicates that type unsafe accesses may occur and thus accesses should be byte-level. In the integer mode, we assume that elements stored in a map do not overlap. Functions *load* and *store* are just wrappers around map selection and update expressions, respectively. For example, the body of function load.i32(M, p) in Fig. 3 is simply M[p]. If the range types of such maps get updated to bv, then all the accesses (*load* and *store*) are rewritten to byte-level versions that use bit-vector extraction and concatenation operations. For example, the body of function load.bytes.32(M, p) in Fig. 5 is $M[p+3] {+}{+} M[p+2] {+}{+} M[p+1] {+}{+} M[p]$, where $++$ is the bit-vector concatenation operator. For the case where a map holds only elements of a single type, map accesses are simply replaced with their bit-vector counterparts that are also wrappers around the map selection or update expressions.

3.2 Program Update

If the precise error trace program *trace'* verifies (see Fig. 4), we know that over-approximation of bitwise operations produces a spurious counterexample and updating the types of relevant variables invalidates it. Then, as a simple solution to prevent such spurious counterexamples, it is sufficient to enable the bit-vector mode. However, we observed that such approach severely limits scalability. Instead, rather than changing the bit-precision of the whole program, we perform a restricted transformation of parts of P (implemented as function update) such that it only prevents the error trace represented by $trace$ from reappearing. Such a transformation contains all the type updates performed on $trace$ that are necessary to block the spurious counterexample. On the other hand, we do not change the precision of bitwise operations that are not related to the trace expressions whose types get changed to bit-vectors. Therefore, our approach has the potential to outperform the bit-vector mode of SMACK or even applying the transformation described in Sect. 3.1 to the entire program.

Function update first generates and solves the type constraints of the entire program to obtain equivalence classes EC^p. Then, it propagates the type constraint solution of $trace$, EC^t to EC^p and thereafter rewrites P. The type constraints of the whole program P are generated slightly differently than of the error trace program $trace$. Recall that for the type constraint generation of $trace$, types of an uninterpreted bitwise operation and its operands are equated to each other and to the type constant BV, according to the first rule in Fig. 6. In contrast, if an uninterpreted bitwise operation is encountered during the type constraint generation of the whole program, types of this expression and its arguments are only equated.[1] Hence, the type constraint solution for the whole program does not contain BV and only indicates which expressions have the same base type.

Propagating the type updates of $trace$ to P works as follows: for each equivalence class $ec^p \in EC^p$ of the whole program, if it intersects with an equivalence class $ec^t \in EC^t$ of the error trace program and $BV \in ec^t$, then BV is added to ec^p. We show next that the propagation ensures the type updates from int to bv in $trace$ are also contained in P. Note that for a type variable tv, if $tv \in ec^p$ of P and $tv \in ec^t$ of $trace$ then $ec^t \subseteq ec^p$. The type constraints generated for the whole program subsume those produced for any error trace programs because the sequence of commands in error trace programs is always a subset of the commands in the whole program. Therefore, to solve the type constraints of the whole program, our unification algorithm could unify type variables that belong to both the entire program and the error trace program, resulting in the same set of equivalence classes. Then, we start with these equivalence classes and continue the unification algorithm, which either expands a class or merges two classes. Both operations produce an equivalence class that is a super set of the original one. Hence, lifted types in the scope of the entire program include those in the scope of an error trace program.

Invoking the verifier on the updated program P' cannot produce $trace$ again. If it would, then the new error trace program $trace''$ would have all the necessary

---

[1] The solution to the type constraints of the whole program is the same for each iteration of function cexg and can thus be cached. To simplify the presentation, we recompute it in the paper at each iteration.

types being bv since P' already contains the type updates of $trace$, and $trace''$ would verify just as $trace'$ does. Moreover, function update updates at least several types in P in each iteration of cexg, which ensures that our iterative approach makes progress. Assume that in iteration i of cexg, update is called if there are uninterpreted bitwise operations in the error trace program $trace_i$ that cause the counterexample to be spurious. In iteration $i+1$, if update is invoked again it improves the precision of some other uninterpreted bitwise operations since those in $trace_i$ and all previous iterations are already precisely modeled. In other words, the number of iterations of our approach is bounded by the number of uninterpreted bitwise operations in the input program, which contributes to the termination guarantee of our approach formalized by the following theorem.

Theorem 1. *Function* cexg *in Fig. 4 terminates if function* verify *terminates.*

Proof. If each invocation of the verifier finishes or exceeds the time limit, then the only potentially non-terminating path in cexg is to recur, which calls function update. Each time update is called, at least one uninterpreted bitwise operation becomes precisely modeled. Since there is only a finite number of uninterpreted bitwise operations in the input program, the number of calls to update as well as cexg is also finite.

4   Empirical Evaluation

We empirically evaluate our approach using benchmarks from SV-COMP [25], which contain several categories representing different aspects of software systems. We leverage BenchExec [6] as the core of our benchmarking infrastructure for reliable and precise performance measurements. Experiments are performed on machines with two Intel Xeon E5-2630 processors and 64 GB DDR4 RAM running Ubuntu 14.04, which are a part of the Emulab infrastructure [11,26]. As in SV-COMP, we set time limit to 900 s and memory limit to 15 GB for each benchmark. We implemented functions transform and update of our approach as a standalone tool, which we invoke from the SMACK toolchain.[2]

We created 4 different configurations of SMACK: *baseline, nobv, allbv,* and *cexg.* Configuration *baseline* corresponds to the SMACK baseline version (release v1.8.1) that uses heuristics for SV-COMP; the baseline has been carefully optimized for SV-COMP benchmarks using manually crafted filters that identify benchmarks that require bit-precise reasoning, and subsequently enabling the theory of bit-vectors on such benchmarks. Configuration *nobv* uses imprecise reasoning in the theory of integers (i.e., bitwise operations are encoded as uninterpreted functions), while configuration *allbv* uses precise reasoning in the theory of bit-vectors. Configuration *cexg* implements our counterexample-guided bit-precision selection approach. Whenever the theory of bit-vectors is used, we tune Corral by enabling several well-known options that improve its performance

---

[2] We made the tool publicly available at https://github.com/shaobo-he/TraceTransformer.

in the presence of bit-vectors. We run every configuration on all SV-COMP benchmarks[3] except categories REACHSAFETY-FLOAT, CONCURRENCYSAFETY-MAIN, MEMSAFETY-LINKEDLISTS, and TERMINATION.[4]

4.1   Used Metrics

We measure the performance of each configuration using the SV-COMP scoring schema, which assigns scores to verification results as follows:

(a) +2 when the verifier correctly verifies a program,
(b) +1 when it reports a true bug,
(c) −32 when the verifier misses a bug,
(d) −16 when it reports a false bug (i.e., false alarm), and
(e) 0 when the verifier either times out or crashes.

We calculate the weighted score of a meta-category (e.g., REACHSAFETY) by again following the SV-COMP rules: normalized score of each subcategory is summed up and multiplied with the average number of benchmarks in that category.

Since a verifier is severely punished for reporting incorrect results, we add *correct result ratio* as an additional metric to complement the weighted score. We define it as the average percentage of correctly labeled verification tasks of all subcategories in a (meta-)category. We introduce the *timeout ratio* and *false alarm ratio* metrics to measure the scalability and precision of the configurations, respectively. Similar to the correct result ratio, the timeout ratio is the weighted percentage of timeouts in a category, while the false alarm ratio is the weighted percentage of false alarms.

We use score-based quantile functions [4] to visualize the overall performance of a configuration. Figure 7 shows an example of such functions for subcategory REACHSAFETY-BITVECTORS. The horizontal axis x represents the accumulated score of n fastest correct verification tasks and all of those incorrectly labeled as false. Therefore, the x coordinate of the leftmost point is the number of all false alarms multiplied by −16 and of the rightmost point is the total score. The vertical axis y is the largest runtime of n fastest correct verification tasks.

---

[3] Benchmark `sleep_true-no-overflow_false-valid-deref.i` from category SYSTEMS_BUSYBOX_OVERFLOWS is removed because an invalid dereference leads to a signed integer overflow error, which is not specified by the SV-COMP rules.

[4] Bit-vector mode must always be enabled for reasoning about floating-points, and it is also not consistent with SMACK's support for Pthreads. Our tool currently does not fully support SMACK's encoding of memory safety properties. Finally, SMACK currently cannot verify termination.

4.2   Results

Table 1 shows the performance of each configuration over all the used metrics. As expected, configuration *baseline* yields the best performance overall in terms of both scalability and precision since it has been manually fine-tuned over the years on these benchmarks. It has the highest weighted score for all the top-level categories and it solved the largest weighted percentage of benchmarks correctly in 3 out of the 4 categories total. Configuration *nobv* times out the least, but it also produces the largest number of false alarms. Note that the scoring system is crafted to mimic users' disfavor of false alarms by deducting a large number of points (16) when a false alarm is generated. Therefore, although *nobv* managed to correctly solve the largest percentage of benchmarks in the SOFTWARESYSTEMS category, its score is less than both *baseline* and *cexg* as a result of its high false alarm rate. In contrast, configuration *allbv* does not generate any false alarms, but at the expense of solving the smallest percentage of verification tasks — in particular in the SOFTWARESYSTEMS category that contains benchmarks from real-world large software systems such as Linux drivers. Moreover, *allbv* also times out much more frequently than other configurations in the MEMORYSAFETY category with mostly small or medium benchmarks. Hence, we conclude that always using the theory of bit-vectors is not practical on real-world benchmarks. Configuration *cexg*, which implements our approach, successfully eliminates most of the false alarms seen in *nobv* without placing a significant burden on scalability.

We focus next on the results for benchmarks that could actually benefit from our approach, meaning those benchmarks where uninterpreted functions appear in counterexamples. (Note that our approach has basically no influence on other benchmarks.) For each of these benchmarks, our approach either produces a correct result or it times out (on the transformed error trace program or the updated version of the whole program). Table 2 shows the experimental data we gathered for subcategories that contain such benchmarks. The results

Table 1. Experimental results for all the SV-COMP categories of interest

Category	Weighted Score				Timeout Ratio			
	baseline	*nobv*	*allbv*	*cexg*	*baseline*	*nobv*	*allbv*	*cexg*
REACHSAFETY	3498	1155	2905	2675	16.6	17.5	29.5	17.7
MEMSAFETY	375	321	179	375	10.9	10.9	57.6	10.9
OVERFLOWS	472	141	450	469	4.2	4.2	7.7	4.2
SOFTWARESYSTEMS	2731	2133	503	2529	46.2	41.8	85.1	44.0

Category	Correct Result Ratio				False Alarm Ratio			
	baseline	*nobv*	*allbv*	*cexg*	*baseline*	*nobv*	*allbv*	*cexg*
REACHSAFETY	81.2	76.3	66.8	79.2	0.00	3.33	0.00	0.22
MEMSAFETY	88.6	87.5	42.2	88.6	0.00	1.10	0.00	0.00
OVERFLOWS	92.3	85.8	91.7	91.4	0.00	5.56	0.00	0.00
SOFTWARESYSTEMS	50.2	54.6	8.8	53.4	0.04	1.79	0.00	0.85

Table 2. Experimental results for benchmarks that could potentially benefit from our approach. #B is the total number of such benchmarks; #TOC is the number of timeouts in *cexg*; #TET is the number of true (i.e., confirmed) error traces; #FET is the number of false (i.e., infeasible) error traces discovered by our approach; #RR is the average runtime ratio between our approach and baseline; #FAN is the number of false alarms in *nobv*; #TOA is the number of timeouts in *allbv*. R, M, and O in the first column stand for categories REACHSAFETY, MEMSAFETY, and OVERFLOWS, respectively. The meta-category prefix (SYSTEMS) is omitted for subcategories DEVICEDRIVERLINUX64 and BUSYBOX_OVERFLOWS.

Subcategory	#B	#TOC	#TET	#FET	#RR	#FAN	#TOA
R-BITVECTORS	20	0	4	16	1.5	14	1
R-CONTROLFLOW	21	2	19	0	3.6	0	21
R-LOOPS	2	0	1	1	4.4	0	1
M-HEAP	8	0	1	7	1.8	6	0
O-OTHER	6	0	0	6	2.3	6	0
DEVICEDRIVERSLINUX64	136	111	22	18	11.6	3	133
BUSYBOX_OVERFLOWS	1	1	0	1	—	1	1

show that our approach outperforms configurations *nobv* and *allbv* in terms of precision and scalability, respectively. It avoids all the false bugs reported by *nobv* and times out less than *allbv*. In general, our approach does not place a significant runtime overhead on the verification tasks such that the time limit is exceeded. However, as the complexity of benchmarks increases, and especially when they become memory-intensive (i.e., containing numerous reads and writes from dynamically allocated memory), our approach may not scale well. Benchmarks in the two subcategories with high runtime overhead, REACHSAFETY-CONTROLFLOW and DEVICEDRIVERSLINUX64, contain many more memory accesses than those in the other subcategories in Table 2. Nevertheless, our approach still outperforms *allbv* on these subcategories. Moreover, for subcategory DEVICEDRIVERSLINUX64 where error traces are usually long and tedious to debug, it successfully rejected 18 spurious counterexamples, 2 of which lead to more precise ones.

4.3   Discussion

We identify memory accesses as the main culprit that sometimes limits the scalability of our approach because type updates are much less contained in their presence. The range type of a memory map is updated to bit-vector if it is involved in a bitwise operation in an error trace, thereby changing the types of all the elements in this map to bit-vectors. This leads to large parts of the program being unnecessarily converted into using the more expensive theory of bit-vectors. Moreover, the imprecision of the alias analysis used for memory splitting can also cause the types of pointer variables to be changed to bit-vectors even though they are not involved in any bitwise operations (due to false aliasing with an integer variable that is involved in a bitwise operation). In this case, we add expensive type cast operations to load and store expressions. Finally, bit-vector extraction and concatenation operations are needed for byte-level accesses to maps containing elements of different types. We conjecture that improving the precision of the alias analysis used in memory splitting would result in better scalability of our approach, but this is beyond the scope of this paper.

Another issue that can limit the scalability of our approach is that the type constraint generation can lead to overly aggressive type changes since all the uninterpreted functions in an error trace are considered, some of which may not affect the correctness of program assertions. Although optimizations are possible as discussed in Sect. 6, the current setup suffices to give correct diagnose when a false alarm arises as a result of over-approximations of bitwise operations. Furthermore, the type analysis is context-insensitive which can also be optimized (e.g., by forking stateless procedures). In the rest of this section, we present two detailed case studies that highlight the strengths and limitations of our approach.

ReachSafety-BitVectors. Subcategory REACHSAFETY-BITVECTORS contains benchmarks that require precise modeling of bitwise operations and unsigned integers (e.g., to model the wrap-around behavior of unsigned integer overflows). Therefore, configuration *nobv* yields a high false alarm rate on this subcategory, reporting 15 false alarms out of 50 verification tasks in total. Moreover, even for the buggy benchmarks the produced error traces are likely to be infeasible. On the other hand, our approach removed 14 of these false alarms. (The only false alarm that is not removed by our approach is due to lack of precise modeling of casts between signed and unsigned integers.) In addition, it also discovered 2 infeasible error traces due to the imprecise modeling of bitwise operations, and it automatically refined them into their precise

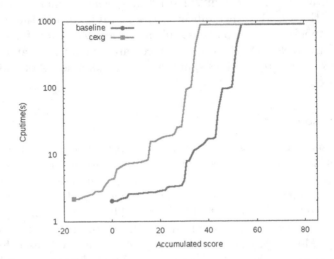

Fig. 7. Quantile functions for subcategory REACHSAFETY-BITVECTORS for configurations *baseline* and *cexg*. The vertical axis uses a logarithmic scale.

counterparts. With respect to scalability, our approach did not cause any verification tasks to time out and it also placed little run time overhead as demonstrated by Table 2. It even outperformed the baseline version on some benchmarks. Figure 7 presents the quantile functions of *cexg* and *baseline*, and we can observe that the two are close in terms of performance and scalability. We find these results to be particularly encouraging because our approach completely automatically achieves almost the same level of precision and performance as the highly-optimized (albeit manually) baseline version.

SoftwareSystems. This category includes large and complicated real-world benchmarks, and hence the results obtained by our approach are mixed.

BusyBox Benchmarks. Benchmarks ported from the BusyBox 1.22.0 Linux utilities are checked for memory safety and signed integer overflows in the SYSTEMS_BUSYBOX_MEMSAFETY and SYSTEMS_BUSYBOX_OVERFLOWS subcategories, respectively. Our approach outscored the baseline version in subcategory SYSTEMS_BUSYBOX_OVERFLOWS by proving 4 more benchmarks while reporting zero false alarms. In SYSTEM_BUSYBOX_MEMSAFETY, although the baseline version outscores our approach, we still report one more correct result. The only remaining false alarm we report is not due to bitwise operations, and is thus out of scope of this work. The SMACK baseline version is not as fine-tuned on the BusyBox benchmarks as it is on the benchmarks from other categories. Hence, the fact that our approach correctly solves more benchmarks proves its potential to enable automatic bit-precision selection that has better performance than manually deciding bit-precision.

Linux Drivers. The subcategory SYSTEMS_DEVICEDRIVERSLINUX64 contains large benchmarks extracted from Linux drivers. This category pushes our approach to the limits of its scalability: only 39.4% of the benchmarks that the baseline version correctly reported as false is also correctly reported by our approach, while 81.6% of the benchmarks times out when Corral is invoked on either the transformed error trace programs or updated input programs. Several reasons contribute to such poor scalability of our approach on this subcategory. First, these benchmarks contain numerous bit-level manipulations over the driver flags that are often defined as C bit-fields, and some even employ bitwise operations in pointer arithmetic. Second, the benchmarks are pointer- and memory-intensive due to the heavy usage of the Linux kernel data structures. Finally, the alias analysis used in memory splitting loses precision more in this subcategory than in the other (sub-)categories, likely due to the existence of external calls and inline assembly.

5   Related Work

The Boogie-to-Boogie transformation used in our approach was inspired by Microsoft's Static Driver Verifier (SDV) [15], which also leverages type analysis to re-type the program and generate a mixed integer and bit-vector program which may precisely model the semantics of bitwise operations. However, SDV eagerly lifts the types of the whole program while our approach lazily updates them based on the feedback obtained from error trace programs. SDV's memory model as well as rare appearance of bitwise operations in the SDV's benchmark suite makes type changes fairly controlled even at the level of the entire programs. On the other hand, even though in our approach the transformation function can be applied to the whole program, verification of the transformed program does not scale on our more complex benchmarks. The proposed selective type updates guided by counterexamples allow us to alleviate this limitation. Moreover, the transformation used in our approach is guaranteed to improve the precision of modeling bitwise operations whereas SDV's may not because it restricts the types of certain expressions as integers in order to maintain scalability.

Our approach is also similar to the framework of *counterexample-guided abstraction refinement* (CEGAR) [8] used in SLAM [2]. Both systems validate the counterexamples produced in the verification process and leverage them to refine the input program. They are different in two aspects. First, the root cause of the spurious witness traces in SLAM is the predicate abstraction on the input program while for this paper it is using uninterpreted functions over integers to model bitwise operations. Second, although CEGAR guarantees progress, it does not necessarily terminate since the input program may contain infinite states. In contrast, the number of iterations in our approach is bounded by that of bitwise operations and thus it eventually terminates given that the verifier terminates when invoked. Furthermore, our approach also guarantees to make progresses in each iteration as discussed in Sect. 3.2.

Others have explored the idea of counterexample-guided abstraction refinement as well. For example, Lahiri et al. [14] present a greedy CEGAR technique that is used to refine memory maps of a program. Babić et al. [1] introduce a technique called *structural abstraction* that iteratively refines a program by analyzing counterexamples and replacing uninterpreted functions with inlined procedures. CAMPY [24] tackles the problem of verifying if a program satisfies a complexity bound expressed in undecidable non-linear theories by selectively inferring necessary axioms in terms of grounded theorems of such non-linear theories and fitting them into decidable theories. This framework could potentially be used as an alternative method to refine the uninterpreted functions that over-approximate bitwise operations. However, for certain programs, especially those in the REACHSAFETY-BITVECTORS subcategory of the SV-COMP benchmark suite, simple axioms over integers and uninterpreted functions are usually not expressive enough to complete the proofs, while complex axioms (e.g., enumerations of input-output mappings of bit-vector functions) may significantly reduce the performance.

6   Conclusions and Future Work

Based on our experience with performing software verification on real-world low-level programs, we identified the need for precise reasoning about bitwise operations as an important issue that is crippling many contemporary software verifiers. On one end of the spectrum, verifiers opt for exclusively bit-precise reasoning, which often becomes a performance and/or scalability bottleneck. On the other end, verifiers opt for imprecise modeling using integers and uninterpreted functions, which often leads to a large number of false alarms. We propose an approach that attempts to strike a balance between the two extremes — it starts with imprecise modeling and gradually increases precision on-demand driven by spurious counterexamples. We implemented the approach by leveraging the SMACK toolchain, and performed an extensive empirical evaluation on the SV-COMP benchmarks. Our results show that it reduces the number of false alarms while maintaining scalability, which makes it competitive with a highly manually optimized baseline on small- to medium-size benchmarks.

As future work, we would like to improve the scalability of our approach on large-scale memory-intensive benchmarks by exploring two possible directions. The first direction is to refine the memory model such that the type updates are more controlled. For example, we could leverage the strict aliasing rules of C/C++ to further split memory regions (maps) by element types since aliasing of pointers pointing to elements with different types is undefined behavior. In this way, we could probably avoid the case where pointers become bit-vectors due to the overly conservative alias analysis. The second direction is to increase the granularity of the refinement. Currently, all the uninterpreted bitwise operations in an error trace program are considered, while in fact some of them may not contribute to the false alarm. Therefore, we could greedily start from one of the uninterpreted bitwise operations and perform the transformation, while leaving the others as uninterpreted. If the false alarm disappears, we propagate the type updates caused by only a subset of the uninterpreted bitwise operations in the error trace program. As an alternative to this greedy technique, we could analyze the model returned by Z3 to identify relevant bitwise operations.

References

1. Babić, D., Hu, A.J.: Structural abstraction of software verification conditions. In: Damm, W., Hermanns, H. (eds.) CAV 2007. LNCS, vol. 4590, pp. 371–383. Springer, Heidelberg (2007). https://doi.org/10.1007/978-3-540-73368-3_41
2. Ball, T., Bounimova, E., Kumar, R., Levin, V.: SLAM2: static driver verification with under 4% false alarms. In: Bloem, R., Sharygina, N. (eds.) FMCAD 2010, pp. 35–42. FMCAD Inc, Austin (2010)
3. Barrett, C., Sebastiani, R., Seshia, S., Tinelli, C.: Satisfiability modulo theories. In: Handbook of Satisfiability, Chap. 26, pp. 825–885. IOS Press (2009)
4. Beyer, D.: Second competition on software verification. In: Piterman, N., Smolka, S.A. (eds.) TACAS 2013. LNCS, vol. 7795, pp. 594–609. Springer, Heidelberg (2013). https://doi.org/10.1007/978-3-642-36742-7_43
5. Beyer, D., Keremoglu, M.E.: CPAchecker: a tool for configurable software verification. In: Gopalakrishnan, G., Qadeer, S. (eds.) CAV 2011. LNCS, vol. 6806, pp. 184–190. Springer, Heidelberg (2011). https://doi.org/10.1007/978-3-642-22110-1_16

6. Beyer, D., Löwe, S., Wendler, P.: Benchmarking and resource measurement. In: Fischer, B., Geldenhuys, J. (eds.) Model Checking Software. LNCS, vol. 9232, pp. 160–178. Springer, Cham (2015). https://doi.org/10.1007/978-3-319-23404-5_12
7. Christakis, M., Bird, C.: What developers want and need from program analysis: an empirical study. In: Lo, D., Apel, S., Khurshid, S. (eds.) ASE 2016. pp. 332–343. ACM, New York (2016). https://doi.org/10.1145/2970276.2970347
8. Clarke, E., Grumberg, O., Jha, S., Lu, Y., Veith, H.: Counterexample-guided abstraction refinement. In: Emerson, E.A., Sistla, A.P. (eds.) CAV 2000. LNCS, vol. 1855, pp. 154–169. Springer, Heidelberg (2000). https://doi.org/10.1007/10722167_15
9. de Moura, L., Bjørner, N.: Z3: an efficient SMT solver. In: Ramakrishnan, C.R., Rehof, J. (eds.) TACAS 2008. LNCS, vol. 4963, pp. 337–340. Springer, Heidelberg (2008). https://doi.org/10.1007/978-3-540-78800-3_24
10. DeLine, R., Leino, K.R.M.: BoogiePL: a typed procedural language for checking object-oriented programs. Technical report MSR-TR-2005-70, Microsoft Research (2005)
11. Emulab network emulation testbed. http://www.emulab.net
12. Godefroid, P., Levin, M.Y., Molnar, D.: Automated whitebox fuzz testing. In: Cowan, C., Vigna, G. (eds.) NDSS 2008, pp. 151–166. Internet Society, Reston (2008)
13. Henzinger, T.A., Jhala, R., Majumdar, R., Sutre, G.: Lazy abstraction. In: Launchbury, J., Mitchell, J.C. (eds.) POPL 2002. pp. 58–70. ACM, New York (2002). https://doi.org/10.1145/503272.503279
14. Lahiri, S.K., Qadeer, S., Rakamarić, Z.: Static and precise detection of concurrency errors in systems code using SMT solvers. In: Bouajjani, A., Maler, O. (eds.) CAV 2009. LNCS, vol. 5643, pp. 509–524. Springer, Heidelberg (2009). https://doi.org/10.1007/978-3-642-02658-4_38
15. Lal, A., Qadeer, S.: Powering the static driver verifier using Corral. In: Cheung, S., Orso, A., Storey, M. (eds.) FSE 2014. pp. 202–212. ACM, New York (2014). https://doi.org/10.1145/2635868.2635894
16. Lal, A., Qadeer, S., Lahiri, S.: Corral: a solver for reachability modulo theories. In: Parthasarathy, M., Seshia, S.A. (eds.) CAV 2012. LNCS, vol. 7358, pp. 427–443. Springer, Heidelberg (2012). https://doi.org/10.1007/978-3-642-31424-7_32
17. Lattner, C., Adve, V.: LLVM: a compilation framework for lifelong program analysis & transformation. In: Dulong, C., Smith, M.D. (eds.) CGO 2004, pp. 75–86. IEEE Computer Society Washington, D.C. (2004)
18. Lattner, C., Lenharth, A., Adve, V.: Making context-sensitive points-to analysis with heap cloning practical for the real world. In: Ferrante, J., McKinley, K.S. (eds.) PLDI 2007. pp. 278–289. ACM, New York (2007). https://doi.org/10.1145/1250734.1250766
19. Linux driver verification project. https://forge.ispras.ru/projects/ldv
20. Leino, K.R.M.: This is Boogie 2 (2008)
21. Rakamarić, Z., Emmi, M.: SMACK: decoupling source language details from verifier implementations. In: Biere, A., Bloem, R. (eds.) CAV 2014. LNCS, vol. 8559, pp. 106–113. Springer, Cham (2014). https://doi.org/10.1007/978-3-319-08867-9_7
22. Rakamarić, Z., Hu, A.J.: A scalable memory model for low-level code. In: Jones, N.D., Müller-Olm, M. (eds.) VMCAI 2009. LNCS, vol. 5403, pp. 290–304. Springer, Heidelberg (2009). https://doi.org/10.1007/978-3-540-93900-9_24
23. SMACK software verifier and verification toolchain. http://smackers.github.io

24. Srikanth, A., Sahin, B., Harris, W.R.: Complexity verification using guided theorem enumeration. In: Castagna, G., Gordon, A.D. (eds.) POPL 2017. pp. 639–652. ACM, New York (2017). https://doi.org/10.1145/3093333.3009864
25. International competition on software verification (SV-COMP). https://sv-comp.sosy-lab.org
26. White, B., Lepreau, J., Stoller, L., Ricci, R., Guruprasad, S., Newbold, M., Hibler, M., Barb, C., Joglekar, A.: An integrated experimental environment for distributed systems and networks. In: Culler, D., Druschel, P. (eds.) OSDI 2002. pp. 255–270. ACM, New York (2002). https://doi.org/10.1145/844128.844152

Author Index

Printed in the United States
By Bookmasters